Traditional Cultures

A Survey of Nonwestern Experience and Achievement

Glenn E. King

WAVELAND

PRESS, INC.

Long Grove, Illinois

For information about this book, contact:
  Waveland Press, Inc.
  4180 IL Route 83, Suite 101
  Long Grove, IL 60047-9580
  (847) 634-0081
  info@waveland.com
  www.waveland.com

Cover: The cover images come from all three of the "Domains" described in this book. From upper left clockwise: Native American dancers represent the New World Domain; a Korean man represents the Old World Domain (Asia); a Fijian warrior represents the Oceanic Domain; a mother and child represent the Old World Domain (Africa). Together they suggest the diverse manifestations of culture in human life: from infancy to old age, from creation to destruction, from anger to joy to serenity.

To the memory of

Edith King

who would have been a treasure in any culture

and to her wonderful friends

James Bennermon

Jane Jackson

and Geri Kilpatrick

Photo Credits

Contents

Part III   The Oceanic Domain   232

Acknowledgments

I am very grateful to the following for their comments on various portions of the manuscript and for providing important resources: Julius Adekunle, Gary DiBenedetto, Hans and Waltraud Hieslmair, Cynthia King, William P. Mitchell, Kenneth Stunkel, Mary Carol Stunkel, and Richard Veit. In addition, Gary DiBenedetto provided invaluable technical assistance. I also appreciate the moral (and, in a couple of cases, immoral) support of those mentioned above.Others who lightened the psychological load were David Payne, David Bramhall, and my good neighbors, Jack and Angie Jackson. Numerous members of the Association for Social Anthropology in Oceania contributed helpful on-line comments, and Richard Scaglion was especially generous in discussing several issues with me and encouraging my project. Members of the VISCOM Listserve were very helpful in my search for photographs.

It has been a great pleasure working with people associated with Waveland Press, including Tom Curtin, Jeni Ogilvie, Wanda Giles, Don Rosso, and Katy Murphy. Jan Weissman deserves special credit for organizing the numerous photographs in the text. Finally, I owe a special debt to the anonymous reviewer who plowed through the entire manuscript in an earlier and messier incarnation. This individual provided an abundance of useful commentary directed toward *my* intentions rather than any agenda of his or her own. This was constructive criticism in its highest form. Not every reviewer of books or papers displays such insight and self-possession.

I also want to stress my great debt to virtually everyone cited in the bibliography. This work is original only in scope and in some aspects of organization and treatment. It would not have been possible without the enormous efforts of my colleagues working in the field and my predecessors in synthesis.

A significant portion of the manuscript was written during a leave of absence from Monmouth University that was made financially possible by Edith King. The final draft was written during a sabbatical granted by Monmouth University, for which I am very grateful.

I depended on Kathleen Weeks and all the other fine staff members of the Ocean Township Library, past and present, for help in maintaining my sanity during this project. In that connection I would also like to acknowledge my debt to Lawrence Block, Parnell Hall, Carl Hiaasen, Tony Hillerman, Stuart Kaminsky, Elmore Leonard, Ed McBain, James Melville, Robert B. Parker, Ellis Peters, and Donald Westlake.

It is obvious but must be said: none of the valiant helpers mentioned above is responsible for any of the continuing shortcomings in my work.

Finally, and most of all, I would like to thank David, Kim, and Cynthia for being my children and my friends.

INTRODUCTION

- The Need to Understand Other Cultures

- Design of This Book

Previous page   Statue of the Golden Buddha (China). To believers in the Mahayana branch of Buddhism, Buddhas are manifestations of God (more theologically, the Dharma principle) who enlighten people on earth and guide them to joyous heavens. Statues such as this one are not idols, but merely representations of the spiritual Buddhas.

The first three chapters will provide a foundation for understanding and appreciating cultural variation. This chapter briefly explains the purposes and organization of the book. It introduces a number of vital concepts that apply to the entire text. The terms for these concepts will be indicated by **boldface**. As you read the book, you can refresh your memory about these and other key terms by consulting the glossary.

The Need to Understand Other Cultures

"GIRL POWER IS SQUELCHED." The newspaper article explained that concert dates for the folk duo called the Indigo Girls had been canceled by several high schools (Strauss 1998). One reason given for the rebuff was that the singers "worship pagan religions," as evidenced by the following lines from one of their songs:

> You had to bring up reincarnation
> over a couple of beers the other night?
> Now I'm serving time for mistakes made
> by another in another lifetime,
> How long till my soul gets it right?

For many people the phrase "pagan religions" conjures images such as blood sacrifice and black magic. Presumably this is the sort of thing that the Girl-bashers meant to imply. To the reader with a basic knowledge of traditional non-Western cultures, however, the implication of the lyrics is very different. The allusion to reincarnation is clearly based on Hindu-Buddhist concepts in which the destiny of the soul from one life to another derives from the ethical value of the individual's behavior. For most believers, the ultimate goal of multiple reincarnations is to end the cycle in some kind of union with God. In other words, contrary to the ignorance or prejudice of certain high school officials, the song in question refers to a deeply moral and spiritual religious tradition that has lasted for thousands of years and that guides the lives of more than a billion people today.

Unfortunately, such problems are not limited to pop music or high schools. A few years ago I heard a professor of philosophy give a public talk at a university in which he referred to the traditional religions of Africa as "beating tom-toms in the jungle." To my amazement the head of African-American studies then praised him for his Christian perspective. The truth is that the philosopher's ethnocentric attitude produced a blatant distortion of African religions. These ritually and philosophically complex systems are comparable to Christianity and the other widespread traditions of Eurasia (Schneider 1981).

Africa also provides a good example of the opposite extreme in cultural misrepresentation. People who call themselves Afrocentrists (allegedly looking at the world from an African viewpoint) paint a glowing picture of ancient Africa as a culture that invented everything good in the world. This is hardly more connected to reality than the ethnocentric portrayal, since traditional Africa had its limitations as well as its real achievements (Lefkowitz 1996). Romanticized views of other cultures are just as misleading as bigoted ones. Furthermore, they carry the seeds of ethnocentrism within them. The Afrocentrist idea that Africans brought the first civilizations to the New World implies that Native Americans were incapable of creating them.

The main point of all this is that an educated person today must have knowledge about cultures other than his or her own. It is a necessary antidote to the distortions that many people purvey, whether for a variety of political and ideological reasons or out of simple ignorance. The purpose of this book is to provide basic, accurate information about cultures around the world in a way that is readable and reasonably easy to remember. It can provide you with a new perspective on much that you encounter in daily life. This includes people that you meet and items that you see on television or in print or on the Internet.

To be more specific, this book surveys the traditional cultures of the non-Western world. Both terms need definition for our purposes. **Western culture** includes Europe and all of its cultural offshoots, such as the United States and modern Australia. All other cultures are **non-Western**. The significance of this distinction is that western countries have wreaked enormous changes in the rest of the world in the last few centuries. Accordingly, I define **traditional cultures** as those that existed just before substantial change due to westernization, modernization, or outright destruction. The end of most traditional cultures, then, is marked by the spread of European colonialism.

In the Americas the decline of traditional cultures began with the Spanish conquest and proceeded rapidly at the hands of many different Europeans. Accordingly, my description of Native American cultures tries to reconstruct them as they were around the year 1500 A.D. The rest of the world, despite prior contact with Europe, did not undergo such drastic changes until the last rush of colonial expansion. Therefore, I describe Asia, Africa, and the Pacific as they were around 1700.

There are a variety of reasons for studying these cultures of the past. One of the most important is that, in an increasingly homogeneous world, they give us a better sense of the enormous range of variation in human cultural experience and achievement. For those who approach human life from a rationalistic point of view, knowledge of cultural variation provides a better understanding of the causes and the possibilities of human behavior. From a humanistic perspective, knowledge of human diversity will help anyone to better appreciate and empathize with the perceptions and feelings of other human beings.

The study of traditional cultures also helps us to understand and cope with events in the world today. Although traditional cultures have been altered and disrupted, they continue to affect contemporary life. A person with an awareness of Confucian ideals can better understand East Asian attitudes toward education. Middle Eastern gender relations are still affected by ancient concepts of the differences between male and female. Ethical and legal debate about casinos on North American Indian reservations may be illuminated by knowledge of the role of gambling in Native American culture. To understand other cultures today, you have to know something about the traditional cultures on which they are based.

Design of This Book

Cultural Units

The book is arranged to avoid redundancy and thus maximize the amount of information presented. That process begins with the next two chapters, which describe worldwide cultural patterns. Presenting them as background makes it possible to avoid repetition throughout the rest of the text. Universal incest taboos, for example, are noted in the second chapter and not mentioned again.

The heart of the book uses the same approach to explore cultural diversity in units of decreasing size that I call **Domains, Zones,** and **Areas**. My Domains correspond to the conventional geographic units known as the New World (the Americas), the Old World (Eurasia and Africa), and Oceania (the Pacific Islands and Australia). Every Domain is divided into Zones and each Zone into Areas. Each of the resulting units is distinctive with regard to a number of important cultural traits.

Note that the words "Domain," "Zone," and "Area" are capitalized above. I do this because the words also denote concepts of space in everyday language. Throughout this text, capitalization indicates my special definition of the terms while the absence of capitals means they are being used in the everyday sense.

With worldwide cultural features established in chapters 2 and 3, the description of each Domain can focus on the traits that distinguish it from the others. Similarly, distinctive features are emphasized for each Zone and Area. For example, some kind of quest for a personal guardian spirit was found in every Area of the Northern American Zone. This cultural pattern will be described in the section on Northern America; it will not be repeated in the sections that cover Areas within that Zone.

To be successful, this approach requires careful study of each cultural unit before considering its subdivisions. Otherwise, the more specific descriptions in the smaller units will be out of context. You must keep in mind that each cultural unit has (previously described) characteristics of the larger ones to which it belongs, as well as its own distinctive features.

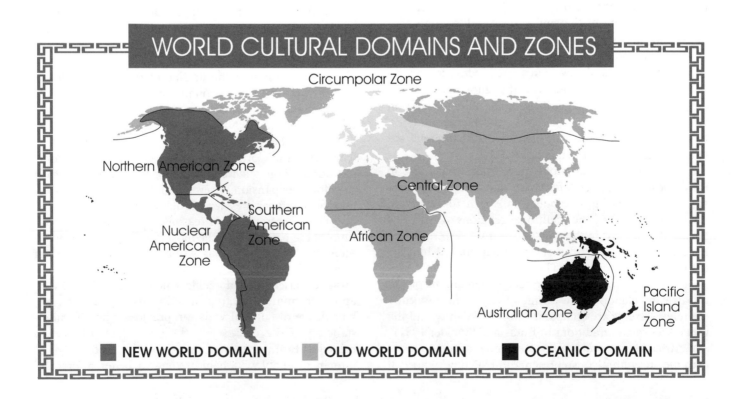

WORLD CULTURAL DOMAINS AND ZONES

Circumpolar Zone

Northern American Zone

Central Zone

Southern American Zone

African Zone

Nuclear American Zone

Australian Zone

Pacific Island Zone

■ NEW WORLD DOMAIN   ■ OLD WORLD DOMAIN   ■ OCEANIC DOMAIN

Categories of Culture

Each Domain, Zone, and Area will be described in terms of the same basic categories of culture. These aspects of culture are **material culture**, **social relations**, and **knowledge and expression**. Arranging the information this way facilitates comparisons and thus makes it easier to learn and remember the differences among cultural units.

"Material culture" loosely encompasses the physical aspects of life. It includes adaptations to the environment, production of goods, and the principles by which goods are distributed among the people in a culture. The "social relations" category includes family, community, and political organization.

By "knowledge" I mean all the things that people in a given culture believe about the universe around them. We can distinguish subjective and empirical knowledge. Subjective knowledge is perceived as reality only by those brought up in a particular cultural tradition—for instance, the assumption that particular heavenly bodies have certain effects on the behavior and life course of human beings (astrology). Empirical knowledge refers to observations that can be confirmed by members of other cultures even though they have different subjective views, e.g. the apparent movement of celestial objects (astronomy). As is illustrated by astrology and astronomy, the two kinds of knowledge can be intertwined in a given culture, and discussing them separately would give a misleading picture of that culture.

Various kinds of knowledge are expressed in ritual and art. Even games and sports often have symbolic connections with various aspects of knowledge. These vehicles for cultural expression also serve personal feelings and motivations. Participants often derive esthetic satisfaction or simple pleasure from their performances.

Modal Patterns in Culture

Descriptions of culture refer to patterns rather than actual events. That is, the description presents the common features of a particular cultural idea or behavior while recognizing that different individuals are likely to have slightly different versions. Some farmers in a particular village, for example, may believe that it is essential to plant a certain crop on a specific day in April while others think that there is some leeway. The anthropologist can record this as a cultural pattern in which the crop is planted in April or in the early spring.

In this book I try to simplify the presentation by using the idea of **modal patterns** for my cultural units. A modal pattern can be thought of as the most common form among several variants. I apply the concept to the most common form of each cultural trait in whatever cultural unit is being described. Consider a society in which people smoke pipes, cigars, and cigarettes. If a substantial

majority smoke pipes, we can consider this the modal pattern for that society. If pipes are predominant in most of the societies within a culture area, then we can say that pipe smoking is a modal pattern for the Area.

If we have an understanding that my descriptions refer to modal patterns, I can dispense with annoying and space-wasting repetition of qualifiers such as "the majority of" and "almost all." Having this understanding, you will know without constant reminders that *there are exceptions to every generalization that I make*. My daughter says that most of you won't read this chapter and will miss this important point. I hope you prove her wrong.

Finally, I don't claim that every aspect of every culture can be legitimately described in terms of modal patterns. I have tried to limit the book to those cultural patterns that do seem to display such a central tendency. Where necessary for the sake of clarity or realism, I depart from the modal principle and describe variation.

Introductions, Closer Looks, and the Glossary

It may be tempting to dive into the main text of a chapter for a realistic, well-rounded description of a cultural unit. However, you should resist the temptation and read the more abstract introduction first. The introduction will focus your attention on the main points in the chapter, emphasizing cultural patterns that have the most pervasive effects on the societies described and pointing out how those patterns distinguish the cultural unit at hand from others that have been discussed previously. A list of "Key features" sums up each of these introductory discussions.

Many parts of the book end with a section entitled "A Closer Look." The topics in that section elaborate the primary material in various ways. In some cases an especially interesting and distinctive cultural pattern is discussed in greater detail. Other instances explore the theoretical significance of a cultural pattern or relate it to a contemporary issue. In some cases, subdivisions of an Area called **Regions** are described. This is done where such a subdivision is too important, distinctive, or interesting to be ignored.

All cultural units are illustrated by maps that are a compromise of many different sources. The boundaries are very rough approximations, intended only to give you a general idea of where the cultural units were located in 1500 or 1700 A.D. Examples of particular cultures also illustrate the cultural units. Most of them were chosen with the idea that you might have encountered them previously, either in the mass media or in courses you have taken, so that you can start reading the pertinent section with some feeling for the subjects.

Last, but far from least, there is the glossary. It can help you to recall basic concepts as you read the text, without going back to the introductory chapters. It is also important because some of the terms used in this book are defined differently by various anthropologists, for example, "tribe" and "chief." The glossary will tell you how I am using such words. My definitions were chosen or developed for their applicability to a wide range of cultures.

WORLDWIDE CULTURAL PATTERNS

2

- Material Culture
- Social Relations
- Knowledge and Expression

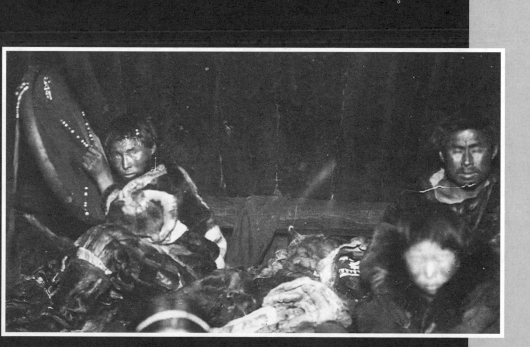

Previous page A shaman (at left, playing drum), a kind of religious practitioner who made direct contact with the supernatural primarily for the purpose of curing the afflicted (Koryak culture, Siberia).

In order to minimize redundancies later on, this chapter describes cultural patterns that existed in traditional societies all over the world. Although worldwide patterns are not the main concern of the book, which emphasizes cultural variation, they provide a context that cannot be ignored. Summarizing them here (and in the next chapter) will allow me to focus more sharply on distinctive features throughout the rest of the volume. To make the strategy work, however, you will have to keep the background generalizations firmly in mind as you continue to read. There are, of course, many exceptions to the broad background generalizations in this chapter.

Many of the cultural patterns described below were modal patterns for the world as a whole. A good example is farming, which played a fundamental role in all three Domains and six of the eight Zones that they contained. It provided food for the vast majority of people in the traditional world.

However, the chapter also describes some widespread patterns that were perhaps not quite world-modal. The reasons for this are illustrated by fishing. Fishing was not nearly as important for the world in general as farming, but it did reach prominence in several parts of every Domain. Equally important for the purpose of this chapter, the basic methods of fishing were the same wherever it was practiced. Therefore, the basic patterns of fishing are described here rather than repeated in several different chapters later on.

Some of the generalizations in this chapter came from Brown (1991) or Ember and Ember (1999) or more specific surveys (e.g., Child and Child 1993; Frayser 1985; Levinson 1989), while others are derived from the research for this book. As in the first chapter, key concepts are emphasized with **boldface**. You may recognize them as concepts that are usually taught in an introductory anthropology course. However, you should remember that some of my definitions may differ from those you have encountered elsewhere. Use the glossary as a quick antidote to any confusion (or memory loss) along the way.

Material Culture

People in traditional cultures wore at least one or two items of clothing and they decorated themselves in various ways. The **loincloth** was probably the modal garment for men. It wrapped around the waist with part of it covering the pubic area and sometimes the buttocks as well. A man, especially when not working, often wore an additional item of clothing on his upper body. He decorated himself with earrings, bracelets, or a necklace.

Women also covered their upper and lower bodies with clothing and decorated themselves with jewelry, but the designs of these adornments differentiated them from

Two different styles of the loincloth, the most basic male garment (Kuene, Angola).

men. Women wore their hair longer than men, usually hanging down, and they added or changed to distinctive adornment when they married.

Both sexes painted their bodies, faces, hands, or feet at least part of the time. They obtained black pigment from the products of fire (soot or charcoal) while red and white came from minerals (iron oxide, clays, chalk). The most elaborate adornments were reserved for special occasions, such as feasts and ceremonies. People also painted themselves for war and for mourning. Some body decorations simply pleased the eye or attracted the opposite sex, but many denoted achievements, personal status, or group affiliation. Whatever their specific purposes, modifications of the body were seen as distinguishing humans from animals.

People made permanent changes in their bodies for much the same reasons. The **tattoo** was the most common means, being applied to men in about one third of all cultures and to women in almost half. A tattooer pierced the skin with a pointed tool and inserted soot or charcoal. The less-common practice of **cicatrization**, which is patterned scarification, was favored mainly by darker-skinned peoples. They often inserted caustic materials in the cuts to make the scars more prominent.

A family used a **dwelling**, a roofed structure, for sleeping and for storage of their possessions. They also used it to take shelter from bad weather but otherwise conducted most of their activities outside. The world-modal dwelling (though present in only about half of all cultures) was a rectangular house with a slanted roof to shed rain. The roof was made of thatched plant material—grass, reeds, or long leaves.

A cluster of dwellings may be called a **village** if it existed for at least several months. If several small settlements of this kind had close social connections with one another, then each one can be termed a **hamlet;** together they constituted a single village. The terms "village" and "hamlet" imply relatively substantial dwellings. When people on the move constructed flimsier shelters to use for a few days or a few weeks, the term **camp** is more appropriate for the whole group.

Making fire with bow and drill (Siberia).

A rectangular house with slanted, thatched roof, perhaps the most common kind of dwelling (Fiji Islands, Pacific).

A **household** included all the people who occupied the same dwelling, or several dwellings in close proximity to one another, and cooperated economically for ordinary subsistence. Fire provided a focus for household activities. A domestic fire burned in a **hearth** lined with stone. Its main use was for cooking food, but it could also provide warmth, illumination, smoke and drying heat for food preservation, and protection from insects and predatory animals. A person made fire with a drill, rapidly rotating a stick with the end against a depression in a hard surface. The resulting sawdust smoldered and set fire to tinder.

People organized many of their tasks by assigning them primarily to men or to women. In this **sexual division of labor** men obtained and worked hard materials: wood, stone, bone, and horn. With such materials they erected the dwellings and any other structures needed by the household. The basic male artifact was a chopping tool consisting of a blade of stone or metal attached to a

wooden handle. In the **axe** form of the tool the plane surface of the blade was parallel with the handle; in an **adze** the blade was perpendicular. Men used these tools for clearing farm plots and for a variety of other subsistence tasks related to wood and bark. They made musical instruments from the hard materials, and they also manufactured rope, cordage, and nets.

Where water transport was significant, men made **dugout canoes** from tree trunks by chopping out the interior and chopping the outside to trim and smooth it. Some boat makers facilitated the hollowing process by alternating chopping with the application of fire. Another technique involved filling the hollowed boat with water and heating it almost to boiling with hot

Making a dugout canoe with an adze (Camayura culture, Brazil).

stones. This made the wood pliable and allowed the canoe makers to stretch and shape the sides by placing cross-pieces of varying lengths between them. After drying, the boat held the new shape. Wooden paddles propelled canoes.

Women spent considerable time in gathering, providing their families with water, plants for food and other purposes, and wood or other fuel for the household fires. They processed and cooked food, made drinks, did whatever laundering was necessary, and carried most of the burdens from place to place. Women produced fabrics and made clothing, which served the community as gifts, religious offerings, and payments of various kinds, in addition to their technological uses.

Women practiced the craft of **ceramics**, shaping clay into pots (wide-mouthed vessels), jars (narrow mouths), bowls (hemispherical), and plates (slightly concave). In the simplest approach, called molding or modeling, a woman formed the whole object from a single mass of clay. A potter who used the coiling technique built her vessel from successive layers of clay and then smoothed them together. Although dried clay vessels could be useful, true ceramics were better. They required firing, hardening by exposure to high temperatures that drove the water out of the clay.

Illustration of the worldwide pattern of burden-carrying by women and of the use of basketry (China).

Making pottery by the coiling method (Zuni culture, North America).

Women made **basketry** artifacts by interlacing fibrous materials such as reeds or vines, producing the same kinds of vessels as ceramics. Again, two basic methods were available. In coiling the woman laid down the foundation by spiraling one of her materials into layers. Then she used the other material to sew the layers together. Using the second method, a woman started with a vertical foundation and then wove the other material through it. In addition to basketry vessels, women made mats, flat items used for many different purposes ranging from sitting to roof construction.

People, especially women, accomplished a great deal of work with one basic tool: the long, straight, sharpened stick. It is often called the **digging stick** for one of its main uses in both cultivation and foraging. It could also be used for prying objects loose and knocking them down from high places. In a moment the stick became a weapon to club or skewer a small prey animal.

The vast majority of people in the traditional world obtained food by **farming,** meaning any regular cultivation of plants. Cultivation took place in two different settings. People raised their staple foods and other important crops in **fields** outside the village. Men cleared the land and prepared the soil, but responsibility for other aspects of field cultivation (such as weeding and harvesting) varied a great deal. Within the village, women took primary responsibility for most of the **gardens** closely associated with each household. Garden crops included secondary foods and plants for other purposes, including craft manufactures and decorations.

Farming peoples also engaged in varying degrees of **foraging**, the subsistence exploitation of nondomestic plants and animals. Foraging includes **hunting** and **gathering**. Hunting, the relatively vigorous pursuit of animals, was the province of men. Men usually hunted alone or in groups of two or three. Both sexes engaged in gathering, the collection of plants and easily captured animals such as shellfish and turtles. Women predominated in gathering, with one exception: men climbed trees and braved bee stings to obtain honey. Farming, hunting, and gathering provided people with technological materials and medicines as well as food.

Fishing was another form of foraging, mostly practiced by men. Whether fishing ocean, lake, or running water, men used much the same array of tools and techniques. One was angling with line and hook, but this only worked for some species in some conditions. Alternatively, the fisher could skewer his prey with a spear or arrow. Those who practiced this method became adept at compensating for the image distortion caused by light passing through the surface of the water. Fishers in shallow water, often women, captured their prey with nets or bare hands. Although worth the effort in the right conditions, these methods brought in only one fish at a time. People obtained greater numbers by using wood or stone to construct a **weir**, a barrier that passed water but channeled fish to their fate. Fishers also used basketry traps, sometimes in conjunction with weirs.

Weirs, one of many methods of fishing (China).

It was rarely possible for one person to be self-supporting, so economic success depended on **exchange**, the mutual transmission of goods and services. According to one basic principle of exchange, **reciprocity**, cultural tradition specified mutual obligations for the people involved. Reciprocity is a broad concept, and the relationships that it covers can be placed on a continuum with two key variables: time and equivalence. In generalized reciprocity one party gives to another with the idea that any return may be a long time in coming and that it may not equal the value of the initial donation. Balanced reciprocity requires that a recipient return something of nearly equal value within a relatively well-defined period of time. Reciprocity governed exchange within a household and between households of related people, often including an entire village.

For unrelated or unfamiliar people, exchanges were more likely to be based on **bargaining**. In this kind of exchange the participants negotiated the terms of each transaction according to desires and conditions current at the time the transaction took place. Sometimes people argued about the relative value of their offerings. This differed from reciprocity disputes, in which one person accused another of not living up to traditional obligations.

People were most likely to bargain when they engaged in **external trade**, exchange with partners outside the community. Trade goods generally varied with environment and technology, but salt played an important role in trade everywhere in the traditional world. The human body requires it, and plants provide little of it. Because of the irregular distribution of salt, those who lived near seacoasts or inland deposits had a special opportunity for profitable exchanges with others.

Social Relations

Marriage established a long-term relationship between a man and a woman that involved reproduction and the sexual division of labor. Parents and other older members of kinship groups **arranged marriages** for their young people, evaluating possible partners and negotiating the unions. They considered their wisdom necessary to judging the qualifications of a prospective spouse, although they often considered the opinions and feelings of the young people involved. Older individuals also took an active role because a marriage united two groups, not just two people. The wedding, the ritual celebration of the marriage, brought together members of both kinship groups and at least some other community members.

Arranged marriage did not preclude the existence or expression of love. Love could develop gradually within marriage on the basis of shared experiences and concerns. Love could also be the basis for premarital or extramarital relationships. People accepted (or at least condoned) premarital sex, but they condemned adultery. Both rules applied to male and female alike, but a husband had greater leeway in punishing his adulterous wife or her lover. Husbands administered beatings and sometimes killed one or both of the offenders. Sex and marriage were both circumscribed by **incest taboos** that prohibited these relationships between parents and children and between siblings.

A reproductively successful marriage gave rise to a **nuclear family**, composed of one man, one woman, and their children. Kinship bonds and common residence with other such groups created an **extended family**. Some extended families were linked by parent–child ties and others by sibling connections. **Polygyny**, the marriage of one man to more than one woman, also linked nuclear families (through the common father). Men who

A contemporary man with three wives demonstrates the persistence of polygyny (United Arab Emirates).

actually practiced polygyny were usually of special economic, social, or ritual status, and even they rarely had more than three wives. Wives in a polygynous family sometimes came into conflict, but they also cooperated to their mutual benefit. Cooperation and harmony came more easily when co-wives were sisters to each other.

Whatever form it took, a family was at the core of a household. Kinship guided cooperative economic effort as well as coresidence itself. Usually a newly married couple took up some kind of **patrilocal residence**, living with or near the family of the new husband. Many households contained one or more extra relatives, most commonly a widowed elderly person. In some cases the household included unrelated individuals.

People expected a marriage to produce children. They believed that conception took place when sexual intercourse led to the mingling of body fluids from the mother and father. Inability to conceive resulted from external supernatural interference: breaking of taboos by other people, or deliberate hostile actions by humans or supernatural beings. The husband was never to blame. A pregnant woman observed a variety of ritual restrictions on her behavior, mostly avoiding experiences that would adversely affect the baby. The health of the baby was the main concern, although there were also observances meant to ease the delivery for the mother.

In most respects a pregnant woman continued her normal activities for as long as possible. When labor pains left no alternative, the expectant mother went into seclusion for the delivery in a separate room or a place outside the house. Men stayed away unless unusual difficulties required a religious practitioner. One or more female relatives or friends attended the birth, and a **midwife** usually took charge. This was a woman who had given birth several times and had special knowledge of both physical and ritual techniques. The family summoned an outsider as midwife if none of the relatives or friends were qualified.

As labor progressed, the pregnant woman assumed various positions in search of comfort and sometimes rose to walk around. One thing she did not do was lie flat on her back. The midwife or another helper massaged her abdomen to facilitate labor. At the delivery, supported by helpers, the woman assumed an upright or semi-reclining posture. Aid during the birth process made survival more likely as well as easing the mother's pain and anxiety. In addition to supervising the mother's well-being, the midwife made sure of the newborn's first breath, cut the umbilical cord, and then bathed and dressed the infant. The placenta and umbilical cord were buried with some ritual in order to ensure the baby's future health.

Sometimes reproduction was terminated at this point, if not before. A pregnant woman could attempt an abortion, or a new mother might practice **infanticide**. Most often the mother abandoned or killed her baby because she was unable or unwilling to raise it. In some cases the precipitating circumstances were general (for example, a food shortage), and in some cases they were personal (such as lack of support by the father). The community might or might not approve of such actions. Children with obvious physical defects were usually killed, and so were one or both twins, because they were considered unnatural. Infanticide was carried out by abandonment or some form of asphyxiation. Use of these methods, leaving no visible marks on the baby, may have eased the emotions of the mother or both parents.

The infant received a name at the time of the birth or within the next month, recognized with some public ceremony. The parents, often just the father, chose the name. This was a significant prerogative because the child's name would help to shape its identity. Most names distinguished gender. They had meaning, often referring to an animal, a personal trait, or an event.

After giving birth a woman returned to her usual work within a few weeks. However, for the sake of the child's health, she observed some ritual restrictions for a longer period. In particular she and her husband followed a **postpartum sex taboo** and refrained from intercourse for the greater part of a year.

Infancy began in a world that was physically and emotionally warm. The newborn spent most of each day in contact with its mother's body, bound to her when she walked. The baby nursed frequently and found its other demands quickly met. During the night, the infant slept in the same bed as its mother, or at least nearby.

A girl carrying a baby represents the worldwide pattern of sibling care (Turkana culture, Kenya).

Soon the baby met other caretakers, but they also provided close physical contact and quickly took care of the baby's needs and wants. These alternative caretakers allowed the mother to work unencumbered or to rest. They included older siblings, especially sisters; grandparents, who tended to be especially indulgent; and other relatives, mostly women. A father might play with his child, distracting it for a while, but few provided serious caretaking.

The period of complete indulgence ended when the infant began to walk and adults insisted that it wear an item of clothing, even in the home. Misbehavior began to have mild consequences in the form of harsh words or an occasional slap while good behavior sometimes brought small rewards. By three years of age an individual was toilet trained and weaned. The learning of language was well underway.

Early **childhood** was a period of considerable freedom. Children played with tops, balls, and dolls, and they made string figures with their fingers. They chased each other and, the boys especially, wrestled with one another. They began to learn about adult culture by imitating their elders' activities and by listening to stories.

Later childhood began with parents imposing gender differences on children at about five years of age, treating boys and girls differently and requiring them to act differently. Boys learned to be tough and girls to be dutiful and submissive. Gender differentiation was facilitated by the spontaneous separation of boys and girls into same-sex peer groups. Older children spent most of their time in company with other children, whether their peers or caretakers.

Parents viewed children of this age as having attained the ability to reason. They had acquired all the essentials of language and lacked only the full development of vocabulary. This meant that they could understand explanations of proper behavior and could undertake some significant chores for the family. Girls especially assumed increasing responsibility, including the care of their younger siblings. Older children maintained informal and affectionate relationships with their mothers while fathers were regarded with respect. The primary caretakers continued to be female, but men became the authority figures and disciplinarians. Mothers disciplined children more frequently, but fathers were regarded as stricter. Bad behavior brought physical punishment; good behavior elicited rewards and privileges.

A ritual marked the transition to **adolescence** at puberty (especially for girls) or before it (often the case for boys). The young person was removed from the parental house to a place where the rites were conducted. Although parents might be present, they did not participate. This was the business of community elders. When all observances were completed, the new adults were ritually reincorporated into the community. Both sexes represented their change in status with added or different adornments. This new stage of learning and participation in community life included intensified gender socialization and more attention to sexuality. A boy moved into

Attempting to spear a rolling disk, boys play a game that also appealed to men throughout much of the world (Native Australian culture).

new sleeping quarters, a separate room or dwelling, away from his mother and sisters. He engaged in some recreation with a group of peers but spent much of his time with his father and other men. He began to participate in adult economic, military, and religious matters.

A girl had less time and maintained fewer friends as she learned the duties of a woman from her mother. She continued to sleep near her parents. People considered the girl's first menses an important event, marking her readiness for an adult life of marriage, sex, and reproduction. Women introduced the girl to behavioral restrictions that she would observe during every menstrual period for the rest of her life. The most important of these were abstinence from sex and some degree of avoidance of men in everyday life.

Such restrictions were based on the belief that reproductive capacity endowed women with supernatural power. The rationale for this belief is a matter of some controversy among anthropologists. The older interpretation is that men considered menstrual blood and other manifestations of reproduction to be evil and polluting. Recently, emphasis has been placed on the idea that the supernatural aspect of reproduction is good, but it is so powerful that it can be dangerous if not managed properly. It is likely that some cultures held one view and other cultures the other. It is also possible that the ideas coexisted in some cultures: cultures are complex and contain internal contradictions.

Adulthood began with marriage. Most of the girls in a community were wives by the age of seventeen. Boys married between eighteen and twenty-one. When the time came, relatives and community members celebrated the wedding together. Economic exchange played a greater role than religious elements in the ceremonial recognition of marriage. In perhaps half of the traditional world the bride's family received considerations from the groom's side. Most commonly they gave **bridewealth**, a gift or series of gifts composed of valuable goods. Although negotiated, bridewealth was not considered a purchase price. It compensated the girl's family for the loss of her services and/or the children she would have. Sometimes the groom performed **bride service** as an addition to, or substitution for, bridewealth. Bride service entailed a period of work for the in-laws, either before or after the wedding.

Some marriages did not last, even though custody issues or the return of bridewealth discouraged divorce. Both sexes reacted against incompatibility and failure of the partner to fulfill domestic obligations. In addition, men rejected wives for not producing children and for adultery. Men approved of a certain amount of wife beating; women accepted it up to a point but left their husbands to escape severe violence.

A person might achieve the status of **elder** as early as the age of 45. It was marked by a gradual reduction in economic productivity and an increase in leadership. Elders supervised important activities, made community

policy, and resolved disputes. In addition to personal experience, they brought to bear their knowledge of tradition and ritual.

People distinguished old age by an individual's appearance, capabilities, and activities. Many elderly people did useful work such as crafts and baby-sitting as well as providing younger adults with the benefits of knowledge and life experience. Aging women, usually after menopause, gained more authority in the community. They were also released from a variety of restrictions ranging from the burden of young children to ritual prohibitions such as menstrual seclusion. However, any woman or man who became inactive and dependent on the young suffered their resentment.

During the course of life many people received names in addition to the ones bestowed at birth. These

An elder in a ceremonial setting (Ainu culture, northern Japan).

were nicknames, most of them given casually by age-mates and carrying derogatory implications. Some were merely humorous, but others served as reminders of mis-behavior that should not be repeated.

Regardless of names, people usually used **kinship terminology** to address one another. This was essential when a person interacted with parents or other older relatives and also in relationships with affines (in-laws). It was required or preferable in many other relationships. A person also used kinship terminology to identify and classify all **kin**. For example, the distinction between **parallel cousin** and **cross-cousin** was probably modal for the traditional world. A parallel cousin is the offspring of a parent's same-sex sibling (that is, a child of father's brother or mother's sister). The parents of cross-cousins are siblings of the opposite sex (father's sister or mother's brother). Distinctions like this were related to appropriate behavior between the relatives in question.

All kinship systems are **bilateral** in the sense that a person recognizes relatives on both the father's and the mother's sides. Using a narrower sense of the term, a bilateral system is one in which the two sides are of approximately equal importance (as in the contemporary West). Such systems were in the minority in the traditional world. The modal pattern was **unilineal descent**, in which relationships through parents of one sex were consistently more important than relationships on the opposite side. Everyone in a patrilineal society, the most common kind, inherited membership in a descent group from his or her father. Everyone in a matrilineal society inherited membership in one of these groups from his or her mother. These groups required **exogamy**, that is, marriage outside the group. Many were **corporate** in the sense that they held some property in common, although this could be of social or ritual significance rather than economic.

The **lineage** was one kind of unilineal descent group and the **clan** another. Each kind of group traced its origin to a single common ancestor; however, all members of a lineage knew their exact kin relationships with one another while many members of a clan did not. Closer relatives in a clan knew their exact connections, but many members considered themselves to be related only because they claimed descent from the same common ancestor (who was usually mythical). Clans could be much larger than lineages, and a clan could contain a number of lineages linked by the clan ancestor.

Families lived in a **community** of several hundred people, defined by physical proximity and regular personal interaction. The community in this sense could coincide with a single village, or it could encompass several of them. On the other hand, a single large settlement might contain several distinct communities. Each of these would constitute a **neighborhood**.

Men predominated in leadership and decision making for the community as a whole. **Situational leaders** coordinated activities in which they had special expertise or skill, such as hunting a particular kind of animal or leading a war party. Factional leaders represented (or formed) subgroups within the community and competed with each other for greater influence over the community. A **chieftain** led an entire community or a distinct subgroup, such as a lineage, neighborhood, or faction. In contrast to situational leaders, a chieftain led in several areas of life, such as economic coordination and dispute resolution.

Leadership involved some balance of influence, power, and authority. **Influence** emanated from an individual's personality and ability; people willingly followed an influential leader because they thought it was in their best interests. **Authority** gave the leader the right, according to some cultural standard, to expect certain kinds of behavior from his followers. **Power** came from having the means to coerce people into following orders.

Conflict arose within the community as a result of disputes between members or behavior that violated community standards. People involved in a dispute could negotiate a settlement, sometimes helped by a third party who mediated. Sometimes an aggrieved person retaliated violently, frequently with the help of kin. Male relatives also sought revenge for the killing of one of their own. Other community members could influence a dispute with gossip or direct exhortations, tactics that were also effective against those who violated the norms. Those who resisted were sometimes punished directly, up to and including execution.

Warfare, defined as organized fighting between independent political units of any size, even single communities, was virtually universal. In **raiding**, relatively small and loosely coordinated parties set out to make a single attack. Some raiding parties were content to ambush a lone person while others surrounded a village, usually at dawn, and tried to kill a number of the inhabitants. The overt purpose of such assaults was to punish a prior injury or death, an insult, a trespass, or a supernatural attack (witchcraft or sorcery, discussed in the next section). Victorious raiders often obtained material benefits in the form of goods, including food, or captives (for marriage, adoption, or slavery). **Conquest** entailed a decisive victory to achieve some kind of economic or political domination, even if only the control of a single resource. It required more organization than raiding. Men who succeeded in either kind of warfare gained prestige in their communities. They displayed their prowess by bringing home trophies: the heads or other body parts of enemies they had killed.

Knowledge and Expression

People believed in supernatural beings that can be loosely grouped into two categories. **Spirits** were numerous, and people tended to think of them in terms of types rather than as individuals. Some ranged freely while others inhabited natural features, but all were connected to this world and in proximity to humans. Although limited in power, spirits could affect human life for good or ill; people made efforts to contact some of them and avoid others. The beings called **gods** were fewer, more powerful, and more individualized. Each had a name or some other specific designation, such as the portion of nature that he or she controlled. Many could be distinguished by their personalities. The term God (with a capital G) designates a supernatural being that was in some way far superior to all others in the same belief system.

A mask represents a spirit (Biwat culture).

Mythology, sacred stories set in the remote past, told about the origin of the gods and explained how the world began and became the way it is. At first there was nothing but an endless primordial ocean; then one or more gods brought about the Creation. Dry land came first and then the separation of the earth from the sky. With those great feats accomplished, life proliferated on the surface of the earth. However, much more would occur before the world took on its familiar forms. Catastrophes—such as universal flood, fire, or darkness—separated the past into two or more epochs. Mistakes by humans or their predecessors brought on these disasters. The world that emerged from the last disaster was the familiar world of ordinary human beings.

One consequence of mythic catastrophe was the withdrawal of some gods to other realms. Among the most important were the culture heroes. A **culture hero**, either a god or a superhuman person, performed one or more great feats that provided the basis for human life. These beings modified the physical environment and made technology available. One of the most important acts of a culture hero was to take fire from a supernatural source and put it in the hands of humans. Culture heroes also established social and ritual life by giving rules or setting an example.

The **trickster** god of myth, invariably male, deceived others to satisfy his greed for food and sex, and sometimes simply to be malicious. Often foolish, he sometimes harmed himself. In other instances tricksters inadvertently benefited others with their actions, and some became culture heroes in this way. A trickster disrupted social life and violated norms, frequently engaging in obscene or blasphemous behavior. People found entertainment in trickster tales, but also food for thought about proper and intelligent behavior. Trickster gods appeared in important myths, often as culture heroes, while lesser tricksters figured in many mundane stories.

Although some gods had become remote, many remained accessible to humans through various means of communication. The numerous spirits were similarly available. People prayed to the supernaturals on many occasions, stating their messages either aloud or in thought. Sometimes they made **offerings** of valuable objects, ranging from food to jewelry. A special kind of offering was the **sacrifice**, in which the killing of an animal was dedicated to the supernatural being. Supplicants based their attempts at communicating with supernaturals on the assumption that both gods and spirits tended to be humanlike in their emotions and behavior. Human sacrifice, though receiving much attention in popular accounts of other cultures, was far from being a modal pattern for the world as a whole.

Communication with the supernaturals could be carried out by individuals or groups, irregularly or on a calendrical schedule. People regularly sought to appease supernaturals or gain benefits from them through communal ceremonies, coordinated religious actions carried out by a group on a specific occasion. Along with direct communications such as prayers and offerings, communal ceremonies featured music, dance, and the appearance of **ritual clowns**. Clowns, a few specially trained individuals, were the earthly counterparts of tricksters in some ways. They parodied the sacred rituals of the occasion, simulated disgusting and immoral behaviors, and did ordinary things backwards. The actions of the clowns warded off evil spirits while providing comic relief during a solemn time. They also reinforced the social order by making deviance seem absurd. In some instances clowns related their antics to real people or events, obliquely criticizing individuals for error, arrogance, or malfeasance.

A communal ceremony was in many cases associated with a **festival**, a period of days or weeks when the community held its ordinary activities in abeyance. The special mood of the festival was marked by temporary public decorations and personal adornments. People participated in games and sports as well as music and dance. Some behavior differed sharply from that of everyday life, sometimes to the point of complete inversion such as members of one sex acting like the other.

The heart of many a festival was a **feast**, but these ritualized meals also served smaller groups and marked lesser occasions. Feasts brought people together for the communal consumption of special foods. Because these special gatherings served to create or maintain important social ties, they were often combined with transactions such as gift-giving or negotiations. Although the issues addressed by a feast were usually male concerns, women provided the food and performed much of the other labor.

Individuals sometimes interacted with supernatural forces through **magic**, which consisted of rituals that people expected to have an automatic and specific effect on events in this world. Supernatural beings had little or nothing to do with the outcome of such performances, which were based on mystical connections between the things to be influenced and the symbols used in the rituals. One set of techniques assumed a lingering connection between objects that had been in physical contact with one another. Thus hair clippings or other residue from a person could be used to magically influence that person. The other important principle of magic was similarity: effects could be achieved by ritual manipulation of an object that resembled a real person or thing, or by ritual imitation of a desired event. Speech and thought, as powerful human faculties, could be used for magical purposes with or without the physical paraphernalia.

A major concern of ritual activity was **spiritual pollution**, a kind of damage to a person's spiritual essence. Human bodily functions could cause pollution and so could violence, blood, and death. An affected person was recognizable by physical or behavioral symptoms. The pollution could be transmitted to other people by touch and sometimes merely by membership in the same kinship group or community. The only solution to this urgent problem was **spiritual purification**, usually achieved by rituals involving water or fire. People routinely purified themselves before any contact with sacred beings or forces.

Every individual was linked to the supernatural realm by a **soul**. This spiritual essence could leave the body during life, especially during dreams, and left it permanently at death. The soul differed from the supernatural life force that animated the body. A person who had just died inspired anxiety in survivors because the newly dead could give rise to ghosts. A **ghost** was a soul or some other spiritual component of a human being that lingered on earth. Although not necessarily evil, a family ghost might be lonely and tempted to take a living relative as company. Ghosts of strangers were not limited by family sentiment; ghosts of murdered people and enemies were likely to seek revenge. The actions of ghosts explained some of the mysterious sicknesses and other misfortunes in life.

People attributed many other ills to **sorcerers**, human beings who practiced evil by supernatural means. The **witch** is a special kind of sorcerer. Ordinary sorcerers were experts in harmful magic that exercised their craft for gain of some kind (e.g., for compensation or political power) or for specific personal reasons such as revenge. Witches were individuals who had intrinsic ability and desire to do evil for its own sake. I classify the witch as a kind of sorcerer because witches often used some magic and, at the very least, performed some specific act to focus their power (such as looking at or thinking about a victim).

Shamans helped other people to cope with the supernatural. A **shaman** had direct control over supernatural power through a relationship with one or more particular spirits. The most common use for shamanic power was the curing of illness, although shamans performed other feats as well. While people recognized the natural basis for broken limbs and many other problems, they attributed more mysterious ailments to supernatural causes. One was the intrusion of alien objects into the body, and another was the loss of the soul. In the former case a shaman cured the condition by sucking the intrusive objects from the victim's body. If the soul had been lost, the shaman sent his helping spirits or his own soul to retrieve it. To contact the spirits, a shaman often went into a **trance**, an altered state of consciousness in which he had little or no awareness of external stimuli.

Priests led groups of people in ritual or performed rituals on their behalf. Unlike shamans, priests had no direct power over the supernatural and depended on special knowledge of how to communicate with it. Many of these practitioners were individuals with other qualifications (e.g., shamans or political leaders) who performed a priestly role when it was required; that is, they were part-time priests.

Most religious practitioners, as well as many ordinary people, performed **divination**. They used a variety of supernatural means to gain information that was otherwise not available, including events in the future, at a distance, or kept secret. Some, especially shamans, obtained information directly from spirits. Others used more magical means, interpreting the results of rituals that may or may not have been influenced by spirits. One such method was to burn a bone or other hard object and interpret the pattern of cracks that resulted. People turned to divination for practical information rather than spiritual enlightenment.

Religion was prominently served by what we call "art." This word is notoriously difficult to define, even within the confines of our own culture. Many other cultures had no equivalent term at all. Fortunately, a general definition is not necessary for the purpose of this book. It is enough to recognize the worldwide distribution of behaviors that we usually classify as art. People decorated their bodies and/or other surfaces and modified objects by carving and sculpting. They preserved oral traditions that included myths, lesser stories, and various forms of humor and wisdom. They danced and played music on percussion instruments, including drums and rattles.

Song blended with poetry and oratory. In some cases a strong melody dominated the words, but in other instances melody was subordinate. Poetry was commonly sung or chanted, and formal speeches displayed strong rhythms and melodic elements. In short, there was a continuum between song and what has been called heightened speech.

The buffalo dance is an example of communal dance and music for a ritual purpose (Hano Pueblo, North America).

People had two overlapping reasons for such activities. They enjoyed them and/or used them to enhance other aspects of culture. Artistic activities played a major role in supporting religion, heightening the impact of rituals, symbols, and expressions of belief. However, art also occurred in the more mundane aspects of life, ranging from the decoration of weapons to the singing of lullabies.

Sports and games also straddled the border between supernatural and secular. Some were accorded symbolic and ritual meaning while others were simply played for fun. Men often wrestled in the context of communal ceremonies or festivals. A match ended when one grappler managed to throw the other to the ground. Men also competed in throwing projectiles for distance or accuracy.

Men wrestling (Camayura culture, Brazil).

People organized time in terms of the natural world, including the cycles of the sun and moon. The lunar calendar of twelve months fell a few days short of the full round of seasons, so people inserted an extra month every few years to bring the lunar and seasonal calendars back into alignment. Major events in community life, both natural and social, provided reference points for talking about the past.

When a person died, relatives and others gathered to express their grief and prepare the body for ritualized disposition. The corpse was washed, dressed in special clothes, and placed on display for the community. Then it was taken in procession from home to a place of burial. People cried, women more than men, some of it real and some simulated. Men often displayed anger at the loss of a kinsman, sometimes at a specific person known or thought to have caused the death.

For some time afterward close relatives wore symbols of their loss, including clothing that was nondescript by virtue of being old or colorless. They avoided amusements and observed ritual prohibitions of some other activities. Unusual treatment of hair also marked mourners, ranging from shaved heads in some cultures to leaving hair long and unkempt in others.

At one or more points during the process of funeral and mourning, people performed tie-breaking rituals that symbolized separation from the dead. Disposal of the deceased's possessions served this purpose, as did a purifying bath to end a relative's obligation to mourn. A communal ceremony brought the mourning period to an end and allowed all the relatives to resume normal life. This final ceremony was often keyed to the economic cycle so that more people could attend. By this time the soul had completed its transition from this world to the next and the danger of ghostly malice had receded.

The soul went to an **afterworld**, a place of the dead where it joined others that had gone before. This required a journey that might contain obstacles and dangers. During the funeral or at the burial, survivors offered the deceased food (and in some cases other goods) to help with the journey. The **afterlife** in the place of the dead resembled life on earth, at least superficially. Some souls went to a different part of the other world based on their status during life or the way that they died.

FOUR WAYS
OF LIFE

- Horticultural
  Communities

- Chiefdoms

- Agricultural States

- Forager Bands

Previous page   **Four ways of life:** a man with an axe represents the work of horticultural villagers (Waorani culture, Ecuador); a contemporary chief displays the symbolism of rank in chiefdoms (Ghana); a hunter represents one aspect of foraging cultures (Native Australian culture); a probable observatory represents the intellectual and architectural achievements of agricultural civilizations (Maya culture, Mexico).

As in the previous chapter, the main purpose here is to eliminate redundancy later on. This chapter introduces more key concepts, presented in **boldface** that will be used but not explained in succeeding chapters. Again I recommend the glossary for jogging the memory as you read.

We now look at four different kinds of society that once existed around the world: the horticultural community, the chiefdom, the agricultural state, and the forager band (Bates 1998; Ember and Ember 1999; Scupin 1995). Horticultural communities and chiefdoms occurred in all three of my Domains. Agricultural states clearly arose in both the Old World and New World, and some have argued that a few small states developed in the Oceanic Domain as well. Forager bands existed in all three Domains, but marginally because the other ways of life supported denser populations that pushed foragers into the least desirable regions.

HORTICULTURAL COMMUNITIES

Examples:

Pueblo and Iroquois (North America),
Munduruku and Yanomamo (South America),
Igbo (West Africa)

The concept of **horticulture** encompasses the simplest methods of farming, which usually wore out the soil and thus forced communities to relocate from time to time. Social values emphasized reciprocity and **egalitarian** relations. The latter meant that people of the same gender were born to the same rights and opportunities. Although born equal, individuals and groups competed, sometimes strenuously, for influence based on wealth and prestige. Unilineal descent groups undertook many political functions, supporting their authority over members with religious justifications. The community usually recognized one chieftain as the overall leader, but with limited authority. Communities often made alliances with one another and sometimes formed more stable unions.

Key features:

- ▶ Simple farming methods
- ▶ Short-term sedentism
- ▶ Egalitarian but competitive
- ▶ Unilineal descent groups
- ▶ Community chieftain
- ▶ Kin-based religion

Material Culture

Horticultural villagers cleared their farm plots with the **slash-and-burn** technique, cutting down the natural vegetation and then burning it. This not only cleared the land but also added nutrients to the soil. Even so, the soil in a particular plot was exhausted after two or three years. People had to fallow the plot for several years, allowing natural vegetation to regenerate in order to start the cycle over. Other than the cutting tools needed for clearing, the main horticultural implement was the digging stick.

Slash-and-burn horticulture: women chant as men burn a field (Cashinahua culture, Peru).

The farmers interplanted one or two main crops with a number of others, often including fruit trees. The varied heights and other features of the plants protected the whole plot against excess sun and rain, erosion, and weeds. If some crops fell victim to a certain kind of pest, others survived. As a result of different growing periods, the farm plot produced food throughout most or all of the year.

Most horticultural activities required group cooperation. This included clearing, planting, harvesting, and storage. Related families reciprocated help, and some jobs brought together most or all members of a larger kinship group or even the whole community. After a while, five to twenty years depending on local conditions, all the land around a village was worn out. Then the villagers moved the community to another place and started over. This pattern of shifting cultivation required a great deal of land and could only support fairly low population densities.

Social Relations

Unilineal descent groups (lineages or local segments of clans) played a major role in community organization, including family matters. Marriage to anyone within the descent group was forbidden. However, marriage to a cross-cousin was acceptable or even desirable. Such unions created multiple bonds between specific groups.

Members of a descent group reinforced their bonds through reciprocal help, gift giving, mutual protection, and joint religious observances. The group chieftain and elders held authority over their people, including disposition of land held in common by the group members. These leaders also negotiated community matters with the heads of other local descent groups.

Feud was a major concern because of the internal solidarity of lineages and the rivalries between them. When hostility led to a killing, lineage mates of the victim were likely to take revenge against any member of the killer's lineage. The other lineage was then likely to retaliate, and so on. When a feud occurred, a village chieftain could make a major contribution to the community with successful mediation. However, a village chieftain's authority and power over community members were limited. His main function was to represent the community to outsiders.

Though each community was autonomous, members had relationships with people in other communities. At the least, they obtained wives from one another and exchanged goods with one another. Sometimes people traded for practical goods, but often they exchanged gifts in order to maintain warm social relations. In some instances villages formed explicit military alliances.

In a significant number of cases communities formed a long-term sociopolitical unit that may be termed a tribe. Often lasting for many generations, a tribe was an aggregation of similar communities united by the existence of one or more organizations with members in several of those communities. Usually pantribal organizations were kinship groups, such as clans, or they were voluntary associations. Less often we find explicitly political institutions such as a tribal council. Membership in a tribe had little effect on the internal affairs of a community. Tribal organization was mainly devoted to coordinating responses to the world beyond the tribe, and in many cases these functions were sporadic.

One writer or another has applied the word "tribe" to almost every kind of cultural unit, from a single forager band to an unorganized ethnic group with millions of people. As a result, some anthropologists have argued for discarding the term. Note that I use it very specifically to distinguish a kind of social system in which communities were politically linked by simple and often tenuous devices.

Knowledge and Expression

Religious ideas and practices linked people to the natural environment and seasonal cycles because these were vital to success in cultivation. Having a simple technol-

ogy, the farmers felt very dependent on the goodwill of supernatural beings. Individuals performed rites for their own crops and joined in groups for ceremonies that marked major events in the farm cycle, such as planting and harvesting.

Much of communal religion revolved around unilineal descent groups, each of which had its own gods, spirits, and rituals. The souls of ancestors maintained a degree of contact with their living descendants and sometimes intervened in human life to reward or punish. In many cases the common ancestor of a clan was a supernatural being who played a role in mythology. A lineage or clan recognized the reality of beings associated with other groups but was concerned only with its own spiritual patrons. Chieftains and other leaders played priestly roles in the ceremonies of their clans and lineages.

Sorcery greatly troubled horticultural communities. Suspicion, if not the actual practice, may have represented tensions arising from long-term coresidence in sedentary communities. Where any amount of wealth existed, sorcery provided some individuals with a means of extorting it from others.

CHIEFDOMS

Examples:

Natchez (North America),
Taino (Caribbean), Maori (Polynesia)

The **chiefdom** resembled a tribe in that it united several separate communities. It differed in having a hierarchical social system in which one person, the **chief**, occupied a well-defined position of leadership over all the communities involved. In this book the term "chief" is applied only to such higher-level political figures and should not be confused with "chieftain," which I apply only to local leadership.

Advanced horticultural practices supported the relatively dense populations of chiefdoms. Reciprocity was important in the economic relations of family and community, but the chief was the focus of more centralized economic processes. The chiefdom was a nonegalitarian society, organized in terms of hierarchies with authority. All but the simplest chiefdoms held some concept of social stratification. Religion played a major role in supporting hierarchy and authority.

Key features:

- ▶ Elaboration of horticulture
- ▶ Centralized economic processes
- ▶ Sociopolitical hierarchies
- ▶ Centralized leadership with authority
- ▶ Religious support for chiefs

Material Culture

Chiefdoms arose in areas with abundant resources. People magnified the environmental advantage by using some techniques of intensive farming, such as terracing and extensive water control. They also developed effective means of large-scale food storage.

The chief played a central role with respect to several aspects of the economy, including privileged access to ritual and luxury items acquired by external trade or from specialized craft workers. The chief used some of these special goods to adorn himself and his large house, symbolizing his unique status. He gave some of them to his high-ranking supporters so that they could aggrandize themselves in the same way.

Cloth played an especially important role in this regard. It had enormous potential for communication through variation in construction, color, and patterning. Its value was multiplied by the fibers and dyes that it contained, the labor necessary to produce it, and the artistry that went into its finest examples. Symbolically, the entwined fibers of cloth suggested the social bonds of those who participated in its production and exchange. As a relatively durable product, cloth could represent the transmission of authority across generations.

A chief had the authority to demand resources from his own people. Those under his direct control paid **taxes** in the form of food and other goods. These were regular assessments from each adult or family or household. Outlying communities of the chiefdom gave **tribute**, assessed to each community as a whole and conveyed by its leader. The chief also had the right to irregular levies for special purposes.

In some contexts a chief practiced **redistribution**, returning most of the goods to his subjects. He regularly used the food he collected to hold great public feasts, and he often displayed generosity to individuals, especially high-ranking people. A chief symbolized his special status through these acts of apparent generosity. However, a principle of **mobilization** also played a role in such societies: the chief kept donations from his people and used them for his own or governmental purposes.

The chieftain of a single village had rights and obligations with regard to his people that were similar to those of the chief. However, the chieftain was more likely than a chief to return benefits to ordinary people in his community because they were his relatives and supporters. Whatever he did with the assessments owed to him, he had the duty of collecting and passing on tribute due to the chief.

Social Relations

Stratification divided a chiefdom into elite and commoner classes. The elite, also known as nobility or aristocracy, shared special privileges and authority. They distinguished themselves from commoners by the clothes and jewelry that they wore. Each individual was born to a specific **rank** in society, depending on his or her kinship group and place in the birth order, but rank was important only among the elite. A chief came to office because he (or she) was a high-ranking member of a particular high-ranking kinship group. He either inherited the office directly or was selected from among candidates made eligible by hereditary status.

The chief had certain kinds of authority over his entire society, such as the right to control economic processes. In addition, he exercised power, especially over commoners. Acting as a judge, he made binding decisions about disputes and accusations of criminal behavior. He imposed punishments ranging from public reprimand to execution. Community chieftains shared in some of these powers.

A contemporary chief displays symbols of rank (Ghana, western Africa).

Women played important roles in the politics of a chiefdom. High-ranking men married wives and married off their daughters to obtain alliances and resources. Women of rank could command respect and obedience from men lower in the social scale. In situations where eligible men were lacking, appropriate women might attain even the highest offices.

Powerful chiefs sometimes organized wars in which they fielded hundreds or thousands of men for a single battle. Some wars resulted in conquest, with the winning chief collecting tribute from the losers for as long as he could continue to dominate them. Large amounts of tribute could greatly enhance the prestige and power of a chief. Unlike the resources that a chief collected from his own people, tribute from the conquered did not necessarily imply that some redistribution or services would be rendered in return.

A simple chiefdom embraced two levels of administrative organization. One was the chief and his assistants, and the other consisted of the community chieftains. Ranking of individuals was strongly graduated, with precise distinctions made throughout most of the hierarchy. A simple chiefdom might contain a few hundred or a few thousand people.

In a complex chiefdom, which could encompass tens of thousands of people, several chiefs owed allegiance to a leader at a third level in the hierarchy. This highest leader is called a **paramount chief**. With so many people, distinctions in personal rank became blurred, especially at the lower levels, and social class became more important as an organizing principle. A paramount chief required more assistants to administer his complex domain.

Knowledge and Expression

A chief symbolized his office and the polity he led by causing extravagant structures to be built by his subjects. At the very least, the chief's house was larger and its furnishings richer than those of anyone else. Large ritual structures also sent a message of wealth and power because of the resources and labor they entailed. In addition, these structures symbolized political unity because large numbers of people could view them simultaneously, often in the context of public rituals.

Large ceremonies that required extensive resources and organization of labor reinforced the message of authority and power, as did the employment of religious specialists closely associated with the chief and the elite class. Human sacrifice sometimes added to the impact of these observances. While the ceremonies justified elite rule, they also invoked supernatural powers for the welfare of everyone in the chiefdom. Priests, or the chief's own priestly performance, supported his leadership in a regular and legitimate way. Sometimes a chief gained power beyond his authority by forming an alliance with a shaman or sorcerer who could threaten or retaliate against the chief's enemies.

During ceremonies and at other times, chiefs and other elite persons displayed their status in the form of finely made ritual and luxury items. A strong chief controlled the distribution of such objects by controlling the artisans who made them or the trading or warfare by which the objects or necessary raw materials were obtained. Using these objects as gifts, he obtained the support of other elite people. They further distributed the goods to their allies and subordinates. In this way the political system patronized the arts and encouraged specialization by artists and craft people.

Rice terraces illustrate an agricultural technique elaborated in chiefdoms and states (Southeast Asia).

AGRICULTURAL STATES

Examples:

Aztec and Inca (New World),
Arab, Indian, and Chinese (Asia),
Yoruba and Ashante (Africa)

By 1500 A.D., the earliest cultural horizon described in this book, the majority of people in the world lived in agricultural states. A **state** is distinguished by a complex government with a **bureaucracy**, a hierarchy of full-time administrative specialists. The state is familiar to every reader because it is the overwhelmingly predominant political form in the world today. However, the state described here is premodern, based on agriculture rather than industry and ruled by a hereditary leader that we will call a **king**.

The elaborate political structure depended on **agriculture**, cultivation by a variety of sophisticated methods that resulted in substantial surplus. Although state economies practiced both redistribution and mobilization, they emphasized mobilization to a much greater extent than in chiefdoms. Surplus production allowed full-time specialization in many activities other than government, including priestly religion and military leadership, that supported the political hierarchy. Specialists tended to concentrate in settlements larger than villages, resulting in a trend toward urbanization.

Living in rural villages, the farmers were **peasants**. That is, they were physically and socially separated from cities and towns even though these urban centers controlled the peasants politically and partly shaped their cultures. It is this peripheral social situation that distinguished peasants from farmers in other kinds of culture. In simpler societies farmers had direct relationships of various kinds with their leaders. In modern societies farmers have access to the same information and political processses as anyone else. In the agricultural state farmers were to varying degrees isolated and yet unable to escape exploitation. The gap between peasants and elite was great enough to create highly distinct subcultures. Those subcultures are treated separately here, as they are in later chapters on agricultural states.

Regularized use of force was a prominent feature in these societies. To consolidate 'social control, governments developed systems of law backed by legitimized force. Highly organized warfare, emphasizing conquest, characterized relations between states. Tribute, as well as taxes, could provide the state with enormous support.

Key features:

▶ Agriculture, urbanization, peasants
▶ Metallurgy
▶ Mobilization economy
▶ Markets and increased bargaining
▶ Bureaucratic government
▶ Pronounced stratification
▶ Laws and legal use of force
▶ Large-scale warfare and conquest
▶ State religion

Peasant Culture in Agricultural States

Material Culture. Peasant farmers used sophisticated methods such as fertilization and water control (drainage as much as irrigation) to keep their fields in production over long periods of time. These long-lasting fields supported very stable communities. Agriculture required long hours, sometimes far from home, which tended to limit participation by women. Excessive expenditure of time took them away from important domestic tasks, and heavy work interfered with infant care.

Within the community most economic relations were based on reciprocity. In addition to mutual support between family members, villagers cooperated in agricultural tasks and other work. They bargained with people from other communities in local markets, and they went

A peasant village (Mali, northern Africa).

Peasants working in the fields (Egypt).

to the nearest town to obtain goods not locally available. A **town** was a large settlement that provided regional administration as well as a larger market. Peasants who lived near a **city** might go there for its even larger market. Others rarely visited cities except to witness major ceremonies or to engage in construction projects as part of their obligation to the government.

Agriculture provided large surpluses of food that supported numerous full-time specialists, including the governmental bureaucracy and the elite class. People gave the government and the local nobility much of what they cultivated and manufactured. The government also required work from men, including construction and military service. When peasant men joined work gangs or became common soldiers in the army, they were supported and rewarded by some of the goods that their families had contributed to the government. Thus mobilized goods turned into buildings and conquests.

Social Relations. Intensive agriculture made children valuable for small, unskilled tasks such as protecting extensive fields from predation by birds. Agriculture in turn produced more food with which to feed many children. As a result, infanticide was rare and large families common.

Farmers in several neighboring communities looked to a nearby town for a market and various services. Further away, a larger town housed regional administrators representing the central government. Though most would never see the king, peasants knew that he sat in a capital city inhabited by many thousands of people. His representatives saw that the villagers provided soldiers for the army and goods to support his government.

The prospect of enslavement shadowed a peasant's life. Free people entered slavery in several different ways. One was capture; in some cases this was a by-product of warfare and in others the specific goal of raiding. A person could also become a **slave** within his or her own

society to compensate for an unpaid debt or as punishment for a crime. However they were obtained, most slaves were similar to their masters in physical and cultural characteristics.

Knowledge and Expression. Peasants viewed religion in practical terms. They visited shamans for cures, and they tried to please the local spirits and gods that were most likely to help and protect them. Communal ceremonies emphasized the agricultural cycle. Though people exerted considerable technological control over the land, only the gods could protect against disaster such as floods and droughts.

Elements of the state religion filtered down from the elite. The government required participation in some observances because these observances rationalized and reinforced the hierarchy. However, the peasants also found some help from the official religion. Its priests could intercede with the most powerful gods to avert disaster and promote fertility throughout the realm. Some priests also provided more personal services such as curing and divination.

Elite Culture in Agricultural States

Material Culture. The main buildings of government and religion clustered near the center of a city, associated with a plaza or avenue used for public meetings and ceremonies. The central marketplace stood nearby. City markets gave people a wider choice of goods than the more localized ones scattered around the countryside, and they met more frequently. Common people found useful items in the urban marketplace, but much of it was devoted to luxury goods that only nobles could afford. These included both finished products and exotic raw materials to be worked by specialized artisans that the elite patronized.

Metallurgy was the basis for several specializations, starting with the workers who extracted and refined the ores. Some artisans made ornaments for the nobility from gold and silver. Others used more mundane metals, such as bronze and copper, to manufacture tools and weapons. Many skilled craft workers created finer versions of artifacts, such as pottery, that were also made by peasants.

Just beyond the city center lived aristocrats and wealthy merchants. Their large houses turned blank walls to the narrow streets. Behind the walls there were luxurious furnishings, large extended families, and numerous servants. Neighborhoods of commoners ringed the city, organized by ethnic group and occupation. In some cases ethnicity and traditional occupation coincided. Limited transportation caused people to crowd together. No residence was higher than three stories, and only nobles lived in such dwellings. Most cities held about ten thousand people, although some of the great imperial centers contained a hundred thousand or more.

An urban scene illustrating the traditional city's pattern of walls and courtyards (Dahran, Saudi Arabia).

Professional merchants brought raw materials and finished goods to the city markets from faraway places. They traveled many hundreds of miles from home to bargain with their counterparts in different states and even different cultures. It was arduous and sometimes dangerous, but the successful merchant could acquire a great deal of wealth.

Social Relations. In addition to several wives, some elite men kept **concubines**. These female slaves provided sexual pleasure and also heirs, if necessary. Men chose some concubines for their individual characteristics, such as beauty or personality. In some cases a concubine gave the master affection or companionship that may have been absent from his politically motivated marriages. Whatever the personal benefits, numerous concubines (like multiple wives) displayed a man's wealth and power to other men.

Urban residence brought numerous advantages to royalty and aristocracy, including ready access to the best of goods and services. It also placed them in close contact with one another, which facilitated communication and reinforced their self-concept as a privileged stratum of society. The urban elite easily dominated all the key institutions of political society, and they were well defended against invaders or bandits who might disrupt their control.

The king ruled from a **palace**, a dwelling that exceeded others in size, complexity, and furnishings. Despite a customary preference for transmission of the office from the previous king to a specific relative, high-ranking nobles exercised some choice among the members of the royal family. Some of their decisions excluded incompetents while others had more to do with their own competition for power.

Most administrators above the community level were drawn from the hereditary aristocracy. The higher nobles supervised a bureaucracy consisting of officials with vari-

ous specialized administrative responsibilities. The state encouraged or required the nobility to marry endogamously, minimizing kinship ties between the classes. With no relatives among the urban commoners or the peasants, an aristocrat could exercise power unconstrained by family sentiments. This social separation contributed to the cultural gap between elite and commoners, a gap that the elite cultivated as a sign of their superiority. Beyond conspicuous consumption of material goods, aristocrats advertised their status with distinctive manners and speech such as the use of numerous honorific terms for one another. They preferred to exclude merchants from elite status because people in business had extensive contact with the lower classes, engaged in social manipulation to achieve success, and threatened the traditional power structure. On the other hand, because the city depended on successful trade, the wealthiest merchants exerted influence that could not be ignored.

The state tried to monopolize authority and power. It created a body of **law**, a formal code of behavior, and granted itself the only legitimate right to enforce the laws. The bureaucracy included a formal legal system in which officials at various levels settled disputes and judged criminal cases in accord with laws set forth or approved by the king.

States found many reasons for warfare with their neighbors. They prosecuted these wars with large and well-organized armies, led by professional officers, sometimes resulting in decisive victories. When a state conquered its neighbors and maintained economic and/or political control over them, it established an **empire**, and the victorious king became an emperor.

Traditional states tended to be flexible about relationships with their imperial possessions. They often left local rulers in place and ignored local customs that did not interfere with imperial goals. One barrier to uniformity was **ethnicity**. Many empires, especially the larger ones, incorporated peoples with diverse cultures. Thus language, religion, and other cultural features became markers of distinct ethnic groups within the same political system. Trade also brought very different peoples into contact and contributed to awareness of ethnicity.

Agricultural states varied greatly in size, spatial organization, and power structure, and this variation has produced controversy over classification and terminology. The term "city-state," for example, has been used to designate polities centered on a single urban area. One problem is that the term was originally applied to a political system in Classical Greece that differed greatly from the ones for which the term is now used. Another problem is that the centers of some such states hardly qualify for the category of "city" by any common criterion. To avoid both controversies, I propose the term **focal state** for any state that has only a single center of population and power, whether it be a city or town or ceremonial complex.

The term **regional state** can be used for a polity with more than one major center within a continuous area and under a single government. This kind of system is familiar as a nation today. Separate major centers tended to specialize in government, ritual, or commerce.

Finally, there is the problem of small units left behind when an empire or large state disintegrated. The ruler of such a residual polity behaved like a king, and his nobles preserved the endogamous class structure. In many cases, however, the polity controlled a territory no larger than that of a chiefdom and a population of fewer than ten thousand people. Probably most of these cases could be placed in the category of focal states as defined above. However, I propose the more precise designation of **remnant state** for polities known or postulated to be the result of a larger entity's disintegration.

Knowledge and Expression.   The **state religion** had a hierarchy of priests that was intertwined with the governmental bureaucracy and elite class. The formally trained priests voiced a theology that accorded divine authority to the ruler, and they conducted regular ceremonies that legitimized his status. High priests came from the same elite stratum of society as the political leaders.

This state religion coincided with the political boundaries of the state or empire. The government required observance by all people, although imperial authorities tolerated local customs that did not conflict with the official religion. Shamans were marginalized and viewed as a threat, perhaps more by the priests than by the political leaders.

Construction of monumental works of art and engineering, such as large statues and buildings, required expert planning as well as highly specialized skilled labor. Full-time specialists also developed complex forms of music, dance, drama, painting, and sculpture. They created and performed these works in service to

The ruins of a pyramidal platform illustrate the monumental work in art and engineering that characterized agricultural states; modern tourists demonstrate the scale (Mayan culture, Mexico).

the government or the nobility. The elite used elaborate art to awe the commoners and demonstrate their own superiority. Perhaps the most distinctive and influential invention of the agricultural state was writing. Its uses ranged from bureaucratic records to the recording of astronomical observations.

Formal education provided the elite with one means to control this complex society. They became literate and familiar with sacred literature. In doing so, they acquired moral and spiritual attributes that set them apart from common people. The elaborate forms of speech that they learned were patterned after written language. Used on special occasions, such as public worship and oratory, speech patterns that commoners could barely understand gave the elite an aura of mystery.

FORAGER BANDS

Examples:

Native Australians (also known as Aborigines), Native Americans such as Cree and Paiute

Foragers subsisted entirely on undomesticated plants and animals unless they obtained other foods in trade. The foragers described below were generalized in the sense that they relied on a wide range of wild foods with none having overwhelming importance. As to foragers who are *excluded* from the generalized category, the Plains Indians of North America provide a familiar example. They were specialized in that they relied on a single unusual resource, large herds of bison. Furthermore, this was made possible by the unusual practice of hunting on horseback.

Dependence on wild foods required low population densities, often well under one person per square mile, so generalized foragers accounted for only a small proportion of the people in the traditional world. Furthermore, foragers had been geographically marginalized by the spread of more numerous and powerful food-producing peoples. On the other hand, despite their limited impact on the world, foragers are significant as the bearers of a highly distinctive way of life. Some anthropologists think that recent foragers provide useful ideas about how our ancestors lived before the invention of farming.

Nomadic pursuit of varied wild plants and animals demanded a flexible social system, which foragers achieved through **band organization**: a relatively stable community (**regional band**) consisted of subgroups (**local bands**) that readily changed in composition and location. Forager society emphasized bilateral kinship, informal leadership, and egalitarian social relations. Shamans played a vital role as the only specialized religious practitioners.

and arrows. They often gathered and ate plant foods to sustain them while on the hunt.

Back in camp, women shared the results of gathering mainly with their own immediate families and perhaps a few other selected individuals. When men killed a sizable animal, they always gave portions to many people in the camp; those who initially received meat passed some on to others until everyone had obtained a portion. Those who received on one occasion would be givers on another. Everyone readily shared other possessions except for a few highly personal ornaments, tools, and items of clothing.

Based on extensive knowledge of the environment, people in a local band decided when to break camp and move elsewhere. In their travels they sometimes met a similar group and camped with them for a while. They knew each other because they all belonged to the same regional band, a community that occupied a large tract of land open to use by all its members.

Boundaries of the regional band were vague, and members were often hospitable to outsiders who asked permission to use the land or even to join the group. These interactions, like those among individuals, were

---

Key features:

- ► Undomesticated food sources
- ► Nomadic movement and low population density
- ► Emphasis on sharing and reciprocity
- ► Band organization
- ► Bilateral kinship
- ► Egalitarian social relations
- ► Informal leadership
- ► Dependence on shamans

Material Culture

People moved from place to place in local bands to exploit diverse resources that changed with the seasons. They spent most of their lives in temporary camps with a fluctuating number of residents. Most often there were four or five couples along with children of various ages and a few widowed elderly. Each couple and their children occupied a shelter of their own with any relative that they had taken in.

A woman gathered for her family, walking several miles in a day with a digging stick in hand and an infant on her back or hip. Women foraged together for company, often accompanied by their older daughters. Men went their own way to hunt larger animals with spears

A hunter represents one aspect of the foraging way of life; gathering by women was equally important (Native Australian culture).

based on reciprocity. Members of a regional band claimed primary rights to the use of their territory and occasionally attacked intruders, but nobody owned the land itself. Reciprocity coincided with a network of friendly regional bands, while exchanges with outsiders were more likely to involve bargaining. This was especially true if the outsiders belonged to a different culture, most often farmers.

Social Relations

Parents arranged first marriages for very young offspring, with the result that many adults divorced in order to choose subsequent partners for themselves. People looked for a prospective spouse beyond the relationship of first cousin, but they often married within the regional band. Almost all families were monogamous because it was difficult for a hunter to provide enough meat for extra wives and children. Even if women provided the bulk of staple foods, they expected their husbands and sons-in-law to augment the quantity and quality of the diet with meat.

Many newly married couples traveled with the husband's male relatives, but there were reasons for a man to choose residence with his wife's family. One was greater availability of resources where the woman's relatives lived. Another was to gain knowledge about more of the land to extend his future hunting potential. And some men, especially younger ones, sought to escape from the authority of fathers or older brothers.

After a child was born he or she quickly got used to a variety of people by experiencing caretakers other than the mother at an early age. Older children, especially girls, spent a lot of time on this task, thus freeing the mother for vital economic activities that could take her far from camp. Other than infant care, there were few serious chores for older children. The work required the strength and intelligence of adolescents and adults. Most of an older child's life consisted of play and socializing.

Most of the people in a regional band were connected with one another through bilateral kinship or marriage. Using these ties to pave the way, individuals and families readily moved from one local band to another. Sometimes they changed regional bands. In addition to considering resources, people joined those they preferred to be with or left those they disliked. The mobility of foragers made this an important way to resolve disputes. When many people left, a local band dissolved; new ones were formed just as easily.

The regional band sometimes persisted for generations or centuries because the constant circulation of its members made it a community. All the members knew one another personally and interacted regularly, even if not on a daily basis. Most or all members of the regional band aggregated in one place when resources permitted, sometimes for several months. These gatherings rein-

forced the existing ties of kinship and marriage and provided an opportunity to seek spouses. They were also exciting occasions for recreation and ceremonies.

All families in a band had equal access to resources and the means to obtain them. They also had equal rights to express opinions in public. Reception of those opinions, however, depended on the reputation gained by a person's achievements. Men had the greatest opportunity to build prestige by sharing meat from large kills. Although women spoke publicly, men had more influence and usually assumed leadership roles.

Facing a group task or problem, such as a cooperative hunt, people usually turned to situational leaders. People respected the elderly for their knowledge and the fact that they had survived. Sometimes a chieftain emerged as leader of a local or regional band because he displayed a variety of skills. Any form of leadership, however, depended on continuing effectiveness.

Warfare was sporadic and minimally organized, arising mostly from personal grievances. Trespass on regional band territory was usually a matter for those residents who were on the scene. Occasionally men from several local bands joined to raid another regional band in response to trespass or some other offense.

Knowledge and Expression

Animals pervaded religious and artistic expression in the forager community. The beings of myth and the spirits in daily life had animal characteristics. The hunter felt a sympathetic bond with the animals that he killed. Ritual life emphasized nature and spirits, the sources of subsistence and survival. People feared that supernatural powers would deny their needs if they offended nature by taking too much or not showing respect.

Shamans were the only individuals who had extensive expertise in dealing with the supernatural. In the fluid context of band organization, a successful shaman could exert a great deal of influence and even power. People owed him respect and gratitude for his services, and they feared his ability to do harm with his supernatural powers.

Foragers placed a value on mobility that went beyond recognizing the need to find food. Many traveled to visit friends, and some just went to satisfy curiosity or relieve boredom. Another powerful value was autonomy. People prized their independence and strongly resisted coercion. They believed that prestige should not lead a person to seek power.

Because reciprocity was a fundamental value, those who benefited knew that they were expected to be equally generous when they could. Though they sometimes grumbled, most people saw the practical sense in such behavior. Technology and the need for movement limited the amount of food that any family could store for themselves, so reciprocity was an investment.

Many people used sharp humor to curb pretentious or aggressive individuals. Much of this was directed toward ensuring that others would share. Despite a preference for avoiding confrontations, people made open accusations of stinginess in extreme cases. Gambling also furthered the circulation of goods.

The New World Domain

circa 1500 A.D.

The New World Cultural Domain, with one major exception, corresponded to the Americas in the geographic and the modern political sense. The exception is composed of the Arctic coast of Canada and the coastal regions of Alaska. The Inuit and Yupik (Eskimo) cultures in these places closely resembled the cultures of Siberia and will therefore be described later in connection with the Siberian cultural unit.

Within a few decades of Columbus's first landing in the Americas, native Caribbean cultures were severely disrupted, the Spanish conquered the empires of Nuclear America, and DeSoto ravaged the south-eastern part of North America. Most other Native American societies succumbed to the European invasion in another century or two. Therefore, this part of the book attempts to reconstruct the traditional cultures of the New World as they existed around 1500.

Northern
American
Zone

Southern
American
Zone

Nuclear
American
Zone

Subarctic
Area

Northwest
Coast Area

Great
Basin
Area

California
Area

Pueblo
Area

Eastern
Area

Mesoamerican
Area

Intermediate
Area

Supra-Amazon
Area

Subamazon
Area

Brazilian
Highland
Area

Tupinamban
Area

Andean
Area

Argentine
Area

NEW WORLD
CULTURAL
DOMAIN
c. 1500 A.D.

MODAL PATTERNS AMONG NEW WORLD CULTURES

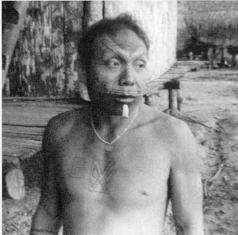

The native people of the Americas paid a great deal of attention to decorating hair and skin. Tattooing and body painting were probably as widespread as any other art forms in the New World, and early European visitors greatly praised the artistry of these applications (Feest 1993).

Every Zone of the New World contained a large number of farmers. Among their major crops were squashes, a large and diverse group that includes pumpkins, and a distinctive genus of beans *(Phaseolus)*. The most important crop was *Zea mays*. Of the nonscientific words for this plant, "maize" is preferable to "corn." The latter term, although used very specifically by modern North Americans, has denoted different staple grains in various other countries at various times (S. Coe 1994).

Hunting played a prominent role in Native American life, to the point of distinguishing the New World from the other Domains (Bourguignon and Greenbaum 1973). Farmers, as well as foragers, placed a high value on meat and accorded high prestige to hunters. The emphasis on hunting and the human relationship with animals shaped many aspects of religious belief and practice.

A large number of New World societies emphasized bilateral kinship and matrilineal descent. Presumably related to the limited influence of patrilineality, many aspects of New World economy and social relations add up to unusual status for women. They enjoyed more customary rights and greater autonomy and influence than women in many other parts of the world.

Two worldwide features of social life seem to have been especially important in the New World Domain. One is a person's name, which was accorded profound spiritual significance in the Americas. The other is grandparents, whose prominent role in both family and community is said to be one of the distinctive features of New World social life (Miller 1993).

"If there is one aspect unique to aboriginal religion in the Americas, it is the ritual use of tobacco" (Paper 1988:3). Many peoples cultivated tobacco, while others traded for it or found it wild. Used in various ways, tobacco provided numerous avenues for communication with supernatural beings. New World people prized personal contact with the supernatural.

Paired culture heroes played a large role in mythology. The anthropological literature often refers to these characters as twins, but in many stories they were no closer than half-brothers, and in some they were not kin at all. Shared adventures defined their relationship.

Key features:

▶ Elaborate adornment
▶ Importance of hunting
▶ Cultivation of maize
▶ Status of women
▶ Religious relationship with animals
▶ Ritual use of tobacco
▶ Personal contact with supernatural
▶ Paired culture heroes

Modal Patterns in the New World Culture

Material Culture

People often treated their hair as a malleable esthetic medium, shaping it or shaving parts of it to form a wide variety of patterns from one society to another and sometimes within a single community. Individuals further distinguished themselves with a variety of painted lines and geometric designs on face or body or both. Red and black

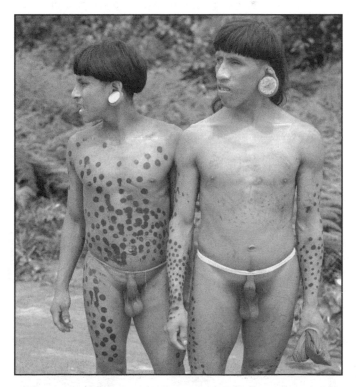

Modes of adornment in the New World Domain: shaped hair, ear ornaments, and body paint (Waorani culture, Southern American Zone).

predominated, augmented by flashes of white, yellow, and blue made from rare materials. Purely for beauty, both sexes plucked the sparse hair from their faces and bodies. Men especially prized feathers for decoration because they represented male spiritual concerns. Feathers came from birds, which were connected with the supernatural world above because they could fly into the sky.

People built substantial houses in the village where they lived during at least part of each year. Farmers lived in a village to stay near their fields, while foragers did it to take advantage of periodic concentrations of wild resources. Farmers as well as foragers left the village on expeditions to increase their opportunities to obtain wild plants and animals. When moving from camp to camp, people used simpler shelters such as windbreaks or tents.

Maize gave farmers an abundant and reliable food supply in many different environments. Numerous varieties gave people choices as to maturation time, resistance to plant diseases, and adaptation to climate. Maize also gave people a variety of flavors. Green maize, at the peak of its taste, was the occasion for ceremonies of joy and thanksgiving. If the ear was removed early, the stalks accumulated a sweet juice. In addition to calories and flavor, maize provided a substantial amount of protein. The particular proteins in maize and beans complemented each other as far as human needs were concerned. Together they provided all the protein required by working men, although not enough for nursing women or newly weaned babies.

A woman knew dozens of plants, perhaps a hundred or more, and how to use their various parts for food, seasoning, healing, dyes, and other purposes. She spent a great deal of time in food processing, grinding or pounding plant and animal foods to prepare them for cooking or storage. By pounding and drying meat, women produced jerky, which could be preserved. Most foods were boiled in a ceramic vessel over a fire. When pottery was not available, women practiced stone boiling with flammable containers made from materials such as bark or skin. The cook repeatedly placed heated stones in the container until eventually the water boiled.

To make pottery, a woman ground her clay into fine powder and mixed it with sand or some other gritty material to act as a temper that prevented the vessel from cracking when it was fired. The potter watered the mixture to make a workable paste from which she shaped the base. Then she built up the sides with a single coil of clay or layers of separate rolls. As she built the sides, the potter thinned and smoothed them. When the vessel was complete, she set it aside to dry. A woman decorated many of her products by cutting designs into them before firing. Then she placed them upside down on stones over hot coals and covered them with earth, shards from broken pottery, or other debris. This kept the heat even during the firing process, which took two or three hours.

After a woman met family obligations with the products of her labor, she had the right to control any surplus. Women also had substantial property and use rights to natural and human-made resources, including houses and farm plots. When women worked away from the household, they usually had no contact with men. Although many female tasks could be done alone, women usually worked together for company. If a task required cooperation, senior women directed it. These work relationships contributed to a female solidarity that could help in gender conflicts that might arise in the community.

Hunter draws bow (Cashinahua culture, Peru).

A man hunted mainly with his bow and arrows, often seeking deer. In some cases weighing as much as a person, a single deer provided a substantial amount of meat as well as hide and other materials for technological use. Smaller animals also fell to the hunter's arrows, and others were taken in traps and snares. When conditions were right, men organized cooperative hunts in which they either encircled their prey or drove them to an advantageous place for the kill. Men recruited women to act as beaters in some of these hunts, especially for smaller and less dangerous animals. People valued meat above fish and virtually any plant food, regardless of the role meat played in subsistence. Prestige accrued to those who acquired it and those who distributed it, usually men.

Despite occasional cooperation, as in some hunts, men and women usually did different kinds of work. Because of this, neither had the competence or the right to give orders in the other's sphere of activity. At most, a person could complain if his or her spouse failed to fulfill the family obligations associated with work.

The people in a community were self-sufficient, but men traded to obtain luxury or ritual items or the materials to make them. A community traded mainly with its neighbors, but some expeditions traveled hundreds of miles, and some objects ended up thousands of miles from their origin. Remote societies tended to inspire suspicion, and their differing ways made bargaining difficult. Most people were content to leave long-distance contacts in the hands of leaders who were knowledgeable about the necessary etiquette, prayers, or other procedures. Such men could gain wealth and prestige from trade.

Social Relations

A senior woman ran the household, and her husband said little about domestic work or childcare. A wife served her husband in certain ways, such as giving him meals, in return for the man's contributions to the household. She regarded such acts as part of the customary division of labor. Sexual obligation was also reciprocal. Before and after marriage, women took pleasure in sex if they could find men who were capable of providing it. A man who was overbearing or abusive ran the risk of losing his family. Divorce was relatively easy, women had as much right to it as men, and mothers retained custody of young children.

A prospective father provided substance for his child's body through repeated acts of sexual intercourse, but life and soul came from the supernatural world. The birth attendants often included a grandmother of the baby. She and her husband would play a large role in the child's life. Their status as grandparents also gave them a larger role in the life of the community.

A new mother remained in seclusion for some time following the birth and continued to observe taboos. After purifying baths for herself and the infant, they emerged, and she presented the baby to its family or to the whole community. In a significant ritual early in life, the child received a name. That name was a part of the self, an essential feature of the person's spiritual being. It was used by only a few people and perhaps known to only a few. In ordinary social settings a person was denoted by a separate public name if not by kinship terms. The first haircut was another important ceremonial occasion, usually attended by relatives beyond the nuclear family. People associated hair with life itself, and they used hair cutting to denote major transitions in life.

While a maturing girl learned her domestic responsibilities, a boy imitated his father's use of weapons for war and the hunt. Later on he received serious training in such skills and learned discipline to go with them. His father and other men subjected him to various ordeals, such as whippings or exposure to biting insects, which built up his strength, courage, and endurance.

A family was surrounded by relatives in the community. Ties of blood and marriage provided the basis for sharing and cooperation. When the community occasionally accepted refugees from violence or poverty elsewhere, the newcomers were incorporated into the system and treated like real kin. People expected community leaders to treat them with concern, kindness, and generosity. Personal qualities and achievements were always important in the selection of these individuals. Significant community actions required that leaders consult with at least some of their followers, a process that usually produced unanimity or at least acquiescence on the part of the unconvinced. In keeping with a general aversion to confrontation, most leaders gave advice and made requests rather than seeking obedience. Often they appealed to religious values or used mythological allegories in order to lend spiritual force to their goals.

When work allowed, people engaged in a variety of recreations. Men smoked tobacco in pipes just for pleasure, although the act could also have great religious significance in the context of ritual. In addition to wrestling, men competed in archery contests in which they shot for distance, speed, or accuracy. Both sexes enjoyed testing their strength and skill in a variety of other sports and games, including footraces and tug-of-war. People competed for distance in sliding a pole or some similar object along a smooth surface, and they tried to hit rolling targets with a pole or weapon. The ring-and-pin game emphasized dexterity: a thong connected the two objects, and the player held the pin and tried to flip the ring over it. In many team sports the players propelled a ball of some kind with sticks, hands, or some other part of the body.

Knowledge and Expression

After a hunter made a kill, he approached his prey with care because it had a soul much like that of a human being. The soul of an animal gave up the body willingly, or at least without anger, to a man who showed respect. He began by ritually offering food and drink to the soul and assuring it that the killing was necessary. When he butchered the animal, whether on the spot or back home, he did it with restraint and prayer. Finally, he buried the remains so that they would not be disturbed. As the hunter showed respect to his animal benefactor, he was mindful of more than a single soul. A game-master god governed and protected that animal and others like it. Some game masters controlled a single species while others ruled in some section of the natural world, such as sea, beach, or forest. Some of these gods were male, some female, and others neuter.

A man on the hunt encountered other manifestations of the supernatural. The animals and plants that he saw owed their lives to the same goddess that endowed women with fertility. A rumble of thunder reminded him that a powerful god lived in the sky. A splash in a body of water might have been caused by a fish or a supernatural being. The latter gave the man a slight tremor because the beings of the water were generally hostile and dangerous to humans. Foremost among them was the giant serpent that was also enemy to the thunder god and others in the sky. Stone, the oldest and most resistant of materials, connected this world with the ancient past. The man knew that many rocks were supernatural beings or contained them. A boulder could represent a god and a mountain was undoubtedly divine.

Men prized personal contact with supernatural beings and searched for ways to achieve it. They secluded themselves from other humans, sometimes going to strange and frightening places. They subjected themselves to deprivation or exposure or pain. Where such things were available, men took substances that altered their consciousness. Some women used similar means to seek supernatural experience, but this was less common. Shamans distinguished themselves from other men by having closer and more frequent contacts with the supernatural. Though men smoked tobacco in social settings for sheer pleasure, they also used it in religion. Because smoke attracted supernatural beings, it facilitated communication with them. In addition, when smoke was blown or fanned across the body, it could ease fatigue, promote healing, or imbue the recipient with spirituality.

A dance mask represents Octopus Hunter, a mythological figure (Kwakiutl culture, North America).

People thought witches in other communities or ethnic groups to be the strongest. However, competition within the community was a frequent source of witchcraft motivations, suspicions, and accusations. People believed that initiation into the realm of supernatural evil required the cannibalistic sacrifice of a close relative. Victims and their supporters often tried to kill witches by supernatural means and sometimes resorted to physical execution.

Communities held ceremonies in which they thanked gods and spirits for blessings received or tried to borrow their power for human purposes. Some celebrants danced in masks and costumes to represent or identify with the supernaturals that they honored and petitioned. Ceremonies often alluded to mythology and especially to the culture heroes who shaped the world. Many culture heroes traveled with a sibling or another individual. These companions usually had contrasting personalities and sometimes worked at cross-purposes. Many culture heroes, especially obstructive companions, displayed trickster characteristics to varying degrees.

Storytellers recited some of the myths in more ordinary circumstances and told many other stories as well. One common tale, which seemed to reflect family tensions, was that of the bird nester. He was a boy who went with a close relative to gather bird eggs. After the boy had climbed a tall tree or cliff, his relative, because of a conflict between them, left him stranded. A supernatural being rescued the boy, who eventually took revenge on his relative.

In one of the most common trickster tales, the twisted protagonist fell in love with his daughter. Telling her to marry a certain stranger after he was gone, the trickster faked his own death. Then, playing the role of the stranger, he married his daughter. The sexual misadventure of Moon also reminded people about the evil of incest. Moon repeatedly went to his sister in profound darkness, so she had no idea who her lover was. During one of these encounters he received marks on his face that told his sister and everyone else what he had done. Now he displays his shame in the sky every night.

When people looked at the moon and the other bodies that glowed in the black night skies, they were sometimes reminded of beings who lived on earth during mythical times. However, the heavens also told them about more immediate and practical matters. The appearance of the Pleiades, for example, marked the changing of the seasons, which foretold changes in the availability of food. The relationship between subsistence and the seasons led observers to emphasize events on the horizon, such as the point of sunrise, and many built structures on the ground that aligned with significant points on the horizon. People also observed and interpreted the world immediately around them. Instead of classifying by physical form, they emphasized associations among living things and the usefulness of those things to human beings. They paid attention to stable similarities but also attached significance to the unusual and the changeable because these were signs of supernatural power.

A Closer Look

Knowledge of Plants

When humans came to the New World, they brought with them generalized techniques for hunting, fishing, and processing animal foods that would continue to serve them well (Driver 1969). In many cases they continued to pursue the same kinds of animals, such as deer and bear. Even new animals required few changes. Small animals of new species, for example, could still be taken in traps and snares. It may have been necessary to learn the habits of a few large species that were unfamiliar (e.g., tapirs in South America), but the old techniques for butchering and hide processing still applied.

It was the vast number of plants unique to the Americas that required a large body of new knowledge (Kidwell 1993). Foragers began the collection of these plants for food, technology, and medicinal purposes. Later in New World history farmers domesticated many of them. Ultimately, the people of this Domain learned to exploit over one thousand indigenous plant species. Since women were the main plant gatherers in all societies and the primary cultivators in many farming societies, they may have been responsible for this explosion of knowledge.

Witchcraft

Since this book is mainly about what distinguishes each cultural unit from others, it is important to note the treatment of New World witchcraft beliefs by Miller (1993). He describes a situation that is at variance with the rest of the world (compare with the discussion in chapter 2). He claims that witches were "tolerated" and even "accepted" as reminders of the "unpleasant consequences" of selfishness. This tolerance might have been easier because witches "always belonged to distant groups." Witches were killed only during times of great stress such as famine in order to "reset the balance of the world" (Miller 1993:327).

However, Walker (1989) reached different conclusions that are more in accord with the worldwide pattern. He found that Native Americans feared witchcraft, from within their communities as well as outside. They usually considered witches subject to execution, even if they did not act on it. Walker's view, which I find more convincing, is based on his edited volume that contains accounts by experts on many different parts of the native New World.

NORTHERN AMERICAN ZONE

5

Areas:

- Eastern
- Northwest Coast
- Subarctic
- Great Basin
- California
- Pueblo

Northern American Zone with Areas and Regions

Alaskan Region

Northwest Coast Area

Subarctic Area

Canadian Region

Coast-Plateau Region

Great Basin Area

California Area

Prairie Region

Iroquoian Region

Eastern Area

Western Pueblo Region

Mississippian Region

Coastal Algonkian Region

Pueblo Area

O'odham Region

Rio Grande Pueblo Region

Northeast Mexico

Previous page   Carving representing the supernatural power of the bear in Northern American belief (Northwest Coast culture).

OVERVIEW OF THE ZONE

Examples:

Cree, Iroquois, Cherokee,
Hopi, Pima, Paiute, Nootka

The Northern American cultural zone largely coincided with the geographic continent of North America, including the arid northern section of Mexico. However, as noted previously, the Eskimo cultures will be described later in connection with the closely related cultures of Siberia (see "Circumpolar Zone").

Native Northern America was distinguished from the rest of the world by the percentage of societies that depended on foraging (Bourguignon and Greenbaum 1973). Hunting in particular was practiced everywhere and dominated subsistence on much of the continent (Driver 1969). Meat provided many people with substantial quantities of calories and other nutrients, and it was highly valued by farmers as well as foragers. The predominant deer in the roster of game was the white-tailed species *(Odocoileus virginianus)*, which stood about three feet high at the shoulder and weighed between 200 and 300 pounds. In the far west it was replaced by the similar mule deer *(O. hemionus)*. The widely hunted black bear *(Ursus americanus)*, actually varying in color from black to cinnamon brown, weighed from 200 to 500 pounds. Plant gathering and fishing varied in significance because of the diverse environments. Fishing could be more pro-

White-tailed deer, the primary game animal of the Northern American Zone.

ductive per acre than either gathering or hunting but was important in less than half the Zone (Driver 1969).

According to Albers (1989), gender relations in native Northern America reflected a degree of "complementarity" not found in many other parts of the world. When the sexes interacted, it was usually in terms of relative equality and reciprocity. The status of Northern Zone women was more than a de facto condition or a grudging acknowledgment by men that women were important. Women received overt respect, and their opinions and suggestions were "highly regarded" (Garbarino and Sasso 1994). They privately influenced their husbands and male relatives, as did women in most of the world, but they also affected public debate. The specific rights of women were numerous, well defined, and important. Men apparently regarded the spiritual power of reproduction as benign even though potentially dangerous. The great power attributed to women resulted in more extensive menstrual restrictions than in most other parts of the world (Frayser 1985).

Many communities contained one or more anatomically normal men who assumed some of the occupations, behavior, and dress of the opposite sex. These individuals, who often played important roles in society, have been termed "berdaches." The word itself is controversial, but I agree with those who consider it the best term available for the phenomenon (see "A Closer Look" for discussion).

The majority of games in Northern America were characterized by the unusual combination of chance and physical skill (Bourguignon and Greenbaum 1973). Gambling was an "integral part" of nearly all games and sports (Vennum 1994) and had economic, social, and spiritual significance (Gabriel 1996).

While tobacco was one among a number of sacred plants elsewhere in the New World, it had no peer in Northern America (Paper 1988). Tobacco was grown separately from food crops and raised by some peoples who had no other crops at all. Northern Americans used tobacco primarily to establish communication with supernatural beings by offering it in formal rituals. Northern Zone culture acknowledged some evil among supernatural beings but regarded most of them as readily helpful to humans if treated properly. This view was epitomized by the idea of the guardian spirit, a lifelong protector. People considered themselves to be part of a "moral order" that unified them with all other living things, including supernaturals, and with the physical features of the universe (Miller 1993).

In the realm of oral literature "the popularity of trickster tales (was) the most characteristic feature" of the Northern Zone (Garbarino and Sasso 1994:373). Trickster gods appeared in myths, but lesser tricksters were especially prominent in secular stories. The more distinctive earth diver character, who took different physical forms in different cultures, played an important role in creation stories.

Key features:

- ▶ Importance of hunting
- ▶ Gender complementarity
- ▶ Extensive menstrual restrictions
- ▶ Alternative genders ("berdaches")
- ▶ Games combining chance and skill
- ▶ Importance of gambling
- ▶ Benevolent supernaturals, especially guardian spirits
- ▶ Spiritual unity of all life
- ▶ Tobacco offerings
- ▶ Predominance of trickster tales
- ▶ Earth diver

Modal Patterns in Northern American Culture

Material Culture

In response to environmental diversity, Northern American dwellings varied more than in the other New World Zones. We can say that a framework of poles was the modal pattern, but size and covering varied a great deal. In moderate weather men worked in loincloths made of deer or rabbit skin, while women covered themselves with aprons, skirts, or dresses of the same materials. Many men and women kept their hair long, often in braids, dressed it with bear fat, augmented it with animal hair, and enhanced it with feathers and down. They also wore headbands, along with ornaments made from a variety of stones and from organic materials such as shell, bone, and claws. In the cold of night or winter men and women swathed themselves in deerskin robes and wore leather footgear.

When not involved with getting or preparing food, a woman spent many hours dressing the animal hides needed for clothing and blankets. First she stretched a skin on a frame or with stakes in the ground and then scraped away all the fat and flesh. Then she rubbed the skin with a paste made from the mashed brain of the animal. To soften the treated hide, the woman repeatedly pulled it across a tree trunk, pole, or taut rope. In some cases she smoked the skin to obtain a tan or golden-brown color. A person who wanted to make rawhide left the stretched animal skin to dry for several days without curing or softening it. The tough and durable material

that resulted was suitable for making containers and had many other technological uses.

Men also worked with animal products, especially bone and horn. Both materials required heating or boiling to eliminate fatty deposits. After that, a man placed bones in the sun to dry and bleach until they were suitable for carving into beads, pendants, or combs. Boiling softened horn so that a man could manipulate its shape, usually to make utensils such as spoons, cups, and ladles. After the new objects cooled and hardened, the artisan polished them with sand or sandstone and sometimes rubbed them with fat or oil to make them shine.

Men made stone tools that included knives, axes, and projectile points. After chipping a flake with another stone, the toolmaker refined his product with a softer hammer of bone, antler, or wood. Finally, he polished many of his artifacts by rubbing them with moist sand held with a piece of leather or a clump of plant fiber. If sand were not readily available, he used an abrasive rock such as sandstone or pumice.

The association of subsistence tasks and other activities with gender was not rigid. A person who gained a competence usually associated with the opposite sex was not stigmatized. In fact, there was relatively equal prestige for men or women who excelled in any kind of task. Women's rights to material property were on a par with those of men, and a woman's domestic authority gave her control of food and other resources brought into the household by men. Controlling the products of her own labor, a woman had opportunities to accumulate whatever her society acknowledged as wealth.

Personal property included intangible items, especially those connected with ritual life, such as names, titles, songs, dances, magic rituals, myths, and group memberships. Ownership of both material and intangible property included the right to give away, sell, or destroy the possession. Children also had rights of ownership to at least some possessions.

Social Relations

People married with little or no ceremony, marking the union mainly with economic exchange. The groom's family gave bridewealth, and the bride's family reciprocated with substantial gifts, sometimes of comparable value. In addition to bridewealth the young man provided some bride service. The main point of exchange seems to have been to cement the alliance between families rather than to establish control over the wife.

Through repeated intercourse in marriage, the husband provided bone and other hard substances for the creation of a child. The mother contributed soft parts of the body, such as flesh and blood. Life, breath, and thought came from the spirits. Among other taboos, the expectant mother restricted her consumption of water and ate little or no meat so as not to offend game animals.

Parents named many babies after distinguished persons in the hope that they would acquire the desirable traits of those adults. An infant spent most of its time in a cradleboard that was a convenience for the working mother. She could place the apparatus on its back, stand it upright, or hang it in a tree. Adults tried to control babies with love, praise, and cajolery because they believed that ill treatment could affect the baby's personality and health or even cause death. They also believed that the baby was still close to the spirits that were partly responsible for its creation.

Adults routinely ridiculed older children for misbehavior and meted out some physical punishment. Parents preferred not to do such things to their own children, so they often enlisted other relatives. In many cases the discipliners disguised themselves as supernatural beings, which dissociated them from the harsh treatment and heightened the impact on the children.

People believed that the behavior of boys and girls around the time of puberty affected the course of their entire lives, and so ritual controls were important. A girl was secluded in a separate hut during her first menses. She received instruction about menstruation itself and performed tasks to demonstrate her motivation to work as an adult. Older women made the girl's seclusion less tedious by joining her for intervals of song and dance. There was also the anticipation of a community feast that celebrated her new fertility when the isolation ended.

A woman went back into seclusion during every menstrual period and for most or all of each pregnancy. While in the hut she observed various restrictions on her behavior, such as scratching only with a stick, avoiding meat, and not weaving baskets. Violation of these prohibitions could cause her physical damage. While the woman was secluded, her husband should not hunt, fish, gamble, or dance. The spiritual power of her reproductive state could endanger men and overwhelm the powers necessary for other activities such as shamanism and hunting. A woman sometimes manipulated her ritual status for personal purposes. For example, she might pretend to be menstruating if she did not want her husband to go to war. Believing that this supernaturally diminished his chances for success, the man would probably stay home.

The social maturation of a boy was closely linked to achievements such as the first kill of an important prey animal. In early adolescence he joined others in a collective religious initiation. Older men prepared the boys for marriage and reminded them that fathering children was a primary responsibility to society. Initiated status for both sexes, but especially for boys, brought the lifting of dietary taboos, the opportunity to wear new symbols, and freedom from adult lectures.

New names symbolized the maturation process. The most common occasions for the bestowal of new names were puberty or initiation ceremonies, success in war or the hunt, and the attainment of supernatural power. Because such names symbolized status, honor, and achievement, their acquisition was marked by solemn rituals, and they were held to be private and even sacred. Nicknames used in daily life were casually acquired and discarded because they were just a convenience and had nothing to do with true identity or self-concept. Thus they were often trivial, ridiculous, or even derogatory.

Adolescents entered a social world in which sex was considered a natural and desirable part of life, perhaps even a gift from the gods. Though good in itself, sex diminished certain male powers, so men often abstained in connection with hunting, war, and ritual. People idealized cooperation and the avoidance of conflict within the community. A person who behaved properly was rewarded with praise, prestige, and gifts. Most deviant acts brought gossip or open ridicule rather than physical retaliation. Only the most extreme provocation justified killing an offender.

Many communities contained one or more berdaches, men who did women's work and assumed some female characteristics such as hairstyle or speech patterns. People regarded berdaches as a third gender, mingling characteristics of the other two. They often provided a sexual outlet for young men and for some married men when their wives were unavailable because of reproductive or other taboos. However, many berdaches also had intercourse with women, and some may have been exclusively heterosexual. Despite their diverse sex lives, berdaches never had sex with one another.

Though often clad in at least some women's garments, many berdaches changed to suit occasions, as when donning male dress to accompany hunting and war

The hand game: a guessing game combining acuity and luck, a favorite pastime throughout Northern America (Paiute culture).

parties. Some of them participated in battle and were noted for their courage. They often competed for prestige and wealth in nonmasculine pursuits such as high-quality craft work. They were generally good with children, especially in educating them. As a result, a berdache often played a central role in his family. While berdaches sometimes adopted children, they never assumed the care of infants.

Although women sometimes used their social or ritual influence to deter men from war, they often supported and encouraged it. A wife prepared rations for a husband to carry on an expedition of any length. Sometimes a few women accompanied a war party to continue this kind of support. Those who stayed behind always prayed or performed magic for the safety and success of their men. Women occasionally engaged in combat, and men admired them when they were successful. Any woman might fight in self-defense when surprised by an attack, but some joined war parties to avenge a fallen husband or relative, and a few went to satisfy a personal desire for the experience.

Amidst work and conflict people found or made opportunities for pleasure. Along with sports and games of skill, men enjoyed games based on pure chance. In many of these they threw marked sticks or other objects to generate random scores. Competitive guessing games were also popular. In the hand game a player hid an object in one hand, and the opponent had to guess which one. People played as individuals or on teams. Women played most of the games and sports. One of their favorites, shinny, was a form of field hockey in which two teams used sticks to propel a ball toward goalposts. Men and women gambled on games whether they were participants or spectators. Sometimes people wagered large amounts of material wealth or even personal services. Whatever the stakes, losers cultivated a dispassionate demeanor.

Women playing shinny, a widely popular sport in Northern America (Dakota culture).

Knowledge and Expression

Humans, animals, plants, and supernatural beings were all "people" in the sense that they all had thoughts and emotions and that they organized themselves into social groups based on gender, age, and ability. Supernaturals and animals could change into various shapes, which included human forms. Human people played a central role in the system, but as mediators with a ritual obligation to contribute to harmony in the universe rather than try to dominate it. The relationship of humans, animals, and plants to the land had a spiritual dimension because the features of the physical environment were inhabited by supernatural beings. Earth itself was a god, usually considered female because it was a source of birth and nurture. Plants came from her surface, game animals emerged from her body, and water ran in her veins.

Dogs played an ambiguous role in this harmonious universe. They had a disturbing ambiguity, residing with humans and yet obviously the close kin of wolves and coyotes. Dogs seemed almost human and yet departed from the human pattern in striking ways. People appreciated dogs as hunters and protectors but associated them with promiscuity and filth. They valued good hunting dogs, sometimes to the point of giving them a formal burial after death, but they often neglected or abused ordinary dogs.

A person connected almost every thought and act with the supernatural because most supernatural beings, other than the malevolent water creatures, willingly helped humans in everyday life and in emergencies. Every man hoped to establish a lifelong personal connection with a particular spirit or lesser god. Although supernaturals initiated a few of these contacts, a man ordinarily had to seek the experience in a vision quest. He isolated himself and fasted and prayed. If a being found him acceptable and took pity on his efforts, it appeared and spoke. Most beings showed themselves in animal form, but some manifested themselves as other natural objects.

The being who responded to a vision quest became the supplicant's personal protector and provided him with one or more supernatural powers. Some men became outstanding hunters or warriors and some received the ability to cure particular sicknesses or injuries. Each man learned symbols that represented the power granted to him. These objects or songs or designs would help him to use his supernatural abilities in the everyday world.

Some individuals received an unusual creative capacity from a vision or from favor shown by spirits at birth. They had special skill or knowledge of particular forms or access to necessary materials. Such abilities often enhanced religious observances. People painted or otherwise decorated ceremonial objects to provide them with spiritual qualities. They played music for the power that it generated and, when music was performed well, they called it "good" rather than "beautiful."

A few men received the great privilege of visiting a home of animal souls during a dream or vision. This was the hidden village or camp where the souls of a particular species lived together in a humanlike society and displayed a humanlike form. They assumed their animal form only when they went into the ordinary world to make their bodies available to hunters. In the animal home a visitor might meet the game master, a god who resembled the ordinary animal form but was larger and had special markings. A man could come away from such a visit with unusual powers.

Other gods were less accessible to individuals, but they watched over human beings in general. Sun and Earth provided the means of human life every day. The thunderbirds made the sounds of the storm by flapping their giant wings while lightning flashed from their eyes. They fought the evil water serpents, and some sacrificed their lives in the battle. The God above all others, remote in the sky or in some more abstract upper world, surveyed contemporary events with minimum involvement. To many who thought about this sexless being, God was like an impersonal universal force.

People sometimes prayed to God, but they devoted little or no ritual to it. For the other great deities they held major community ceremonies. These festivals, conducted by religious specialists, marked the beginning or the end of the subsistence year and were devoted to the renewal of the world and of life. Communal ceremonies emphasized gratitude for well-being in general and food in particular. Communities and families made offerings of the first products of the year from all kinds of subsistence activities. Participants also used the occasion to make personal prayers for the cure of disease and future good health.

People sometimes called on berdaches to assist them in their spiritual pursuits, both domestic and communal. The spirits must have taken extra care to create such special persons and so must be unusually close to them. The ceremonial activity of berdaches was both extensive and intense; some berdaches may have been endowed with special supernatural powers, including shamanism. When they accompanied hunting and war parties, it was usually for spiritual purposes.

There were many polarities in the universe, such as sky and earth, plant and animal, water and fire. Mediators existed for all such polarities, and berdaches were the mediators for male and female. They were natural go-betweens in disputes between men and women. Even more important, the male–female distinction was of great religious significance, and so berdaches were also mediators between flesh and spirit, combining the spiritual powers of male and female. The berdache was a reminder of the kinship among various kinds of humans, other kinds of "people," and the universe that they all inhabited.

Any person who approached the supernatural, whether as an individual or as part of a group, engaged in

A berdache posing in women's clothing (Zuni culture).

certain basic preparations and ritual procedures. Purification was fundamental. People often bathed for the purpose or used an emetic, a substance that caused vomiting. The most important means of purification was the sweat lodge, a special structure that accommodated one or two individuals. Steam was produced inside by sprinkling water on stones that had been heated in a shallow fire pit; the resultant perspiration removed polluting influences from the body. People often used the sweat lodge on nonritual occasions to promote general health. The sweat lodge connected humans with the universe around them: the structure itself represented the cardinal directions by its orientation with the entrance to the east and by the use of poles in multiples of four. The purifying ritual frequently concluded with the incantation "All my relations," acknowledging the other kinds of people in the universe.

Ritual use of sacred objects also made the supernatural more accessible. Most of these objects represented the power and mystery of nature, and the eagle and the bear were particularly important sources. People used the bones and claws of both animals in their rituals but considered the feathers and down of the eagle to be of the greatest significance. Sacred objects were often kept in a "medicine" bundle, prized as a locus of supernatural power (which is the meaning of the term "medicine" in this context). Some bundles belonged to individuals and others to groups.

People offered tobacco to the supernaturals in various ways. They placed it near sacred features such as trees and rocks. They directed it to particular beings by throwing it into the air or onto water or by placing it on the ground. Sometimes tobacco was burned like incense, in a fire or on hot coals. More often it was ingested because people recognized the stimulation that it provided. Most importantly people produced smoke, which the supernaturals loved but could not make for themselves. It pleased them when humans offered smoke and made them more receptive to human requests.

When a man sang, as he did in any ritual, he created the sound deep in a tightened throat. The song had a simple melody and irregular rhythms like those of speech. When men sang together in a communal ceremony, they all followed the same melody without harmonizing. The singers or other participants accompanied the vocal performance with complex rhythms from various kinds of drums and rattles.

Women sang in an open-throated manner, considered to be more feminine. They also danced differently and apart from the men, using a restrained style with small steps and arms close to the body. Women never took the same roles as men in public rituals, and in some cases they were excluded from the ceremonies themselves. In private life women used the sweat lodge less often than men and never along with them. Women were also less likely to seek a supernatural guardian.

Limits on a woman's ritual life followed from her intrinsic supernatural power, which was capable of disrupting and overwhelming the religious efforts of men. While men sought spiritual guardians, organized rituals, and tried to purify themselves in the sweathouse, women carried supernatural powers within themselves because they were the bearers of life. Thus women were restricted in public ceremonies for the same reason that they were secluded during menstrual periods and pregnancies. Everyone regarded female spirituality as good for the community, but only if handled properly and with care. Despite the restrictions, women played important roles in a wide variety of ceremonies, especially those associated with food and health. Life depended on the pairing of male and female powers, just as God encompassed both male and female characteristics. The lesser gods, so important in daily life, included many with female names and attributes.

In ceremonies that referred to the beginning of things, someone mentioned or recited the myth of the earth diver. When nothing existed but the primordial ocean, supernatural animal beings took turns diving to the bottom in search of something more. Finally one of them came up, dead or nearly so, with a bit of mud. Another of the animal beings expanded it, creating the earth.

People usually told stories about tricksters in more secular settings, such as an evening gathering around the fire. The trickster took the form of a small mammal, such as a coyote or a hare. He was involved in some mythological events, most notably making death an irrevocable part of human existence. However, most of the trickster's storied exploits were petty deceits that had no effect on the world except to damage himself and those around him. In addition to a great deal of entertainment, these tales gave people emotional relief from social frustrations and deflated the pompous individuals among them. The stories also provided an oblique way to communicate about sex, selfishness, and other issues that people considered sensitive.

When not laughing at a trickster, people often heard the tale of the bird nester. He was a young man who was interested in the same women as his father. To get him out of the way, the father stranded him when he climbed up to a bird's nest to get eggs. He was saved by another and got revenge. A more tragic story recounted the fate of a man who tried to bring his beloved wife back from the land of the dead. After an arduous journey, he found her and received permission to bring her back to the living if he obeyed several taboos. Unable to do so, he lost her forever. In the hands of some tellers, this explained how death became a permanent condition during mythic times.

Despite careful attention to ritual obligations, men and women sometimes fell ill. In some villages the sufferer could find a person, most often a man, who had received supernatural power to cure that particular condition. Alternatively, there were persons who offered herbal cures, sometimes accompanied by magic and prayer. Women seemed to have more knowledge than men in this field. However, if the illness were the result of soul loss, there was no recourse but a full-fledged shaman. Whatever conditions other people might cure, only a real shaman could send out his own soul to recover that of another person.

When life ended, the soul tried to reach the place of the dead by traversing the Milky Way. Those killed by childbirth, lightning, or drowning could expect a better afterlife than other people. Souls of those who did wrong might perish on the way to the next world or remain on earth as ghosts. Many people believed that a soul could be reincarnated on earth, but their ideas about how and why this occurred were vague. Sometimes people in the same village held contradictory views on the matter.

A Closer Look

Berdaches

The word "berdache" is said to be misleading and prejudicial (Jacobs, Thomas, and Lang, eds. 1997). Unfortunately, critics have not provided an alternative that is applicable to the traditional culture of the Northern American Zone as a whole. Words from native languages are too specific while the new phrase "two-spirit people" lumps together biological inclinations and a variety of culturally prescribed roles. "Berdache" remains the best general term for the traditional, culturally defined roles (Roscoe 1998).

No single explanation covers every manifestation of the phenomenon. Berdaches have been characterized as averse to an aggressive male way of life. However, some were violent people while some nonberdaches did not fight. Furthermore, berdaches existed in some peaceful cultures and not in some of the most warlike (Callender and Kochems 1993; Williams 1986). The use of women's

clothing suggests transvestism, but it may have been variety of dress that really distinguished berdaches. In one culture, for example, they dressed like old men regardless of their real age (Williams 1986). "Institutionalized homosexuality" fails to take account of the complexities in berdache sex lives and the tolerance for sexual diversity in the lives of ordinary people (Williams 1986). One of the more common features of berdaches is that they were spiritual people; if so, the assumption of feminine traits may have symbolized the assimilation of female supernatural power.

EASTERN AREA

Examples:

Massachusett, Iroquois, Cherokee, Natchez, Powhatan, Illinois

The Eastern Area encompassed the Mississippi River Valley and extended from there to the Atlantic Coast. Its northern and southern borders approximated those of the United States today. A northeastern nucleus of lush temperate forests faded into prairie grassland toward the west and into coastal lowlands in the east and south. The rainfall of approximately forty inches per year, well distributed across the seasons, supported about 130 species of deciduous trees. Watered by large rivers with numerous tributaries and streams, the East provided its human population with an abundance of plant and animal resources.

Eastern peoples cultivated the standard New World staples: maize, beans, and squashes. Wherever possible, they planted in soft valley soil that was easy to work and had its fertility renewed by silt from the river. Those who lacked this resource practiced more conventional slash-and-burn horticulture in the forests.

Eastern society was distinguished from most other Northern American Areas (and most of the world) by the widespread incidence of well-defined matrilineal descent groups and permanent matrilocal residence. Political leadership was marked by dual organization: One leader and/or faction took primary responsibility for internal matters and another for war.

Unlike others on the continent, Eastern Area people valued warfare for its own sake and it pervaded their lives. Some referred to it as their "beloved occupation" (Hudson 1976). Elaborate torture of prisoners further dis-

tinguished Easterners from other Northern Americans (Driver 1969). The signature game of the Eastern Area, lacrosse, was often called "little war" or "younger brother of war" (Vennum 1994).

When Easterners offered smoke to the gods and spirits, they used a two-piece pipe associated with highly formal ritual and complex symbolism. Their concern with the supernatural included two powerful gods, one good and one evil. Although reminiscent of some companion culture heroes elsewhere, these Eastern gods were active in the affairs of living humans rather than existing only in myths.

Key features:

▶ Horticulture
▶ Matrilineal and matrilocal
▶ Duality in political organization
▶ High value on war
▶ Torture of war captives
▶ Lacrosse
▶ Good and evil gods
▶ Sacred pipe

Modal Patterns in Eastern Culture

Material Culture

Green forest shaded the large village on one side, and a sparkling river flowed past it on the other. The circular stockade of upright logs enclosed more than a hundred brown rectangular houses. Patches of green among them marked the gardens. Outside the wall, stalks of maize lined the bank of the river for a mile on each side.

Along the river and its tributaries, many smaller villages dotted the land between the large ones. The unfortified smaller villages consisted of scattered houses that varied greatly in number, some fewer than ten and some many more. A cleared area separated each community from the forest. Wood and brush had fed the household fires, and the space that resulted made a surprise attack a little more difficult.

Each house in the village was at least twenty feet long. To build one, men rooted saplings in parallel rows and then joined the saplings in each row with horizontal crosspieces. They stood on the crosspieces at each level to make the next level until their weight bent the saplings together at the top. They lashed them together and then covered the structure with bark or reed mats, overlapping the units to shed the rain. Inside they built foot-high platforms along the walls to sleep above the damp and the fleas. A sleeper found comfort with mats or hides for a mattress, hide blankets, and a wooden pillow. On shelves above, the family kept most of its ceramic vessels and the eating utensils made from wood and bark.

As individuals and through matrilineal groups, women owned houses along with gardens and farm plots, organized farm labor, and determined the distribution of much of the produce. To cultivate the fields, a woman used her digging stick and a hoe with a blade made from wood, flint, or an animal's shoulder bone. She planted maize seeds in clusters. When the maize began to grow, the farmer piled dirt into a hill around each cluster of stalks and planted beans in the mounds. Sometimes she added squashes so that the maize stalks

supported their vines. In the gardens by their houses women grew sunflowers for the oil from their seeds and gourds to make containers that were lighter and more durable than pottery. They also gathered wild plants, including a variety of berries.

Women used maize to make soup, the favorite food, and also succotash, hominy, cakes, and bread. They made beverages from parched maize, berries, sunflower seeds, and sassafras roots. If there was a scheduled meal, it was eaten in the morning. Men ate before women. A visitor always received a meal and so did any person who had just finished work. Otherwise, people snacked whenever they were hungry.

Men left the village for long expeditions at various points throughout the year to fish, hunt, trade, and make war. They hunted frequently throughout the winter when snow made animal tracks easier to find and slowed the larger animals down. Hunters especially sought white-tailed deer for meat, cooperating to take a large number when conditions were suitable. They also prized the black bear, more for its fat than its meat. People used the oil for cooking and to rub on their bodies as insulation against cold and as a base for paint. In the early spring men took advantage of large numbers of fish swimming up the rivers to spawn. At other times some men went on long trips by land or canoe to trade. One of the most prized materials was copper for ornaments.

A farm plot lasted an average of about ten years until it had to be left fallow. When all the nearby land was exhausted, along with the firewood, and the houses were seriously deteriorating, the village would move. This occurred at intervals of ten to twenty years. Most shifts were probably limited to a few miles.

The clothing and birchbark canoes in this village scene represent the temperate adaptations of the Eastern Area. The huts are typical of the Algonkians who occupied the east coast. The baby in the cradleboard (front, right) illustrates a modal pattern of the Northern American Zone.

Social Relations

A young man with a bride in mind had a choice as to how to proceed. He could ask one of his relatives to propose the match to the other family, or he could try to attract the girl first so that she could influence her family. In either case there would be a negotiation process. At some point, if the young man proved worthy, the girl's family accepted the couple's sexual relationship. Eventually, if all went well, a wedding took place. It began with a private exchange of gifts between the spouses and between their families, symbolizing the reciprocal nature of the marriage. Then the families publicly announced the new status of their offspring with a feast for the whole community. The young couple expected a lasting monogamous relationship, perhaps for a lifetime. An ordinary man would take another wife only if he inherited her from a male relative, though a few prominent men took extra wives to help them with their community duties or ambitions. If either event took place, the original wife was considered first among equals.

A new husband went to live with his in-laws to do bride service, which often ended in permanent matrilocal residence. Since a man spent much of his time away from home, children grew up under the influence of their mothers and matrilineal relatives. If praise or shame failed to control the behavior of children, the withdrawal of maternal affection had a powerful effect.

Adolescent girls were quickly incorporated into the highly organized female kinship group. Boys sought special friendships with each other to provide mutual support in adulthood. Boys who had potential for political or religious leadership underwent a special, arduous initiation process in which they were ritually killed and then resurrected as adults without childish thoughts.

Every village had a chieftain who took responsibility for peaceful matters such as relations within the community, welcoming visitors, and organizing trade. Eligibility for the position of civil chieftain came from membership in a particular descent group. A woman sometimes took the position, though often in special circumstances such as lack of eligible males in the appropriate kin group. The prominent men in a village formed a council that advised this civil chieftain.

Every village also had a war chieftain. Some attained the position through achievements in battle; however, many of these leaders came to office like civil chieftains, selected in the same way and often from the same kinship groups. Civil and war chieftains often disputed the question of whether to make war. The reluctance of civil chieftains was probably a combination of concern for their men and anxiety about the amount of influence wielded by war leaders and successful young warriors.

Young men went to fight eagerly because it was one of the few ways that they could achieve immediate status in community life. Moreover, they knew that political opportunities in later life were based on at least some success in war. Even civil chieftains, so often the advocates of peace, had past war records that brought them respect.

War chieftains occasionally organized war parties of several hundred men. More often a prominent warrior invited men in the village to participate in an ordinary raid. To prepare themselves for the expedition, men sang and danced. They also ate dog meat, perhaps symbolizing the enemies they would kill. A volunteer could withdraw from the expedition at any time, particularly if he had a dream or vision that predicted his death.

Warriors began an attack on a village with their arrows, but for close fighting they switched to a club with a special head—a spike, beak, or stone ball. They were supposed to be brave, but not foolhardy. Ideally the war party took no losses; the death of a single man was reason for the whole community to mourn. As he fought, a warrior looked for a chance to take a prisoner. Women and children were to be incorporated into the community to increase its numbers. Men, especially older men with significant war honors, were desired for ritual torture at home.

Abuse of a male prisoner began on the return trip, but much worse awaited him. When a captive arrived in the village, people began preparations for a ceremony surrounding the torture. The victim anticipated hours of beating, stabbing, mutilation, or burning. At some point he would probably be shot with arrows. Torturers proceeded carefully in order to keep the victim alive for hours or even days. When he fell unconscious, they revived him and continued. During the ordeal, the victim struggled to live up to the expectations of his own people and his captors by remaining brave and defiant. He sang his own songs and taunted his tormentors. Eventually they killed him with a single blow, giving him peace and an honorable death.

Because so many men died in war, an occasional captive was spared to replace the husband of a widow. In this status he could become a full-fledged member of the community. More often widows and other women participated fully in the torture, which they regarded as revenge for their losses to the enemy. There may have been deeper causes. Torture might have dissipated tensions caused by the persistent state of intense warfare or by social life within a complex community.

When men were not at war, they imitated it in the game of lacrosse. Ritual preparations for a lacrosse match were essentially the same as those for battle, including the use of red paint on the players and their equipment. They donned the feathers of war and simulated the movements of a raiding party as they approached the field. As they lined up before the match, the men voiced war cries.

In the game players used sticks with thong pockets to carry and throw a ball made from wood or stuffed buckskin. A team scored when the ball touched the opponent's goalpost or passed between a pair of them. Field length varied up to a mile or more, and team sizes were proportional. War cries continued during the game as players legally rammed and slashed one another. Respected older men tried to limit serious violence, but injuries were common. Players reacted stoically to legitimate tactics, but a perceived deviation could start a real fight. Teams often played rematches to ease the hard feelings that resulted.

Many lacrosse games were major social events, arranged by civil chiefs well in advance, that pitted two communities or larger political entities against one another. The players may have numbered in the hundreds and the audience in the thousands. The occasion allowed people to renew personal friendships and to identify with the larger social groups to which they belonged.

Lacrosse: an Eastern Area sport, here played in the southern style, with two sticks (Cherokee culture).

Knowledge and Expression

The community tried to maintain a ritual balance between two powerful gods, one largely benevolent and the other dangerous. The sky god was the source of all good things in life but tended to be remote. The underworld god, often manifested in the water serpent, fomented evil in the world through spirits or witches. However, the underworld god was also a potential source of power for ordinary men. People gave thanks to the benevolent god but spent as much or more time in appeasing the dangerous one. They also had to acknowledge dozens of other deities, especially the gods of war and maize.

The community held a number of important ceremonies at various points during the year. Most had to do with food, especially the crops. People celebrated maize at the time of the main harvest in late summer or fall, usually a period of abundance. Another major festival gave respite from the dreary winter. Such communal celebrations emphasized thanksgiving and renewal. They included feasting, games, dancing, and singing. Many songs had syncopated rhythms and took the form of a dialogue in which a solo performer chanted one part and was answered by a chorus.

Chieftains and other people acted as priests by maintaining ritual paraphernalia for the community and by leading ceremonies. Many ritual leaders had characteristics of the shaman as well as priest: they had visions and other direct contacts with the spirit world. The sacred pipe played a role in all important observances. The holder offered the pipe to all of the cardinal directions, including zenith and nadir, and it was passed among the participants in a social communion. Smoke could be blown toward a particular spirit and could be spread over the smoker or others as a blessing. The rite concluded with a tribute to "all my relations," the other beings in the universe. Through repeated use in contacting the supernatural, some pipes became such powerful objects that only people with special capabilities could handle them.

The two parts of the pipe, bowl and stem, were kept apart except during ceremonial use. The bowl was composed of stone, associated with the earth, while the wood of the stem came from trees that grew toward the sky. Thus the instrument combined the greatest forces in the universe. The long stem made it easier for people to hand the pipe around as they shared the ritual. Even more important, the long stem allowed the supplicant to show deep respect to another person or to a supernatural being by offering the pipe with both hands.

Although men and women sat on opposite sides of the circle when the sacred pipe was passed, everyone received it. Not only was the sacred pipe shared by men and women, but its symbolism represented their complementary nature. The bowl was considered to be female and the stem male: the pipe became powerful only when the two were joined. The pipe was usually offered to the Sky (male) and to the Earth (female).

Many lacrosse games were highly ceremonialized and expressed religious beliefs. In a game played for a specific ritual purpose, sacred numbers determined the size of the teams; often they were small. People believed that the spirits determined the outcome of a lacrosse match.

Lacrosse was also a major venue for gambling by both players and spectators. Higher stakes resulted in harder competition among the players. For spectators the act of betting was more important than the amount involved because it made them active participants in the event. Betting was incorporated into the relevant myths and celebrated in song. A common reason for rematches was to give losers a chance to recoup. Thus the duration of a series of games was often determined by the pattern of gambling losses. As a result, the long-term economic effects were minimal.

In mythical times only one family had maize because the senior woman produced it from her own body. She allowed herself to be killed and, amidst her remains, maize sprouted from the ground. From these plants everyone obtained seeds that they could cultivate for themselves. This major myth emphasized the importance of maize and its association with women.

The antics of the trickster, often embodied in a rabbit, delighted people but rarely came to anything significant. Another entertaining fiction explained the origin of the Pleiades. As hungry children danced, they became light-headed and rose into the sky to become stars. Another version derived the constellation from fasting adults. People associated the Pleiades with hunger because they appeared in the sky during winter. In the more personal romance of the sky maidens, a man happened to see several young women descending from the sky. He captured one of them and married her, but eventually she left him and returned to her own realm.

A Closer Look

The Eastern Area was a large cultural unit that encompassed some significant environmental diversity. Despite profound common features, such as dual organization and lacrosse, the culture varied in very important ways. Some of the most significant can be summed up in a regional survey.

The Mississippian Region

Anchored in the valley of the Mississippi River up to the border of Minnesota, this Region stretched across the southeast to the Gulf Coast and the Atlantic. My name for it comes from the archeologists' term for the spectacular culture that pervaded the Region before Europeans arrived. The Natchez represented that culture, and peoples such as the Creek and Cherokee were derived from it. The Mississippian Region displayed the greatest elaboration of tattooing in North America. Both men and women were tattooed over most of their bodies. Warriors and other important men displayed the most elaborate designs to symbolize their achievements.

Stratified paramount chiefdoms dominated the Mississippian Region. A chief resided in a fortified town with a thousand or more inhabitants (but see Williams 1995 for another view). Commoners lived in small, nuclear-family houses like those of people in the villages. Nobles had larger dwellings, and the chief's was the greatest of them. Some or all of the elite homes rested on earthen mounds. The temple also sat atop a mound. This building contained images of gods, a perpetual fire that represented the sun god, and the remains of deceased chiefs. Priests tended the temples and their contents. Along with their religious duties, they received tribute that people brought for the chief.

A Mississippian chief carried on a litter (Natchez culture).

The paramount chief was a semidivine being who had virtually absolute power, at least in theory. In practice he seemed subject to the influence of relatives and other powerful people and governed with the aid of a number of officials. Whatever the limits of power, the trappings of office were striking. The chief wore and carried numerous badges of honor and received tribute and special salutes from his people. Wives, guards, and others were sacrificed at his funeral.

In contrast to most other Northern Americans, Mississippians believed that animals were basically enemies of humans and quick to take offense at mistreatment. This came about in mythological times because the animals perceived humans as becoming too numerous and destructive (Underhill 1965). As a result, animals became a major source of illness. For curing, people frequently turned to the realm of plants, who were generally friends of humans and rarely took offense (Hudson 1976).

The mythology held that human beings had emerged from the earth. The one great adventure of the trickster, Rabbit, was to steal fire from the gods and make it available to humans. Having talked his way into a ceremony, Rabbit saw to it that part of his costume caught fire. Then he ran away and scattered the flames. The gods tried to douse the fires with rain, but people found some of them and learned how to use them.

The Iroquoian Region

The famous Iroquois and others of closely related speech and culture, including their Huron enemies, inhabited the dense forests of New York, Pennsylvania, and adjacent Canada. Men created a variety of hair patterns by partially plucking, shaving, or burning hair from their heads. A stiff longitudinal ridge (known as a "roach") was perhaps the most common style; it gave us the "Mohawk" haircut. Iroquoians lived in "longhouses," the largest houses in the Eastern Area. Some exceeded 100 feet in length and held more than a hundred people.

The core members of such a household belonged to a matrilineage or a local segment of a matriclan that had members in several villages.

The Iroquoians differed from the Mississippians in being essentially egalitarian. However, some kinship groups were privileged because of their generosity, war prowess, or their right to provide chieftains to a larger group. Each descent group in a village selected a chieftain from among its eligible members. These men had little authority but possessed some significant privileges, such as control of trade. Usually one chieftain emerged as leader of the village, but chieftains consulted with each other and with a council composed of the most prominent people.

Iroquoian villages formed tribes that were integrated by two institutions. First, matriclans had members in more than one village, thus connecting them with bonds of kinship. Second, a tribal council included representatives from every village. The council made nonbinding decisions about the external affairs of the tribe, based on unanimity. The council pattern was repeated for the federations to which most tribes belonged. The League of the Iroquois is a famous example. These federations were devoted to keeping internal peace and trying to agree on common external policies. The Iroquois became so successful that they dominated the entire Region and affected the neighboring Prairie and Coast Regions (see below). One of their feats demonstrates the potential economic consequences of Eastern warfare. Through repeated long-distance raids, the Iroquois cleared Ohio of its earlier inhabitants and used it for a hunting ground. Some people have argued that elements of the United States Constitution are based on Iroquois principles, such as impeachment and checks and balances.

In Iroquoian religion the good and evil gods were close relatives who lived somewhere on earth rather than in the sky and underworld. This view of cosmology is tied to the origin myth of the woman who fell from the sky. After she fell, because of a real or an imagined sexual transgression, the earth diver made the world for her. She then had a daughter, who in turn gave birth to male twins. As the story went on in various versions, one of the boys became the benevolent god while his brother, mother, or grandmother became the evil one. Religious life included curing societies whose members performed in masks or other disguises. Women either participated in the rituals or maintained the paraphernalia. The prominence of these curing societies diminished the importance of shamans.

The Algonkian Coast Region

Algonkian-speaking people occupied the Atlantic coastal plain from New England through North Carolina. They made extensive use of the shore and rivers to obtain food, leaving their villages for extended periods. Accounts of kinship and postmarital residence are mixed, perhaps representing the effects of powerful matrilineal/matrilocal neighbors on an earlier culture more inclined to bilateralism or paternal bias. There is little doubt that the coastal Algonkians were organized into stratified chiefdoms with chiefs who inherited office matrilineally. Temple religion resembled that of the Mississippians, though it was much simpler. Shamans played a major role in religious leadership and exerted a great deal of influence in political matters.

The Prairie Region

This Region encompassed two major groups: Algonkian speakers between the Great Lakes and the Mississippian Region (e.g., the Illinois and the Miami) and Siouans to the west of the Mississippian Region (e.g., Dakota and Omaha). These peoples shared a habitat in which the forests thinned into short-grass plains where they could hunt bison ("buffalo"). Prairie people were the antecedents of the Plains Indians, who abandoned the farmlands completely and based their livelihood on mounted hunting of the bison. The Prairie adaptation was based on a summer village composed of medium-sized houses with several families in each. After harvesting their crops, people camped away from the village as they pursued a cycle of foraging that culminated in a cooperative buffalo hunt.

Both boys and girls sought a vision at puberty, which suggests equality, but only women were subject to severe punishment for adultery. Residence was patrilocal, and personal kinship terminology was consistent with a patrilineal system. People belonged to patriclans with ritual functions. The clan held the rights to a set of names for its members, maintained a medicine bundle, and conducted war rituals. Instead of torturing war captives in elaborate ways, Prairie people burned them to death.

NORTHWEST COAST AREA

Examples:

Tlinkit, Kwakiutl, Salish, Tillamook

The Northwest Coast Area extended along the Pacific shore from southeastern Alaska to northern California. Warmed by the Japan Current, the environment provided people with moderate temperatures and abundant marine resources. Dense coniferous forests, supported by heavy rainfall, provided men with the basis for highly developed woodworking skills.

The inhabitants of the Northwest Coast depended completely on wild foods, yet they had some of the highest population densities in the Northern American Zone. They led a relatively sedentary way of life that included rank, stratification, and slavery. All of this was possible because they were specialized foragers in a bountiful environment. Marine resources were crucial, especially salmon and other fish that lived their adult lives in the ocean but swam up the many rivers in large numbers on a seasonal basis to lay their eggs.

Individuals and kinship groups prized wealth, which included natural products and fine manufactured goods made by specialized craft workers. Northwest Coast people held strong concepts of ownership and fought feuds and wars for economic reasons. Wealth was intertwined with hierarchy and leadership: the elite displayed wealth to justify their position, most notably in rituals called potlatches. This concern with hierarchy and wealth is reminiscent of chiefdoms. However, the key leader in Northwest Coast culture was the chieftain of a village or kinship group. In no case was there a true chief with authority over several distinct communities.

Key features:

- ▶ Foragers specialized in marine foods
- ▶ Skilled woodworking and craft specialization
- ▶ Wealth highly valued and displayed
- ▶ Potlatches
- ▶ Rank and stratification
- ▶ Hereditary chieftainship
- ▶ Slavery and slave trade
- ▶ Feuds and wars for economic reasons

Modal Patterns in Northwest Coast Culture

Material Culture

A dim spring sun pushed through sky the color of whale skin and illuminated one winter village after another. In some places a single large wooden house stood alone, but most villages consisted of several clustered together. Each house was anchored by heavy corner posts that supported the long planks of the walls and the pitched roof.

Inside a dwelling, families rose from their sleeping mats and warmed themselves by the central fires. They ate meager breakfasts from shallow wooden dishes, mindful that the winter stores of dried food were running

A Northwest Coast chieftain's plank house with totem poles in front (Tlinkit culture). Although the planks in this house are vertical, horizontal planks were the modal pattern for the Area as a whole.

low. In preparation for the day, some people renewed the paint on their faces, a brief task because they wore only simple designs or a single solid color. The paint pleased the eye, but its main purpose was to protect against salt air, wind, and sun. Simple tattoos added a bit more color, and so did ear pendants made from dentalium shells. Most individuals wore a pin through the pierced septum.

The people went out to see what the new spring offered them, women in their skirts and men nude as they were in almost every kind of weather. Men went inland to hunt and trap, the most likely spring game being beaver, mink, and bear. Women went to the shore, where they gathered masses of seaweed and filled baskets with clams, mussels, and abalones. They used their sticks to pry the shellfish from rocks and dig them out of the sand. Back in the village, women began the long process of cooking by the stone-boiling method in watertight baskets or boxes. Sometimes they baked food in earth ovens.

Later in the spring people began to leave the village and go to separate camps to exploit fish and sea mammals. Each household or kinship group owned certain sites where members hunted or fished at various times of year. Men began to refurbish their dugout canoes or make new ones, using wood-handled chisels with blades of stone, elk horn, or clam shell. It took many days to finish the larger canoes, some as long as fifty feet and as much as eight feet wide. As soon as the surf permitted, men put to sea in their canoes to harpoon seals and sea otters and angle for halibut and salmon.

A relatively small canoe that illustrates the Northwest Coast style of manufacture.

At the same time, women began to gather plant foods, emphasizing the young shoots. They also picked berries and dug up roots and bulbs, the first of a succession of species that would continue appearing throughout the summer. People ate the fresh berries plain or with oil. Toward the end of the summer women would begin to dry them for storage as winter food.

During the summer, people moved again to take advantage of the fish that came up the rivers. They prized the five kinds of salmon the most. The great chinook carried the most flesh, some individuals weighing as much

as eighty pounds. Smaller species spawned in smaller rivers, which allowed people to spread out and increase the efficiency of the harvest. Some kinds of salmon provided extra fat while the lean ones were most easily dried to store for the next winter. As tons of fish came into the camps, women worked hard to process it all. They cooked for daily needs but, more important, they preserved most of the fish to provide food for the winter.

Men took some time from the salmon to engage in trade. Calm summer weather encouraged long voyages along the coastline, some a hundred miles or more. Canoes themselves were important trade items because a few peoples made extremely fine boats. Similarly, some wove good robes and capes to keep off the rain.

An elk, also known by the Native American name of wapiti.

As fall set in, people donned their rain gear on many days. The fish runs fell off, and men spent more time inland to hunt elk. Finally, with little new food available, people gathered again in the winter village. During winter days women had a great deal of time to make their finely twined baskets. They wove colored strips into them to form angular geometric designs. Men made wooden boxes with curved contours, steaming and bending the wood. People used cedar bark fiber to make arm and leg bands and low turbans for ceremonial use. Above all, winter was the time for social relations and ritual.

Social Relations

The families in a household were closely related but distinguished by rank. Proximity to the direct line of descent from the group's ancestor determined the inherited statuses of the blood kin at the core of the group. The chieftain was the oldest man in direct line of descent from the common ancestor. Each adult in the group was married to an outsider of about equal rank. The household also contained the slaves of higher-ranking members.

In addition to having personal ranks, free people were categorized as nobles or commoners. Heredity and wealth were the criteria for high status and mythology justified the system. Inherited status had little significance for commoners, but they could improve their social standing with achievements in the crafts, war, or shamanism.

Members of a kinship group shared in its possessions and prestige. Material possessions included the house, fishing stations, and hunting areas. Ceremonial possessions included personal names, canoe names, songs, dances, and rituals. Above all the group prized its crests, visual symbols of its identity and privileges. The chieftain was the custodian of these possessions.

Wealth was an essential feature of leadership and high rank. It was measured precisely in standard units such as hides, blankets, and slaves. A chieftain inherited wealth and accumulated more as the organizer of subsistence activities and exchanges. His status was marked by displays such as fine clothing and release from ordinary labor. He had one or more assistants to facilitate his work and contribute to his prestige.

Although a chieftain held considerable authority, he had little formal power. Some allied with a shaman or sorcerer to afflict dissidents and enemies. The supernatural practitioner benefited by greater prestige and wealth than he could otherwise achieve. Thus the role of shaman was less independent than in many other cultures, but it provided a major route to upward mobility in a hierarchical society.

At the birth of a child family members observed the rituals and taboos known to everyone. They also used privately owned magic to promote long life and success in some particular endeavor, such as canoe making or gambling. When girls reached puberty, they went into seclusion so as not to offend the spirits of salmon or game.

Marriages of the nobility were carefully arranged in accord with the social standing of the individuals and families involved. The groom's family made a gift to that of the bride that was as large as possible. This was a matter of prestige. The bride's family retained their connection with her and continued to be concerned with her welfare.

A chieftain held ceremonies called potlatches that confirmed his status and reflected glory on his group. The specific occasion for a potlatch was a change in the leader's status, such as death or recognition of an heir. Another group was invited to feast and to receive gifts that comprised the chieftain's personal wealth and donations from his people. The more that was given away, the greater the prestige of the givers. The host handed out gifts to his male guests in a fixed order, according to the ranks of the recipients. The host's wife or sister

A chieftain with a copper, an important symbol of wealth in the Northwest Coast Area (Kosksino culture).

made the presentations to the women. Potlatch gifts rewarded the guests for validating the proceedings by witnessing them.

During a potlatch, individuals other than the chief might have their status raised or enhanced by the public acquisition of new rights, privileges, or ritual names. Commoners received honors for their achievements in the crafts or war.

Defense against economic exploitation by neighboring groups was a major concern. Some conflicts were ter-

Chieftain distributing blankets at potlatch (Kwakiutl culture).

ritorial while others focused on specific resources. Some encounters were serious battles with substantial casualties. War captives were made into slaves, and this was the main goal of some raids. Relatives, disgraced by the abasement of one of their own, quickly ransomed the more fortunate captives. Others were sold in trade along with canoes and other goods. Slaves were kept by noble families and did ordinary domestic work. Some were treated fairly well, but only at the whim of their masters because they had no rights. Whatever life was like, a slave always faced the possibility of a sacrificial death, especially when the master died.

Knowledge and Expression

The salmon spirits lived together under the sea in a society much like that of humans. Each summer they assumed the bodies of fish, which they intended to give to humans. As the salmon arrived at each important place along their routes up the rivers, the humans were assembled to welcome their benefactors. At each site a chieftain or a priest honored the first salmon caught by speaking to it as he would a visiting chieftain. Then he performed a complicated ceremony known only to those who had studied it. The rituals belonged to a particular family, but they allowed them to be performed for the benefit of the community. Obligation to the salmon spirits did not end there. All the bones of consumed fish would have to be returned to the sea. Otherwise, some of the salmon spirits might not have complete bodies to bring them back the following year. Such an offense could anger all the spirits and cause them to stay away. People believed much the same thing about other important fish species and honored them with similar practices.

When they settled in the winter village, the inhabitants turned their attention to the spirits and gods of the land. At the potlatches and other great ceremonies, men danced in masks to celebrate their contacts with super-

natural beings in the forest. These beings, some animal and some monstrous, were dangerous and frightening, but occasionally they deigned to be a man's guardian or give him power. In some cases the beings specified that a man could bequeath this spiritual connection to his descendants, giving them the exclusive right to perpetuate the associated songs, dances, and crests.

Ceremonial songs were long and complex, filled with half notes that made them seem eerie to outsiders. Dancers wore carefully carved masks with naturalistic features. They performed in front of wooden panels painted with crests. The intricate and stylized pictures were mainly in red and black with occasional patches of blue or green.

Masked dancers representing two powerful mythological birds (Kwakiutl culture).

Outside the house stood the most spectacular manifestation of the crests, carved into tall poles. The figures that accompanied the crests on a pole came from the same myths that explained the group's privileges and possessions. The poles in front of a house declared the group's status to all who saw them.

Between the ceremonies that punctuated the winter, storytellers dramatized the myths and legends. After the formal opening a teller imitated the characters, sang their songs, and repeated events and objects in accord with sacred numbers. Some of the myths he recounted were private to the kinship group. Others were known to everyone. Most of the common myths described culture heroes who made the world as it is today. The myths concentrated on the physical features of life, ranging from geography to the existence of death. Explanations of human behavior and customs were rare, and many stories described the actions of ordinary people in familiar cultural settings. Raven, the trickster god, displayed an enormous appetite for food and sex, but he lacked the interest in wealth that characterized so much of human life.

When death came, the body of the deceased was removed from the house through a hole in the wall so that nobody had to follow in his path. The remains were placed in a wooden box lodged in a tree or on a pole. At the death of a chieftain, his successor gave a potlatch, and a new crest pole was erected as a memorial.

A Closer Look

This "Closer Look" divides the Northwest Coast Area into several Regions for two different reasons. The Alaskan and Canadian Regions of the Area represent two versions of the fundamental Northwest Coast culture that contrast in several important ways. The third Region, the Coast-Plateau, is marginal in that it lacks some key features of the Area. Some authorities would classify the Plateau as a culture area in its own right while others would divide it among several Areas.

The Alaskan Northwest Coast

This Region coincides with the strip of modern Alaska that extends southward from the main body of the state. Traditional societies of the Region resided on both the coast and the nearby mainland. The predominant ethnic groups were the Tlinkit, Haida, and Tsimshian.

Social organization was based on matrilineal descent and avunculocal residence. A matrilineage occupied a house or a village of its own and held material and spiritual property. Often associated with matrilineality, avunculocal residence meant that a man went to live with his mother's brother at or before his marriage. The result was that he left his father's matrilineal kin for those of his mother. In this Region a boy moved when he was seven or eight years old, and his maternal uncle trained him for manhood. When the boy married, his wife came to live with him. Eventually their sons would leave to reside with their mother's brothers.

The potlatches of the Alaskan Northwest Coast were concerned mainly with death and succession. When a lineage chieftain died, his people invited other groups to attend a potlatch in which they mourned the deceased and installed his successor. The art style also distinguished the Region. It was highly standardized and emphasized symmetry and the rhythmic repetition of conventional forms. Carving tended toward shallow relief, even on the poles.

The Canadian Northwest Coast

The inhabitants of this Region lived on Vancouver Island and the adjacent mainland, near the current border between Canada and the United States. Kwakiutl, Nootka, and Bella Coola are examples. These peoples combined bilateral kinship with a flexible rule of patrilocal residence. Close kin of any kind were forbidden to marry, with any connection of less than four generations being out of the question. In connection with marriage an approximately equal exchange took place between the two families.

The Canadian elite gave more potlatches for more different occasions than their counterparts to the north. Potlatch occasions in the Canadian Northwest Coast included mourning and replacement of dead leaders, but other life passages were at least as significant. One of them was marriage, but the most important occasions may have been those marking the maturation of children. Rosman and Rubel (1986) suggest that this was related to the uncertainties of recruiting children to kinship groups in these bilateral societies. A particular group asserted its claim, so to speak, by giving a child several potlatches during the course of his or her maturation.

Artists of the Canadian Northwest excelled in three-dimensional art. They created full-fledged sculptures in wood as opposed to the relatively flat carvings of their northern neighbors. For ceremonies carvers made marionettes and masks with movable parts to represent supernatural beings. A variety of other mechanical devices and illusions made rituals highly dramatic.

The Coast-Plateau Region

The Oregon coast was the center of a Region that extended north into Washington, south into a small portion of California, and west into the uplands known as the Plateau. The inhabitants included the Tillamook, Tolowa, and Yurok. Most people lived in houses made from vertical planks rather than the horizontal ones to the north. Postmarital residence was patrilocal. The potlatch seems to have been absent, but the Region fits with the Northwest Coast in that wealth was an important aspect of rank and stratification. People counted wealth in woodpecker scalps and dentalium shells. To measure the shells, they tattooed marks along their arms. Winter ceremonies featured songs that shamans and others had learned from their guardian spirits.

SUBARCTIC AREA

Examples:
Kutchin, Dogrib, Cree, Montagnais

The Subarctic Area encompassed almost all of Canada and Alaska, excluding the coastal sections occupied by Inuit and Yupik (Eskimos). This was nearly one third of the North American continent.

The land was vast but the people few and scattered because of an extremely cold environment that provided little food. The bitter winter that lasted for about eight months was crucial in shaping the culture. At these high latitudes, winter days shrank to six hours or less while summer daylight extended to eighteen hours or more.

For humans there were few edible plants in the Subarctic. At best some westerners were able to gather significant quantities of berries in late summer while some eastern people made a lichen into a nutritious soup to help them through food shortages (Rogers and Smith 1981). Fishing provided more food than plants, but opportunities varied with season and habitat.

The key game animals were two unusual deer species. The caribou or reindeer *(Rangifer)* stood about five feet tall at the shoulder and weighed up to 700 pounds. The moose *(Alces)* was a foot taller and often double the weight. Field studies indicate that, in the subfreezing temperatures of winter, each person required between 4,500 and 5,000 calories each day (Rogers and Smith 1981). Only big mammals could provide the necessary quantities of meat. They also had large amounts of fat, which yields more calories than flesh and contains essential acids. The voluminous entrails of big animals added more nutrients to the diet. As native people say now, one can starve to death while eating rabbits. Furthermore, smaller animals were harder to find and catch, especially in winter.

People adapted to the Subarctic with a distinctive technology that included sewn clothing, toboggans, and snowshoes. In contrast to tropical and temperate foragers, because of the emphasis on hunting and fishing, the men provided virtually all the food. However, because subsistence took so much of a man's time and energy, women were all the more vital for food processing and other domestic work. Environmental demands made many of women's tasks more difficult than elsewhere; for example, the manufacture of more elaborate clothing.

Subarctic people would not have survived if they had not maintained a very low population density. From their point of view there was a stringent limit on the number of nonproductive people they could sustain. This meant that, in addition to infanticide, they had to abandon the sick and elderly with unusual frequency. The latter practice is called senilicide or gerontocide.

Even more than in other Northern Zone cultures, individualism characterized Subarctic society and psychology. This extended into the realm of religion, where beliefs were very personalized, gods unimportant, and communal ceremonies essentially secular.

Key features:

▶ Heavy dependence on animal food

▶ Emphasis on big game: caribou and moose

▶ Cold weather technology: sewn clothes, snowshoes, toboggan

▶ High rates of infanticide and senilicide

▶ Highly individualistic society and religion

Modal Patterns in Subarctic Culture

Material Culture

Three small dwellings stood near each other in deep snow beneath towering trees. It was dark, as it would be for most of the winter day. The dwellings were wide conical structures covered with bark. At the top of each one, the poles that formed it emerged from the bark cover and the sinews that lashed them together were visible. Smoke rose from the small opening there. Snow was packed up against the sides except where an animal hide covered the low doorway.

The moose, an essential game animal of the Subarctic Area.

Some dwellings held as many as twenty people. Inside, the people wore little clothing despite an external temperature far below the freezing point. The central fire kept them warm because the house was well insulated by the snow piled against the outer walls. Reed mats and bear hides shielded the family from the cold ground beneath.

A woman cut hides into pieces and sewed them together with sinew and a bone needle. She made bags from hide, but most importantly she made clothes: moccasins, leggings, loincloths, dresses, coats, and hats. Clothing was rather thin, composed of one layer of scraped hide, but a person who went outside in winter would either make a short trip to a neighboring dwelling or engage in vigorous activity. Hunting methods entailed a great deal of movement, placing a premium on supple and durable clothing. The availability of wood made large fires possible during times of rest.

When men donned their clothing for a winter hunt, they also strapped on snowshoes made from wooden frames laced with rawhide thongs. Winter was the time to go after moose. Their tracks were obvious in the snow, and hunters on snowshoes followed them easily. Because moose were solitary, the hunt required no more than a small party. Because the huge animals floundered in deep snow, even a lone man on snowshoes could spear one to death. In a year when moose were scarce, men turned to small game and fish in near desperation. Taking small game and fish required a great deal more labor in winter than at other times of year.

Women stone-boiled meat in a container made from bark or animal skin or a large animal's stomach. The process was long and tedious, so people ate much of their meat nearly raw. The raw meat probably provided them with needed vitamin C. Women flavored animal foods with small amounts of berries, roots, or other plant products. People put further variety into the diet by eating virtually all parts of animals in varying combinations. Only the lungs and genitals were ignored.

Women preserved extra meat by smoke-drying it on a rack. The length of the treatment depended on how long they expected to keep the meat. If the stores ran out and hunting failed, the group would have to put all their goods on toboggans and move to another locality. The toboggan was made from two thin boards, joined by crosspieces and turned up at the front. A person pulled it with a line across the chest. People eased the task by moving across ice whenever possible. In a bad winter local bands split up, and each family camped alone. During such times the family was most likely to abandon a sick or feeble individual. At the end of a bad winter starvation threatened, and occasionally some people resorted to cannibalism in order to survive.

Liberated by spring, small bands joined to form a larger camp with enough hunters to take large numbers of caribou from migrating herds. First they built a chute, as long as three miles, from brush or poles. At the end

Men in snowshoes, a vital element of Subarctic technology; carcasses of caribou, the other essential game animal of the Subarctic besides the moose.

they constructed a corral and laid it with snares. Then they drove a herd of caribou through the chute and into the corral, where most of the animals became tangled in the snares. The men speared some of the tangled individuals and killed the rest with arrows.

During the brief summer, people came together along waterways in the largest camps of the year. In the relative warmth they constructed simple shelters of a few poles and hides. They hunted the animals that came to drink, and they added fish to the food supply. With streams thawed and many land areas now swampy, people used birchbark canoes to go on visits, trading trips, or raids. Life was generally good, except for the numerous biting insects. As autumn set in, the caribou migrated again. During this season, the most effective hunting method was to spear the animals at water crossings. After these hunts, carrying stores of caribou meat to help them survive, people dispersed for the long, dark winter.

Social Relations

The household within a dwelling consisted of two or three related nuclear families. In most cases they were linked by men—father and son, brothers, or brothers-in-law. Often there was an elderly dependent and sometimes a young man doing bride service. They were connected to the other households in a winter band through close kin ties or friendship. This was the group that went through a harsh winter with the horrifying possibility of cannibalism in their minds. If they actually faced the issue, some would prefer starvation, some would wait for the death of others, and a few might commit murder.

Problems with food and travel at any time of year could require the elimination of some group members, but winter was the most critical. People pulled the infirm on toboggans as long as they could but recognized a hopeless situation when it arose. They usually sacrificed infants first but sometimes had to give up older children, the sick, or elderly relatives. People respected age because survival implied knowledge and wisdom. That wisdom led elderly individuals to sacrifice their lives willingly for younger relatives, and it may be that many such deaths were really suicides.

As local bands moved through the seasons, they joined in the largest groupings permitted by local resources. In most cases aggregants belonged to the same regional band. Sometimes this involved meeting a few strangers because people could shift from one regional band to another fairly easily, especially if they married across the vague boundary. At the summer gathering, people often had the chance to renew their bonds with all other members of the regional band.

However large the group became, individuals insisted on their autonomy. They valued personal independence and kept authority to a minimum. However, these values were not exercised in a way that was selfish or harsh; people readily cooperated and shared with each other. The appropriate response to conflict was restraint or avoidance. In extreme cases an entire camp moved in order to leave a deviant individual behind.

Knowledge and Expression

Because life itself depended on hunting, a man did everything possible to please the animal souls and game master gods. If he hunted a bear, the most awesome of animals, he performed extra rituals for the hunt itself and for the disposal of the remains. While he walked through the forest, especially in the dim light that prevailed throughout most of the year, the hunter's thoughts inevitably strayed to other spirits that might help or harm him and to the half-human monsters that sometimes attacked people. Any gods that might exist were remote.

The man's view of the supernatural world was very much his own, as was true of everyone else in his society. He had learned things from his family as he grew up, and then he exchanged ideas with other people who had learned different things. There was no need for people to agree on details; each individual used what worked for him or her. Though most ritual was personal, people in a camp or village sometimes gathered for a feast to mark a special occasion. Most of these were sponsored by a particular family in connection with a transition in the life of a member.

On the rare occasions when personal knowledge was insufficient, people went to a shaman. In addition to curing, he predicted the future, giving special attention to the weather because it could drastically affect hunting possibilities. The shaman could also find or summon game when it was scarce. One method, which could be used by nonspecialists, was scapulimancy. A person placed the shoulder bone of a large animal in the fire and then used the resulting cracks to divine the location of game.

A Closer Look

Fear of the Supernatural

A key modal pattern in the culture of the Northern American Zone was belief in a benevolent supernatural realm. While acknowledging the existence of some helpful spirits, Subarctic people tended to be more fearful of the supernatural than others in the Zone. Particular beliefs varied.

West of Hudson Bay were speakers of Athapaskan languages, including the Kutchin, Slavey, Dogrib, and Chipewyan (not to be confused with the Chippewa). The ideas of these people may have been influenced by neighboring Eskimo. They regarded many spirits as indifferent or hostile to human beings, and even the helpful ones were not entirely reliable. The prospect of ghosts lingering near human habitations terrified the westerners. They made extensive use of amulets and magic to protect themselves, and they observed many taboos for the same reason (Vanstone 1974). Their mythology (Bierhorst 1985) emphasized a "deliverer" who destroyed many man-eating animals or monsters. These antagonists tried to trap the deliverer and eat him, as did a variety of stupid giants, but he overcame them all.

Lack of confidence in animal spirits may explain the prevalence of "Dog Husband" stories in the western Subarctic. The fictional man's human wife or lover had children who could shift between human and dog forms. To some this was just a folktale, but several cultures made it a myth that explained the origin of human beings. Such a close identification of humans with the dog, rather than wild animals, was unusual in Native America.

People in the eastern Subarctic, exemplified by the Cree and Montagnais, spoke Algonkian languages. Their beliefs and mythology were more typical of the Northern Zone and displayed resemblances to the lore of Iroquoians and other southern neighbors. However, they transformed their fears of cannibalism into a monster that ate human beings. It was called *windigo*, or some variant of that term, in many of the languages. A person who succumbed to starvation cannibalism turned into such a monster, and so did some mentally disturbed people. It was necessary to kill an individual who showed signs of such a transition.

Great Basin Area

Examples:

Shoshone, Paiute, Ute, Yavapai

The Great Basin Area occupied a large part of what is now the Western United States, primarily in Utah, Nevada, and eastern California. It was desert in a broad sense, encompassing a variety of very dry habitats at moderate to high altitudes. There was substantial plant cover, which was the main source of food for the foragers who inhabited the Area.

The Basin environment combined aridity with wide fluctuation in temperatures from place to place, from year to year, and through daily and seasonal cycles. To cope with cold winters the inhabitants developed a woven cape that has been called their "most significant technological invention" (Beckman 1996).

Though Basin people used virtually every kind of food available to them, they sustained only a sparse and highly nomadic population. The plant foods in this dry environment were mainly hard or tough, so women made extensive use of grinding and parching to process them. Gathering and processing these items required a variety of skillfully made basketry artifacts.

People depended mainly on small game for much of their animal food, but two kinds of deer provided occasional prizes. In addition to the mule deer, typical of western America, Basin hunters went after pronghorn "antelopes" *(Antilocapra)*. Both animals had about the same shoulder height, approximately three feet. At 100 pounds the pronghorns weighed half as much, but they ran in herds that facilitated cooperative hunting and multiple kills. Even so, people probably obtained more meat from communal rabbit hunts.

Key features:

- ▶ Generalized foragers
- ▶ Pole and brush houses
- ▶ Winter cape
- ▶ Exploitation of virtually all available foods
- ▶ Skilled basketry
- ▶ Extensive use of grinding and parching
- ▶ Cooperative hunting of antelope and rabbits

Modal Patterns in the Great Basin Culture

Material Culture

People never knew which of their food sources, if any, would provide an abundance. At best, this occurred every third or fourth year for any particular plant or animal. Nor did people know where an abundant, or even adequate, supply of food would appear. Survival depended on knowledge, alertness, and flexibility. Accordingly, a person spent most of the year in a small nomadic band of relatives; in the worst years single families wandered alone. When they were near water, people gathered turtles, fish, and shellfish. On land they hunted, trapped, or gathered virtually every animal, including lizards, snakes, rodents, and the larvae and eggs of insects. Most importantly, they gathered seeds, nuts, roots, and other plant foods.

In the fall separate groups converged on the places where pinyon nuts grew on a species of pine tree. Although many people congregated where the pinyons were abundant, the harvest was a family activity. Families reached an understanding as to which would work where, and perceived violations sometimes resulted in conflict. The pinyon was the most important single food, and a man helped his wife to harvest as much as possible. They used basketry artifacts that the woman had made with great skill. They removed the seeds from plants with seed beaters and collected them in tight conical baskets.

Back in camp a woman used more of her basketry products to process the pinyons. She winnowed them in a triangular tray and parched them with live coals in a flat basket. During the parching she kept the contents of the basket in constant motion to prevent burning. After this she turned to her stone grinding tools to make flour and then concluded by using another basket to stone-boil the flour into the mush that was a staple food. Women applied these same methods to most of the foods that they prepared throughout the year. When they gathered the bulbs of agave plants, it eased the burden a bit. They baked the bulbs in an earth oven, simply leaving them mixed with hot rocks under the ground for several days.

Though families worked separately in the pinyon harvest, the large group in the vicinity made it convenient to organize a communal rabbit hunt in the late fall. A man who was recognized as an expert organized the effort. Families brought out the big nets that they carefully kept in repair and passed down from one generation

Great Basin family group with grinding tools (mano and metate), basketry, clay pots, and infant in cradleboard (Southern Paiute culture).

to the next. Made from grass twine, some of these nets were three hundred feet long.

When they were ready for the hunt, people hung the nets from bushes and sticks pushed into the ground. Then men and women, sometimes helped by children, spread out and drove as many rabbits as possible into the nets. As the animals piled into the trap, people closed the ends to encircle them and then killed them with clubs or arrows. In a good year the rabbits could provide more meat than anything else and contribute substantially to survival during the coming winter.

For the winter about fifty people settled into a village. They built or restored conical or domed houses formed from a framework of poles covered by grass thatch, brush, or bark. Here people maintained grass-lined storage pits to preserve their dried foods.

Men often hunted mule deer and bighorn sheep with their bows. In a year when pronghorns seemed to be sufficiently abundant, men organized a major game drive in which they herded the animals between funneled walls into a corral made of brush and reinforced by stones and poles. Inside the corral the hunters ran the pronghorns until the animals were exhausted and then killed them with arrows or clubs.

Just as men and women shared the work of the pinyon harvest, they both played a role in the provision of

Pronghorn "antelope," a distinctive and important game animal of the Great Basin Area.

meat. In addition to helping with the rabbit hunts, women set their own traps for small animals throughout the year. In camp they had the responsibility for distributing the meat from both their own kills and those made by men. Men and women also combined with delight in the occasional windfall provided by a swarm of grasshoppers. They captured large numbers of the insects by driving them into a pit. For immediate consumption people boiled or roasted the grasshoppers. If there was a surplus, they parched them like pinyon nuts and made them into a dry paste for storage.

Though virtually naked during much of the year, people protected themselves from winter with a rabbit skin cape that tied around the neck and hung to the knees. At night it became bed and blanket. The thick garment, furry both inside and out, was made from strips of rabbit skin. The garment maker cut each skin into a single long strip and then twisted strips together to form a kind of yarn. Finally, she wove the yarn into a cape on a simple loom.

Social Relations

Strong ties existed between families, usually on the basis of marriage. People preferred to arrange marriages through the exchange of siblings. The only limitation was that the spouses could not be related through an ancestor within the last three generations. A new husband traveled in the local band of his wife's family and performed bride service for them. Matrilocality was also desirable because it allowed the wife's maternal grandmother to assist with the birth of her first child. To protect and benefit the baby, mother and father observed similar ritual practices. These included food taboos, especially pertaining to meat, restrictions on normal activities such as subsistence work, and the ritual bath concluding the period of confinement.

People called their band chieftains "talkers" because oratory was a major feature of the role. Having no real authority, a chieftain exhorted his people to good behavior in elaborate public speeches. A good talker entertained listeners with his verbal skill. Chieftains were all men, but some attained the position with the help of kinship ties to women. Other than exclusion from chieftainship, women participated in the limited political processes on much the same footing as men.

The regional band, rarely exceeding 150 people, was little more than an idea. Members usually assembled into several small winter villages rather than just one. These villages varied from year to year as to size, location, and personnel. Boundaries were vague, and people readily transferred from one regional band to another. Extensive visiting and resource sharing took place between members of friendly bands, as well as cooperation in communal hunts. After the occasional raid against an offending group, the victors took scalps for display in communal celebrations rather than as symbols of personal achievement.

Knowledge and Expression

The name of a deceased person came under a permanent taboo because fear of ghosts was strong. Nevertheless, there were some individuals who sought supernatural power from ghosts rather than animal spirits. However, the majority obtained supernatural capabilities in dreams rather than on vision quests. They dreamed of a power itself rather than a spirit or ghost. Many of these powers were highly specialized, such as control of rain or the ability to cure rattlesnake bite, but a person could accumulate several different capabilities. Women had equal access to supernatural power, and female shamans attained much the same status and prestige as males. There seem not to have been any restrictions on supernatural practice related to menstruation or any other female characteristic.

In addition to the oratory of chieftains, people enjoyed the words of storytellers. Tales about Coyote seemed to be endless. He was the main culture hero as well as the main trickster. Coyote frequently associated with Wolf, who was consistently benevolent and identified with God. Coyote and Wolf were antagonists in some tales and worked together in others.

On major social occasions, mainly animal drives and some harvests, people engaged in games. They also performed their only communal dance, the Round Dance, around a pole. Men and women, especially the young, alternated with each other in a circle, arms linked, facing inward, and danced clockwise. Some believed that the Round Dance could bring rain, but it was also recreational and an occasion for courtship. Basin people sang with a distinctively smooth technique, involving no vocal tension or pulsation. When music accompanied them, rasps and rattles provided percussion because drums were absent. Melodic instruments were used only for personal purposes.

A Closer Look

Northeast Mexico

We now skip some geographic space to a cultural unit that occupied what are now the states of Chihuahua and San Luis Potosí in Mexico (Griffen 1983), and included a portion of western Texas (Newcomb 1974). Often ignored in surveys of Northern America's native cultures, this unit is discussed in the current chapter because of many similarities to the Great Basin with regard to material culture and related aspects of society. It is tempting to consider Northeast Mexico as a Region of the Basin Area even though there is some spatial separation between them. On the other hand, there seem to have been some profound differences in other social features as well as in religion. Thus Northeast Mexico could be considered a small culture area in its own right. I leave the decision to someone else.

Northeast Mexicans, exemplified by the Chichimec and Karankawa, looked different from Great Basin people because they decorated themselves extensively with face and body painting, tattooing, and scarification. Although they exploited a variety of seeds and nuts with techniques like those of the Basin, the staple plant food of the Mexicans was the agave bulb. They also made extensive use of cactus apples and mesquite beans. Hunters included peccaries in their wide range of prey. In cooperative pursuit of mule deer and pronghorns, they often used fire to drive and to trap.

It seems that Northeast Mexicans were able to maintain local bands of 20 to 50 people on a semipermanent basis. Each band had several chieftains who may have inherited the positions patrilineally, but who also had to display bravery and ability. Female infanticide, in addition to patrilineal inheritance of leadership, suggests a male bias in society.

Northeast Mexico contrasted sharply with the Basin in its emphasis on warfare. Huts were often hidden and sometimes fortified. Victorious warriors underwent a purification ceremony after battle in which they danced with trophy heads and scalps and sometimes tortured and cannibalized captives. Such practices may have been borrowed from more complex societies to the northeast and the south. Other ceremonies presaged war, celebrated war alliances with other bands, and occasionally marked peacemaking. People took the hallucinogen peyote in curing and war ceremonies.

CALIFORNIA AREA

Examples:

Shasta, Pomo, Miwok,
Yokuts, Chumash, Cahuilla

The California Area of native America coincided almost exactly with the modern-day state.

The geographic space covered by California is rather small for a culture area. One justification for distinguishing it is pragmatic: it is hard to classify California culture with any other (some things don't change much). This is not to say that the culture was entirely unique; rather, similarities to other Areas are almost equally divided. The California Area was like the Great Basin in much of its material culture while it resembled the Northwest Coast in many aspects of social relations. California was most distinctive in its varied patterns of religion.

Another reason for distinguishing native California as a culture area is that it contained a great many people, even though they were foragers. The dense population, as well as a relatively sedentary lifestyle, was largely based on the use of the highly nutritious acorn as a staple food. This required a technological achievement, however, because people had to remove tannic acid from the acorns. Another technological achievement that distinguished California, also the Area's greatest artistic achievement, was the elaborate basketry manufactured by women.

Although the native California community has been portrayed as unique (termed the "tribelet"), it can be seen as a variant of the regional band found in other foragers. The California community consisted of 100 to 500 people within a common territory. It was unusual in having one or more permanent villages, but people left the villages during part of every year to extend their food-getting activities.

Californians differed most from other foragers in the elaboration of their political systems. Resemblances to the adjacent Northwest Coast included the intertwining of wealth and status and a community chieftain with numerous duties and privileges. A special form of ritual clown, much like the jester in medieval European royal courts, reminded the chieftain of his fallibility.

Ceremonial systems linked large numbers of communities together. Two surprising negatives marked expressive behavior: the absence of drums and the lack of ritual significance for the sweat lodge.

Key features:

- ▶ Semisubterranean houses
- ▶ Acorns
- ▶ Elaborate and artistic basketry
- ▶ Regional band with permanent villages
- ▶ Hereditary chieftain
- ▶ Wealth and stratification
- ▶ Jester clown
- ▶ Intercommunity religious systems

Modal Patterns in California Culture

Material Culture

The family lived in a house that was partly beneath ground level. Logs or poles formed its basic structure, and bark or tules completed the external covering. Similar dwellings were scattered nearby, numerous because this was the central village of the band. Another village existed in the band territory, but it was small and its people came here for ceremonies and other important events. All able people left the villages for seasonal camps during part of the year to increase the quantity and diversity of their diet.

Woman manufacturing a basket (Mono culture).

An earth lodge, the partially underground construction that served much of the California Area for dwellings and communal houses (Maidu culture).

Men provided an abundance of fish from lakes, rivers, and the ocean, and shellfish added to the bounty. However, it was largely due to the acorn that people led rather sedentary lives. Three inches long and plump, the acorn was a filling and highly nutritious staple food. However, people had learned that it contained something that could make them sick and kill their babies. They subjected acorns to a lengthy process of grinding, leaching, and parching before making them into food. Ground acorn meal was placed in a basin made of sand and lined with leaves. A cover of small branches evened the flow of repeated pourings of spring water. Women baked some of the cleansed acorn meal into cakes and mixed the rest with warm water to make mush. A cook enhanced flavor and nutrition by adding fruits or dried meats to the mush.

California women used basketry methods similar to those of the neighboring Great Basin, but they created a

greater variety of baskets and excelled in technique and design, raising the craft to the artistic level. Their skill was displayed in objects that had as many as sixty stitches to the inch, some so small that the stitches can be distinguished only under a magnifying glass. Many items were elaborately decorated with tiny, bright feathers and beads or carried intricate designs. Such creations were sometimes used as gifts; many had no practical function and were significant only as products of skill and art.

Some individuals specialized in certain economic activities such as trading, basketry, or manufacture of the shell ornaments used to represent wealth. Some were born to family occupations while others specialized because they had displayed talent or gained access to the necessary training. Specializations often brought prestige and wealth to their practitioners.

Basketry, the outstanding craft and art form of Native California ("Mission Indians").

Social Relations

When a child was born, the mother and father both observed many restrictions on their behavior in order to ensure the child's health. People celebrated a girl's puberty with dancing, sometimes lasting for several days. A boy took a major step toward adulthood when he was initiated into a religious secret society.

Parents chose their children's spouses carefully, especially with regard to kinship. Any connection between the two should go back beyond three generations. People of wealth and status were also greatly concerned that their children marry equals. The community was composed of three strata: the wealthy and prestigious elite, the commoners, and the poor. Restrictions on the choice of a marriage partner often made it necessary to find one outside the community.

A man measuring shell money, one sign of wealth in the California Area (Tolowa culture).

Marriage was monogamous, but many men divorced and remarried several times during their lives. Divorce was harder for a wife to obtain, although either partner could leave for a good cause. People recognized that the community chieftain should have several wives because they helped him to fulfill his duties.

The main village of a band rarely exceeded one hundred inhabitants and satellite villages could be as small as one or two extended families. A hereditary chieftain coordinated economic activities within the band and represented it to other communities. The chieftain brought wealth to his position or gained it quickly through his role as economic administrator. He lived in a larger house than other people and displayed his status with the abundance in his house and the extravagant clothes and insignia that he wore. He rarely did ordinary work.

Several assistants helped the chieftain carry out his duties, especially those that involved communication with the people. The chieftain himself sometimes under-

took the important role of ritual manager, organizer of the community's elaborate ceremonial life. No matter how many responsibilities a chieftain assumed, an assistant who played the clown confronted him. This individual acted disrespectfully, satirized his superior, and sometimes explicitly pointed out his failings to the public. As the only person who treated the chieftain this way, the clown served to emphasize the leader's special status. At the same time, he provided a reminder of fallibility.

A chieftain's main duties concerned the food supply. In addition to coordinating internal economic activities, he tried to forestall occasional crises by establishing ties with other communities. This was done by means of gift giving, intermarriage, and ritual alliances.

Conflicts between communities sometimes arose from claims to important resources. Battles were relatively rare, usually brief, and involved few fatalities. In some cases a duel between champions settled an intercommunity dispute. Community administrators appointed war leaders and peace negotiators as needed. People expected their chieftain to favor peace whenever possible.

Knowledge and Expression

Social and ceremonial gatherings took place in a community house, which often served as a men's house and a sweat lodge. The California sweat bath used direct exposure to fire rather than steam. It was a group affair, indulged in for physical comfort, and had little religious or symbolic significance. Tobacco also lacked some of the intense meaning it had elsewhere in North America. It was offered to the spirits, but pipe smoking had little to do with social ritual.

On the other hand, individuals used tobacco to achieve a trance state for the purpose of contacting the supernatural. People also used jimsonweed (Datura) for that purpose. This is a powerful hallucinogen, and experienced men controlled and guided youths through their early encounters with it. A young man took jimsonweed for his initiation ceremony after a period of fasting. It caused nausea and then a trance state with visions that might bring spiritual enlightenment. The most important result of this experience was the acquisition of a guardian spirit. Shamans experimented with the drug in order to achieve refined control over the way it affected them.

The larger religious ceremonies integrated neighboring bands because the rules required that ritual leaders from other groups participate. The greatest occasions drew thousands of people from more than a hundred communities. Participants took the opportunity to engage in economic exchanges, and some of the rituals affirmed the rights of particular persons or groups to specific goods and services.

Shamans prepared the ceremonial places with ritual cleansing. During the festival they displayed their powers to the spectators and sometimes competed with each other. Chieftains and their assistants acted as priests. Secret societies also played a prominent role in these ceremonies. The opportunity to join such a society, and the status achieved within it, depended on the individual's birth, wealth, and skills. Membership was essential to achieving any secular leadership position. Singers, usually a chorus with a leader, provided music for ceremonies. Only rattles and whistles supported them. Rattles were made from deer hooves, cocoons, and split sticks. Whistles were carved from bone or wood.

People cremated their dead in connection with elaborate funerals. Anniversary ceremonies were even more elaborate than the original funerals. Other major observances included the offering of first fruits to the spirits, especially acorns.

PUEBLO AREA

Examples:

Hopi, Zuni, Keresan, Tanoan

Struggling with arid conditions, the Pueblos preserved an ancient complex culture based on farming. By the year 1500, drought had largely restricted them to the plateau of northern Arizona and New Mexico. However, even within this small range, the distinctive and influential Pueblo way of life demands recognition as a Culture Area. The southwest of today is largely associated with the Navaho and Apache, but in 1500 their migrating ancestors were just starting to arrive there. This section describes only the Pueblos and other indigenous farmers.

To survive as farmers in their arid habitat, the Pueblos used natural water sources and irrigation ingeniously. Along with the standard Native American crops, they raised cotton and made it into clothing that suited the environment. With little wood available, they built substantial homes of stone. The adobe walls of today were introduced by the Spanish.

In contrast to the Eastern Area, men were the primary cultivators in Pueblo farming. The male role also included gathering wood and weaving cloth, activities assigned to women in most other cultures. Perhaps this was connected with the relative unimportance of hunting and the negative valuation of warfare. Emphasis on peace fitted in with a general search for harmony in external and internal relations. The Pueblos developed a view of life that was unique in Northern America and perhaps in the New World. They idealized the sacrifice of individuality for the sake of harmony with their neighbors and membership in a tightly knit community.

Pueblo religion conformed to the ideal. It emphasized the cooperative and mechanistic performance of ritual and downplayed the modal North American pattern of personal contact with the supernatural. Several basic beliefs also differentiated the Pueblos, including a female creator and emergence of the original human beings from beneath the earth.

Supernatural beings called kachinas were prominent in ceremonial life. (An alternative spelling, katsina, more accurately represents the pronunciation of the word [Adams 1991].) The fact that a ritual dancer became one with a particular katsina when he put on its mask is the "unique aspect of katsina ritual that distinguishes it from all other masked dancing among Indian tribes in North America" (Adams 1991:15). Thus, within the highly formalized and communal religion of the Pueblos, each man had the opportunity for a personal religious experience. It seems that their unique idea of masked dancing brought the Pueblos close to the emotional religious experience more typical of other Northern Zone natives.

Many preparations and ceremonies took place in special chambers called kivas. Ritual clowns were frequent participants in the public ceremonies. The clown role was probably more prominent and elaborated among the Pueblos than anywhere else in Northern America.

Key features:

- ▶ Men the primary cultivators
- ▶ Cultivation of cotton
- ▶ Stone dwellings
- ▶ Little trade
- ▶ Submergence of individuality
- ▶ Negative value on war
- ▶ Highly communal religious system
- ▶ Kivas, katsinas, ritual clowns
- ▶ Female creator and emergence myth

Modal Patterns in Pueblo Culture

Material Culture

At first glance the village seemed to be composed of several piles of brown blocks. The mud-plastered houses in each section were built up against each other and had no visible doors or windows. Some houses rose above the others in several terraced levels. A network of ladders showed how people got to each level and then descended through the roof into a house. With the ladders pulled up, the structure provided an effective defense against raiders. Within the village, but separate from the houses, the tops of several kivas were visible. Ladders provided access to these underground chambers where men carried out secret rituals.

Part of a Pueblo village, including a corner of the plaza where public ceremonies were performed (Zuni culture).

On days when no major ceremonies were in progress, people worked on various mundane tasks in their ordinary cotton clothes. Men dressed in loincloths or kilts, women in skirts or dresses. Some men brought firewood to their homes while others sat at vertical looms and wove cotton cloth. Women made the cotton clothing, some of which they decorated with vegetable dyes. They also sewed the rabbit skin robes and blankets that people would use when the cool nights brought relief from the desert heat.

Throughout the village, containers provided splashes of color against the dusty browns of the soil and the houses. Women wove colored fibers into their basketry and painted their pots with vegetable juices and minerals. On round jars and hemispheric bowls they inscribed geometric units, subdivided them to create complex designs, and filled in some of the units with black or white.

Pueblo pottery, displaying both craft skill and artistry (Cochiti and Sia cultures).

On some days women left the village to gather plant foods. This was not a crucial task unless weather or warfare seriously diminished the crops. Then the hardy mesquite bean became a staple food, and cactus fruits were a particularly welcome supplement. Men provided most of the food, as well as cotton, from the fields that they cultivated. Hunting was also significant. In some areas rabbits, because of their abundance, rivaled deer as game animals.

Social Relations

The members of each monogamous nuclear family occupied a room or small house of their own, but they were never really alone because their closest relatives lived on each side of them. Together they formed a kinship group that was the basic economic and social unit. However, this did not mean independence. Every kinship group participated constantly in the tightly knit community.

When a baby was born, the family performed its own ritual of formally presenting the newborn to the sun god. Thereafter, most ceremonial experiences would be devoted to making the maturing person a cooperative member of the community. Indulgence ended around the

A room in a pueblo, showing a roof entrance as well as a doorway.

age of two, when parents began to lecture about hard work, frugal use of food, and acceptance of discomfort without crying. They spoke of ogres and giants who carried away bad children, and they allowed the toddlers to catch glimpses of the village disciplinarians as they made their rounds. These individuals, who wore frightening masks and carried whips, paid intimidating visits to incorrigible older children at the request of their parents.

Between the ages of six and ten boys and girls were initiated into one of the ceremonial organizations of the community. During the training period the child underwent rigid physical and dietary restrictions. Some young men accepted further discipline in order to gain the highest levels of religious knowledge. Those who did so looked forward to greater prestige in the community and the opportunity to assume priestly offices that brought political authority.

Because the village chieftain was also the high priest, people expected him to be above social strife and other ordinary affairs. He delegated day-to-day political functions to lesser priests and secular officials. The chieftain could hold his office for life, but he was subject to discipline or even removal by a council composed of lesser priests and other village leaders.

Despite early training and continuing social pressure, some individuals resisted conformity. First, the offender might find himself singled out and ridiculed by the ritual clowns who performed in many ceremonies. If he persisted in antisocial behavior, people would begin to murmur that he might be a witch. When the priests made that judgment official, they whipped him. Finally, the presumed witch was liable to execution if the community blamed his actions for some disaster.

Though they prized peace, men sometimes went to war. Occasionally they fought other Pueblo communities over farmland or accusations of witchcraft. More often they defended themselves against raids by nomads or more warlike farmers. Sometimes they mounted retaliatory attacks on the villages of these raiders. Whatever the cause of a battle, men who killed underwent a long period of ritual purification. Success in war did not bring lasting personal glory.

Knowledge and Expression

Reluctance to wage war was part of a larger worldview that emphasized peace and noncompetitiveness. People tried to live in harmony with other people and with nature. They regularly performed or witnessed ceremonies that were carried out in an orderly communal fashion and devoted to perpetuating rain, sun, and other cycles of nature. One major ceremony followed another throughout most of the year, and the most important ones could last a week or more.

Most men and some women joined one or more of the varied associations devoted to ritual life. The hunting

society worked for the fertility of game animals and the success of hunters. Men who had taken scalps united to ensure the success of warriors and purify those who killed, protecting them from the ghosts of their victims. Clown associations ridiculed deviants and provided entertainment, but their activities also enhanced human fertility. Curing societies healed people, although other groups also had some curing rituals. Women's associations cared for enemy scalps and promoted human fertility. Through the efforts of the katsina society, the village welcomed supernaturals who brought rain and general well-being. Although associations took turns in bearing the primary responsibility for ceremonies, it was common for two or more to cooperate for a particular occasion. Whatever the primary theme of a specific ceremony, its performance was believed to enhance all the major ritual goals.

When the members of an association began preparations for their ceremony, they met in a kiva. They entered through the roof of the underground chamber and climbed a ladder down to the flagstone floor. Cottonwood poles supported the roof, benches lined the walls, and niches held offerings. Society members shared the pipe and offered smoke to supernatural beings. They prayed and planned. When the time came for their ceremony, they performed secret rituals in the kiva. Some involved individualistic dancing that contrasted sharply with the staid performance that the whole village would see.

Priests emerging from a kiva (lower right), the underground ceremonial chamber of the Pueblo Area (Oraibi village, Hopi culture).

The public ceremony was intended to honor the gods and spirits in the manner they had prescribed. Having received their due, they would provide rain and otherwise enhance the food supply, protect the community, and provide long life. Recitations and dance steps were precisely prescribed, and people believed that ritual errors could have serious consequences. A person who made a mistake received bitter criticism and in some cases punishment.

A dance of the katsinas, benevolent gods and ancestral spirits of the Pueblos (Hopi culture).

During part of the year the katsinas danced in the village. These diverse supernatural beings had in common their connection with water and their concern for the well-being of humans. People believed that at least some of the katsinas were souls of their ancient ancestors. According to myth, the actual supernatural beings once visited the village. When they stopped, they gave men permission to impersonate them in the ceremonies. Each masked dancer united his own soul with that of the katsina he represented. All together, the dancers presented the villagers with a grand spectacle of feathered headdresses, bizarre masks, and colorful costumes as they danced in a circle with rattles clacking on their legs.

Costumed clowns, representing spirits, played a prominent role in many ceremonies. Their antics provided comic relief in the midst of intensely solemn rituals as they simulated forbidden behavior, such as incest or eating filth, and parodied people in ways that would have destroyed harmony under ordinary circumstances. But even these outrageous acts had serious purposes. They impressed upon the audience the absurdity of antisocial behavior by humans while reminding them that supernatural beings were above human constraints.

During ceremonial periods and at other times, people communicated with the supernatural by means of prayer sticks. Carved with rudimentary human features and adorned with eagle or turkey feathers, a prayer stick was like a surrogate human sacrifice. People put them in special places as offerings.

The journey to this spiritual life on the earth's surface began when the creator goddess brought the world into existence. In the beginning human ancestors lived underground. Helped by two brothers, the war gods, people gradually climbed through several levels and emerged through a mist onto the surface. Then they migrated in different directions and became the peoples of today.

Pueblo clowns at a corn dance ceremony (Santo Domingo culture).

A Closer Look

The Western Pueblo Region

The Western Pueblos, including the Hopi and Zuni, lived in villages consisting of parallel rows of stone houses. With no rivers in their environment, they depended on rain and wash-off to water their fields. Each family maintained several separate plots, carefully located to maximize the reception of water while minimizing rain damage.

The extended families were based on matrilocal residence, and women owned the houses and land. Matrilineal exogamous clans were represented by lineages in each village, and members of the same lineage occupied contiguous rooms. These groups played major roles in subsistence, community affairs, and religion. Village political offices, for example, were associated with specific households or lineages. The village chieftain always came from one particular clan. This rarely caused any conflict because his authority was relatively limited.

Clans or lineages also controlled the ceremonial associations (although association members did not have to belong to the descent group). A lineage directed ceremonies performed by particular associations. Each lineage or lineage segment had its own ceremonial room where ritual paraphernalia were stored under the supervision of the female head of the descent group. At such a time the male lineage head, usually the senior woman's brother, put up an altar in the ceremonial room and placed sacred objects on it. The most important was the fetish that symbolized the group itself, an ear of maize wrapped in cloth and feathers. Members of that lineage, or of the same clan, came to visit, smoke the ritual pipe, and pray.

The ceremonial associations included one devoted to rain, which reflected a distinctive religious emphasis on weather control. Every man was initiated into one of the main associations, and so were some women. In addition there were a few all-female groups. The katsinas received a great deal of ritual attention. Boys and girls were introduced to them between the ages of six and ten, although only boys received the most intimate knowledge and only men could dance as katsinas.

The Rio Grande Region

Tanoan speakers occupied the valley of Rio Grande River where it flowed from north to south through New Mexico. These Pueblos channeled water from the Rio Grande and its tributaries to irrigate their fields, resulting in more communal effort and less food anxiety than among the Western Pueblos. Rio Grande villagers built their houses around one or more plazas. Bilateral kinship defined the extended family as the basic economic and social unit. Sons as well as daughters inherited land, usually when the senior member of the family became nonproductive.

Rio Grande communities had a quasimoiety system that divided each community into halves that were defined by varied criteria. Although parental membership was often a factor in recruitment to these groups, it was never a simple matter of unilineal descent. In some cases, for example, a wife changed to her husband's group when she married. Each division fulfilled a number of public functions by coordinating the activities of affiliated associations, including those dedicated to war, clowning, curing, and hunting. Among their responsibilities were cleaning and constructing irrigation ditches, organizing and directing planting activities, nominating and installing secular officials, repairing the community kiva or constructing a new one, keeping a solar calendar and announcing dates for ceremonies, cleaning the plaza for communal ceremonies, and organizing the ceremonies.

A village also had several associations that were not connected with the quasimoities, even though their interests overlapped. The hunter society held small dances between the major ceremonies and arranged a ritual rabbit hunt. The warrior society also held small dances and organized communal ritual races. Rio Grande Pueblos placed greater emphasis on war than those to the west did.

The Rio Grande chieftain was exempt from ordinary work. He and his priests compelled people to perform communal duties, both secular and ceremonial. They had greater power than the Western Pueblo leaders, subjecting the disobedient to physical punishment or confiscation of possessions and banishment.

The O'odham Region

To the west and south of the Pueblos the lands of the O'odham (Pima and Papago) extended from Arizona and New Mexico into the northwestern Mexican state of Sonora. Around 1500 A.D. the O'odham seem to have been emerging from the decline of a more complex and Pueblo-like culture. Whether by common origin or diffusion, the O'odham and Pueblo cultures displayed a number of significant similarities.

Their social organization tended to be loose and flexible (Kehoe 1992), perhaps reflecting the relative importance of food gathering, which provided at least 40 percent of the diet under ordinary conditions. People lived in simple homes of wood, brush, and turf, strung out along streams or irrigation canals. Families aggregated in a summer village governed by a council.

The council chose a chieftain to minister to the social and ritual concerns of the village with the help of several assistants. The chieftain lived in a special house, larger and apart from the others, which also housed sacred objects.

His helpers included a village crier, who announced the decisions of the council. The Keeper of the Smoke was the main ceremonial official, and others took charge of specific ceremonies and festivals (Baldwin 1973).

The desired state of harmony was symbolized by abundance of maize, deer, and eagles. Eagles were especially significant in this desert environment because they could fly to the clouds from which the rain came. A distinctive ritual was the solemn drinking of fermented cactus juice, a purificatory action that ensured rain. Smoking of tobacco in cane cigarettes was another important ritual act.

O'odham differed from the Pueblos (and were more typically Northern American) in their pursuit of personal supernatural power. Ordinary people had visions and power dreams from animal spirits. Shamans were significant religious figures and (again in contrast to the Pueblos) subject to no more wariness than anywhere else.

SOUTHERN AMERICAN ZONE

Areas:

- Subamazon

- Tupinamban

- Supra-Amazon

- Brazilian Highlands

- Argentine

Southern
American
Zone

with Areas
and Regions

Supra-Amazon
Area

Western
Subamazon
Region

Subamazon
Area

Brazilian
Highland
Area

Tupinamban
Area

Argentine
Area

Fuegan
Region

Previous page   Interior of a typically large house in the Southern American
Zone; women preparing for a ceremony (Waorani culture, Ecuador).

OVERVIEW OF THE ZONE

Examples:

Jivaro, Kayapo, Tupinamba, Taino,
Tewelche, Yahgan

The Southern Zone stretched from the Bahamas to the tip of Tierra del Fuego and from the eastern foothills of the Andes to the Atlantic Ocean. This cultural zone differed from the geographic continent of South America in that it included the Caribbean islands and excluded the Andes. The bulk of the land and the vast majority of people were located in tropical latitudes. Thanks to relatively low altitude and high rainfall (in contrast to the adjacent Andes), the environment itself was truly tropical. The mosaic of vegetation incorporated various forms of forest and grassland. The modal way of life was that of the horticultural community, based on slash-and-burn farming. Only in the narrowing funnel at the end of the continent, did tropical habitats give way to a temperate regime that harbored only foragers.

Generalizations about this Zone carry less weight than many others in the book because South America is "the least known continent" (Lyon, ed. 1985). Much progress has been made recently (e.g., Roosevelt, ed. 1994; D. Wilson 1999), but the judgment still rings true. One thing we do know a great deal about is manioc, the distinctive staple cultigen of the Zone. It was a root crop well suited to wet tropical conditions. The term "cassava" may specifically denote dough made from manioc, but it is often applied to the plant as well. Southern American cooks spiced this bland staple with chiles, which are often misleadingly lumped with another plant under the name "peppers" (S. Coe 1994). Chiles are the pungent fruits of several *Capsicum* species.

The tapir, a large game animal of the Southern American forests.

Manioc, familiar to some of us as the basis for tapioca, is a very starchy plant with little protein. Cultivation of maize and beans added some protein to the diet, but these crops had limited potential in many Southern American environments. Protein scarcity made animal foods important. Men hunted deer, but it is difficult to find any designation of the species in ethnographic accounts. Presumably the pampas deer *(Ozotoceros)*, the most common in South America (Nowak 1999), was the usual prey. It was a relatively small deer, weighing 50 to 80 pounds. Among other animals hunted, some armadillo and peccary species exceeded 100 pounds (peccaries are wild relatives of pigs). The largest land animal was the tapir *(Tapirus)*, a hornless distant relative of the rhinoceros that weighed up to 500 pounds. Because tapirs were rare, people obtained more meat from numerous large rodents that ranged up to 25 pounds and three feet in length. The biggest and most famous rodent, the hundred-pound capybara *(Hydrochaeris)*, was a less common prey.

The capybara, one of many large rodents that provided food for Southern Americans.

The sparse vegetation, due to the canopy allowing little sunlight to reach the forest floor, limited mammal populations in the forests. People often turned to the streams, rivers, and oceans for sustenance. The larger the body of water, the more likely that fishing would equal or exceed hunting as a source of food. However, the waters did offer one mammalian bonanza: the manatee *(Trichechus)*, a walruslike animal (without tusks) about ten feet long and weighing at least a ton.

Although descent tended to be patrilineal, men went to live with their wives' families to provide bride service, and in some cases matrilocal residence was permanent. This may have contributed to tensions that men expressed in ritual and folklore. The most famous example is the varied birth practices loosely classified together as the "couvade." In the extreme case the father imitated the process of labor and birth and then underwent a period of "recovery" while the mother quickly resumed her ordinary activities. This was rare. In the modal pattern of the couvade for this Zone, father and mother observed similar restrictions on behavior.

Southern Zone women had much the same autonomy as those in Northern America, but not the same respect. Men expressed negative stereotypes about women in everyday life and asserted their superiority in myth and ritual. Following Murphy and Murphy (1985), Kensinger (1995) argues that Southern Zone cultures defused gender hostility with ritual. He sees significance in the fact that such rituals pitted men and women against each other as groups rather than as individuals. This explains how couples could lead a calm and even affectionate existence in an atmosphere of gender hostility. On a larger scale it may account for the fact that "some sources describe women as their husbands' slaves, others as their companions" (Lowie 1948:30). The former view may stem more from indigenous male ideology and the latter from real life.

Humans shared the South American continent with one of the most imposing big cats in the world, the jaguar *(Panthera onca)*. The head and body length of a male could reach six feet and the tail added another three. Weighing over 300 pounds and decorated with large spots, this was a terrifying enemy and an awe-inspiring role model. The jaguar played a prominent role in Southern Zone myth and ritual that contrasts with the Northern focus on eagle and bear. The dominant cat of the Northern Zone (called cougar, puma, or mountain lion) was much smaller than the jaguar and drably colored. Southern America differed from the Northern Zone in two other aspects of expressive behavior: gambling was virtually absent, and shamans used tobacco to achieve the trance state. Numerous physical and behavioral characteristics of the Southern shaman can be explained by heavy use of high-nicotine tobacco (Wilbert 1987).

The jaguar, an impressive big cat of the Southern American forests.

> ### *Key features:*
>
> ▶ Horticultural communities
> ▶ Communal houses
> ▶ Manioc and sweet potatoes
> ▶ Fish and rodents for protein
> ▶ Basketry by men
> ▶ Bride service and matrilocal residence
> ▶ Couvade
> ▶ Symbolic significance of jaguar
> ▶ Tobacco shamanism
> ▶ Ritual cannibalism

Modal Patterns in Southern American Culture

Material Culture

In a land of tropical forests interspersed with patches of savanna, villages occupied cleared areas near rivers and streams. Those that stood near their enemies huddled within wooden stockades or circles of thorny vegetation, and a few had moats. Within its defenses a village consisted of elongated houses made of palm thatch, arranged around a flat dirt plaza. Gardens accompanied the houses while staple crops grew in cleared plots in the forest.

As dawn approached, the doors of each house were still blockaded against enemy infiltration. Inside, the building's structure was more obvious. Heavy posts supported the roof and anchored the walls. Between the wall posts stretched a lattice of poles covered with thatch like that of the roof. The house pillars and other posts supported several dozen hammocks, in which people still slept.

A woman stirred and opened her eyes to see the thatched roof that peaked above her at several times the height of a person. From the roof came rustlings that occasionally ended with a plop on the floor nearby, followed by scuttling sounds. The roof was inhabited by insects and mice and by the spiders and lizards that preyed on them. It was visited by snakes that were interested in all of the other denizens. Worse, the thatch was disintegrating and the structure weakening after about four years of assault by tropical sun, rain, and wind. Soon the villagers would build a new settlement, probably just a few yards away from the present one because the fields continued to produce enough food. When they had exhausted all the arable land in the vicinity, they would move further.

Swinging out of her hammock, the woman noticed others doing the same around the perimeter of the house. She looked away quickly so that they would not think she was too interested in their affairs. Although the dwelling contained no internal walls, people tried to give each other some privacy. Each family clustered in the area marked by their own small hearth and their possessions. Some, including a variety of ceramic containers, stood on the floor along the nearby wall while bows and arrows protruded from the thatched wall itself. Other items hung from a post or rafter in baskets or nets.

The people who began preparation for the early tropical morning wore virtually no clothing, but their bodies were bright with decoration. Everyone wore cotton bands on their legs, usually below the knee, and many wore armlets and bracelets of bark or beaded string. Red and black designs on their faces and bodies protected against certain supernatural forces as well as conveying social or ceremonial meanings. Men stood out in bright feather hairdressings and bracelets. They also wore labrets, plugs that penetrated the flesh below their lips. Warriors took pride in the necklaces of human teeth that signaled their successes.

A woman peeling manioc, the staple root crop of Southern America (Cashinahua culture, Peru).

After rising, a woman revived the fire that had made the night drier and warmer for her family. During the day, she used it to cook. She boiled meat in a ceramic pot and baked manioc bread on a ceramic griddle. The bread took the form of a wide, flat, circular loaf. Processing manioc took a great deal of time, especially in communities that depended on the bitter variety. This form of the plant contained an acid that women removed by means of an arduous leaching process. They began the treatment by shredding the roots on a studded board or a roughened slab of pottery. Then they used a lever to squeeze the pulp through a long basketry cylinder. Finally, they toasted the manioc into cakes or dried it into flour. Either one could be eaten immediately or

stored. People accepted the extra work associated with bitter manioc because it produced high yields.

On many days women gave time to making beer from manioc. They chewed the tubers and spit the mash into large ceramic pots in which it fermented and could then be stored. A woman also had several crafts to occupy her, one of the most important being the manufacture of hammocks for her family. She spun cotton thread and then wove it. In addition to hammocks, she made leg bands from the cotton.

Woman making a hammock, Southern America's distinctive invention for resting and sleeping (Camayura culture, Brazil).

A woman occasionally went to the forest to care for the fields of staple crops, which included sweet potatoes and maize as well as manioc. More often she tended the garden near the house, where she raised pineapples and other fruits, along with squashes, chiles, beans, peanuts, and gourds. The gardens also contained nonfood plants that were useful in a variety of ways. When people wanted paint, they went to the gardens and picked berries for the red pigment and larger tree fruits for the black. The berries yielded soft seeds that could be crushed with the finger to provide red paint for immediate use. However, people boiled some of the juice with oil to make a paste that they could keep for times when the berries were not in season. The tree fruits required a few minutes in hot embers. Then a person could cut off the top, squeeze the sides, and dip a cotton brush into the black paint. These pigments stayed on the body for a week or more.

A man made most of his family's basketry with vines and leaves. Using different weaving patterns, he produced a variety of items with a pleasing appearance. When some strands had been dyed, usually black, the result was a design that brightened baskets, trays, mats, and fans around the household. Men also made carrying baskets and manioc presses for their wives to use. An important basketry item for male work was the fish trap.

A man making a basket, distinctively a male job in the Southern American Zone (Waorani culture, Ecuador).

Spider monkey, one of several large monkey species that provided Southern Americans with meat.
    *   used blowguns

One of a man's major tasks in the village was the shaping and conditioning of his bow from a single piece of wood, a process that took time and patience. He made the string from vegetable fiber. Stood on end, the completed bow exceeded the height of its maker. The arrows were almost as long.

On the hunt a man searched the trees for monkeys and birds and looked for deer or large rodents on the ground. The rodents, covered with coarse, brownish fur, had stocky bodies, blunt heads, and short tails. The hunter shot an armadillo when he could catch it in the open; otherwise, he had to dig the animal from its burrow and club it. Although the exhausting job sometimes took several hours, it could result in a lot of meat when the animal weighed as much as a person. Occasionally hunters encountered the greatest prize of the land, a tapir. Lumbering through the forest alone, an adult tapir presented little danger to men; however, a cornered animal would try to bite, and its bulk alone could cause injury.

Peccaries traveled in groups, some containing a dozen animals and some containing more than a hundred. Armed with long tusks and often aggressive, they could be very dangerous to human hunters. Men were safer and more successful when they attacked peccaries cooperatively. Cooperative hunting could also be effective with smaller animals. From time to time a group of men would set fire to savanna grass to drive a large number of animals together. Sometimes the hunters waited

for the fleeing animals at a particular place; other times they surrounded them.

There were many days when a man took special arrows, with multipronged heads, and went to a stream or river. From the bank or in a canoe he shot large fish. They provided a great deal of food even though people did not prize the flesh as much as meat. Sometimes the waters provided abundance in the form of a manatee. Men in a canoe easily spotted and caught one of these grayish-brown giants as it paddled along at about three

The peccary, a major game animal of the Southern Zone.

miles per hour within ten feet of the surface. They could wait for the manatee to surface for breath, which it did several times each minute, and then propel their arrows or spears into it. Since it was a plant-eater with blunt teeth and flippers, only the animal's bulk presented any serious danger. Once wrestled ashore and butchered, the carcass provided large quantities of meat and oil.

Periodically a group of people, men or women or both, cooperated to capture smaller fish in large numbers. Sometimes they drove the fish into shallows and grabbed them by hand, which could be a hilarious occasion. An easier and more productive method was to drug a pool of water with a plant extract so that the stunned or dead fish floated to the top. Fishers cornered their prey in natural pools when available, but they often built weirs from upright poles.

Men and women also gathered turtles and tortoises, which could be kept alive for long periods until needed. Even without food or water the reptiles sometimes survived for a week or more. They provided little meat compared to mammals, but people enjoyed eating the organs. During breeding season, thousands of turtle eggs became available in the soft sands by the water.

People spent less time gathering plants than in other subsistence pursuits, but they obtained some important materials that way. They collected insect larvae and honey for food and augmented their crops with wild fruits and vegetables, many from palm trees. Nuts and seeds provided convenient and nutritious food (handy for snacks or traveling) and also oils for various purposes. Women cooked in oil, and they used it to preserve red dye. People gathered materials for craftwork, and every few years they turned to wild leaves and vines for the construction of new houses. Periodically a large group, sometimes everyone, left the village for days or weeks to increase their foraging opportunities. Some of these treks were long hunting expeditions and others, usually determined by season, emphasized plant foods.

Social Relations

Marriage required bride service. A young man spent several years in the house of his new or prospective wife, hunting on behalf of her parents and providing them with other help. Most men hoped to marry a cross-cousin or niece so that they could live among kin. A man preferred a bride from his mother's kin in order to establish or maintain a bond between that kinship group and his own patrilineal group. Matrilocality was permanent for some men, but others shifted to patrilocal residence later in the marriage. A husband was more likely to receive permission to go back to his own kin if they provided a wife to his brother-in-law, resulting in an exchange of brides between the groups.

During a pregnancy, the father and mother observed similar taboos to ensure their child's welfare. They avoided eating, or even touching, certain animals and plants with characteristics undesirable for humans so as not to transmit those traits to the baby. They refused certain other foods in order to prevent a difficult delivery. The parents also refrained from activities that could do magical harm: if a parent went into deep water, the child might drown; handling a cutting implement could cause injury to the unborn baby. People explained the prominence of the father in these rituals in terms of his powerful bond with the infant's soul. By observing the rituals, a man made the community aware that he would take responsibility for the child.

At the time of birth the father undertook additional limitations. He took to his bed for several days and refrained from heavy work for some time after that. Thus the baby was not magically weakened at a crucial time. Parents continued to observe the prenatal taboos until some time after the birth, at least until the umbilical cord fell away naturally.

Children remained closely attached to their mothers for six or seven years, undertaking few responsibilities. They walked on stilts and played with a ball made from maize leaves, catching it or batting it back and forth with the palms of their hands. Their dolls were made from wood, clay, wax, gum, bone, or straw. In later childhood a boy underwent the first in a series of more or less ritualized events that marked his path to manhood, such as the perforation for a labret and receiving a genital covering for everyday wear. Youths formed teams to play the rubber ball game in which they advanced the ball by hitting it with parts of the body other than the hands. As adults they would continue to wrestle and play the ball game. A girl's time for childhood games ended with a puberty ritual that included some painful physical ordeal. In some cases the puberty rituals concluded with the girl's marriage, especially if she had been betrothed as a child.

Marriage brought more restrictions to a woman than to a man. A husband might beat his wife for adultery, and in many cases he engaged in a violent conflict with her lover. Despite such outbursts, the lives of many couples went smoothly because they had feelings for one another or simply because they spent little time together.

If people needed leadership in their work, they turned to the chieftain of the house. When necessary, he coordinated cooperative production activities, including farming, hunting, and fishing. The house chieftain was an older man with several wives, admired for his generosity and skill. As a close male relative of the previous leader, he had been exempted from matrilocal residence and bride service. Living among close male and female relatives, he could exert a strong influence over the entire household. A chieftain obtained his wives through bride wealth or by virtue of his prestige.

The chieftain in charge of the entire village, often one of the household leaders, had the same advantages but somewhat different duties. He organized feasts and ceremonies, which overlapped with his responsibility for receiv-

A man prepared for a festival. His decorations—feathered headdress, cotton armbands, and body paint—are elaborations of everyday adornment (Waorani culture).

ing visitors to the settlement. An event attended by people from other villages was a matter of prestige for the hosts.

Some of these events were linked to conflict between villages. Some were intended to make peace while others led to quarrels that became feuds. War meant a series of raids between the villages involved and any allies that might join them. The men who joined a war party had varied ideas in mind. Revenge was paramount to those who had recently lost close relatives to the enemy, whether in previous combat or through sorcery. Other men hoped to acquire women for wives or concubines. All expected to gain prestige in the community if they were successful.

Before an expedition the village held a ceremony that roused the warriors and provided them with supernatural help. Then they set out, carrying their clubs and their spears or arrows. Some of these tense journeys lasted for just a few hours. Others took several days and required the men to carry food as well as weapons.

The ideal was to surprise the enemy near dawn while they were still in their hammocks. As the attackers approached the village in darkness, they moved with great care to avoid the traps that had been set for them. These could include sharp objects scattered on the ground, covered pits with stakes at the bottom, and spears or arrows set in a bent sapling or pole. Those who survived these obstacles surrounded the village and began a barrage of spears or arrows. With luck they killed

some of the inhabitants and drove the others out in disarray. Then they killed more and took some captive.

After a victory the warriors set about severing the heads and limbs of their victims. Display of these trophies at home would bring prestige to those who had acquired them and ease the feelings of relatives who desired revenge. The heads would be put on display, the teeth made into men's necklaces, and the long bones into flutes.

Knowledge and Expression

Men cared for gardens of tobacco because they were the sole or primary users of the plant. After drying it, they used various plant wrappings to roll large cigars that approached a foot in length. Smoking gave a man a great deal of pleasure during his leisure time. The act was often a social one as men in a group passed the cigar around.

Tobacco transported shamans to the trance state in which they interacted with the supernatural world. From cigars that were even larger than those used for pleasure, a shaman inhaled far more smoke than a casual user. Some shamans puffed very rapidly while others smoked a number of cigars in rapid succession. As the tobacco took effect, the shaman began to breathe heavily. He gagged several times and then vomited. Sporadic vomiting continued while more severe symptoms appeared. The man lost control of his body and slipped to the ground as tremors seized him. The tremors became more intense and ended in convulsions. Finally, the shaman lay stiff and paralyzed, apparently not breathing, seemingly dead. During his trance the shaman entered a world of flashing lights and a giant sun. Sometimes he heard voices chanting or giving messages. He saw various supernatural beings. With the help of his own familiar spirits, the shaman recovered the soul of the sick person if necessary.

After several long minutes the shaman regained control of his body and slowly began to treat his patient. Many cures involved application of tobacco to the subject, either by blowing smoke or by pressing wet leaves against the skin. This made it easier to remove alien objects lodged in the victim's body. Absorbing some of the strong tobacco, the patient at least felt better. The drug also killed botfly larvae that burrowed under the skin; people envisioned many of their supernatural enemies as being similar to such natural parasites.

Tobacco made it possible for anyone to become a shaman. It took only the will and physical ability to endure rigorous training and lifelong use of tobacco. Most of the seekers were men, but a few women made the spiritual journey. The prospective shaman sought tutelage from an experienced practitioner, who taught his protégé about the supernatural world and supervised the necessary fasts and other rituals. Most important, the master gradually developed the novice's ability to use tobacco.

After months or years of supervised progress, the novice first achieved the ritual death necessary to exerting control in the other world. By experiencing death and rebirth, he acquired the power to protect other people from death. He learned to control his use of tobacco so that, whenever called upon, he could achieve the transition from this world to the next and back again.

Death became part of the shaman's life in many ways, including his appearance. As he grew gaunt and pale from eating little, he better understood the idea that tobacco was food for the spirits. It acted like food in diminishing his hunger, as well as dulling his taste, and yet it did not sustain him like real food. Therefore, it must be sustenance for the supernatural beings associated with him.

The shaman became active at night, the time associated with the Underworld and death. He walked surely in the dark, seeing things that other people could not. Heavy tobacco use causes a form of amblyopia in which sharper night vision is combined with dimming of daylight vision and decline in color perception. These symptoms, along with a high level of nicotine stimulation, may have inclined shamans to be unusually active at night.

A great shaman identified himself with the jaguar, a power of the night and a symbol of the Underworld. He could become a jaguar and did so in order to perform his most difficult feats. The distinctive singing voice needed to communicate with the spirits, a guttural and raspy sound like the voice of a jaguar, began to develop after weeks of heavy smoking during apprenticeship. In addition to the raspy voice and nocturnal proclivities, tobacco shamans gave off a pungent body odor and reported a roughness of the tongue. The symbolic association be-

The face of the jaguar, the animal of the night with which the greatest shamans identified.

tween shaman and jaguar was further reinforced by the spotted appearance of the tobacco plant.

Though well acquainted with death, a shaman sometimes plunged into the midst of life by officiating at communal ceremonies. These rites celebrated the farming cycle, placated the most powerful supernaturals, and provided support and recognition for the efforts of the warriors. Here, too, the shaman brought to his people the power of tobacco, often by blowing its smoke on the participants. Men danced during every ceremony, shuffling in a line or circle, each dancer with a hand on either or both of those nearest him. Others played flutes or trumpets of shell, clay, and wood. They shook gourd rattles and sang.

It was difficult to control spirits for the benefit of people because most of the spirits were hostile to humans or easily offended by them. The forest abounded with such beings, eager to frighten or harm people. Beyond the spirits there were evil gods with far greater powers. Tobacco was vital in dealing with all these supernaturals because they needed it for food. By feeding them, a communicant could harness their powers. The shaman's familiarity with this use of tobacco made him indispensable to the community.

Feeling anxiety about so many supernatural beings, people delighted in stories concerning the culture heroes who had helped humans in various ways. Some of these beings were not much better disposed toward people than the contemporary spirits, and many of their benefits to humanity were accidents. However, the culture heroes were distant in the mythological past or in another world to which they had retired after concluding their activities on earth. Their works remained while they posed no danger.

Many people knew the stories, in varied versions, but it took a gifted teller to bring the mythological time to life. People were glad to have one in the house or at least in the village. In the evening they lay in their hammocks or sat on the floor and watched the elderly artist, usually a man but sometimes a woman, re-create the ancient world. His quick gestures made the story livelier as he spoke in the characters' voices and imitated the sounds of animals. The listeners laughed and interrupted with questions.

In myths the world already existed; nobody knew how it came to be. Culture heroes transformed the original world into its current state. Some brought forth the waters by breaking into a container that held them. Some caused the separation of night from day and established the heavenly bodies. Some created people, animals, and plants.

One of the most important myths described the origin of the relationship between humans and jaguars. A boy who had been abandoned by a male relative ended up in the village of the jaguars, who still had human characteristics. The boy was menaced by a jaguar and retaliated by killing one or more of them. Then he sought and found the relative who abandoned him. In different versions these events had varied effects on human beings.

Myths told of the differences and conflicts between men and women. The sexes had been created separately, and their joining was difficult. Mythical women, some in monstrous form, had attacked men, stolen from them, or tried to control and oppress them. Somewhere on this earth, on an island or deep in the forest, a village of women excluded men. According to one common story, the prior origin of men made them superior to women. Another common myth described an ancient world in which women dominated men and behaved irresponsibly; men rebelled and established the order that exists today. Women rejected these claims and expressed their own negative stereotypes about men. They also vented their feelings in public rituals, either satirizing the pride and pretensions of men or physically attacking them with weapons such as stinging nettles.

When a person died, men dug a grave in the floor of the communal house and placed the body within, covered by cloth to avert contact with the soil. In the near future they would recover the bones and give them a ritual reburial. Then the deceased might make a final gift to the living: people often found wild tobacco on graves (and at the sites of abandoned houses), which they saw as a sign that the plant came from the ancestors. Tobacco grows well in disturbed soil.

A Closer Look

Cannibalism

The Southern Zone has been depicted as a center of cannibalism. The word itself is derived from one of the Zone's ethnic groups, the Caribs. However, according to an influential study (Arens 1979), stories of cannibalism were nothing but lies spread by European conquerors to justify their treatment of native peoples. Although there is certainly some truth in this assertion, experts are convinced that cannibalism really did occur (e.g., Bruhns 1994; Conklin 2001; Dole 1985; Ralegh 1997). On the other hand, it is likely that it was practiced only by a minority of the cultures in the Zone; thus it was not a modal pattern. We consider cannibalism here because of the combination of popular attention and scientific controversy and because it was a distinctive cultural pattern that was practiced widely (if thinly) in the Southern Zone.

More accurately, Southern American cannibalism included two cultural patterns: (1) exocannibalism was practiced against outsiders in connection with warfare; (2) endocannibalism (also called mortuary or funerary cannibalism) was part of the funerary or memorial rituals for a member of the participants' own community. Within each category the form and meaning of the practices varied from one culture to another. However, both forms were largely symbolic. Many peoples consumed only a small portion of the deceased to express a profound sentiment or achieve a supernatural goal.

In some societies warriors ate small portions of flesh as a way of expressing contempt for the enemy. Others did it to ward off the ghost of the deceased. In still other cases people ate a particular part of the body to obtain a special benefit; most often warriors consumed the heart to acquire qualities such as courage or skill. Many societies incorporated exocannibalism into a ceremony or festival. Participants killed a prisoner for the purpose, often regarding the act as a sacrifice to the supernatural.

Mortuary cannibalism was for many practitioners a symbolic way to maintain contact with the dead. In this respect it followed the same principle as the communion ritual in Christianity: renew the connection with a departed spiritual entity by incorporating the entity's essence into your own physical body. The particulars varied from one culture to another as to who was to be consumed (if there were any restrictions at all), preparation of the body, and which mourners would participate.

In the most common practice mourners cremated the body or the defleshed bones and mixed the ashes into a ritual drink. The most common purpose was to preserve something of the deceased: the essence of a relative, the energy of the ancestors, the courage of a warrior, or the power of a shaman. Even if the spiritual essence was gone, the ritual was a way to honor the person and provide a warm resting place for the remains. Some peoples clearly viewed burial in the ground as cold and even degrading.

There were some cultures in which people ate the flesh of the deceased rather than taking ashes in a drink. The best available information (but from only two societies) indicates that flesh eating was restricted to adults and performed by in-laws rather than blood relatives (Conklin 2001). In such cases people often consumed only a small symbolic portion. Many regarded the act as a disagreeable ritual duty (Dole 1985).

Subamazon Area

Examples:

Jivaro, Tukano, Cashinawa, Moyo, Munduruku, Mehinaku

For want of a better term I name the Subamazon Area for its location. Most of the Area was south of the Amazon River, and the westerly part encompassed the remote headwaters of the Amazon.

An important feature of Subamazon social life was the men's circle: men of a village met regularly in the same place, usually in the plaza, to socialize and conduct most of their regular activities. Beer played an important role in social and ritual life. While some beer parties were purely social, every major ritual occasion included such a celebration.

Subamazon men strongly emphasized their presumed superiority to women. They rested their claim in large part on the supernatural power in sacred musical instruments that they possessed. The instruments are usually termed "flutes" or "trumpets" in the anthropological literature. However, these large and simple instruments bore little resemblance to what most of us think of as flutes or trumpets, so I refer to them by the loose generic term "horns."

Key features:

▶ Men's circle

▶ Social and ritual importance of beer

▶ Sacred horns

Modal Patterns in Subamazon Culture

Material Culture

A woman slept in a hammock below the level of her husband's, in accord with his view of her status. When she rose in the morning, she tended the pepper pot that would boil throughout the day to provide food for snacks and meals. The ceramic pot contained manioc juice that had been boiled with chiles. The woman frequently replenished the food supply in the pot with bits of meat or small fish and added ants when large ones were available. She used a mortar and pestle of wood to process foods.

A wife served regular meals in the morning and evening. Each meal included manioc bread and, ideally, large pieces of meat. Sometimes women boiled the meat in water; sometimes men barbecued it on a grill made from horizontal sticks supported by three or four legs. Everyone washed their hands carefully before eating and did so again afterwards. Men and women ate separately, women serving the men.

Although her pepper pot and manioc bread provided an adequate diet, a woman always hoped that her husband or male relatives would bring home a large animal to eat. Because women prized meat as much as the hunters did, hunting was a prestigious activity. Even so, women sometimes found it necessary to remind the men of their responsibility—occasionally questioning their masculinity in the process.

In addition to dugout canoes, men made rafts from balsa wood to provide platforms for fishing or for hunting aquatic creatures. They also made canoes by heating and shaping a single large sheet of bark. These light craft maneuvered easily in shallow water. They were also easy to carry around rapids and waterfalls or from stream to stream. Bark canoes facilitated long-distance travel for war or trade.

Men traded for a few essential items such as salt or poison for projectiles. However, they spent more time exchanging raw materials or finished goods related to self-decoration and ritual. Some common trade items were pottery, cotton products, ornaments, and raw materials for ornaments. In many cases they obtained manufactured items that they could have made for themselves. Furthermore, in many trade relationships, recipients had to take what was offered, and they could defer repayment for a year or longer. It seems that the main purpose of trade was to facilitate relationships between individuals in different communities and interdependence between villages for alliances or at least nonaggression.

Social Relations

In the morning men sat together in their place apart from the family houses. Some were preparing to leave the village for various tasks; others would stay all day and do craft work or just relax. Some of the men gossiped idly while others talked about more important matters such as hunting and war and ceremonies. In this same place they conducted more formal discussions when communal decisions were necessary.

Having come from elsewhere to live with their wives, the men in any given village could be strangers or even enemies to one another. The men's circle gave them a chance to create a feeling of solidarity and reinforce their view of themselves as superior to women. Women tended to observe the forms of male dominance in everyday life, and they probably had good reason to do so. It is likely that frequent warfare enforced a degree of real dependence on men, especially because enemies often lived nearby. Without protection by their own men, women ran an almost continuous risk of being raped, captured, or killed by enemies.

Women were quite conscious of their position and made use of the solidarity that came naturally in a matrilocal village. They supported each other openly and, where necessary to circumvent male control, duplicitously. In situations where men were likely to close ranks against a female threat to social order, as in the case of a blatantly promiscuous woman, gossip and criticism from other women often brought the violator under control before the men acted.

The morning talk in the men's circle was interrupted by the loud voice of the village chieftain as he approached and harangued them to work hard and get along with one another. They resumed their discussions as the chieftain moved on through the village to give his message to the women. Some mornings were quieter, but often that just meant that the harangue was coming in the evening. Because a chieftain had little authority over his villagers, he depended on personal characteristics such as oratorical skills to exert influence. The strongest chieftains had shamanic powers, which tended to intimidate people.

One of the village chieftain's more important functions was to coordinate preparations for a beer party. This was a small matter if contained within the village but an occasion for great excitement when guests from other settlements were invited. Then women labored for days or weeks to accumulate huge quantities of beer in large ceramic jars or wooden containers. A successful party enhanced the prestige of the whole village among its neighbors.

On the day of the party the villagers watched eagerly for their guests, hoping that none had rejected the invitation because of a suspicion of sorcery or some unexpected grudge. Their anxiety eased as the first group of guests approached the settlement and walked in with stiff dignity. The male hosts offered them a formal greeting while women and children enjoyed the brilliant feather headdresses, intricate body painting, and other finery. The hosts' satisfaction grew as contingents from additional villages entered in the same way.

Soon they were serving their seated guests with large gourds of beer as musicians began to play and people began to dance. Each guest swallowed his beer as quickly as possible, had it replaced almost instantly, and downed it again. Soon one of them staggered away to vomit, and others followed. Their hosts plied them with more beer as soon as they returned, and pursued the reluctant ones to the dark corners of the village. When some passed out, their hosts revived them and offered more to drink. It was a matter of prestige to provide more than enough beer to make everyone drunk. It was a matter of courtesy and honor for the guests to drink as much as possible, facilitated by vomiting.

Women drank less than the men or nothing at all, but they participated vigorously in the singing and dancing. Part of the time they danced with the men, often close to them and in a flirtatious way. Some, including a few married women, had an affair with a particular man in mind. In the crowd and the growing darkness, amidst the swirling sounds of horns and drums and song, with many of the male hosts drunk along with their guests, there would be opportunities to get away for a while. The revelry would continue throughout the night and perhaps for several days thereafter.

Some people with more restraint, especially chieftains, watched for trouble. A husband could take offense at his wife's real or imagined flirtation with another man. Another might take the occasion to retaliate for a past adultery. Some men were on edge because of the implied competition in providing and consuming beer. A careless word could be taken as a threat to do sorcery. Suddenly two men were shouting at each other and then grappling as chieftains or women tried to intervene.

People recognized that grievances might come out at a drinking party. Sometimes the result was desirable. The men traded blows or wrestled and put an end to their conflict. Other occasions saw a new rift created or an old one made more bitter. In the worst case, allies of two antagonists joined the fight before others could control it. Then a village might split or two villages become enemies.

Knowledge and Expression

The men's circle controlled religious knowledge and organized communal ritual observances. The major ceremonies were times to invite guests from other villages and to have beer parties. By taking leave of their ordinary senses through massive drinking, men gained access to the spirits.

Men in the circle had seen the sacred horns, musical instruments kept hidden from women and children. The horns embodied powerful supernatural beings who were well disposed to those who cared for them. The men brought the horns out and played them for ceremonial occasions, either to honor the supernaturals they represented or to enhance some other kind of ritual. Women had to withdraw from the vicinity of the horns on these occasions. If a woman so much as saw the sacred instruments at any time, she was subject to severe punishment and possibly death.

The rationale for hiding the instruments was that women once used them to control men and might do so again. According to myth, the contemporary social world originated in a transfer of power from women to men. Women had been dominant because they controlled secret religious knowledge that was associated with the sacred horns. Eventually men discovered the secret and turned the tables. When they obtained the ritual prerogatives, they gained control of society. However, they had to be careful to keep the secrets from women, or their positions might be reversed again. Men further justified their ritual precedence with a creation story in which they emerged from underground and occupied the earth before women appeared.

Mythology explained many other features of the world through the exploits of figures who were both culture heroes and tricksters. They rarely, if ever, acted on behalf of humanity, and any benefits they provided came accidentally. The most prominent culture heroes were two half-brothers from the same womb, one of them fathered by the highest god and the other by a trickster. Pregnant with the first one, the mother was abandoned by her divine husband. While searching for the god, she was seduced by the trickster and conceived the second brother. The mother died in the village of the jaguars but the brothers survived. When grown, they avenged their mother's death and then searched for the godly father. At first he refused to acknowledge his sons, but they earned his acceptance by finishing several tasks and ordeals that he set for them.

Then the brothers set out on their own and experienced several adventures that had a profound impact on humans. Seeing someone tap a tree for bath water, they chopped the tree down and unwittingly released a great river. Then they created fish to go in the river. One of the brothers feigned death in order to steal fire from the vultures. When the birds gathered around and lit their fire, the hero scared them away and saved an ember, with the result that people have fire and vultures do not. One of the brothers was informed that he could revive a dead person by eating the body. Instead he absentmindedly ate a peanut growing on the grave, and death became the permanent fate of human beings. When the brothers opened a mysterious container, night spilled out and became part of the daily cycle.

A Closer Look

Meanings of the Drinking Festival

The obvious social implications of the Subamazon beer festival were explored earlier. Its symbolic and ritual significance is more difficult to fathom, but Sullivan (1988) offers a number of interesting interpretations. From his account it is not clear how explicit these meanings are for

the participants themselves. Nor is it clear which, if any, are modal patterns for the Area. Nevertheless, these interpretations are drawn from a number of different cultures, and they make sense of ritual occasions that are obviously more than just parties to the participants.

According to Sullivan, these festivals restaged the "transformative acts" that marked the boundary between the mythical world and this one. The ideology of the beer festival in many cultures alluded to destruction, most often destruction of the primordial world by a great flood. By drinking a liquid that symbolized the primordial flood, men took control of its chaotic power. This explains forced drinking: to consume the bulk of the primal flood, men had to go far beyond pleasure or any other personal preference. In this context drinking as much as possible might be regarded as a duty.

Why not just drink water to carry out this symbolism? Perhaps because alcohol facilitated other important symbolic behaviors. To recall the primordial world was to recall conditions and behaviors that were no longer accessible or legitimate. Sullivan emphasizes allusions to incest in festival ideology, the idea being that symbolic representation of the behavior in a restricted ritual context can help to curtail its ill effects in mundane life. Perhaps the same idea can be applied to the nonincestuous, but ordinarily illicit, sexual relations that were a common feature of the festivals. The reduction of inhibitions by alcohol may have facilitated this aspect of the occasions.

Alcohol consumption eventually produced unconsciousness, or perhaps a more complex state of altered consciousness in at least some cases. People perceived this as a kind of death, an interpretation supported by a widespread analogy between the ritual drink and the venom of a snake or a scorpion. Sullivan seems to see this as an individual manifestation of the destructiveness of the primordial liquid. Perhaps awakening from this state was a further representation of victory over primal chaos.

The altered state produced by alcohol also had religious significance in that it provided an opportunity for direct contact with the supernatural. The individual's soul might leave the body, or spirits or souls of ancestors might appear and communicate. Like tobacco, and hallucinogens in some regions, alcohol was an answer to the desire of men to contact greater powers.

Some of these interpretations may be rather speculative, but they are consistent with important themes of culture in the Subamazon Area and even the Southern Zone in general. It may be that no single meaning of the drinking festival is a modal pattern for the Area. Taken together, however, they may explain why the festival itself was a modal pattern.

The Western Subamazon

Some important cultural patterns, several of them well known, distinguished a Region in the western part of the

Subamazon Area. This Region stretched from Brazil's Madeira Valley in the east to the Andean foothills of Peru, Ecuador, and Colombia. From there it curled around the headwaters of the Amazon to encompass the origin of the Rio Negro. An isolated single house was the modal pattern and, for some at least, the ideal. The most distinctive traits of the Region included the blowgun, taking tobacco as snuff, hallucinogens, and certain features of endocannibalism.

Hunters used the blowgun to take small animals, especially in the trees. Monkeys and birds were the most frequent victims. The blowgun was a long tube made from bamboo. A cotton plug on the end of the dart sealed the chamber so that a puff of breath could propel the missile. Since the dart carried little weight, it depended on curare or some other poison for its effect.

Shamans and others took tobacco as "snuff" in a manner quite different from what the word now implies in western culture. They rapidly inhaled a large quantity of tobacco powder through a tube made from bamboo or the hollow leg bone of a bird. Many tubes were doubled or forked so that both nostrils could be used at once. In some cases one man blew the powder into the nostrils of another.

Seekers of the supernatural also used a hallucinogenic drink made from the bark of *Banisteriopsis*, a woody vine. It is now widely known by several of its native names, most notably ayawaska, yahe, and cayapi. Men sometimes gathered to take the hallucinogen together. Older men helped the younger during these times, but each man had his own personal experience with the spirits.

Practitioners of endocannibalism engaged in extensive consumption of flesh, which may have been related to protein shortage, and some explicitly took pleasure in the eating (Dole 1985). Some Western Subamazon people also differed from other Southern Zone people in regarding mortuary cannibalism as a way to *banish* the soul or memory of the deceased rather than keep them in communion. Ghosts were frightening and the memory of a lost relative painful.

Rape As Punishment

On the Mato Grosso plateau of central Brazil, the most distinctive cultural feature was the use of gang rape as a punishment against women who offended male values (Gregor 1985; Murphy and Murphy 1985). Such data are relevant to current controversy in our own society as to the nature and implications of rape. One view is that rape exists because it is an effective way to intimidate women and keep them in a subordinate status.

Men of the Mato Grosso considered gang rape the appropriate response to sexual promiscuity and to encroachment on ritual prerogatives, especially the secrecy of the sacred horns. According to Mehinaku tradition, all the men would die if they did not administer the rape punishment when appropriate. Nevertheless, some men admitted to a recent ethnographer that they would not report a violation if they saw one (Gregor 1985).

Tupinamban Area

Examples:

Tupinamba, Guarani, Tenetehara, Urubu

This Area stretched along two thousand miles of the Atlantic Coast from the mouth of the Amazon River to the southernmost part of Brazil, where it curled westward into Paraguay. The name comes from the predominant ethnic group, the Tupinamba, represented throughout most of the Area. The next most prominent ethnic group was the closely related Guarani of Paraguay.

Tupinambans used high-yielding bitter manioc, maize, and rich marine resources to support relatively dense populations. They lived in houses the length of football fields, grouped in villages that harbored as many as several thousand people. Tupinamban society and religion revolved around intense warfare and exocannibalism (Metraux 1948). They ate the flesh of their enemies in an elaborate sacrificial ceremony. Many aspects of the ceremony strikingly resembled the treatment of war captives in eastern North America (see chapter 5), including the enthusiastic participation of women and the responses of the prisoner.

Also reminiscent of North America was the relatively high status of women, perhaps related to a high percentage of permanently matrilocal marriages. There was no men's circle. Men did keep sacred musical instruments hidden from women, but details of the pattern differed from the Subamazon. The instruments, which were rattles rather than horns, attained their power through blessing by shamans rather than from some ancient connection with male dominance. The matriarchy myth seems to have been absent from Tupinamban culture.

The Tupinamban Area also differed from the Subamazon in several other matters of myth and belief. Tupinamban mythology told of the sibling culture heroes who encountered the jaguars, but Tupinambans attributed their further adventures to different characters. Shamans functioned much as they did elsewhere in the Southern Zone but attained greater social influence. Of particular importance was the Grandfather god who created an earthly paradise as well as a celestial one. Searches for the earthly paradise may have stimulated lengthy migrations by some Tupian groups, bringing their culture into neighboring Areas.

Key features:

- ▶ Dense populations, large villages, large houses
- ▶ Bitter manioc, maize, marine resources
- ▶ High status of women
- ▶ Exocannibalism in elaborate ceremonies
- ▶ Socially powerful shamans
- ▶ Grandfather god and earthly paradise

Modal Patterns in Tupinamban Culture

Material Culture

A seemingly endless strip of tropical forest paralleled the ocean shore. Along most of that length, the forest's western edge fragmented against the escarpment that bounded the highlands. Hills emerged from the forest and villages sat atop many of them in the fresher air. Most villages consisted of four to eight long rectangular houses around a square plaza. Many villages were enclosed by a stout double stockade.

Close up, one could see the apertures in the stockade that allowed defenders to shoot arrows at besiegers. The houses were low, about twice the height of a person along the midline. Inside a house the hammock clusters of the families lined a communal passage that connected the doors at each end. For those with quarters by one door, some people at the other end of the long house were hard to distinguish as individuals even though they were kin.

Outside, in a settlement with a thousand people or more, some really were almost strangers. This was particularly true of men who had just joined other houses to do service for their brides. However, adornments provided information about the social status of villagers. A young man wore only a string on the penis while an older one wore a sheath of leaves. Each man communicated his success in war by the extent of the geometric tattoos on his body. Some important men wore a long coiled necklace of shells, others a string of black wooden beads. On the other hand, some decorations were common to all. Every man had shaved his hair to extend the forehead and wore a stone labret in his lower lip and bone ornaments in his ears. A woman wore nothing but the tattoos from her initiation ritual on her back, buttocks, breasts, and stomach. With her hair tied up for work, the woman displayed the shell cylinders dangling from each earlobe.

As hunters scattered into the forest each day or so, they checked their camouflaged pits to see if a tapir or jaguar had fallen in. Occasionally they formed a large group to drive rodents into a ditch, where they could club many of the animals. Otherwise, they cooperated only when they went to the river or the sea. In the water some men stretched out a large net while others drove fish into it by beating the water with sticks. In more confined places they herded the fish into a tipped canoe. At certain times of year fish provided the main part of the diet, especially when certain species swarmed up the river to spawn. During other months, whole villages left their homes and camped at the seashore to gather oysters. They ate their fill and preserved much more by smoking the shellfish on grills.

Women spent time in the village spinning thread and weaving cloth by the simplest methods. They also coiled their pots and then baked them in a shallow pit covered by fuel. Old women were best at making the numerous different forms and sizes. They painted many pots with red and black pigments.

Men built dugout canoes of various sizes. They used the larger ones, which held as many as sixty people, for the occasional trading expedition in which they obtained luxuries such as feathers and crystals. Some bark canoes were forty feet long and held thirty men. Paddling in a standing position, men used these boats to go on raids against their enemies.

Social Relations

Two or three years of matrilocal service brought a young man permission to marry his intended bride. His service continued after the marriage unless he escaped by giving bridewealth to his wife's father or a bride to one of her male relatives. A father did all that he could to accumulate sons-in-law in his household. In addition to hunting and other valuable domestic services, they assisted their father-in-law in war. They carried his equipment and fought by his side. Most importantly, they helped him to subdue the prisoners that brought him prestige.

When marriage produced a child, the importance of its name required discussion at a special meeting. Usually the name of an ancestor was given. Beginning with the piercing of the lower lip around age five, boys entered the first of five stages in male life. Although youth was exciting, later life had its own satisfactions. Elder men of about forty years did no hard work and contributed to society by deliberating in the village council. Even the last part of life was worthwhile because very old men were treated with respect.

A woman also went through five stages of life after infancy. She experienced a major ritual transition at puberty. After having her head shaved and her body tattooed, she fasted for three days. Then she was free to have sexual relations unless she was betrothed to a chieftain. A man could not severely punish his wife for extramarital sex unless he was a great chieftain or she a war captive. More important to the average woman, divorce was easy for her (as well as for her husband) on almost any grounds. A woman could become a shaman, an extremely powerful role, although few did.

With little authority over a household of one to two hundred people, the chieftain strove to organize everyday tasks effectively and give eloquent exhortations to do good work and follow the example of the ancestors. At least one of the house chieftains, sometimes two or three, rose to the position of village leadership. When people recognized more than one village chieftain, conflict was minimized by the fact that most of the important decisions came from the council. It consisted of all the house chieftains, the elder men, and the greatest warriors. They met in the plaza where they sat in hammocks or squatted on the ground, arranged according to social status. Smoking large cigars, they spoke in turn about the organization of major activities, relocation of the village, treatment of visitors, and, most importantly, the planning of warfare. It was in matters of war that the council and the chieftains had the greatest authority over other people.

The purpose of a raid was to avenge a previous attack and to take captives for sacrificial rites. Preparation for a war party included the reading of omens and performance of magic. Then the warriors, accompanied by women, set out for the enemy village in one or more large bark canoes. When the target was a stockaded village, the attackers surrounded it with their own barrier of thorny bushes. This protected them and impeded any who tried to escape. A siege might work if the settlement were short of supplies, but often the warriors tried to burn out their enemies. They set fire to cotton on the tips of their arrows and shot them into the thatched roofs. If the defenders came out, the attackers killed some with their arrows and others with their clubs. Most important, they tried to take prisoners. It usually took several men to seize an enemy warrior, but he became the possession of the first one to touch him. Deferential sons-in-law were of great value here.

After a successful attack, the warriors roasted and ate some victims at the scene. Then they took heads and genitals for trophies and brought them home with their captives. On the way they stopped at friendly villages where they displayed their prisoners. The local people insulted the prisoners, who replied with contempt. Prisoners also expressed pride in meeting the fate of brave warriors. On arrival at home the victors released their captives to the women, who danced around them and sang of their impending execution. They forced the prisoners to dance in front of the hut holding the sacred rattles. Then a cotton rope was placed around each man's neck, which he would wear as long as he lived in the village.

A captured man knew that he would eventually be sacrificed and eaten in an elaborate ceremony. However, that day might not come for weeks, months, or even years. Meanwhile, he moved freely about the village. There was no point in escaping because, if he avoided the honorable fate of a warrior, his own people would kill him as a coward. Attached to the family of his captor, a prisoner assumed a place in the community much like that of a son-in-law. He was welcome at social events such as drinking parties. People sometimes insulted him, but he was never physically abused. The captive's owner treated him well and gave him a wife. However, any children that resulted from the marriage would inherit the status of their father and suffer the same fate.

Female captives were less desirable than males because they could not play the role of warrior in the sacrificial rites. However, a woman was occasionally kept in much the same captivity as a man. If she married and had children, they became full-fledged members of their father's community. Their mother, however, was eventually sacrificed.

Knowledge and Expression

Only shamans smoked tobacco in the bamboo pipe. Through tobacco and beer a shaman achieved the trance state in which he communicated with the evil spirits that he controlled. Spirits first entered the rattles when a shaman chanted over them and fumigated them with tobacco smoke. In addition to such public services shamans cured, divined, and made rain. People admired and feared them because they provided the only access to the supernatural world. This gave them a great deal of political power. A shaman came and went as he pleased, often extending his practice to other villages. Some even traveled into enemy territory with impunity.

During a sacrificial ceremony the tethered war captive sang and denounced his captors until he was finally killed with a club. Then his body was dismembered and cooked, and parts were given to designated people to eat. Although the practice had ritual significance, people also expressed a liking for human flesh. One purpose of the sacrifice was to sustain the power of the sacred rattles by feeding the spirits within them. These instruments resided in a small building that hid them from the view of women. The rattle spirits granted people favors in return for offerings. Men took the rattles out and used them during the sacrifices and all other ceremonies.

An early European impression of the ritual killing of a captive by Tupinambans.

During such ceremonies, the men danced formally. They stayed in a circle, each man mostly in the same spot. Fruit shells or rattles tied around their legs added to the rhythms of the small drums and the bamboo stamping tubes. Women danced separately, with more exaggerated movements.

During a major social event people drank beer for three or four days. Both men and women danced with greater freedom than on ceremonial occasions, and some lost control of themselves. The blasts of conch trumpets cut through the tumult from time to time, and musical background came from flutes made of wood, bamboo, or the long bones of enemies. People sang to accompany the dances, repeating the words of the individual who started and led each song. Composers of lyrics, which concerned myths and the heroics of war, earned a great deal of prestige.

The myths of which people sang concerned beings long gone from the earth, such as the hero siblings who killed the jaguars. They came from the same womb at the same time but had different fathers. One was the great culture hero and the other was Opossum, the trickster god. The hero father acknowledged them after they performed difficult tasks and underwent ordeals. The father's boons to humanity came about accidentally. For example, agriculture began after he dropped fruits and tubers to the earth during a beating. Then some ungrateful people murdered him. The flames originated lightning, and the first thunder was the sound of the hero's head exploding.

The Grandfather was a more benevolent being, who had created a paradise for the living somewhere on earth. Some peoples had migrated with hope of finding it. Only in death did people find peace with the Grandfather in his supernatural realm.

SUPRA-AMAZON AREA

Examples:

Tapajos (Santarem), Yurimagua, Omagua, Taino

This Area, which I have slightly misnamed for convenience, included most of the Amazon River Basin as well as the lands north of it. The Basin formed the Area's longest dimension. From the Amazon the Area extended up to eastern Venezuela and the Guianas, taking in the extensive river system of the Orinoco. To the northwest, in the Caribbean, the Area encompassed most of the islands in the Greater Antilles.

Complex chiefdoms controlled the richest environments along the large rivers while autonomous horticultural villages were scattered through the hinterlands. The inland villages very likely shared many cultural features with the horticultural communities of the Subamazon Area. Some of those cultural patterns may also have characterized the commoners in the chiefdoms, but we have little information about their everyday lives. The description below will emphasize elite culture in the Supra-Amazon chiefdoms.

Those complex societies benefited from the renewal of their farmlands with fertile soil deposited by regularly flooding rivers. They made the most of it by adding a variety of sophisticated techniques to basic slash-and-burn farming. Along with their crops, the chiefdoms depended heavily on abundant aquatic resources.

The mode of subsistence, combined with a rich environment, supported large villages and towns, with the populations of many settlements numbering in the thousands. Craft specialization, at least on a part-time basis, is suggested by the quality of work in ceramics, gold, and precious stones. Both raw materials and finished products circulated through a trading network that united the entire Area and linked it to the chiefdoms of the northern Andes.

Complex chiefdoms, containing ten thousand people or more, sharply distinguished the Supra-Amazon Area from its neighbors to the south. A powerful chieftain controlled each village, and paramount chiefs had divine characteristics. Priests served the gods in temples.

Key features:

▶ Heavy use of aquatic resources

▶ Craft specialization

▶ Large permanent villages and towns

▶ Matrilineal descent

▶ Complex chiefdoms with temple religion

Modal Patterns in Supra-Amazon Culture

Material Culture

Large oval mounds of packed dirt lined the riverbank almost continuously. On the flat top of a typical mound stood five to ten oblong thatched houses, the homes of several hundred people. Perched ten to twenty feet above river level, the houses were safe from the regular floods. The height also made an attack more difficult. Some mounds, higher and larger, stood out from the others. On such a mound stood more houses, arranged around a plaza, and distinct neighborhoods were apparent. In such a town many people wore the gold ornaments that distinguished the nobility.

On any given day in a village many people were engaged in special tasks. Women wove cotton into various garments, including beautiful robes for ceremonies. They also created fine ceramics with elaborate painted designs, and shaped gold and jade into ornaments for the nobles. Men often tore down deteriorated houses and erected new ones, rebuilding on the same site or just a few yards away. A village could stay in the same place for hundreds of years because the river renewed the soil for crops and provided a constant supply of animals for food.

Farmers constructed mounds of soil about three feet high and nine feet around. These heaps of soft alluvial dirt retarded erosion and improved drainage, allowing longer storage of mature root crops in the ground. They also facilitated weeding and harvesting. Where necessary, the farmers dug ditches for irrigation or drainage.

When a man went hunting, he took to the river more often than the land. On the way to his canoe he passed large pens, partly on shore and partly in the water, holding thousands of live turtles and iguanas. Along with maize and dried fish, these easily captured animals provided the village's reserve food supply. On the river in a dugout canoe, the hunter used a spear with a spear thrower to subdue large aquatic animals. In addition to

manatees and caimans, men took fish that weighed several hundred pounds.

Since men conducted many of their activities on water, the construction of dugout canoes was one of the most important skills. Larger craft could take as many as one hundred people on a long trip, such as a trading expedition organized by a chief. Traders often traveled hundreds of miles from home and made contact with a variety of people in different river systems and even in the mountains. The goods exchanged included cloth, pottery, rice wine, hallucinogens, and above all, gold to validate political authority.

Social Relations

A young man left his matrilineal household to do five years of bride service for his wife's family. When a child was born, parents flattened its forehead to make it more beautiful. Later in life, both boys and girls underwent lengthy initiations that included ordeals. These included ceremonial whippings for the boys. A common practice for a pubescent girl was to hoist her in a hammock to the top of the house. There she stayed for days or weeks, subjected to the rising smoke from the household fires. Perhaps such rituals prepared young people, especially commoners, for lives of constraint. The village chieftain had the authority to sentence rebellious individuals to whipping or death, and some of the other nobility had the same rights.

Elite ranking was based on descent from deified ancestors. In everyday life it was represented by goods and symbols that came from specialized artisans at home and from long-distance trade. In addition to gold ornaments, the elite wore elaborately decorated clothing for ceremonies. Only they had the right to sit on stools rather than on the ground. Chieftains and other nobles further set themselves apart from commoners by speaking their own dialect of the common language. Elites in different societies recognized their shared interests by forming religious groups that cut across ethnic lines.

The status symbols of the village elite came from the district chief and the paramount chief. Chiefs controlled local resources, such as metals and clay for fine ceramics, and the long-distance trade that brought in raw materials and artifacts not locally available. The domain of the paramount chief took in more than a hundred miles of the main river and extended along several of the tributary streams. Although he lacked direct political power over most of his subjects, he had a godlike status. This supported his authority to require food and military service from his subjects.

When a man was called to battle, this usually meant an expedition into the forest to attack a village of the interior people. One purpose was revenge for a prior raid; the other was to take slaves. If successful, the warriors from the chiefdom killed most of the adults and took heads for trophies. They captured as many children as they could to make them into slaves. Some were to be traded, but others would be incorporated into families and put to ordinary domestic and farm work.

Occasionally the paramount chief assembled a force to attack another chiefdom. Then most of the men in the village took to the large canoes and joined their neighbors on the river. As they paddled along the river, they saw strangers from their own chiefdom moving in the same direction. Eventually a fleet of more than a hundred canoes assembled and went on toward the enemy. Since it was difficult to keep such movements secret, the initial engagement was often settled in a shower of arrows between two fleets.

Chiefs organized these battles to contest the key resources and trade routes that kept them in power. Some sought to conquer other chiefdoms and subject them to tribute or political control. However, it was difficult to win a war on such a scale, and many chiefs preferred diplomacy. They arranged alliances with their neighbors, using devices such as political marriages.

Knowledge and Expression

The greatest of the communal ceremonies took place in towns where chiefs lived, which were characterized by plazas and shrines. A shrine building might stand by itself or be part of a chief's house or a temple. When priests entered the shrine, they were surrounded by symbols of supernatural power. The remains of deceased chiefs represented the ancestral line that justified the living chief's authority. These ancestral spirits watched over the polity, and the people worshipped them. Some shrines also contained remains of the priests who had served them. Large painted images represented the gods who had power over water, crops, animals, and war. These beings could reward or punish people and required ritual attention. Along with representations of the greatest supernaturals, a shrine contained ritual and military equipment.

During communal ceremonies the priests brought the appropriate images out of the shrine, along with the paraphernalia needed for the celebration. The chief or the priests sniffed a powdered drug that allowed communication with the gods and the ancestors. People drank beer that had been made from crops collected by the chief. At some ceremonies war captives of high status or great courage were sacrificed to the gods. Their heads were severed and kept in the shrine. Although women were excluded from some of these public rites, they could become diviners and curers if they were of high rank.

In addition to images of the gods, art included ceramic figurines and large effigies of humans that were elaborately painted, modeled, and incised. At death people other than chiefs were placed in large urns and buried in cemeteries near their houses. One or more wives and slaves accompanied a nobleman to the next world. Some

time after a burial, relatives recovered the bones and consumed some of them in an alcoholic drink.

A Closer Look

The People Who Discovered Columbus

An ocean-oriented variant of Supra-Amazon culture was displayed by "the people who discovered Columbus." William Keegan (1992) applies that term to the Taino because they were the first Native Americans that Christopher Columbus encountered. The culture of the Taino people centered on Hispaniola and Puerto Rico and extended to Jamaica, the Bahamas, and most of Cuba. It may also have included parts of eastern Central America (Lange 1996). In addition to mounding and irrigation, Taino farming techniques included terracing and the use of potash and urine as fertilizers (Steward and Faron 1959). However, they used the slash-and-burn method to cultivate maize in the forest. Lacking large land mammals, hunters drove numbers of rodents into corrals and kept them alive until needed.

Taino traveled by sea whenever possible, in dugout canoes that carried fifty to one hundred people (Wilson 1990). Individuals and groups made long trading voyages, and certain districts excelled in particular products for that purpose. Some mined gold nuggets and beat them into small plates that were used to inlay wooden objects and to overlay clothes and ornaments. People also carved wood, stone, bone, and shell.

Chieftains were carried on litters and slept on wooden platforms. They wore headdresses of gold and feathers, and a pendant in the form of a human mask also conveyed rank. The chief's house on the plaza was larger and better than others. He organized daily activities, as well as feasts and dances, and oversaw the storage of surplus in special buildings. He hosted visitors and handled relations with other villages. His canoe, the largest in the village, was used for the public.

Groups fought each other to avenge murders and to resolve disputes over hunting and fishing rights. Another cause of war was a chief's failure to provide a woman after receiving bridewealth from another chief. Only chiefs and nobles participated in war meetings where one chief was elected to lead the attack in the company of a noble bodyguard. Human sacrifice was minor and trophy display rare.

Taino society was matrilineal as well as matrilocal. A chief ordinarily bequeathed his position to his sister's son. Elite women played an important role in the ritual welcome of outsiders (Wilson 1990). The origin myth displayed concern with women and the "great role assigned to them" (Radin 1969). It reflected the high status that is typical of women in matrilineal and matrilocal societies.

The Taino recognized two major deities: one was the lord of manioc and the sea; the other, his mother, attended to fresh water and fertility. People made idols and fetishes from the remains of their ancestors or from natural objects inhabited by powerful spirits. One person might own as many as ten idols, which he could give, trade, or bequeath to others. Most people kept their idols in niches or on tables in their homes, but some chiefs kept theirs in temples. The village paid homage to the chief's spirits annually in the plaza. Assisted by priests, the chief presided over rituals that included singing, drumming, and rattling. Communal religion affected individual prac-titioners: shamans cured the sick in the presence of priests. Communion with the supernaturals required puri-fication by fasting or vomiting and the taking of halluci-nogenic snuff in order to see them. The goal was to learn the wishes of the spirits rather than try to control them.

In village plazas and on special courts, the Taino played a rubber ball game in which the ball could not be touched by the hands or feet. People placed bets on ordi-nary games, and chiefs wagered when villages played against each other. Some matches were connected with the making of public decisions. Women played the game separately from men.

BRAZILIAN HIGHLANDS AREA

Examples:

Timbira, Kayapo, Shavante,
Bororo, Kaingang

The heart of this Area is the extensive uplands of eastern and southern Brazil. It was framed by the Subamazon in the west and the Tupinamban Area in the east. Virtually all native peoples in the Brazilian Highlands spoke lan-guages classified as Gê (pronounced Zhuh).

Highland culture lacked several items that were prominent in most neighboring Areas: hammocks, beer, canoes, and pottery. The last two can be explained in terms of a largely savanna habitat that favored foraging on land. Though headquartered in a village with farm plots nearby, people spent much of the year trekking: moving over long distances from one foraging camp to another. They traveled on foot and made relatively little use of aquatic resources. The mobile way of life also pre-cluded pottery.

Despite their nomadism, the Highlanders main-tained a relatively elaborate social structure that included "a number of kinship divisions, moieties, age grades, associations, and sexual dichotomies unequaled in South America" (Steward and Faron 1959:362). Above all they emphasized dual organization, dividing every society into at least one set of two opposing sub-groups (Maybury-Lewis 1979). These are often loosely called "moieties"; however, they varied in the criteria by which they recruited members and were not necessarily exogamous. Matrilocal residence was stronger than in neighboring Areas, being permanent rather than a func-tion of bride service.

Although Brazilian Highlanders engaged in little worship of supernatural beings, their complex social groupings provided the basis for a rich ceremonial life. The elaborate festivals included unique competitive sports. Unlike their neighbors, the Highlanders did not enhance either social or religious experiences with beer or hallucinogenic drugs. Many, perhaps most, seem to have lacked tobacco.

Sun and Moon in human form played prominent roles in the distinctive Highland mythology. The culture hero brothers were absent; a different character, Bird Nester, encountered the jaguars.

Key features:

▶ Extensive trekking

▶ Absence of canoes, pottery, hammocks, beer

▶ Permanent matrilocal residence

▶ Numerous and varied association groups

▶ Dual organization

▶ Elaborate festivals with sports

▶ Tobacco rare and no other drugs

Modal Patterns in Brazilian Highland Culture

Material Culture

The village stood in a cleared area amid tall grass. Nearby, a long strip of green tropical trees marked the passage of a stream. On the other side of the village the savanna stretched into the distance, interrupted irregularly by thickets of thorny vegetation and stands of deciduous forest. The houses formed a semicircle around the plaza where the men's house stood; in large communities the circle was completed. Inside each house people slept on mats, some of them atop simple wooden platforms. A man rose early and made his way to the men's house to talk or sing or prepare for the day. His wife brought him a breakfast of leftovers from the previous night's meal. If it was insufficient, he ate some of the nuts that would sustain him throughout the day.

When people left the village for work, they used small roads that extended as far as ten miles. Women went to the gallery forest that bordered the stream. There they could work in the fields, cultivating sweet potatoes and yams along with some manioc. More often they gathered roots, nuts, and fruits, which provided at least as much food as the crops.

Sometimes men went to the forest. From the bank of the stream they could shoot fish with arrows or scoop them up with a net. Hunting was good because the shade and water attracted animals, and the hunter who wanted a deer could wait in a tree that the animals habitually passed. However, pursuit through the tangled vegetation on the ground was unpleasant and often frustrating. Men preferred an exhilarating chase in the open savanna.

When hunters brought meat home, women baked it in an earth oven on a bed of leaves, covered with ash and soil. It was a slow process, and hungry people sometimes took the meat out too soon. When thoroughly cooked, the meat could last for as much as a week. Whether there was meat or not, women used the earth oven to cook palm shoots.

After planting their crops, people left the village for a long period of foraging in the savannas. Women carried household goods in baskets and made small houses for their nuclear families at each camp. They also gathered a great deal of food because the treks were calculated to take advantage of the availability of particular fruits or nuts. Men kept busy hunting because animals were much more common away from the village.

Since the larger villages had close to a thousand people, trekkers often split up into separate bands. They kept track of one another by watching the smoke from the fires that they used to clear their campsites. Sometimes a band camped overnight, and sometimes they stayed at a rich site for a week. The whole trek lasted for at least six weeks, and some people stayed out for several months. During many years, at least some villagers went on two or three of these trips.

Social Relations

When a young man married, he crossed the village to live in his wife's house for as long as the union lasted. Because the settlement was large and socially complex, it was often not necessary to go outside it for a spouse. Marriage was regulated by membership in descent groups or other subdivisions of the community. Initially a man engaged in ritual avoidance of his parents-in-law, with whom he had a tense relationship. These restrictions eased after his wife had borne children and people considered the marriage to be stable. Nevertheless, with his own kin in the same village, a man continued to perceive himself as part of a group in opposition to his in-laws.

At birth or at some time in childhood, a person became a member of a moiety, one of two groups in the village that organized various activities. This affiliation became more important later in life, especially for males as they became involved in the political and ceremonial life of the community. Age grades organized the maturation of a boy. At puberty he received the penis sheath, which symbolized adult status, and he began to acquire secret knowledge, including ceremonies that excluded women. Of more immediate importance, a series of rituals joined him with other boys in an age set that occupied the warrior grade. All men participated in warfare, but this was the primary concern of the warrior grade. It was an exciting time of life that brought automatic prestige. After a number of years all the boys in the age set would become mature men, married and full participants in the adult men's circle. Eventually, they would be elders.

Girls went through comparable age grades, but they had less community significance. Puberty ritual introduced them to the many menstrual taboos that they

Men crossing a savanna in the Brazilian Highlands (Camayura culture, Brazil).

would observe until menopause. In addition to the prohibition of sex, menstruating women were forbidden to practice horticulture, wear decorative dress, and engage in certain recreations. Girls were married around the time of puberty, if not before.

"Wantons" did not marry but had sex with various men who helped them to survive. They were forced into this status because they engaged in premarital sex that was inappropriate or because they had no relatives to arrange a proper marriage. Sometimes one followed from the other. Refugees, orphans, and captives lacked family to arrange a marriage.

In village life a man was always ready to defend himself, either verbally or physically. Although the groups that divided the community had complementary functions, they also provided a framework for factional competition. Many conflicts were worked out in the political arena of the men's house, especially if the leaders of various groups and subgroups were effective and disposed to peace. One or two village chieftains might override troublesome factional leaders. However, there were times when anger or ambition led to bloody conflicts that caused a village to split. In the best case, the losers in a sublethal brawl packed up and left. At worst, survivors fled a massacre.

Men also went to war with neighboring villages and with other ethnic groups. They used stone axes and lances in addition to bow and club. Sometimes they decapitated their victims, but they never brought home the heads or any other trophies. They did bring home women and children to be incorporated into the community. The women became wives or wantons, and the children were adopted. A warrior who killed an enemy went into seclusion for several days and observed restrictions on food and activities. The period ended with a ritual bath.

Knowledge and Expression

Each village had a variety of subgroups such as moieties, clans, and voluntary associations. These groups organized an elaborate ritual life. Whenever people were reunited in the village after trekking, they joined in numerous communal ceremonies. These were social events more than spiritual ones, manifesting a relatively casual attitude toward the supernatural.

A communal hunt began most ceremonial periods. Sporting events played a prominent role in the festivities, and log races were the foremost among them. For a log race men from several groups went to a place distant from the village. There they began a race back to the village carrying carved tree sections that were in many cases the weight of a man. Usually several runners from the same group took up the burden along the way.

The most important myths were those that explained the origins of ceremonies and of personal names. In most of these stories a human was abducted by supernatural beings. They taught him a ceremony and gave him names that he took back to his village.

The Bird Nester myth told of a boy who was abandoned by his brother-in-law and trapped in a tree while trying to gather macaw nestlings. He was rescued by Jaguar after giving him all the birds. After a time in Jaguar's village, the boy took some meat and went home to his family. He drove out the brother-in-law who had betrayed him and gave meat to all the people. They liked it so much that they went back to Jaguar's house and stole the fire that had cooked the meat. Jaguar was so angry that he vowed to become an animal and eat people from then on.

Sun and Moon went through numerous adventures together, each trying to get the better of the other. Moon was usually the fool or the clumsy imitator. Some incidents were simple, as when Moon complained that Sun was keeping roasted meat to himself. In his annoyance Sun threw a piece of hot meat and hit Moon in the stomach, causing the burn spots that we can still see today. Other such incidents had greater consequences. Envious of Sun's red headdress, Moon obtained one from Woodpecker; however, he found it too hot to hold and dropped it, setting the earth on fire.

In their last modification of the world, the two companions took gourds they had cultivated and threw them into a creek in pairs; the gourds rose to the surface, transformed into men and women. In a final act of mischief each of the culture heroes used magic to make some of the other's creations defective. Then they made a village for the new humans, placed them on opposite sides to create the first moieties, and married them. Having established human society, Sun and Moon agreed to rise into the sky.

Told individually, these stories provided no more than entertainment. However, some tellers related them in cycles that showed progress from ignorant self-gratification to some degree of awareness if not responsibility. Though Sun and Moon were figures of fun in their ancient appearance on earth, some people prayed to them in their celestial incarnation.

People gave little respect to the few shamans among them. Many people knew cures for various ills, and few of them involved contact with spirits. Numerous cures used plant products, and some employed mechanical means such as deliberate bleeding.

When a person died, members of the opposite moiety or some other group took the body to the cemetery near the village and buried it with ceremony in a sleeping mat. Some time later the bones were recovered and given a secondary burial. Souls of the previously deceased came to guide the new one to the place of the dead under the earth's surface or at the foundation of the sky.

ARGENTINE AREA

Examples:

Tewelche, Pwelche, Ona, Yahgan

This Area included the geographic regions known as the Pampas and Patagonia. It coincided with what is now Argentina except for the omission of the Argentine portion of the Gran Chaco (assigned to the Subamazon in this work) and the inclusion of modern Chilean territory from Chiloe Island to Tierra del Fuego. The traditional culture of the Area is little known because it left few archeological remains and because it was thoroughly transformed by the introduction of the horse in the eighteenth century. The best-known ethnographic representatives of the earlier culture were marginal peoples of the far south who never adopted the horse (Steward and Faron 1959). Recently, archeological knowledge has advanced significantly despite the great obstacles (McEwan, Borrero, and Prieto, eds. 1997).

This was the most divergent Culture Area in the Southern Zone because the temperate grasslands prohibited horticulture. The Argentine natives were nomadic foragers who depended heavily on hunting guanaco (a relative of the camel) and rhea (a large flightless bird). It is difficult to interpret old (and somewhat contradictory) literature about their social organization, but much of it is consistent with the general model of forager band organization described earlier (see chapter 3).

The southernmost cultures in the Argentine Area are famous for a matriarchy myth, which resembled that of the Subamazon. However, the male rebellion took a more violent form. Men commemorated the event with an extremely long and elaborate ceremony associated with initiation. This cultural complex may have been widespread in the Area, but it is well documented only for the island of Tierra del Fuego. Therefore I discuss it in the "Closer Look" section.

Key features:

- ► Forager bands
- ► Hunted guanaco and rhea
- ► Extensive use of animal skin
- ► Violent matriarchy myth (?)
- ► Elaborate male initiation ceremony (?)

Modal Patterns in Native Argentine Culture

Material Culture

The camp consisted of a dozen windbreaks made from poles and animal skins. Behind their shelters people slept between more animal skins. When they left their blankets on a cold morning, hide clothing kept them warm. At first glance men and women looked alike, hunched in ankle-length robes and wearing moccasins stuffed with straw. Everyone wore necklaces and bracelets and displayed tattoos when they extended their arms. However, a man fastened his mantle with a belt and wore nothing but a pubic covering underneath. A woman fastened her robe at the breast, and her movements revealed a wrap underneath that covered her from armpits to knees.

Native Argentine man and woman inside a tent (Tewelche culture).

Women spent a great deal of time in camp processing hides and sewing them together to make clothing, blankets, and windbreaks. They used eyeless needles and animal sinews for sewing. Women also made bags from skins to augment their other containers, a few simple baskets or ceramic pots. One use for containers was the gathering of mushrooms, grass seeds, roots, and berries. Women ground the seeds on stone metates. Sometimes they also made flour from roots, but these could be cooked or eaten raw.

Men provided most of the camp's food with their bows. Some made their own, but others obtained them by trading with men who were particularly skilled in making bows. Although such craftsmen lived slightly richer lives, they still had to hunt to support themselves and their families. When men hunted guanaco, they sometimes decoyed their prey with a tame young member of the species. They stalked rheas wearing feathers for camouflage. Digging large rodents from their burrows, on the other hand, took more muscle than ingenuity.

People shifted camp often, with women carrying the gear on their backs. Men planned band movements largely in relation to the availability of guanaco, the most important game. The two-hundred-pound animals provided both meat and hides. Guanacos followed a predictable seasonal pattern of migration within small ranges that allowed the hunters to ambush entire family groups of the animals in favorable situations.

The band incorporated the seashore into its annual nomadic cycle. Men fished with spears and nets, and they killed sea lions at the breeding grounds where the animals gathered in large numbers. Sea lions provided capes as well as meat and fat. Marine birds were another source of food at the shore, and women gathered shellfish.

Social Relations

The sixty people in the camp constituted the entire regional band. They traveled as a group when possible but broke up into local bands when necessary. Some neighboring bands with a hundred or more members found this hard to do. For others, with as few as thirty people, it was easier. The chieftain of the band had no authority and received advice from all adult males in the group.

A man and his nuclear family occupied one or two windbreaks in the camp. Following the preferred pattern, he had found a woman he liked in another band, and she had accepted him. The man lived among relatives because women joined their husbands after marriage.

Men and women joined to celebrate a girl's puberty. After a period of seclusion, she feasted with the adults. They expected her to be chaste until she and a boy agreed on marriage. Although she then went to live in her husband's band, she and her family would see each other on many occasions. Bands came together regularly for ceremonies and joined sporadically at unusual food sources such as a beached whale.

Hostilities could override the connections. Each band identified a hunting territory as its own. The chieftain, representing the group, usually granted access to any outsider who asked permission. However, a trespasser was liable to attack, and intrusions commonly led to feuds between bands. Murder, kidnapping of women, and accusations of sorcery also led to sporadic raids. Men fought only for revenge. They took no trophies, and captives were incidental. Men settled some disputes less violently, with a wrestling match or with an arrow duel in which two parties took turns shooting harmlessly toward one another.

Knowledge and Expression

God, more powerful than any other being, caused the world to be created as it is today and established the proper way for humans to live. God was remote from people's everyday lives, but they sometimes prayed to it, especially in times of crisis such as a critical illness. They feared that God would punish them for misbehavior, afflicting the wrongdoer's entire group with disease.

The culture heroes of the mythological past were ancestors of living people, human beings rather than supernaturals. Two brothers, one more benevolent than the other, were responsible for many features of human life. The older brother accidentally discovered fire by playfully striking rocks together. He suggested that they keep the flame burning forever, but his younger sibling said that people should work to keep fire going. The older then instructed people in how to do it. Similarly, the younger brother insisted that men use weapons to hunt rather than just killing game with a look. Eventually the brothers grew old and became stars in the sky.

Neither God nor the beings of myth received any kind of ceremonial recognition. People devoted ritual activities largely to propitiating evil spirits or achieving protection against them. Otherwise, ceremony commemorated the periods of transition in a person's life. People buried their dead on hills and hoped that the souls would reside with God.

Shamans led ceremonies as well as curing people. A shaman, usually a man, bequeathed the position to his son and trained him for it. The practitioner's helping spirits were the souls of dead shamans.

A Closer Look

The Fuegan Region

Named for the island of Tierra del Fuego at the tip of South America, this Region occupied the cold south and west where the continent narrowed and the sea was always near. The inhabitants made more use of marine resources, especially sea mammals and shellfish, than any other peoples in the Culture Area (Borrero 1997; Steward and Faron 1959).

Fuegans hunted with harpoons rather than the bow. They used shell knives and depended heavily on bone in their technology. Despite the orientation toward the sea, Fuegan life was anchored to the forests of beech trees that provided wood and bark for artifacts ranging from canoes to buckets (Borrero 1997).

Men expected women to be subservient. This patriarchal ideology formed the basis for much of myth and ritual. Moon was a goddess who symbolized the dangerous qualities in women. Sun, her husband, was ultimately responsible for the establishment of a patriarchal society that controlled the baser tendencies of women. According to myth, women once dominated men and controlled society. However (in contrast to the Subamazon story of sacred horns), this was done by impersonating evil spirits that intimidated the men. After discovering the trickery, men killed all the older women because they had been initiated into the secret knowledge.

Men commemorated their rise to power, and reinforced it, with elaborate initiation rituals for boys that could last for weeks or months. Because many groups came together for the ceremonies, their duration depended on the food supply. Women were excluded from the ritual performances, which were held in a special structure. They were not supposed to know that the masked and painted performers were men rather than the spirits they impersonated. This secret was imparted to the boys as part of the initiation. During the ceremonial time, male spirits periodically emerged from the ritual house to humiliate and assault women, sometimes beating them.

The presence and occasional manifestation of a savage female spirit reminded the men and taught the boys about the need for male dominance. The spirit was not even a friend to women. Gluttonous and cannibalistic, she ate any women or children who came too close to the ritual house. In the end she symbolically killed the male initiates, whose rebirth completed their transition to adulthood.

As noted in the introduction to this section, the southernmost Region of the Argentine Area is famous for a form of the matriarchy myth and for an elaborate initiation with which it is associated. There is only a hint of the myth in a more central portion of the Area (Bierhorst 1988) and no indication of the ceremony. No conclusion can be drawn about the distribution of either because we have very few data about expressive behavior in most of the Area.

NUCLEAR AMERICAN ZONE

Areas:

- Mesoamerican
- Andean
- Intermediate

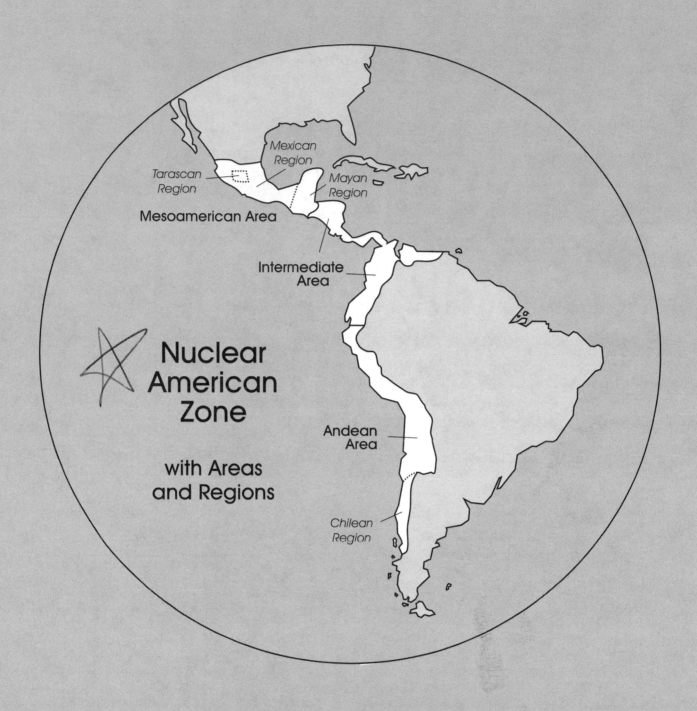

Nuclear
American
Zone

with Areas
and Regions

Tarascan
Region

Mexican
Region

Mayan
Region

Mesoamerican Area

Intermediate
Area

Andean
Area

Chilean
Region

Previous page   Part of the capital city of a medium-sized Nuclear American
state (Cakchiquel culture, Guatemala).

OVERVIEW OF THE ZONE

Examples:

Aztec, Maya, Inca, Aymara, Muisca (Chibcha)

The Nuclear Zone encompassed the native civilizations of the New World. The term "Nuclear" connotes both the central location of the Zone and the extent to which it influenced its neighbors. The elongated Zone stretched from what is now central Mexico along the Pacific Coast of Central America and down the western rim of South America. It was dominated by plateaus and mountains that were flanked by lowlands, some dry and some wet. The complex terrain offset the largely tropical location of the Zone and divided the land into many distinctive natural regions with varied ecologies and resources (Carrasco 1982).

Agricultural states with elaborate civilizations dominated both ends of the Nuclear Zone, separated by chiefdoms in what are now Colombia and Central America. Generalizations in this chapter emphasize the civilizations for several reasons. First, they have left profound influences on contemporary cultures of the Americas (Collier 1982). Second, they are of great interest for comparison with the early civilizations of the Old World (e.g., Trigger 1993). Third, reconstruction of the cultures between the Nuclear American civilizations is highly controversial (Graham, ed. 1993).

The farmers of Nuclear America domesticated a wide variety of plants for food and other purposes. People in one Area alone cultivated about seventy different crops, almost as many as all of Europe and Asia combined (Wilson 1999). Maize was the basis for Nuclear American civilization, providing the calories needed to sustain dense populations. For protein, maize and beans were supplemented by the avocado *(Persea americana)*, which contained at least double the amount in other fruits. Avocado also helped balance a relatively low-fat diet with flesh that was up to 30 percent oil (S. Coe 1994). Chiles, the fruits of *Capsicum* plants, spiced a largely bland cuisine.

The endogamy of peasant communities was unusual compared to the rest of the world. Perhaps even more distinctive was the use of cradles for infants rather than keeping them in contact with the mother's body. This may have been related to women's work patterns.

Cloth production by women was important in many civilizations, but it seems to have reached its apex in Nuclear America. Both peasant and elite women made cloth that figured in economic, political, and religious relationships. Nuclear American culture recognized the complementary nature of male and female social roles without the hostility of Southern America or the symbolic celebration of Northern America (e.g., Silverblatt 1987; Schroeder et al., eds. 1997). The relationship can be characterized as "gender parallelism" because in some ways it involved a greater separation of the sexes than elsewhere in the New World. Most notably, there was a tendency toward unilineal inheritance for both men and women.

The concept and treatment of spiritual offenses in the Nuclear Zone resembled the Old World concept of sin in several ways. However, ancestral spirits played a greater role in Nuclear America than in the Old World civilizations.

Key features:

► Agricultural states
► Extreme importance of textiles
► Community endogamy
► Gender parallelism
► Cradles for infants
► Concept of sin
► Ancestral spirits

Modal Patterns in Nuclear American Peasant Culture

Peasant Material Culture

A peasant family lived in a one-room hut about ten feet along one side and twenty on the other. A thatched roof peaked above adobe walls made of mud-bricks that had been dried in the sun. Some families covered the single doorway with a plain coarse blanket, while others left it open. Stepping from the dark interior of her home, a woman saw another just like it across an open space and another on one side. Together they enclosed a courtyard that the families, linked by kinship, shared for work and recreation and ceremonies. Scattered across the nearby landscape were similar clusters, some with as many as six houses. Associated with each cluster were mud-walled storage bins that held each family's long-term supply of food.

As the woman began her work, she wore her usual long skirt along with a cloak to ward off the remaining chill from the night. Much of a wife's day was spent in food preparation for her family, including the cooking of gruels and stews that had maize and beans as their main

A contemporary peasant house indicates what traditional Nuclear Zone dwellings were like (Peru).

ingredients. The cook spiced most of the dishes with chiles and often added salt. People considered these condiments so important that they were always part of the sacrifice during religious fasting. Squashes were another important food source, and people welcomed the variety and sweetness provided by berries or other fruits. Gourds and calabashes facilitated cooking and other work. Hollowed out, these hard-shelled fruits or vegetables made excellent containers for drinking, storage, and other purposes.

In addition to cooking, a woman devoted a great deal of time to spinning yarn and weaving cloth. She spun by hand on a twirling stick, an activity that was easily picked up during any free moment. To weave she used a portable loom that could be attached to a wall or post or any other stable object. Leaning against a strap across her back, the weaver created the necessary tension. From the cloth she made blankets and clothing, taking special pride in this contribution to her family. Finer cloth contributed to her husband's status because it could be used for impressive gifts.

The woman's husband went to the fields in a cotton loincloth and simple ornaments and wearing a cloak if needed. In his hand he carried the simple long-handled tool that he would use for working the soil. Some of the fields were on terraces that ascended the hillsides. Such terraces, formed from soil held by stone retaining walls, turned slopes into flat agricultural plots. The ditches that watered or drained these fields, depending on the season, belonged to a larger system that included dams, dikes, and canals. Men cooperated in keeping the structures repaired and the channels clean.

The farmer had worked with other men to create the terraces, as well as other fields in different circumstances. In some fertile river valleys they had only to clear level land. Other locales required construction of raised fields, which were either ridges or individual plots that had been built up to surmount standing water or seasonal floods.

On larger projects the farmer worked with men from the other villages. Linked by kinship and marriage, these villages formed a community that shared the rights to land, water, and other resources in the vicinity. Dispersal was generally an efficient way to use and protect essential resources that were irregularly distributed.

The farmer and his family spent much of their time producing food and goods for their own needs. However, there were some in the community who spent extra time making pots or engaging in other crafts for external trade. The need of craft people for raw materials made extraction an important economic activity in communities near the resources. Materials taken from the earth included metals, clays for ceramics, and stone of various kinds. Salt, more mundane but in great demand, was obtained from land deposits as well as from the sea. Where these resources were abundant, local people often became experts in their extraction.

Peasant Social Relations

A man lived among close male relatives. He had established his home in his father's house cluster, and so had his brothers. By the same patrilocal rule he would eventually share the compound with nephews and male cousins and grandsons. Some men built separate compounds, although usually near their relatives. Reasons for separation included lack of space, more efficient use of resources, or minimization of strains in family relations.

In his home a man had a complementary relationship with his wife. The wedding ceremony emphasized that both partners had obligations to fulfill to each other and to their children. To a large extent they fulfilled these obligations by playing the distinct roles defined by society. The man cultivated the land, represented the family in community matters, and gave military service to the state. The woman wove cloth and took care of the household.

Although wives came to live with their husbands, a woman maintained ties with her blood relatives. In many cases they lived nearby because people preferred marriage within the community. Aside from sentiment, a wife valued the connection with her natal family because she could inherit land or other property from her mother and perhaps from her father. Her mother was the more likely source because women emphasized descent relationships with women and men with men. Having inherited from either source, a woman had the same rights as a man to sell or bequeath her possessions or use her resources to acquire more.

A young married woman looked forward to creating her own family and, when she became pregnant, prayed for success. Shortly after a birth the mother placed her infant in a cradle, where it would spend much of its time until it began to walk. Soon after learning to walk, a child began to perform the simple domestic and agricultural tasks that would occupy much of its time until adulthood.

Parents with a boy entering his later teens began to look for a suitable wife. After negotiations that sometimes lasted for several weeks, the families agreed on the goods to be exchanged between them or bestowed on the new couple. At last the couple gathered with their close relatives and other guests for a formal ceremony. The guests brought gifts that would help the young people to establish their new household. After a ritual joining and speeches about the responsibilities of adulthood and the obligations of marriage, everyone feasted and many drank alcohol in festivities that were as elaborate as the family could afford. People sang and danced to express both the joy and the sacred nature of the occasion. At some point a priest blessed the couple. Within a few days they settled into their own small house in the compound of the husband's father and began life as adult members of the community.

One of the most stringent obligations of the spouses was appropriate sexual behavior. Because it threatened the family, people regarded adultery as a severe offense against society as well as the victimized spouse. The result could be death for an adulterous wife or her lover or both. For the same reason, people despised homosexuality and punished it with death.

All members of the community were kin or at least regarded and treated each other as if they were. Marriage, ideally between members of the same community, contributed to close ties. The senior man of each household represented the family in community matters. Councils of respected people considered some issues of common interest, but one or a few officials from within the community attended to most of the important matters. They apportioned land to families on the basis of need, settled disputes, and judged minor criminal matters. They also coordinated cooperative labor on local projects, including the construction of buildings, development and maintenance of irrigation systems, and performance of intensive agricultural tasks such as land clearance or harvest. Ultimately, the community was the responsibility of a particular aristocrat or noble family.

Community leaders, supervised by the local lord, organized the fulfillment of obligations to the outside world. Peasants cultivated lands held by elite individuals and institutions. Women wove cloth for the elite. Men served as soldiers and as laborers on public construction projects. Sometimes, during the agricultural off-season, the government summoned men to build huge stone structures in a city or to fight in a faraway battle.

A man marched to war with others of his community. They were divided into units, each led by an experienced and successful warrior, and the local noble commanded the entire contingent. Groups from different communities joined to form a state army of thousands. In great campaigns for the emperor the soldiers numbered in the tens of thousands.

As two armies approached each other, a soldier was surrounded by the pounding of drums and a rising tide of shouts. Then he heard the first blasts from shell trumpets that would be used to signal the troops at key points in the battle. No other commands would be audible during the battle, so the soldier followed the veteran warrior leading his squad and, if possible, he kept an eye on the feathered wooden helmet of his community's noble officer.

When the front lines came within a few hundred yards of each other, slingers began to whirl their egg-sized stones overhead and release them toward the enemy. A bit further on, the archers stopped and pulled their bowstrings. Able to stand closer together than the slingers, they released a more concentrated fire. As the enemy hurled back similar barrages, some men fell, but most successfully protected themselves by raising their circular leather shields. Thick quilted cotton tunics saved others from serious injury. To negate the effect of the flying missiles, the armies now rushed toward each other and joined in hand-to-hand combat. Nobles, highly trained in the use of heavy slashing weapons, engaged each other in the midst of the battle. Commoners harassed the enemy's relief troops with their stones and arrows and tried to hold the flanks with spears or clubs.

Some commoners made the most of any opportunities to kill or capture enemy soldiers, knowing that they could better themselves in this way. At the least a valorous commoner received proud insignia or valuable gifts from his superiors. The most successful achieved a status like that of minor nobles, which allowed them to own personal land, have extra wives, and hold some political offices.

Peasant Knowledge and Expression

Worried about war and other dangers, as well as health and fertility, peasants turned to a variety of supernatural beings for help. Each family made offerings and simple prayers to its own spirits for protection of the household and the fields. Each small settlement directed group observances to its special god or spirits, as did the community to which the settlements belonged.

All people gathered regularly to worship the rain god, who provided the moisture on which the crops depended. They thought of him as a manlike figure carrying a weapon that produced lightning. Although frightened by the power of lightning, villagers also saw it as a sacred creative force. They worried more about the rain god's deliberate punishments for their transgressions: flood, drought, or hail. Several deities governed maize, the most important product of rain. They were young and attractively human in form. People gladly expressed their gratitude to these benevolent beings during ceremonies that marked the yearly cycle of the crop.

Drums marked the place where a ceremony would be performed because music and dance were essential to communal ritual. Each drum was made from a single hollow log with animal hide stretched across one side.

With the drums set upright on the ground, the players used hands or sticks to set up the basic beat. Other musicians, holding small drums or gourd rattles, added their rhythms, and singers chanted a hymn. Dancers embodied the music in simple steps as they moved in procession, often around a circle. The jangling objects on their anklets added to the music. Groups of men performed some dances and women others. When appropriate to a particular celebration or deity, men and women danced simultaneously and sometimes formed a single group.

The villagers knew of many powerful gods other than the ones that they worshipped in the community. However, these beings were less involved with the immediate concerns of ordinary people. They received their due from priests and nobility in temples and in the great public celebrations of the cities.

A sick person had access to several kinds of healers; which of them would be best depended on the nature of the problem. Herbalists, who knew the properties and effects of hundreds of plants, treated many ordinary complaints. The shaman dealt with stronger supernatural causes, including souls that had been dislodged by a sudden shock or fright. An affliction was all the more frightening if caused by a sorcerer. In such a case, the victim had little hope of a cure except by consulting another sorcerer. This was hard to do because practitioners of evil magic, unlike shamans, worked in secret. They faced execution if discovered by the authorities.

Many sick people needed the help of a priest because they had offended a supernatural being or engaged in some other sinful behavior. If a god, spirit, or ancestor had sent the affliction, the victim provided an appropriate sacrifice as specified by the priest. The priest also prescribed one or more acts of ritual purification. These included confession, physical punishment or some form of abstinence, and bathing in a stream. Bathing concluded almost every treatment.

Besides impurity, sin caused imbalance and loss of harmony. This applied within the victim's body and also to his or her relationship with society and with the entire cosmos, including the supernatural worlds. Because of these far-reaching consequences, priests conducted regular communal ceremonies to restore purity and harmony.

Most of the dead went to the Underworld, at best a dreary place, where they might encounter the frightening skeletal gods of death. Some could hope for the most desirable afterlife, in company with the sun god, which was reserved for people of distinction. Whatever their destiny in another world, the dead somehow stayed in contact with their living descendants. They protected and helped where possible and expected offerings of food and drink in return. If neglected, or offended by other behavior, they punished the culprits with disease. Founders of kinship groups or communities received the most ritual attention.

Modal Patterns in Nuclear American Elite Culture

Elite Material Culture

In the morning an aristocratic family awoke in bedding much like that of the peasants. However, their one-room house was larger and better constructed. The rich furnishings included cotton textiles and objects of silver and gold. Even the plates, cups, and utensils were of precious metals. Much of the everyday food was similar to what ordinary people ate although elite families were more likely to enjoy products of the long-distance trade, such as pineapple, papaya, and other tropical fruits. The family took pride in the seats that distinguished them from peasants, who sat on the floor in their huts.

The nobleman emerged from his house into a courtyard surrounded by numerous buildings. Several housed his secondary wives and their children while others held the families of married sons and other relatives. In some of the nonresidential buildings the noble received respected visitors and carried out administrative duties connected with the urban neighborhood for which he was responsible. His rural counterparts took care of sprawling peasant communities in the same way.

While her husband involved himself in political matters, the aristocrat's wife spun and wove. She spent more time at it than a peasant woman did because secondary wives and servants took care of the mundane aspects of cooking, childcare, and other domestic tasks. Her husband used the fine textiles as political gifts to his superiors and to actual or potential allies in the constant competition for status. He also used some to reward his loyal followers.

The aristocrats in the streets wore clothing that was brightly colored or woven with striking designs. In addition to representing wealth, high-quality clothing designated social class and specific ranks through decoration and iconography produced by dyeing and embroidering. Ornaments of gold and silver, augmented by rare stones and feathers, adorned them. A few people of highest rank rode on litters, carried by drab servants or slaves. The urban commoners dressed plainly, like peasants. Wealth determined some differences in clothing and ornament, but the law enforced many distinctions.

Sometimes harsh sounds of construction rose above the ordinary drone of human activity as gangs of peasant workers fulfilled their duty to the government. The elite who planned these monuments to state and religion turned the massive construction jobs over to specialized architects and engineers. They in turn directed the intensive work of thousands of men, who used levers, pulleys, ropes, rollers, and ramps to bring stones from their quarries to the cities and turn them into imposing and beautiful structures.

Near the large rectangular plaza at the heart of the city, the highest government officials lived in compounds guarded by soldiers. In a capital city the greatest was that of the king. Inside the walls the layout resembled that of a minor noble's home, but on a much larger scale and with several courtyards. Large buildings served a variety of official functions. The elite family lived in a lush setting of decorative gardens and trees with access to special bathing facilities. It was especially important for the king, embodiment of the state, to maintain ritual purity as well as physical cleanliness. His servants and other attendants, numbering in the hundreds or even thousands, lived outside the royal area.

A bath for the purification of the elite (Inca culture, Peru).

The main temple complex was another great compound in the heart of the city. Though finely crafted, the sanctuary buildings were small because only priests and some nobles entered them. Inside the sanctuaries, images of the highest gods rested in the presence of magnificent decorations. Public ceremonies took place in the courtyard or in the city's main plaza. Gold and silver objects made by specialized artisans were offered to the gods, and they decorated the temples as well as the homes and bodies of the aristocracy. The craftsmen employed charcoal furnaces for the initial working of the metals. They created delicate pieces with the lost-wax method, in which a mold was made around a wax figure and the wax then displaced by molten metal.

Stone workers also produced fine pieces, such as figurines, as well as heavy practical items like war clubs. They augmented their chipping tools with the use of sand and water for precise shaping and polishing. Some potters used the coiling method to make finely shaped and highly decorated wares for the elite and the temples. Others used molds to mass-produce pots and other ceramic items.

Merchants supplied the city markets through great effort and risk. Some traveled along overland routes, using roads and suspension bridges, while others took to rivers and the sea by means of large canoes and rafts. Emphasizing exotic goods such as gold, feathers, and seashells, merchants provided the elite with status symbols, rewards for underlings, and symbols to reinforce religious institutions that supported stratification. Exchange was based on local and regional specializations in crops, crafts, and mineral extraction.

Elite Social Relations

A noble married his first wife with a celebration similar to those of ordinary people, though grander in gifts, food, and finery. He began his secondary marriages with little or no ceremony. In everyday life secondary wives obeyed the directions of the primary one. Although the children of secondary wives were considered legitimate, the sons of the first wife usually took precedence in matters of heredity. An aristocrat's reasons for taking additional spouses ranged from personal attraction to political considerations. Many of them married cousins or other relatives to enhance the solidarity of the kinship group to which they belonged because this group vied with others for power and wealth. Some unions promoted alliances between kinship groups.

Beyond the advantages of wealth, the law gave nobles the exclusive right to wear distinctive clothing and ornaments and to construct buildings with extra stories in their compounds. However, elite status carried a sense of responsibility as well as privilege. A nobleman spent a great deal of time in public service because the aristocracy held all the highest positions in government, religion, and the military. Nobles held ideals about refined and dignified behavior. Moreover, the law declared that, for some crimes and sins, nobles should suffer punishments equal to or greater than those inflicted on ordinary people.

Grudgingly recognizing the need for special services from commoners, the aristocracy gave them opportunities to rise above their origins by serving the state or a noble household. Success in war was the most common means of advancement, but artisans who produced luxury goods could also attain special status. Some nobles appointed trusted servants to positions of authority. Elevated commoners received gifts such as wealth and secondary wives. They were allowed to wear emblems of their achievements and could hold some military or government offices.

A king and his advisors ruled the state from its only real urban center. They and other nobles derived subsistence and luxury from the surrounding towns and rural communities and from the work of urban commoners. The ruler was an earthly representative of the gods and their foremost worshipper. He also derived authority from leadership in war. The strongest states created extensive empires, from which they extracted enormous wealth.

From the greatest palace in the realm, the emperor ruled as the earthly counterpart of a celestial god. Before his public coronation he had fasted and meditated for several days in a special house built for the occasion. He had contemplated his role as the supreme religious, political, and military leader. He had also considered the customary obligation to care for and protect his people.

The emperor cared for his subjects as a father would his children because he was far superior to them. During every moment of his day, the luxurious symbols of his unique status surrounded him, from the murals on the walls to the delicacies that he ate. Secondary wives, many taken for political purposes, thronged the royal courtyards along with their numerous children. In other parts of the palace compound, government officials did the business of the empire.

The ruler received information and advice from a small number of people, including a few dozen of the highest nobility. More important, he had chosen a few of his closest male relatives as the inner council. Even these individuals rarely penetrated the emperor's exalted isolation, exchanging communications with him by messenger. During the occasional audience, the emperor sat on a raised seat with a special covering. The visitor, even if one of the greatest lords, approached barefoot and wearing some symbol of inferiority. A subject did not look into the emperor's face. When the ruler appeared in public, usually for a major ceremony, special bearers carried him on a litter above the crowds.

In expanding the realm, the imperial government usually attempted diplomacy first. Negotiators plied the local elite with gifts and extolled the benefits of alliance in terms of wealth and protection. At the same time they made clear the dire consequences of resistance. The thousand or so troops in the emperor's guard constituted the only standing army; however, trained full-time officers, drawn from the nobility, stood ready to maintain order and coordination among commoners called up for military service. Although some warriors fought for personal glory and advancement, all subordinated themselves to the goals and orders of their superiors. Trophies such as heads were accumulated for the aggrandizement of the empire and its ruler.

The government grouped conquered polities into new provinces to facilitate the collection of wealth, which was placed under the control of imperial officials. Tribute in the form of cloth and many other goods arrived in the capital on a regular schedule, ranging from once to four times each year. This solidified the subsistence base of the dominant state and provided luxury goods that supported elite political power as well as enhancing their quality of life.

Perpetuation of empire depended on the threat of force, but also on the benefits received by the conquered and on their eventual assimilation. Imperial authorities were often satisfied with indirect rule, as long as they received material support and warriors to help with further conquests. Local rulers became related to the imperial dynasty by marriage, and they or their sons visited the capital for ceremonies. The sons were also sent to the capital for education, which served the dual purpose of holding them hostage and assimilating them to the dominant culture or at least co-opting them to the political goals of the dominant state. When these mechanisms worked smoothly, imperial authorities gave material rewards to loyal subjects and permitted a great deal of internal autonomy to subordinate states.

Imperial organization extended to the community level in order to ensure the fulfillment of obligations and to prevent disruption of order. Petty officials were appointed to supervise groups of households on the order of 10 or 20, 50, and 100. They were responsible for the local production of tributary goods and recruitment of men for government service.

Application of the law also began at the community level. A local government official judged ordinary cases, civil and criminal, such as land disputes or assaults. He heard both sides, including witnesses, and then rendered a verdict. In deciding the consequences of a criminal act, the judge considered all circumstances, such as intent and severity. Penalties ranged from public humiliation to physical punishment. Serious cases were referred to a regional court under a noble official. The offenses included murder, adultery, theft, treason, and violation of the sumptuary laws that prescribed the privileges of the elite. The procedures in a regional court were like those at the lower level, but the sentence was frequently death by stoning, hanging, or clubbing.

Elite Knowledge and Expression

The priest in charge of a large urban temple occupied a high place in the religious hierarchy. The lesser priests in his temple, most of them nobles like their leader, held varied ranks associated with their seniority and functions. They made astronomical observations and kept the calendars. They took confessions, performed divinations, and prescribed cures. The lowest, novices and commoners, took care of routine maintenance in the shrine buildings and throughout the temple compound. The novices also pursued their studies, assimilating the vast body of knowledge that made the priesthood a full-time profession.

Aspiring priests had to learn in detail about the origins of the world and humanity and how these events linked them to the gods. Mythology divided the past into sharply distinct ages, separated by catastrophes with supernatural causes. A great flood destroyed the previous world and its inhabitants, who had been people significantly different from those of today. The ultimate Creator of the present world, who combined male and female aspects, was often depicted as very old, perhaps to connote wisdom. Other gods assisted the Creator in various ways. One or more of the creators visited humans in the role of culture hero, introducing farming and various social customs. The Sun, another of the greatest gods, was associated with rulers and justified their power. The rain god, so important to peasants, was also worshiped at the national level because everyone recognized dependence on the crops.

Priests preserved legends and history, including the story of how the ruling class had originated elsewhere and migrated to their current place under divine guidance. Thus they justified control of the state and the empire. As nobles, the priests identified with elite interests and had many relatives in the government. The highest priests were closely associated with the emperor and his advisors.

The education of the priests included a vast amount of ritual knowledge. Only they, and a few of the highest secular officials, could enter the small buildings that served as shrines to the gods. Finely constructed and decorated with the richest materials, these shrines housed stone and wooden images of the deities. They also contained the regalia used outside in public ceremonies. Priests performed some of these ceremonies in the temple courtyard for aristocratic audiences. Others, usually in one of the city squares, welcomed commoners.

Religion emphasized the parallel importance of the sexes. An androgynous Creator gave rise to the separate descent lines of men and women. Many of the other deities preferred that people of their own gender play the leading role in worshiping them. Thus hierarchies of priestesses paralleled those of priests. Women were symbolically associated with water, night, dark, cold, and the Underworld; men with dryness, day, light, heat, and the sky.

Sanctified women worked in royal and temple compounds to produce the fine cloth needed for sacrifices to all the gods. Like peasant women they prayed to the patron of weaving, who was very much attuned to female life because she was also the goddess of reproduction.

Great public ceremonies, many related to the agricultural cycle, took place on a monthly basis. Others were performed in response to special events such as war or catastrophe. People fasted in preparation for a major ceremony. When it began, hundreds or thousands of people joined in processions and performed ritual dances while many thousands more watched. The priests offered goods and food to the gods, including animal sacrifices. They also sacrificed humans, children as well as adults. Priests made this greatest of offerings for the most important regular ceremonies and in times of great stress or danger, such as famine or the death of a king. One technique involved cutting out the heart. If blood was drawn by any means, it was smeared on the image of the god to whom the sacrifice was devoted.

Ceremonies were occasions for grand expressions of art. The many musicians were skilled professionals who were likely to be punished for a mistake. Performers recited epic narratives that reminded listeners of the Creation, the gods, and the glorious history of the state and its rulers. Dances, songs, and narratives were interspersed with dramatic performances in which a few actors carried on a dialogue supported by a chorus. Most important of all, the highest priests chanted poetic prayers and hymns in which they used beautiful language to celebrate the gods and their gifts to humanity. In the privacy of their homes elite individuals composed more modest and personal poems. They meditated on love and friendship and extolled the beauty of the natural world, often linking the two realms with metaphor. Such poems were often sung or recited to music.

Priests kept annual and monthly calendars that guided the cycle of ceremonies and the agricultural cycle that was the reason for many of the ceremonies. The solar calendar was based on the rising and setting of the sun at particular points on the horizon. Specialists used pillars or other markers to keep precise track of these events. Astronomers also noted the movements of other heavenly bodies and constellations that they believed to have influence over human affairs. Foremost among these were the moon, Venus, and the Pleiades.

People viewed irregular celestial events, such as comets, as ill omens. Eclipses of the sun and moon were particularly frightening because they affected prominent heavenly bodies that represented important deities. Many thought that an eclipse was caused by the attack of a supernatural beast. They tried to frighten it away by making as much noise as possible with shouts and musical instruments. Some abused their dogs in order to add their howls to the din.

Mathematics served astronomy and calendrics. It was also essential to the more mundane calculations needed to administer the state and tax its inhabitants. Mathematics, astronomy, and religion combined in architecture, engineering, and city planning. The city itself represented the spiritual dimension of life. Some streets existed for ritual rather than practical reasons. Urban structures, as well as layout, represented religious ideas. The political leaders who planned construction emphasized concepts such as access (or denial of access) to special places, astronomical orientation of structures, and relationship to topographic features. Numerous topographical features, such as particular rocks and caves, were sacred.

When the life of an aristocrat ended, many people came together for an elaborate ceremony. Attendants covered the body in the finest clothes and ornaments available and prepared it in a flexed or sitting position. They provided equipment and gifts to facilitate the journey to the next world. Sacrificed wives and servants accompanied the highest of noblemen.

A Closer Look

Nuclear American Crops and the World

Nuclear Americans domesticated a wide variety of plants for food and other purposes. The following list samples a few of the most widespread and important crops (note that several entries refer to genera or larger groupings rather than to single species).

Amaranth *(Amaranthus paniculatus)*
Annona *(Annona spp.)*: fruits, including sweetsop and soursop
Avocado *(Persea americana)*
Beans *(Phaseolus spp.)*
Berries (various)
Chiles *(Capsicum spp.)*
Cotton *(Gossypium spp.?)*
Gourds and calabashes (diverse genera)
Guava *(Psidium guajava)*
Maize *(Zea mays)*
Manioc *(Manihot enculenta)*
Papaya *(Carica papaya)*: fruit of the pawpaw
Pineapple *(Anaus comosus)*
Squashes *(Cucurbita spp.)*
Tomato *(Solanum lycopersicon)*

Several Nuclear American crops have profoundly affected other parts of the globe. The Spanish quickly recognized the virtues of maize, which soon became the third most important crop in the world, after wheat and rice (S. Coe 1994). Within a century of Columbus's first landing in America, maize was under cultivation in Europe, the Middle East, and central Africa. Within another century it was in China.

The avocado enjoyed rapid acceptance in Europe. Among Old World products, only olives and coconuts could compete with its distinctively oily quality. The pineapple had no competition at all. As one monarch declared, it was the most delicious thing he had ever tasted. There was no such luck for the poor tomato. Initially its odiferous vine repelled Europeans, and some thought it might be poisonous. Nevertheless, it endured and conquered and "today the food of the world is overwhelmed by this red tide" (S. Coe 1994:29).

Some Nuclear American foods had social class implications in the Old World. Certain squashes were prized because their seeds could replace almonds in the making of marzipan, a highly prestigious dish. On the other hand, chiles may have led to the decline of highly spiced foods as a status symbol. In contrast to expensive imported spices, European peasants could raise chiles cheaply.

The Ecology of Civilization

There is chronological gap between Old World and New World civilizations. The earliest Old World civilizations arose around 3500 B.C. while those of the New World began about 2,000 years later. The Nuclear American cultures of 1500 A.D. were roughly equivalent to the Greek city-states and the Roman Empire of Classical Europe. This is the sort of thing that some people are apt to explain in terms of varying racial capabilities. A more plausible alternative provides a lesson in the ecology of civilization.

Maize was the foundation of New World civilization, the Native American equivalent of wheat and rice. However, this could not have been predicted by anyone in the beginning: "Wild corn was a primitive and unpromising plant, and one wonders why it was selected for development in the first place" (Adams 1991:34). When people first ate maize, each cob (not kernel) was about the size of a small thumb (S. Coe 1994). A person chewed a handful of the tiny cobs and spat out the resultant quid. Refinement of this minor dietary item to the bountiful crop of recent times was a long process. It was made longer and more complex by various genetic and reproductive factors.

The sparseness of wild maize and the problems involved in its selective breeding contrast sharply with the characteristics of wheat in the ancient Middle East. Wild wheat grew in abundance even before domestication, and its breeding pattern made artificial selection relatively easy. Early abundance and rapid improvement of wheat facilitated the early development of civilization in the Middle East.

Another possible ecological factor was the absence of large, strong, domesticable animals (Adams 1991). The fauna of Nuclear America provided no equivalents to the cattle and horses of the Old World. With no animals to ride or to pull plows and heavy loads, the Native Americans suffered serious disadvantages in agriculture and transportation.

This is not to say that ecology explained all differences between New World and Old World civilizations. Although social, political, and economic developments proceeded with equal rapidity in both Domains, a gap in technology persisted: "In the New World technology was much less important and essentially Stone Age" (Adams 1991:22). In contrast (according to Adams) technological development in the Old World was almost continuous; despite halts here and there, stasis was never complete and the systematic accumulation of empirical knowledge continued.

The implication seems to be that Nuclear America developed to a technological plateau necessary for civilization and then throttled back. The fact that they reached the plateau implies that this was not due to a lack of ability. More likely, it was a matter of placing intellect and energy in other areas. The elaborate ceremonial life of Nuclear American cultures suggests that religion was the cultural choice that they made.

MESOAMERICAN AREA

Examples:

Aztec, Maya, Zapotec, Mixtec, Tarascan

The Mesoamerican Area included central and southeastern Mexico and adjacent portions of several Central American countries: Belize, Guatemala, Honduras, and Nicaragua.

In the early sixteenth century Mesoamerica harbored close to one hundred focal states (so-called city-states; see chapter 3). Many were controlled by empires, most notably those of the Aztecs, Tarascans, and Quiche Maya (Pollard 1993). Other sections of the Area were "balkanized" into small states (many with fewer than ten thousand people) that were frequently at odds with one another, e.g., the Yucatec Maya (Adams 1997). The description below is largely based on the abundant evidence from the Aztec and Mayan cultures, but much of it is known to apply to other Mesoamericans. It is also based mainly on the larger empires, because they are better known and because they affected the lives of the largest number of people.

A form of free enterprise flourished in Mesoamerica, connecting marketplaces large and small. The marketplace gave women an opportunity to gain wealth, and it gave even greater opportunity to male professional merchants. The merchants may have been largely responsible for creating the Culture Area itself by carrying cultural traits across the boundaries of states, empires, and Regions. The elite prestige system that the merchants served led to a "comprehensive economy" that rose above political fragmentation, as in early capitalist Europe and in the global economy of today (Blanton et al. 1993; W. P. Mitchell, pers. comm.). Trade goods included distinctive minerals for highly skilled craftsmen. Specialists used obsidian, a volcanic glass, to make tools with edges sharper than modern steel. Others fashioned luxury goods from "jade" (actually jadeite, serpentine, and other green minerals).

Religion emphasized duality: complementary oppositions essential to the working of the universe. Divination and ceremony were regulated by a complex calendrical system that meshed solar years with shorter ritual cycles. Ceremonial life joined religion and sport, most notably in a ritual ball game that combined rigorous physical activity with profound symbolism. The rubber ball game was played for 2,000 years over an area of more than one million square miles (Scarborough and Wilcox, eds. 1991).

Key features:

- ▶ Unusually fine stone work
- ▶ Marketplace system
- ▶ Economic opportunities for women
- ▶ Professional merchants
- ▶ Duality in religious concepts
- ▶ Elaborate and precise calendrical system
- ▶ Ritual ball game and volador

Modal Patterns in Mesoamerican Peasant Culture

Peasant Material Culture

Rising from their woven sleeping mats in the morning, a peasant family heard the ducks and turkeys that provided some flesh for their diet. When they went out to tend the fowl, they also saw to the silent hairless dogs that they bred for meat. Unlike the gaunt canines that guarded the house, the silent dogs were force-fed to fatten them. Many people gave them maize, and some limited them to vegetable foods, in order to improve their flavor. On some days family members took honey from the hives of stingless bees kept near the house. People made the hives from hollow logs with the ends covered by mud.

A village woman spent up to six hours each day processing maize to make food for her family. First, she removed the kernels and placed them in water with white lime to steep overnight so as to loosen the hulls. The next day she boiled the kernels, skinned them, and ground them into flour between a stone roller and a stone surface. Then she was ready to cook.

For the morning meal the woman prepared a gruel, either spicing it with chiles or sweetening it with honey. She made tortillas for the main meal in the afternoon by baking them on a clay griddle. Family members rolled the tortillas and used them as spoons to dip into beans, sauces, or stews. Some days the cook varied the routine with tamales, which she made by steaming balls of maize dough.

Every few weeks women of the community gathered in the marketplace to exchange surplus foods and craft products. The latter included pottery and obsidian tools. A variety of cutting tools made from obsidian, a volcanic glass, were the mainstay of every household's technology. In the marketplace women met others from parts of the community that they rarely visited. They exchanged news and enjoyed the company.

Contemporary women suggest what a day at the market might have been like in the traditional Mesoamerican Area (Mayan culture, Guatemala).

Occasionally village women took their goods to the nearest urban center, which offered a market every five days. There they obtained items brought in by professional merchants, such as obsidian and salt, as well as manufactured items not available in the home village. Midwives and healers offered their services in the marketplace, and so did prostitutes. In these larger markets government officials enforced rules, settled disputes, and collected taxes. A god, represented by a shrine, watched over the market.

Women bartered their goods in some market transactions and used money in others. Cacao beans served as units of exchange because, imported from tropical areas, their value was established by rarity. A woman had to be careful that the beans she received were legitimate. Some unscrupulous traders mixed shriveled beans with good ones, and others filled the skins of discarded beans with sand.

When a man was not summoned to build or fight for the state, he did most of his daily work in the main fields away from the house where he tended to the maize and other staples. From time to time he went hunting to provide his family with additional meat. He took his bow and arrows in hope of shooting a white-tailed deer or a peccary. More often he would find a small animal—such as a rabbit, gopher, or armadillo—in a trap or snare that he had previously set.

Peasant Social Relations

When a pregnant woman went into labor, a professional midwife came to the house to attend her. Soon after a successful birth, parents concerned themselves with the ritual calendar, which represented cosmic forces that shaped the infant's soul and thus its destiny. The father consulted a specialist to learn the details of his child's prospects. If the baby had been born on an unlucky day, there was a possible remedy: performance of the naming ceremony on a particularly auspicious day. Sometimes parents delayed the rite for this purpose. Ordinarily, the naming ceremony took place soon after the birth on a day that the astrologer declared to be fortunate. One important ritual was a purifying bath for the infant. Sometime during these early days, he or she was presented with implements appropriate to the role of man or woman.

A child's life was filled with speeches; parents and others lectured on responsibilities and morality. Despite the oratory, and household work, children found some time for play. Their toys included rubber balls and dolls of wood or clay. Older boys went to a local school to learn about war and train for it. Some of them learned about sex with prostitutes, who were despised but tolerated. Girls stayed close to home and learned from their mothers about running a household. They also guarded their virtue; virginity was one of the most important prerequisites for marriage.

Parents used a go-between to find and negotiate marriage for their children. When a match was likely, they consulted an astrologer. He told them whether or not the marriage was likely to succeed and determined the most auspicious day for the wedding.

Peasant Knowledge and Expression

The house was a sacred place. The fire in the hearth represented the fire god and symbolized the continuity of life and of the world itself. The sanctity of the household fire was manifest in the ritual foundation of three stones. It had the same significance as the fires that burned continuously in the great temples.

Life in the house began with spiritual events. At the moment of birth a wild animal was born somewhere that would share the baby's fate. When one died, the other would too; this relationship explained many cases of sudden death in humans. Between the birth and the naming ceremony the baby received the soul, centered in the head, that determined temperament. This was the soul that would leave the body during dreams or visions. Illness and death could result if this soul were forced from the body by shock, impurity, or sorcery. Early in life the connection between body and soul was tenuous, and the infant needed special protection. Spiritual emanations caused by the jealousy of outsiders were particularly dangerous at this time.

Eventually two other souls became part of a person. The one in the heart governed mental functions such as understanding, memory, imagination, and will. The liver housed the force of desires and other strong feelings. If an individual failed to restrain powerful emotions, this soul produced dangerous emanations with the breath. They could sicken the person or his family, cause the death of their animals, or result in material losses such as rotting food.

A few persons could consciously control the emotional soul and project its force into some other entity: an object, an animal, even another human. People did not consider this power to be intrinsically evil, but they viewed it with suspicion because the potential danger was great.

Modal Patterns in Mesoamerican Elite Culture

Elite Material Culture

Walking the narrow alleys in the central part of a great city, a person glimpsed stone pyramids rearing above the ordinary buildings in stepped tiers. At the wall of a temple compound containing several pyramids, the viewer craned his or her neck to see the top of the highest one. On the level top sat a temple, its boxlike structure made elegant by the colorful crest that surmounted it. A long, steep stairway ascended the front of each pyramid; some had additional stairways on other faces. Priests, and sometimes nobles, used these stairs to reach the temples that only they could enter.

After the awesome sight of the main temple complex, the city's marketplace provided a different kind of excitement. Many thousands of people thronged the large open area, seeking goods and services, talking with friends and acquaintances, arguing with the government officials who supervised the activities of the market and the behavior of its patrons. A large number of the buyers and sellers were women. This was an opportunity to enhance the well-being of their families and to accumulate some personal wealth.

As a prospective buyer circulated through the market, he or she passed clearly defined sections in which different goods were grouped: all the pottery here, the clothing there, and the woven mats further on. In addition to these and other crafted goods, sellers offered natural products such as fresh food, firewood, and lumber. A person could spend the whole day in the market because cooked foods were also available. Much could be done in one day since the arrangement of the goods made it easy to find desired items and compare the deals being offered. This arrangement also facilitated the collection of market taxes by government officials.

Besides the utilitarian items that everyone needed, some sections of the market offered luxury goods purchased mostly by nobles or their servants. These

A Mesoamerican pyramid, topped by a temple that would have been even more impressive in traditional times when it was painted and had a high roof comb (city of Chichen Itza, Toltec-Mayan culture, Mexico).

included ornate clothes, gold ornaments, precious stones, tropical bird feathers, and slaves. Nobles also bought large quantities of cacao beans to make into a chocolate drink; regular consumption of chocolate was an important status symbol. Local peasants produced a few of these luxury goods, but professional merchants brought most of them over long distances. In the marketplace merchants found porters to carry their goods. Barbers, carpenters, and artisans also offered their services to those who could afford them.

People accomplished most of their exchanges through barter. However, some used cacao beans or cotton capes as money. One cape was worth a great many beans. Judges sat in the marketplace to resolve disputes and to punish criminal behavior such as theft or counterfeiting.

Those who made and sold obsidian artifacts did a great deal of business. All people prized the volcanic glass for the sharpness that lent itself to work such as wood carving. Highly polished, it provided wealthier people with mirrors. The elite valued jewels made from obsidian with a green tint. They prized jade and attached similar significance to turquoise. In addition to their beauty, these materials were mystically associated with water and therefore with life itself. Jade equaled gold and silver with regard to symbolic importance.

Elite Social Relations

In a noble household, slaves did most of the hard work. Although reduced to similar circumstances, they came to their status in varied ways. Most were products of poverty, some having gambled themselves into unmanageable debt while others had been afflicted by famine or other events beyond their control. Those in the latter situation had been sold by their families or had sold themselves. A few slaves were war captives, and a few more were suffering punishment for theft or other crimes.

The head of the household had obtained his slaves from a trader in the market. Occasionally he purchased one for a religious sacrifice rather than for service. No such acquisitions were needed to work the land on his rural estate. There he had serfs to cultivate his crops. He did not own them as individuals, but they were bound to the land that they worked no matter who held the estate.

With thousands of slaves in his palace, the emperor had no concerns about adequate domestic service. He worried about administrative service because the imperial structure was better suited to tribute collection than to political organization. Even the most successful empires found it difficult to exercise consistent political control far from home. This had several implications for interactions among states. One was the extensive use of terrorism in war, such as the complete destruction of towns, as a cheap way to conduct competition for power.

Another response to imperial uncertainties was the development of stable patterns of diplomacy. These included elite marriages between states and exchange of presents among rulers. Ambassadorial contacts occurred regularly, and the emperor invited other rulers to major ceremonial events. Diplomacy included intimidation, as in cases where foreign dignitaries attended ceremonies in which large numbers of war captives were sacrificed. When diplomacy failed, war was conducted according to generally accepted rules.

Between great empires there were sections where small independent states, some hardly more than chiefdoms, squabbled among themselves. These petty states grouped and regrouped into various alliances and federations. In some cases one king was the figurehead leader of a federation. If he gained real power, the line between federation and state or petty empire became blurred. The great imperial governments often left these regions alone because they were too remote for conquest or held no attractive resources or made their resources readily available through trade.

Elite Knowledge and Expression

The priesthood told of at least four ages in the earth's history. The Feathered Serpent, a reptilian being decorated by plumes, played a major role in the creation of the current age and acted as a culture hero by giving humans their most important customs. One of the most benevolent deities, the Feathered Serpent was a patron of the political elite. Another reptilian god, connected with the crocodilelike caiman, was associated with creation and sustenance.

Other gods had more frightening aspects. Those who physically supported the world were malevolent and threatened to end the world at certain times. Some deities devoted themselves to violent death and execution. The image of the earth goddess, humanoid but monstrous,

A sculpture of the Feathered Serpent, one of the most important gods of Mesoamerica (city of Chichen Itza, Toltec-Mayan culture, Mexico).

displayed a fanged mouth that led to the Underworld. A powerful goddess wearing a serpent headdress presided over death and destruction as well as birth and creation.

Certain special interest groups, such as merchants and the various craftsmen, had divine patrons of their own. The long-nosed merchant god was especially associated with cacao and militarism: cacao beans were a premium trade item and militarism expanded trade opportunities.

To the commoners it seemed that there were hundreds of gods. To the priests this was largely the result of each major god having several aspects. Manifestations of the same god, often with variations on the same name, were distinguished by gender, by association with the cardinal directions, and by differing manifestations in the Upper World and the Underworld. The Sun, for example, became Jaguar when it went below the horizon and into the Underworld each night.

Gender ambiguity and night–day transformations represented the fundamental role of duality in philosophical thought. People saw day as the human time of stability and order while gods and demons came alive at night. They viewed solar eclipses with great fear because the disappearance of the sun seemed to be the defeat of the day by the night. Nevertheless, as with gender and other dualities, the relationship of the components was considered to be complementary. Both sides were important to existence because the energy of the supernatural night revitalized the ordinary life of the day. In the beginning of the current age, a god from above had to penetrate the Underworld to obtain the substance from which human beings were made to live in daylight on the surface of the earth.

Though diverse in nature, the deities required similar forms of worship. Many practices involved the sacrifice of blood and flesh, which nourished the gods. The priests regularly offered their own blood, using a sharp instrument to penetrate soft parts of the body, such as the ear lobes, tongue, and penis. During the great monthly ceremonies, rulers and nobles performed these acts as an obligation to society. For extra penance they drew a reed or straw or cord through the hole to increase the bleeding. In some cases they smeared the blood on a particular idol. In others they spattered it on a piece of paper and then burned it, carrying the offering skyward.

The ultimate sacrifice, human life, highlighted each of the great monthly ceremonies. During such a rite, the brightly robed priests and a painted man slowly climbed the long, steep stairway to the top of a temple pyramid. The man was an enemy aristocrat who had been captured in battle. In front of the temple the sacrificers stretched the warrior across a stone altar. A priest plunged a stone knife into the man's chest, made a quick and skilled incision, and pulled out the heart. He placed the heart, still beating, in a sacred vessel and smeared some of the blood on a godly effigy. Then the body was taken off the altar and rolled down the pyra-

This skull rack represents the long-term emphasis on human sacrifice in the Mesoamerican Area (city of Chichen Itza, Toltec-Mayan culture, Mexico).

mid steps. At the bottom certain individuals took some portions of the body for ritual consumption. The head was kept as a trophy.

Other gods and rites demanded different practices. The priests often sacrificed women and children. For a few rituals decapitation was the appropriate mode of death. In some cases a priest danced while wearing the flayed skin of the victim. When merchants or some other group had the opportunity to offer a sacrifice, they purchased a slave for the purpose. Whatever the occasion, the ultimate purpose of all sacrifice was to give the gods the motive and ability to perpetuate life. To die in this way was considered a great honor and a pathway to the most glorious afterlife. People told stories about war captives who, having been spared, demanded to be sacrificed. In lesser ceremonies priests offered dogs, turkeys, and quail.

Regular ceremonies, as well as divination and administrative schedules, were organized by a complex calendrical system. One calendar was a sacred almanac of 260 days, formed by the combination of twenty names and thirteen numbers, which diviners used to foretell an individual's fate. The astronomical calendar was com-

An observatory atop remnants of complex Mesoamerican architecture (city of Chichen Itza, Toltec-Mayan culture, Mexico).

posed of eighteen months of twenty days each with a final period of five days. Combination of the two calendars yielded a fifty-two-year cycle, marked by the points in time at which both calendars ended simultaneously.

The importance of the calendar was symbolized in the volador ritual. Four men, dressed as birds, attached themselves with coiled ropes to a movable platform atop a tall pole. When the men leaped off, the platform rotated and they "flew" around it as the ropes unwound. The length of the ropes was adjusted so that thirteen revolutions brought the men to the ground. Multiplied by the four participants, this made 52 revolutions to symbolize the number of years in the calendar round.

The ritual ball game also gave physical expression to religious ideas. Two teams of nobles played the formal game in a stone court shaped like an I. Forbidden to use the upper body, the players propelled the rubber ball with hips, knees, or buttocks. They scored by placing the ball through one of the stone rings mounted vertically on the sides of the court.

A symbolic ball game was played on elite courts like this one (Teotenango, Mexico).

The ball symbolized the world, and the game itself represented a mythological or political struggle. Some Mesoamericans regarded the game as a way to communicate with the gods by reenacting a myth of supernatural conflict. In other cases it was used as a kind of divination: the outcome of the game prompted a major decision or predicted the outcome of an important event. Either interpretation could lead to a human sacrifice to redress an undesirable outcome (one that was contrary to the mythological rationale or that made an unfavorable prediction).

The ball game also had more ordinary implications. Heavy betting resulted in significant transfers of wealth or territory as well as the reduction of some losers to slavery. Since the nobles took the leading role in battle, the game may have been important for maintaining their conditioning. Some games may have been used as a substitute for military confrontation or as a means to settle conflicts within a political unit.

Scribes recorded information in pictographs. They carved some messages into stone. They drew others in

books made of paper or deerskin that were folded accordion style. Maize received artistic as well as ritual attention. People personalized maize itself, glorified it in poetry and song, and used elaborate terminology when they discussed it. Much of the poetry, however, expressed sorrow or resignation about the transitory nature of life.

Ideally a person anticipated death with confession to a priest, but the afterlife had little to do with morality on earth. Various fates awaited the dead, depending on factors such as social status in life and the manner of dying. Commoners were usually buried while nobles, and those who accompanied them as sacrifices, were likely to be cremated.

A Closer Look

The Mesoamerican Area readily divides into several Regions with important cultural distinctions. Two of these cultural units are represented by famous cultures, the Mayas and the Aztecs. A third demands recognition for its sharp contrasts with the rest of Mesoamerica.

The Mexican Region

This Region occupied the heart of the modern country of Mexico from the central valley north to the Gulf and south to the Pacific. In the early sixteenth century there were fifty to sixty focal states, most of them dominated by the vast Aztec Empire. The empire hinged on a federation between two huge cities, Texcoco and Tenochtitlán. The latter, the seat of the emperor, had a population of nearly 200,000 people. The Aztecs, and others like them, acknowledged a long tradition of great empires in the Region and used mythologized connections with their predecessors to validate their own standing.

The Aztecs, and probably other societies in the Mexican Region, conducted trade mostly by land with human bearers. Aztec merchants occupied a complex role in society. They served the government as spies and warriors, and in some cases their alleged mistreatment provided the pretext for declarations of war. Some merchants earned great honors and wealth, giving them influence and power that rivaled the lower nobility. To offset the resultant hostility from the aristocracy, merchants cultivated a modest public image.

The Aztecs seem to have practiced human sacrifice on a scale never seen anywhere else in the world (Berdan 1982). Their need for victims led them to invent the concept of "sacred war" (Adams 1997) and a special category of ritualized warfare, the "flowery war," devoted only to the capture of men for sacrifice. Although the flowery wars did provide numerous sacrifices, they may also have had long-term political and military significance as a means of testing and pressuring formidable opponents (Hassig 1988).

Ritual cannibalism followed some Mesoamerican sacrifices. The Aztecs regarded the victims as divine and the cannibalism as a way to commune with the god with whom the victim was identified (Berdan 1982). In a parallel practice they ate god images made from amaranth dough in order to assimilate the god's essence. Because of the association with cannibalism, Harner (1977) suggested that protein and fat deficiencies in the Aztec diet were the underlying reasons for human sacrifice. Some critics have taken this idea as a contradiction of the religious explanation for the phenomenon, which is a mistake. The conscious motivation for the practice is independent of any ecological explanation that we might discover as objective outsiders. The religious significance of sacrifice for Mesoamericans is obvious; the question is whether it also had ecological significance. Although animal nutrients may have been an issue for Native American civilizations, this seems an unlikely explanation for Aztec ritual cannibalism: the flesh went to nobles and warriors who needed it least, and the torsos were not eaten at all (Berdan 1982).

The Mayan Region

This Region was and is inhabited by people speaking Mayan languages. It is composed of the Yucatán peninsula and the adjacent highlands of Mexico, Guatemala, Honduras, and Belize. In large sections of the tropical lowlands slash-and-burn farming was common and produced the bulk of food for many people (M. Coe 1993).

The mostly balkanized Mayan states of the sixteenth century were remnants of larger and more distinctive polities. Indigenous ruling classes had been replaced by Mexican invaders or by Mayans that had been heavily influenced by Mexican culture. Traditionally, scholars have judged these Mayans to be less accomplished than their predecessors in fields ranging from art to construction. However that may be, the Maya showed continued vigor in their commercial and political activities.

Merchants in this Region did not suffer the social ambiguities of their Mexican counterparts because the Mayan merchants were nobles. Their bearers brought goods to the shore, but most of the journey was made by sea. The great canoes employed crews as large as two dozen men. A major factor in this continuing success was that the Mayan Region contained the most important sources of salt in Mesoamerica. According to one expert, "it was probably the smooth business operations" of the Mayan traders "that spared the Maya from the Aztec onslaught that had overwhelmed less cooperative peoples in Mesoamerica" (M. Coe 1993:169).

Mayan pictographs constituted a true writing system because they were actually hieroglyphs. That is, they represented syllabic sounds rather than memorized concepts. Thus the reader could "sound out" a particular representation. There were other ways in which the Mayan intellectual heritage stood out from the rest of the Area and the rest of the New World. For example, their astronomical observations were the most precise and their calendars the most accurate. Much of their astronomical expertise was devoted to Venus, a deity in the sky who received considerable prayer and sacrifice. Beyond the cyclical calendar system, they established a linear "long count" that was anchored in the year that we designate 3114 B.C. Many scholars think that the Maya invented the important mathematical concept of zero as a placeholder, although some have doubts (Kidwell 1993).

The Tarascan Region

This Region was distinguished by people who spoke a language unique in Mesoamerica and related to Zuni in North America and Quechua (the tongue of the Incas) in South America. They built mainly in wood and erected unique keyhole-shaped pyramids for the Sun.

The Tarascans built an empire to the south and west of the Aztecs and showed remarkable resistance to their aggressive neighbors. The highly centralized state placed unusual emphasis on ethnic unity, disseminating Tarascan culture and language to conquered peoples. This degree of imperial organization probably helped them to resist the Aztecs. They were also highly militarized and defended by well-placed border fortifications. The placement of the forts may indicate that the Tarascans had conceptualized their state as one with national boundaries. Such a perspective would have contrasted sharply with the typical focal-state view of political control as gradually waning with distance from the capital.

Tarascan religion had fewer and different gods than the rest of Mesoamerica. The Creator, who was a female god, also controlled rain. Moon, her daughter, was responsible for birth and fertility. The third major god, the culture hero of the Tarascan state, was male. There was little indication of duality in the gods or other religious concepts, and the Feathered Serpent was absent. The Tarascans also lacked the ritual calendar, writing, and books. Considering their distinctive language, the cultural divergences may be explained by a relatively recent arrival in Mesoamerica.

ANDEAN AREA

Examples:

Inca, Aymara, Chimu

The Andean Area revolved around the central section of the Andes mountain range and encompassed large parts of what are now Peru, Ecuador, Bolivia, and Chile. Although the people had to cope with the second largest and most rugged mountain range on earth, they created agricultural states. Perhaps because of the environment, they repeatedly constructed empires that diversified the resources available to ruling groups.

By the beginning of the sixteenth century the Inca people from Cuzco in Peru had welded the entire Culture Area into a single polity. It was the largest on earth at the time and "one of the largest empires ever to arise in the preindustrial world" (Moseley 1992). Rivaling the Roman Empire in length at about 3,300 miles (5,500 km), the Inca polity encompassed at least 10 million people. Even more remarkable, the government was more centralized than those of smaller realms in Mesoamerica.

Andeans kept domestic guinea pigs *(Cavia porcellus)*. They also had the only large domestic mammals in the native New World, known collectively as camelids because they are relatives of the Old World camels. The New World species lacked humps but resembled camels in their facial features and, according to numerous reports, in their proclivity for expectoration. Llama and alpaca (both genus *Lama*) stood about three feet tall at the shoulder; however, the llamas weighed twice as much, with a range of 200 to 300 pounds. Both species provided people with meat and other resources as well as sacrifices for important ceremonies. Andeans also exploited two wild camelids. The guanaco *(Lama guanicoe)* was the species ancestral to the domestic forms. Slightly smaller than the llama, it yielded a significant amount of meat. The slender vicuna *(Vicugna vicugna)* weighed only 70 to 130 pounds. It was used as a source of soft fleece.

Because of sharp variations in temperature and precipitation, the resources available to humans differed significantly at different altitudes in the mountains. People integrated these resources with a strategy called verticality, in which a given group maintained holdings in several distinct ecological settings. In many cases these holdings were physically separated from one another, like islands, and formed a "vertical archipelago."

In many respects Andean technological ingenuity exceeded that of Mesoamerica. Andean superiority manifested itself in greater practical use of metals (especially copper and bronze), precise assembly of massive stone structures, and a 20,000-mile road system that conquered the mountains. For the peasants, there was a domestic grain mill that required far less labor than those of Mesoamerica. Lacking any form of writing, the Inca kept their records with a clever memory device, the *khipu* (also spelled quipu), consisting of knotted strings.

Some features of Inca royal life differed sharply from those of Mesoamerica. One was incestuous marriage. The Inca emperors extended the aristocratic tendency to marry relatives to its extreme, favoring a sister as the first wife. Even more distinctive was the custom of split inheritance, which gave a new ruler the office of his predecessor, but not his material wealth.

Key features:

▶ Verticality

▶ Domesticated camelids and guinea pigs

▶ Practical metallurgy

▶ Engineering expertise

▶ Extensive road system

▶ High degree of political centralization

▶ Split inheritance

▶ Incestuous royal marriages

▶ Record keeping with knotted strings

Modal Patterns in Andean Peasant Culture

Peasant Material Culture

A peasant family slept in blankets on the floor of their small, dark house. Several large jars held their spare clothing and the food to be cooked soon. Cooking utensils, tools, and other objects sat in niches or hung from hooks set in the walls. A small clay stove marked the kitchen side of the house. Around it dozens of guinea pigs rested or scuttled across the floor. Unable to climb, they were contained by low barriers. These shaggy rodents, breeding rapidly in the household setting, provided small amounts of meat for the family and sacrifices for ordinary religious observances.

Guinea pigs in a contemporary house (Ecuador).

The cluster of houses that shared a courtyard were further united by the wall that surrounded them and provided only one entrance to the compound. Compound walls were composed of stone or adobe. People made them rectangular where possible, but in some cases they had to accommodate to the mountainous terrain. Beyond the enclosure, the other house clusters of the community were scattered in response to the irregular distribution of resources.

Waking in the cold morning, a woman fastened leather sandals to her feet with elaborate wool ties. Then she draped a large cloak over her long dress and fastened it in front with a large and decorative copper straight pin. She also wore a necklace of beads made from shell or bone. Preparing food for her family, the woman used a mill that made the work fairly easy. Kneeling in front of a level stone slab about eight inches high, she crushed grain with a rocker that measured one to two feet across its flat top. The weight of the rocker made heavy pressure unnecessary, and operation was simple enough to leave to young girls.

A woman often cooked on the clay stove in the house, which had several holes on top for pots and a small stoking hole in the front. She kept the fire small because wood was scarce and hard to collect. She could also cook outside, in a corner of the courtyard. Her cooking pots were made with legs that allowed them to stand in an open fire. During a meal men and women sat on

the floor or ground, back to back, with the women facing the cooking. They ate from ceramic plates and drank *chicha* beer from wooden tumblers.

Making beer was another important domestic task for women. They began by chewing the vegetal material, usually maize kernels, sometimes seeds or fruit. Then they spat the pulp into a large jar of warm water. After several days the mixture began to ferment, and it became increasingly alcoholic as more time went by. Beer was the drink of everyday life and also played an important role in ceremonies.

A man wore a tunic with slits for his head and arms. It was decorated with an inverted triangle at the neck and broad bands across the waist and hem. In the morning he donned sandals like his wife's and a large cloak that he tied across his chest or one shoulder. A bag slung across his chest held small tools, amulets, and other items he wished to carry. He wore bracelets for decoration and, if he had been recognized for a feat of war, a metal disk around his neck or on his head.

Stepping outside his compound in the valley, a farmer could look up the mountainside and see long terraces with fields that he and other villagers worked. Stone markers separated the fields devoted to the community, the state, and the official religion. Stone irrigation channels kept the crops watered. The man climbed stone stairways to reach the fields, carrying the footplow that was his basic tool. It was a six-foot pole with a bronze point, a footrest near the point, and a handle at the top.

On many days the farmer was accompanied by his wife, carrying her hoe. The hoe had a chisel-shaped bronze blade that extended directly outward from the haft. During planting the man dug holes with his footplow while his wife broke clods of dirt with the hoe and threw seeds or cuttings into the holes. The hoe was also used for weeding.

At lower altitudes people raised maize, squashes, chiles, and red berries. Higher elevations only accommodated hardy tubers like potatoes, along with special seed plants such as quinoa. The upper reaches of the mountains permitted only one good harvest every three or four years.

The farmers coped with periodic food shortages by storing surplus crops. They made use of the cold mountain environment by freeze-drying potatoes. The potatoes were softened in water, then ground up and left to freeze at night. During the day, they were thawed and the pulp dried. The process was repeated until the potatoes reached a state in which they would not spoil. A similar procedure was used on strips of meat and fish. One remarkable crop lent itself to storage without such treatment: a species of squash remained fresh for as long as two years when kept in the right conditions.

Above the agricultural lands, people of the community tended flocks of llamas and alpacas. Some herders were young men who rotated the pastoral duty. Others were whole families who lived with the animals most or all of the time. They exchanged the products of their work for those of the farmers. Llamas served as pack animals, and their wool was made into cordage, while the alpacas provided softer fleece for ordinary clothing. Farmers used the dung to fertilize their crops and burned it as fuel when wood supplies were inadequate.

A llama herder playing a flute (Peru).

All economic activities—farming, food preservation, weaving, herding—were performed for government and religion as well as family. All Inca taxes were paid in the form of labor. Food came from work by both men and women on imperial land. Some of that land belonged to the gods, and its produce supported both local and imperial religious institutions. The rest of it belonged to the emperor and provided for him and for government officials and their families. Crops raised for the state also supported the armies and government craft specialists. Products of the herds followed the same principles. In addition, peasant men and women labored to fulfill the textile tax. Using material provided by the government, men made cordage and rope from coarse llama wool. Their wives then wove the cloth that was used to reward people for government service.

Men regularly left the village to fulfill their labor obligations to the government. In addition to war and construction, they sometimes participated in mass hunts organized in the name of the emperor, who held title to all hunting land. Thousands of men from different villages assembled at the hunting site, and officials organized them into a ring many miles across. Then they closed in, driving animals before them, and forming concentric circles as they crowded together. In the end designated hunters entered the human enclosure to kill the targeted animals: guanacos and deer provided luxury meat for the nobles; carnivores such as mountain lions and foxes were killed in order to eliminate threats to domestic animals.

During some of these hunts the peasants were required to capture vicunas alive for shearing. They had

to stand firm as the animals galloped toward them, their fear-crazed eyes level with those of the men. The vicunas were long-necked and slender, but they still weighed as much as a man. When a struggling animal was finally pinned to the ground, some men restrained the animal while others cut off its soft fleece to provide nobles with the finest clothing. In other hunts, aimed solely at the vicunas, the pursuers drove the animals through a fenced area into a narrow gorge. The vicunas were always released after they were shorn.

Peasant Social Relations

Young men and women who were prepared to marry had to await imperial validation. Once each year prospective couples gathered for betrothal by a local leader in the presence of a visiting Inca official. The leader joined the hands of each couple; then they were free to marry by local custom. If there were disputes, the Inca official resolved them.

A pregnant woman confessed her sins to a priest and prayed to the *wakas*—sacred objects and places—for a successful birth. When the birth came, she was fortunate if the village contained a midwife, a woman with a religious calling to help others bear the fruits of fertility. Afterward the new mother went to a stream to bathe herself and her infant. Four days later she placed the baby in a cradle, where it would spend much of its time. The mother was aware of the imperial decree that the young should not be touched very often so as not to be spoiled by tenderness. However, in the privacy of her house she may have exercised her own ideas about the matter.

The baby had no name until it was weaned. Then people gathered for the hair-cutting ceremony. The child's oldest male relative cut off a lock of its hair and bestowed the name. In early adolescence a person received a permanent name during another important ceremony. At about age fourteen, boys participated in a public rite in which each of them received a loincloth made by his mother. This typical garb of a man symbolized the transition to adulthood.

A girl celebrated her first menstruation in a family ceremony. After fasting for three days, she emerged to a gathering of relatives, wearing new clothes and with her hair braided. She served her kin and then received gifts from them. Her most important male relative bestowed the permanent name and lectured her on her duties to her parents.

Sometimes a community separated into more than one village, especially when the verticality strategy demanded that community members colonize other ecological zones. Whether the community was localized or dispersed, its identity focused on a network of kin, descended from a founding ancestor, that provided members with rights to land and herds. The colonists retained full privileges in their home villages.

Whatever its spatial organization, the community was divided into two subgroups, each with its own leader. Subgroups joined together for community work and religious observances, and they may also have provided a basis for division of social roles, with political posts placed in one subgroup and religious ones in the other. One was known as the "upper" group and took precedence in seating and speaking in public situations; in some cases its leader represented the whole community to outside authorities.

The imperial government of the Incas regimented local organization. The family belonged to a group of ten families who were the responsibility of an official. Another official governed a grouping of fifty families. These were local men appointed by the chief in charge of one hundred families. Beyond him were several more levels of administration leading to the state and ultimately to the emperor in the sacred city of Cuzco.

Peasant Knowledge and Expression

Mother Earth was the most benevolent of the many forces of nature that could bring fortune or ill health to human beings. People prayed to her and offered her coca leaf and beer at all major agricultural ceremonies. The goddess, like other female deities, was particularly receptive to worship led by women. Even as she dropped seeds into the holes made by her husband during planting, a woman prayed to Mother Earth. Women had a similar relationship with Earth's daughters, the goddesses of maize and other crops. They also found spiritual support in the moon goddess, the wife of the Sun. Women prayed to her for successful births and revered her as the patron of weaving. To the benefit of all, the Moon provided the basis of a calendar that regulated essential activities.

A man, as head of a household, saw to the worship of the rain god. He maintained a family shrine on a mountaintop near the village. As he climbed the mountain for one of his regular visits to the shrine, a man was aware that the mountain itself was imbued with supernatural power. The higher the mountain, the greater the power. He also saw the streams that integrated the mountains with a larger divine system that supported human life. Water, the symbolic blood of agriculture, flowed from the mountains down to the ocean. From the ocean the water rose to the celestial river (the Milky Way), and from the sky it descended to the mountains again.

A person back in the village was surrounded by lesser spiritual powers that anyone could visit at any time. Most of them resided in rocks and springs, some in hills and certain buildings, and a few in other natural or human-made objects. In most cases someone had constructed a small shrine for such a *waka*, usually attended by an elderly man no longer able to perform his customary work. At one or two local wakas with unusual powers, a trained priest presided over a small temple.

A person who visited a waka to ask for supernatural help or guidance performed the standard gesture of reverence. He or she stood in front of the object and bowed from the waist with both arms extended forward, then brought fingertips to the lips and kissed them. The person explained the purpose of the visit in an extemporaneous prayer and made a sacrifice. Most people killed a guinea pig. The very poor, who had nothing else to offer, drew sacrificial blood from their earlobes or offered hairs from their brows and lashes. A person with a very serious request went to a temple and asked the priest to pray. These priests also heard confessions.

During some important communal rituals in the village, people sacrificed a llama. Beer played a vital role in every ceremony. Libations were poured on the ground, and people bonded with each other by offering and accepting alcohol. Intoxication was the ultimate goal of drinking on important ceremonial occasions. Appointed servers ensured the proper flow of drink, sometimes for several days and nights.

The shamans who treated some illnesses and divined information had received their calling in a dream. After making initial contact with the spirits, some invoked them with sacrifice and others with a spell. Some met them in a stupor produced by alcohol. A midwife learned her destiny in a dream or by having an unusual birth, such as twins or a baby with a physical abnormality. People buried their dead in caves or grottos. The souls of those who had led virtuous lives went to be with the Sun.

Modal Patterns in Andean Elite Culture

Elite Material Culture

An Inca nobleman prepared for his day by donning colorful clothing made of soft vicuna wool. His hair was short and bound up in a woven band. In his distended earlobes the man placed the golden ear plugs, two inches across, that marked him as a member of the conquering and ruling elite. Noblemen also wore earplugs of silver and other precious materials.

In the walls around him there were trapezoidal windows, with the wider side below, and niches of the same shape for household goods. He stepped through a trapezoidal door into a compound where the walls of the buildings formed the same contour. This theme prevailed throughout the city. Walking the alleys and streets, the aristocrat passed walls constructed in two different styles. One used symmetrical rectangular blocks. The other employed irregular polygonal blocks that had been carefully shaped and fitted together. For important buildings the artisans had achieved perfect fit by painstaking work with stone and bronze tools, abrasives, and water. With this technique they could build massive walls, even fortifications, without mortar.

A glance at the mountainside above the city was inevitably drawn to long rows of large government storage houses that held food, cloth, and other goods. Each storehouse was ventilated by a system that admitted air through an underground channel and let it out near the top. Although many of the stored goods were used in the ordinary workings of the empire, some food was kept in reserve. Famines could quickly arise from the vagaries of mountain weather or unpredictable disasters like earthquakes. The conspicuous structure and location of the storehouses reassured the populace as well as impressing them.

Beyond the storehouses, somewhere on the mountain, bronze artisans worked at their craft. They took advantage of mountain winds to generate high temperatures in their furnaces. Their understanding of the effects of varying proportions of tin in the alloy allowed them to produce effective tools for a variety of purposes.

When he had to leave the city, usually to perform administrative service or lead a military contingent, the aristocrat entered into a road system that linked the

A contemporary building incorporates the fine stonework of the Incas (Cuzco, Peru).

Remains of massive Inca stonework at the fortress in Saksawaman (Cuzco, Peru).

entire empire. Some stretches of roadway were built up steep slopes. Some were paved with stone to reduce the effects of flooding. Along the sides of many roads, stone walls three to six feet high protected agricultural lands from traffic. Suspension bridges with fiber superstructures spanned gaps in the terrain. The greatest highland route was the highway between Cuzco and the city of Quito in Ecuador, which varied in width from ten to fifty feet. Inca engineers had elaborated a road system inherited from their predecessors, ultimately extending it to about twenty thousand miles.

The Incas built stone steps like these within their cities and as parts of their road system (Machu Picchu, Peru).

Travelers on the roads saw the small huts that housed government runners, prepared to take messages by relay to any part of the empire. Those on a long journey passed each night in government-built lodgings. These varied from a small isolated inn to a building in an administrative city. Government storehouses were associated with many lodging places.

Any traveler was likely to see a long train of llamas bearing goods on their backs, up to about 130 pounds each. Men in imperial service guided the caravans in accord with the Inca policy of controlling as much exchange as possible. The government maintained large herds throughout the empire and used them to collect food and goods from the peasants, to supply military expeditions, and to carry gifts from the government to local rulers and nobility to maintain their goodwill. Some caravans went to the coast, where they transacted business with the only professional merchants that the Inca tolerated. These traders transported the goods north to the independent polities of Ecuador. There they obtained unique local products, especially the spondylus seashells that the Inca prized for ritual reasons.

Part of a llama train that recalls the massive use of the animals for transport by the Inca empire (Peru).

Elite Social Relations

Like commoners, Inca aristocrats married only with the approval of the emperor. In the upper levels of society, women were crucial to succession and became the focus of alliances among men. Royal status for a woman increased the wealth, power, and prestige of her male relatives. This enhanced her standing among them, especially when the family was not of the nobility.

Girls celebrated puberty rites in a family setting. Those of boys were communal and led by a priest. Ceremonies for noble boys were long and complex demonstrations of manhood, emphasizing endurance and skill. Noble boys received schooling in the record-keeping system, as well as language, religion, and history. The Inca regarded their ordinary subjects as being like children, with no need for formal learning.

Among the servants in a noble household were *yanas*. Some were recent gifts from the emperor to recognize personal support or to reward specific service to the government. Others had inherited the status from their parents. The emperor decreed yana status for individuals that his officials selected from newly conquered populations. They chose many for their outstanding intelligence or talent and some for their standing in local aristocracies. Whatever their origin, yanas were removed from any contact with their home communities and placed in the service of Inca nobles, who gave them positions of great responsibility inside and outside the household. Yanas were becoming a social class that filled many and diverse social positions.

The Inca nobility lived in the central part of Cuzco, the imperial capital. This was the sacred city of the sun god, father of the Incas, designed to be a spectacular symbol of imperial power. All the people classified as Incas considered themselves to be the descendants of the original conquerors, the population of a tiny focal state that was centered on Cuzco when it was really no more than a town.

The initial conquests by the Inca assimilated a number of ethnic groups in the area surrounding Cuzco. Their new rulers made the aristocrats of these conquered societies "Incas-by-Privilege" and granted them many of the prerogatives held by the true Inca nobility. Incas-by-Privilege were allowed to live around the central city of Cuzco.

Despite its special status, Cuzco was divided into "upper" and "lower" subgroups according to the same principle of duality that applied in small communities. This principle was even used at the imperial level: new acquisitions, even whole provinces, were reorganized along dual lines.

The Inca government had constructed about eighty ethnically distinct provinces and made heavy use of the road system to maintain and expand the sprawling empire. The relay runners could carry a message to a far corner of the realm in just a few days. Sometimes officials, even the emperor himself, traveled far to take up administrative posts or gather information. Armies moved quickly to protect Inca lands or to secure new territory.

The economic organization of the Inca was also important to their military victories. Traditional Andean warfare revolved around hilltop forts with high walls and dry moats. Taking such a position by storm often resulted in very high losses. The Inca supply system allowed them to win these confrontations with sieges that sometimes lasted for many months.

The Inca consolidated control of the empire by placing their own officials over local rulers, permanently if necessary. Sometimes they replaced them. If loyalty were a crucial issue, the emperor could appoint one of his yanas as ruler. This was a person who had no local ties to conflict with gratitude to his patron. As a kind of slave, he did not command the reciprocity that the emperor owed to a hereditary king. A hierarchy of lesser officials functioned as tribute collectors, judges, and inspectors for a province. They supervised taxpayer units of ten thousand people and five thousand people and so on, down to community subdivisions of fifty and ten.

Where necessary, the Inca built their own provincial and rural administrative centers, ranging from way stations to cities. The government also moved populations for various reasons. They settled loyal people in newly acquired territories in order to stabilize them, and they scattered rebellious groups among loyal subjects.

A highly specialized cadre of government officials maintained and interpreted the records kept on the *khipu*. A great deal of information could be encoded by varying patterns of knots in strings of different lengths and colors. The system enabled the government to record the annual census that it conducted throughout the empire.

Every year in every part of the realm, government officials selected young girls to become "Chosen Women." They had to be virgins and physically beautiful, both outward signs of spiritual purity. They went to the provincial capitals, where they learned from older women already in service how to work for the government by preparing food and beer for ritual purposes and by spinning and weaving fine textiles. The cloth rewarded men for government service, including the army; on occasion army units had threatened mutiny because they had not received their allotment. Chosen Women were closely guarded to ensure their continued virginity.

Eventually the best of the Chosen Women were sent to Cuzco, where their ultimate role was determined. Some became human sacrifices, and others went into the service of the sun god or other imperial deities. The emperor took some of them as his own wives and gave others to men that he wished to reward for their achievements on behalf of the empire.

For his principal wife the emperor married his full sister. He was the only man in the realm allowed to do so. His divine status as a descendant of the Sun required that he keep the royal bloodline pure, which could be accomplished by producing an heir with his closest relative. Ideally he chose the most competent of his sons to inherit the throne. However, because there was no clear rule of succession, competition among potential successors could escalate to civil war.

The status of the empress paralleled that of her husband. He was a son of the Sun; she was a daughter of Moon, the sun god's wife. As such, she represented the women of the empire, politically as well as spiritually. During the major festivals, women kissed her hand while men kissed the hand of her husband. The empress had her own lands and other resources, which she used to give great feasts like those of the emperor. She was attended by young noblewomen, who learned from the experience about society and government.

The empress was chosen from the emperor's sisters on the basis of her responsibility and potential for leadership. She advised her husband and sons with regard to matters of government. She addressed serious issues on which the inner council could not agree. When her husband left the capital for war or to inspect the realm, the empress governed in his place.

Under the rule of split inheritance a new emperor received his predecessor's throne but none of his wealth. The dead emperor's estate came under the control of a *panaka*, composed of the sons of his secondary wives, leaving the new ruler with a need for resources. The potential in the existing Inca polity was limited because property was already owned and taxpayers already burdened. Further conquest was one answer, and this may have contributed to the vast expansion of the Inca Empire. Another profitable enterprise was control of a major waka. The emperor could take over existing wakas or create new ones.

Each panaka evolved into a corporate group of the deceased emperor's male descendants. These royal men held most of the empire's highest positions in administration, the military, and religion. Panakas competed with each other for power. Daughters of a panaka played an important role in the competition, some marrying the emperor or other important men and some of them becoming priestesses of the Moon. Occasionally different panakas supported rival claimants to the throne.

Elite Knowledge and Expression

In Cuzco, in the great temple of Koricancha, six chambers around a square courtyard honored the foremost deities of the empire. The chamber ornamented in gold harbored the image of the sun god while the icon of his wife, the moon goddess, occupied a silver chamber. The temple also recognized the Creator, the rain god, and other celestial deities.

The Creator and culture hero, having no name, but commonly titled Wirakocha, placed all peoples where they belonged and saw that they were taught their various ways of life. However, the Inca had elevated the sun god to the highest place in their pantheon and given him new meaning, based on a revelation to the emperor Pachakuti. He had learned that the original Incas were direct descendants of the Sun who gave them, as the possessors of the first civilization and the true religion, the mandate to conquer the rest of their world.

Further representing the relationship between religion and empire, the great temple also housed the most sacred objects of the conquered provinces. The Inca respected the religions of their subjects, but only in subordination to their own, which justified their overlordship. Just as subject peoples were required to submit their own most sacred objects to the custody of the conquerors, they were expected to give precedence to the Inca religion of the Sun in their own lands.

Beyond these ideological measures, the Inca politically co-opted some existing cults and shrines. Perhaps the most important was the ancient oracle of Pachakamak on the coast, which had established far-flung branch temples before the rise of the Inca. The Inca used the oracle's branch temples to support the spread of imperial ideology and as the basis for an intelligence service.

Inca political centralization placed limits on art. Craft workers were tightly controlled and constrained to official styles of ceramics and textiles. Architecture was similarly standardized with regard to both style and construction. Sculpture was simple and of limited variety: occasional reliefs, containers for offerings, and elaborately carved rocks.

Part of an Inca-built compound in the conquered city of Pachakamak. The trapezoidal form of the niches (which may have held images) was typical of Inca architecture. Some experts suggest (and others doubt) that this was a compound for Chosen Women (Hyslop 1990).

The empress, daughter of the moon goddess, prayed to her for the well-being of all women in the realm. In Cuzco and in temples elsewhere priestesses maintained the worship of the Moon. From the adoration of the Moon came the lunar calendar that regulated most activities in the empire. It directed the timing of agricultural production, presentation of taxes and tributes, conducting of the census, and selection of special women for service to the government. The calendar even specified the times when subject peoples could marry.

Survey and interpretation of the skies revolved around the celestial river (the Milky Way). Its apparent movement during the course of the year can be seen to form two axes, dividing the sky into quarters. The Inca used this as a reference grid for observing the movements of other celestial phenomena, which they in turn used to predict earthly cycles of great importance: fauna, water, and flora, including crops and their needs. The symbolic importance of quarters was extended to the terrestrial world, where it became the basis for conceptually dividing the Inca Empire. Imaginary lines emanating from Cuzco and extending beyond the horizon divided the Land of the Four Quarters.

Animals served for regular and large-scale sacrifices. This was yet another role for the llama, and thousands were offered to the gods on some occasions, along with guinea pigs and birds. Each year two human infants were sacrificed in each of the most important temples. There were no human sacrifices in lesser temples, although woodcarvings representing humans were burned. Children of both sexes were sacrificed by various methods at the coronation of an emperor, and boys were left high on the mountains to die of exposure for the mountain gods. Children, as well as adults, were given alcohol before their deaths.

The nobility, including the royal families, mummified the deceased, kept them in houses, dressed them, and treated them as if they were alive. Mummies of the emperors were paraded on litters for special occasions. Thus the wealthy and powerful gave the fullest expression to an ideal of ancestor veneration that was fundamental at all levels of society. Whether as mummies or in the grave, the ancestors were kept close. The bodies or graves were used to document the rights and responsibilities of the living.

A Closer Look

The Coastal Region

This was a narrow strip along the Pacific coast of Peru. In this desert environment people watered their crops with large irrigation systems, using the rivers that flowed from the mountains above them. They also depended heavily on the sea for subsistence, taking the Sea Mother as one of their most important gods. Development of distinctive bodies of subsistence knowledge led to ethnic specialization in fishing and farming with concomitant exchange of the products. The trend to specialization reached the point where different farm communities raised different crops (Moseley 1992).

Verticality was less important along the coast than it was to the mountain people. Some coastal empires had penetrated the mountains up to an altitude of about 6,000 feet (c. 2,000 meters). However, this was of limited significance because the coastal population already lived in the most productive tier of the Andean ecology (Moseley 1992). Accordingly, most of their political conquests had extended along the shoreline rather than into the mountains.

In contrast to the pervasive government control of exchange in the highlands, markets and professional merchants seem to have been important along the coast. Peruvian merchants sailed large rafts as far as Ecuador in order to trade. There they obtained *Spondylus* shells, which the Inca regarded as sacred. Perhaps this particular part of the exchange was responsible for Inca tolerance of coastal commercialism, since the Inca never conquered the Ecuadorian shores from which the shells came.

The Chilean Region

The Chilean Region included the northern and central parts of the modern country. It contained the southernmost section of the Andes Mountains and the adjacent coast. Inhabitants included the Diaguita and the Picon. The Inca conquered the Region in the latter part of the fifteenth century and incorporated its chiefdoms into the empire in the standard ways (Villamarin and Villamarin 1999). The rulers adopted (or may already have had) Andean customs like feasting their workers. Even before the conquest, extensive trade with the empire had opened the door to Inca influences. The native Chileans had combined intensive maize agriculture with llama pastoralism and traded their loom-woven fabrics to the north. Further south in the Region, simpler social organization prevailed. The Mapuche, for example, lived in autonomous farm communities.

Symbols of Power

Several distinctions between the Andean and Mesoamerican Areas can be linked (speculatively) to their political differences. While Mesoamericans built ever more spectacular pyramids, the Incas abandoned them except for low pyramidal platforms as foundations for some buildings. It seems that Inca construction emphasized practical symbols of power, such as fortresses, storehouses, and the road system (W. P. Mitchell, pers. comm.). It may be that the loosely organized Mesoamerican empires

needed spectacular religious symbolism to reinforce their influence while the bureaucratically successful Inca required only mundane reminders of the power that they exercised in their subjects' daily lives.

A similar interpretation can be given to differences in human sacrifice, which apparently declined under Inca hegemony (Hultkrantz 1979) and which involved no cannibalism (the Inca tried to abolish cannibalism among the forest tribes that they encountered on the eastern slopes of the Andes). Mass sacrifice and cannibalism (practiced in connection with great pyramids) have been explained as terrorist tactics designed to intimidate enemies (Berdan 1982). The Inca, more secure in their highly organized political system, gave up the building of large pyramids, practiced less human sacrifice than their predecessors, and rejected cannibalism.

The Zekwe System

The Inca capital of Cuzco was the center of the "most complex ritual system yet identified in the ancient New World" (Bauer 1998:155). It is known as the zekwe system (an earlier spelling, ceque, is still commonly used). It is "one of the most widely debated, and perhaps misunderstood, aspects of Andean studies" (Bauer 1998:10). To the Inca it consisted of 42 imagined lines extending outward from central Cuzco in a radial pattern. Most of them originated at the main temple, the Korikancha. The lines were physically marked by more than three hundred wakas (shrines) of various kinds. Some were natural, such as caves, boulders, springs, trees, and mountaintops; others were artificial, such as houses, fountains, canals, or intricately carved rock formations. All required prayers and offerings.

A widely accepted hypothesis explained the system as being related to astronomy and the calendar. The lines were interpreted as sight lines used to connect celestial phenomena on the horizon with particular days of the year. For example, the rising of the sun at different points marked the times for planting at different elevations (Aveni 1993), distinctions that were essential to the subsistence strategy of verticality. It has also been claimed that clusters of lines symbolized lunar months while each waka represented a day of the year. The latter idea is based on the assumption that there were 328 shrines in the system, but there may have been as many as four hundred (Bauer 1998). The astronomical hypothesis is likely to be correct for some zekwe lines, but recent research indicates that many had other meanings.

One possible symbolic parallel for the radial shrine system was the radial pattern in the flow of underground water: "people believed that the reception of the underground water was part of their birthright, and that it came directly from their ancestors who resided in the body of the earth-mother" (Aveni 1993). Bauer (1998) emphasizes the social meaning of the system, pointing out that maintenance and worship of the shrines was apportioned among all the kinship groups in Cuzco. These included the ten royal panakas, and ten communities of non-royal people. Each group took responsibility for the wakas located on one or more of the zekwe lines. Some of the lines ran toward or in the vicinity of resources controlled by those groups. It is very likely that certain shrines were land markers and possible that the lines defined boundaries. When a group (or its representatives) traversed one of its zekwe lines and worshipped at its shrines, it also affirmed its economic and social position in relation to others. Contrary to the astronomical interpretation, many of the lines were not straight. This may indicate that groups altered them from time to time, perhaps expanding their holdings. In a court case of the Spanish colonial period, one indigenous group complained that another had encroached on their land by moving the location of one of their shrines.

The zekwe system of Cuzco may represent a modal pattern for the Andean Area. Documentary and archeological evidence suggests the radial distribution of shrines and possible conceptualization of zekwe lines at several other sites in the Inca empire. The famous lines on the Nazca Plain in Peru (notoriously attributed to "ancient astronauts") may represent an earlier version of such thinking. They seem to have performed similar functions with regard to resources and calendar. Many of the Nazca lines began and ended at water sources and some pointed to the place where the sun rose when water began to run in the rivers and canals (Aveni 1993). Studies of twentieth century communities in Bolivia and Chile report continuing use of ritual lines and shrines. It may be that "over the past several millennia systems of radial lines have represented a core concept in indigenous religious practices" (Bauer 1998:154).

Taking a broad view, the success of the Inca empire is attributable in large part to "the strict order and the high degree of organization that was built into every component of it." The zekwe system played a central role in achieving this order because it "served to unify Inca ideas about religion, social organization, calendar, astronomy, and hydrology" (Aveni 1993:138). All citizens of Cuzco, and perhaps other places, were made part of the system by both ideology and ritual action. Bauer adds that the system was flexible. It could be adapted to social and territorial changes and incorporate those changes into the ritual order.

Coca and Cocaine

One topic related to the high mountains is worth bringing up because of its contemporary significance: the use of coca, which is the basis for cocaine. Faced with extreme cold and oxygen deficit, Andean peoples found a remedy on the forested eastern slopes in the form of the coca leaf. When chewed with lime, coca acts as a mild stimulant that combats fatigue and chill. It contains calcium, iron, phosphorus, and vitamins A and B-1, all difficult to obtain in an environment where green leafy vegetables are scarce (Allen 1988), and it may also facilitate carbohydrate metabolism. Coca was a key offering in many religious observances. The Inca limited consumption of coca to the nobles, who carried the leaves around with them in a bag. After the Spanish Conquest it spread to ordinary people and became an emblem of ethnic identity.

Coca has become extremely important to the rest of the world because it is now made into cocaine. In connection with this problem, it is worth knowing about indigenous attitudes toward coca. In recent times many Andean peasants have continued to associate coca leaf with religion, ethnicity, and beneficial physiological effects.

INTERMEDIATE AREA

Examples:

Chibcha (Muisca), Cauca Valley, Tairona, Cuna

The cultural territory between the Nuclear Zone civilizations has usually been designated the Intermediate Area. Although rather ugly and pedestrian, the term is thoroughly ensconced in the anthropological literature (e.g.,

Allaire 1999), and I have no viable alternative. Serious doubts have been raised as to the existence of a Culture Area here (Graham, ed. 1993; Lange, ed. 1996). However, recent research indicates significant cultural continuities from Costa Rica through Panama and Colombia to coastal Ecuador (Allaire 1999; Villamarin and Villamarin 1999). Though the boundaries may be very fuzzy, a distinctive Area did exist between the civilizations of Mesoamerica and the Andes.

The societies in the Intermediate Area were chiefdoms, some of them paramount chiefdoms with tens of thousands of people. Men cultivated the fields with tools like those of the agricultural states in neighboring Areas, and in some cases with similar advanced techniques.

Chiefs in the Intermediate Area held many of the same prerogatives as kings of agricultural states. Chiefs in the larger polities placed the same value on conquest and tribute as did the kings.

In detail the Intermediate Area displayed features in common with each of the civilized Areas and with the tropical cultures to the east. For example, people wore cotton clothing and went to marketplaces like those of Mesoamerica. They chewed coca leaf like Andeans and mummified the bodies of their chiefs. Many of them cultivated manioc along with maize, as tropical people did, and at least some of them practiced cannibalism in connection with warfare. There are also some traits distinctive to the Intermediate Area, although it is in many cases difficult to tell if they are modal patterns. One striking example is the stuffing of enemy skins to keep as war trophies.

Key features:

- ▶ Agriculture
- ▶ Craft specialization
- ▶ Extensive and intensive trade
- ▶ Complex chiefdoms
- ▶ Political importance of gold

Modal Patterns in Intermediate Area Culture

Material Culture

Most people lived in small villages or hamlets, in wood-framed houses with thatched roofs. Men cultivated permanent or semipermanent fields, in some cases terracing, irrigating, or constructing raised fields. The most important crops included the familiar combination of maize and beans along with peppers, fruits, and gourds. Where warmer and moister conditions permitted, the farmers raised manioc, sweet potatoes, and coca. Domestic cotton provided material for clothing.

A chief lived in a compound surrounded by one or more walls. His house was built in the same way as those of ordinary people, but it was larger. He maintained a large store of food, which provided for feasts and gave him a reserve in case of siege. The chief also maintained a temple building of the same construction as houses but larger. The chiefly village tended to be larger than an ordinary one and to display more organizational features, such as streets and a plaza. Sometimes a wall of wood or stone surrounded the whole community because warfare was frequent.

People traded their goods in markets that met regularly. Some communities specialized in the extraction of local resources, and some craft workers spent most or all of their time in manufacturing. Many of these products went into the long-distance trade and were transported hundreds of miles on the backs of slaves or in large dugout canoes. Trade connected distinct polities and peoples in varied ecological settings. Major trade items included gold and gold objects, jewelry, cotton, textiles, cloaks, fish, peccaries, and salt. Some of the merchants who conducted the trade may have been full-time specialists. In at least one culture they had their own gods.

Social Relations

The village of a chief was usually larger than others because many of his kin lived with him along with his numerous wives or concubines, noble retainers, and slaves. Some of the population may have been involved with the long-distance trade, which the chief controlled. Some chiefs also controlled important crafts such as the manufacture of gold objects. They used these goods to aggrandize themselves and reward their supporters.

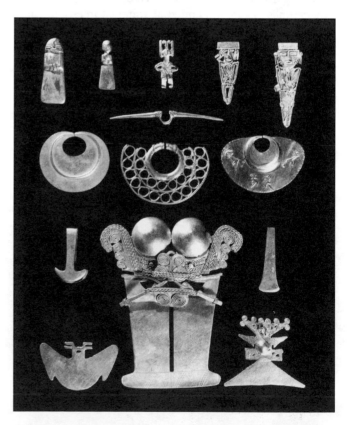

Gold objects like these were vital in the long-distance trade and in the symbolization of elite status in the Intermediate Area; the items include nose rings, figurines, tweezers, and a chisel (Colombia).

Chiefs wore ornate dress and decorated themselves with gold. Some were carried in hammocks or on golden litters. In addition to the benefits of trade, a chief received food and other support from his own people and tribute from subordinate groups elsewhere. Tribute goods were much the same as those in the long-distance trade.

A chief's duties included coordination of ceremonial activities and the administration of justice. He had the right to punish those who committed crimes such as theft or rape. A chief also had to manage relations among the communities within his realm and with other chiefdoms. Most chiefs had numerous wives for diplomatic reasons. In some cases relations between allied polities were good because siblings ruled them. Chiefs also used siblings in subordinate positions, such as command of troops. Large numbers could be summoned for organized battles, and a few polities may have maintained a standing body of troops.

Victorious chiefdoms held or gained territory, established tributary relationships with other polities, and obtained captives for religious sacrifice. Leadership in war was associated with high social status, and in some cases commoners bettered themselves through success in battle. Warriors kept trophies, including skulls and whole skins that were stuffed with ashes or straw. At least some of the cultures practiced cannibalism in connection with war.

Knowledge and Expression

Religion emphasized deities of the sky and nature, such as sun, moon, earth, and rain. Full-time priests served the gods, who were represented in the temples by idols of wood or stone, adorned with gold. The priests held public ceremonies for the public good and sacrificed human beings in the most important ones, an act that was followed by ritualized cannibalism by priests or chiefs.

A Chibchan origin myth may be representative. The first chief and his nephew created human beings, a man from yellow earth and a woman from a reed, and then the sun and moon. Common people were given the duty to pray to those deities while their chiefs served as intermediaries.

When a chief died, the body was preserved by mummification or desiccation. Then he was buried in his compound along with wives and retainers who had been poisoned or drugged. Nobles were buried in deep shafts with side chambers, often sunk into hillsides or artificial mounds.

The Old World Domain

Europe was and is part of the Old World, and many of the statements in the following portion of the book would apply to Europe at various times in its history. However, the book is about non-European cultures, and so the term "Old World" in this context effectively means Asia and Africa.

Most of the major cultures on these continents were in varying degrees of contact with each other and with Europe during a long period of trade, warfare, and reciprocal diffusion of culture traits. Until the last few hundred years, Western influence was no greater than that of any other culture. However, Western countries began to take control at the end of the seventeenth century when the British and Dutch advanced into India and Indonesia. From then on severe disruption of Asian traditional cultures became increasingly common. Comparable disasters overtook Africa in the nineteenth century.

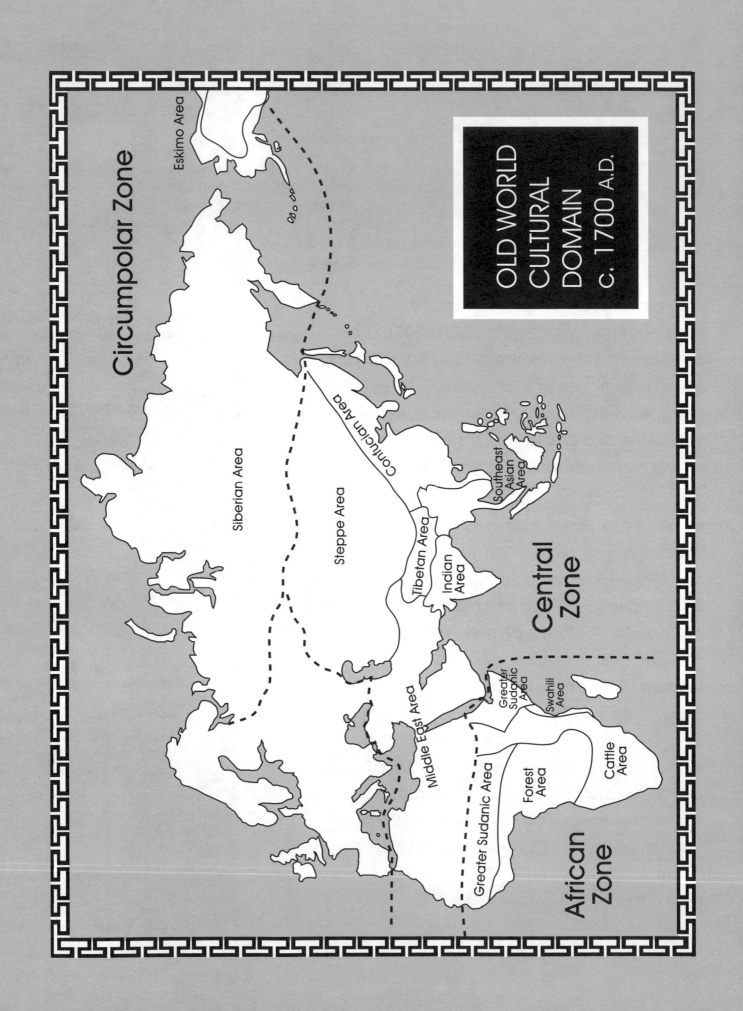

OLD WORLD
CULTURAL
DOMAIN
c. 1700 A.D.

Circumpolar Zone

Eskimo Area

Siberian Area

Steppe Area

Confucian Area

Tibetan Area

Indian Area

Southeast Asian Area

Central Zone

Middle East Area

Greater Sudanic Area

Swahili Area

Greater Sudanic Area

Forest Area

Cattle Area

African Zone

MODAL
PATTERNS AMONG
OLD WORLD
CULTURES

Farming, practiced by an overwhelming majority of the Domain's population, dominated at least half the land area of Asia and Africa. The Old World had no single crop to match the combination of ubiquity and importance of maize in the Americas. By the year 1700 maize itself was spreading rapidly, along with tobacco, but indigenous crops persisted where maize was unavailable or unsuitable. The most widespread of those native plants were the millets, a group of several similar genera (including *Panicum, Eleusine,* and *Setaria*) and sorghum *(Sorghum).* One or more of them ranked among the staple cereal crops in many parts of the Domain. High in carbohydrates, millets had a protein content that varied from 6 to 11 percent.

Old World farmers kept a variety of large mammals that provided them with various products and services. The highly adaptable goat *(Capra hircus),* sometimes called the poor man's cow, was found almost everywhere, and sheep *(Ovis aries)* were almost as common. Although harder to maintain, cattle *(Bos taurus)* attained great importance in favorable circumstances. People derived food and clothing from all of these animals. As naturally herd-living species, they all provided the potential for keeping large numbers. In a very different realm of material culture, Old World people made extensive use of iron. They learned to control the quality of the metal with techniques that varied the amount of carbon it contained.

Agricultural states dominated almost all of the Old World. The greater importance of slavery tended to distinguish them from comparable societies in Nuclear America. They were also affected by the development of universalistic religions.

The Old World gave rise to universalistic religions, distinguished by the idea that their beliefs are equally relevant to all human beings rather than limited to just one society. These religions crossed the boundaries of culture areas and zones and continue to be powerful today. Such religious systems have been characterized as *great traditions* because they entail more than rituals and supernatural beliefs. They are associated with literacy, scholarship, and philosophical sophistication emanating from the elite levels of complex societies.

The great tradition of Islam will be described at the end of this chapter because it had spread through much of Asia and into Africa by 1700 A.D. The Hindu–Buddhist tradition, though encompassing several culture areas, had a more limited distribution and will be discussed in the appropriate chapters later on.

Possession played an important role in many different Old World religions. As in the Pentecostal branch of Christianity today, supernatural beings entered the bodies of humans and controlled them. This should not be confused with a shamanistic performance in which the practitioner goes into a trance to make contact with spirits over which he has some degree of influence. In possession, the supernatural being completely controls the human.

Finally, domestication of large mammals provided the basis for a unique adaptation. Called *nomadic herding* or *nomadic pastoralism,* this way of life depended primarily on sustenance from the animals. Dependence on the animals meant that people had to maintain large herds, and this meant that they had to engage in nomadic movement to feed and protect the herds throughout the year. These unique cultures posed unique problems to the farmers and states of the Old World.

Key features:

▶ Millet and other cereal crops
▶ Large domestic mammals
▶ Iron working
▶ Patrilineal descent
▶ Predominance of states
▶ Prominence of slavery
▶ Universalistic religions
▶ Supernatural possession
▶ Nomadic herding

Modal Patterns in Old World Culture

Material Culture

Checking on a plot of maturing millet, a farmer saw stalks that reached as high as four feet with edible seeds clustered at the tops. Unlike many other crops, the millet rarely succumbed to sudden disasters because it completed its growth in less than eighty days. In a drought it had the ability to go dormant and then grow again when the rains returned. After the family harvest a woman processed the seeds and made them into porridge or flat bread. Millet could not be leavened.

Goats, "poor man's cattle" (East Asia).

Almost anyone could keep a number of goats. They were agile and hardy, and they ate bitter vegetation that other domestic animals refused. They did well at high altitudes or in hot climates where other domestic species could not survive. They were also prolific, gestating in five months. A growing herd of goats added little to a farmer's workload because he could assign his small children to look after the easily managed animals. In return for minimal attention, the family got milk that was nourishing and easy to digest, well suited to infants and the elderly. They also obtained a little meat, along with skins for clothing. Goatskins made lightweight water containers, especially important in dry regions.

Sheep herded by a woman (Iran).

Many families also maintained at least a few sheep. Like goats they provided meat, milk, and skins. Cattle, larger and less adaptable, required much more care than sheep or goats. It was difficult for a farm family to maintain more than one of these animals, and many had none. Only the affluent, who owned a number of cattle, could occasionally slaughter one for meat and hide. For most people, milk was the main subsistence product of cattle. Where trees were scarce, their manure could provide fuel.

People used implements made of iron, which they obtained from the smith. Iron workers smelted the metal in a furnace, modifying the temperature and flow of air to alter the quality of the metal. Wrought iron was easy to work but soft, while cast iron was very tough but difficult to shape. Steel was a compromise. These options allowed artisans to form iron ornaments and sculptures as well as tools and weapons.

Social Relations

Modal features of social relations are harder to find in the Old World Domain than in the New World. Regarding two of the most obvious patterns, the difference between the Domains is essentially quantitative: agricultural states and patrilineal descent groups were much more common in the Old World. It can also be said that slavery was highly developed in this Domain. It encompassed a large number of people on a long-term basis and was governed by elaborate institutions. The marketing of slaves as a commodity particularly sets the Old World apart from the other traditional Domains.

The farmers and agricultural states of the Old World faced a unique problem in social relationships: nomadic herders. At both levels of society the relationship tended to be complex and shifting. Village farmers sometimes traded with the nomads and sometimes lost goods to them in raids. Governments tried to co-opt the nomads if not control them outright. Sometimes nomads conquered agricultural states and became the government. Although the nomads were only a small proportion of the population, they strongly influenced the history and culture of many farming societies.

Knowledge and Expression

A universalistic religion envisioned God as a single supreme supernatural entity. It contemplated salvation, a release from ordinary human life that culminated in a superior state of existence involving proximity to God. Achievement of this goal involved adherence to strong moral rules. The elite leaders of the religion organized these rules into a systematic and abstract code.

As it acquired numerous believers across a wide area, a universalistic religion experienced sectarian divisions. Some arose from theological differences and others from social competition. Sometimes the two were difficult to distinguish. Divisions also occurred because the abstract rules and theological formulations of religious specialists often provided little help or comfort in everyday life. Disappointment gave rise to devotional and ecstatic cults that emphasized emotion over doctrine.

An alternative response for commoners, especially peasants, was the retention of religious ideas that their ancestors held before the advent of a great tradition. These *little traditions* or *folk traditions*—simpler, less organized, and more localized—placed people in closer contact with the supernatural. The little traditions had less moral content and a more pragmatic quality. They addressed an array of minor gods, spirits, and ghosts that were largely ignored or denied by the great tradition. Along with witchcraft and sorcery, they feared special afflictions such as the evil eye. Those with the latter power could harm other people or their animals with only a glance. Most often they acted out of envy, so people tended to hide their good fortune. They were especially careful to shield healthy and beautiful infants from the evil eye. Shamans played a prominent role in rural society, and other specialists, as well as ordinary people, used magic to achieve various ends.

Although most adherents of a great tradition considered it superior to peasant religion, great traditions and little traditions had some beliefs and practices in common. One of the most important was *spirit possession*. During a trance state, made visible by convulsive behavior, a god or spirit took control of a human being's mind and body. In some cases the supernatural being's intent was evil, but more often it was benign. In some instances the possession was a purely personal experience, but often the supernatural being spoke to others through the possessed individual.

A Closer Look

Nomadic Herders

Beyond the towns and villages, nomadic people herded large mammals through lands that were too dry or too cold for cultivation. Specialized in animal husbandry, they led lives of cyclical movement determined by the seasonal appearance of pasturage in separate areas. In some habitats with unreliable vegetation, the movement pattern had to be opportunistic. In other places it took the form of transhumance: the herders made a limited number of moves each year, often just two, among predictable pasturages.

Sheep were the economic mainstay, but pastoralists also kept goats and a variety of other animals. These species all fed on grass or bushes, so pastoralism was an efficient way to use natural grasslands that were not accessible to other forms of human subsistence. The pastoral species have gregarious tendencies that facilitate human control, which the herders enhanced by castrating most of the male animals.

Each pastoral culture had a "key animal" that provided more than subsistence or transport (Barfield 1993). It excited the imagination of the people and was used as the standard for wealth. It also provided other satisfactions, including esthetic ones. The key animal displayed four characteristics: (1) it was well adapted to the environment so that large numbers could be kept; (2) it was a necessary component of everyone's holdings, or there would be no basis for comparison; (3) its ecological requirements took precedence over those of other stock; and (4) it was used to define the people's social, political, or economic relationship to the world. Numerous beliefs and rituals marked the key animal in any herding culture.

Nomads consumed the milk and blood of their animals, as well as meat, and used the hides and hair in their technology. Nevertheless, they were also dependent on farming. Some did their own, while others interacted with sedentary farming people and the states that governed them. These interactions included trade, raiding, extortion, smuggling, military service, and wage work.

Nomadic herders with camels (Bedouin culture, Sudan).

Pastoralism entailed peculiar benefits and risks. Farmers can increase their output only by more intensive or extensive labor while pastoralists can hope for their animals to reproduce themselves at an exponential rate. On the other hand, farmers can store surplus safely while extra animals are always at risk from the environment or other people. Consequently, pastoralists usually have a strong incentive to make use of surplus animals through slaughter, trade, or social exchange such as bridewealth.

The local group, somewhat like the local band of foragers, consisted of mobile households with a great deal of autonomy, including the ability to shift from one band to another. The combination of herding and mobility shaped the patterns of warfare among pastoralists. Having wealth in animals tempted the herders to raid among themselves: being highly valuable and mobile made the animals a particularly attractive target. Raids elicited defense, counterattack, and a perpetual state of hostility, creating a tradition in which warfare was positively valued and warriors had high status. These aggressive tendencies were readily directed against agricultural and mercantile neighbors for profit and sometimes for political control.

The Great Tradition of Islam

Like its predecessors, Judaism and Christianity, Islam envisioned a personified male God. Numerous ritual requirements included specific dietary prohibitions, such as a ban on pork. The most important tenets of the religion were enshrined in the Six Articles of faith and the Five Pillars of ritual.

The Six Articles of Islamic Faith

1. There is no God but Allah, and Muhammad is his final Prophet.

2. The prophets have revealed the will of God.

3. The Koran is the word of God as revealed to Muhammad.

4. Angels are the instruments of God's will.

5. Every soul will be consigned to paradise or hell.

6. God has determined everyone's fate, but obedience to His will is still the responsibility of all.

Islam placed strict emphasis on monotheism and viewed Muhammad himself as no more than a human being. Muhammad was the last and most important of the prophets, but his great predecessors included Adam, Noah, Abraham, Moses, and Jesus. There have also been twenty thousand lesser prophets, for every people throughout the world.

The Five Pillars of Islamic Ritual

1. Statement of the creed that Allah is the only God and Muhammad is his Prophet.

2. Public prayer five times daily, and private prayer.

3. Obligatory and voluntary contributions to charity.

4. Daylight fast during the month of Ramadan.

5. At least one pilgrimage to Mecca if possible.

To become a Muslim, a person simply stated his belief in one God and the Prophet. A person born into an Islamic community usually did this at an early age. However, converts were welcome to confess the faith at any time. Additional knowledge was desirable, but the first pillar was enough to make a person a Muslim.

The obligation of prayer represented the personal nature of Islam. Although the believer received knowledge of the religion from learned men, he or she spoke directly to God. At the same time, Islam stressed social responsibility, as indicated by the requirement of charity. Fasting during all the daylight hours of the month of Ramadan commemorated Muhammad's reception of the word of God. The pilgrimage to Mecca brought a person to the Prophet's birthplace. Many expended all they owned out of desire to make the pilgrimage, but it was not required of those for whom it caused great hardship.

Arabic calligraphy on the wall of a mosque; Arabic is the language of the Koran and, therefore, of Islam (Middle East).

CENTRAL ZONE

Areas:

- Middle East
- Indian
- Confucian
- Tibetan
- Steppe
- Southeast Asian

Turkish
Region

Steppe Area

Confucian Area

JAPAN

Persian
Region

Tibetan Area

CHINA

KOREA

Middle East Area

Indian
Area

VIETNAM

Arab Region

Mainland
Region

Southeast Asian Area

Insular
Region

INDONESIA

Central
Zone
with Areas, Regions,
and Key Countries

Previous page This elegant dancer and her costume represent the artistic
achievements of the Central Zone (Balinese culture, Indonesia).

OVERVIEW OF THE ZONE

Examples:

Arabic, Persian, Indian, Chinese, Japanese, Tibetan, Mongol, Thai

The Central Zone of the Old World was formed in eastern and southern Asia, several thousand years ago, by the emergence of literate urban civilizations. It expanded into northern Africa via Arab invasions that began in the seventh century A.D. Eastward, it extended across the islands of Indonesia. To the north it encompassed the steppes of central Asia.

The modal patterns of the Zone were represented most clearly in three Areas that contained the great majority of the population: the Middle East (Southwest Asia and North Africa), the Indian Area (which largely coincided with the contemporary country), and the Confucian Area (including China, Korea, and Japan). The Tibetan, Steppe, and Southeast Asian Areas diverged from the core Areas (and from each other) in some important ways.

People in the Central Zone wore more clothing than others in comparable climates and seem to have engaged in little scarification, tattooing, or body painting. Farmers cultivated wheat *(Triticum)* and barley *(Hordeum),* along with other grains. At its best in temperate climates, wheat raised in dry conditions had a protein content of 11 to 15 percent. The greatest value of barley was its ability to adjust to a wider range of climates than any other grain.

Central Zone farmers eased the burdens of cultivation and marketing in a way that was unique in the traditional world: they used large domestic mammals to pull plows and wheeled vehicles. The civilizations of Nuclear America knew the wheel, but, without a strong draft animal, they used it only in toys. Size and power placed cattle *(Bos)* foremost among the Old World draft animals. The donkey *(Equus asinus)* served well as a pack animal, cart puller, and occasional mount. It was used extensively where horses *(Equus caballus)* did not thrive or were too expensive (Caras 1996). Farmers had a similar range of uses for the mule, the powerful hybrid of a male donkey and female horse.

Two major patterns of subsistence crosscut the culture areas in the Central Zone. In dry regions farmers depended primarily on millet, barley, and wheat. The main pack animals in many of these dry regions were camels, the one-humped dromedary *(Camelus dromedarius)* in the west and the two-humped bactrian *(Camelus bactrianus)* in the east. The species were similar in most respects, six to seven feet high at the shoulder, seven to ten feet long, and weighing between 600 and 1,500 pounds. The humps contained fatty tissue that provided

an energy reserve. Contrary to popular beliefs, there is no evidence that the humps or the stomach lining stored water. However, camels had numerous other adaptations to dry climates. They could, for example, get enough water from desert vegetation to survive for weeks, and they could drink brackish or salt water if necessary (Nowak 1999).

The camel, an essential animal in many of the arid parts of the Central Zone.

In wetter climates, mainly in the southern and eastern parts of the Zone, the staple was rice raised in flooded paddies. Farmers added other cereals where possible. Under these conditions water buffalo *(Bubalus)* often supplemented or replaced cattle. This true buffalo should not be confused with the genus *Bison* of North America or Europe.

Some inland peasants used fishing to supplement agriculture. Coastal fishers usually specialized in that pursuit, and some of them included maritime trade or boat building in their subsistence base. Beyond subsistence activities, the socioeconomic organization of fishers tended to parallel that of peasant farmers; accordingly, they are sometimes included in the peasant category (Clammer 1993).

Families owned land rather than deriving it from larger kinship groups. As a result, poorer families were forced to engage in transactions with landlords in order to have farm plots. People idealized the extended family as a residential group that held land across the generations. Most often it took the form of a *stem family*; that is, there was no more than one nuclear family in each generation (Sorenson 1993b).

A high level of male dominance expressed itself in the unusual ideal of isolating women in the home. Community government depended more on the interaction of prestigious individuals than it did on the leadership of any single person. Factionalism often played an important role. Beyond the community there were several levels of administration in a complex national system. Elite culture was heavily influenced by written language. Contrasting with most other parts of the world, slavery was predominantly "closed." This meant that slaves could not be incorporated into the families that owned them.

Consistent with the control of mythology by universalistic religions, Central Zone tricksters were human (or at least humanlike) figures that appeared only in folktales. In many cases mastery of disguise replaced the supernatural ability to change shape. The rebelliousness of these tricksters often took the form of challenging the stratified authority, religious as well as secular, that characterized the Central Zone. Beyond that, their pranks and verbal skills could lead people to some kind of profound enlightenment about the world around them.

Key features:

▶ Agricultural states

▶ Wet and dry subsistence patterns

▶ Plows and wheeled vehicles drawn by animals

▶ Potter's wheel

▶ Corporate stem families

▶ Male dominance and sexual segregation

▶ Complex government

▶ Closed slavery

▶ Elite literacy

▶ Philosophical trickster

Modal Patterns in Central Zone Peasant Culture

Material Culture

A peasant family lived in a house composed of three or four rectangular rooms. People in some places built their homes from mud bricks, either baked or unbaked. Other peoples used stone or some combination of mud and stone. In dry regions builders made the roof simple, a flat layer of earth or mud on top of a framework of poles. Wet climates called for sloped roofs of tile or thatch. More affluent peasants lived in similar but larger houses. Some had as many as ten rooms, and a few rose to two or even three stories. In many multistory houses the ground level

was used to shelter animals. The rooms inside a house included one for receiving guests, though not necessarily exclusive to that purpose. There were also one or more bedrooms, each used by an adult couple and their children. Many houses contained a kitchen, but some people cooked outside or in a separate shed.

A man broke the soil in his fields with a simple wooden plow pulled by an ox (a castrated bull or buffalo). More fortunate farmers owned a team of two or even more. The less fortunate man had no draft animal at all. He had to rent one from a neighbor or obtain its use in return for his labor or some other reciprocal consideration. One of the most important functions of these large animals was to produce quantities of manure to fuel fires and to fertilize the fields.

A man plowing his field with oxen; the plow was one of the most important inventions of the Central Zone (Rajasthan, India).

Many families used a donkey for ordinary transport, such as taking goods to the local market. The donkey differed from its close relative the horse in having a thin, upright mane and a tufted tail. A brownish-gray coat faded to white on its underside. The small animal, less than five feet tall at the shoulder, stood quietly as a person loaded its burden; aside from occasional stubbornness, it had a docile disposition. Sometimes the load rose high and spread wide because a donkey could carry over two hundred pounds. It could do so for several days with little food, and it could go longer without water than a horse, withstanding any temperature that the human alongside it could survive. With long and narrow hooves the donkey moved slowly and surefootedly on almost any surface, including undulating rocky terrain that endangered the limbs of a horse. Mules also served well for such purposes. They resembled donkeys but were usually larger and stronger. A mule had greater strength and stamina than a horse of the same size.

Sheep resembled their cousins, the goats, only in their facial features. People had bred the sheep to produce thick, woolly coats that provided finer material for textiles than the coarse hair of the goats. The white color of the wool was attractive in itself but also took dyes very well. Given such raw material, weaving was a very important craft.

Another important craft, among many, was the manufacture of ceramics using the potter's wheel. Turning the horizontal wheel with a foot-operated device, the experienced potter shaped the object on it quickly and evenly. The wheel increased the efficiency of the work and the symmetry of the products, but it demanded a high level of skill. Some people made ceramics or other craftwork their primary occupation and supplemented it by farming or fishing. They provided goods for community use, local trade, and wider trade. A great deal of trade was carried out in marketplaces.

Families owned the cultivated land. Some owned enough to support themselves completely and perhaps even prosper. Others had to rent additional land in order to get by. Some of the poor were tenants, sharing their crops with a landlord or otherwise compensating him for the right to cultivate. The poorest lacked the resources to own or rent and had to make a living as hired labor.

Villages assumed two main settlement patterns, depending on local conditions. In a *compact village* houses clustered amid the fields. In a *linear village* they lined a road or a stream that served transportation purposes. Many villages approached a population of one thousand, and some exceeded it. In the large villages subgroups based on residential area or kinship formed the communities in which people lived their everyday lives.

In dry habitats farmers depended mainly on wheat, barley, and millet in various combinations. They built their villages near water sources and dug irrigation systems to provide for the crops. Because the main job was handling large animals, men did most of the farm labor. Women worked at home.

Paddies like these were the central feature of wet rice cultivation wherever it was found in the Central Zone (Chinese culture).

Tropical temperatures and monsoon rains supported an agricultural pattern devoted primarily to wet rice. This labor-intensive pattern began before the rainy season with the planting of rice in small seedbeds and the cleaning of the main fields, including the leveling of the muddy soil before planting. Then women performed the arduous labor of transplanting the seedlings from their nurseries into precisely spaced field rows, which made each plant accessible to individual treatment. The fields received thorough raking and weeding while the water supply was carefully regulated with a system of ditches and dikes that required maintenance. If conditions permitted, people cultivated wheat, barley, or millet while the rice seedlings matured in the nurseries.

A peasant planting rice seedlings in a paddy; this picture conveys the backbreaking nature of the work (China).

Wet rice agriculture tied people closely to river valleys, where water renewed the nutrients in the soil. In this environment families could sustain themselves indefinitely on small plots of land. However, there were limits on the animals they could keep. They kept pigs and chickens, which can scavenge human leavings, and some ducks. Fish provided the bulk of the protein. Farmers caught them in nearby streams and in the flooded rice fields and sometimes traded for fish caught on the coast. Vegetables and fruits, planted on land unsuitable for rice, rounded out the diet.

Farmers in wet regions used cattle if necessary, but water buffalo were more effective. Weighing a ton, with horns nearly four feet across, a bull was immensely powerful in hauling a plow or a heavily laden cart. Buffalo cows gave three times the milk of cattle. Richer in fat, it could be made into a hard, greenish-white butter that resisted spoiling. However, the buffalo required muddy water in which to wallow every day to counter the heat and acquire a muddy coating to protect them against insects.

Social Relations

People idealized the extended family as a corporate body that controlled property. The family head attained his position through a clear rule of succession and played a role with specific rights and duties that were independent of his personality. Membership boundaries were clearly defined because membership conferred property rights. The importance of the corporate family can be attributed to highly productive plow agriculture on permanent fields. Differential access to limited land correlated with great variation in wealth and status. Thus the acquisition and transmission of control over property became central family concerns, as did productive efficiency.

All but one child left the household when they married. This effectively preserved corporate wealth because most or all of the inheritance went to the child who remained in the household. It also meant that the family head maintained full authority until death or retirement because there could be no agitation by multiple heirs for immediate division of the legacy. These stem family systems favored sons and made a sharp social distinction between the heir and other sons. One child was designated to care for the aging parents, a role that was often combined with succession and inheritance.

The combination of patrilocality and corporateness shaped personal relationships within the extended family. Mother and son were usually very close because they were lifelong companions within the family. In addition a woman looked to her sons for prestige and support. In contrast the father–son relationship, based on authority and inheritance, was often distant and formal. However, these were all issues for successful families. The poor had no resources to support a large household in the first place and no inheritance to protect by fostering family solidarity. Lacking control over a family estate, the senior member of a poor family also lacked authority.

Men (and perhaps many women) considered the sexes to be profoundly different and of unequal worth. They celebrated the birth of a boy far more than that of a girl. People pitied or blamed mothers with several daughters and no sons. Men were the ritual, intellectual, and moral superiors. Women, emotional and irrational, were potentially disruptive to family and community, especially with regard to sexuality. Male relatives provided the direction, control, and protection that women needed; transgressions by women thus affected the reputation of the family or even a larger kinship group. Females learned deference and obedience to males from childhood on.

Men at a wedding illustrate the sexual segregation that characterized the Central Zone (Bedouin culture, Saudi Arabia).

The sexes were segregated in order to prevent misbehavior. Ideally, women were secluded in the household, and male relatives closely supervised any external activities. Poorer women were often less restricted. Many contributed to the economic upkeep of the household with outside work, in the fields or for wages. Permissible activities depended on a variety of social criteria, including age, generation, birth order, rank, and class.

The senior woman in a family could become quite powerful, especially if she had many sons. As manager of the household, she controlled younger women and influenced men's decisions. However, it took a long time to achieve such status. The patrilocal family regarded junior wives as potentially disruptive intruders and compelled them to show great modesty and respect. A husband and his family held the ultimate advantage in a marital relationship. He had numerous grounds for divorce while his wife had few or none, and he was likely to retain custody of their children. Widowed men could remarry, but this was rare or impossible for women; they were expected to continue serving the marital family.

Kinship groups beyond the extended family were organized by patrilineal descent. Corporate features were minimal or lacking in these lineages and clans. Their main role was to regulate marriage and alliance. They also tended to play some role in political relations within the community and beyond. A council of wealthy and influential men governed the internal affairs of a neighborhood or community.

Knowledge and Expression

Peasants shared some of the beliefs and practices of the universalistic religion practiced in the cities and by the elite. However, their access to this knowledge was limited by the amount of time they spent in work and by lack of the reading skills necessary to appreciate the literature of the great tradition. Some aspects had become part of their own little tradition, but priests and scholars remained the ultimate arbiters of religious obligations and rewards. For many practical purposes peasants turned to local gods and spirits. Some of these they feared, such as the dangerous spirits of water and darkness.

Tales about the trickster lightened the spirits of ordinary people. Although some of his humor was directed at individuals like themselves, much of it was reserved for religious and secular authorities. Often found in a royal court, the trickster challenged the king himself. In some cases he undermined the ruler, in other instances he enlightened him. In addition to playing pranks, the trickster was literate, eloquent, and witty. Through both word and deed he illuminated people about the world around them. He led them to consider matters such as the use of language, the variability of perception, and the nature of reality itself. Thus the trickster stories raised issues that could be pondered by the elite as well as the peasants.

Modal Patterns in Central Zone Elite Culture

Material Culture

Within a walled enclave near the center of the capital, the ruler lived luxuriously with his entourage of family and relatives and their numerous servants. Also within the compound, administrators manned important government offices. Near the palace enclave the city's major religious complex welcomed the populace. The complex contained temples for worship and courtyards in which the less affluent public could meet or relax. A few major avenues linked these power centers with the rest of the city and the outside world.

Commercial sections alternated with the residential neighborhoods. Artisans plied their various crafts, some selling from their own shops. Merchants maintained shops in which they sold goods from many sources. A successful business made it worthwhile to put up with taxes and government bureaucracy. Others took a simpler way and displayed their wares on the ground or hawked them from stalls, booths, or carts. They offered passersby cooked food, fruits, drinks, clothes, and trinkets. Somewhere in the city a market received goods from the peasants of the countryside and from the merchants who controlled the long-distance trade. The marketplace concentrated on luxury goods and expensive items such as weapons. There was little standardization in commercial practices, and many sellers adulterated their products if possible.

The bustle of affluence ended at the massive city walls. The poorest people lived in squalor outside. Among them were many immigrants who had been lured from near and far by the pleasures and opportunities that the city seemed to offer. The fortunate ones made contact with relatives, fellow villagers, or members of the same ethnic group who had already established an economic foothold.

City wall and gate (Dali, China).

Other kinds of cities followed much the same pattern but with different emphases. The marketplace dominated a city devoted to commerce, taking in goods from hundreds or thousands of miles away. Overland caravans provided a significant portion of trade goods, but well-located seaports handled the greatest volume and became the largest and wealthiest cities. Their populations ranged into the hundreds of thousands. Commercial cities were most likely to have large ethnic minorities, each with its own residential section. Religious centers were the most distinctive, lacking the frenzied pursuit of power or wealth. Most religious cities harbored major shrines that summoned pilgrims in a spiritual state of mind.

Social Relations

The elite achieved family ideals more often than peasants did, housing extended families together and keeping women in seclusion. However, such successes were not necessarily permanent. Extended families became nuclear families through the deaths of members, or they dispersed because of bad fortune or internal disputes. Some lost status because of economic reversals or political disfavor.

A slave occupied a hereditary position and could achieve legal freedom only through manumission by his or her master. Some slaves did heavy work such as agriculture and construction, but most performed menial domestic tasks. Slavery was largely a status symbol for the wealthy. Owners could sell their slaves, give them away, and bequeath them to heirs like any other property. However, masters were responsible for health care and funeral expenses. Sometimes they arranged marriages for their slaves.

Ethnicity was another important basis for social differentiation. People used a variety of markers to distinguish categories and groups to which they assigned themselves and others. These included geographic location (e.g., hills, jungle, desert), subsistence economy (e.g., nomadic herders versus farmers), religion (especially sectarian divisions), and language (including dialects). People noticed variations in skin color and other physical features but attached relatively little importance to them.

A monarch ruled the state with religious support or justification, leading to complex interactions between rulers and religious scholars. Centralized control by secular means was never a certainty in the long run because rulers often had to confront recalcitrant aristocrats, usurpers, or rebellious tribal people in marginal areas.

Knowledge and Expression

Literacy in the higher levels of society had numerous ramifications. First, it facilitated governmental, legal, and economic administration. Second, it provided a vehicle for religious and philosophical scholarship that affected government as well as moral and spiritual thinking. Third, it allowed systematization of empirical and intellectual pursuits such as geography, natural history, medicine, mathematics, and astronomy. All these interests were intertwined in a unified intellectual world. Astronomy, for example, lent itself to practical achievements such as calendars but was also closely associated with astrology.

Literacy gave a new dimension to poetry and other forms of literary arts. Music theory also appeared in books. Sophisticated classical traditions in music were distinguished from the folk music of the countryside and the popular songs of ordinary city dwellers. Among the diverse instruments played, stringed instruments had the highest prestige. People performed music solo and in small ensembles. Although their product was highly valued, professional musicians were usually of low status. Only the gentleman amateur was admired. Sculpture, painting, architecture, and other arts also flourished.

MIDDLE EAST AREA

Examples:

Arab, Persian (Iranian), Turkish, Berber, Kurd

In terms of contemporary countries the Middle East Culture Area is most clearly represented by Turkey and Iran, and the numerous Arab nations of northern Africa and southwestern Asia from Morocco to Saudi Arabia. Some would include Afghanistan and Pakistan (Eickelmann 1998), but these countries are borderline cases that can easily be assigned to neighboring Areas (Bates and Rassam 1983).

From a human viewpoint the Middle Eastern environment revolved around oases (Gulick 1976). Sharp local contrasts between arable and nonarable land constitute "one of the most striking environmental characteristics of the Middle East" (Bates and Rassam 1993). These scattered patches of water and vegetation, varying in size and nature, provided refuge from predominantly arid climates. They included the stereotypical desert spring along with desert rivers and mountain valleys and meadows. The Area was distinguished by the extreme predominance of men in farm work (Bourguignon and Greenbaum 1973), which was perhaps related to a particularly strong application of the Central Zone rule of female seclusion.

Clustering in the oasis areas, Middle Easterners formed unusually large villages that often exceeded a thousand inhabitants (Bourguignon and Greenbaum 1973). The real communities were neighborhoods within the large settlement, often inhabited mainly by kin. Middle Eastern culture was characterized by heavy emphasis on the solidarity of patrilineal kin groups, represented by the very unusual preference for marriage between close patrilineal relatives. Such groups adhered to concepts of honor and shame that distinguished the Area by the extent to which they were reflected in social institutions and formed the basis for social action (Bates and Rassam 1983). Propriety in the behavior of women was the foremost concern.

Nomadic herders were numerous compared to other parts of the world (perhaps 15 percent of the population). The camel was the key animal in desert sections while sheep were most important in the mountains. Herders affected the economic and social lives of peasants because they depended on the farmers for plant foods and other goods. Well organized into tribes and chiefdoms, the herders also had profound effects on national governments, sometimes supporting them, sometimes destabilizing them, almost always frustrating them. Government officials in Morocco called the tribal areas "the land of insolence."

The nomads, along with religious sects and other groups, displayed strong and persistent resistance to central authority (Gulick 1976) that distinguished Middle Eastern political systems from others in the Central Zone. Perhaps related to political resistance, Middle Easterners held an egalitarian ethic that also distinguished them from other Central Zone cultures. In this respect they resembled the Western world of today (Lindholm 1996).

In its Middle Eastern homeland, Islam had a powerful and pervasive effect on the behavior of individuals and the organization of society. Nevertheless, peasants retained folk beliefs. One of the most powerful was the jinni, the source of the Western word "genie" and pronounced the same way. However, the frightening jinnis of Middle Eastern tradition differed from recent Western stereotypes. They seem to have been psychological projections of strong human emotions (Gulick 1976).

Religion was the single most important source of individual and group identity (Bates and Rassam 1983). The vast majority of people were Sunni Muslims, but Sunna was subdivided; and there were other major Islamic sects, as well minorities of Christians and Jews. Sedentary people and nomads were distinguished everywhere, with the nomads sometimes accorded romantically high status.

Key features:

- ▶ Oases
- ▶ Large villages
- ▶ Prominence of nomadic herders
- ▶ Marriage of patrilineal relatives
- ▶ Family honor and shame
- ▶ Resistance to central authority
- ▶ Egalitarian values
- ▶ Pervasive influence of Islam

Modal Patterns in Middle East Peasant Culture

Material Culture

The Koran, the holy book containing God's revelations to Muhammad, instructed believers in the essentials of household relationships. While setting forth the rules of property and inheritance, the book implied the right of every family to live in its own enclosed space. Each extended family in the village occupied a walled compound in which the rooms or houses of several nuclear families faced a common courtyard.

After people put away their sleeping mattresses for the day, there were few furnishings in the house except for the sitting cushions. Every room could serve multiple purposes, including sleeping and eating, except for the kitchen and the storage facilities. The separation of men's and women's quarters was the most important division of space. When a couple left their private sleeping room in the morning, the wife went to the women's area in the rear of the house or the compound to be as far as possible from the public world and the chance of a dishonorable encounter with an unrelated man. Men spent their domestic time in the more exposed areas, often receiving male guests.

Dinner in a Middle Eastern home (Saudi Arabia).

Unless desperately needed to help with farming, women spent most of their time in the household. They sewed sheets, pillow covers, towels, quilts, napkins, and prayer mats for domestic use. Women also devoted a great deal of attention to cooking, since people valued good food. Family members ate a simple breakfast after the dawn prayer and looked forward to a big supper in the late afternoon or after the sunset prayer. The cuisine emphasized fresh ingredients with subtle seasoning by herbs and spices. Meals could be taken anywhere in the house.

A household stood among many like it with the closest in many cases abutting its walls. Beyond the crowded village of perhaps a thousand people the cultivated fields gave way to a dry wilderness that harbored nomadic herders. Some raided the village for loot and some came to trade. The nomad men rode horses when possible, especially for battle. Milk provided them with a major source of food, supplemented by some meat from their goats.

Beyond the wilderness the owners of village land lived in towns and cities. Most of the men in the village cultivated fields owned by others. The state claimed much of the land but rarely bothered to administer it. The ruler granted some of it to powerful men in return for their services, and they held the land as private estates. The government turned other tracts over to tax farmers. These men paid a set fee for the right to collect and retain taxes that otherwise would have gone to the government. Still other lands were held by trusts. Some of these were private, intended for the perpetual support of a family. Other trusts were religious foundations devoted to public works and charitable causes. With the income from their holdings they built things ranging from drinking fountains to mosques.

Whatever the ultimate destination of the crops he shared or, less often, the money he paid, the farmer worked for a landlord. When a single individual represented the ownership, he formed a patron–client relationship with the farmer. However, many owners were exploitative and prepared to expel peasant families from the land if there were some profit in doing so.

hand, related nuclear families cooperated very closely even if separated by a considerable distance. Related heads of several families formed a local patrilineage. Members of these groupings felt deep concern about collective reputation based on honor and shame. A prestigious origin was one source of honor. So were recent actions of the group, including generosity and piety. Prowess, power, and wealth also brought honor when used morally.

However, control of female kin was the single most important basis for honor. By the same token, the greatest shame came from a breach of the sexual code. The worst insults were those that referred to sexual misbehavior by a man's mother or sister. Concern about sexual behavior tended to make many husband–wife relationships uneasy and even hostile.

While both men and women were thought to have strong sex drives, men believed that women had less control and were more likely to behave dishonorably. The mosque was forbidden to them because it was a place for men to gather, so they worshipped in the household. A woman who went outside the household should have a male escort and be dressed appropriately in shapeless clothing and a veil. Even within the house a woman usually covered herself in the presence of any man not forbidden to be her husband, such as her husband's father and elder brothers. The educated knew that the Koran enjoined women to nothing more than modesty and morality, but most people considered seclusion and the veil as fundamental symbols of Islam. A man had the right, or even duty, to kill a female relative for sexual misbehavior.

A Middle Eastern marketplace, or bazaar (United Arab Emirates).

Middle Eastern women in typically modest clothing.

Social Relations

Ideally all members of an extended family lived together in the same walled compound, but most sons had the ambition of heading their own households. On the other

Ideal restrictions on women were not fully observed and may not even have been desired by all men. Possible breaches were often minimized or even ignored. Veiling was flexible and depended on trust. Women might remain unveiled in front of men regarded as trustworthy or not dangerous, such as religious figures and servants.

Affinal men could come into this category and so could male family friends (at the discretion of family elders). On the other hand, if a woman came to mistrust a close male kinsman, she might start veiling in front of him. Because of the marriage of patrilineal kin, some women could be unveiled much of the time because they were among close and trusted relatives. The main concern was the danger to honor posed by outsiders, so avoidance was strictest beyond the household.

As a man matured, he developed a bilateral network of kinsmen for personal support and protection. However, his marriage reinforced patrilineal bonds because the preferred partner was a patrilineal relative. He and his wife both hoped for many sons. People loved children and rejoiced at every birth, but both men and women favored boys. Gender distinction meant little to the children until around the age of seven, when a boy was dressed in special clothes and taken in a procession around the neighborhood. Back in his house, he underwent a ritual circumcision. Though not mentioned in the Koran, this act was regarded as an essential feature of the faith. It symbolized the transition from household to community and from the women's world to the men's world. It also anticipated mature sexuality; the boy was often prepared for the ritual as if he were a bridegroom.

People celebrated circumcision but regarded the first menses as shameful. From about the age of seven the focus of a girl's development was the marriage that would take place shortly after puberty. While learning all the skills of a woman, the girl emphasized the sewing of the various domestic items that would form her trousseau. A good mother relentlessly pursued a favorable match for her daughter.

A young bride could hope for a happy life if she had a husband who was kind, honorable, or in love with her. Otherwise, marriage placed the woman in a precarious position. Unable to work outside the home, she had limited resources. Although Islam guaranteed a woman's inheritance, her rightful share of family property was half that of a brother. In a poor family she was unlikely to receive that much. Her husband could easily divorce her by pronouncing his desire in front of witnesses, and custody always reverted to the father when the children reached a certain age.

Various descent groups handled everyday governmental matters. Households were linked together in small patrilineages; these were in turn joined together in larger patrilineages or clans, each with a chieftain. Many peasants and all of the nomads were organized into tribes based on patrilineal descent. A putative common ancestor joined maximal lineages or clans as a tribe. A chief led the tribe as a whole, but he was often a figurehead or functioned mainly in coordinating external relations. The tribe was segmentary in nature, especially among pastoralists, with kin groups at each level capable of entering into hostilities with each other or uniting against outsiders. "I against my brother," they said, "my brother and I against my cousin, my cousin and I against the outsider." A tribe as a whole controlled land, water, and trade.

In the ideal stratification system, prominent ancestry conferred membership in the upper strata. Direct descendants of Muhammad were at the top and likely to wield local power as a result of their moral authority. Next were the descendants of prominent Islamic scholars and holy men, who might be scholars in their own right but might also have mundane occupations such as tending shops. Nomads claiming long descent lines from tribal heroes were accorded high status. The mass of ordinary people had no special descent claims.

Knowledge and Expression

Every individual communicated directly with God through prayer. At the same time everyone knew that God's Word had provided an elaborate written guide for human life. It began with the Koran, the direct revelation to Muhammad, but included much more. The Traditions (Hadith), composed of numerous stories about the Prophet's words and actions in various situations, provided additional information. Finally, scholars had drawn upon both sources to create the more systematic code known as Divine Law (Shari'a). Aware of this great body of written literature, ordinary people knew that they needed the advice of scholars in many matters.

Some of these learned persons taught themselves, but most studied with established scholars. The scholars, setting themselves apart with their special robes and turbans, broadly agreed on certain rules for recruitment and ranking. Status among the learned came from scholarly achievement, personality, the opinion of peers, and the endorsement of the community. Scholars received financial support from trusts set up by wealthy donors. They themselves administered these rural lands and urban properties.

Ordinary people acknowledged the need for Islamic guidance, but many found legalistic orthodoxy unsatisfying. They turned to one of the Sufi movements, most of which emphasized love and emotional spontaneity. The ultimate goal was to escape from individual consciousness and achieve complete union with God. Each Sufi movement revolved around a specific spiritual path specified by a founding saint. Together they constituted a vast array of beliefs, rituals, and institutions. Choice was limited only by local availability. In most Sufi movements the initiate sought renunciation of worldly concerns through physical and spiritual exercises. He or she went through stages of development assisted by personal teachers. Sufi provided one of the few paths to status and power for women. Many of the movements accepted them as equal participants and allowed them to become leaders and even saints.

Other villagers held beliefs that were even less orthodox than Sufi, such as the evil eye. Jinnis were on the borderline. These powerful and dangerous spirits frequented dark and damp places in the wilderness. They could take animal or human form, either normal or fantastic; however, one feature, such as hooved feet, always gave them away. Those who believed in the jinnis knew many magical spells to placate or counteract these fearsome beings. Not everyone believed in them because, though mentioned in the Koran, jinnis were not part of the essential faith.

The trickster in the villagers' tales was a religious teacher who often played the fool. He entertained the listeners with odd behavior, such as riding his donkey mounted backwards. Other escapades, however, taught lessons about matters such as effective communication. When a man asked the trickster how long it would take to reach the next town, he received no answer until he began to leave. The trickster then explained that he could not answer the question until he had seen how fast the man walked.

Modal Patterns in Middle East Elite Culture

Material Culture

A wealthy merchant and his wife rose from the mattresses in their private room and dressed for the day. The woman carefully arranged her richly patterned gown and chose striking ornaments of silver and gold. She intended to receive some friends in the guest room of the women's quarters, and all of them would be elegantly dressed, each according to her personal taste. The fine

Gold objects in an urban marketplace (Syria).

appearance of elite women reflected on the status of their families. The patriarch of the family dressed more modestly for his day's work. When they were ready, the servants entered to serve a light breakfast and put away the mattresses.

As the man walked through his spacious house, he encountered his eldest son and new bride emerging from their room, the nervous girl with a veil across her face. In one of the many family rooms his lazy youngest son still slept, and in another his two daughters ate their breakfast sitting on fine embroidered cushions. Expensive textiles hung everywhere, dividing large rooms into cozier spaces, curtaining doorways, and decorating walls. Motifs on ceramics, boxes, and other household items reflected the textile patterns. As in most elite homes, the rooms, stairs, balconies, terraces, and courtyards swirled together in a unique configuration.

Leaving the house, the merchant glimpsed more domestic beauty. Some of the brickwork in the compound used checked and striped motifs derived from weaving patterns. Stone facing covered other brick walls, and still others were plastered and painted. The buildings were interspersed with gardens in a carefully balanced way. When he stepped through the modest door in the outer wall, the merchant entered a different world. He walked down the narrow, crooked, dirty streets that separated the blank walls of houses. At least they provided shade from the hot sun.

Turning into one of the few major avenues of the city, the merchant walked among many other men. A few escorted well-covered women while many others controlled animals pulling or carrying loads to the market. The merchant passed one of the city's main mosques which offered courtyards for public meetings and gardens to be enjoyed by those who had none at home. Briefly he glanced up at the minarets, the tall and slender spires that rose above the avenue's turmoil. From the balcony of a minaret, the chant of a muezzin reminded people when it was time for prayer.

A little further on the merchant saw the palace walls in the distance. Behind them, he knew, was a sprawling compound with gardens more beautiful than his. However, the architecture was haphazard: in that governmental center, buildings were often added or adapted to serve varied and changing purposes.

Turning into another section of narrow streets, this one commercial, the merchant passed his wife's shop. Like some other elite women, she had purchased a business of her own. Unlike some of the more daring ones she never visited the place herself but used agents who came to the house for orders. At last he arrived at his shop, one of several that he owned, and prepared to support his elegant lifestyle.

A mosque with elaborately decorated dome and several minarets (Iran).

Close-up of the top of a minaret, from which the muezzin calls people to prayer.

Social Relations

The merchant's wife was his cousin. Their marriage conformed to an ideal based on the marriage of Muhammad's daughter to his cousin. Actual practice varied widely, but cousin marriages often joined influential families. Such unions prevented the dilution of wealth and status and made it easier to obey the Islamic law prescribing that spouses be of equivalent social background. A cousin marriage signaled the family's enduring importance to the community.

Personal friends, who could also be relatives, played an important role in life. The merchant's wife went to one of the numerous public bathhouses once a week, even though the family had a private bath in their house. A full day at the public bath gave the woman a chance to socialize with many friends and to enjoy the elaborate and relaxing services provided by the attendants. Men also went to public baths, but for shorter visits that involved brisk scrubbing and vigorous massage. To relax, the merchant went to a coffeehouse or teahouse to enjoy conversation along with the beverages. Many such places also offered musicians, dancers, and storytellers.

A city as a unit had no more government than a village or a tribe. In a sense an urbanized area was not a city at all, having little political or social integration. The Middle Eastern city was not a legal entity, being administered by the state ruler or his regional governor. Neighborhoods were sharply separated from one another, sometimes to the extent of being walled. Each had its own leader, who maintained order, collected taxes, and acted as a liaison between the citizens and the government. Gangs of youths acted as a kind of police force.

Some wider integration was provided by religious scholars and their schools of law, which offered moral guidance, physical relief, and leadership. Every member of the city population was affiliated with one of these schools. To a large extent the religious leadership supported the city through charitable endowments funded by income from agricultural properties. They maintained public buildings and lesser structures such as fountains and paid the salaries of those associated with these structures.

Islam forbade debt slavery, so slaves could only be obtained by capture and purchase. Although slaves were rarely assimilated into families, they could rise to great prominence in family affairs and beyond. Some became agents of their families, handling the most important and confidential matters, including foreign business. Such slaves were often raised with the same care and education as adopted children and, even if freed, they remained close to their former masters. Other slaves assumed trusted positions in the military or rose to high levels in government administration. These were considered servants of the ruler rather than chattels. The Koran acknowledged slavery but conferred rights on slaves and urged kindness.

Despite slavery and kingship, all men were considered equal before God. Inequities arose from competition among equals and received little acknowledgment in interpersonal behavior. Men greeted each other with the wish "Peace be upon you," and they shook hands or embraced. Even a king was confirmed in office by handshakes from his advisors and religious scholars. The Muslim scholars endowed a ruler with the legitimacy of Islamic law, but the ruler himself had no divinity. The Prophet was only a human being, and no man can be more. Since the king was constrained by Islamic law, which pertained to almost every aspect of society, the scholars were politically influential.

Many states were forced into complex relationships with nomadic tribes, which often formed powerful federations. Sometimes the tribes contributed to the government and the military; in other instances tribal dynasties controlled the state. In some cases the government successfully played the tribes against one another; in others it simply coexisted with them, exerting minimal control. If the tribes were under control, dissidents might rally around charismatic religious leaders or powerful local landlords. Governments tended to exploit rural areas on behalf of the cities and, overreaching, they fomented resistance that was often effective.

Knowledge and Expression

Forbidden the mosque, because men worshipped there, women prayed in their homes. Men also prayed at home frequently because the small mosques in residential areas opened only at midday or for special celebrations. If they cared to walk the distance, they could go to one of the few great mosques that remained open all day. Whatever the setting, the prayer of elite urban people differed from that of commoners only in the beautiful prayer rugs on which they knelt.

In an educated household men and women both read, wrote, and did calligraphy. They started together as boys and girls, either in the home or at a school, learning reading, writing, and the Koran. They received the same instruction until gender segregation began around the age of seven.

Despite the concern about illicit activity, sexual expression was celebrated in both religious and literary writings. Islam supported sex as a gift to be enjoyed by men and women, who were both thought to have strong sex drives. There was no spiritual value to celibacy and no association between pleasure and sin. Rather, sex was viewed as a powerful force that could disrupt society and thus was restricted to the appropriate context of marriage.

Because books were copied and illustrated by hand, they were rare. Literacy was limited to a small minority of the population, a very few of them scholars who had mastered one or more languages. Scholars took pride in abstract learning, enjoyed the respect they received from the general population, and circulated and discussed books among themselves. These books included biographies, histories, and grammatical treatises. Other literates were proficient in ordinary usage as a matter of profession, for example, scribes, clerks, and accountants. The less accomplished handled government records, legal papers, correspondence, and the like.

The ceramically decorated wall of a mosque conforms to the rule that prohibits images of living things, lest they become objects of worship (Jerusalem, Israel).

The visual arts were limited by broad and literal interpretation of Koranic injunction against making "graven images." There was also some feeling against nonreligious music and dance as being frivolous, but people of all social classes enjoyed them. Wealthy people kept musicians in their homes. Classical music was controlled, reflective, and entailed lengthy improvisations. The popular songs played in the coffeehouses and at family celebrations were more emotional—romantic, mournful, or jovial. In the written literature only poetry expressed personal feelings.

The sciences integrated ancient Greek and Persian thought with an Islamic view of the world. Physics, the study of things that change, was essentially Aristotelian while geography made no sharp distinction between empirical descriptions and sacred symbols. In medicine, which had long influenced Europe, the physician was expected to be a virtuous and deeply religious man. Islamic astronomers corrected some of the shortcomings of Ptolemy, considered the possibility that the earth revolves around the sun, and made mathematical analyses of planetary motion. The pure mathematicians provided new concepts and computational methods while developing algebra, geometry, and trigonometry.

A Closer Look

The traditional Middle East included three Regions identified with large ethnic groups that remain prominent in the contemporary world.

The Arab Region

This largest Region of the Middle East stretched across all of northern Africa and encompassed Southwest Asia except for Turkey and Iran. Along the coasts of the Mediterranean Sea people lived in a climate much like that of southern California and raised abundant crops, including fruit orchards along with their grains. However, most of the Arab Region's geography fitted Western stereotypes about deserts and camels. Merchants needed camels to take their great cargoes of salt and gold across the Sahara and Arabian deserts. With the camel as their key animal, nomadic herders could live in those same deserts. Suited to any dry environment, camels were especially well adapted to the loose sands of the Arab Region. Long lashes protected their eyes from the sand, and broad hooves kept them from sinking despite their great weight.

The usefulness of camels offset their other characteristics. They all tended to be bad-tempered and the males, standing seven feet at the shoulder and weighing up to three-quarters of a ton, could be extremely difficult and sometimes dangerous. Not very intelligent or responsive, camels were hard to train. And even those who loved them admitted that they smelled bad.

As suggested by the decorations, the camel was the key animal of nomadic herders in the Arab Region.

The Arab Region gave birth to Islam and remained its center. The true Koran is in Arabic, and Mecca, Muhammad's birthplace, is the prime goal of Muslim pilgrims. However, though steeped in religion, Arab scholars also produced many of the Middle East's greatest scientific and mathematical innovations.

The Turkish Region

Invaders from the Steppes (see p. 176 ff.) who settled in what is now Turkey formed the Turkish Region. By 1700 A.D. the Turks dominated most of the Middle East through the Ottoman Empire. Much of their culture was derived from the Arabs and Persians, but they developed or kept distinctive forms of their own. One example was the *victory letter*, ostensibly a report on a military triumph but actually a long and elaborate narrative celebration (B. Lewis 1963). This literary direction is in accord with a generally militaristic ideology that may derive from their Steppes origin (Bartholomew 1995). The linkage is more obvious in the specific symbols that Turks used in decorating their carpets. Sufi movements were particularly strong in the Turkish Region and often influenced the government.

The Persian Region

The Persian Region, centered on the country of Iran, combined an ancient indigenous civilized tradition with Islamic culture derived from the Arabs. In this mountainous environment the sheep was the key animal for nomadic herders. Each city was the center of an economic network that encompassed dozens of towns and hundreds of villages.

The Shi'a sect of Islam predominated. Its emphasis on martyrdom derived from the heroic death of its founder in pursuit of the leading position in the early Islamic world as the successor of Muhammad. Shi'a was (and is) organized into an elaborate hierarchy that exercised great

Man in modern clothing preserving an ancient Persian art by weaving a carpet (Iran).

authority over its followers. This system contrasted strongly with the Sunna ideal of egalitarian religion.

Ancient Persian customs persisted, represented by the weaving of beautiful carpets and by miniature paintings with ancient themes. The Persian artists painted with brushes made from kitten hairs and refused to accept the Sunni stricture on making human images (Mackey 1996).

Female Genital Operations

Recent controversy has acquainted the Western public with the existence of female genital operations, usually done in childhood or early adolescence. Although more common in part of the African Zone (see chapter 10), such operations were also performed in parts of the Middle East. Scattered Middle Eastern societies practiced clitoridectomy, removing part or all of the clitoris; in some cases part or all of the labia were removed as well. This was not a modal pattern for the Middle East Area or for any of its Regions.

Lengthy and painful, the operations also posed the danger of serious infection. Their main rationale was to reduce or eliminate the sexual motivation of women to ensure that they would behave honorably (Gulick 1976). This was an extreme manifestation of a strong Middle Eastern concern for proper sexual behavior in a woman and the concomitant honor of men in the woman's kin group.

Female genital operations are still performed today, resulting in an international controversy. Many see the practice as nothing more than a way of brutalizing and oppressing women. On the other hand, some argue that it is an emblem of ethnic and religious identity (paralleling male circumcision) and that Western objections are ethnocentric. To keep the matter in perspective it is important to remember two things: genital operations on girls were never widely distributed in the Middle East and official Islam never approved of any of these procedures. The Koran does not mention them; rather, the practice seems to contradict the holy book's assertion that women are entitled to sexual pleasure with their husbands.

INDIAN AREA

Examples:

Aryan (northern India),
Dravidian (southern India)

The Indian culture area, largely defined by Hinduism and the associated social stratification known as the caste system, nearly coincides with the contemporary country of India. Parts of several small neighboring countries also belong. Pakistan and Bangladesh display a significant number of Indian cultural traits; for example, aspects of the caste system (Maloney 1974). However, being predominantly Muslim, they diverged from Indian culture in important ways.

All of India was tropical in temperature because the Himalayas blocked the cold winds from the north, and the Indian Ocean moderated the climate. However, the incidence of rainfall had a profound effect on agriculture. The monsoons, heavy seasonal rains, were highly variable in timing and intensity, often resulting in crop destruction by drought or flood or high winds. Millet, wheat, sorghum, and rice were widely cultivated.

Islam had a powerful impact in the heart of the Indian Area. A long history of invasions by various Muslim peoples culminated in the formation of the extensive Mughal (Mogul) Empire. Nevertheless, independent Hindu states existed outside the Empire, some rulers within it were Hindu, and the Mughal emperors themselves adopted some aspects of Indian culture, such as the idea of divine monarchs. By 1700 A.D. the Empire was in decline and challenged by independent polities, both Muslim and Hindu.

Caste, an ideal system of stratification, affected every aspect of Hindu life at every level of social organization. However, the word itself can lead to a misunderstanding of these effects. It is a term of western origin that loosely refers to two kinds of groups. *Varnas* were broad categories with highly idealized characteristics: Brahmans (priests and scholars), Kshatriyas (warriors and rulers), Vaishyas (merchants), and Shudras (groups associated with the performance of various services). A *jati* was any kind of subgroup within a varna, but the most important application of the concept concerned Shudra subgroups that were defined by the services they traditionally performed. Theoretically outside the system were the outcastes or Untouchables.

Varnas and jatis were ranked according their degree of ritual purity or pollution. Though Hinduism is known for its multiple gods and concept of reincarnation, purification can be considered the "defining feature" of Hinduism (Tapp 1993). Perhaps the most distinctive application of these concepts held that all products of the cow, a sacred animal, were pure. This facilitated the use of cow manure for a variety of important practical purposes.

Hinduism recognized different ways to achieve closeness to God. The path of *bhakti* (love) has been the basis for numerous movements comparable to Sufi in the Middle East. These cults may have provided "psychological consolation" to those oppressed by the caste system. Many were vehicles for egalitarian sentiments that rejected the caste structure in whole or part (Tapp 1993).

Language was an important ethnic factor in the Indian Area, which harbored at least sixteen major linguistic groups. Regardless of language, people of the plains contrasted themselves with the less-civilized hill people, who were in many cases organized tribally. Despite a substantial Hindu majority, religion also differentiated the population. Muslims were numerous and politically dominant in the Mughal Empire. Other minorities included Buddhists and regional offshoots of Hinduism. Sikhism, a sect that mingled Hindu and Muslim beliefs, dominated the Punjab in northwestern India. Jains, whose founders rebelled against Hinduism's negative view of earthly life, were concentrated in Gujarat and Bombay (Twedell and Kimball 1985).

Key features:

- ▶ Diverse uses of cow manure
- ▶ Preference for joint family
- ▶ Importance of dowry·
- ▶ Veiling within the household
- ▶ Caste system
- ▶ Hindu religion
- ▶ Religious significance of cattle
- ▶ Medicine and mathematics

Modal Patterns in Indian Peasant Culture

Material Culture

Driving two oxen before them, a man and his grown son walked through the narrow dusty streets of the village on the way to their fields. Moving in the other direction, several boys of the household escorted other cattle to pasture. Each man had a cloth covering wrapped around his head and wore a loose shirt over a heavy cotton loincloth. All items of clothing could be adjusted for the changing temperature, and the shirt and headcloth could be removed if necessary.

Behind the men and youths the rising sun lit the baked-brick walls of their prosperous house. The slanting rays highlighted the carvings that decorated the wooden door as well as the mural above it that gave color to the entranceway. Behind the walls were several rooms that surrounded a courtyard in which the women of the household worked. Having put away the wood-and-rope cots used for sleeping, they ground grain for the day's meals. Rough cotton garments covered their bodies and legs, but they left their faces exposed because all the men were away. They wore jewelry, some made from silver, on their necks, arms, and ankles.

The women finished the grinding after about two hours and went on to other chores. One swept the floors while another went to get water and the third collected cow manure from the animal enclosure. The cow manure, a pure substance because it came from a sacred animal, had important practical uses. First of all, it provided fertilizer to renew fields that had been worn out by thousands of years of agriculture. Second, it could be used to plaster floors and also the verandas that fronted some houses. Finally, dried cakes of dung gave people fuel in a land where forest clearance had made wood scarce.

Even with wood available, the dung had its advantages. Burning slowly, it gave a cook a chance to do other tasks or visit with neighbors while her vegetables or curry simmered. The low temperature of the flame allowed her to cook in a ceramic vessel, a necessity if the family could not afford copper. The contents of the pot would be served with flat bread made from grain. The cook enhanced the meal with butter or buttermilk, but members of a higher and purer jati ate no meat.

The woman who had gone for water carried two clay jugs on her head. She moved briskly through the village, confident that all the men had gone to the fields with their oxen and all the youths had taken the other cattle to pasture. After passing a number of brick houses similar to her own, she came to the small well reserved for members of her jati. There she repeatedly lowered the leather bag at the end of a rope until she had filled her containers.

People of the Indian Area in front of the decorated wall and doorway of a prosperous house (between Agra and Jaipur).

Beyond the well was a poorer neighborhood in which most of the houses were mud huts containing one or two rooms. Some of the inhabitants had constructed their walls from mud bricks, but others had simply piled and shaped the mud. Many people in the neighborhood kept goats and chickens. As members of an impure jati, they ate meat and eggs. They also sold their goats in the town market or within the village to someone who wanted to make a blood sacrifice to a god. In other parts of the village members of higher jatis lived in similar mud houses, but without the animals. Purer spiritual status did not guarantee prosperity.

To fulfill many needs, the farmer and his household turned to jatis that specialized in particular products and services. These included pottery, carpentry, and barbering. Those who provided such help received shares of the farmer's grain after harvests. Some of these people lived in the village, but others were summoned when needed or visited regularly. Since the system was hierarchical, these relationships were affected by social status. The lower-ranking partner owed unstinting service, day and night if he lived nearby, while the superior was expected to be generous in his rewards. Service specializations provided

Indian women getting water from a village well.

the basis for exchange throughout the village. Reciprocity was emphasized and there was often no immediate return. Untouchables performed the most polluting tasks, such as sweeping the streets and removing dead animals.

Local merchants offered the peasant credit, trust, and advice. Itinerant peddlers provided trinkets and cooking utensils, and also news and gossip that may have been valued more than the trade goods. Many peasant villages were not self-sufficient, using towns to market their crops and acquire urban products. Weekly markets in small towns were serviced by traveling merchants. Larger towns and cities offered permanent markets with lower prices and greater variety.

Social Relations

The ideal household contained a patrilocal joint family, with all married sons remaining in residence. This was particularly hard to maintain in the face of personal conflicts, competition, and demographic processes. Families of higher status observed strict exogamy based on patrilineages. Thus marriage extended kinship ties, a desirable thing because it opened more social and economic opportunities. People considered power and wealth morally acceptable as long as they were used to benefit kin.

For parents, allowing a daughter to remain unmarried after her first menses was the equivalent of abortion. As a result, girls were considered extremely burdensome because they married and left home just at the time that they were becoming useful. Marriage arrangement was a complex matter. In addition to caste and kinship, it took into account age, appearance, horoscope, and insistence that girls not marry below their social level. Hinduism idealized the free gift of a daughter, so families in the upper strata of society did not ask for bridewealth and usually gave dowry. Bridewealth was important to lower-status families for economic reasons. People considered divorce a moral evil, but they also avoided it because it disrupted so many social and economic transactions. Men had some valid grounds for divorce while women had none.

When she arrived in her new home, the young woman was expected to treat her husband as a god, regardless of his behavior, and be completely subordinate to her in-laws. The sexual behavior of the young couple concerned their elders. Sex was a major source of ritual pollution, which was more of a problem for men because they were more pure than women. In addition, men regarded the loss of sperm as potentially debilitating and tried to set limits. Women were regarded as more sexual than men and therefore likely to tempt them into excess. Young husbands were considered particularly susceptible and wives often veiled themselves in front of their husbands (a practice that would have made no sense in the Middle East).

Sexual dishonor outside the family was also a concern. Some women had to perform chores outside the house while most used the markets as a valid reason to leave home. This gave them one of the few opportunities to visit with their relatives. Women had to be properly dressed for these occasions.

The senior woman in an extended family could accumulate considerable power and influence, but the rewards of later life were fleeting. People despised a widow and often blamed her for her husband's death. *Suttee* was the ideal solution to the problem: she should throw herself on her husband's funeral pyre. A woman who actually did this might be revered as a minor god. Those who did not were likely to live in a degraded subordinate status for the rest of their lives.

The peasant village had a nominal identity, but a man gave his primary loyalties to family and jati. The community was divided into hamlets representing different jatis. An appointed or hereditary head of the village administered external law and organized tax collection, but his influence depended on force of personality. Internal affairs were the province of a council composed of elders and influential men belonging to landowning castes. Usually one caste was dominant, but there was always competition. The council, operating by consensus, took care of secular disputes, ritual offenses, and intercaste violence. Penalties and fines were the common punishments, but more serious offenses incurred deprivation of village services or expulsion from the community.

The varnas constituted the ideal stratification of society. Hinduism justified the separation of endogamous groups on the basis of ritual purity. Everyday manifestations of ritual distance included refusal to take food from the hands of an inferior. Although the system was theoretically immutable, this really applied only to the top and bottom, the Brahmans and the Untouchables. Jatis in other varnas maneuvered for position based on shifts in wealth and power. Some even rose into a higher varna or fell into a lower one.

Knowledge and Expression

A God without gender manifested itself in three major forms: Brahma the creator, Vishnu the preserver, and Shiva the destroyer. Brahma was remote, but the masculine Vishnu and Shiva had intense meaning for ordinary people. Vishnu was entirely benevolent; his earthly manifestations, avatars, devoted themselves to the needs and welfare of human beings. Shiva governed fertility, as many phallic symbols represented, but he had a dark side in his associations with time, death, and war. Most worshippers concentrated their attentions on either Vishnu or Shiva, although they were not required to be exclusive. Certain avatars of Vishnu were widely favored.

Goddesses were essential to the spiritual world because they embodied divine energy *(shakti)*. Every male god had a female consort to provide this energy. Mortal women, on the other hand, were excluded from temples because they were more polluted than men. The bhakti movements probably offered them the best hope for spiritual fulfillment. These cults emphasized ecstatic union with goddesses as well as gods, and their egalitarian sentiments may have extended to women.

Ornate carvings and sculptures decorated many Hindu temples, but worship was simple. After purification in an associated pool or nearby stream, the worshipper walked around the inside of the temple, made a brief prayer, and then sat down to observe whatever might occur. Temple events included the care of the god's icon by the priests. They fed it, bathed it, entertained it with music, and honored it with garlands. On feast days they took the image through the streets. Other observances included daily rites of purification, sacraments of the life cycle, reading of scriptures, participation in annual festivals, and pilgrimages to holy sites.

Hinduism teaches respect for all living things, but cows received a degree of reverence comparable to that of a senior family member or even a lesser god. They were not to be killed or eaten, and animal hospitals existed to care for them in old age. Reverence for cattle came from their ubiquitous presence in religious symbolism and ritual. At the highest cosmological level, all but one of the gods lived in the body of a cow. Krishna, the most important avatar of Vishnu, was the cowherd god, often depicted in pastoral settings. Lesser gods included Kamdhenu, the cow that grants all desires. The Five Products of cattle (milk, curds, clarified butter, urine, and dung) were vital in ritual, magic, and medicine. The bull was the sacred vehicle of Shiva and appeared at the entrance to each of his temples.

Peasants gave a great deal of ritual attention to goddesses. The earth itself was a goddess, usually worshipped in connection with planting and harvest. A mother goddess of the village provided protection from disease and other calamities. Some goddesses were important to the fertility of women and cattle, as well as crops. Others were concerned with health, many of them specifically associated with dangerous diseases such as smallpox and cholera. Health anxieties also made curers and exorcists prominent in the little traditions.

Animal sacrifice was common, although regarded as unclean by orthodox theology. Higher-caste people in the villages condoned it because they believed in the deities to which it was directed. The possibility that a soul might become a dangerous ghost also called for sacrifices to ensure passage to heaven. Many believed that souls experienced heaven and hell between reincarnations while the idea of an ultimate union with God was an extremely distant prospect.

According to an Indian proverb, "The man who knows nothing of music, literature, or art is no better than a beast." Peasants danced in their ceremonies for the smallpox goddess, and they were entertained by wandering minstrels and troupes presenting dance-dramas with music and song. Dramas told bawdy stories of seduction and abandonment and other tales based on traditional stereotypes such as greedy landlords and monstrous mothers-in-law. The highly stylized dance-dramas

of the elite were based on the religious epics. They included devotional songs and a complex language of hand gestures and body movements. There were, for example, twenty-two poses for the head and neck.

Music was melodic and rhythmic but lacked harmony and counterpoint. The classical music group consisted of three to six instruments, including the sitar, tabla drum, and a multistringed drone. Although largely improvisational, each musical piece *(raga)* had a dominant mood: heroic, pathetic, tranquil, or erotic. Audiences involved themselves in performances by beating time, shaking their heads, and expressing their feelings by gestures such as smacking their lips.

People greatly appreciated storytelling, a tradition that went back to the great religious epics. Brahman bards entertained villagers with tales of gods, demons, heroes, and villains. Some plays were based on the epics, but others told human love stories, and there were also comedies and dramas set in the present. Devotional poetry expressed adoration of the gods.

Villagers entertained each other with stories of the trickster, a Brahman who had lowered himself to become jester in a royal court. He displayed his propensity for wordplay, and offered a lesson in communication, in a dire situation after offending the king. When the ruler announced the trickster's death sentence by asking him how he wished to die, the latter replied "Old age." The amused king absolved him. In another story a prank taught the lesson. When the king requested a ceremony to turn him into a Brahman, his jester arranged for them to take a walk and encounter a man obsessively scrubbing his donkey. Questioned by the king, the man said he was trying to make his donkey into a horse. The startled ruler took the point that something born into one state cannot be forced into another.

Contemporary urban women in saris but unveiled (Delhi, India).

Modal Patterns in Indian Elite Culture

Material Culture

The rectangular bulk of the king's palace buildings marked the heart of the capital city. The major temples nearby rose toward the sky, each composed of a series of spires shaped to resemble mountains. Some temples recalled Mount Kailasa, the home of the great god Shiva; others represented Mount Meru, the center of the universe. Together they seemed like a small city of their own. Also in this central part of the city, large three-story residences housed the most prominent families—those of priests and other Brahmans, courtiers, and wealthy merchants. The palaces, temples, and houses all displayed the finest metalwork, carving, and textiles. Open squares provided space for festivals or the muster of armies, both being frequent events. Farmers lived in congested neighborhoods away from the urban center in houses of varying modesty. The mud hovels of untouchables marked the edge of the city.

The sprawling palace complex provided space for numerous animals, many of them essential to war. Some high officers rode elephants into battle and horse-mounted cavalrymen played a vital role. Mules and oxen pulled carts where possible, but camels were needed for operations in desert areas. In addition to the ordinary materiel of war, the pack animals transported the heavy tents of silk or brocade that any traveling aristocrat required. Nobles kept similar establishments on their rural estates because their main obligation to the king was military service.

Many economic exchanges in the city followed the pattern of reciprocity between members of different jatis. However, the marketplace saw some transactions based on money, copies of Greek coins issued by the government. Caravans of oxcarts brought a great variety of practical and luxury goods into the city: diamonds and other gems, silks and other fine cloth, indigo for dye, pepper and salt, iron, copper, and lead.

Most caravans consisted of two-wheeled carts pulled by oxen. They were faster and cheaper than camels and carried more goods, so camels were used only in desert regions. River transport was slow and many rivers unnavigable for large parts of the year. The greatest problem encountered by most caravans was likely to be a confrontation with another caravan heading the other way. Because they could not pass abreast on many of the narrow roads, fighting for priority sometimes ensued. The group that made way sometimes waited three days for a long caravan to pass.

Many caravans originated in port cities. The walls of an important port city enclosed several square miles and tens of thousands of people. Almost as many lived outside the walls. Having no palace association, the main Hindu temples clustered at a distance from the city. Brahmans had their own area within the walls, as did religious groups such as Muslims, Jains, and Parsis. Artisans also lived in their own neighborhoods. Lower jatis were located outside the walls, including those of oil pressers, fishers, potters, bricklayers, washers, butchers, fodder dealers, and hired farm workers. The untouchables lived apart from everyone else.

Goods came to the port by sea in the boats of Muslim merchants. They brought the varied products of every part of India. Once they had also brought cargoes from the Middle East and Indonesia. However, Europeans had gradually taken away the overseas trade during the past two centuries.

Social Relations

The Indian state followed an ancient tradition of monarchy in which the ruler represented social order. An ancient text admonished that "a man should first select a king" or else be at risk for any wives or wealth that he might accumulate. A bad king was better than none. Ideally, however, the ruler would heed the advice of priests and scholars to control his impulses for the good of his people.

Although of the warrior varna, the king was at least partly divine and linked to the most important gods. He was particularly close to Shiva, and thus to the creation of the universe, and to Indra, who sat atop Mount Meru at the center of the universe. Charisma and spiritual prowess justified the king's rule, and asceticism symbolized his closeness to Shiva. He mystically embodied the prosperity and fertility of the state, symbolized by his numerous wives and children.

The religious status of the monarch made him the focus of state rituals, and his many wives brought him political alliances. Both were essential to his power in a feudalistic system characterized by local rulers with their own armies. The political process entailed constant competition in which the goal was to weaken actual or potential opponents and then incorporate them into one's own domain.

The king legitimized and empowered selected subordinates with grants of land and titles and with invitations to participate in the highest levels of state worship. Given the symbolic feudalism of the state and the focus on a charismatic king, bureaucracy was weak and the concept of borders undeveloped. Using vague and often impractical legal codes, kings and nobles kept order with harsh and sometimes inconsistent punishments.

Because of their domestic work, most slaves had to come from clean castes. A master could not abandon an aging slave nor beat a slave worse than he would his own wife or younger brother. Some law books permitted slaves to own and inherit property, and manumission was encouraged as a pious act. Some people entered slavery as punishment for certain sexual offenses.

Knowledge and Expression

Sophisticated Hindus contemplated a God that was universal, eternal, and formless. Shiva, Vishnu, and all their avatars were simply manifestations of this ultimate reality. Hindus recognized Four Paths to God. These were Knowledge (realization of one's inner divinity), Work (daily performance of duties), Meditation (psychological activities), and Love (devotion and intimacy). To those with time and resources, release from the cycle of reincarnation and union with God seemed to be within reach.

The caste system expressed deep concern about ritual purity and pollution, including the second birth ceremony for "twice-born" males of the three highest varnas. Bodily processes—such as eating, sex, and bleeding—caused pollution, resulting in spiritual concern about matters such as sharing meals and the frequency of sexual relations. Such concerns accounted for the low status of jatis dedicated to activities such as washing. Pollution also came from life passages, such as birth and death, which therefore required ritual attention. A funeral pyre counteracted the pollution of death.

A major temple, like the minor ones, was a place for worshippers to focus on their personal prayers and meditations. Outside the temple a worshipper removed his sandals and purified himself with ablutions. Then he went through the entrance on the western side and proceeded toward the main shrine under the eastern tower. On this journey through a series of dim chambers, many people asked the blessings of minor deities whose icons they encountered. Finally the worshipper arrived at the main shrine, where the greatest god resided. He gazed at it from outside the sanctuary because only the ritual priests who attended the deity were allowed within. Some people came to ask the god a favor or fulfill a vow, some to receive grace by partaking of food that the priests distributed after offering it to the god. Most simply wished to experience the deity by viewing its image. The worshipper eventually walked around the inner sanctuary, stopping at each cardinal direction to touch hand or forehead to the wall, in order to honor every aspect of the god.

The gateways, towers, and walls of a temple were carved with mythological figures and events. Sculptures of guardian deities stood at thresholds to frighten away demons. Throughout the temple, niches contained images of auspicious symbols such as the lotus and the banyan tree. Temples, rulers, and monastic orders patronized sculpture in stone and bronze. The anonymous artists improved their karma by depicting the gods.

One striking feature of these representations was the multiple limbs and eyes of the gods. These symbolized the fact that the deities had so much to see and do. Another feature was the sensual nature of many images, with gods and humans often naked and in sexual embrace. The association of religion and sex had more than one meaning. On the one hand, climax was compared to the ultimately sought union with Brahman. On the other hand, the truly devout proved their spiritual strength by viewing the sensual images without being distracted from their religious focus.

Medicine, the oldest empirical field of knowledge, used a holistic approach based on exercise and diet. This included the avoidance of meat and the use of honey and garlic to prolong life. Doctors applied herbal cures and performed surgeries that were based on the dissection of corpses. Consonant with the religious attitude toward animals, veterinary medicine was also highly developed. Kings supported hospitals for their horses and elephants and also supported care for cows and other animals.

Scholars pursued the linguistic study of Sanskrit grammar. However, their greatest contributions were in the realm of math: place notation and the concept of zero, the decimal system, geometry, algebra, and trigonometry. Mathematics was applied to astronomical studies.

A Closer Look

Variation in Gender Relations

Northern Indians spoke Indo-European languages that represented an ancient intrusion into the subcontinent from the north and west. They associated themselves with exogamous local patrilineages. Marriage to any close relative was forbidden. Parents ideally arranged marriages between complete strangers, thus keeping the husband closer to his mother and sister than to his wife. The new wife was extremely subordinate to the husband and parents-in-law.

Southern Indians spoke Dravidian languages. They followed the tropical pattern of agriculture, transplanting rice seedlings from nurseries to the main fields. This arduous work, often done in the rain, was assigned to women. Because South Indians preferred cross-cousin marriages, a new wife was likely to be on lifelong intimate terms with the family that she joined and so was much less intimidated (Maloney 1974). Gender roles in general were less polarized than in the north, and women had more freedom of movement.

CONFUCIAN AREA

Examples:

Chinese, Japanese, Korean

The Confucian culture area is named to represent the extensive influence of Chinese ideology, especially the social philosophy of Confucius and his successors. The Area included about one fourth of what is now the People's Republic of China (the western and northern parts of that country belonged to the Tibetan and Steppes Areas). In addition to China, modern countries that represent the Confucian Area are Taiwan, Japan, Korea, and Vietnam.

The Confucian Area depended mainly on the cultivation of wet rice, usually in combination with barley, millet, or wheat. Maize, introduced in the sixteenth century, had established itself in peripheral regions along with potatoes. This was perhaps the only culture area in the world where peasants were explicitly valued rather than held in contempt. Elite ideology placed them on the second rung of the social scale, above artisans and merchants. However, the lot of real life Confucian peasants resembled the experience of their counterparts elsewhere in the world: poverty, exploitation, and oppression (Dunn 1972; Smith 1994).

According to Temple (1998), the Chinese were the first in the world to develop inventions and ideas that included the iron plow, cast iron and steel, the wheelbarrow, the spinning wheel, strong beer (called *sake* in Japan), playing cards, endocrinology, decimals, the compass, the seismograph, paddle-wheel boats, tuned drums, gunpowder and guns. Temple also claims that the Chinese were the first in the Old World to invent the concept of zero, although this is more often attributed to the Indian Area. By 1700 A.D. many Chinese inventions had spread throughout the Confucian Area and to other parts of the world. This chapter emphasizes a few important items that continued to distinguish the Confucian Area from the West (e.g., porcelain) or from its neighbors (e.g., printing).

Confucian social relations were characterized by close attention to hierarchy in personal as well as political relationships. An emphasis on tight emotional control in social interactions is undoubtedly the basis for Western stereotypes about the so-called inscrutability of East Asians. Government was based on extensive and highly organized bureaucracy associated with the unique trait of qualification by examination.

The great tradition of the Confucian Area was woven from two main strands. One was Confucianism (more accurately, neo-Confucianism), which emerged from centuries of elaboration on the master's philosophy. It emphasized rules of social order and proper ceremonial behavior, including ritual veneration of ancestors. To peasants this usually meant literal worship of ancestral souls. Household spirits of nonhuman origin also figured prominently in peasant life.

The other main strand of the great tradition was Buddhism. The Mahayana form of Buddhism conceived of God as a universal being or force that is unpersonified and neuter. The human soul underwent a series of reincarnations, advancing as a reward for moral behavior. According to the Law of Karma, actions in every lifetime affected the person's destiny. The ultimate goal was release from the cycle of reincarnation and eternal union with the universal entity. Belief in the unity of life devalued the killing of any animal, and so vegetarianism was preferred. The Buddhist tradition allowed for belief in many gods, or at least many different manifestations of the one God.

Religious ideas in the Area also included nature-oriented mysticism (e.g., Taoism in China, Shinto in Japan). Religious practices included self-improvement through meditation and proper breathing (e.g., Taoism in China, Zen Buddhism in Japan). Such disciplines were intertwined with highly developed forms of martial arts that used both bare hands and weapons.

The tricksters of the Confucian Area differed from the rest of the Central Zone in taking animal forms. Those of Japan and Korea, the fox and the tiger, were greedy and vengeful like tricksters in other parts of the world. In contrast, Monkey (or the Monkey King) of China was humanlike in form and behavior. He was also benevolent and taught spiritual lessons. However, unlike other tricksters inside and outside the Central Zone, he tended to be obedient to secular authority and was chastened in his attempt to challenge the highest religious authority. Only Monkey will be described in this section.

Key features:

- ▶ Printing
- ▶ Porcelain ceramics
- ▶ Hierarchy in personal relationships
- ▶ Extensive bureaucracy
- ▶ Emphasis on emotional control
- ▶ Confucian philosophy
- ▶ Mahayana Buddhism
- ▶ Ancestor veneration
- ▶ Household spirits

Modal Patterns in Confucian Peasant Culture

Material Culture

When not working in the rice fields a woman might spend a great deal of time in a small room of her house devoted to silkworms. There she fed the larvae with mulberry leaves and tended their other needs. After they had spun their cocoons, she chose some to breed the next generation and dropped the rest into boiling water. Some people killed them by exposing them to the sun. A single cocoon could provide up to 500 yards of silk to be sold at market or to the local elite.

Other families engaged in different enterprises for profit. Some specialized in certain crops, such as tobacco, tea, or the mulberry bushes that provided food for silkworms. Some processed wine, vegetable oils, sugar, tea, or tobacco. Some manufactured silk or cotton cloth, leather products, or iron utensils. Women were important in most of these home industries as well as in the fields. Some families prospered from them.

Peasants traded some of their products with each other, but they also supplied the elite. This meant contacts with the local gentry as well as many trips to markets. Through the market systems, peasants received and accepted influences from other parts of the country. Contacts with the elite impressed them with social and ritual values that they followed to the best of their economic ability.

Seating for a meal precisely reflected the hierarchy in the family. People often ate beans with their rice and, when fortunate, obtained some protein from a few bits of fish. Many meals included fresh or pickled vegetables, and vegetable oils provided essential fats. Warm wine usually accompanied the meal. A peasant family looked forward to eating meat at the next festival, a time when people were supposed to eat their fill of special foods.

After the meal a man might relax by smoking tobacco in his water pipe. Or he might go to the teahouse to socialize. There he could choose from several varieties of tea, some of them known throughout the country. He might also patronize an establishment that served strong beer. This drink was made from ground, partially cooked wheat grains that had been allowed to go moldy. Addition of this material to grain cooking in water produced a drink with two or three times the alcoholic content of ordinary beer.

Social Relations

Both bridewealth and dowry validated marriage in all social classes. Dowry was linked to the status of wives, as in India. As long as the couple remained in the patrilocal extended family, the dowry was supposed to be under the girl's control. It was merged with her husband's resources after he received his inheritance. Most families used bridewealth to finance the marriage ceremonies and gave the balance to the bride. Substantial dowry encouraged an elite family to accept a bride of lower status. The offer of a powerful social or political alliance could bring high bridewealth.

The poor sometimes minimized dowry and used bridewealth to obtain wives for their sons. Proper marriage was impossible without dowry, and very poor women sometimes became commodities. People used the language of gifts and reciprocity to speak of marriage exchanges, but market idiom applied to the acquisition of maids and concubines.

The lives of Confucian women were subject to the Three Obediences: to father, husband, and son. Just as men were subservient to their rulers, women were subservient to men. Age offered improved status to women, including the veneration of all elderly people as symbols of wisdom. Widows rarely remarried because of continuing obligation to the family of the deceased husband and because they were unwanted by other men. Widowhood therefore meant that the woman would never again be under the control of a husband. Despite the principle of obedience to her son, a woman in reality could exercise family power when she was the senior survivor.

Hierarchy in personal relationships was a major theme of Confucian society. The Seven Obligations were those of official to emperor, son to father, wife to husband, younger brother to older brother, younger person to older person, host to guest, and friend to friend. Even the most intimate friendship entailed superior and subordinate roles. There were no concepts of freedom and equality, so subordinates in all relationships complied without any damage to ego. Hierarchy gave people a sense of order, and they were uncomfortable without it.

The concept of *face* referred to each individual's position in a formal structure of rights and duties. An individual lost face by failing to discharge social obligations. A personal embarrassment did not necessarily cause a loss of face, but a loss of face was always embarrassing or worse. The ideal of harmony required that social relationships proceed smoothly, and courteous lies were a legitimate way to preserve harmony. These social ideals applied only to the inner world of established relationships, so outsiders could be treated rudely. Deceit was a legitimate way to protect oneself and one's family from outsiders.

Knowledge and Expression

Household spirits were of particular importance to peasants. They inhabited every part of a house. One, often associated with the kitchen, was predominant. Others included fertility and childbirth spirits, dwelling in the more private parts of the house, and a guardian who stayed outside but within the walled compound. These spirits required ritual attention such as regular food offerings.

To peasants one man's ancestor was another man's ghost; souls of outsiders could be dangerous. People who left no descendants to venerate them were ghosts to everyone. The little traditions made use of various forms of magic, including numerous methods of divination. Shamans, many of them women, were prominent and often operated by means of spirit possession.

Conventional religion supported male dominance of women. Confucianism and Taoism portrayed women as inclined to do evil. Moreover, a woman could not achieve the status of venerated ancestor except through her affiliation with a man. Buddhism was perhaps less harsh, but it also endorsed the idea of moral inferiority. A woman's only hope for spiritual advancement was to be reincarnated as a man. Women were more prominent in domestic and community ritual. They propitiated the household spirits or ancestors, and some of them became shamans. Beyond ordinary society, many secret religious movements espoused gender equality.

Confucianism, primarily a system of social philosophy and ritual, was dominant because of its association with government. Developed by scholars, Confucian ethical principles revolved around family and social order. They envisioned a society governed by a bureaucracy of virtuous educated men and headed by an emperor who ruled with a mandate from Heaven. Heaven was conceived by some as an abstraction, but others interpreted it as a celestial counterpart of the ruler. Confucianism interpreted many aspects of the world in terms of balance between *yin* and *yang*, the female and male principles.

Buddhism and Taoism offered more truly religious ideas with broader appeal. However, their priesthoods were uncentralized and materially poor, and they did not extensively sponsor charity or education. Buddhism held that life is suffering, which can only be ended by renunciation of worldly desires. It perpetuated the Hindu ideas of reincarnation and ultimate release but rejected the caste system. In the Mahayana form of Buddhism, the Buddha was a god who responded to the prayers of believers. Additional comfort and guidance were provided by bodhisattvas. These were individuals who had reached the stage of enlightenment where release from the cycle of reincarnation was possible but who chose to remain distinct entities in order to help suffering humans.

Taoism was a nature-oriented mysticism that developed through a series of revelations and eventually deified its founder as the incarnation of a heavenly lord. It taught that divinity resides within every individual and can be cultivated by proper meditation, breathing, and diet. Perhaps its most influential idea was the goal of a long and happy life in this world. Buddhism and Taoism offered monastic life, either permanent or temporary.

The trickster, Monkey, was a humorous prankster with a serious side. Many of his adventures took place during an epic journey with several companions to obtain religious scriptures for the imperial government. He used his cunning and verbal skills to protect his companions, as on the occasion when they entered the realm of a king who killed Buddhist monks. To save his monk companion, Monkey penetrated the royal court during the night and shaved the heads of all the nobles in the manner of monks. In the confusion the trickster and his friends escaped. In a land plagued by drought Monkey used his eloquence to persuade the king that his own misbehavior had elicited punishment from Heaven. Monkey's tractability traced to an experience with Buddha, to whom he confided his desire to rule the universe. Buddha told the trickster that his wish would be granted if he could jump to the end of the universe. Monkey did so and wrote his name there as proof of his feat. When he returned, Buddha held out his hand and showed Monkey the name he had written.

A Taoist altar (China).

Modal Patterns in Confucian Elite Culture

Material Culture

Inside its moat and wall, the city was a diversified place. Its landmarks included the magistrate's office, the military barracks, the examination hall, and the drum and bell tower. Scattered throughout the city were Confucian temples and temples for the city god, most of them providing open spaces for gatherings of the communities they represented. People from every segment of the city came together in the marketplaces. Also ubiquitous were restaurants, theaters, and the lodges of ethnic associations. Separate neighborhoods harbored businesses, including numerous pawnshops, the small houses of the poor, and the fine homes of elite families.

Gleaming lacquer surrounded people in an affluent household. A varnish derived from the sap of a tree, lacquer was used to coat wood, bamboo, and cloth. It conferred enormous strength and durability on any object, resisting acids, alkalis, and heat. Those who could afford it owned lacquered furniture, screens, pillows, and boxes. Coated vessels worked as well as bronze for cooking, and lacquered utensils constituted the standard dinner service for the wealthy. Artisans also treated items of weaponry such as bows, shields, and scabbards. Often they inlaid the lacquer with gold, silver, or tortoiseshell. The monetary value of lacquerware exceeded that of bronzes, and the emperor often rewarded his officials with lacquered objects. Aside from the coating, many wooden objects in elite households represented the finest craftsmanship. Woodworkers produced artifacts with interlocking pieces, avoiding glue and nails wherever possible to produce a more esthetic effect.

Porcelain also represented wealth and good taste. The white translucent pottery was shaped into graceful curves and decorated with varied designs. Using a unique Chinese clay, the artisans fired the vessels at a very high temperature. The resulting surface glaze created an object of great beauty that also prevented any leakage. Porcelain manufacturers profited from the elite market in their own part of the world and also from the frantic demand emanating from Europe.

In such beautiful surroundings many a scholar or tasteful merchant settled down to enjoy a book. Printers used carved woodblocks, usually with one page on each side, to create the sequential pages for a bound volume (these had replaced scrolls long ago). A small private printer usually kept the blocks for a few works over a long period of time, sometimes bequeathing them to his heirs. The small printer usually produced a few dozen copies of a book at a time, avoiding risky expenditures on paper and the possible destruction of inventory by

A courtyard in the Forbidden City, home and headquarters of the Chinese emperor and government (Beijing, China).

worms. However, other printers made a larger business of it. One man employed up to twenty carvers to produce a hundred thousand printing blocks representing six hundred titles. The government published thousands of volumes of several editions of the imperial encyclopedia.

Social Relations

An elite wife was primarily a vessel for paternity, and legal measures to reinforce womanly virtues fell most heavily on royalty and the upper classes. Elite men took concubines for a number of reasons, including romantic love and social status. Some men bought and sold them almost as a sport. Sex was somewhat problematic, at least for a younger man, because it could sap his yang, the vital force of males. A safer recreation was gambling, common among all social classes.

The ruler was considered at least semidivine and he reigned with the approval of Heaven. Application of Confucian ideals began with loyalty to the emperor as a filial duty. Symbolic assertion of authority was essential because the larger states and empires had less direct control than they claimed. In the actual process of governing, monarchs and their officials tended to give way to bureaucrats who shared authority and made group decisions. These professional bureaucrats did most of work and held much of the real power. This shared authority gave rise to hostility among various factions.

According to Confucian philosophy, education demonstrated that a man was virtuous and entitled to govern other people. Bureaucrats qualified for their positions through formal examinations in subjects such as history, philosophy, and art. As a result of Confucian ideals, scholars received great respect. Otherwise, the ideal stratification of society was based largely on productivity. Below the warrior rulers, peasant farmers ranked high because they were primary producers. Artisans, as secondary producers, came next. Merchants were at the bottom because they were considered parasitic. In the real world most peasants remained poor and powerless while merchants increased in wealth and power.

Chinese slavery was unique in its concentration on children under ten years of age, most of them sold by poverty-stricken parents. Although they performed menial household chores, male slaves were rigidly excluded from the house itself. Their status as slaves was unchangeable. Females worked inside the house and were subject to drastic changes, sometimes ending up as concubines or even wives.

Knowledge and Expression

The Buddha and his successors elaborated on the knowledge and behavior that led to salvation. These teachings have been encapsulated in the Four Noble Truths, which say that life is full of sorrow, that sorrow arises from self-ish desires, that the elimination of desire eliminates sorrow, and that this can be achieved by following the Eightfold Path. The Eightfold Path prescribes correctness in attitude, speech, behavior, occupation, effort, perception, consciousness (self-examination), and concentration (meditation). Through these practices and disciplines a person can see through the illusions of this world. Eventually one may break the cycle of reincarnation and achieve a perfect state called nirvana.

The Mahayana school of Buddhism emphasized social morality over austere individualism. A person could live the right kind of life by expressing faith, doing good works, and showing compassion toward others. Mahayana offered help to seekers of Enlightenment in the form of ritual, numerous benevolent manifestations of the Buddha, and a complex metaphysics with many heavens and hells. It gave hope of final rebirth in a paradise ruled by a radiant Buddha.

The *bodhisattva* was the central ideal of Mahayana Buddhism. The term has two meanings, but both revolved around spiritual altruism. Broadly, a bodhisattva is a being who strives for enlightenment in order to benefit others rather than himself. More specifically it is a being who is on the verge of nirvana, but foregoes that reward to continue offering help and spiritual power to those who are suffering. Though short of nirvana, the bodhisattva has overcome all personal suffering.

Secluded residence in a monastery facilitated the pursuit of enlightenment by monks and nuns. The monastery also served as a temple for worship by lay people. Some monasteries were open to the general public, but many served a particular clientele.

While many people pursued personal salvation, the emperor maintained harmony among the worlds of nature, humanity, and the supernatural. At various times of year he made sacrifices to Heaven, Earth, the Land and Harvests, and the imperial ancestors. These major ceremonies required ritual bathing and sexual abstinence. The emperor had to kneel and prostrate himself and sacrifice animals without blemish, including oxen, sheep, and pigs. Correct performance of all ritual acts was essential. Only government officials participated in the ceremonies, excluding the priests of any religion. Bureaucrats in lower levels of the hierarchy performed similar rites for local gods.

Literacy and printing encouraged literary creation. Many people, especially in the cities, enjoyed poetry and novels. However, calligraphy (hand painting of language characters) was preserved as an art. Some painters continued traditional themes such as landscapes while others catered to a merchant clientele with subjects such as contemporary urban scenes. Performing arts included music, theater, and puppet shows. Itinerant troupes created a bond between the performing arts of city and village, elite and commoners.

A character in the Chinese opera, exemplifying the elaboration of performing arts in the Confucian Area (Hong Kong).

A Closer Look

Two Regions of China

Two major Regions within China can be recognized in the work of Naquin and Rawsky (1987). The North China Region was located between the Manchurian border in the north and the Yangtze River Valley in the south. A variety of peoples were attracted to the Region around 1700 A.D. because it contained the imperial capital, Beijing. Most notable among these were the Manchu, a Tungusic people from Manchuria, who had recently conquered China and established the Ching (Qing) dynasty. Despite diversity, the great majority of North China inhabitants belonged to the Han ethnic group. Each minority was small in numbers, so there was less violence between groups than in the South.

Other than Beijing, North China displayed little urbanization. Farmers lived in small nucleated villages. Because of the dry and temperate climate, they concen-trated on crops such as millet, barley, and wheat. Women made these grains into noodles, gruels, or breads. They added fresh vegetables to the diet on a seasonal basis. Floods and droughts made the harvest unpredictable. As a result, hired labor was much more common than tenancy. Landowning families brought in help to deal with abundant harvests and kept all of their meager production during times of scarcity.

The South China Region included the lower and middle reaches of the Yangtze River Valley and extended south to the Vietnamese border. It also included the island of Taiwan. Among the many prominent cities, commercial centers were as important as administrative ones. People joined a variety of voluntary associations that ranged from occupational guilds to secret societies. The long coastline encouraged overseas trade and emigration.

South China was a Region of many conflicts. Ethnic diversity was a factor almost everywhere. In the cities workers struggled with their employers for better conditions. In the countryside powerful lineages feuded with one another. They made extensive use of feng shui in aligning graves in order to enlist powerful ancestors in the conflicts. Finally, the Region contained several factions that sporadically resisted the central government.

Korea

Korea has been called the "most Confucian" of countries. The culture has in some instances applied the social principles of Confucianism with an intensity that surpassed that of the philosophy's Chinese homeland. Male superiority and aloofness tended to isolate a man from his own wife as well as other women. Ancestor veneration was elaborated to the point that death almost seemed more important than life (Osgood 1951). One reason for this may be that Buddhism did not achieve the same consistent importance that it did in other parts of the Area.

Despite this dedication to Confucianism, the Koreans have sometimes been called "the Italians of the Far East," referring to a greater display of emotional expression in personal life than in other Confucian countries. This was manifested publicly in the intensity of singing, dancing, and drinking. This interpretive theme might also apply to the highly spiced national cuisine and to a virtual national pastime involving two teams throwing rocks at each other (Osgood 1951).

Finally, the cultural history of Korea provides a balancing perspective on the political conflict that has characterized the country for the last half century. While formidable defensive fighters, Koreans have not shown the same enthusiasm for conquest as many of their neighbors (as well as other countries around the world). Furthermore, "It is a singular fact that a thousand years of national unity passed unblemished by civil wars" (Osgood 1951:337).

Japan

The Japanese corporate family *(ie)* was essentially bilateral. The mode of succession to the headship was not important and could be affected by individual desires and pragmatic considerations. A male head was preferred, but a female was possible. Large houses granted a proportion of the inheritance to nonsuccessors, who started branch houses. The branches were subordinate to the main house and provided services when asked. Branches participated in ancestor worship at the main house, which was directed toward generalized house ancestors with little regard for genealogy.

The Japanese monarch, though descended from a god, was purely a figurehead. A military leader, the shogun, was the real head of government. The Japanese elite resisted the Confucian ideal of advancement by education because of their firmly entrenched emphasis on privilege by birth.

Although all the major religions of China came to Japan, indigenous Shinto beliefs persisted. This animistic system included nature spirits, clan gods, and some powerful deities such as the sun goddess who gave birth to the first emperor. People honored them with offerings, prayers, and festivals. Shinto also stressed ritual purity.

Japan developed a distinctive form of Buddhism in Zen, which emphasized meditation and perception. The quintessential ritual was the tea ceremony, quiet, precise, and beautiful. The tea ceremony was associated with the samurai, who had a profound effect on Japanese ideology. They were medieval warriors who subscribed to a strict code of behavior that emphasized courage, stoicism, and loyalty. By the year 1700 they had become the mainstay of the government bureaucracy. In modern Japan the mantle of the samurai has been claimed by groups as diverse as police, gangsters, and baseball players.

Although women were held to be inferior for social reasons, the division of labor in household and folk religion was flexible. Either men or women could propitiate the household spirits and ancestors or become shamans (Kendall 1985).

The Vietnamese and the Vietnam War

In terms of geography and politics the modern country of Vietnam is usually associated with Southeast Asia. Culturally, it is a mixture of Southeast Asian and Confucian traits. The Confucian traits were imposed during a long period of Chinese military and political domination. They are strongest in the north and fade toward the south.

The connection with the Confucian Area provides important perspectives on the role of Vietnam in recent history in relation to its neighbors and to the United States. The assimilation of Vietnam to Chinese culture alienated the Vietnamese from their Southeast Asian neighbors. However, since the assimilation was the result of repressive imperial rule, it did not result in warm relations with China.

Had American policymakers considered this background carefully, the Vietnam War might have been avoided. The domino theory provided a rationale for the U.S. involvement in the war: if Vietnam went Communist, then so would all the other nations of Southeast Asia. "Red China" would rule that whole part of the world through the Vietnamese. However, as we might have predicted from the cultural gap between them, Southeast Asians vigorously resisted Vietnamese hegemony. Also not surprising, considering the historic tension between them, Vietnam and China had a falling-out as soon as the American threat was withdrawn. Contrary to the domino theory, only the countries originally involved in the war—Vietnam, Laos, and Cambodia—became Communist. And the Vietnamese were soon at war with the Communist, but Southeast Asian, Cambodians.

TIBETAN AREA

The Tibetan Area largely coincided with what is now the country of Tibet, which became politically integrated in the eighteenth century under Chinese influence (Carrasco 1959). Bhutan may be included in the Culture Area, as well as sections of some neighboring countries, for example, Nepal (Samuel 1993). Lhasa is now famous as the capital of Tibet, but in 1700 it was the center of just one (albeit the largest) of numerous states in the Tibetan Area.

Tibetans created agricultural states in the highest mountains in the world, the Himalayas. In this they were helped by the incorporation of nomadic herders into the economy of the state. The herders survived in that environment because they had the yak, a local species of cattle *(Bos grunniens)* well adapted to the high, cold mountains. They also had a distinctive breed of sheep. The yak was the key animal but, as in so many other places, the sheep had the greatest economic significance. Tibetan herders ate more meat than most other pastoralists.

Information about local social organization pertains mostly to feudal estates. These were based on land osten-

The Himalayan Mountains, tallest in the world, in central Tibet.

Modal Patterns in Tibetan Peasant Culture

Material Culture

The valley of a small river huddled beneath towering, jagged mountains. From the lower slopes a person could see large farmhouses scattered across the valley. Each one harbored an extended corporate family with rights to the land around it. Such peasants were known as taxpayers because they held the land from the government, owing services and a share of their crops in return. Around a farmhouse clustered the cottages of subordinate peasants, including servants, craftsmen, herders, and hired farmworkers who had little or no land of their own. This establishment and neighboring ones formed an estate under the direct control of an elite group. Aristocratic families held some estates while Buddhist monasteries managed others.

In most of the agricultural fields stalks of barley waved in the wind, impervious to the altitude and cold. Farmers also cultivated wheat, peas, and radishes. Terraced lower slopes extended their holdings, but the irregular rainfall made irrigation essential. The farmers built dams across mountain streams and guided the water to their fields with long canals and conduits. People fertilized the soil with cattle manure where that was possible, but the first priority for the dung was its use as fuel. The alternative fertilizer was human excrement mixed with ashes and earth. Good land was kept in almost continuous use, but poorer plots were fallowed as often as every other year. In addition to being sources of fertilizer and fuel, cattle pulled the plows, carried loads, and provided meat, milk, and hides.

On the slopes and plateaus above the valley, nomadic herders used land that could not be farmed. Like the farmers, the pastoralists were associated with

sibly granted by the central government to nobles and Buddhist monasteries. Prosperous peasants ran farms on these estates. They apparently formed communities among themselves, but little is known about how those communities were organized.

The Tibetan Area is famous for an unusual incidence of polyandry, the marriage of one woman to several men. Researchers are at odds as to just how common and stable these unions were. Tibetan farmers devalued their women in much the same manner as elsewhere in the Central Zone but accorded them significantly more freedom of action than in the other Areas. The herders held women in higher regard than the farmers did.

A distinctive form of Buddhism (Lamaism) prevailed in the Tibetan Area. It combined Tantric Buddhism (an offshoot of Mahayana) with indigenous beliefs about spirits and shamans. Much of Tibetan art represented the syncretic relationship between Buddhism and shamanism.

The Tibetan trickster could change his shape, but often fitted into society as if he were fully human. His voracious sexual appetite made him more similar to the archetypal trickster of the world than was true for comparable figures elsewhere in the Central Zone. He was especially known for his association with excrement, but in a way that was typical of the Central Zone. By treating excrement as a powerful and respected object, he called into question the rigid categories that people impose on the world (Christen 1998). This is a version of the cognitive enlightenment offered by most Central Zone tricksters.

Key features:

- ▶ Domestic yak
- ▶ Feudal estates
- ▶ Polyandry
- ▶ Lamaist Buddhism

Yaks, the distinctive domestic animal of the Tibetan Area, harnessed to a plow.

estates. The estate owned the lands of nomads and had rights to their labor, but the nomads owned their own animals and managed them as they saw fit.

The nomad herds included many yaks with shaggy black coats, the males up to five feet high at the shoulder. Long slender horns curved away from their low-slung heads. The yaks were agile on the slopes and strong in the snow. One way to clear a blocked pass was to run the yaks back and forth until enough snow had been removed for other animals and humans to go through. The herders referred to their yaks as "wealth." More numerous were the "high-pasture" sheep. Heavy-bodied and long-legged, their coarse wool did not reach their heads or limbs. Able to bear thirty pounds over long distances, the sheep helped the yaks carry human goods from camp to camp. The herders used both animals for meat, hides, and hair. They tapped the blood of the yaks and made their milk into butter, cheese, and yogurt. The few horses were prestige animals, used mainly for warfare. As the seasons changed, the herders took their animals up and down the mountains to keep them in pasture. When in the lower altitudes, they renewed a regular subsistence trade with the farmers.

Social Relations

Although theoretically tenants, taxpaying peasants could in fact transmit their land freely to male heirs. When the inheritance was passed on before the death of the senior male, the family elders could select any of their children to care for them in old age, but a daughter was the most popular choice. The family, tightly knit and sharing within, was adamantly independent of others. Continuity of family and household were the greatest concerns, and ties to patrilineal descent groups were weak.

Sometimes several brothers married the same women in order to avoid splitting up their inheritance. People expressed great admiration for a woman who could keep several husbands content. Junior brothers who were not kept in the family by polyandry could join a Buddhist monastery or seek adoption into another family. Dependent peasants obtained some land from taxpayers or held none at all; having little property and no reason for polyandry, they lived in nuclear families created by informal unions.

Farmers spoke demeaningly of women, perhaps because they brought small dowries, but did little to restrict their behavior. Traditional values emphasized independence of individuals as well as families. Women had fewer opportunities than men but exercised considerable freedom in their own spheres of activity. Herders accorded women higher status. Among them, dowry was substantial, controlled by the woman, and returned in case of divorce.

Both farmers and pastoralists had considerable freedom as long as they fulfilled their obligations to the lord of the estate. Some hired temporary replacements to do their work. Thus relieved of their responsibilities, people left the estate to go visiting, trading, or on religious pilgrimages.

Knowledge and Expression

A farm family spent a great deal of time attending to their relationships with supernatural beings. First there were the spirits of the household, including the male spirit associated with the men and the defense of the house. His shrine rested on the roof where incense could be burned. A shrine inside the house honored the female spirit who looked after the well-being of the family, especially the women and girls. The spirit of the hearth was easily upset by polluting events, such as the overflow of a cooking pot. Located outside the home, the storehouse spirit caused people less anxiety.

Beyond the house a variety of malevolent spirits lurked in various places. Less hostile, the spirits of the soil and the waters could be punitive when their realms were disturbed. Greater in power, the gods of the mountains could be helpful. However, having arisen from the souls of evil kings, they were capricious and dangerous. All of these beings had been partly tamed by the Buddhist gods and monks, but it was still wise to maintain a good relationship with them.

People used two main rituals to appease the supernaturals and to ask their favor. One was to build cairns of stones near their abodes, especially in the passes high in the mountains. Everyone who passed added a stone and recited a bit of religious text. Some considered the cairns homes to honor the supernaturals while others thought they might be prisons to control them. The other main ritual involved the burning of incense, especially juniper, and a recitation of the names of local gods and spirits. Sometimes the worshippers planted a prayer flag to invoke Buddhist protection.

Offense against spirits or gods caused most misfortunes. To apply ritual remedies, people had to know which supernatural had been offended and how. When this was not obvious, they consulted a medium, who revealed the answer while possessed. Some mediums, while possessed, could contact other spirits that helped them to heal people.

Buddhism had given people the tantric gods as the ultimate recourse. These gods arose through the meditation of enlightened individuals, expressing spiritual potentials that existed within human beings and in the universe as a whole. Some had become externalized and available for appeal from any human being. The tantric gods were completely benevolent. People were also dimly aware of the gods in the Buddhist heavens, but these played no role in everyday religious observance.

People enjoyed the bawdy tales of the trickster, Agu Tomba, which almost always involved sex. In addition to satisfying his own sexual appetite, Agu Tomba often helped others attain satisfaction. When he encountered a farmer whose cursed fields produced only penises, the trickster gathered them up and delivered them to a Buddhist convent. Although the nuns were forbidden sex with men, there was no rule against intercourse with a disembodied penis. While extolling sexual satisfaction, the story of the nuns also ridiculed the religious establishment.

Agu Tomba delighted in undermining political authority. In the following tale he used his favorite tool, excrement, to achieve that purpose. While acting as secretary to a king, the trickster incurred the punishment of spending a freezing night on the palace roof without any clothes. When he awoke to find that his bowel movement had frozen, he covered it with white lime from the roof, wrote on it, and dropped it through a skylight onto the lap of the king. The illiterate king was forced to summon his secretary from the roof to interpret the object. Warmed and fed, Agu Tomba told the ruler that the object was a gift from the gods and that he should eat some of it to gain the fullest benefits.

Modal Patterns in Tibetan Elite Culture

Material Culture

Cities were few in the mountains, and an ordinary one contained perhaps five to ten thousand people, far short of the twenty thousand or more that populated the fabulous Lhasa. Any city included market stalls, artisan shops, and the homes of aristocrats and merchants. One or more offices harbored a city magistrate and perhaps other government officials. Foreign minorities occupied several neighborhoods.

Merchants and foreigners represented the fact that many cities grew along trade routes, to send and receive or

Central part of the city of Lhasa, current capital of Tibet and, in traditional times, the capital of the largest of the independent states of the Tibetan Area.

to sustain the caravans that struggled through the mountains. The caravans carried necessities from one small, isolated valley to another. They also brought luxuries from faraway places such as China and India, along with continuing cultural influences from those civilizations.

Many urban structures reminded people of the Buddhist religion at the heart of Tibetan society. Most prominently, a temple stood near the urban center. A large monastery was located outside the city. Isolation was preferable for a place of meditation; nevertheless, because a great monastery required considerable financial support to build and maintain, proximity to nobles and merchants was vital. In some cities the presence of a great lama's palace completed the religious presence.

Palace of the Dalai Lama, the reincarnate monk who was the supreme religious figure of traditional Tibet and the head of the Lhasa state.

Social Relations

The nobility held hereditary family estates from the government in much the same manner as the taxpaying peasants were obligated for their land; however, the service owed by the nobles was the fulfillment of government offices. Formal training, short terms, and promotion by seniority characterized these offices. There was no hereditary connection between particular offices and particular families; each individual served in a series of different offices during his lifetime. In most cases he was part of a team that held joint responsibility for the office. Hierarchical authority was diluted somewhat by a tendency to diffuse power at each level.

The same bureaucratic responsibilities rested on monk officials from the Buddhist monasteries. Having arisen from the ranks of ordinary monks, these officials differed from the aristocracy in possessing no personal estates. Nevertheless, they had the landed power of the monastic estates behind them. The largest states and some of the smaller ones were headed by such religious figures. In theory they had absolute power over all lands and people. However, this image was really just a symbol of the collective and theocratic nature of the state.

The ruling class was the top layer of Tibetan stratification; below them were the taxpaying peasants and then the dependent peasants. Lower still were traders, shopkeepers, and artisans. They were considered to be outside of "normal" society, perhaps because many of them were foreigners. At the bottom were endogamous castes of smiths, ferrymen, fishers, and butchers. Perhaps the last two were accorded low status because they violated the Buddhist ideal of not taking life.

Knowledge and Expression

Tantric Buddhism, derived from India, emphasized sacramental action. Merit could be accumulated through the repetition of verbal formulas or rote prayers *(mantras)*. The emphasis on repetition was translated into mechanical means. Physical movement of a printed mantra was regarded as sufficient to gain merit. Hence the proliferation of prayer cylinders, flags, and barrels. Cylinders were turned by hand while flags fluttered in the wind, and barrels were turned by water.

Large prayer "wheels" in a monastery.

Man with a prayer "wheel," actually a cylinder, a mechanical means for repeating a prayer.

Sacramental action included *mudras*, special gestures and postures used to communicate with deities, most of which originated in the pre-Buddhist religion. Each spirit required its own particular mudras. The complexity of Tibetan rituals, and the reluctance to make them general knowledge, made spiritual teachers *(gurus)* a necessity.

Buddhist religious practice centered in the monasteries inhabited by celibate monks. The most important monks were lamas, religious teachers. The highest lamas were reincarnations of previous great lamas, manifestations of deities, or both. The most important application of this doctrine was to the selection of the Dalai Lama and Panchen Lama of the Lhasa state. They (and others like them) inherited property from their predecessors that had accumulated for centuries, making them extremely wealthy. Often discovered as children, reincarnate lamas underwent thorough training in secluded circumstances, and some died young. Thus the spiritual status that provided the greatest lamas with their authority also limited their opportunities to exercise that authority.

Buddhists accepted the deities and shamanic practices that had preceded their doctrine. Temples were adorned by shamanic symbols such as the divine arrow, the magic mirror, and fine rock crystal. The theatrical costumes used in Buddhist dances were based on the shaman's clothing, and priests wore similar attire when they became oracles through possession by shamanic deities. The gown was trimmed with fur, bone, and feathers and bore the symbols of the sun, moon, and cosmic tree. Monks even addressed

A young Buddhist monk in Lhasa.

the nature gods in some of their ceremonies, although they threatened as well as appeased them. Some monks were mediums who served as oracles when possessed by gods. Religious and governmental authorities regularly consulted them.

Acceptance of Buddhism confronted Tibetan pastoralists with unusual problems. The doctrine of respect for all life forbade killing, but the Tibetans consumed a great deal of meat from their herds and supplemented their food supply with hunting. Communities or tribes paid priests to accompany them if they could afford to do so, and many elderly individuals took to the religious life in order to make amends for these sinful deeds. Women were not ritually degraded because they took only milk from the animals, not meat or blood, thus doing no violence.

STEPPE AREA

Examples:
Mongol, Khazak, Uighur

Along the northern frontier of the Central Zone the treeless plains (steppes) of central Eurasia extended from the Black Sea to the Pacific Ocean. In modern terms the Zone encompassed Inner and Outer Mongolia and the Islamic republics of the former Soviet Union. Many peoples came and went on the Steppes over thousands of years, but the predominant ethnic groups by the eighteenth century were Mongols and speakers of Turkic languages (Barfield 1993).

The Area is unique in that it was inhabited only by pastoral nomads. The thick soil resisted traditional farming implements, and the severe winter and low rainfall made any cultivation unprofitable (Barfield 1993). The Steppe Area people differed from other nomads in several ways. They placed unusually high symbolic value on their sheep (Khazanov 1994) while idealizing the possession of multiple species for economic purposes (Barfield 1993). They made multiple use of each species, including the consumption of more meat than most other pastoralists (Khazanov 1994). On their horses Steppe men formed armies that conquered civilizations in China and Europe. Elaborate shamanic traditions persisted when Steppe societies formed states, not only in rural areas but in the royal courts.

Key features:

► All nomadic pastoralists
► Mounted warfare
► Conquest of civilizations
► Sheep symbolism
► Persistence of shamanism

Modal Patterns in Steppe Culture

Material Culture

In an environment that ranged from grassland to scrub and semidesert, herds of domestic animals sustained human life. People tried to maintain sheep, goats, horses, cattle, and camels. All species were milked, and each was used for other purposes. Sheep were most important for subsistence, followed by goats. Horses provided transport for peaceful travel and the basis for mounted warfare. Camels were most useful in the driest parts of the Steppes while the usefulness of cattle was limited because they were poorly suited to being driven long distances. People had to make lengthy movements to find sufficient pasturage for the animals at all times of year.

In the winter camp a family lived in a circular tent with a domed or conical top, covered with felt made from

Girls representing the Uighurs, one of the Turkic-speaking ethnic groups of the Steppe Area (western China).

A yurt, the typical felt-covered dwelling of the Steppe nomads (Mongol culture).

sheep's wool. Around them were hundreds of other tents because people had aggregated in a southerly location that offered water and good fodder. The site, usually a valley or flood plain, also provided some shelter.

When the spring rains came, people dispersed in smaller bands to take advantage of seasonal pools and blooming grasslands. They carried their tents with them after removing the felt mats and collapsing the wooden lattice framework. In the spring camps the sheep gave birth, and people welcomed the restoration of fresh milk to the diet.

With the advent of summer the herders spread out further and settled in camps that contained no more than a dozen dwellings each. When they erected their tents, people covered them with reed mats so that the breezes

A Mongol mother and daughter.

would cool them. During summer women spent a great deal of time processing milk. They fermented mare's milk into an alcoholic drink, and they mixed the milk of other species to form the basis for butter, cheese, and yogurt.

Fall was the time to shear sheep and for women to turn wool into essential products. They used most of it to make felt for the tents, but they also made cloaks, boots, and saddle blankets from the fleece of lambs. Men calculated the probable survival of their animals during the coming winter and made decisions about selling them to outsiders or slaughtering them. Smoked meat could be preserved for the winter.

When their pastoral responsibilities were satisfied, men turned their attention to raiding sedentary people along the margins of the steppes. Fall was a good season for raiding because the horses were strong and the farmers had just completed their harvests. These raids made a significant contribution to nomad subsistence.

A Mongol man riding a horse, the key animal of the nomadic culture of the Steppes.

Social Relations

Each extended family, headed by its senior male, occupied several tents. People tried to arrange things so that the other families in the camp were related to them patrilineally. Ideally all male members remained with the family, although any married son had the right to leave with his share of the herds. In the end the youngest son cared for his aging parents and inherited their share of the family estate while the oldest son received his father's social rank.

Marriage required substantial bridewealth to be paid in animals. However, this was partially offset and sometimes equaled by the bride's dowry. A person married outside the patriclan; men particularly sought wives in their mothers' clans in order to maintain an alliance between the two groups.

Each clan was divided into nested patrilineages that had political functions. At a minimum, patrilineal groups were responsible for the control of land and resources. In some cases kinship legitimized authority in chiefdoms or even federations. At the higher levels of political organization, kinship was largely fictive. Individuals and groups who came to power reworked the genealogies to support their new positions. Subordinates who joined them claimed the same origin and, as a result, affiliation with a successful group was more like ethnicity than kinship.

Larger political units concerned themselves entirely with external relations, most fundamentally the control of basic resources that might be challenged by other nomads. It was also advantageous to coordinate the exploitation of sedentary people, which included control of trade and the extraction of tribute. The most powerful leaders pursued conquest, assimilating other pastoralists and establishing dynasties over civilized peoples in China, Europe, and the Middle East. The mobility of the nomads was a great advantage when they challenged states. In favorable circumstances their cavalry attacks were highly effective. When put on the defensive by massed forces, they easily escaped to the safety of the steppes.

Knowledge and Expression

The bond between human and sheep began in winter when a child received a newborn lamb to take into the family tent and keep warm for the first ten hours of its life. The child learned to distinguish this lamb from the hundreds of others and took special care of it. Its young formed the herd that the child received upon marrying.

A ram was sacrificed at the wedding and the flesh of the lower hind limb consumed jointly by bride and groom. The defleshed tibia was placed under their bed to enhance fertility. Other important ceremonies required sacrifice of a ram, including annual occasions such as the New Year. A family always brought in an outsider to kill their animals, and the associated rites resembled the funeral of a human being.

One ram in each family herd escaped such a fate because the owner considered it his alter ego. The ram's illness or death foretold the same catastrophe for his human counterpart. Given the best of care and wearing talismans for supernatural protection, the symbolic ram augured peace and wealth for the family.

Shamans provided another way to deal with illness and death. When in trance, they could fly to the sky that symbolized harmony and power. For the sick, the shaman focused that power on healing. For the dead, he or she escorted the soul to the other world. Chiefs and kings coveted the authority that came from heaven, so they sometimes employed shamans to support their regimes. The shamans also performed acts of more immediate practical value, such as healing and divination.

Gradually shamanic beliefs and practices were submerged by religious influences from neighboring civilizations. Buddhism had some impact, but ultimately Islam prevailed throughout most of the Steppes. Sufi movements were largely responsible and so, for ordinary people, the symbolic status of mosques was rivaled by the tombs of "saints" and the houses where "adepts" met and prayed. Some of the sufi orders eased the transition to Islam by incorporating indigenous shamanistic practices.

SOUTHEAST ASIAN AREA

Examples:

Thai, Khmer, Lao, Burmese, Malay, Javanese, Balinese

The Southeast Asian Zone included most of geographic Southeast Asia but excluded Vietnam, which was heavily influenced by China. The major contemporary countries are Thailand, Burma, Laos, Cambodia, Malaysia, and Indonesia (the Philippines were already a colonial possession of Spain when the eighteenth century began).

The terrain was marked by alternation of mountain chains and wide riverine plains. In the wet monsoon climate temperatures varied between 80 and 100 degrees

Fahrenheit. This tropical environment encouraged extensive use of wet rice cultivation and bamboo technology.

Southeast Asia displayed many of the basic characteristics of the Central Zone. It was a land of old agrarian civilizations where peasants supported elites by turning the soil with wooden plows. Monarchs ruled over stratified states and empires containing cities with political, religious, and commercial interests. The great traditions mingled in Southeast Asia, albeit in a complex and ultimately divisive way. Initially Hinduism united the Area with its influences on political organization and the arts. Then, between 1000 and 1500 A.D., two Regions became increasingly distinct as one accepted Buddhism and the other turned to Islam.

Regardless of religious patterns, several interrelated features of social organization united the Southeast Asian Area and set it apart from the rest of the Central Zone. These distinctions revolved around kinship, family, and gender relations. Southeast Asians considered gender distinctions to be fundamental (Brenner 1995; Keyes 1995), but they emphasized complementarity rather than opposition (Ong 1989).

Key features:

- ► Wet rice cultivation
- ► Bamboo technology
- ► Nuclear family
- ► Neolocal or matrilocal residence
- ► Bilateral kinship
- ► Independence and status of women
- ► Theravada Buddhism and Islam

Modal Patterns in Southeast Asian Peasant Culture

Material Culture

The houses of a peasant community either lined a waterway or clustered on higher ground amidst the rice fields. Each house was raised several feet above the ground by stilts or stone pilings as protection from seasonal floods. The rectangular structure had windows and a steep thatched roof to shed the rain. Behind the front porch, one or two rooms contained a few furnishings and a variety of tools and containers.

The frame of the house was made from large pieces of bamboo, and the walls and floors were lined with mats produced by splitting and unrolling smaller bamboo stalks. People also used bamboo to make baskets and torches, and they cooked some foods inside hollow bamboo tubes. Iron tools were essential for working the bamboo and also for clearing the forests to make room for agriculture.

After the backbreaking work of replanting rice seedlings, people enjoyed the harvest. As families worked near each other in the small fields, they sang and joked. During the dry months that followed, they made and repaired tools, engaged in craft work, and participated in social and religious activities. Some villagers added to their income by providing services in the realm of the supernatural: they were shamans, astrologers, sorcerers, and mediums. Others developed skills in metal and woodworking. In some cases whole communities specialized in making pottery, cloth, bricks, hats, umbrellas, jewelry, or paper.

People, mainly women, traded their surplus rice and fruits and craft products in periodic village markets and in permanent town markets. They sometimes found coastal people who had brought fish—fresh, dried, or made into paste. Some men left their villages to become peddlers who took products from the coast on regular routes through the inland areas. Foremost among these was salt, but they also brought items such as imported iron and bronze objects. Peddlers had to pay tolls and taxes, but some accumulated enough wealth to gain an advantage when they settled down to village life. A thriving maritime trade provided most of the imported objects. By the eighteenth century this trade was dominated by outsiders such as Arabs, Indians, Chinese, and Europeans.

Less respectable than peddlers were wandering troupes of professional musicians and actors. Still worse, banditry offered a living to some ordinary men. It attracted those who were in trouble, unwilling to abide by normal social restrictions, or displaced by war. Bandits were organized into groups with their own customs under leaders who dominated with bravado and magical powers.

Social Relations

Wedding ceremonies were modest. After negotiations, the groom's family provided wealth to the bride's, but this was partly to help with the wedding expenses. The bride's family also gave gifts to the new couple. Many households consisted of a single neolocal nuclear family. However, matrilocal stem families formed for several reasons. One was a general tendency toward matrilocal residence for at least a short time after marriage. Another was the facilitation of mother–daughter work relationships. A third was the preference that a daughter care for her aged parents. Women in neolocal households often lived near their mothers, sisters, or other female relatives. Even though the burden of parental care was placed on one child, all inherited equally.

Bilaterality governed personal kin relationships; there were no lineages or clans. Each person had many relatives in the community and the vicinity and either chose to cultivate some or simply associated with those that chance placed in proximity. Specific kin terms stressed generational distinctions and relative age within each generation. Presumption, ingratitude, and disrespect met with intense disapproval.

These emphases in the kinship system represent a more general concern with hierarchy, distance, and respect. Southeast Asian languages elaborated pronouns that distinguished rank and provided peasants in particular with a vocabulary of self-abasement. They used such language frequently because most peasants existed in a patron–client relationship with a wealthy and/or aristocratic person or family. In such a relationship the peasant served his patron in various ways. In return he received physical protection from outsiders, assistance in disputes, and sometimes an opportunity for advancement.

Men accepted the competence of women in economic matters, both inside and outside the household. Wives controlled routine household finances while men helped with other domestic tasks. Women moved freely in public, without escorts, doing most of the buying and selling in local markets. Property ownership further enhanced the economic position of women. All siblings, including daughters, had equal inheritance rights.

Women going to a ceremony, an indication of the public freedom of women in the Southeast Asian Area (Indonesia).

When conflict arose in the neolocal nuclear family, the husband did not have the immediate and automatic support of a patrilocal extended family: disputes were one on one. If either spouse had an advantage, it was likely to be the woman because her female relatives lived nearby. Violence by husbands was rare because the ideal male role emphasized self-control. Beyond the household, husband and wife had recourse to equivalent networks of bilateral kin. There was no well-organized cohort of patrilineal relatives for the husband to call upon. Nor was there a patrilineal group of wife's relatives to sympathize with the problems of a fellow man or to worry about returning bridewealth in case of a divorce.

Either sex could obtain a divorce and incompatibility was usually sufficient grounds. Divorce was socially acceptable, apparently based on the feeling that, for all concerned, separation was better than perpetual strife. The woman usually kept immature children and had no restrictions on remarriage. In addition to her personal economic potential she was entitled to equitable distribution of all property associated with the marriage. This, combined with her personal economic potential, gave the divorcee a great deal of independence.

Although women often participated directly in village decision making, men held positions of authority. The leader of a village came from among the villagers

and acted as an intermediary between them and the higher levels of government. His main duties were the coordination of tax collection and the mobilization of services. He depended largely on his personal qualities and the voluntary cooperation of the community. Local customary law was well developed and a matter of pride.

Knowledge and Expression

Peasants directed a great deal of ritual activity toward rice. The rice goddess stood at the highest level of this religious complex and received ceremonial appeals for agricultural fertility. The seeds, the rice crop, and the land all contained spirits or some kind of spiritual essence. Depending on the identity of such supernatural components, people provided ritual nurturance, exorcism, or appeasement.

Peasants also concerned themselves with numerous spirits that inhabited specific localities throughout the countryside. The most benevolent were community guardians, who received regular ritual attention. They symbolized the identity and stability of their villages. Other spirits were well disposed to people, but some could be dangerous if offended and all required ritual propitiation.

Every person had a spiritual essence, conceived of as multiple particulate souls or a more generalized substance or energy. Loss of this spiritual essence, often under attack by an evil spirit, was the most common cause of illness and death. Another serious problem was disharmony with the environment, either the heavenly bodies or earthly features such as topography. The wrong food (for the particular person or for the time when it was consumed) could also cause illness. Although people believed in witches or sorcerers, they seldom used them to explain misfortunes.

Shamans cured some diseases by contacting their spirit helpers while in a trance. However, magical or ritual specialists treated many conditions. One kind, for example, adjusted the individual to restore harmony with the environment. Another exorcised evil spirits. Diviners and mediums discovered the actions needed to appease neutral or benevolent beings that had been offended.

Men defined their social role in terms of potency, a power that included the ability to fertilize women but which extended to control over other men and one's own behavior. Male potency related to the mastery of personal desires, expressed in a demeanor that remained calm and moderate regardless of circumstances. Potency gave men supremacy in political and religious matters. Women could become shamans or mediums, roles in which self-control was not necessary and could even be detrimental.

Hinduism influenced many beliefs and rituals. To some, for example, the rice goddess was equated with the wife of the Hindu god Vishnu. Elements of Hindu ritual were prominent in ceremonies of royalty, curing, and marriage. In marriage, for example, the couple was represented as an Indian king and queen. Hindu elements were also present in rituals associated with pregnancy, birth, a boy's first haircut, and death. Southeast Asians used Indian sacred symbols such as numbers in multiples of four.

Hinduism greatly influenced Southeast Asian arts, including the style and content of literature and mythology. Stories derived from the Hindu epics provided the basis for performing arts such as puppet theater and dance-dramas. Sculpture also displayed Indian influence. Dance and puppet theater graced the royal courts, but they also entertained peasants when presented by local puppeteers or traveling troupes of performers. Other recreations included cockfighting and kite flying.

Stories of the trickster were heartening as well as entertaining, because he had risen from his peasant birth to challenge powerful officials with his intelligence and wit. However, he was also quite capable of harming ordinary people. The trickster was particularly notorious for turning people's words against them. As a child, he threw everything out of his house in response to his parents' instruction to make it "spotless." As an adult, he became a ruthless swindler and sexual exploiter who could always talk himself out of any punishment.

A monkey mask represents Hindu influences on the performing arts in Southeast Asia (Java, Indonesia).

Modal Patterns in Southeast Asian Elite Culture

Material Culture

An affluent urban family lived in a house made from the same bamboo and other materials as the homes of commoners. However, the elite house was larger and stood higher on its stilts or stone pilings, the height of a man or more. The family inside ate from gold dishes and hung their home with fine, colorful textiles for the entertainment of guests and for other special occasions. Larger and more magnificent than any other dwelling in the city, the palace of a great ruler rested on a platform at least twenty feet high.

Buildings of brick or stone dotted the city. While preferring the comfort of bamboo houses in life, the elite constructed durable and impressive tombs to shelter them after death. Many of these tombs adjoined the compounds of temples built from the same materials. Elsewhere, brick warehouses preserved the goods of the city merchants.

Elite and commoners wore the same basic cloth wraparound garment as peasants. However, nobles used the finer materials reserved for them by law and displayed their varying ranks with different colors and patterns. The law also dictated the amount of gold jewelry that people of different status could wear. A few people wore shirts or tunics that had come from far away by sea or caravan.

Even though the kingdom's main crop after food was cotton, and cloth the main manufacture, the demand was so great that textiles constituted one of the most important imports. This was especially true of luxury cloth, such as Chinese silk and the even more popular fine cotton of India. Gold was available from nearer places, but people considered it their main form of wealth. The ornaments that they wore were made from very soft gold so that they were easily reworked or cut for commercial sale.

In some parts of the city specialized craft workers manufactured the clothing, gold ornaments, and numerous other products. The craft master used his household for the work, adding dependent relatives or apprentices to his family. Wary of unnecessary expense and destruction of inventory, he usually worked his craft only when given a specific commission.

Social Relations

Above the rural communities a hereditary elite controlled provincial government. In the larger and more complex states the province was more subordinate to the central government. The bureaucracy, in some cases composed of hundreds of narrowly specialized officials, existed mainly to facilitate the collection of taxes and mobilization of services. The capital sent officials to supervise such activities while provincial rulers visited the capital to report rather than exert influence. A provincial ruler was often a relative of the previous man in that position and of others who had been appointed to lesser posts. Thus he inherited a network of family connections as well as a set of clients. However, there was a great deal of conflict over succession because primogeniture was not well established, and polygyny produced many claimants.

Southeast Asians borrowed the traditional Hindu form of the state. The king was supposed to have spiritual charisma and ascetic warrior virtues through association with the god Shiva. Royal ritual was largely Brahmanic, and the palace represented Mount Meru at the center of the universe. With walls and moats the palace kept lesser people at a distance.

Along with similar structure and rationale, the Southeast Asian state also tended to have the fluid competition and dynastic instability of its Indian counterpart. Beyond the closest provinces royal authority diminished with distance. Rulers of tributary states rebelled against central control and sometimes usurped the throne. Attack by independent neighbors was also a constant danger.

Local lords mobilized peasants for war on the same basis as labor service. The peasants brought their own food, equipment, and weapons, and went into battle as local or provincial units under their own leaders. Because of chronic underpopulation, the main goal of war was to obtain manpower. Casualties were accordingly low, but crop destruction led to famines. Internal wars of succession had the same result, so warfare was extremely destructive. This presumably created a feedback system in which wars to compensate for underpopulation led to greater underpopulation.

In some cases victorious rulers transplanted thousands of peasants from the defeated state to their own lands. In other cases they made them into slaves. States also conducted raids against hill people to obtain slaves. Within a state some people went into slavery because of an official judgment of criminality or failure to repay a debt. Some debt slaves could be redeemed. Laws regulated the treatment of slaves in some important ways. Slaves might be permitted to marry, for example, and the killing of a slave was regarded as homicide.

Ultimately, Southeast Asian political systems were based on control of manpower rather than land. Kings or local lords claimed control of the land, but this was a rationale for taxing the services and products of the subjects. Warfare served to capture more manpower rather than conquer land, and this was augmented by slave raiding.

Knowledge and Expression

The government orchestrated much of the state's ceremonial life and entertainment. The ruler took advantage of almost every royal and religious occasion to demonstrate his power and splendor, presenting himself to the people as the hub of society. These occasions included coronations and life-cycle rituals for members of the royal family, ceremonies to ensure the fertility and well-being of the country, and the reception of foreign ambassadors. Sacred days of the great tradition occasioned the most spectacular celebrations, with one exception. That was the Sending Away of Waters at the end of the rainy season. Association of the king with the change in season hinted at the magical powers that his predecessors had once claimed.

Thousands of people took part in a major festival. The ruler engaged in a grand procession accompanied by courtiers, government officials, soldiers, and subjects. Sometimes he went by water in a galley with hundreds of rowers. A version of the Indian dragon-serpent decorated the boat. The procession was followed by boat races and other contests, animal fights, and theater.

Just as peasants delighted in cockfights, the audiences at royal festivals were entertained by battles

A Thai dancer: comparison with the Balinese dancer on p. 143 suggests similarities that are largely due to Hindu influences.

between larger animals. The most important fight pitted a tiger against a buffalo or elephant. The tiger symbolized danger, disorder, wilderness, and enemies. It had to be defeated by the animal representing ruler and state, so the tiger was often tied to a stake for the fight.

Theater presentations always intertwined drama, song, music, and dance. In the main stories the heroes of Hindu religious epics populated the local legendary past. There they became the progenitors of society and especially of an orderly monarchy. The masks worn by the characters were artistic, and the dances provided a model for aristocratic bearing. The higher a person stood in the social scale, the more it was expected that he emulate the elegant dance movements that were once attributed to the gods.

Sanskrit was the first written language in Southeast Asia and hundreds of words found their way into the languages of the Area. The lunar calendar came from an Indian model, as did the week in which each of seven days was named for a deity. The calendar was the basis for the ceremonial cycle and for astrological forecasts.

A Closer Look

After a long period of Hindu influence, Southeast Asia became divided by the effects of two very different universalistic religions. These effects and other important variations can be summarized in terms of two well-defined Regions.

The Mainland Region

The Mainland Region roughly coincided with the modern countries of Thailand, Burma (Myanmar), Laos, and Cambodia. It had little coastline, so its societies were oriented toward the large river systems. Many distinctions of Mainland culture can be linked with the acceptance of Buddhism and more particularly with the Therevada form of the religion.

The use of domestic animals for food was limited by Buddhist strictures on the taking of life, although people did make some distinctions. Peasants hunted and gathered small animals such as birds, lizards, squir-

A Buddhist temple in the Mainland Region of Southeast Asia (Laos).

rels, frogs, snails, and freshwater shrimp. They readily slaughtered chickens for feasts or for honored guests, but they avoided the killing of larger animals. Eating meat was not in itself proscribed, so people sometimes enjoyed a pig or an ox that they caused to be slaughtered by a non-Buddhist (e.g., a Muslim or a pagan hill person). Nevertheless, all of these were more or less luxury sources of protein compared to the reliable supply of fish.

Villagers raised hot peppers, which they included in many of their dishes. They made beer and whiskey from some of their surplus rice. Men drank alcohol on festive occasions while women rarely indulged at all. Coconut liquid provided an enjoyable drink for everyone in ordinary times.

Beyond the peasant world and its ubiquitous water buffalo, elephants were used for heavy labor such as moving logs. They provided battle support and enhanced royal ceremonies. Elephants also played a role in the caravan trade with China and Vietnam, along with oxen, horses, and mules. Through these exchanges Southeast Asia obtained silver, tobacco, hill cotton, and forest produce. Royal trade monopolies increased the wealth of kings and subjects that they favored.

People tried to influence their children's marriages and perhaps succeeded among the elite where there was much to be gained or lost. Ordinary young people usually made their own choices after participating in elaborate courting customs. Feasts and cooperative labor parties provided boys and girls with the opportunity to associate. Groups of young men sometimes serenaded their favorites on ordinary nights during the dry season when work was leisurely. Sexual relations sometimes resulted from these contacts, but certain spirits found this offensive. If a girl became pregnant, her lover married her and paid a fine to the appropriate spirit.

The Hindu form of the state was syncretized with Buddhism. While maintaining the characteristics of Shiva, the king was also supposed to be the protector and exemplar of Buddhist values. Thus Buddhist monks had displaced Hindu Brahmans as his advisors. Mainland kingdoms exerted some direct control over the labor of their subjects rather than depending entirely on mobilization by local lords.

The great tradition was Theravada Buddhism. It was an austere philosophy, which held that only a few could achieve the enlightenment that allows nirvana. With the only supernatural entity in Theravada belief so remote, ordinary people were stimulated (and permitted) to rely on folk religions, which gave them immediate and intimate access to many supernatural beings. Belief in these beings explained misfortune and gave people hope for improvement in this life.

The Buddhist interpretation of karma gave ordinary people another spiritual focus. According to the Law of Karma, there was an impersonal cosmic balance that

A statue of Buddha (Thailand).

linked the actions of human beings with the amount of their suffering. This balance was carried across the threshold of reincarnation so that a person could work toward betterment in the next life even though the ultimate reward, nirvana, was remote. The idea of spiritual merit brought the abstraction of karma into the everyday world. Anyone could reduce future suffering by performing meritorious actions and retain that merit by avoiding negative behavior. Meritorious behavior was based on the virtues of charity, wisdom, and equanimity exercised mainly in connection with religion.

Charity was displayed by giving to a Buddhist temple, as little as one meal for a monk or as much as the construction of a new building. Ordination as a monk was also a kind of charity because the monk sacrificed his participation in the world, though often not permanently, and his parents sacrificed his connection with their family. Wisdom and equanimity could be expressed in several different ways. One was the giving and hearing of sermons on dharmic subjects. Another was acts of veneration toward the Buddha, the dharma, or the monastic order, which could be carried out at the local temple or a distant shrine. There was also meditation, especially performed by the elderly preparing for death.

People tried to share their merit. Every ritual act of merit ended with the performer pouring a libation of water and asking the earth goddess to carry the merit to all sentient beings. At funerals the mourners engaged in meritorious acts to better the rebirth of the deceased.

Behavior that detracted from merit resulted from the vices of greed, anger, and delusion. The major acts to avoid were taking life, stealing, lying, improper sexual acts, and ingesting substances that caused "heedlessness." There was some disagreement as to whether the occasional festive use of alcohol fell into the last category.

To Mainlanders a man's potency included the power to reject the world (Keyes 1995), placing him at a superior spiritual level with regard to Buddhist ideals. Only males could be ordained as monks, a sacrifice that gained more merit than almost any other act even if the stay in the monastery was temporary. One consolation offered to a woman was the possibility of being reincarnated as a man.

Women were endowed with a nurturant quality that had spiritual overtones. They shared this quality with the Earth and with rice, both regarded as feminine and represented by goddesses. Human and divine females were imbued with the ability to provide physical and spiritual well-being to others. A woman's equivalent to a man's ordination was the reproductive rite of lying by the fire. She stayed by a fire for at least several days after the birth of a child. People believed that this helped to dry the uterus, get rid of bad blood, heal wounds, and stimulate the flow of milk. However, it also had the symbolic implication of ripening or cooking. Lying by the fire after bearing a child, a woman reached maturity.

Mainlanders believed that the spiritual essence or life force was a part of every human being as well as rice and certain animals, including buffalo and elephants. It had to be securely attached to the body, or illness, death, or social failure might follow. Periodic rituals ensured this connection. Comparable rites were performed when a person underwent a major transition in life, such as a change in status or residence. Loss of the essence required a specialist to retrieve it and tie it to the body.

People had less control over fate, the random effect of cosmic elements in their lives. Heavenly bodies, topography, the directions, the oscillation of day and night, the components of the human body, all had an impact. However, this was limited to one's current life. Basic suffering, especially across the boundary of rebirth, was controlled by karma.

The village temple was a center of art and knowledge. It contained paintings that represented cosmological themes or the life of the Buddha. The most common was "Buddha calling Earth to witness," in which he is in the meditational posture that leads to enlightenment. Tempted by a demon, who offers worldly pleasure and comfort, Buddha calls on the earth goddess to witness his steadfastness.

The monks offered formal language instruction to make boys literate in order to prepare them for entry into the monastic order. Some of these boys continued their studies elsewhere, emphasizing sacred language and religious interpretation, and a very few went on to high positions in the capital city. Although basic study utilized texts that taught religious and moral values, most monasteries kept libraries that offered non-Buddhist knowledge. The subjects included customary law, herbal medicine, astrology, love magic, control of the spiritual essence, and exorcism of evil spirits.

Buddhist monks and an acolyte (Bangkok, Thailand).

The Insular Region

The Insular Region included what are now the countries of Indonesia and Malaysia. It diverged from the Mainland with the acceptance of Islam. However, the effects of Islam were moderated by Southeast Asian traditions, resulting in distinctive patterns and conflicts. The Area was culturally diverse but numerically dominated by the closely similar Javanese and Sundanese ethnic groups. The description that follows is largely based on their culture, although much of it is also pertinent to the Malays, the third-largest group, and to many smaller minorities.

Consisting of a thin peninsula and many islands, the Insular Area was largely oriented to the sea. Many villagers specialized in fishing, while the coastal states supported themselves by taxing passing ships and the merchants doing business in their ports. The Insular fishing village was distinctive in a number of economic and social patterns (Steinberg, ed. 1987). It was small, composed of a dozen or so families. Fishing methods varied, at least in part because some villages fished small streams, others the rivers, and still others the oceans. However, it was usual for many people to pool their resources to acquire the needed materials and to cooperate in the maintenance and use of nets or boats. A village contained one or more groups of fishermen, each headed by a man with either superior technical knowledge or the ritual skills needed to enlist the spirits.

Parents arranged marriages, but divorce was available to women as well as men. Islam altered the rationale of monarchy somewhat, since a human could not be a god in any sense. Nevertheless, a Muslim king held himself to be God's representative on earth, a source of holy light. Below the king, the same aristocrats and bureaucrats continued to administer the territories of the peasants.

Men did not place a high value on economic activity, so the financial and marketing work of women may not have brought them a great deal of respect (Helliwell 1993). Nevertheless, men tolerated the work even though it entailed a degree of freedom unusual for Muslim women. Many women fulfilled the requirement of public modesty with no more than a symbolic gesture such as a scarf on head. Even many strict Muslims made no attempt to seclude their wives and daughters.

Everyone believed in Allah and in the judgment that he rendered, sending the souls of good people to heaven and those of the evil to hell. They knew that a sacred book of Islam existed, though some did not know its name. Almost every male performed the first ritual Pillar of the religion by making the confession of faith at his circumcision ceremony.

Santri Muslims adhered strictly to all of the Five Pillars and to other doctrines, such as the taboo on pork. They looked down on the loose observances of others and on their retention of more traditional religion and magic. Santri existed at all levels of society, urban and rural, but they predominated in the commercial class. They constituted a large minority of the population.

Kejawen Muslims prayed only on special occasions, ignored the Ramadan fast, had no interest in a pilgrimage to Mecca, and saw no reason to avoid pork. Their relationship with Allah tended to be an emotional one, based on "intense belief" (Koentjaraningrat 1975). The Kejawen incorporated many Hindu–Buddhist concepts into their religious system, including fate, reincarnation, veneration of sacred graves, and emphasis on life-cycle ceremonies (Koentjaraningrat 1975). Deviating from Islamic monotheism, they recognized a god of time and death, equivalent to the Hindu Shiva, who governed sickness and disaster. They equated the rice goddess with the wife of the Hindu god Vishnu. Kejawen readily perpetuated "pagan" religion as well, incorporating good and evil spirits into life-cycle ceremonies and other rituals. They consulted shamans and other such religious specialists and looked for magical power in objects like amulets, heirlooms, and sacred musical instruments.

The aristocratic/bureaucratic class practiced a sophisticated version of Kejawen with an elaborate philosophy of fate, death, and disaster. They placed great value on mysticism and sought God within themselves. Under gurus, they meditated and denied their physical needs as far as possible.

The central ritual of Kejawen was a sacred communal meal intended to promote emotional calm in which no misfortune occurs. Associated with the major transitions of an individual's life, these feasts were held by a household and included no more than the closest relatives, neighbors, and friends. The feast helped the person's soul and prevented harm from supernatural causes. Santri Muslims attended these feasts and even held their own, though less often than the Kejawen.

AFRICAN ZONE

Areas:

- Forest
- Cattle
- Greater Sudanic
- Swahili

African
Zone
with Areas
and Regions

Greater Sudanic Area

Sudanic Region

Guinea Coast Region

Nilotic Region

Ethiopian Region

Somali Region

Forest Area

Congo Region

Great Lakes Region

Cattle Area

Swahili Area

Southern Savanna Region

Cattle Area

Previous page Though dance was important in many cultures, it may have
had its greatest significance in the traditional African Zone (Kenya).

OVERVIEW OF THE ZONE

Examples:

Yoruba, Ashante (Asante), Zulu, Xhosa, Masai

The Sahara Desert and the Mediterranean strip north of it belonged to the Central Zone as a result of Arab conquests in the eighth century A.D. (see chapter 9). The African Cultural Zone occupied the continent south of the Sahara and is often referred to as sub-Saharan Africa. To distinguish the indigenous cultures of Africa in this way is not to say that they were isolated. They had long-term contacts with the Middle East and their relations with Asia extended as far as Indonesia and China (July 1998). Portuguese ships arrived in the fifteenth century and other Europeans followed. The traditional cultures of the African Zone incorporated influences from all these peoples while maintaining their distinctive cultural identity.

Between 1600 and 1850 Europeans explored African coastal areas and the immediate hinterlands. More importantly, they instituted the Atlantic slave trade. Over 10 million people were taken to the Americas from western and central Africa, and at least 5 million related deaths occurred. Meanwhile, about 7 million eastern Africans were lost to the Arab slave trade. The toll in personal suffering was great, but the cultural consequences not as drastic. African societies, especially in the interior of the continent, retained their independence and the basic features of indigenous culture. Even the major changes that took place during the slave-trading era had their roots in pre-European times, including the increasing size of political units, more intensive environmental exploitation, and increased external trade. Despite slaving and other external trade, internal production and exchange continued to predominate in the economy (Keim 1995). When compared to other external sources such as trade in raw materials, profits from slaving probably did not exceed 10 percent of the native African income (Isichei 1997). After 1850, Europeans quickly penetrated the interior of Africa, conquering and arbitrarily partitioning the continent. These conquests, and the colonial era that followed, caused far greater cultural disruption than the slave trade (Keim 1995) and ended the traditional period of African culture.

Rain forest (the "jungle" of Western popular imagination) covered no more than a fourth of the African Zone. The rest of the Zone consisted mainly of various kinds of savanna; that is, habitats with at least some grasses in the vegetation. Some savannas are almost completely open (exemplified by much of the famous Serengeti Plain in East Africa) while others include varying degrees of bush and tree cover. In these diverse tropical environments Africans obtained most of their sustenance from horticulture. The savannas were hospitable to native grains such as sorghum and several varieties of millet, but people preferred maize wherever it could be grown. Other recently arrived crops of American origin, brought by European ships, also played a role. So did earlier imports from the Pacific, such as taro.

Metallurgy affected the material, social, and ideological aspects of African culture. Copper was the luxury metal, occupying a position much like gold in the western world (Herbert 1984; Isichei 1997). Iron products included the practical as well as the artistic. African smelters came up with a number of innovations, including the crucial one of producing carbonized steel directly from the furnace. They invented a greater variety of furnaces than did any other part of the world, and the most efficient of these made bellows unnecessary.

One of the most striking features of traditional Africa was the abundance of land in relation to an expanding population. Some fundamental aspects of culture seem to follow from these basic ecological facts, revolving around the value of people in comparison to land (Iliffe 1995). Land was readily available, but it was useless without a sufficient number of people to cultivate it. Polygyny and slavery were ways for particular men or kinship groups to add to their wealth in people. Although the majority of the world's cultures permitted polygyny, it was more common and more idealized in Africa than almost anywhere else. Slavery may also have been more common among traditional Africans than elsewhere in the world (Bourguignon and Greenbaum 1973).

Patrilineages dominated social organization. Clans had many of the same functions as lineages (Siegel 1996). They may have been a recent development, at least in some places, to carry out activities such as labor organization on a large scale (Isichei 1997). As in most patrilineal societies, African women were under extensive economic, social, and political constraints. However, these were mitigated by various factors, including the women's own resistance (Morrow 1986). Systematic separation of activities by gender gave women a great deal of autonomy, especially since marriage did not merge the goals of husband and wife. African women were deferential to men in some contexts and assertive in others (Morrow 1986).

In every part of Africa egalitarian and hierarchical polities intermingled. The populations of states ranged from a few thousand to several million. Hierarchical societies also included chiefdoms with paramount chiefs who had much in common with the kings of full-fledged states. Largely because of the complex hierarchical societies, "Africa is one of the homes of advanced legal institutions" (Bohannan and Curtin 1995:95), manifested in civil and criminal courts.

Some say that tribute provided rulers with "rich incomes" (Lamphear and Falola 1995). Others claim that it was nominal, noting that the chief or king returned a substantial portion of tribute to his people in the form of religious sacrifices and public celebrations (Bohannan and Curtin 1995). These interpretations parallel the variation described for other powers attributed to African rulers. Cross-culturally, the most consistent attributes of these rulers were symbolic and religious.

Although the term "ancestor worship" is often applied to African religion, "veneration" (deep respect) may be a better term (McCall 1995). Deference was due to living elders as well as ancestors. As subjects of ritual, the ancestors were in many cases treated as intermediaries between the living and God (Moyo 1996). Beyond such basic ideas there was little orthodoxy in African religion. People held many versions of basic beliefs and acknowledged several ritual and moral ways to achieve any purpose (Bohannan and Curtin 1995). The flexibility of religion may be related to a more general theme of practicality in the African philosophy of life (see Iliffe 1995).

Distinctively structured music played a vital role in African life. The structure can be described as mosaic rather than linear: "The delight in conflict, in clash of parts, draws from a different source of order than does much of Western music" (Stone 1995:264). Musical performance was "transactional" in the sense that a part could only be understood in its balance with another part, as in the call and response pattern that was eventually carried to the Americas.

Key features:

▶ Agricultural states and chiefdoms

▶ Sophisticated horticulture

▶ Patrilineal/patrilocal society

▶ High rate of polygyny

▶ civil and criminal courts

▶ Open slavery

▶ Ancestor veneration

▶ Elaborate music and dance

Modal Patterns in African Peasant Culture

Material Culture

Rainy and dry seasons alternated, but temperatures stayed warm throughout the year. People wore clothing mainly for social and esthetic reasons. Varying with available resources, the materials included goat leather, bark cloth, and woven palm cloth. Patterns of scars adorned faces and bodies, some purely decorative and others having social and ritual meanings. The cicatrices of many women tended to cluster on the abdomen, especially around the navel. Explanations of this pattern usually related to a woman's child-bearing capabilities. However, these abdominal scars, as well as other patterns on the chest and back, also had erotic value. Men were attracted by the sight of them and enjoyed the tactile stimulus during intimate encounters.

A polygynous man lived in a small house alone while each of his wives, with her children, maintained her own dwelling and cooking place. The small homes were made of perishable material such as mud, wood, and thatch. People knew they would have to move in the near future because even the most fertile lands would not sustain them for more than a decade or so.

Farmers cultivated by hand in the poor soil, using an iron-bladed hoe, augmented by digging stick and machete. The basic method was slash-and-burn, enhanced by a variety of tactics, including irrigation, fallowing, and the use of manure for fertilizer. Farmers chose their crops for labor efficiency and for viability in local conditions. They designed interplantation to spread labor requirements over time as well as to spread out the harvests. Interaction among some of the mixed plants produced higher yields, and rotation of crops benefited both plants and soil.

Women performed all routine farm activities, which kept them busy on a year-around basis. Men harvested and threshed, sometimes along with the women, in addition to preparing the fields. Men felt that affection interfered with a woman's important labor, but husbands were constrained to give their wives some consideration if they were to work efficiently. It was probably because of their economic significance that divorcees and widows were valued and quickly reintegrated with society. Slaves worked alongside family members to enhance production. The more affluent peasant families owned enough slaves to free them for other activities. People harvested a surplus in some years, but famines and seasonal hunger also occurred. Farmers supplemented their diet with hunting and gathering and used domestic goats and sheep for meat.

Specialized artisans held the secrets of smelting and smithing. Ironworkers made a variety of tools and weapons, including fishhooks and the blades for hoes, machetes, spears, and knives. Artisans shaped copper into jewelry, sculptures, and other works of art. In these forms, or simply as ingots, copper represented wealth and was an important item of exchange.

Tradition provided ideal exchange rates for trade, but people often made adjustments with reference to the general availability of the goods involved. In other words, they engaged in a certain amount of subtle bargaining. Usually they bartered, but in some instances they paid

Women, like these farmers in a sorghum field, were the mainstay of cultivation throughout the African Zone (Saracolle culture).

special purpose money. This means that a particular currency could be used only in certain kinds of transactions; for example, one currency for bridewealth and another for food. Types of money, which varied from place to place, included livestock, metal bars, and slaves. Cowrie shells often served for small amounts.

When people arranged a transaction, they gestured as they spoke. The gestures repeated the numbers they were saying, a useful habit because some trade took place between people who spoke different languages. For some transactions involving large numbers, such as taxes or bridewealth, people used sticks or other physical markers to represent the items in question. If those items were living things, such as slaves or animals, the discussants had to distinguish carefully between the symbols they were using and the actual people or animals. To count living things directly could cause them to sicken and die.

The number system was based on five and ten. People added to the base numbers, or multiplied them, to represent larger quantities. To keep a long-term numerical record of anything, people notched sticks or tied knots in string. The subject of such record keeping ranged from specific kinds of possessions to the number of days on a trip.

Pounding grain, an essential job of women throughout the African Zone (Nigeria).

Social Relations

Though highly active in marriage arrangement, sometimes consulting an oracle for advice, parents hesitated at forcing children into marriage because adamant young people sometimes eloped. By giving bridewealth, men obtained various rights in their wives, including labor, sexual access and exclusivity, and affiliation of her offspring with the father's kin group. The children became legitimate successors to the status and property rights of the father and his group. Until a new wife began to bear those children, her husband's group considered her a stranger. Bridewealth could also be viewed as a loan of capital in return for the woman's services.

The economic aspect of marriage seems to have been a source of tension and hostility between affines, particularly between the husband and mother-in-law. Siblings-in-law had a ritualized joking relationship that was inclined to insults and obscenities. These hostilities tended to lessen over the years with growing certainty that the exchange had been fair. Despite the potential for friction, marriage was the basis for alliance between kinship groups. The marriage exchange symbolized their social status: a large bridewealth could give the receiving group prestige, but it also reflected well on the wealth and generosity of all the groom's relatives who contributed. In a case of divorce, the bride's relatives returned the bridewealth, less a portion for each child that remained with the husband's group.

Although men sought polygyny, they entered into it with some misgivings. Failure to administer the household effectively could bring a great deal of personal grief and social disapproval. The path was smoothed somewhat by traditions that spelled out a husband's specific obligations to multiple wives and appropriate ways to treat them. The behavior of the husband was not the only potential source of trouble. Co-wives came into conflict, especially with regard to real or imagined slights against their children. On the other hand, the women could also be friendly, cooperative, and mutually supportive. Then the women exchanged childcare and shared the services they owed to their husband. Some women stayed in unsatisfactory marriages because of their relationships with their co-wives. In some instances co-wives benefited by forming a united front against a husband who was abusive, stingy, or lazy. One factor that helped was a senior wife or a mother-in-law with management and diplomatic skills. The fact that each woman could retreat to her own house also buffered conflicts.

Most polygynous men had no more than three wives, and an ordinary man often acquired his extra wives only through inheritance from a relative. However, some prominent men acquired many more than three through their own efforts. Because women were economic producers, a man with more wives could be more generous with actual or potential followers.

People regarded children of either sex as an unmixed blessing. At an early age they relieved their elders of simple subsistence tasks. Later in life they provided aging parents with security and protection. Then they gave their parents proper burial and memorial rituals as well the continuing sacrifices that ancestral souls needed. Finally, children would ensure that the kinship group continued in the future. "Without children you are naked," some people said while another proverb asserted that "a race is as fragile as a child." Lack of offspring was the worst fate that anyone could imagine. People pitied childless couples, or they feared them because their bitterness might make them destructive.

After giving birth, a mother abstained from sex for as long as two years. Most women had children about three years apart, and a person who gave birth less than two years after her previous child earned the contempt of the community. People had strong ideas about maximizing the survival chances of every baby.

Circumcision was a pivotal rite for boys; in terms of the magnitude of ritual and the numbers of people involved, initiation into manhood was the most prominently observed transition. Adolescent boys were partially or wholly segregated from the community, grouping together to hunt, herd, or carouse. Girls were kept closer to home and prepared for marriage.

Because of the need for substantial bridewealth, many men could not afford to marry until about the age of thirty. Those that did marry earlier rarely acquired a second wife until they were well past thirty. As a result, women often married men a great deal older than themselves and expected to be widows at a fairly early age. Many remarried, but some pursued alternate life courses.

Slaves worked in households and on family farms, often alongside their masters. They were considered part of the family, in a sense, and some of them assumed highly responsible household positions. They could marry and possess slaves of their own. To call attention to a slave's status was a grave insult that justified physical retaliation by the slave, even with a weapon, sometimes joined by his master.

Localized patrilineages, up to seven generations in depth, provided identity and support for members, organized political and ritual activities, and determined inheritance. These lineages were also corporate groups that controlled access to land based on the claim that they were the indigenous occupants or the original settlers. Their most common activity was probably mobilization of men for short-term, highly labor-intensive projects such as clearing land, weeding, house building, ritual, and military service.

Lineage members also protected each other and took revenge in cases of homicide. Revenge of any kind could lead to a feud, but an alternative existed in the form of bloodwealth, payments made to a person or surviving kin for injury or death. Disputes within the group could also lead to the payment of bloodwealth, with the killing of distant relatives bringing the largest amounts. A close relative required less, probably because the affairs of close relatives were intertwined, so that a high fine would have ramifications for the receivers as well as the givers. Though accorded less social value than men, women were considered significant. This was reflected in the bloodwealth for a woman, less than that of a man but still substantial.

Besides lineages, people belonged to clans with a depth of ten or more generations. Clan members felt a special bond even though many could not trace their exact relationships with each other. Each clan had a name and was associated with a totem, a symbolic animal or plant. Clan members avoided the totemic species or treated it with other signs of respect. However, the degree of attachment to particular totems is unclear since clans sometimes abandoned them. Lineages and clans provided opportunities to manipulate the social world at various levels. Both were exogamous, resulting in ties between organized groups. People deliberately modified the genealogies of both to achieve a variety of personal and political ends.

An age set united males who were born during the same year or some other designated time period. When these boys reached adolescence or early adulthood, ceremonial recognition formalized the group. They remained members throughout their lives, feeling a strong bond with one another and providing mutual support for ritual purposes and aiding each other during times of crisis. Age sets fulfilled community functions such as defense and government. These functions were organized in terms of age grades: group statuses that an age set occupied sequentially, e.g., youths, warriors, mature men, and elders. The system also served to organize some aspects of education and economic cooperation.

Specialists in curing, religion, and other fields formed more restricted organizations that protected the interests of their members and maintained the standards of their professions. Metalworkers occupied a special social category with positive connotations. In some societies they were wealthy or closely associated with chiefs; in others they were credited with introducing the skills of civilization or believed to possess dangerous supernatural power. In all cases metalworkers possessed secret knowledge that allowed them to work with great supernatural forces.

Villages were governed by chieftains and/or by councils composed of lineage heads and/or elders. Though elders were of relatively advanced age, they were not necessarily old in a physiological sense; they were men who had many children and who set an example of community standards. Elders had great authority but rarely used it in a heavy-handed way. Wealth also added to a man's influence.

Knowledge and Expression

God created and sustained the universe. The power and abstraction of this being were beyond the contemplation of humans. People could only comprehend the supreme being through concrete manifestations, such as the water that sustained all life. Social propriety dictated distance from God because direct approach to a superior as petitioner or penitent was extremely disrespectful. This principle, applied strictly to mere parents and rulers, was imperative in dealing with the supreme being. People appealed directly to God only in cases of sudden personal danger such as drowning, lightning, or a wild animal. Because of God's close association with water, an appeal by the community for deliverance from drought was also appropriate.

Ancestral spirits, the focus of most African ritual, provided the people with intermediaries between themselves and the supreme being. Prayers and sacrifices made to the ancestors ultimately reached God, and every right of passage implicitly celebrated God's gift of life to human beings. The recently dead were perceived as individual spirits and required regular ritual attention until they settled into their new status; the ancient ancestors, the founders of descent groups and political units, were thought of in collective terms. All were concerned about their living descendants and involved in their affairs.

The living and their ancestors were still kin and formed a social coalition. Ritual attention to ancestors was an extension of the respect owed to parents and elders. Elders were viewed as people on the verge of becoming ancestors. The involvement of ancestors and descendants represents a philosophy of time in which the past and the present were not sharply distinguished. Death was not an end, nor even a complete separation from the living world. By the same token, there was great concern for leaving descendants who would provide the proper ritual veneration.

As the Creator, God arranged the universe so that justice and goodness could triumph. The means to good life was the vital force, a kind of spiritual energy. Because heaven and earth were morally neutral, the spiritual energy that prevents social and cosmic disaster and enhances the lives of human beings had to come from the efforts of humans themselves. They had to worship and sacrifice and, even more important, lead righteous and generous lives. The ancestors expected to be honored, and they required that the living behave properly toward each other. Since the ancestors possessed more spiritual energy than living people, their approval could result in an increase for the living.

Just as humans were responsible for good in the world, so they were responsible for evil and misfortune. Selfishness accounted for much that went wrong. A person brought punishment on himself by failing to honor the ancestors or by misbehaving toward other humans.

People were also harmed by others through sorcery or witchcraft. Sorcerers were outsiders, usually male. Witches, mostly female, cursed or poisoned members of their own descent groups. The latter apparently reflected social tensions in these tightly knit groups. Whether a person was afflicted by his own failings or the malevolence of another, evil was always traceable to human action.

When a person prayed, he or she usually made a generalized request for well-being accompanied by an avowal of innocence of evil intentions. Sacrifice, the more potent act of worship, usually involved killing an animal (most often a chicken) on the assumption that taking life was necessary to get in touch with the source of life. The blood was smeared on any beneficiary of the sacrifice and on emblems of the supernatural beings. Members of a beneficiary group shared the flesh of the animal. Human sacrifice, though rare and regarded as an act of desperation, was often imitated with a symbolic animal, such as a dog, or a human corpse. Real human sacrifices, often slaves, accompanied the death of kings and other important persons.

Heads of kinship groups or political leaders often undertook the role of priest. Some more specialized priests attended to the shrines of various gods and spirits. Mediums were more powerful supernatural practitioners than priests. Mostly women, they were possessed by their family or clan ancestors and conveyed messages to the living. Men excluded women from many rituals, although their dependence on women was one of the things symbolized in the rituals. Men tended to think of women as witches because they so often worked against male interests.

Diviners used many different methods, including the casting of dice or other objects and the reading of animal entrails. Divination was important in establishing the guilt of a witch or other offenders who had not been accused by witnesses. It was also vital for telling people which particular rituals to perform in order to cope with their problems. Most diviners were highly intelligent men, many of them physically handicapped, with high-strung personalities. They had an intuitive knowledge of society and the courage to point out areas of conflict.

Becoming an adult entailed gaining some proficiency in music and dance. People noticed, admired, and shaped sounds, including the noises of everyday activities. Musicians chose from several scales, including those with five and seven notes to the octave. The transactional element in the music applied to the playing of instruments as well as to the vocal pattern of call and response. Musicians also practiced more complex fragmentation, such as the construction of a piece of music from numerous instruments, each of them playing only one or two notes. The music was highly polyrhythmic, using five or six different rhythms at the same time (European music uses two rhythms and occasionally three). Dance followed music, with different parts of the body reflecting different rhythms and the dancer responding to changes in tempo.

Traditional women's dance (Mozambique).

People thought of musical instruments as being like humans and interpreted their sounds as voices. They spoke of an instrument's components in terms of body parts and sometimes carved them with humanoid features. The degree of humanness attributed to a musical instrument depended on the particular role that it was playing at the time. Wind instruments—flutes, whistles, horns—were considered to be the voices of spirits. Ancestors and other spirits were invited to attend many events; their presence enhanced the playing of the music.

Men controlled carving and metal sculpture, the most prestigious arts, while ceramic work was the province of women. Plastic art emphasized masks, figurines, body decoration, and the shaping or augmentation of mundane objects such as furniture, weapons, ceramics, basketry, and clothing. Artists worked mainly in wood, using the adze. They did not expect their creations to last indefinitely; on the contrary, renewal was considered desirable. Art objects were used in many rituals, especially initiations, and they were also used to accumulate and activate spiritual energy.

Myths educated people about their place in the universe, especially in relation to the ancestors, but they had little narrative structure. Narrative skills were more apparent in the creation and performance of lesser stories to admonish, instruct, recall, and entertain. Many of these tales featured tricksters in the form of small animals. The tricksters often used their ingenuity to confuse and disturb rich and powerful people.

Proverbs played a serious role in African society, as evidenced by continuous quotation in everyday life. They were also employed in solemn settings such as courts of law and regarded as the core of any meaningful discussion. Proverbs were set apart from ordinary discourse by the frequent use of archaic terms. Less serious, riddles (couched as statements) always attracted an audience.

They entertained people while challenging them to a contest of wits. Among the most popular amusements was a board game much like checkers in which the pieces were of equal value. A player tried to capture his opponent's pieces and add them to his own.

Modal Patterns in African Elite Culture

Material Culture

The capital town of the kingdom had more buildings and people than any other settlement. It was built of long-lasting materials and inhabited by merchants and craft workers as well as farmers. The ruler's court formed a village in itself, with enough dwellings to house the king's many wives, children, officials, retainers, and the servants and slaves that they all needed. One official devoted himself to provisioning and maintaining the organization of the court as a whole. Another performed comparable functions for the royal wives. A third supervised maintenance of the extensive regalia that symbolized the ruler's status.

Members of the court, like other powerful and wealthy people, wore many items of heavy copper and brass jewelry. These included earrings, neck rings, bracelets, and anklets. Design varied a great deal: solid or hollow, twisted or smooth, closed or open, cast or wrought. Women wore the most jewelry, up to thirty pounds of it, most conspicuously in the form of bracelets on their legs. These forced the women to walk in a ponderous way that signaled the ultimate dignity, that they were above physical labor. Thus they displayed both wealth and status at the same time.

Numerous other copper and brass items rested within the king's buildings: utensils, tools, weapons, musical instruments, and so on. Any object could symbolize power if made from copper. Sumptuary laws limited ownership of many such objects. Rulers gave them to each other and to favored subjects as gifts, and sometimes they were included in bridewealth.

Subjects supported the royal lifestyle with taxes and tribute. The ruler of a large state also used slaves to support his court by selling them or putting them to work on his plantations or in the mines that produced metals and salt. Gold and slaves brought great profits through the long-distance trade that linked the kingdom with the coast and ultimately with the world beyond Africa.

Social Relations

The king had absolute power in theory but was actually limited by numerous checks and balances, beginning with his accession. He came from a royal lineage but was subjected to some degree of selection by a traditionally designated individual or group. Once in office he delegated many of his functions to a central bureaucracy and up to five levels of rural authority, revolving around chiefs or appointed governors responsible for one or another kind of subdivision of the state (e.g., tribes, districts, villages, or kinship groups).

Within his own court the king had to cope with government officials in hereditary positions. His close relatives also had advice for him, especially the royal mother and sisters who held some authority of their own as well as having the king's ear. Councils representing factions in the kingdom, groups with ritual power, and nongovernmental institutions, such as various kinds of associations, also tended to prevent abuses of power.

A hereditary chief was the king's delegate to the people but also the people's representative to the king, so he had to be acceptable to both. Tribute and taxes, collected by chiefs and passed up through the hierarchy to the king, symbolized authority. A chief who challenged his king's legitimacy withheld tribute, and a king who was dissatisfied with a chief refused the tribute that the chief offered. On the other hand, strong rulers sometimes increased tribute as a punishment for an unsuccessful rebellion.

To the extent that a king could appoint his own bureaucratic officials and governors of subordinate districts, he increased his own power. Oral tradition named the ruler who first claimed such a right. Appointed governors often came from the royal family, while the king usually chose central government officials from among attendants he knew at the palace. Fathers offered their sons for palace service in the hope of such advancement. Stories told of lowly free men, and even the occasional slave, who rose to the highest positions.

Peasants considered the rule of law and orderly resolution of disputes as important returns for the taxes they paid. Highly organized courts heard both civil and criminal cases, the latter defined as challenges to governmental authority. Witnesses testified, and judges rendered verdicts in public proceedings. Often the chiefs and kings acted as judges, so their political hierarchy functioned as a hierarchy of appeals courts. However, a ruler was frequently assisted by a panel of other judges. In civil cases the disputants might engage in some kind of contest, either consensual or forced, to decide the issue. Supernatural methods were also used, especially in cases that involved witchcraft. Some chiefs and kings had oracles that revealed the knowledge or will of supernatural beings. Ordeals ranged from risking spirit punishment by taking an oath on a shrine to ingesting poison that magically spared the innocent.

For war a king required his chiefs or governors to raise troops from the communities that they supervised. Some wars of conquest evicted populations from their homes or destroyed their societies. Others created states from chiefdoms and empires from states. An important result of war was to provide slaves for the king's mines and plantations or for trade to other societies.

Knowledge and Expression

The ceremony to install a king was perhaps the most important to a society. The well-being of the state and all its inhabitants depended on having a king of proper descent, consecrated to the office by the proper rituals. The inaugural ceremony endowed the new ruler with the spiritual power to carry this burden. It invoked the blessing of the ancestors and gods who watched over society and symbolized the king's legitimate connection with his predecessors. In specific rituals, such as washing and head shaving, the new ruler shed his old status of one among many royals so that he could rise above the rest. The ceremony included an explicit statement of the king's obligations to his people. Representatives of all the main groups in the society participated in the ceremony, committing all the people to the new regime. Periodic rituals thereafter served to purify the king and the office of kingship, ensuring that obligations would be properly fulfilled.

Religious and moral values constrained the king's behavior because he and his lineage derived the right to rule from the ancestors of the nation. Given the prominence of ancestral spirits in African religion, this was a profoundly spiritual charge. The kingship was a divine office, with sanctity in the royal emblems (e.g., crown, umbrella, drums, trumpets) or even in the body of the ruler himself. The king performed essential religious duties for the state and was surrounded by religious taboos. The latter tended to create isolation and enforce the delegation of political functions.

Numerous symbols served as daily reminders of the monarch's special status. Copper denoted wealth, but other substances also symbolized a king's power. Although iron was used for mundane purposes, artistic and luxury objects made from iron suitably represented royal strength. Another prestigious medium was elephant ivory, the strength and power of the animal symbolizing human leadership. The skin and claws of the powerful leopard also aggrandized a ruler, and he was entitled to receive the remains of any leopard killed by any of his subjects. Musical horns, especially when made of copper or brass, were associated with royal courts.

A Closer Look

Polygyny

We have noted the unusual frequency of polygynous marriages in Africa. Twentieth-century data suggest that at least 35 percent of married men were polygynous (Dorjahn 1959). "Competition for wives in polygynous societ-

ies made conflict between male generations one of the most dynamic and enduring forces in African history" (Iliffe 1995:95). Competition was regulated by the fact that men married rather late in life, sometimes in their thirties. This in turn may have generated more specific devices such as segregated regiments of young warriors who were permitted sexual activity but not marriage.

An erroneous idea about polygyny is that it increases the birth rate. This is a dubious proposition in general terms because women are the limiting resource as far as reproduction is concerned. One man can fertilize a large number of women while each woman can bear only a small number of children. Beyond this basic demographic fact, African polygyny coexisted with long periods of postpartum sexual abstinence. Polygyny maximized the reproductive potential of certain men and their kinship groups but did not increase the overall birth rate.

The Quality of Slavery

Some authorities have emphasized the differences between African slavery and that practiced by Europeans (Bohannan and Curtin 1995). African slavery was "open" in the sense that the enslaved or their descendants were assimilated by the kinship groups of their owners, integration usually being achieved by the second generation. Debt slaves were usually redeemed and freed. These distinctions have sometimes been romanticized to the point that traditional African slavery seems little more than a form of domestic service.

Goody (1980) reminds us that the conditions of capture and transfer "at times rivaled the horrors of the Atlantic trade" (p. 31). Once placed in a new community, the slave was a person without kin, a pathetic condition in traditional Africa. Finally, the path to eventual freedom came to a literal dead end for the slave who was sacrificed at the funeral of his master or a political official. Even the hope of freedom or family assimilation had unfortunate implications. These eventualities created the perpetual need to replenish the slave population from the outside, encouraging a cycle that included warfare and personal tragedies (Goody 1980).

Woman–Woman Marriage

Although probably not a modal pattern, marriages between women took place in numerous societies across the African Zone. Commonly, perhaps universally, this distinctive practice was a legal fiction. It used a traditional institution as a way to organize activities that were unusual for women. To obtain greater authority as an individual, a woman might assume the male role by symbolically marrying another woman. This was also a form of economic investment. If she acquired profits from her own activities (e.g., farming, trade, inheritance, or divination), a woman could invest them as bridewealth. In addition to making her wealth safe, she could obtain other advantages, such as control of a production unit or an heir to political office. Because of its socioeconomic nature, woman–woman marriage did not imply a sexual relationship.

FOREST AREA

Examples:

Mende, Yoruba, Ashante (Asante),
Igbo (Ibo), Mongo, Kongo

The Forest Area was characterized by tropical rain forest of varying density. It occupied the heart of the African continent with its western edge on the Atlantic and extended further west along the north shore of the Gulf of Guinea. It encompassed, among others, the modern nations of Congo-Kinshasa, Nigeria, and Sierra Leone.

The wet tropical climate of the Area encouraged the cultivation of root crops. Manioc, recently arrived from the Americas in 1700 A.D., challenged the indigenous yams for preeminence. Taro, an earlier import from Asia, served as a staple crop for many societies. Farmers also raised grains where possible, including native species and maize. Palm trees played an important role in material culture, especially the oil palm *(Elaeis guineensis)* and the raffia (several species of *Raphia*). They provided oil, food, drink, and construction materials. Another important tree *(Cola acuminata)* provided seeds that Africans chewed, but which others turned into a worldwide drink. Sleeping sickness carried by tsetse flies placed stringent limits on large domestic mammals, especially cattle.

The forest presented many of its inhabitants with major ecological problems, the first being the need to find or clear enough space to raise crops. Crop failures could be caused by excessive unseasonal rains as well as by droughts in some sections. The forest also harbored numerous diseases, many chronic and debilitating and some deadly. Despite these conditions, the Area gave rise to many states and chiefdoms along the fringes of the deep forest (including the seacoasts) and in places where its continuity was broken by rivers, plateaus, or other physical features.

Craft specialization resulted in highly skilled works of practical and spiritual significance. Forest Area people worked in diverse media, including metals and wood. From the latter they made masks and figure sculptures for ritual use. Africans created such items to accomplish specific goals, but the West now considers them to be great art.

The economy of the Area revolved around complex systems of regularly meeting markets. Most of the participants in markets were women. Because their trade profits belonged only to them, they were in a stronger economic position than women in most other traditional cultures in Africa or elsewhere. This translated into influence in the community as well as the family. Beyond having influence, women were regarded as legal adults with extensive rights.

Polygyny reached its greatest prominence in this Area where female farmers provided the bulk of the food. Lineages were more important than anywhere else in Africa, probably due in large part to two factors. First, farming depended on large-scale cooperation. Second, large numbers of kin could live near each other for long periods because Forest Area societies were relatively sedentary.

A variety of associations elaborated social relations. These included occupational groupings, organizations of religious practitioners, and title associations in which people purchased titles and emblems to add to their prestige. Cult associations devoted themselves to particular supernatural beings and/or particular powerful charms. Many cult associations were *secret societies* in the sense that their membership was not public knowledge or the identities of ritual performers were not known to spectators or they performed some ceremonies that were attended only by members. Secrecy heightened the impact of rituals and kept sacred knowledge from the uninitiated. In many cases a single group combined elements of cult and title. Occupational associations sometimes displayed elements of the other types.

Key features:

▶ Palm products and cola seeds

▶ Tropical tubers

▶ Market systems

▶ Craft specialization

▶ Cult associations

▶ Elaborate wooden masks and figures

Modal Patterns in Forest Culture

Material Culture

The man emerged from his small house into a dim and dappled world. Tall forest trees blocked most of the rising sun's light from the clearing in which the village stood. Near the man's dwelling stood two similar ones that housed his two wives and the children that each had borne for him and his lineage. The children played while their mothers prepared for the day's work. One of the women spoke to a small child who brought the man his breakfast, thick porridge on a broad leaf. He ate it quickly with his fingers, as did the two mothers with their children.

After the women left for the fields, their husband went to the grove of oil palm trees that he considered his private property. He anticipated a strenuous day as his gaze traveled up the first tall, thin tree to the spray of fronds at the top. There he would find the nuts that he

A young woman displays some of the traditional dress of the western part of the Forest Area (Ashante culture, Ghana).

needed. He placed his climbing ring around the tree, planted one foot on the trunk, and began his arduous climb. At the top, steadying himself with one hand, he took his machete in the other and hacked away the fronds that hid the palm nuts. He found four clusters, the usual number, which he cut loose and dropped to the forest floor. On some days the man performed this procedure fifteen times.

Back in his compound the man placed the palm nuts in water for processing. Some boiled them while others whipped the water with a small stick. In either case the result was an oily froth on top of the water that was easy to scoop out and place in a container. When the oil-making process was done, a man's wives took charge of the nuts themselves. After drying them, the women broke the shells to get the kernels inside. The kernels could be eaten or marketed and the shells provided a fuel that made brisk fires.

While the husband processed palm nuts, his wives used previously made oil to cook dinner. Pouring the yellow-orange oil from a gourd into a more open container, a woman made it into a stew with hot peppers and other ingredients. She could use greens or seeds and always included bits of meat or fish when they were available. People obtained some meat from a small number of goats, but chickens were the main domestic source. People used the stew as a dip for taro porridge or manioc bread. After eating, the diners drank large quantities of palm sap whenever it was available.

Obtaining the sap from oil palms was easier and safer work than climbing for the nuts, but it was also time-consuming. A man began in the morning by boring holes into the trees, and he returned at midday to clear out the same holes. In the evening the tapper collected some sap, cleaned some of the old holes, and made some new ones. Each tap was good for three or four days. Once the process had begun, the man collected the greatest amount of sap during the morning visit. The cloudy white liquid had the consistency of water. When placed in a stoppered calabash and set in the sun for just a few hours, it became an alcoholic drink with the strength of a strong beer.

A man could also obtain oily nuts and sap from raffia palms, but this was very much a second choice. The main attraction of the raffia was the very long and wide fronds that sprouted from its short trunk. They were excellent material for roofing and their strong stalks did well as a basis for walls and other construction.

Yet another tree that concerned men was the cola tree with its dome of long, thin leaves topping a vertical trunk covered by smooth green bark. In season they opened its pods to take seeds that were about one inch long and thick, colored either red or yellowish-green. People chewed them to ward off sleep, thirst, and hunger. Taken fresh, they had a somewhat bitter taste, but dried ones were milder. In preparation for storage people fermented the cola seeds in heaps for five days and then washed them. After this treatment they could last for several months.

A man's contribution to the staple crops entailed little more than clearing the main fields, but the large forest trees made it an arduous job that required iron cutting tools. Usually it got done in a day or two because a man called upon twenty or so of his relatives and friends to help. Of course he was then obligated to help them with their fields. Men sometimes burned cleared land, but this was often unnecessary because yam cultivation did not require it. When a field had been cleared, women hoed the soil into mounds and then planted a variety of crops in each one.

Though a woman spent most of her time in the fields and at the cooking fire, she also went to market on a regular basis. She could attend any or all of several marketplaces within walking distance because they met on different days, every fourth or eighth day. The smallest market drew perhaps a hundred people on a busy day while the largest often attracted more than a thousand. In addition to its economic benefits, the market gave busy wives a chance to renew or maintain friendships and to exchange information. It was a place to learn new things or simply be fascinated because markets, especially the larger ones, transcended ethnic, political, linguistic, and cultural divisions.

At the market a woman exchanged the products of her own labor and often those of her husband. She benefited personally because she had the legal right to control profits from her own labor as long as she fulfilled all obligations to her husband and children. Wealth accrued to the individual, not the family, and spouses pursued their own goals. Along with every kind of food grown in the vicinity, the market offered a wide variety of craft items. They included tools, utensils, weapons, furniture, pipes, and adornments. Specialized artisans had made many.

There were always some men among the many women in the marketplace. Some were local, but others were professional merchants who undertook long and arduous journeys between widely separated markets. They stopped at some markets simply to provision themselves and the numerous slaves in their caravans. Local people along their routes profited from raising surpluses for them, especially manioc, which was filling and could be preserved well.

The ultimate destination of the great traders was the coast. There they dealt with white people from across the ocean. The merchants provided the whites with luxury materials, such as ivory and gold, and with slaves. In return they obtained European manufactures, including firearms and gunpowder. While at the shore, the traders obtained salt to bring back with them.

Social Relations

The beating of drums announced a gathering of cult association members outside the village and warned the

A contemporary woman trader represents the market role of women in the Forest Area (Nigeria).

uninitiated to stay away. This was a particularly solemn occasion to honor the charm and the god that gave the association its powers. First the charm was displayed: a combination of materials from the forest that represented a forest creature. Then the god danced in front of the assembled members. The large mask and raffia costume hid the body of a senior official of the association, but it was the god who inhabited the mask and performed the dance that assured his followers of his patronage. Even when placed back in storage, the mask commanded fear and respect because it belonged to the god.

Several other cult associations existed in the village. These associations took a great deal of responsibility for socialization of children and for the maintenance of social order. Their rituals invested basic cultural values with emotion and reinforced the moral basis for the community by placing values and morality in the spiritual context of the ancestors. Members underwent an initiation followed by a period of training. Participation created a bond among people who in some cases had no other connection.

In the secular realm, cult associations sometimes administered physical punishment to those who violated community norms, a source of social control that was especially important in egalitarian societies with no other general authority. Cult associations also compensated for imbalances in the power of lineages. In hierarchical societies, they could check the abuse of power by rulers. This was possible because their religious charter gave them spiritual power that was even greater than that of chiefs or kings.

Knowledge and Expression

Farmers relied on nature spirits for the fertility of their crops and on the priests who propitiated these beings. Nature spirits sometimes communicated directly through a medium. The forest loomed large in people's minds as the opposite of civilization. Associating the forest with witchcraft and sorcery, they carried out important human activities, such as burial, in the cultivated areas. Boys were initiated in the forest because it symbolized their raw state; after the ritual they returned to the clearings and the villages to take their places as civilized human beings. The axe that cleared the forest was a compelling symbol in many contexts.

While most people feared the forest, some found ways to channel its power to human use. Herbalists, for example, used forest vegetation to cure some diseases. Sometimes they combined domestic and wild plants, drawing on two different sources of power to make the most effective medicines.

In the village clearing a carver sat down to the block of wood that he had prepared by hacking out the parts that would become head, torso, and legs. With his knife he began to refine the features. The iron blade of the tool was soft, but it took a sharp edge that allowed the artisan to carve the hardest woods. A skilled practitioner, he had a clear vision of his final product without recourse to any model or sketch. He also had vital knowledge of the rituals needed to placate the spirit that had inhabited the tree before it had been cut down.

Despite the carver's skills, visitors to the compound felt free to make remarks and give advice. Each had his or her own opinion about the features that would make the statue effective for its religious purpose. Once it was done, that effectiveness would speak for itself. People would judge whether the individual or group that possessed the figure had received the anticipated good fortune or power. Everyone agreed that the figure should be cool, that it should portray composure by restraint in facial expression and gesture. This was an ideal for human behavior as well, an ideal that people often tried to convey during dance.

The figure shaped by the sculptor faced forward as all statues did; nevertheless, the artisan also took care with the profile view. He made the head proportionately larger than in adult human beings. This infantile trait was appropriate in the representation of an ancestor because newborns were close to the ancestors, having just arrived from the supernatural realm. In other figures the infantile head may have symbolized the intense desire for children that all people shared.

The carver made some statues that were complete creations in themselves; others had parts left unworked. The latter were to be dressed in clothing made from the same materials that dressed humans. Sculptures had varied destinies. Some commemorated ancestors; others became temporary containers for visiting gods or spirits; still others were made into charms by a medicine man's spell. The audience for a completed work also varied. Some figures were constantly visible in family shrines, though often partly dressed or wrapped. Others were revealed only to the initiates of cult associations or seen only by the priests who administered major shrines.

While one carver completed a statue, another worked on a wooden mask. In addition to visualizing his finished product, he had to imagine the circumstances in which it would be used. The mask had to blend with a dance costume woven from raffia and make an impact on the viewers while in motion. For some masks the sculptor had to imagine how they would look by torchlight during a ritual dance. The various cult associations used some of the masks. Others represented gods who danced for the whole village on major ceremonial occasions.

The horns of sacrificed animals, mainly goats, were attached to some statues and masks. They represented devotion to the deity. Also, being hollow, they sometimes held magical substances. Snail shells sometimes served the same purpose.

A Closer Look

The recognition of Regions in this Area is more important than in almost any other place. Despite the profound modal patterns described above, the Forest Area included three sharply distinct cultural units.

The Guinea Coast Region

The Region is named for its long coastline on the Gulf of Guinea. It extended from the Ivory Coast to the eastern border of Nigeria, including the countries of Ghana, Togo, and Benin. Here the tropical forest was interspersed with savannas and swamps, providing subsistence opportunities that supported the highest population densities in the African Zone.

Many features of the Forest Area were expressed most intensely in this Region, including craft specialization. Artisans included mask makers, dyers, brass casters, and weavers who made the cotton cloth for the region's highly distinctive clothing. Associated with the high level of craft specialization was the prominence of craft associations, some of them much like the guilds of medieval Europe. In training apprentices, masters took on economic and quasi-parental responsibility for their charges.

Guinea Coast market systems were the most complex in the Forest Area. People used cloth as the main currency in ordinary marketing, value depending on particular styles and qualities (Bohannan and Curtin 1995). Rulers taxed, regulated, and policed the markets. Market courts settled trade disputes, and regular courts sometimes met at the market because it was a convenient gathering place.

Commerce with the Europeans now overshadowed the older relationship with the Muslims to the north. However, Muslim caravans still made their way into the forests on a regular basis. In addition to slaves, they prized the cola seed, one of the few stimulants that their religion permitted them to use. Trade was at least partly responsible for the fact that the Guinea Coast had the only real cities in sub-Saharan Africa. These cities, harboring tens of thousands of people, were also the capitals in which kings held court. Peasant farmers who cultivated surrounding lands comprised a large portion of city inhabitants.

Forest kingdoms kept many slaves because their productive importance went far beyond subsistence (Goody 1980). Large numbers of slaves worked on plantations, mined salt and metals, and carried the loads of the caravans. Slaves also assisted in various craft enterprises and even took charge of some small-scale tasks.

High-ranking and prestigious men used wives to establish alliances and to produce food and goods with which to obtain the goodwill of their subjects. The political significance of polygyny may account for its maximization in the complex societies of the Guinea Coast Region, where 43 percent of married men had more than one wife (Dorjahn 1959).

Women had specific public roles, including semiautonomous political structures parallel to those of the men. A variety of female associations also provided mutual support for members and input into political processes. With or without formal recognition, women used various strategies to limit male power and advance their own interests. This included informal mobilization to seek redress and sanctions for specific abuses and assaults, especially sexual ones.

Many children were fostered with grandparents or other relatives. One reason was the belief that it taught them to get along with a variety of people. Also, given the extreme psychological and social consequences of being barren, it was acceptable for a woman who had no children to ask a relative for a child to adopt.

Guinea Coast peoples believed in pantheons of powerful gods who were below the Creator but far greater than ordinary spirits. Some of these were similar throughout the region, including the thunder god, the god of war and iron, and a trickster god different from the animal trickster of folklore. Most people gave their allegiance to the cult of one particular god, although they acknowledged and sometimes petitioned others. Everyone respected Earth as a generous living thing, if not actually a god.

The Region was also distinguished by belief in fate. Although human actions had consequences, supernatural forces sometimes conferred undeserved fortune or misfortune. One source of fate was the destiny established before birth. Some believed that the individual made choices in a prior existence that had unpredictable consequences; alternatively, God decreed a fate for every human being before his or her life began. People also were subject to the fickleness of lower gods. The trickster god in particular might do good or evil for a person out of carelessness or malice. However, divination, prayer, and sacrifice could counter damaging intrusions on an orderly moral life.

The Congo Region

This Region encompassed the densest rain forests in Africa. In modern terms it consisted mainly of Congo-Brazzaville and northern Congo-Kinshasa. A wide variety of social adaptations, including rather ephemeral chiefdoms and kingdoms, were based on a common and distinctive system of village life that emphasized competition for leadership (Vansina 1990, 1999). Some Congo peoples, such as the Mongo, seem to have departed little from this original system.

Farming provided only about 40 percent of the food supply in a balanced system that included gathering, hunting, and trapping. People used hundreds of plants and dozens of animals from the forest. They coordinated foraging with farming in a seasonal round that produced a consistently well-balanced diet. The staple crops were yams (*Dioscorea cayensis*) and the oil palm. The hoe was absent and only digging sticks were used in cultivation.

Each large, rectangular house held between twenty and forty people. At the beginning of every dry season all able people left the village for a trek in the forest. Over the following month or so they made a series of camps from which they conducted a variety of foraging activities. Men especially looked forward to joining in cooperative hunts with nets. With all the men of the village participating, these hunts generated excitement and camaraderie that made up for the unpredictable and often disappointing results. Women usually provided more animal food from their gathering activities, including crabs and shellfish from the shores of ponds and streams. With their children they caught fish with dams, traps, scoops, and drugs. In the forest they gathered ants, larvae, and snails along with fruits, roots, leaves for food greens, and cola nuts.

However successful and enjoyable the trek might be, the requirements of farming brought people back to the village. They had to clear new fields in time for the vegetation to dry before the next rainy season set in. The men of a communal house prepared a single major field every year, using their stone axes to cut down large trees and trim wood for a strong fence to protect the crops from animals. The women of the house joined the men to plant the yams and secondary crops. The latter included beans and other legumes, peanuts, hibiscus, amaranth, gourds, and calabashes.

Women weeded the field several times and harvested the faster-growing secondary crops while men planted stakes for the yam vines when the time was right. Finally, after ten months, everyone harvested the yams together. Then, except for a few secondary crops in a small section, they left the field fallow for up to ten years.

The growing season was interspersed with other subsistence tasks for both sexes. Each woman cultivated greens, peppers, and medicinal herbs in a small garden next to the house in which she lived. She rotated her crops and sometimes experimented with new ones. Men took responsibility for tree crops, including raffia palm, several fig species, plum, and cola. They also manufactured and set a variety of traps outside the fenced fields. They knew which animals were attracted to which crops: bushpig to yams, for example, and antelope to the leaves of the bean plants. Trapping provided more meat than the enjoyable but unreliable cooperative hunts of the dry season. A few men hunted alone or in small groups occasionally throughout the year. Most of them were youths or semispecialized experts. During short seasons of abundance, people went back to the forest for caterpillars, termites, mushrooms, and honey. They camped in the forest at the height of the fruiting season.

Along paths through the forest and navigable streams people carried raw materials and manufactured items to other villages for trade. These included crops, salt, metals and metal objects, raffia cloth, pottery, canoes, palm oil, and fish. Some of the fish came from men who systematically worked the large rivers with specialized equipment.

The chieftain was the focus of his house because its inhabitants had been brought there by his leadership and generosity. They included his wives and children, kin on his father's and mother's sides, friends, clients, and slaves. They spoke of themselves as a family and the chieftain as their father. House chieftains competed with each other

for followers. A few large houses had more than a hundred members. The smallest, with perhaps as few as ten, were in danger of extinction. The need for cooperative labor during the dry season placed a lower limit on the house population.

The issue of marriage deeply concerned the chieftain because it related to the strength of his house. He had to make sure that the membership included enough men and women to carry out all necessary tasks. To this end he frequently intervened in marriage arrangements and facilitated unions by various means that included bridewealth, sister exchange, capture, and the reception of women in exchange for peacemaking. Sometimes he attracted young men to the house by giving them some of his own wives for consorts.

Within the village the domain of each house was clearly marked. However, the village also displayed signs of unity in the plaza and clubhouse where public activities took place. People acknowledged the leadership of the chieftain who had founded the village. They showed him respect in everyday life and gave him his due from the killing of special animals such as leopards. He in turn shared leadership with a council composed of the community's most important men. Every few years villagers joined for the collective rite of circumcision. After preparatory schooling in the main principles of social life, the eligible boys made the transition to adulthood together. The resulting bond united men of different houses.

The solidarity of the village had its greatest significance in mutual defense. Communities often fought all-out wars in which the victors burned the village of the losers. Tribal alliances provided further protection. An alliance emerged when neighboring villages came to rely on each other for mutual defense, trade, and intermarriage. They formalized the connection in terms of a clan relationship. Discovering a common ancestor, they took a common name and developed an origin story and a shared food taboo. Conflicts occurred between villages within a clan, but they were restricted by rules. Disputants made a formal declaration of war and agreed to meet near the border for a battle. Elders from one side or the other stopped the fight after one or two serious casualties.

Many objects used for curing and other purposes were charms, which worked only if the correct spell was combined with the correct ingredients. Most importantly, the creator and the user both had to observe the right taboos. People treated charms as tools to be used for specific purposes. Some belonged to individuals while others were collective. The purposes of the latter included rain control, success in warfare, and control of witchcraft. Some diviners used charms to detect witches while others consulted oracles or saw the malefactors in dreams or trances. The accused was subjected to the poison ordeal in which the innocent vomited the poison and lived. When guilt was apparent, people killed the witch and burned the body. Men generally suspected women, clients, and slaves of witchcraft because these people of low status had no other reliable means to redress their grievances.

The Southern Savanna Region

This cultural unit has been variously and confusingly referred to as Central Africa, the Southern Sudanic region, and the Matrilineal Belt. The term "Southern Savanna" combines relative simplicity and accuracy. It distinguishes the Region from the northern savanna (in the Greater Sudanic Area) and the eastern savanna (Cattle Area), both described later in this chapter. Prominent cultures in the Region included the southern Kongo and Luba. By 1700 the Lunda had established an empire that affected virtually the entire Region.

The environment of the Region varied from northwest to southeast. The fringe of the deep forest gave way to increasingly scattered pockets of forest and finally to extensive grasslands. Gallery forests occurred wherever the rivers were sufficient to support them. Thus tropical crops like manioc, peanuts, and sweet potato persisted through much of the Region.

Nevertheless, a common environment was hot savanna with low bushes and scattered trees. The soils were even poorer than those elsewhere in Africa and required unusual elaboration of horticultural practices. Even with crop rotation a farm plot lasted only two to four years and then needed a fallow period of up to twenty years. Farmers cleared and burned new fields annually and applied unusual techniques such as *chitimene*, in which branches were cut from trees in a much wider circle than the plot being prepared.

Farming problems seem to have been related to other features, the most obvious being the value placed on hunting. Cult associations placed great emphasis on fertility. The extra labor needed in farming probably placed a premium on the use of slaves; this led to frequent warfare that provided large numbers of captives for enslavement.

Although sometimes called the "matrilineal belt," the Southern Savanna actually harbored many bilateral societies as well as matrilineal ones. The defining feature in contrast with the rest of Africa is the scarcity of patrilineal systems. Bilaterality and the emphasis on recent ancestors might be explained in terms of the mobility of families. Matrilineality and bilaterality enhanced the status of women. On the personal level gender relations could be tense and divorce was common, probably because of the assertiveness of women. Ideologically, respect for women and for femininity was represented by symbols ranging from rich graves to serene sculpted figures.

Residential preference was virilocal: residence with the husband's father or his mother's brother was preferred. However, either because of bilateralism or a wife's matrilineal ties, people made intricate and flexible arrangements. Because of the great mobility of the population, kinship was often less important than personal political attachments. People readily moved from one village chieftain to another and even from one chief to another. Political leaders tended to see kinship as a competing principle of organization.

Kinship may have been weakened by inability to deal with heavy demands for labor. There was an unusually high incidence of hereditary slavery because of the high labor demand. Large numbers of slaves were obtained by capture in war, a process supported by militaristic values. However, despite the prevalence of military force, the state tended to be sprawling and loosely organized with emphasis on tribute rather than political control.

Individuals made private prayers to God and sometimes offered first fruits. Priests dealt with nature spirits and elders with the ancestors. There were also special religious associations devoted to fertility. Perhaps because larger political entities were so loosely organized, the spiritual role of rulers took on distinctive form with state cults that centered on royal graves. Religion combined with art in the form of figurines with attachments such as mirrors, horns, shells, beads, nails, and herbal medicines. These were intended to harness spiritual power.

CATTLE AREA

Examples:

Zulu, Xhosa, Ganda, Tutsi, Masai, Nuer

People kept cattle in various parts of Africa and accorded them social as well as economic significance. The Cattle Area was distinguished by (1) the extent to which cattle replaced slaves and trade goods as the medium for accumulating, storing, and reproducing wealth (see Iliffe 1995), and (2) the extent to which cattle entered the religious, esthetic, and symbolic sensibilities of the people. Cattle constituted the key animal for nomadic herders in the Area, but many people who were primarily farmers valued cattle in ways similar to the pastoralists.

Cattle are economically attractive in a savanna habitat because they require relatively little work. Compared to the cultivation of land, maintenance of a herd takes fewer people and less effort. However, though hardy and adaptable, the small hump-backed cattle of this Area produced relatively little milk and meat. Blood, usually tapped from a neck vein, was also used as a food but was not sufficient as a staple. Having limited food value, these cattle were more important as a form of wealth and played a major role in prestige and exchange.

More specifically, wealth-in-cattle seems to have partially replaced the African Zone's modal pattern of wealth-in-people. Polygyny was less common in the Cattle Area than anywhere else in Africa, with perhaps only one fourth of married men having more than one wife (Dorjahn 1959). A man with many cattle could acquire a wife when and if he needed one.

Also, slavery was of relatively little importance. Little effort was made to secure slaves: most of them were people who had voluntarily given up their freedom in order to escape famine (Iliffe 1995). The insignificance of slavery may have been due to the lack of prominent trade networks (Iliffe 1995) and/or the availability of cattle as large-scale portable wealth (Schneider 1981). Slaves and cattle were both economically productive and provided alternative ways to accumulate value for use in social exchanges.

The Cattle Area was characterized by a *house-property complex* in which each mother–child house stood on its own plot of land, dispersed from the others in a polygynous family. Women had some domestic authority and some influence on men (Morrow 1986), but their status was low in many ways compared to that of women in other parts of Africa (Iliffe 1995). According to Macquet (1972), the men concentrated on "aristocratic values" that glorified themselves as individuals and groups. It is not clear whether this differed greatly from pastoralists elsewhere in the Old World. Restraint in artistic performance supposedly represents this aristocratic elegance.

Key features:

▶ Dispersed household (house-property complex)

▶ Prominence of age grading

▶ Relatively low status for women

▶ Insignificance of slavery

▶ Ritual and esthetic significance of cattle

▶ Restrained art styles

Modal Patterns in Cattle Area Culture

Material Culture

Both farmers and nomads made cattle their key animal but also kept sheep and goats, sometimes in greater numbers than cattle. They regularly slaughtered the smaller animals for meat while preserving cows for milk, steers for social and ritual purposes, and a few bulls for breeding. While milk was the main food product of cattle, people considered their blood a delicacy. Some consumed blood directly, some roasted it, and others mixed it with milk or porridge. Blood was also used as an emergency food when the milk supply was inadequate. Despite economic and cultural restrictions, pastoralists also obtained a significant supply of meat from cattle. They consumed cows that died of natural causes and they frequently performed rituals for which the sacrificial slaughter of steers was required.

Cattle management was based on the maintenance of the largest herds possible, even at the expense of weight and productivity. There were several reasons for this. First, the particular breeds of cattle used were able to survive in difficult conditions. Second, large numbers compensated for the low productivity of individuals. Third, large numbers hedged against periodic losses to drought, disease, and raids. Fourth, people regarded cattle as social wealth and used them in numerous exchanges. Finally, placing symbolic and esthetic value on cattle, people delighted in their quantity and variety.

The herders followed a seasonal round in which they dispersed their herds during the rainy season and clustered them around waterholes during the dry season. The daily routine was based on fixed compounds (widely called *kraals*) to which the animals were returned every night. Construction of these fenced compounds entailed a great deal of work, and their use limited the mobility that was essential to finding sufficient pasturage. The presence of numerous large carnivores made substantial fences necessary.

Social Relations

Each married woman lived on her own plot of land, apart from any other wives that her husband had. She and her sons formed a unit for the inheritance of land and cattle. The mother managed the property for her sons until they were of age. Wives engaged in little cooperative or reciprocal effort, and warm personal relationships were uncommon. Sons felt strong loyalty to their mother and tended to be competitive with half-brothers.

Bridewealth consisted mainly of cattle, preferably in large numbers. The groom's family eased its burden by

Like his counterparts throughout the Cattle Area, this boy watches cattle for his family (Kenya).

Young warriors were a vital part of the nomadic herding way of life in the Cattle Area (Masai culture).

accumulating the cattle from a wide range of relatives and friends who could be gradually repaid. Pressure was also diminished by the African pattern of late marriage. A girl was trained to serve all the men and the older women of the household into which she married. A woman had no right to land or even to the grain that she had cultivated, except through men. She was a legal minor who had access to judicial action only through male representatives. In a divorce she lost all rights to her children, a sanction that men used to enforce unusually stringent chastity. Women were kept away from cattle and did not share the male attachment to them.

Age grading emphasized young warriors. This was partly due to high levels of warfare, but it may also have been a device by which older men controlled the younger. Junior warriors were often placed in military outposts and forbidden to marry until they reached their thirties. For old men, control of cattle probably prolonged the period of life when they remained respected and influential.

Knowledge and Expression

Water was a paramount concern in the dry grasslands and rainmakers were important religious practitioners. Some rainmakers played that role because it went with being a high political official. Others were specialists in the field.

Cattle constituted the most important religious sacrifices, but other animals were also used. The symbolism of cattle pervaded ideology and society. Men identified themselves with cattle in very specific ways that often facilitated personal and emotional attachment. This particularly applied to the prize steers that were associated with every life-cycle ritual. Men named these animals, decorated them, and sang their praises. They also praised themselves for qualities such as courage, self-confidence, and pride, contributing to a feeling of collective superiority over other groups.

A young woman displays the elaborate personal decoration that characterized the Cattle Area (Pakot culture).

Art focused on personal items, including clothing, ornaments, and the body itself. People wore beads and bracelets and dressed their hair in various ways. They carved and decorated clay pipes and shields and weapons. They furnished their houses with skins, mats, and pottery. Art styles emphasized simplicity and order. Visual art was characterized by quiet, linear motifs. People often played percussion instruments solo or sang with the accompaniment of a zither or a musical bow. They recited concise poetry with vocal expression, but without gestures. The spear was glorified in historical recitations, as well as poems and songs, but the latter also dealt with love and cattle.

A Closer Look

The Great Lakes Region and Ethnic Politics

The Great Lakes of east central Africa provide a convenient reference for delimiting the subdivisions of the Cattle Area. The largest of the lakes are Victoria, Tanganyika, and Nyasa—all touching the borders of the modern country of Tanzania. In 1700 A.D. the strongest states of the Cattle Area existed among the Great Lakes and to the east of them. They included Bunyoro, Buganda, and Rwanda. Great Lakes kings consolidated their states by marrying women from every clan in the realm. This was more than a symbolic gesture because every male child of these relationships was a potential successor to the throne. At least some of the kings consolidated empires by appointing military leaders as governors of conquered lands.

The ethnic and political structure of these traditional states is relevant to modern political problems, especially in the countries of Rwanda and Burundi. It was previously thought that the traditional states were structured by a simple caste division between oppressive pastoral conquerors (e.g., Tutsi) and indigenous farmers (e.g., Hutu). Current thinking is that the groups intermingled in complex ways and that the state facilitated beneficial exchanges between farmers and pastoralists (July 1998). The ruling dynasties certainly came from the herders, but officials and other personnel of the state included indigenous farmers. Furthermore, the form of the state was largely based on indigenous traditions (Meeker 1989).

What about the Zulu?

The Zulu are among the most famous of African peoples. During the nineteenth century, they built a powerful empire in the southern part of the Cattle Area. However, their ancestors in 1700 A.D. were submerged in a simpler and more fluid political system. The basic units were chiefdoms that grew or fused into small kingdoms that soon fell apart. Oral traditions explained these processes in personal terms, such as conquests by a hero or conflict between rival princes. Population growth in a very dry environment probably accounts for much of the political volatility (Isichei 1997).

Whether chief or king, a ruler had more cattle, wives, and children than other people. He also controlled the use of cattle by other people. Control of people and cattle conferred power, and power made it easier to gain more people and cattle. However, at least two major factors could interrupt this upward spiral. First, the ruler's subjects were mobile. Those who felt oppressed could move away and, because the polities were small, they did not have far to go in order to escape. Second, because rain-making was a principal ritual duty of the ruler, a drought provided a powerful reason for others to challenge him.

The Nilotic Region

Speakers of Nilotic languages dominated the Nilotic Region in the northern part of the Cattle Area. They are called "Nilotic" because they originated further north,

in the vicinity of the Nile River in what is now the country of Sudan. Nilotic culture differed from the rest of the Cattle Area in that women, far from having cattle tabooed to them, regularly milked cows. Age grades were especially prominent here because a high degree of nomadism often weakened lineage solidarity and made residential groups unstable. Since many unrelated young men were initiated into the system together, a man could usually find other members of his age set wherever he went.

In religion the Nilotic people distinguished themselves from all the rest of Africa. They thought of God as a formless spirit, manifested in natural phenomena such as sun and wind, rather than as an anthropomorphic deity. Ironically, this unhuman god took an unusual interest (for Africa) in everyday human affairs and therefore received frequent prayers and sacrifices. Correspondingly, people paid less attention to the ancestors than elsewhere in Africa. To a large extent they attributed evil and misfortune to ritual impurity. Thus the usual goal of sacrifice was ritual cleansing rather than communication with supernatural beings.

GREATER SUDANIC AREA

Examples:

Hausa, Fulani, Bornu, Amhara,
Oromo (Galla), Somali

The Greater Sudanic Area combines two of anthropology's more conventional cultural units. These are commonly called the Sudan (which I retain as a Region) and the Horn (which I split into two Regions). The Sudanic Region occupied a belt of savanna between the Forest Area to the south and the Sahara Desert to the north and ran from the Atlantic Ocean in the west to the border of the modern-day country of Sudan in the east. Unfortunately the nation of Sudan does not belong to the Sudanic cultural unit, being split between the Cattle Area and the Middle East. This is confusing, but the term "Sudanic" for the cultural unit is deeply entrenched in the anthropological literature, and no better alternative is available. To complete the confusion, my Greater Sudanic Area is discontinuous. Its remaining two Regions lie east of the nation of Sudan.

Why create this geographic monstrosity? Because its component Regions shared numerous traits of material

culture and several striking features of social organization. The latter included caste distinctions and female genital operations. Slavery in this Area contrasted with other parts of Africa in that it was a hereditary status. Slaves and the offspring of slaves had no hope of joining the master's kinship group.

An essential feature of the Sudanic Area was the intermingling of diverse groups, particularly the influence of Middle Eastern cultures and Islam on native African traditions.

Key features:

▶ Grain cultivation

▶ Various domestic animals

▶ Markets

▶ Long-distance trade

▶ Nomadic herders

▶ Occupational castes

▶ Female genital operations

▶ Hereditary slavery

▶ Middle East and Islamic influences

Modal Patterns in Greater Sudanic Culture

Material Culture

The small farm village consisted of round huts with conical thatched roofs. The mud walls of the huts lasted for a reasonable length of time in the dry climate. Villagers raised sorghum and other grains as their staple crops. Every family kept some animals and the more fortunate had a full complement of chickens, donkeys, sheep, goats, and cattle. Women tended the smaller animals while men took primary responsibility for the cattle. However, women milked the cows and made some of the milk into butter.

A village scene in the Greater Sudanic Area features typical round, mud-walled huts with conical thatched roofs (Mali).

Outside such villages nomadic herders kept the same animals in much larger numbers and drove them long distances to keep them in adequate pasturage. Women tended the cows in camp, milked them, and sometimes sold their dairy products in market. However, men herded the cattle and celebrated symbolic and emotional ties with them.

Farmers and nomads bartered their goods in local and regional markets that met on a regular schedule such that one was within reach every day. At a large market or on the road, people sometimes encountered a caravan of long-distance traders. Often the slaves, who were to be sold themselves, carried other goods such as gold, ivory, and salt. Many merchants used pack animals, either donkeys or camels, depending on the terrain to be covered.

Social Relations

An important family occasion was the performance of a ritualized genital operation on a daughter. This involved removal of part or all of the clitoris. Often it was followed by infibulation, in which the labia were sewn or, if partially removed, fused together. Only a small opening for urination remained until the genitals were reopened in preparation for marriage. People explained the operation in various ways, but the consistent result was to reduce the sexual activity of the subject. Intercourse was physically impossible before marriage. Extramarital sex held little appeal due to removal or impairment of the clitoris while marital sex was performed as a duty.

Several groups of craft workers lived apart from other villagers. People regarded those who worked in iron, leather, and wood as being inferior and refused to intermarry with them or even eat with them. All the stigmatized groups were forbidden to bear weapons. They were also exempt from enslavement and from codes of honor. Many people believed that the unusual skills of these specialists came in some way from evil spirits.

Islam enjoined kindness to slaves, but the slaves had no legal rights. Some left slavery because their masters released them, but they continued to occupy a low status in society. Some found more favorable destinies by remaining slaves. Able male slaves could achieve wealth and influence by service to prominent men. If attached to nobility or royalty, they might attain high office. Because their status was thought to check ambition and ensure loyalty, qualified slaves were given high administrative posts. Women who became concubines saw a better future for their children, who were free persons and legitimate offspring of the master.

Knowledge and Expression

Traders from the Middle East had first acquainted the local people with Islam, and preachers had followed. Many nomadic herders accepted the new religion wholeheartedly and tried to spread it further. Others were less enthusiastic or less orthodox. Some resisted strongly. Even those who became staunch Muslims tended to preserve features of indigenous African religion.

A Closer Look

The Sudanic Region

After clearing his land with fire, a farmer planted his first crops when the rainy season began and continued to plant at intervals thereafter. Along with interplanting and crop rotation, this conserved the ungenerous savanna soil as long as possible. The periodic harvests resulting from sequential planting reduced the possibility of starvation. Whether men or women cultivated the crops, they joined for the communal harvests. They preserved the grains in pits lined with straw or in large urns made from mud that

Women selling sorghum (Mali).

they elevated for protection from termites. Women processed the grain and made it into flatbread that they served with green vegetables raised in their gardens.

In 1700 A.D. the greatest impact of Islam on the Sudanic Region lay a century away. Villagers knew that a religion called Islam was gaining converts around them. They had heard that the king subscribed to at least some beliefs and practices of the new faith. Many of the nomads accepted it and tried to convey its basic tenets to the farmers. From time to time the villagers encountered an itinerant preacher who provided a somewhat more learned viewpoint. These clerics gained some converts, but their rigid orthodoxy alienated many people. They frowned on the African version of checkers, which was played quickly, publicly, socially, and noisily. Some even preached against traditional music and dance. Most of the villagers continued to worship the old gods and the ancestors in the old ways.

Diverse people and ways of life mingled behind the walls of a city. In some sections round huts with thatched roofs housed members of the native population. Elsewhere, foreigners lived in rectangular houses of stone or mud with interior courtyards. These were Arabs and other Muslims, who also built mosques in the city. Well-clothed Muslims, many of them merchants and scholars, walked the narrow, crowded streets. They contrasted sharply with local farmers driving their loaded donkeys toward the marketplace and ragged desert nomads trying to control their camels. The Muslims felt varying degrees

of outrage at the sight of lightly and brightly clad women walking the streets on errands of their own, not to mention the occasional naked servant girl on an errand for her master. Occasionally a squadron of the king's cavalry pushed through the mob.

Proponents of religious rigor tried to introduce Middle Eastern constraints on women in everyday life but encountered strong resistance. Along with those who maintained traditional African ideas, many converts rejected seclusion and even veiling. Some women who were secluded managed to engage in traditional African activities such as trade by various devices, including the use of their children as agents. Divorce was a viable option for women because they retained important ties to their natal kinship groups.

Merchants conducted an elaborate trade across the savanna that connected the southern forests with the desert and the seashores beyond. In addition to porters and pack animals, traders used dugout canoes on rivers. Along with other valuables, they brought cola seeds from the forests to provide devout Muslims with the only stimulant that their religion allowed them. Traders made complex deals that required shipments to be split and recombined in various ways as they found their way to many destinations. The great merchants maintained agents at points along the trade routes to keep track of market trends, political events, and the competition.

Savanna kings and nobles coveted large warhorses from the Mediterranean coast and Arabia. Though expensive, the horses facilitated capture of the slaves that paid for them. Trade in slaves and horses was brisk because both suffered high mortality rates. The introduction of warhorses created a fairly exclusive new social class and profoundly affected military and political activity. A powerful kingdom had thousands of horses. The cavalrymen cultivated codes of honor that emphasized self-glorification and widened their separation from the general population.

A horseman (Saracolle culture).

During battles between armies, horsemen were often held in reserve behind the foot soldiers. However, they played a vital role in the economy by maintaining a steady supply of slaves. Every dry season, the cavalry raided non-Muslim people of stateless societies to the south. Small units swooped down on children in the fields and threw them into bags as they rode away. A larger force surrounded a village and burned it, taking most of the survivors prisoner immediately and riding down those that fled. The new slaves were taken back to the savanna in files bound to the horses' tails.

Many slaves passed through the grassland kingdoms, but many were retained. The males took on a variety of roles that included servant, porter, laborer, craftsman, and miner (especially in the Saharan salt mines). Male slaves were also used as ordinary soldiers and as mounted retainers to cavalrymen. Masters had many male slaves castrated because the menials often performed traditionally female tasks. However, savanna masters favored female slaves over males. They used the women as domestic servants and concubines.

As states and empires rose and fell, the great cities came under the domination of one or another but usually retained a degree of independence because of their importance. They were centers for trade, government, religion, education, literacy, and science. Because most rulers found Islamic law to be an efficient basis for administering their sprawling domains, they retained literate and educated Muslim advisors. Though mostly clerics, the advisors had a stake in the status quo and rarely advocated the rigorous faith of rural proselytizers. Kings continued to take the throne on the basis of matrilineal descent, to accept advice from royal women, and to enjoy an aura of spiritual power.

While glad to benefit from Muslim law and advisors, kings varied a great deal in their observance of the religious beliefs and practices. Some devoutly performed the Five Pillars, including the pilgrimage to Mecca. Others were casual about ritual and tolerated traditional customs in the countryside and even at court. Some kings ignored calls for holy war against pagan neighbors, and some even persecuted certain groups of Muslims although all in the faith were supposed to be brothers. The rulers were aware that they benefited from the traditional aura of spiritual sanction even though they could no longer overtly accept divine status.

While getting varied results with monarchs, Muslims gradually but steadily brought their culture into the urban world of the grasslands. They built mosques in the cities and universities in some of them. In those places they propagated the religion and also the literacy, arts, and sciences of the Islamic tradition.

The Ethiopian Region

This Region consisted largely of the highlands in the central and western parts of what is now Ethiopia. In the northeast it extended to the shore of the Red Sea. The environment was somewhat arid, but altitude produced complex local variations. The Region contained three major ethnic groups: the Amhara, the Tigray, and the Oromo (Galla). They shared certain features of peasant economy and ideology.

A farm village consisted of a few homesteads dispersed on a hillside above potential floods. Ideally a homestead contained a patrilocal joint family. Some of these peasants owned their own land while others had to survive as tenants on the lands of the wealthy. Farmers turned the soil for their grains with iron-tipped plows drawn by oxen. A large number of cattle brought prestige. Regular local markets allowed people to trade the products of diverse habitats. The pivotal geographic location of the Area encouraged substantial long-distance trade by caravan and by coastal shipping.

Gender ideology revolved around a cult of masculinity in which the preeminent value was to display prowess by killing animal and human enemies. Men esteemed hunting as a display of courage even though they disparaged the members of the hunting caste and the use of wild animals for food. Killers received an exalted status reflected in special privileges and insignia. They boasted of their own accomplishments, and their deeds were recited at their funerals. Special genres of verse goaded men into aggression and celebrated their victories.

The masculine ideology did not value sexual prowess or idealize women in any way. Sex was considered dangerous to men, either polluting or depleting. Women themselves were considered treacherous, unreliable, and weak. Men expressed little appreciation for any female characteristics and used many idioms of contempt for real or imagined female traits. Considering women inferior, men excluded them from most public assemblies and important rituals.

Some supernatural beliefs were characteristic of the African Zone, such as spirit possession and animal sacrifice. Others, like the taboo on pork, clearly came from the Middle East. There was also a widespread belief in jinnis associated with natural locales such as trees, hilltops, and water places.

The Amhara ethnic group formed the nucleus of a long-lasting kingdom with a feudal social structure. Dependent peasants lived as serfs on the land of an aristocratic overlord. The noble held his land from the king in return for military service. The Amhara subscribed to Monophysite Christianity, which allowed them three forms of marriage. Most people entered into civil marriage arranged by their kin, with perhaps a priest to bless the union. Divorce was possible, with property and custody negotiable. Nobles and priests had church weddings that gave them no right to divorce. Some men made a contract with a woman for a temporary marriage in which she functioned as a wife for a specified period of time in return for the same wages as a housekeeper.

The woman had no right to inherit from her temporary husband, but any children of the marriage could make a claim. A girl married as young as age fourteen to ensure that she was a virgin at the wedding. Youth also made a new wife easier for the husband to control.

Amhara Christians attached little significance to Christmas, viewing it mainly as a time for young men to play and boast about a favorite game that resembled hockey. Epiphany was a more important religious holiday, but it also marked a sporting season. At this time young men jousted on horseback with blunt wooden lances. At the Easter feasts after Lent, groups of men drank beer while priests prayed.

Sick people turned to herbalists or to shamans linked with the church. They also had the option of the *zar* cult, in which most of the practitioners were women. They pitted their own possessing spirits against the evil ones afflicting their clients. Many men considered the cult effeminate and visited the healers secretly at night.

The Oromo ethnic group (until recently known as the Galla) invaded the Ethiopian plateau in relatively recent times. They emphasized cattle keeping but raised enough crops to sustain kingdoms and perpetual warfare. They also profited from slave raiding. Traditional Oromo social organization was based on a complex series of ten or eleven age grades. A boy entered the system when he was initiated, forty years after his father's initiation. The age grades provided the basis for democratic local government. However, war leaders tended to gain a great deal of personal power and institute hierarchical relations culminating in the state. Oromo religion, expressed in a rich oral literature, espoused a creator God much like that of the Old Testament.

The Somali Region

In the arid lowlands along the Red Sea and the Indian Ocean, most of the Somali people lived as nomadic herders. Women and children tended the same livestock kept by the highland farmers. However, Somali men herded and milked the animal most important to them, the camel. The Somali Region contrasted with the rest of the Greater Sudanic Area in maintaining a largely tribal level of organization. In many ways the Somali herders resembled the Nilotic pastoralists in the northern part of the Cattle Area. They differed in the use of camels and in varying degrees of adherence to Islam.

SWAHILI AREA

The Swahili people lived in a narrow band along the east coast of Africa from southern Somalia to northern Mozambique. No specific examples are given here because no communities or subdivisions of the Swahili are generally known among Westerners. The name (which they did not use for themselves) comes from Arabic for "coast." They claimed Arabic or Persian origins; however, this was a device to distance themselves from their slaves, who were Africans from the interior (Middleton 1992). Although Muslims, the Swahili displayed a number of African cultural traits. These included relative freedom and equality for women, ceremonies for town purification, and non-Islamic practices for healing and protection from witches and sorcerers. With regard to this syncretism the Swahili resembled the Muslims of the Sudanic Area. The two Areas differed in that Islam was universally accepted by the Swahili while some ethnic groups of the Sudanic Area rejected it.

For almost two thousand years the Swahili played a pivotal role in trade between Africa and Asia by acting as middlemen. After 1500 A.D. many settlements declined under domination by the Portuguese, but some continued to thrive (Kusimba 1999). This account describes the thriving settlements that represented the heights of Swahili achievement.

Key features:

▶ Coastal settlements

▶ Intercontinental trade

▶ Islam

▶ African religious practices

Modal Patterns in Swahili Peasant Culture

Material Culture

A screen of palm fronds protected the privacy of the household. The buildings inside were all small and square with mud walls and roofs thatched from palm fronds. Some people used palm mats for the walls as well. Private gardens between households harbored coconut and mango trees, along with green plants. The trees provided both food and technological materials.

The primary mosque, a modest building much like a house, marked the center of town. Near it stood the Islamic school. Several other mosques were scattered throughout the sprawling town of perhaps a thousand people. Other public buildings included shops, coffeehouses, and meeting halls. People also met at the markets, wells, and washing places.

In the fields beyond the town, women cultivated rice and sorghum, the staple crops, along with a variety of other food plants that included tubers as well as grains. The fields provisioned the farmers, and the surplus went to the nearby harbor town, where elite people lived. Women also engaged in small-scale trade and manufactured coconut products. Many men went to the ocean to fish or to the harbor town for wage work. People considered the work of men and women to be complementary and the sexes to be equal in most respects.

A young Swahili woman, presumably rural, in typically African dress (as opposed to the Muslim customs of the towns).

Social Relations

The town was physically divided between moieties, and each half was divided into neighborhoods. A neighborhood was composed of bilateral kin who formed a corporate and landholding unit. In these groups, where female ties were as important as male, women were the equals of their male kin in most matters.

People preferred cousin marriages in order to retain land rights within the kin group. Marriage required bridewealth, part of it from the groom himself and part from his kin. The bride's kin provided a dowry, and the husband went to live with them.

A group of boys underwent an initiation ceremony that began with circumcision. Afterward they went into seclusion for two or three weeks. During this time they sang special songs, ate special foods, and received moral and sexual instruction. Girls went through an initiation of comparable complexity that emphasized sexual pleasure rather than procreation.

Senior men and women held authority in everyday life. A council of men with representation from every ward made decisions for the town. Two officials had special functions. One accepted and controlled tenants, using their rents to support the mosque and sacrifices for the spirits. The other official, often a woman, specialized in ritual. She placated spirits when new fields were cleared, and she opened and closed the planting seasons. She used sacrifice and medicines to treat the sick and fight against witches and sorcerers. She also organized the non-Islamic portion of the New Year celebration.

Knowledge and Expression

All the people considered themselves to be orthodox Sunni Muslims, although visiting Arabs would have questioned a number of their practices. People prayed five times daily, men attended the mosque every Friday, and children received Islamic education in the school near the mosque. The town observed regular Islamic ceremonies such as the fast of Ramadan and the feast that concluded it. However, they also placed great emphasis on a non-Islamic ceremony that opened the New Year by purifying the town. Men and women led a bull around the town in a counterclockwise direction. Feasting followed the ritual slaughter of the bull. During the festival, people symbolically dismantled and rebuilt key structures in the town. These town ceremonies expressed the feeling of the population that they were civilized, as opposed to the barbaric peoples of the interior. Literacy further reinforced this view. Most people could read and write, and they highly valued the written records that chronicled their history and religion.

Spirit possession was considered "African" rather than Islamic and was associated with women. However, the women who practiced it considered themselves to be orthodox Muslims. Furthermore, most men regularly patronized these practitioners, and men controlled most of the associations that united the mediums. Some male doctors also practiced possession, along with herbal cures and Islamic methods. They provided people with a way to deal with spirits and sorcerers.

Modal Patterns in Swahili Elite Culture

Material Culture

In the central part of the stone town stood the large houses made from coral blocks that gave this kind of settlement its name. Some rose to two or even three stories, dimming the narrow streets and alleys that separated the blank sides of the houses. Inside such a house the wealth of the owners was displayed by the quality of the symmetrically arranged beds, chairs, stools, cushions, and wall hangings. Gardens also brightened elite life. Outside the wall that ringed the town center, the poor and slaves lived in palm mat houses like those of rural towns. Beyond the town slaves worked large plantations, growing grain for export. Food for townspeople came from rural farmers.

A variety of ships rode at anchor in the harbor, some from as near as Arabia and others from as far away as Indonesia. Smaller boats waited for cargo to be carried along the African coast. From the interior came caravans of human bearers with the goods that the ships would take on board. These goods included slaves, gold, ivory, hides, gums, and rhinoceros horns for magical use. The town itself provided grain, mangrove poles, and cowrie shells from the sea. Among the imports were textiles, beads, firearms, jewelry, luxurious household furnishings, and porcelain from China.

The merchants of the town provided the facilities and organization necessary for the exchange between caravaneers and shippers. They maintained a safe, deep harbor and warehouses. They arranged contracts and credit, sometimes breaking cargoes for separate shipments from their own town or from others along the coast. They made provisions available to caravans and ships and saw to the repair of ships when necessary. Hotels lodged the travelers. Successful merchants combined mathematical and other technical knowledge with diplomatic skills. Although business required formal arrangements, all dealings were between individuals who knew each other personally.

Social Relations

The stone town, like its rural counterpart, was divided into moieties and wards. The moieties provided one basis for governmental organization of the thousands of people who inhabited the town. The two groups symbolized their separation in ritual fighting and poetry competitions.

In contrast to the bilateral grouping of commoners, an elite ward was composed of a patrilineal clan segment or a lineage. The lineages were the corporate groups that owned houses and businesses. Ranking of the clan segments depended on their antiquity of settlement in the town. Wealth also played a major role in social standing. The town rarely saw violence, but elite society was rife with intrigue and spite. Families expressed their rivalries and alliances in many ways, including the choice of a mosque for Friday worship.

Marriage was vital to relationships between families, and a wedding was the most elaborate ritual in an individual's life, much more so than among the lower classes. The firstborn daughter should marry a paternal parallel cousin in a monogamous union. In accord with elite observance of the shari'a, the Muslim law, the girl had to be a virgin when she married and had to submit herself to seclusion and the veil thereafter. Her husband had a right to divorce, while she had none. However, these marriages rarely ended in divorce. The other daughters of a wealthy family should marry cross-cousins, especially in neighboring towns, for the commercial ties that resulted. For the same reason, a family occasionally arranged a marriage with an Arab trader. Many younger daughters entered into polygynous unions, and divorce was common.

The elite viewed the initiation practices of rural people as African rather than Islamic. For the elite, circumcision of a son was a small family matter without other rituals. A daughter underwent a brief period of seclusion after her betrothal in which she received sexual instruction.

Every household contained slaves from the interior. They had a personal relationship with the master, who sometimes allowed them to do wage work for themselves. They became sailors, fishers, artisans, and port laborers. Part of the earnings went to the master to compensate for the time away from his service. Although the lineage owned these slaves, they had no hope of ever joining it. Owners often freed slaves as an Islamic act of charity or penance, but slave origin carried with it perpetually low status. Slaves outside the elite center cultivated plantation grain for export. They lived in poor housing and depended on Islamic injunctions against cruel treatment. Slaves constituted one quarter to one half of the town's population.

A chief, male or female, headed the town's autonomous government. Having a sacred status, the chief's main internal function was symbolic. However, he or she could play an important role in relations with the outside world, including the maintenance of peace and trading federations with other towns. Despite these efforts, commercial interest often led to war that placed events in the hands of hereditary military and naval leaders.

Knowledge and Expression

A large town often harbored several mosques that were built and administered privately. It was a popular charitable enterprise for the wealthy. It also provided an opportunity to crystallize factional distinctions and to try to humble opponents. Though priding themselves on orthodoxy, especially as compared with the peasants, elite people had their own mixture of Islam and other practices.

People regarded poetry as the highest art. It utilized diverse and complex forms to express devotional and historical themes, the latter relating to the founding of towns and subsequent events. Men, women, and even slaves composed poetry. Lesser arts included the carving of elaborate wooden doors and furniture and furniture and the creation of gold and silver jewelry.

CIRCUMPOLAR ZONE

Areas:

- Siberian
- Eskimo

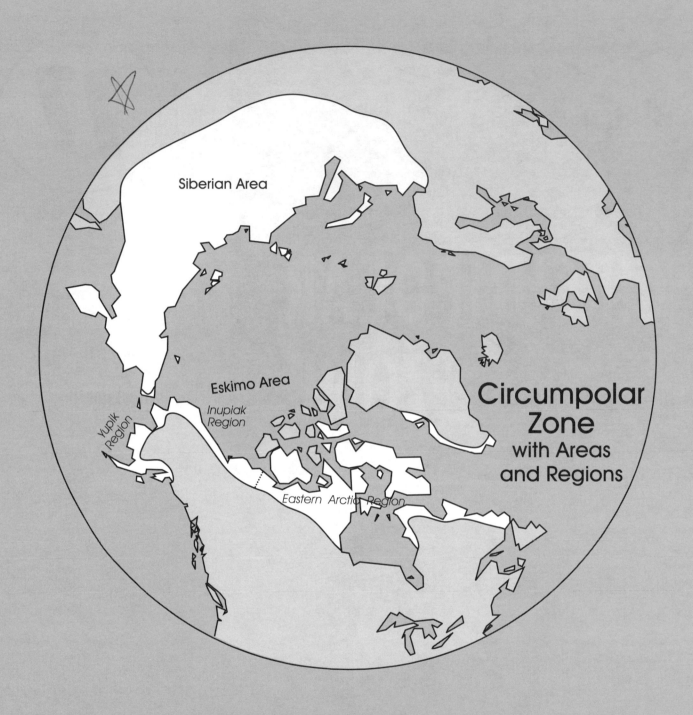

Siberian Area

Circumpolar
Zone
with Areas
and Regions

Eskimo Area

Inupiak Region

Yupik Region

Eastern Arctic Region

Previous page   A hunter wears the evidence of his frozen environment
(Inuit culture, North America).

OVERVIEW OF THE ZONE

Examples:

*Samek (Lapp), Yupik,
Evenk (Northern Tungus), Inuit*

This Zone encircled the North Pole, spanning the northernmost parts of Asia and North America. I place this chapter in the Old World section of the book because the people and their common cultural features originated in the Asian part of the Zone (Siberia). The extension of the culture into Northern America by the Eskimo is a relatively recent phenomenon.

At these high latitudes the summer sun stayed above the horizon for almost twenty-four hours every day. By the same token, darkness prevailed for most of every day during three or four months of winter. Winter lasted half the year and, even where mitigated by coastal waters, temperatures plunged toward minus sixty degrees Fahrenheit.

These unusual conditions brought forth unusual adaptations. Men provided most or all of the food, primarily by hunting large mammals. The most consistent target was the animal known as reindeer in Asia and caribou in North America *(Rangifer tarandus)*. We have already met the caribou as a major game animal in the Subarctic Area of Northern America. The manufacture of warm tailored clothing was a woman's crucial task in the circumpolar environment. She also cooked and maintained the home, like women in all other traditional cultures, but in extremely difficult circumstances.

The phrase "arctic bilateralism" has been applied to kinship in the Circumpolar Zone, but the distinctiveness of the pattern is not clear (if it is distinctive at all). The arctic peoples were foragers (primarily hunters), and foragers all over the world were inclined toward bilateral kin ties to increase social and ecological flexibility (see chapter 3). Arctic tendencies toward patrilocal residence and patrifiliation within the bilateral system also paralleled those of foragers elsewhere. The context for all this was a regional band much like that of other foragers, averaging between 100 and 200 people with outer limits of about 50 and 300. Circumpolar societies differed from those of most foragers in their tendency toward community justice. Although the basic patterns of self-help and revenge by kin were present, these communities also recognized certain offenders as a problem for everyone and took group action.

Animism, loosely defined, means the belief in supernatural beings. Circumpolar cultures took such beliefs further than perhaps any others, attributing some kind of spiritual component to virtually everything in the visible world. Foremost among these beliefs were ideas about hunter–game relationships that closely resembled those described earlier for the Americas (they probably derived from the same historic roots in Asia). Humans partook of the animistic complexity in that every person had several souls. Most spiritual entities other than souls were regarded as dangerous

To deal with this complex other dimension, people engaged in numerous ritual practices. They also turned to a system of shamanism that was among the most elaborate in the world. Shamans used devices such as ventriloquism to convey their experiences with the spirits, and they sent their souls to other worlds to gain information or confront supernatural beings. A distinctive musical instrument, the tambourine drum, was essential to the shaman's performance. It was also the basic instrument for all other musical performances.

Caribou, a vital game animal throughout the Circumpolar Zone.

Key features:

► Subsistence based on hunting
► Tailored clothing and boots
► Bilateral kinship, patrilateral tendencies
► Community justice
► Extreme animism, many dangerous beings
► Benevolent animal souls
► Multiple human souls
► Elaborate shamanism
► Tambourine drum

Modal Patterns in Circumpolar Culture

Material Culture

Wearing a bulky outfit of caribou skin, a man trudged through shallow snow toward the large mound of earth that was his home. Inside, the warm glow from oil lamps illuminated the timbers of which the house was constructed. The house was partially beneath ground level, and the roof had been covered with sod to insulate against the bitter cold of deep winter. Each lamp was a shallow trough of stone or clay with a moss wick atop oil derived from animal fat.

The man put his bow in its place and took off the quiver of arrows that had found no mark. Then he removed his outer coat, boots, and pants, all of which went on the drying rack near a fire. The shirt and pants that he wore underneath had the fur side turned inward while outer clothes were worn with the fur to the outside.

As the hunter rested, his wife worked on the clothing that she sewed for the entire family. Like much of the technology, her awls and needles were made from the bones of caribou, birds, and fish. She used a heavy awl to make holes in the caribou hides because the needles were easily broken. She wore thimbles of animal skin to protect her fingers.

Ready to start a new line of stitches, the woman twisted a length of thread, dampened it with her lips, and slipped it through the hole that had been drilled in her needle. Some thread was made from plant fiber or fish skin, but the best for most purposes came from caribou tendons. To make caribou thread, a woman removed tendons from the spine or legs of the animal, scraped off the fat and bits of flesh, and set the tendons to dry. When one of these sinews was ready, she rumpled it until it was pli-

able and then separated it into the strands that she would use as thread. At the conclusion of her sewing, often not until time to sleep, the woman carefully put away her needles. She pushed them into a strip of hide that would prevent breakage and placed them in a cylindrical case, which her husband had carved from bone or ivory.

A woman made new clothing for her family every fall. She had two reasons to start sewing during that season. One was that the hides were easier to manipulate in cold weather. The other was that the best hides were available in abundance as a result of caribou hunts during the late summer and fall. During that time the animals formed large herds as they migrated to their winter grounds. The coats that they had grown for winter also provided excellent protection for humans.

Toward the end of the long winter, women turned their sewing skills to the repair or manufacture of skin covers for the tents that the families would use when the weather eased. Spring brought new subsistence opportunities, and people left the winter village to camp at the most favorable sites. There they constructed tents with poles and covered them with animal skins or bark. In the moderate weather, they often cooked outside over open fires. When new resources became available, the people were ready to pack up their tents and move again. Camp size varied with the seasonal round, usually ranging from one to ten dwellings.

Spring was the time for migrating waterfowl. Men killed large numbers of geese, eider ducks, swans, and other birds with bow and arrow or with darts hurled from a throwing board. Everyone eagerly gathered eggs. When the water birds were gone, the ptarmigan remained. A kind of grouse, the ptarmigan was less elusive than the other fowl and could be killed with a thrown stone.

During summer women foraged for whatever food they could, including berries and other plants. When near water, they gathered shellfish. Sewing, however, was still their main concern. This was the time to make clothes that needed smoking, such as boots, mittens, and stockings. After sewing these items, a woman hung them over a smudge fire inside the tent. She added fungi or some other material to the fire to generate extra smoke.

Elaborated footwear displays the combination of craft and art in the Circumpolar Zone.

Migrating caribou.

At the end of the summer, men joined together to take migrating caribou in large numbers. Where the terrain was right, the hunters organized a drive in order to concentrate the animals at the most favorable place. They often constructed a channel for the deer, made from two rows of stone piles or wooden structures to simulate people. Some of the men, frequently helped by women and children, frightened the herd into the channel and kept them moving. At the end the hunters waited in ambush, sometimes in shallow water that slowed the movements of their prey. A successful hunt provided a great deal of meat, much of it to be preserved for winter, and started the women on a new annual cycle of their vital sewing activities.

Social Relations

A nuclear family shared the winter house with one or two others, sometimes more, each group with its own sleeping space. In most cases they formed an extended family, based on a living father or on the continuing relationship among several brothers. Many of the people in nearby houses were also related through male ties. When a man considered all of his relatives, he included many on his mother's side; however, a man considered the links with his father's relatives to be the strongest and preferred to live near them. Wives lived with their husbands. When people took to their tents in spring, the nuclear family occupied one of its own, but close relatives usually camped next to each other.

A newly pregnant woman entered the most restrictive phase of her life. Numerous taboos barred her from varied foods and behaviors until she gave birth in a small tent or hut, apart from the residence. After that the restrictions gradually eased. The baby received the name of a deceased relative, either a recent family member or a more remote ancestor. People expected the name to exert an influence on the child's personality; some attributed this to reincarnation. Children were indulged in virtually every way, even after weaning. Although young children played at adult activities, their elders did not expect them to do any serious learning until age seven or older.

Along with their subsistence tasks, maturing individuals learned that indulgence did not continue in adulthood. They would be independent and self-reliant in all matters that concerned only them and their own families. However, an offense against others could have dire consequences. The right to take revenge for insult or injury included killing the offender. Nor did that necessarily end the matter, because revenge sometimes led to feuds. In some instances the men of one kin group formed a party to ambush members of the other. Occasionally a stand-up fight between two lines of bowmen took place. Personal vengeance was not the only concern of a would-be offender. The community regarded certain

matters, such as several murders by the same person, as meriting collective punishment without the option of retaliation by kin.

Knowledge and Expression

Spirits and gods filled the universe, around and above and below the people. Some of these beings moved freely; others resided in objects. Virtually every physical object and natural phenomenon was either inhabited by a spirit or had a soul of its own. Many of these beings were hostile to humans or at least quick to take offense at human actions. As a result, human life was filled with protection against the spirits. People carried amulets with them wherever they went, attached to their clothing or worn around their necks. They used anything that suggested the possibility of favor toward humans, including carved figures, feathers, and bits of animal hide. People also tried to protect themselves with spells and other magic, by observing taboos, and by making offerings to the supernatural beings.

Game master gods controlled large segments of the world, such as the forest or the sea. People regularly sacrificed to them so that they would provide food and do no harm. Less powerful spirits abounded, including evil ones that people feared. They also sacrificed to these spirits, or they warded them off with amulets, spells, and other forms of magic. Of greatest significance for human survival were the souls of the major game animals, which resembled those of people. The animals gave themselves willingly to human hunters, but only if humans responded with proper treatment. This entailed ritual preparation for the hunt, signs of respect for the fallen animals, and community ceremonies to give thanks for the sustenance the animals had provided and to induce them to continue.

When ordinary ritual measures failed to maintain sustenance or health, people called for a shaman. Usually a man, the shaman performed in a darkened room with an audience around him. He began with his tambourine drum, made from animal skin stretched over one side of a narrow circular or oval frame. Holding the drum by its handle, he beat it with his other hand. Then he sang songs with magic power, songs with many words that the listeners could not understand because they came from long ago or the shaman had made them up. As he fell into a trance, the shaman made contact with his helping spirits. However, for any important matter, he went far beyond that. He detached his own soul from the body and sent it to a realm of spirits or gods somewhere above or below the ordinary world. There he gathered information that he needed, or he confronted supernatural beings who were causing human problems. During this performance the audience heard strange sounds coming from various parts of the room, apparently marking the presence of the supernaturals.

SIBERIAN AREA

TRADE

Examples:

Samek (Lapp), Samoyed,
Khant, Evenk (Northern Tungus)

The Siberian Area extended from northern Scandinavia, where the Samek people became famous as the "Lapps," across the northern section of Russia for which the Area is named. A small northeastern portion of the continent belonged to the Eskimo Area, which will be discussed in the next section.

Throughout most of the Siberian Area the environment was taiga, subarctic forests with many species of mammals for hunting and trapping. These were the main source of food for people. The prey animals included reindeer and another large deer *(Alces)*. The latter demonstrates the need for technical terminology to avoid confusion, because it is called "moose" in North America and "elk" in Europe.

Siberians traded luxury furs to outsiders such as Russians and Chinese for a variety of manufactured goods. In particular, the pelt of the sable *(Martes zibellina)*, a distant relative of the mink, had been "avidly sought since ancient times" (Nowak 1999). In the late eighteenth century several hundred thousand sable pelts were traded annually in just one Russian city.

The most distinctive feature of Siberian culture was the control of reindeer. By "control" I mean varying degrees of taming and domestication. In some societies people did little more than follow semitame herds and capture the animals when they wanted to use them. In other cases the animals were controlled and protected part of the time, but let loose on a seasonal basis. In still other societies people closely controlled and cared for the deer. They kept the animals in enclosures and moved individuals in halters. Although controlled reindeer were not the main source of food, they provided people with other resources and services.

The words "clan" and "tribe" are often used in the literature on Siberian societies, but clear definitions are hard to find (see, for example, Levin and Potapov, eds. 1964). Since the clan is usually described as a territorial unit, it seems to coincide with the regional band. By the same token, it does not conform to the strict definition of a descent group. The so-called tribe appears to be either a military alliance or a system of intermarriage between two or three "clans." Either way, our stricter definition of "tribe" does not apply.

One of the most dramatic and distinctive traits of the Area was a bear cult, which honored the bear and its mythological relationship with human beings. The cult is said to have existed in Northern America as well, but it is hard to find ceremonies as elaborate as those of Siberia. The symbolism is not well understood, but it seems to have had a lot to do with male power.

Key features:

► Hunting economy
► Fur trade
► Control of reindeer
► "Patrilineal clans"
► Bear cult

Modal Patterns in Siberian Culture

Material Culture

During the long winter, people lived in sod-covered houses in the forest. The trees gave some shelter from the wind but little protection against the bitter cold. Women diligently sewed all the clothing that kept people alive, but they gave special attention to boots. As the item of apparel that made contact between the wearer and the earth, boots had spiritual significance. When a woman made boots, she gained strength for a prosperous life. She applied some of her more elegant artistic touches to boots, such as sewing long white hair from the throat of a caribou into the seams.

Moisture was one of the practical problems with footwear. People solved it with plant materials, such as powder made by crumbling rotted wood from birch or larch trees. A person shook the substance inside the boots for a few minutes, allowing it to absorb the moisture, and then poured it out. This method was used with new boots, those that were worn daily, and those that had become exceptionally wet.

People varied their appearance by wearing fur hats or kerchiefs on their heads. Some displayed tattoos, geometric patterns that had been applied for decorative purposes or as part of a curing ritual. The tattooer made punctures with the jaw of a garfish and inserted soot.

Men put on their skis to hunt in the snow. They checked the traps where they had left spring-loaded bows and looked for signs of animals they could pursue with their hand bows. The most dangerous game and the biggest single prize was a moose, ten times the weight of a man. Wild reindeer were half that size. However, in the right time and place, a group of men could intercept a migrating herd and kill a large number of them. During mating season, the hunters made some easy kills by using tame female reindeer to lure wild males.

Smaller prey were also important. The skins of squirrels and other animals could be made into clothing or artifacts while foxes and sables gave a man furs to trade. The slender sable was about two feet long, varying in color from grayish-brown to blackish-brown. Whatever an individual's color, it bore a winter coat of long, thick, silky hair. From the outsiders, or middlemen who dealt with the outsiders, such furs brought tea and iron kettles in which to prepare it, iron pots for cooking, and various other goods.

Somewhere near the camp a family's herd of perhaps thirty reindeer foraged. They pawed through the snow to reach the lichens that provided their only food during a large part of the eight-month winter. On their own, or urged by men, the animals had to change their foraging ground every few days because their trampling hooves would eventually make the snow too hard to penetrate.

As night approached, men and dogs made sure that the herd came back to the camp, where they found protection from wolves and wolverines. Usually there were few problems in the process. Whether or not they understood how they were protected, the reindeer were attached to the camp by the various sources of salt, including human urine. Sometimes a dried fish was enough to lure a recalcitrant animal. The reindeer readily scavenged bits of fish and meat in camp, and occasionally they chased and ate small rodents.

In spring the reindeer added shrubs and dwarf willows to their diet. However, the forest soon became inhospitable as streams swelled and joined to form extensive marshlands in which the mud was often several feet deep. Using some of the animals to transport their goods, people joined the reindeer in migrating north to the tundra. There the pastures provided lichens, willow shoots, reeds, and some grass. However, mosquitoes and flies annoyed the humans and ferociously attacked the deer. The herders built smudge fires to drive the insects away, adding fungi to the fires to make them smoke. When it was necessary to change pastures, or travel for any other reason, people did so at night in order to avoid the insects.

For travel, including seasonal migrations, some peoples rode reindeer and packed goods on them. A strong animal could carry 175 pounds and walk forty miles in a day. Others hitched the deer to sleds on which they rode along with their goods. Using the reindeer for transport allowed people to hunt and trap over a much larger territory than if they walked and carried their own burdens. The deer also provided milk, meat, and hides. When the animals were next to camp, women looked after the sick ones and otherwise tended the herd. Milking deer was also a woman's job.

Man riding a "reindeer" (the Old World term for caribou). Note his position above the shoulders (Lamut culture, Siberia).

Social Relations

In preparation for a boy's marriage, his father amassed bridewealth consisting largely or entirely of reindeer. The size of the gift affected the prestige of the givers. If the father's resources were inadequate, he turned to his relatives for help. If that was not enough for the girl's parents, they might accept three or four years of bride service.

When the bride came to live with her husband, she brought a substantial dowry that in some cases approached the value of the bridewealth. It consisted of domestic utensils, clothes, often a sled, and perhaps some reindeer. The dowry remained under the woman's control throughout the marriage; she retained it after the marriage ended, whether by divorce or the death of her husband. These possessions offset the fact that a woman could not inherit any property from her father or her husband.

Patrilocal residence meant more to a man than living with his relatives. It meant participating in the life of his clan. The men in a regional band liked to think of the group as a patrilineal clan descended from an ancient ancestor. If some men or their fathers had joined the group and adopted the ancestor, this mattered little. All the men were bound together by the territory and resources that they shared, the activities in which they cooperated, the clan rules and leaders that they followed, and the ceremonies they carried out for the clan ancestor.

The clan occupied and, if necessary, defended a range that contained hunting and fishing sites and pasturage for reindeer. Clansmen readily cooperated in large-scale enterprises such as a caribou drive. The group was also bound by obligations of mutual aid, including revenge for offenses against members. Within the group, heads of families formed a council to deal with matters that concerned everyone. Usually one or more of them emerged as leaders. Community concerns included the coordination of economic efforts and the maintenance of order. The clan punished the most serious offenses, such as incest, murder, and refusal to obey elders. Penalties included a beating, expulsion from the group, or death.

The men of a clan preferred to intermarry with just one other clan. Many men specifically sought a cross-cousin for their sons. When clans grew close, they readily used one another's resources and became allies for military purposes. However, they also sought temporary alliances for particular conflicts. An offense against another band, real or perceived, could elicit an attack by hundreds of men in light armor.

Knowledge and Expression

Clan members shared more than social and political bonds. They traced their common origin to ancestral souls and a heroic founder that they commemorated at a sacred site. There they sacrificed to effigies of their predecessors. They left valuable goods, such as furs, and sometimes they killed reindeer. Clan members also shared the gateway to the other world, the group's cemetery, where only members could rest.

Beings other than ancestors also demanded respect and sacrifice. Beyond the vital animal souls, there were the game masters who protected the animals. Beyond the game masters were two great gods who affected the lives of humans. Although they were related to each other (some said blood relatives, others thought spouses), one was benevolent toward humans while the other brought them bad fortune.

The shamans who dealt with such powerful forces wore special clothes marked by numerous metal pendants, tassels, and other emblems. Metal rods symbolized the bones of a skeleton, representing the ritual death and rebirth through which the shaman had entered his or her profession. Feathers and other bird symbols reminded others that the shaman could rise to worlds above. The pathway was a supernatural tree that had its roots in the underworld and spread its branches in the sky. This tree was featured in many myths. A special cap was essential to the exercise of shamanic powers, along with the tambourine drum.

The bear, lord of the forest, possessed a soul with great power. Though dangerous, the power could also be used for healing. People treated injuries by stroking them with a bear paw or rubbing them with bear fat. Myths showed that bears and humans were closely connected. They told of transformations between bear and human, marriages and kin relations between bears and humans, and bears sacrificing themselves for the benefit of humans.

People expressed their connection with the bear in a communal feast in which one bear was ritually consumed. Men treated the animal with courtesy and restraint while butchering and eating it. Afterward they disposed of the remains in a special way, usually placing them in a tree or on a platform. The head, the most sacred part, was given a separate and especially prominent position. Taboos on contact with the bear and its products strictly limited the role of women in the feast. However, they participated in the dancing, singing, and other recreations that climaxed the festival.

The music that accompanied celebrations was played on the tambourine drum and perhaps the mouth harp, a small lyre-shaped piece of metal. The musician placed the narrow end in his mouth and vibrated it with his tongue, which made the oral cavity into a sound box.

A female shaman, playing a tambourine drum, wears the distinctively elaborate clothing of a Siberian shaman (Yakut culture).

One form of the Siberian bear festival (Amur River).

Thc twanging sound that rcsultcd could be modified into simple melodies.

Oral literature provided more elaborate entertainment and art. It included epic adventures, presented in a poetic style, that sometimes lasted for several evenings. Some described great heroes who battled evil spirits or human enemies; others depicted women of unusual courage and resourcefulness. Military heroes also appeared in ordinary stories, some of which were quasi-historical in recounting the clan's past. Simpler tales, many describing the antics of anthropomorphized animals, just made people laugh.

When a man died, some of his property went to one or more of his sons, with other clan members as the alternative. The kin of the deceased muffled the bells of their reindeer as a sign of mourning. They stayed silent five days for a man or four days for a woman, reflecting the sacred numbers associated with the sexes. Family members took the dead man to the clan cemetery to join his ancestors. Every effort was made to accomplish this for a man who died far from home. At the cemetery the mourners sacrificed a dog or a reindeer. They left the man's sled and other important goods by the grave, broken to release their souls so that they could accompany the owner into the next world. That journey required the help of a shaman, who sent his soul to guide those of the deceased and sacrificed animals to the appropriate afterworld. Eventually that soul, or another that emanated from the same person, was reincarnated in a member of the same clan.

A Closer Look

Old-timers and Recent Immigrants

The most fully indigenous Siberian adaptation was represented in a western region that extended from northern Scandinavia into the valley of the Yenisey River in Rus-

sia. The best-known examples are the Samek, widely known by Westerners as the Lapps, and several ethnic groups loosely labeled the Samoyeds. In this culture people usually hitched their reindeer to wooden sleds for transport, though they sometimes used them for riding or pack. They used the sleds at any time of year. Two or three animals sufficed on winter snow, but it usually took five of them to haul a sled through spring marshes or across summer grass. In the fall people slaughtered surplus reindeer, more for the hides than for the meat.

"Dolls" played diverse and important roles in the western culture (Oakes and Riewe 1998). Some of these little figures served the memory of the dead. For several years after a relative's death, five for a man and four for a woman, his or her effigy sat in the social part of the house. People sometimes offered it food and drink or included it in conversations. Other figures stood guard at the entrance to the home, keeping evil spirits out. The play dolls of children also betrayed the concern about evil spirits; they never had faces or hands because a spirit might inhabit a full replica.

The two major ethnic groups of eastern Siberia displayed signs of rather recent migration northward from the steppes. The Evenks (northern Tungus) used sleds less often than the western Siberians did, usually packing their belongings on the reindeer. They treated the deer much like the horses of the steppes, making extensive use of their milk and riding on them. They placed saddles on the shoulders of the reindeer because their backs could not bear a man's weight. They wore coats that were open in front, probably more flexible in riding but not well suited to the winter cold. The Evenks and other eastern peoples considered their animals too valuable to kill and rarely did so unless faced with starvation. In their music they distinguished themselves by adding an instrument with one or two strings made of moose sinew, played with a hunting bow. The idea of a stringed instrument probably camc from China or Japan.

The Yakuts in the Lena River system, numbering several hundred thousand people, were the largest ethnic group in Siberia. Speakers of a Turkic language, they were the most recent group to migrate north from the steppes and retained more striking steppe traits than the Evenks. The Yakuts insisted on keeping cattle, which they had to bring into their houses to survive the winter. They also kept horses, which they often ate. The Yakuts lived in chiefdoms and fought wars of conquest with each other. They became part of the Siberian Area by adopting the Evenk pattern of reindeer herding.

The Tundra Region

The Tundra Region was a narrow strip, a few hundred miles wide, along the northern margin of Siberia, bordering on the Arctic Ocean. No trees grew in the extreme cold, and wildlife was scarce. The few people who lived there all year, like the Nganasan, became true pastoralists. Unlike the hunters south of them, the tundra people organized their lives around the needs of their herds. These reindeer herders were the only true nomadic pastoralists in the world to keep just one species of herd animal.

Their migrations were seasonal and oriented north-to-south. Summer movements were sometimes affected by supplementary foraging and avoidance of blood-sucking insects. Tundra diet emphasized the meat of the reindeer, but blood was also important. People added to the food supply by fishing and hunting birds and obtained some plant foods and other items by trading with the people to the south.

ESKIMO AREA

Examples:

Yupik, Inuit

For a long time it was an article of faith for many anthropologists (including me) that the word "Eskimo" came from an Algonkian Indian word that meant "eaters of raw flesh" and was intended as an insult. It turns out that "Eskimo" is actually of Montagnais origin and refers to snowshoes (Fienup-Riordan 1995; Issenman 1997). The Eskimo of Canada and Greenland have adopted the term "Inuit" for themselves because it is derived from dialects spoken by some of them. However, this is not appropriate for Alaskan and Siberian Eskimos, who differ significantly from the Inuit in language and culture. There is no native name that covers all the Arctic peoples to be described in this chapter; nor has anyone proposed a new nonnative term that would cover all of them. While waiting for a viable alternative, I use the (noninsulting) word "Eskimo" to encompass all of the people who inhabited the culture area that stretched from northeastern Siberia across coastal Alaska and arctic Canada to Greenland.

Eskimos hunted caribou, but the pursuit of sea mammals defined the Eskimo Area. It was the primary means of subsistence and formed the basis for a unique complex of ecology and technology. It also represents a massive accomplishment in human terms as well as technological ones. The easy prey for these hunters was the ringed seal *(Phoca hispida)*, four feet long and weighing 100 pounds. Averaging twice that length and four to five times the weight, the bearded seal *(Erignathus)* was a more difficult catch. Beyond those species, we speak of the sea hunter's most common game in terms of tons. A male walrus *(Odobenus)*, ten feet long and five feet tall at the head, could weigh one and a half tons and had tusks two feet long (females weighed half as much but also had long tusks). Almost all Eskimo hunted the creamy white

A ringed seal, one of the important marine prey animals of the Eskimo Area.

beluga whale *(Delphinapterus)*, about the same size as a male walrus (but more attractive). Some dared the black bowhead whale *(Balaena)*, which attained fifty feet and 100 tons.

The Eskimo developed three vehicles to help them traverse the arctic seas and land. One of them, the umiak, was a fairly ordinary boat. The other two vehicles were highly distinctive and became well known to the rest of the world: the kayak and the dog sled.

Bilateral kinship stood out in the Eskimo Area because the Area lacked the patrilineal groups of Siberia. In order to extend personal support beyond the kindred, Eskimos used a variety of criteria to establish dyadic (one-to-one) relationships with unrelated or distantly related individuals. The term "partnership" has sometimes been applied to all of these relationships, but it is probably a misleading label for some that are less formal and practical.

The Eskimo are famous for lending or exchanging wives for sexual purposes. Some prefer to call it spouse exchange, but in the native culture it was a male prerogative and was done for male purposes (Merkur 1991). The practice often had to do with establishing or maintaining important social connections between men, such as partnerships. It should also be noted that there were nonsexual reasons to exchange wives. More casual sexual exchanges also took place.

Eskimos combined social control and creative expression when they settled disputes with song duels. The antagonists performed pertinent songs of their own composition with the community looking on. An elaborate oral literature provided another means of expression. One subject was Raven, who was often cast in a positive light that contrasted with his mythological treatment elsewhere in the world. Myth also described the origin of the sea goddess and the moon god, who were vital because they controlled the game animals. Regarding their own spiritual essence, Eskimos clearly conceptualized three different souls for each human being.

Key features:

- ▶ Maritime hunting
- ▶ Kayak and dog sled
- ▶ Bilateral kinship
- ▶ Dyadic nonkin relationships
- ▶ Wife lending and wife exchange
- ▶ Song duels
- ▶ Sea goddess and moon god
- ▶ Prominence of Raven in folklore
- ▶ Three human souls

Modal Patterns in Eskimo Culture

Material Culture

The hunter of sea mammals depended on the kayak, a one-man closed-deck canoe. He sat in the single tight opening and, if he deemed it necessary, completely integrated himself with the boat by wearing a waterproof garment that he lashed to the frame of the cockpit. A man constructed his kayak's long, slender frame from wood or the bones of large animals and covered it with sealskins sewn together by his wife. This was mainly a hunting vehicle, fast but unstable and tiring to propel with the double-bladed paddle.

A man could hunt seals on the ocean alone, but he joined a group to pursue the larger animals. When a hunter saw the blunt whiskered head of a walrus break the surface, he knew that there was a body ten times the

The kayak, one of the ingenious inventions of the Eskimo.

size of his own underneath the water. He quietly paddled his kayak as close as he dared and then, with a long-practiced technique and all of his strength, he plunged his heavy harpoon into the huge body. With luck the animal lunged away from the boat rather than crushing it or ripping the boat apart with its tusks. As the walrus swam, the floats and drag on the harpoon line began to take hold. The floats were inflated sealskins that kept the walrus from diving, and the drag was a skin stretched over a hoop that slowed and tired the animal. The other men, who had been searching nearby, soon caught up and tried to place their harpoons in the walrus. Some of the experienced ones anticipated where the animal would surface after one of its impeded dives. At the end the men towed their kill to the shore together.

Hunters used the same technology and techniques to pursue beluga whales, about the same size as the walrus, and even the giant bowhead whales. At times the walrus and beluga gave men an alternative because the animals came close to the shore in bays. Then the kayakers could drive a large number of the animals into the shallows or onto the beach, where they became easy targets for hunters on foot. Some drove the prey simply by throwing rocks, but others used a device that sounded like the killer whale, the predator that the animals feared most.

During the spring, seals and walrus presented themselves to the hunters by hauling up on ice floes and beaches to sun themselves. On these occasions stalking

Seal mother and pup resting on the ice (harp seals).

was the key to success. One technique had the man crawling toward the animals behind a white blind, stopping whenever they looked toward him. An alternative was to wear a sealskin and imitate the sounds and movements of seals. Any approach required intimate knowledge of the prey. When the hunter came as close as possible, he rose for a sudden rush and drove his harpoon into the nearest animal. Others who had been hanging back rushed to help him haul on the rope and keep the prey on land, which was helpful for taking seals and essential for walrus.

In the spring or the fall anyone could fish at ice holes if he or she wanted to. It was easy to poke a hole through the thin ice that covered the sea and the lakes at these times of year. Then the fisher could drop in a hook and line and wait. Men more often jiggled a lure with one hand and speared the fish with the other.

When families left the winter village for warm weather camps far away, they took a water route where possible and used the umiak. It was a large open boat that could hold as many as thirty people along with their dogs, tents, and other possessions. It could take several households a long distance to the best available hunting or fishing site. People called it the women's boat because women always propelled it with long, single-bladed paddles.

The dog sled, another vital Eskimo invention. Note the fan pattern in which the dogs are hitched.

When the snow flew again, the dog sled became essential for moving the family and for taking the hunters to their game. Most men owned only two or three dogs, and very few had more than six, because the animals required a great deal of food. They were attached to the sled in a fan pattern rather than in a line. Sometimes, if the load was heavy during a family move, people got off the sled and walked alongside. In difficult conditions they helped the dogs to pull.

Occasionally in winter a man decided to go after a polar bear. When he did, his life depended on his dogs.

The distraction they provided allowed him to make the repeated harpoon thrusts necessary to bring the prey down. Polar bears were too rare and too dangerous to hunt for food. The white pelts made a beautiful addition to clothing, but the main reason for killing such a huge and powerful animal was to gain prestige. Although Eskimos rarely boasted, they were highly aware of how others perceived them.

The dangerous polar bear, hunted for prestige.

Social Relations

Many parents arranged marriages for their children when they were infants, but these agreements were seldom firm. Young people engaged in premarital sex and some formed attachments that led to marriage. A young man performed bride service for his in-laws and then brought his wife back to live with his parents. An extended family was based on a father and his younger married sons. The older ones set up their own households as soon as possible, although most of them stayed near their parents.

After sharing a long period of parental affection and indulgence, boys and girls began to diverge into adult life. The boy became a hunter as the family mounted small celebrations for his first kill of any kind and, much more important, his first killing of a seal. He also learned about the need to extend his social connections beyond the standard network of kin.

There were many ways for a man to establish new relationships with other men. Having the same name gave them a spiritual affinity because the soul that governed an individual's personality was connected with the name. Some men entered into a singing relationship in which they performed publicly for one another whenever they met. Each man composed a new song for such an occasion and danced while his wife drummed and sang the song. Singing and joking often overlapped because men in a joking relationship sometimes performed songs and rhymes in public. However, they emphasized insulting humor that made frequent sexual references.

Whatever the basis, true partners recognized their relationship in a formal and sometimes ritualized way. Such a bond lasted for a long time, often for life. Partners expected to help each other in various ways and to share generously. In some cases they defended each other, and a man might seek vengeance for his partner's death as if he were a close relative.

Since the purpose of partnerships was to extend a man's social network, he usually chose to enter into special relationships with nonkin. However, the institution could also be used to strengthen the relationship with a distant kinsman. By doing so through a nonkin bond, a man avoided creating unwanted obligations to other relatives who were equally distant.

Some partners exchanged wives for periods ranging from one night to several weeks. In addition to providing sexual pleasure, the practice epitomized the close and generous relationship that partners were supposed to have. Sometimes sexual pleasure deferred to practical considerations, as in the case of a man exchanging a wife in late pregnancy for his partner's wife before going on a long trip to trade or hunt. The key features in such an exchange were safety for the pregnant woman and more vigorous help for the traveling man. Some wife-exchange relationships were brief while others lasted a lifetime. Some ended in a loss of interest, but others created jealousy and enmity that sometimes led to violence.

A husband might lend his wife to any other man with whom he was on good terms. Some men looked for sexual pleasure mainly in their marriages, but others thought it strange to be satisfied with one woman. Men considered it an honor to a woman to be desired by many men, but women may not have shared this view.

A man usually asked his wife to accept an exchange, and she usually agreed. Occasionally wives initiated the process, but more often they hinted to their husbands about it. Sometimes a woman refused and was beaten, on the theory that a wife should obey her husband. However, men had to keep in mind that a wife could obtain a divorce just as easily as a husband.

Knowledge and Expression

Villagers gathered excitedly in the ceremonial house for a night of contests. Like all festive times, it began with music and dancing. A man began to beat his tambourine drum and sing with a rhythm much like that of speech. Others sang and danced for a while, and then the music

An Eskimo drum dancer.

stopped. Two men stepped into the middle of the circle of people for a wrestling match. It was over quickly when one man threw the other to the ground. Several more matches followed, and then the music and dancing began again. After a while the group quieted for a punching contest. Two men took turns hitting each other until one of them, staggered, decided to accept defeat. If he had continued, the match would have ended when he fell. Finally, there was a song duel. Two men with a joking relationship had agreed to match wits in front of the group. They took turns beating their drums and describing each other's habits and appearance in scurrilous songs of their own composition. The singers sent their audience home to their sleeping platforms in a good humor.

This had been a night of pure entertainment, but sometimes the contests took place in order to resolve disputes. A serious conflict between two men always carried with it the possibility of a homicide. To the community this meant more than the loss of one hunter, because homicide required retribution. Therefore, most people preferred a nonlethal settlement. Furthermore, some disputants did not care to risk their lives despite their anger. Contests provided an alternative, based on the customary rule that the result of the contest ended the dispute. Wrestling and punching resulted in clear-cut victors through surrender or inability to continue; the audience made an informal judgment about the winner of a song duel.

As winter daylight approached its minimum length, people began to prepare a special feast. At the celebration men danced in masks or with soot-blackened faces. They danced naked or with phallic attachments to their costumes, and at some point they paired with women other than their spouses to have intercourse. On various festive occasions following this feast, people engaged in the less ritualized practice that they called "putting out the lamps." After communal dancing and singing, someone extinguished the oil lamps, and the participants found random sexual partners in the darkness.

When hunting turned bad, people called on a powerful shaman. Drumming and singing himself into a trance, he sent his soul to visit a game master. One was the sea goddess, who lived under the ocean and controlled all the sea mammals. Another was Moon Man, who governed the land animals but also influenced the ocean because of his connection with the tides. A third major god was Weather, an amorphous being that most people thought of as female.

Contact with the sea goddess could prove difficult because, as myth explained, she was a bitter woman. As a human girl, she had been thrown into the ocean by a man who rejected her. The sea mammals that she governed originated in the process. The Moon Man, on the other hand, tended to be relatively benign despite his frustrating origins. In mythical times, as a human, he came to his sister in darkness and had sex with her. The curious woman used soot to mark her lover and, when

she saw that it was her brother, snatched up a torch and ran out into the night. He followed, also with a torch, and the pursuit took them up to the sky, where the sister became the sun and the brother the moon.

When the shaman treated an individual for illness, he used his power to contact the spirits; however, he also emphasized the behavior of the victim. He interrogated the sick person, seeking remembrance and public confession of a taboo violation. When the admission was made, the onlookers responded with words of forgiveness. Often, though, the shaman required additional corrective behavior from the patient. Sometimes this was merely the consumption of some herbal remedy. In other cases some kind of penance was required, a practice that the shaman could abuse. He might, for example, command a desirable woman to have sex with him or even become his wife. If the community became convinced that a shaman was abusing his power, an execution might result.

A Closer Look

The people known to the rest of the world as Eskimo occupied just one sparsely populated section of the Eskimo Area. It is essential to put the stereotypical Eskimos in perspective by comparing their culture to that of the more numerous peoples of Alaska. We begin with the two Alaskan Regions.

The Yupik Region

Yupiks, whose language belonged to the Yupik branch of the Eskimo family, occupied the Chukotka Peninsula of Siberia and the Alaskan coast from the Yukon River delta to below Kuichak Bay. They lived in their winter villages for nine months of the year and generally used only one other locality during the summer. The subarctic abundance of the Region required little nomadic movement. During most of the year, men hunted sea mammals in their kayaks; and women gathered berries, tubers, roots, seaweed, and shellfish. However, the plant foods were most abundant in fall and the shellfish most important in winter, when storms and animal migrations diminished hunting opportunities. In the summer men went deep-sea fishing for cod and halibut.

Southwest Alaskans lacked the clans of their fellow Yupik across the Strait, but they shared the use of Iroquois terms for cousins. The postmarital residence pattern of Southwest Alaska was unusual compared to other Eskimos and to the rest of the world. The new bride stayed in the house where she was born while her husband went to live in her father's men's house. At about the age of five a boy left his mother's house to join his father. When the boy married, he started the cycle again. Women served meals in the men's house and brought firewood.

Community leadership came from the heads of the largest and most respected families. War parties raided other bands and sometimes engaged in stand-up battles. Fighters wore walrus-hide armor and used special bow techniques. A band tried to form alliances with others.

The Moon Man was the most prominent among numerous male spirits. Credited with control of human as well as animal souls, he was the master of game. Individuals and families offered first fruits of many kinds to sustain hunting and fishing. The community held the Bladder Feast to honor and perpetuate the animals that had been killed for sustenance. The bladders of the animals, which housed their souls, were saved for celebration at the feast. Afterward, they were returned to the sea. The Messenger Feast, named for the means of invitation, was a social occasion that brought communities together. Its main purpose was the exchange of gifts, but the masked dances of the occasion also pleased the animal spirits. A community held at least one memorial feast every year to honor the preceding year's dead. Some held a Great Feast of the Dead at intervals of four to ten years, which freed the souls from the earth forever.

The Inupiak Region

Hugging a long and curving stretch of coastline that spanned Alaska and Canada, this Region is named for the branch of Eskimo language spoken by all of its inhabitants. From the shores of Norton Sound on the Bering Sea, the Inupiak lands extended around the Alaskan coast to encompass the MacKenzie River delta in Canada.

A man of the Inupiak wore two labrets, one near each corner of his mouth, representing the tusks of the powerful walrus. Men and a few women wore pendants from their pierced ears. With or without his family, a man traveled to a trading fair to meet his partner from the interior. They exchanged oil in sealskin bags for caribou hides and sometimes other coast and interior products. With business done, they enjoyed the many entertainments of the fair. Among these were numerous competitive contests.

Male competition was expressed in many walks of life. Prominent men enhanced their prestige by arranging the messenger feasts that brought communities together. Whaling captains built large men's houses and distributed meat to the entire village. During ceremonies before and after the hunt, a captain and his wife acted like priests.

The East Arctic Region

This is the land of the stereotypical Eskimo, driven into popular imagination by the mass media. The key features of the Region are defined by the Iglulik, Netsilik, and Copper Eskimo who lived to the west and north of Hudson Bay. Similar cultures occupied the peninsula of northern Quebec and the coastlines of northeastern Canada and Greenland.

An Inupiak woman displaying her version of the tailored clothing that allowed people to survive throughout the Circumpolar Zone.

A very fine example of carving in soapstone.

One element of the stereotype that holds up is the igloo. The word itself may call up images of a rounded snow-block dwelling, but that is incorrect. The word simply means "house." However, the East Arctic family did build a snow house as the main winter dwelling, with windows made from ice rather than gut. Villagers also built a larger communal house of snow, which they used regularly for work, games, dances, and shamanistic performances. It was also the site of the midwinter feast, the only major celebration of the season. The promiscuous sex that took place on this and other occasions may have been an especially important distraction in a setting where darkness prevailed throughout most of every day for several months, temperatures approaching sixty below kept people inside cramped quarters for long periods, and the threat of starvation loomed ahead.

An Inuit man pulls a seal through the ice after enlarging the breathing hole through which he harpooned it.

During part of the winter, hunters replenished the food supply by hunting seals at their breathing holes. A seal kept many holes open in the sea ice so that it could breathe regularly while seeking fish. After finding one of these holes, the human hunter poised himself above it and waited, sometimes for hours, silent and virtually motionless. When the seal arrived, he had one chance to harpoon it firmly before it swam away. The larger seals weighed up to 700 pounds, and a man hunting alone might need his dog team to pull the animal through the enlarged hole. This phase of the foraging year ended when the seals migrated away, or when the weather closed in, and people depended on their stored foods to survive the rest of the winter. In the worst of years some people died of starvation while others survived by cannibalism. This did not happen often, but the possibility always existed.

East Arctic people spent more time away from their winter houses than other Eskimo because the sparse

resources of the high arctic environment required a more nomadic life. The combination of sparse and fluctuating resources with the need for extensive travel conspired against the weaker members of society. At times the rates of infanticide and senilicide may have exceeded those of any other culture. "Senilicide" is probably a misnomer; most such cases were probably assisted suicides, usually by hanging (Balikci 1989).

Leadership was less formal than among western Eskimo and more typical of foraging societies. The oldest active man led each household. Heads consulted informally on the few community decisions. When chieftains emerged, their prominence was based on the organization of hunts, planning of seasonal movements, oversight of game distribution, and arbitration of quarrels.

Desperately dependent on sea mammals for survival, the Eastern people placed the sea goddess at the head of their pantheon and told the most dramatic story about her origin. Her father, enraged at her choice of a lover, threw her from a boat into the water. When she tried to grasp the side, he cut off all her fingers. The fingers became the various sea mammals as the incipient goddess sank to the bottom. When a shaman visited, one thing he did to appease her was to comb the tangled hair that she could not maintain for herself.

Inland Hunters

To conclude this survey of Eskimo variation, it is worth noting that Eskimos pushed inland in two places, the interior of northern Alaska and the west side of Hudson Bay. The Hudson Bay people bear a name that would be appropriate for both groups, the Caribou Eskimo. They both abandoned the hunting of sea mammals and depended primarily on caribou for survival. The sea goddess and other such beliefs disappeared. In other respects, however, the rather simple life of the inland hunters resembled that of their coastal cousins.

Aleuts and Anatomy

The Aleut people occupied the western part of the Alaskan Peninsula and most of the Aleutian Island chain that stretched from the Peninsula toward Siberia. There was a population of perhaps 16,000 scattered across that thin 1,250-mile tongue of land, living almost entirely from the resources of the sea. They all spoke a language related to those of the Eskimos, but so distinct that it suggested a separation of the two groups around 1000 A.D. Even so, the Aleut culture was much like that of their Yupik neighbors: "The Aleuts show what a people with a basically Eskimo culture living in a rich hunting and fishing area could achieve in wealth and social differentiation" (Lantis 1983:167, 169).

Though most of their cultural features fitted into the modal patterns of the Yupik Region, the Aleuts displayed several fascinating distinctions. For one thing, "The crowning achievement of Aleut society was silence, whenever it was necessary to maintain privacy and individual equilibrium" (Laughlin 1980:60). If they had nothing worth saying, they kept their silence. This was true self-possession rather than habitual taciturnity: storytelling was "one of the great arts" of these people and some of their tales took two hours or more to tell.

For some students of the Aleut, the most noteworthy feature of the culture was an extensive knowledge of the anatomy of humans and animals, manifested in a lengthy and specialized vocabulary. This knowledge came from a variety of sources, some rather unusual in themselves. For example, the Aleuts achieved a close acquaintance with corpses because, unlike so many people in the world, they had no fear of the dead. On the contrary, they wished to preserve their dead and keep them close for as long as possible. The process began with the removal (and perhaps examination) of internal organs through an incision in the lower abdomen. After the corpse was cleansed in a stream, dried, and stuffed with grass, it was placed in a large cradle and hung from a roof beam over the place where the deceased had slept. After an appropriate period, sometimes a month or more, the remains were dressed, wrapped, and removed to a dry cave. This was the final resting place, but communion with the living did not end. Some people sought advice from the "departed one" and the best whalers sometimes took a finger joint or some other small part to enhance the hunt with the spiritual power of the dead.

Some Aleuts pursued anatomical knowledge in a more systematic way, by performing autopsies on the dead in order to find out why they died. They developed a comparative anatomy by dissecting sea otters, which they considered to provide the closest parallel to the human body. Further detailed knowledge of anatomy came from the practical use of animal tissues that other cultures ignored, such as the skin of a whale's tongue.

Aleut health practices also facilitated precise awareness of anatomy. They cured various ailments with massage, acupuncture, and bloodletting. Some think that the last was learned from the Russians. However, like other traditional health and ritual practices, Aleut bloodletting focused on the joints.

Binding of all the joints was important in the rituals of first menses and widowhood. Conversely, it was important to dismember a killed enemy or other dangerous person. The immediate concern in all these cases was to avert pain and disease of the joints. However, there seems to have been a deeper symbolism related to the spiritual force of humans: binding preserved the force while dismemberment allowed it to dissipate. When a whaling captain took a small part of a corpse, he acquired some of the spiritual force of the dead.

The Oceanic Domain

circa 1700 A.D.

The Oceanic Cultural Domain included the native cultures of Australia and most of the Pacific islands north and east of Australia. It excluded those near the Asian coast that were dominated by Old World civilizations (most notably Japan, Taiwan, the Philippines, and Indonesia). Also excluded were the tiny islands that hug the coastlines of western America and belong to the New World Domain.

Native Australia remained free of serious disruption by Europeans until the British established their first settlements in 1788. Invasion of the Pacific Islands began earlier but proceeded more slowly and haphazardly. Initial contacts were scattered across the sixteenth century and continued to occur on various islands until some inhabitants of highland New Guinea first saw white people in the latter part of the twentieth century. European exploitation of the islands emphasized trade and provisioning until the Spanish began to establish colonial control of the Marianas in 1670, consolidating their hold by 1690. Other imperialist ventures followed, but most traditional cultures continued to function independently into the eighteenth century and beyond (Quanchi and Adams, eds. 1993).

PART III

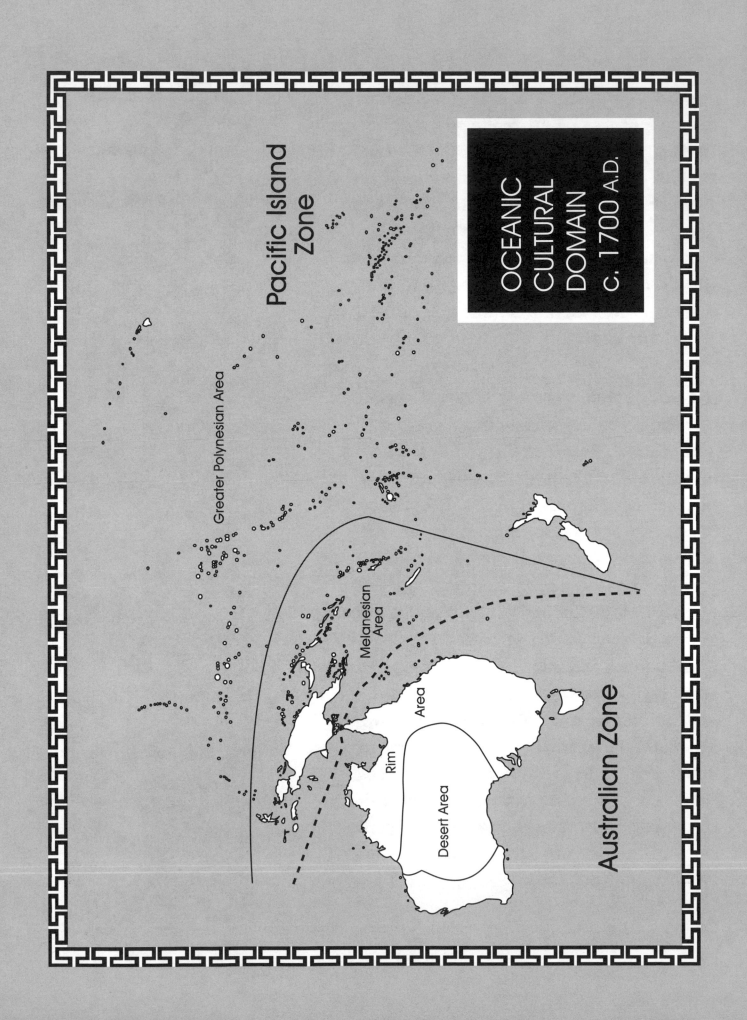

OCEANIC
CULTURAL
DOMAIN
C. 1700 A.D.

Pacific Island
Zone

Greater Polynesian Area

Melanesian
Area

Australian Zone

Rim
Area

Desert Area

MODAL
PATTERNS AMONG
OCEANIC
CULTURES

The two Oceanic Zones seem to have been neatly divided between Pacific Island farmers and Australian foragers. However, their shared features included important elements of subsistence. One was the yams (several species of the genus *Dioscorea*) that people exploited in both Zones and every Area. Aquatic foraging and fishing were also important in both Oceanic Zones. People obtained resources from the sea and from fresh water; and many without access to any significant body of water obtained aquatic resources by exchange.

Several aspects of Oceanic technology are noteworthy, mostly because of their universal importance in the Domain. None were very distinctive, especially when compared with tropical cultures elsewhere in the world. These include maintenance of continuous fires, the prominence of the stone chopping tool (axe or adze), manufacture of varied artifacts from netting, and the technological use of teeth and toes.

Oceanic people engaged in considerable exchange beyond the community. This has often been called "ritual" or "ceremonial" exchange, which is somewhat misleading. Some interactions were ritualized, but others were quite informal. Some objects had ritual uses, but others were luxuries, and still others had very mundane uses. The most important distinction is probably the one that applies in many other traditional cultures: some exchanges took place mainly to establish or maintain social relationships while others involved goods that the participants wanted and could not obtain elsewhere. The former may have paved the way for the latter.

This kind of social exchange existed in other parts of the world. So did formal battles with sportive elements. However, both seem to have been elaborated to a greater extent and practiced with more intensity in Oceania than anywhere else.

Gender relationships in this Domain have received a lot of attention. Interaction between brother and sister was a prominent feature of social life that imposed responsibility and constraint. On the other hand, Oceanic people are famous for the diversity and freedom of their sexual practices. There is truth to this stereotype, although it has often been exaggerated.

The community had a spiritual connection with the land that it occupied. Land embodied the group's history and connected them with the supernatural world. Culture heroes played an important role in linking people with the land and the supernatural. The very specific spiritual connection between a particular community and its land differed from the more generalized reverence for the environment found elsewhere, most notably in the Northern American Zone.

Key features:

▶ Yams and other tuberous food plants
▶ Aquatic resources
▶ Elaborate social exchanges
▶ Brother–sister responsibility
▶ Sexuality valued
▶ Spiritual connection with land
▶ Elaborate formal battles

Modal Patterns in Oceanic Culture

Material Culture

Obtaining yams often required considerable work, either in preparation of a field or finding them wild, and in digging them up. However, the best species rewarded effort with large, starchy roots that contained many calories. Another desirable characteristic of yams was that they could be stored for months.

Women, often with varying help from their children, gathered shellfish and crabs from the seashore and from rivers and streams. They also used hand nets to dip fish from pools or shallows. Women and men sometimes joined for a drive, beating the water as they moved forward in a line, herding many fish toward a confined place where they were easily caught. People set traps, angled, and in some places used drugs to stupefy fish in pools. Men speared fish from the land, and they used canoes to pursue large prey such as sea turtles and sharks.

Because the methods for making a fire were slow and tedious, each family tried to keep one going at all times. Even travelers carried a smoldering source with them. Most days were warm, but nights could be chilly or damp or both, so people relied on small fires for warmth. They also welcomed the light at night. However, they seldom cooked over a fire. People prepared meals by heating the food with hot stones or ashes under a cover of soil. They usually ate some foods, especially shellfish, raw.

A man spent several days in making the chopping tool, an axe or adze, that was his most important implement. After shaping the stone head, he attached it to a wooden handle with numerous coils of twine or sinew. Then it was ready to use for chopping down trees, hewing firewood, and doing at least the preliminary carving on a variety of wooden utensils such as bowls and trays. Additional important tools were knives and scrapers made from stone flakes and various bone tools used as chisels or to bore or punch holes.

Fishing in the lagoon between reef and shore (Tongan culture, Greater Polynesia).

People made their work more convenient by using teeth and toes along with their hands. With their teeth they held, cut, tore, and ground a variety of technological materials. They used their toes for holding and picking up objects. Climbing trees for food required additional skilled use of the body. In some cases the person held the trunk with the hands and soles of the feet and progressed by hopping. Other climbers used a cord around the tree that they looped around their feet, held with their hands, or both.

People twined or braided various fibers and made them into netting. They turned the netting into carrying bags for objects ranging from gourds to honey. They also made nets to capture fish and land animals.

Net fishing (French Polynesia).

Many men engaged in economic transactions with those in neighboring communities; some traveled hundreds of miles for exchanges. Some exchanges were executed by bargaining while others were phrased as gift giving. In most transactions each participant valued both the goods received and the social relationship with the other person, often a kinsman. Some participants offered raw materials not available to their counterparts or artifacts made from those materials. In other cases men exchanged the products of craft specialization based on local tradition rather than resource availability. Particular seashells ranked among the most desired commodities and some were traded across very long distances. Other major items included coloring materials for artifacts or the body and stone for tools, especially chopping tools. Some communities had the fortune to be near a supply of good stone while others had none, so some men traveled up to a hundred miles to a major quarry to obtain stone.

Social Relations

A person spent many days within a small group, a local band or a hamlet, that usually numbered fewer than forty people. This was a subdivision of the community, which in most cases contained a hundred or so people. Many married couples chose residence on the basis of economic or social advantage, but patrilocality tended to predominate, so that each community contained a core of related men. This was encouraged by a spiritual attachment to the land itself.

A man had a special responsibility for his sister. He had to make sure that her behavior conformed to social proprieties. At the same time he had to observe constraints in the way he acted toward her and in her presence. With other women, sexuality was a major interest. Sex was a highly desirable activity, and the positions used for intercourse enhanced pleasure for women as well as men. Restrictions emphasized social propriety and ritual issues rather than being moralistic.

Men desired prestige and sought it in various ways. Knowledge of the supernatural provided advantages in social life. Some men knew various forms of magic while others had detailed knowledge of ritual and provided essential leadership. Prestige could also come from conflict. Men fought formal battles in open areas, confronting each other in roughly parallel lines. Often the battle lines were deep because scores or even hundreds of men fought in a single engagement. Many such battles were prearranged and limited by rules. They fulfilled a variety of purposes. Those that were pure sport and exhibition often took place in connection with ceremonial gatherings. Other battles had the serious purpose of settling personal disputes, but these often ended with no fatalities. Still others, part of warfare between different communities, were intended to achieve a revenge killing or even a decisive defeat. Many participants took pleasure in these conflicts, some enjoying even the more serious ones.

Knowledge and Expression

The core members of a community felt a spiritual bond with the land that they occupied. Physical landmarks reminded them of their history, ancestry, and origins. Culture heroes accounted for major features in the physical environment and at least some aspects of human life. Though in the past, the actions of ancestral culture heroes had generated spiritual power that remained alive and effective among humans. When people performed ceremonies, they tapped that power from mythic times in order to live successful and moral lives. Fertility was one of the great themes of these rituals.

On ceremonial occasions a community invited its neighbors to join the festivities. In addition to religious rituals, people came for visiting, games, and social exchanges. The hosts for such occasions made every effort to make them memorable and to treat their guests generously. They expected the visiting communities to reciprocate at a later date.

When someone died, close relatives gathered around the body to wail and gash themselves with a variety of sharp objects. Women were most demonstrative, but it was important for all concerned to show strong feelings about the loss. Otherwise, a disgruntled ghost might remain to cause harm and even death. An important purpose of the funerary rituals was to send the soul to its rightful place in another world. Details of burial varied with age, gender, and other aspects of departed person's position in society. Almost every death raised suspicion of sorcery and led the survivors to consider retaliation.

PACIFIC ISLAND ZONE

Areas:

- Greater Polynesia
- Melanesia

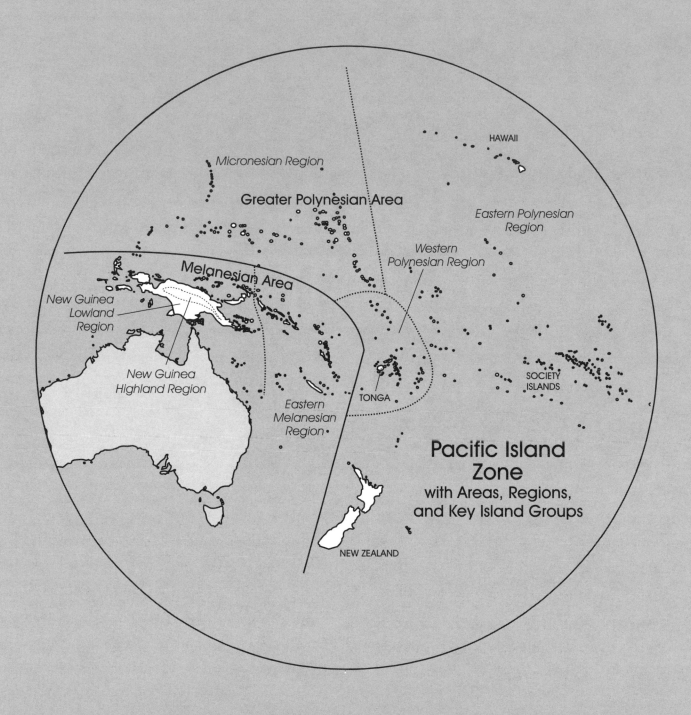

Micronesian Region

Greater Polynesian Area

HAWAII

Eastern Polynesian
Region

Western
Polynesian Region

Melanesian Area

New Guinea
Lowland
Region

New Guinea
Highland Region

Eastern
Melanesian
Region

TONGA

SOCIETY
ISLANDS

**Pacific Island
Zone**
with Areas, Regions,
and Key Island Groups

NEW ZEALAND

Previous page   A village and a canoe with triangular sail, illustrating the
shoreline culture basic to the Pacific Island Zone (Hawaiian culture,
Greater Polynesia).

OVERVIEW OF THE ZONE

Examples:

*Samoa, Tahiti, Caroline Islands,
New Guinea, Solomon Islands,
Vanuatu (New Hebrides)*

This Zone consisted of all the inhabited islands in the Pacific Ocean east of Indonesia and Australia except for those along the American coasts. About a half million square miles of land harbored 3 million or more people (Hays 1991). There may have been many more; some argue that drastic depopulation after contact with Europeans has not been taken into account (Kirch 2000). Although many Pacific people inhabited the inland parts of large islands, this account will emphasize the distinctive cultural features associated with communities that occupied the coasts and small islands.

The most familiar examples of Pacific Island societies, such as Hawaii and Easter Island, belonged to the Greater Polynesian Culture Area. The Melanesian Area, located between Indonesia and Polynesia, is less known to the public. However, although it covered a much smaller part of the ocean than Polynesia, Melanesia had many more people, perhaps five times as many (Hays 1991).

The inhabited islands included three types: (1) small, low coral atolls formed from the calcium skeletons of tiny animals and plants that had been attached to other islands, (2) higher volcanic islands produced by the cones of upthrusting volcanoes, and (3) high continental islands resulting from the movements of continental plates. On the larger islands higher altitudes modified the basically tropical climate. Droughts and typhoons endangered people throughout the Zone, and availability of fresh water was a potential problem for most Islanders.

Like other tropical peoples, Pacific Islanders cultivated root crops, the most important being taro *(Colocasia esculenta)* and yams. More distinctively, they used a variety of tree crops for food and technological materials. The coconut palm *(Cocos nucifera)* was the most widespread. Despite the presence of domestic dogs and fowl, people obtained most of their protein from the sea. The pig, the most important domestic animal, was prized mainly for social and ritual reasons. Pigs were absent from several sections of each Area in the Pacific Zone, but pig keeping characterized the majority of ethnic groups and the majority of the population in the Zone.

Pacific cultures are especially noteworthy for seafaring. Those dwelling on the coasts and small islands used a fairly simple technology to make boats that took them across the sea to colonize, trade, and make war.

Social exchanges between groups often had a competitive element, and coordination of exchanges was related to political leadership. The relationship between brother and sister was stronger and less ambivalent than parallel-sibling connections (sister–sister and brother–brother) and also overshadowed the husband–wife relationship.

With regard to knowledge and expression, there was little that distinguished the Pacific Zone as a whole from the rest of the world. Islanders attached ritual and esthetic significance to farming activities. Other than that, art was mainly directed toward religion. Men sculpted in wood and a wide variety of other, more localized, materials. They regarded the artistic forms of previous generations as "examples" rather than rigid guidelines and displayed a high degree of "judgment and innovation" (Newton et al. 1987).

Key features:

- ▶ Tree crops
- ▶ Protein mainly from fishing
- ▶ Social and ritual use of pigs
- ▶ Seafaring
- ▶ Competitive social exchange
- ▶ Brother–sister bond

Modal Patterns in Pacific Island Culture

Material Culture

The small squarish house was about ten feet wide and perhaps a bit more than that in length. Early morning light crept through the low doorway and joined with the small fire inside to illuminate the structure of lashed timbers and the thatched roof above. In addition to light and warmth for the night, the fire provided a place to dry fish and do occasional light cooking.

Among the shadows a woman swept the dirt floor that she and her family had slept on, using a bundle of stiff plant fibers. She wore her everyday clothes, consisting of a skirt made from plant material and a necklace with seashells in it. Her small children were already at play outside, and her husband had gone to his work. The sweeping, which the woman did every few days to clear away the debris of family life, took only a short time. Then she went outside for her main work of the morning. She joined several of her neighbors in the shade of a large tree, and they talked as they worked. Some made baskets and others made mats, but they all plaited their artifacts from strips of pandanus or coconut leaves.

There were only a few houses nearby because irregularities in terrain and resource availability encouraged people to disperse. However, other hamlets were only a few hundred yards away. The entire community of a hundred people or so defended a territory of several square miles against intruders and enemies. In case of a raid, shouts of warning and cries for help were easily heard from one hamlet to another. When warfare intensified, the people of a community sometimes came together in a single compact village and fortified it.

From time to time a man strolled by in his everyday garb, a pubic covering hanging from the waist. Several of the men carried adzes, which were essential to every kind of woodworking. Depending mainly on availability, the blade of the tool was made from shell, usually that of the giant clam, or from stone.

Some men checked their traps or went after free-swimming fish. Those who sought eels mostly used nooses. Boats increased fishing opportunities. In a safe environment such as a lagoon, a man often used a simple raft as a platform for angling or spearing. To fish in less-sheltered places, including the open sea, several men went out in a boat that consisted of a dugout hull and a stabilizing outrigger of light wood attached to the hull by several booms. In the right wind they raised a triangular sail with its point down, setting it so that the outrigger and booms balanced the wind's force on the craft. Lacking wind or desiring greater maneuverability, the men paddled.

Fishing from a boat, men had several options. One was to use spears or lines in the usual way, although with the prospect of taking larger fish. Sometimes it was better to troll, dragging lines from a boat in motion. They could also drag a large net. When not used for fishing, a boat contributed to the food supply by taking people to gardens that were too distant for walking or inaccessible by land because of rugged terrain.

The bulk of the food came from root crops. Growing throughout the year on shady and well-watered slopes, taro provided food whenever people wanted it. The edible part of taro was the corm, the thickened underground part of the stem. Harvest of a particular plant took place seven to twelve months after it had been started by placing the top of a corm into a shallow hole. People kept close track because taro roots had to be taken close to the time of maturity. Then the perishable plant had to be eaten soon because it remained palatable for only a few days, even after cooking.

Yam cultivators maintained well-drained soil by mounding the earth or digging drainage ditches. They also trained the growing vines to climb trees or poles, exposing their leaves to more sunlight. In contrast to taro, yams rewarded the laborers only on a seasonal basis. However, yams had the advantage of being storable for six months or more.

Coconut palms stood in clusters along the beach and inland at lower altitudes. It was the job of men to climb them for their hard fruits. One way to do it was to use a cord around the tree; another was to grasp it with hands and feet and hop up. Some coconut palms had given food to the grandparents of the men who now climbed them. A tree began to produce about five years after planting and continued without any seasonal changes for up to sixty years thereafter. Immature nuts contained a tangy

A small canoe, showing the outrigger device used on many Pacific Island craft (Fijian culture, Greater Polynesia).

A man in modern clothing showing how to climb a coconut tree to obtain one of the significant foods of the Pacific Islands (Samoan culture, Greater Polynesia).

liquid that people drank for a snack, but a man usually took mature nuts for their solid white meat. After being shredded, the flesh was mixed with a starchy food for cooking. Alternatively, cream was pressed from the shreds and used as oil in the preparation of other foods.

By the middle of the day people were hungry. They had started out with only a light breakfast, often cold leftovers, and snacked on a tuber or a small raw fish or some other item taken from the work at hand. Family members returned to the house for a major meal served in the afternoon. Cooked in an earth oven, it often took several hours to prepare. The cook built a fire in the pit and then raked it out after the stones had been heated. Then he or she placed wrapped food on the hot stones and covered it with leaves and earth.

The heart of the main meal was a starchy vegetable such as taro or yams. One or more side dishes consisted of greens, coconut meat, fish, or some other kind of animal flesh. Men and women ate separately, children with the women. Each individual ate from his or her own leaf plate or wooden platter or bowl. The diners skewered some items, especially hot ones, with sharp sticks and ate the rest with their fingers. The main condiment was salt from the sea or from saline springs inland. With the food they drank fresh water, which they appreciated because it was often hard to obtain. For some people it was simply scarce; others had to walk long distances to get to a source.

In the afternoon the family's pigs came wandering home from foraging in the countryside. The gray-haired animals were thin, long-legged, and long-snouted. With garden plots fenced against them, the pigs had fed only on rough wild forage that was not enough to sustain them. Family members gave them scraps left from meals or meal preparation along with rejected food items such as substandard tubers. The pigs themselves did not figure in ordinary meals because they were slaughtered only for special occasions. After feeding, the pigs settled down to rest in the shade of their owners' houses.

The chickens that wandered around the settlement and roosted nearby also received some scraps, but no other care. They were small, similar to their wild relatives, and people rarely ate their tiny eggs. Occasionally a family varied the flesh diet with a chicken, but people used the birds mainly for decorative feathers. Those from the neck and tail of a rooster were the most valued.

Social Relations

An ordinary man had one wife unless he had taken another because of a kinship obligation such as widow inheritance. In the company of other men the husband sometimes participated in talk about the inferiority of women, their weakness, their lack of intelligence or self-control. When he was with his wife, the man noticed her work and thought about the ways in which her products contributed to his standing in the community. Their relationship had also allied the two families and given the man in-laws to whom he could turn for various kinds of help. Because of advantages like these, men of status and ambition sought extra wives and gained prestige by having them.

The husband had to be somewhat cautious about daily interactions with his wife. Since women were a source of spiritual pollution, too much contact could diminish a man. Excessive sex was particularly dangerous to physical and ritual well-being. On the other hand, a man took great pleasure in sex, and a woman expected sexual satisfaction from her husband. Often couples used sexual positions that gave the woman freedom of movement. Married people had to achieve a balance between the desires of both parties and the dangers that women posed to men.

Childbirth increased the danger because of the polluting blood involved. After birth in a special hut the new mother remained in seclusion with her baby, on whom she lavished the greatest care. In addition to physical attention, she made every effort to keep it away from the harmful spirits to which it was especially susceptible. She and others performed ritual acts to strengthen and protect the child. At the end of seclusion the mother brought her baby into a community of warmth and indulgence. The only imposition that a mother might make on her baby was the introduction of some solid foods as early as the first few months. As the child developed skill in walking and talking, its social world changed. Adults began to withdraw their affection and protection. Those entitled to do so began to administer serious punishments for misbehavior—sometimes disdain or outright ridicule, sometimes a slap or even a beating.

A boy of six had already begun to sleep apart from his mother and sisters. Girls spent more time in adult tasks with their mothers while boys roamed in groups, playing and mock fighting. Eventually the nudity of childhood was covered by clothes that represented the beginnings of adult propriety. With puberty came the possibility of sexual adventures, except for girls who had already been betrothed. The affairs of the young sometimes narrowed down to a choice for marriage, but family decisions overruled many preferences.

Marriage connected families and the descent groups or communities to which the families belonged. Hence the wedding was a time for celebration by the groups involved. They feasted and exchanged goods. At two moments in the festivities, each representing a basic aspect of the new relationship, bride and groom became the focus of attention. First, the couple engaged in a food-sharing rite. Later, they initiated their marital sex life in a symbolic setting such as a new house or a garden.

A man who caught his wife in adultery was entitled to kill her lover, but killings could lead to feuds that disrupted the community or to wars with other communities. More often the husband accepted material compensation from the other man. The husband could and sometimes did beat his wife for betraying him. A wife confronted with her husband's adultery could only talk about it, either to the man or to the rest of the community. Few people sought divorce because of adultery.

There were various other reasons for divorce, which was available to both parties. When a couple separated, the mother kept young children with her. Older ones might stay with the father, but in any case they could choose where to live when they became adults. People who divorced were free to marry again. The likelihood of divorce lessened as a couple grew used to one another and to their in-laws and as they shared in lavishing affection on their babies.

Rarely, if ever, did a husband and wife become as close as brother and sister. If spouses parted, they remarried and went on with their lives. If one died, the grief of the other was assuaged by remarriage no matter how powerful the feeling had been. But a sibling could never be replaced. After a loss, the memory and sorrow lasted for a very long time. Unlike spouses, brother and sister were never troubled by different goals or allegiance to different groups. Having come from the same familial substance, they were like halves of a single whole. They were complementary to one another, the sister representing a spiritual aspect and the brother acting as her secular protector. Many signs of honor and respect marked their relationship. From puberty onward they showed great restraint in their behavior toward one another and observed some degree of avoidance. Above all, there was to be no hint of sexuality in their relationship. It was a terrible insult, perhaps the worst, to accuse a man of a sexual connection with his sister. Ideally, siblings of the same sex were also close, sharing and cooperating with each other and providing mutual support in all matters. However, people recognized that same-sex siblings were more likely to compete and quarrel with one another.

Women usually came to live with their husbands, so most of the men in a hamlet were relatives. With other men in the community they belonged to a descent group that owned the land that they cultivated. The group's identity was intertwined with the land, which was alive with the history of the group. Named localities represented their origin as human beings or their initial settlement in the territory and also the major events that had taken place since that beginning. Sometimes the members spoke of themselves in terms of their common descent and sometimes in terms of the land that they shared.

Although the men of a descent group were deeply attached to their land, they shared use rights and sometimes even ownership with others. Some men settled with their mothers' or wives' groups because of land scarcity or disputes with their male relatives. Sometimes refugees from a military defeat sought safety among various relatives. Everyone had land rights of some kind in several groups, which they could activate by residence and participation. Most groups welcomed immigrants because they added to the group's strength.

Mundane life was frequently punctuated by events in which a family, descent group, or community invited one or more others for feasting and gifts. Life changes, such as marriage and death, occasioned many of these observances. Others were held on a seasonal basis, at a harvest time for example. A great deal of time and effort went into planning and executing these events. There had to be enough food, including pork and other special feast foods, to reward the helpers and to sustain all the guests. There also had to be gifts for the visitors, such as live pigs and valuable ornaments. At a minimum the largesse had to be enough to honor the guests; in some cases the intent was to humble them with quantities that they could not match when they gave a reciprocal feast.

Some men enjoyed unusual prestige or power within the community and even beyond. Exchange provided one important avenue to such status. Leaders sponsored, organized, and contributed to events involving their relatives or the community in general. To make contributions they used wealth accumulated from their followers or from success in their own personal exchanges, including external trade. Also associated with prestige and leadership were ritual knowledge and success in warfare.

Although the community might be at peace for a year or two, a reason for warfare arose sooner or later. Even minor offenses were sometimes magnified by men eager to gain prestige as warriors and by leaders who saw opportunities to gain reflected glory and extend their influence. Often two alliances of several communities confronted each other. Within such a setting enemies fought formal battles in open areas involving dozens or hundreds of men on each side.

A man who set out for such a battle could never be certain about the course of events or the levels of violence that might be reached. At the beginning, the warriors followed rules and casualties were minimal. The two sides gathered several hundred yards apart and no fighting occurred until both were ready. Sometimes the ordinary men became spectators as great or would-be great warriors from each side stepped forward to harangue the enemy and challenge specific individuals. In some cases a series of duels followed that might or might not be conclusive.

With or without the preliminary duels, most battles began with the two sides standing well apart and hurling insults, boasts, and projectiles at one another. Men with youthful agility or battle experience easily dodged most of the missiles. Occasionally a man went down, usually stunned or wounded rather than killed, and his enemies attempted to reach him and finish him with their clubs. Most often his comrades were able to protect him and remove him from the field. Many battles went on for hours without any fatalities, and some ended after only one or two deaths.

There were other battles in which many fighters joined in hand-to-hand combat. If the casualties mounted or the weight of a rush swept one side back, the battle could become a rout. When the victors followed, massive destruction ensued. They slaughtered the enemy warriors if they could catch or contain them. They destroyed one or more enemy settlements, along with their crops, trees, and animals. They massacred the inhabitants, including women and children. On a few occasions allies organized a large-scale sneak attack that had mass destruction as its goal from the outset. It was rare for the victors to occupy the land that they had cleared so violently. Usually they were satisfied to create a no-man's-land that increased their security.

Many conflicts ended with less-drastic consequences as the two sides negotiated a truce based on various compensations. This was most likely to occur if the fighting had been damaging but inconclusive or if the enemies were related in some way. Thus the course and outcome of warfare depended on many different factors, including the relationship between the principals, the events of battle, the original reason for the war, the motivations of leaders, the emotions of the combatants, and the ecological circumstances.

Knowledge and Expression

Farming entwined with the spiritual and the esthetic. People told myths about the origins of the staple crops and, associating specific spirits with the crops, they offered supplications and thanks. They also used magic to enhance their own gardens and destroy those of their enemies. Farmers took pleasure in the precise contours of their fences, the regularity of plant spacing, the alignment of the plots, and the uniformity of vine poles. However, people maintained a more pragmatic attitude toward much of the natural environment beyond their fields.

They shared the world with a variety of supernatural beings. Many of the gods were patrons of particular communities or kinship groups. Some were associated with particular activities, such as fishing or war. Gods had emotions like those of humans. They often assumed human form, although they were capable of others. Men turned to gods for success in war. They appealed for help before any significant military expedition and tried to divine the likely results. Ancestors were also important to families and larger kinship groups. They sometimes helped their living descendants if the living honored them with offerings and rituals. Some ancestors attained great individual power and were deified.

The need to honor gods and ancestors prompted men to create objects beyond the ordinary. The most prominent were ceremonial buildings with elaborate woodcarving and decorations. Men also carved ritual objects such as masks and figurines and enhanced many of these objects with paint. They used them to make a spiritual connection with supernatural beings. Largely excluded from religious knowledge and ritual, women had little to do with such art although they did play a role in ritual dances. Song, drums, and flutes accompanied the dances.

The spirits of the bush and the sea were a concern for individuals rather than groups. Humans might receive benefits from some while avoiding those that were mischievous or malevolent. Because spirits could usually be avoided, people considered sorcerers the greater danger. They carefully disposed of all body wastes because these were the basis of the most common magic used by sorcerers. Even so, many deaths were attributed to evil magic.

Close relatives, especially women, greeted death with loud wailing. Some mourners put on old and ragged coverings and some blackened themselves with soot or charcoal. Burial was not necessarily final. In at least some cases relatives recovered the bones of the deceased, especially the skull. The bones might be kept in a ritual setting or hidden away in a cave where they would not be disturbed. Having been sent to the appropriate place by the proper ceremonies, the dead watched over their descendants and sometimes helped them. The dead in turn continued to benefit from celebrations in which the living remembered and honored their ancestors.

GREATER POLYNESIAN AREA

Examples:

Tonga, Samoa, Fiji, Hawaii,
Tahiti, Maori (New Zealand)

There is general agreement about Polynesia as a valid culture area in the Pacific (Hays 1991; Kirch 2000). Conventionally it was enclosed by a rough triangle with its corners at Hawaii, Easter Island, and New Zealand. I make two significant additions to this Area; hence the term "Greater Polynesia." One addition is the Fiji archipelago, often classified as part of the Melanesian Area (see next section). The other addition is the archipelagoes east of the Philippines that are collectively termed Micronesia. They used to be treated as a distinct culture area, but support for that view is declining (e.g., Linnekin 1997a). In my account the Micronesian islands are a Region in the Greater Polynesian Area.

Although the islands of Greater Polynesia sprawled across most of the Pacific Ocean, they added up to little more than 4,000 square miles of land (less than the state of Connecticut). The number of people supported by this land is subject to wildly varying opinions. The conventional view puts the precontact Polynesian population at about a half million (Hays 1991; Oliver 1989c). Some consider this much too low, arguing that many estimates have ignored inland settlements and/or depletion by disease (Kirch 2000). Recent reconstructions of the Hawaiian population, for example, have resulted in estimates ranging from 120,000 to almost 1 million.

The breadfruit tree *(Artocarpus altilis)* rivaled taro as a source of food and exceeded it in a number of populous archipelagoes. Women made cloth from the inner bark of trees and wove mats from pandanus leaves. Both served utilitarian purposes and also played major roles in social exchange. Polynesians epitomized the seafaring capabilities of Pacific Zone culture. Their largest canoes, double-hulled, held as many as 600 people and took them across hundreds of miles of open sea. To navigate those distances, men used subtle and extensive knowledge about the sun, stars, wind, and waves.

The taste for tattoos in the modern Western world can be traced largely to Polynesia, which was a major center of the practice (the English word is derived from the Tahitian *tatau*). Polynesian tattoos have been characterized as "the most artistic" in the traditional world (Allen and Gilbert n.d.). They were once thought to simply represent high status, but this is now doubtful. Instead tattoos varied between cultures and among individuals according to complex relationships with the social and spiritual characteristics of the tattooed people (Gell 1993; Thomas 1995b).

Adoption and peer socialization played vital roles in Polynesian culture. At least one fourth of the people in any population were adopted at some point during their lives and the figure approached 100 percent in some societies. In Hawaii in recent times almost one third of native persons were adopted (Howard and Kirkpatrick 1989). Polynesian society differed from any other with regard to the nature and the social and psychological ramifications of adoption. Also distinctive compared to the rest of the traditional world was the extent to which the children, natural or adopted, distanced themselves from adults and underwent socialization by their peers (Ritchie and Ritchie 1989).

A hereditary chieftain led each Polynesian community. Virtually all communities were integrated into chiefdoms, although the power and authority of the chiefs varied. In many cases paramount chiefs exerted some control over several chiefdoms. Leadership at all levels emerged from a pervasive system of rank. Distinction of

at least two strata, commoners and aristocrats, was universal, but the social gap between the two classes varied. One tool for status contestants was an ambilineal descent system in which an individual could affiliate with the kin group of the father or mother or both. A person could create the genealogy that conferred the highest rank.

The concept of *mana* was "central to Polynesian worldview" (Shore 1989), but anthropologists have disputed its meaning. Many viewed it as a supernatural force analogous to electricity (Handy 1985), but this monolithic interpretation is now in doubt (Keesing 1984; Shore 1989). Mana was associated with many different persons, things, places, and acts. Above all, Polynesians emphasized its active manifestations in the visible world. It seems that two things were shared by all manifestations of mana. One was origin with the gods; the other was its role in creation and growth of all kinds (Shore 1989). Thus it is probably best for us to think of mana as a category of powers connected by godly origin and by the potential to facilitate creation and growth. This was the Polynesian version of Oceania's spiritual force derived from mythical times.

Mana was associated with *tapu*, another complex concept. Because of danger inherent in the power of mana, a concentration of it created a state of tapu. This required ritual restrictions on those responsible for the concentration of power and avoidance by others. The term also applied to sources of ritual pollution, such as corpses, that required special treatment or avoidance. I use the Polynesian spelling to avoid confusion with the English *taboo*, which is derived from the Polynesian word but often implies that a thing is evil, illegal, or merely naughty.

In contrast to other peoples of Oceania, Polynesians devoted a great deal of ritual attention to powerful gods. To glorify chiefs and gods they created elaborate, poetic chants on which their music was based. Dances also derived from the chants. Specialists ensured that these creations were adequate to their great purposes.

Key features:

► Breadfruit

► Fine mats and bark cloth

► Tattooing

► Extensive adoption

► Peer socialization

► Ambilineal descent

► Chiefdoms

► Powerful gods

► Mana and tapu

► Word-determined music

► Specialists in arts

Modal Patterns in Greater Polynesian Culture

Material Culture

The hamlet consisted of small houses on low stone-faced platforms. Inside one of them a family of commoners rose from their sleeping mats. The husband's loincloth and his wife's skirt were both made from bark cloth. Emerging from the house, they greeted neighbors who were similarly attired and also similarly decorated. All the adults bore modest tattoos in shades of black and gray, and almost everyone wore a necklace. Most of the necklaces were made from small shells and flowers, but some displayed the teeth of a porpoise or small whale.

The woman checked on some pandanus leaves that were steeping in salt water because they were too tough to plait. Later she would pound them to make them even more pliable. For now she took strips that had already been prepared and settled down with some friends on a shaded house platform to make mats. Often she varied the pattern of plaiting to produce designs. Another way to decorate the mats was to use strips of two different colors, either natural or dyed. When there were enough mats on hand, a woman sometimes made baskets or fans from the pandanus strips. People used the fans to cool themselves and to discourage flying insects.

As some women worked on pandanus artifacts, they listened to the sound of others pounding bark cloth. This was a woman's most important job other than mat making. The bast (inner bark) of the paper mulberry tree provided the best material for cloth although the bark of breadfruit or banyan could also be used. The quality of the product also depended on the age of the tree and the amount of time spent in beating the cloth. The mallet used in cloth making had a stone head that had been laboriously grooved.

After scraping the outer bark away with a sharp shell, the cloth maker soaked the bast in fresh water. When it was ready, she spread a large piece across a log or a carved anvil. Keeping the bast moist, the woman pounded it with the mallet, thinning and stretching it, and folding it periodically so that it would be thick enough not to tear. The final product was somewhat stiff, but it became supple and comfortable with wear. Some of the cloth was decorated with dyes.

New skirts and loincloths were needed frequently because the material was fragile and because a woman replaced soiled sleeping mats every time she swept the house. The manufacture of the finer mats and bark cloth brought women prestige because they were used in social exchange and in ceremonies. The finest items were offered to chiefs and gods.

A Polynesian woman performs one of her most important tasks, making bark cloth (Hawaiian culture).

Because women spent so much time on their textiles, men usually tended the farm plots and the groves. Twice each year they climbed the tall breadfruit trees to harvest elliptical fruits, some of which reached ten inches in diameter. People cooked both the meat and seeds but sometimes ate the seeds raw. If they wanted the breadfruit fresh, they had to eat it almost immediately because it spoiled quickly. However, they could preserve breadfruit for months or even years by placing it in a covered pit where it became lightly fermented.

When men remained at home, they often worked on nets, using the bark of hibiscus trees. A man scraped the bark, shredded it, and rolled it between palm and thigh to produce the cord. Some seine nets were more than a hundred feet long and ten to twenty feet high. The makers attached wooden floats to the top and weighted the bottom with stone, coral, or shell. For turtles and sharks men made stronger nets of coconut fiber.

Men fished from boats beyond the reef, sometimes in deep sea and sometimes near another island. They used extensive knowledge about the locations and habits of the prey, as well as their tendencies to take various kinds of bait. The fishers also had to consider edibility. Some species were poisonous at all times and some only during particular periods. Deep-sea catches included grouper and tuna. Although the men could not preserve the flesh, there was little waste because they shared with others in their own hamlets and with inland relatives who did less fishing. The inland people presented their coastal kin with food from their trees and gardens.

A double-hulled Polynesian fishing boat (Tahitian culture).

If a man paused on the beach after a fishing trip, he could see the hamlets of some of his relatives on the inland slopes. He also saw groves of food trees, patches of cultivated plants, and wild vegetation that changed in color and pattern as it ascended the steep hillsides. The swathe of sea and land that belonged to his community ran from the reef behind him to the center of the island. Its diverse resources provided for most of the inhabitants' needs and wants, as did the similar territories that ringed the island.

When it was time for the main meal of the day, men went to the cooking shed that several households shared. It was simply a thatched roof supported by four poles, enough to keep off the sun or rain. Men prepared their own meals because a tapu prevented them from taking food from a woman. People ate shellfish and many scaled fish raw, but other foods were steamed in the earth oven. People sometimes added fowl to their meals, but more often flesh came from the rats that they snared.

The house of a high-ranking family was larger than those of commoners. A layer of coarse mats and another layer of fine ones covered the floor of coral pebbles. The timbers of an elite dwelling were well dressed and accurately fitted, and the thatch was carefully laid. A prominent family could afford to compensate a professional builder. A community chieftain's house was larger than those of any lower-ranking people, and his compound usually contained numerous relatives.

In addition to the housebuilder, two other kinds of craftsmen catered especially to the elite and often lived well on compensation from their clients: the canoe builder and the tattoo artist. When the canoe builder had a commission, he recruited a crew to help with the arduous task and spent most of his working time on it. When not engaged, he fished and farmed like other men. The tattoo artist worked more steadily because high-ranking

A partially constructed house, with men on top for scale, makes it easy to understand why house-building was a specialized skill in Greater Polynesia.

people came to him for the creation and maintenance of numerous tattoos. His basic tool was an instrument like a small, sharp-pointed rake. To create complex geometric designs, he used several instruments of different sizes. The first step was to draw the design on the skin. Then the tattooer dipped the appropriate instrument into a solution of water and soot and tapped the points into the skin with a small stick or stone. As he worked, he followed a ritualized procedure hedged with tapus. Usually he could create a component about the size of a hand in an hour. After perhaps a week of healing, the client returned for more work. Sometimes one complete tattoo took several months. The tattoos of aristocrats were often not visible in public because they wrapped themselves in clothing of bark cloth or fine mats. Both tattoos and clothes were ways of controlling mana.

Occasionally men went on a trading expedition. However, most islands had a uniform environment, so the inhabitants had little reason for practical trade beyond familial exchanges of fish and plant foods. Other archipelagoes might have different resources, but they were far away. The greatest spur to trade was variation in trees on different kinds of islands. People with large quantities or high quality of bark cloth exchanged it for various other goods. They also traded various kinds of wood suitable for tools, weapons, or canoe parts.

Social Relations

With one son already married, a man contemplated building another house and hoped for an old age in a large compound with many grown children to make his life easy and grandchildren to make it pleasant. Of more immediate concern, the man had just adopted a girl of six years from his cousin's family. Having no daughters as yet, he and his wife needed someone to help with the female chores in the household. They also felt a lack of balance in their lives; people liked their families to be complete. The arrangement benefited the girl and the family from which she came because their trees and gardens had done poorly in the last few years. The girl's family also gained prestige because giving a child to others was a generous act. Beyond immediate returns, the adoption strengthened the friendship between the two families.

The numerous adoptees throughout the community had come to their new families at ages ranging from infancy to adulthood. Several lived in the households of specialists to learn the arts of canoe building, tattooing, and the priesthood. Several more were refugees from the other side of the island where a storm had caused severe food problems by destroying numerous trees and canoes. One old man had avidly sought his adopted child as an heir for land that would otherwise go to relatives that he despised.

Adoptees continued the relationship with those who gave them birth. The involved adults shared parental prerogatives and responsibilities, usually a simple matter because this was an arrangement between blood relatives. It extended the basic principle that natural parents shared their rights with other relatives.

Before and after a birth, many rites were performed to protect the baby, its mother, and her helpers. Those for the baby gave it life, strength, and purity. Following the birth, mother and infant were washed in fresh water. Great care was taken in disposing of the umbilical cord in order to prevent sorcery and give the child long life. Naming was a very important religious event because the name became a part of the being. Having a name from the family genealogy gave the child rapport with living kin, the ancestors, and the gods. Other names would be added during the life of an individual, such as an adoption name or a nickname bestowed with tattoos. Some would formally exchange names with intimate friends while successful warriors took the names of their slain enemies as a way to increase their spiritual power.

Whether born to the family or adopted, children were treated in the same ways. Infants were indulged, and older children learned to cope with a much less tolerant social world. In order to behave properly, they had to learn the terms that organized their kin relations. These emphasized gender, generation, and seniority. Within their own generation they distinguished others according to relative age, and they would do the same with their own children.

Subject to significant punishments, older children learned to anticipate the moods and behavior of their seniors. Both girls and boys removed themselves from their elders as much as possible, forming peer groups in which they learned to get along with others. The members of a peer group played, danced, and sang together. Confinement to the house alone was one of the worst punishments that a parent could impose on an older child. The peer group itself sometimes imposed punishments on its members. Boys especially learned to cooperate and compete in ways that anticipated the politics and status seeking of adulthood. When the peer group proved to be inadequate or overly punitive, a child had recourse to the warm relationship with its grandparents. Sometimes older people adopted one or more of their grandchildren.

In later childhood, usually when he felt himself to be ready, a boy went to a specialist to receive his superincision. The man used a thin piece of wood to raise the boy's foreskin and then slit it longitudinally to reveal the head of the penis. Although lacking any ceremony, this operation was considered an essential step toward manhood. Without it a young man suffered the stigma of a serious deviation from custom. Girls would consider him unacceptable for sex or marriage. The next major step in social maturation, which was observed with some ceremony, was the boy's first tattoo.

Everyone belonged to a ramage, a descent group with a single ancestor. People chose to affiliate with the ramage of father or mother, depending on the economic and social advantages that they offered. Sometimes there was no choice because both parents belonged to the same group. Men and women of the same ramage could marry, as long as their personal relationship was not too close, and people preferred to find their spouses nearby.

One basis for choosing ramage affiliation was economic advantage, especially land availability. Another was rank, which depended on descent. An original ramage retained the highest rank as others branched off from it; related ramages were ranked according to seniority. Every person within a ramage was ranked according to descent and seniority, including elder and younger siblings. Given the complexities of the system, a person could sometimes attain higher rank by affiliating with the mother's descent group. These manipulations were of greatest importance for the aristocracy, the people of higher rank who had access to power. Such people could recite genealogies, containing both male and female links, that covered twenty generations or more.

The number and intricacy of tattoos distinguished some persons of high rank. An individual might go back to the tattooist every three to six months until a large part of the body was covered. Prestige came from the wealth needed to finance the operations and the endurance to withstand the pain. However, extensive tattoos also marked a person as playing a more secular role in the elite system. To this end, tattoos isolated and bound the individual's mana. The most sacred personages bore few or no tattoos.

Aristocratic families were less permissive than commoners about premarital sex for their daughters. They were more likely to veto a young member's choice of a spouse, or to select a specific partner and arrange the marriage. The wedding of a firstborn was vital as the initial step toward worthy representation of the family in the next generation. The families exchanged gifts, feasted together, and chanted their genealogies. Abundant food, erotic dance, and sexual license represented the fertility that people wished for the newlyweds. Fertility and well-being were also sought through offerings and prayers.

Among the local aristocracy, the most important individual was the community chieftain. He was the highest-ranking man in the senior ramage. Ideally the office passed from a man to his son or another close male relative. However, other aristocrats saw to it that an incompetent was replaced or made into a figurehead. The chieftain organized work that required more than the ordinary cooperation among families. This applied especially to large-scale fishing and the building of religious structures. People expected the chieftain to keep order by whatever means he had, whether the power of his personality or the willingness of some men to enforce his will. He had the authority to place a kind of tapu on particular places and things, such as a crop reserved for

Tattooing customs varied greatly throughout Polynesia. The culture of the Marquesan Islands emphasized the lower body.

some special use. People expected a chieftain to exercise his power and authority with restraint and in the best interests of the community.

The chieftain received the first fruits of one or more community harvests. He redistributed some of this produce to his people and, acting as the community's ritual representative, offered some to the gods. The remainder went to the chief. A concept of common origin and the need for defense of land united the communities of a chiefdom. The chief acted as his people's representative to the highest gods because his ancestry originated with those gods. He received first fruits from the communities and made additional levies to support ceremonies and other public functions. Assistants of high rank administered the chief's decisions and sometimes dissuaded him from rash acts against his own people or outsiders.

Most chiefs sought land, power, and tribute through military conquest. Thus conquest or alliance connected chiefdoms to each other. A notion of common ancestry often facilitated alliance but did not eliminate conflict among related chiefdoms. In most cases the larger grouping was headed by a paramount chief. He made the same demands on his subjects as did the chiefs below him, including levies of material support and labor for ceremonies and public works.

People hoped that chiefs and paramount chiefs would show the same concern for their subjects as did ramage and community chieftains, but this rarely held true. Chiefs, especially paramounts, usually kept and used more than they gave back to their subjects in any form. They seldom resolved quarrels for the benefit of their subjects, and the only crimes that they punished (very harshly) were those that threatened their power. Chiefs ruled largely by coercion and faced recurring rebellions by their subordinates.

A paramount chief and his wife. Paramount chiefs wore elaborate clothes and other symbols of office; noble women played important roles in public life (Hawaiian culture, Greater Polynesia).

A younger brother of a chief often sought to usurp the office. Apart from his own ambition, he saw steadily decreasing prestige and privilege for his descendants if he kept his position. Their ramages would be even further from the main line to the divine ancestors. One counterstrategy of senior aristocrats was to encourage their juniors to engage in extensive premarital sexual relations with commoner women. This delayed marriage and social maturity and lessened the number of offspring: sons that might support a man in challenging his betters and daughters he could use to recruit supporters through marriage.

A man expected that every few years his community chieftain would summon him to war. He could refuse, but he had to consider how this would affect feelings toward him on the part of the chieftain and other people. On the other hand, success in war could bring him prestige, satisfaction, and perhaps some material spoils. Some men, especially among the well-trained nobility, looked to war for opportunities.

In some cases the chieftain organized his own people for a skirmish with a neighboring community over a local issue such as land. In other instances the chieftain had consented to raise troops for the chief above him. Sometimes it was the paramount chief who had persuaded several subordinate chiefs to support him in war. When a chief called, it might be to avenge an insult from another chief. It might be to defend against a usurper who had drawn significant support from other leaders. Or it might be a major campaign against another chiefdom to destroy a competitor or gain some kind of control over him. Control could mean a simple acknowledgment of dominance, regular payment of substantial tribute, or political incorporation.

A battle began with throwing spears or stones. Many men were especially skilled with stones. Everyone was alert for the first enemy to go down; he would be an important offering to the war god, whether dead or alive. In many battles the two sides closed in with lances and clubs. As the casualty rate climbed, many left the battle. Ordinary men were brave as they charged into the fight, but saw no reason to risk their lives in a losing cause. Only nobles and dedicated warriors stood firm in adversity. Sometimes those who defected suffered serious consequences. They could be caught and slaughtered in a rout and, if nearby, their communities laid waste.

The victors cooked and ate the enemy dead as an act of revenge. The mutilation of the bodies was in itself a humiliation. By turning them into food, which was an ordinary thing rather than sacred, the winners destroyed the mana of their victims. Sometimes they perpetuated the insult by making the bones into utensils associated with food; a skull into a bowl, for example.

Knowledge and Expression

A man, head of his household, was worried because his son's pregnant wife had felt sick for several days. There were several possible causes, including an offended god or spirit or an attack by a ghost or demon. Demons were ghosts that had grown more powerful and less human over time. Sorcerers, sometimes using demons, also caused sickness and death. The man had a relative who could sometimes see things by gazing into a pond or a bowl of water. However, taking the option most people preferred, he had summoned a medium to diagnose the problem.

The medium arrived at the house in the evening, and the family gathered around for the séance. As the night darkened, the medium gazed fixedly at a small wooden image of his familiar spirit and quietly slipped into a trance. The spirit took over his body and spoke. At times the voice came from the man's mouth, and sometimes it seemed to come from another part of the house. The spirit voice explained that the sick woman had violated one of the pregnancy tapus, offending the family god.

Next morning the household head walked to the nearby shrine that held the remains of deceased family members. There he prayed and made an offering to the deified ancestor who watched over the family. He had performed these actions many times before in order to gain divine support in births, deaths, and other private matters. The god was represented by a small wooden image carved in human form. In some families the image represented an animal form that the god liked to assume.

As the man turned from his completed ritual, he noticed the refuse pit next to the shrine and reflected on how much more difficult this situation might have been. The pit held discarded objects that a sorcerer could use for magic, meaning anything that had been in intimate contact with a family member's body. By placing such objects under the tapu of the shrine, people protected themselves from the kind of supernatural assault that they feared most. Nevertheless, sorcerers were clever and people got careless. If that had been the cause of the young woman's illness, the man would have tried to get a more powerful practitioner to send the curse back to its originator. Or, if the attacker's identity had been revealed, a bribe might have been more effective. Demons were not quite as big a problem. They could usually be exorcised with spells, heat, and bad-smelling herbs.

A few days after his daughter-in-law recovered, the family head learned that his cousin, a master canoe builder, needed workers. The man hesitated because he knew that everyone involved would be tapu for however long the job took, and this would place many restrictions on their behavior. The tapu was necessary because any successful enterprise entailed control of creative power. This was all the more true when a number of men had to cooperate.

At the outset the canoe builder went to the shrine dedicated to the patron god of his occupation and made offerings and prayers for success. With his workers gathered, the master performed ceremonies that made them, their tools, and their place of work tapu. Thus everything associated with the task was purified, insulated from common influences, and endowed with mana. As the work proceeded over many days, the canoe builder watched for omens of its success, giving the greatest weight to errors in the work. If the task seemed doomed, he abandoned it. His knowledge of ritual matters was just as important as his practical skills in carpentry.

When the canoe was done, the master protected it with rituals like those performed for a newborn baby because, like an infant and like any newly manufactured object, the canoe had a soul and life that needed strengthening. The builder also made an offering to thank the gods whose mana had made his creation possible. The concluding ceremonies removed the tapu from the canoe, so that it could be used, and from the workers, so that they could resume normal life. Then it was time for a feast prepared in an earth oven, a celebration of success and an additional thanksgiving to the gods and ancestors that made it possible.

Any enterprise that subjected a group of men to specialized leadership went through a similar sequence of events. This included planting, fishing, house building, and war. In return for successful planting or fishing, men offered the gods a portion of what they had produced. In war they offered the first slain enemy or captured a live enemy for a formal sacrifice.

Worship of the gods followed a similar pattern because it too was a cooperative enterprise led by specialists, the chieftain and the priests. At the sacred ground of the community they appealed to greater gods than those of families, often deified souls of past chieftains. Commoners ringed the periphery as their ritual leaders chanted prayers and spells known only to them. The recitations had to be rhythmic and accurate. The chanters used devices such as sticks or pieces of leaves to help them remember the longer prayers. A mistake sometimes caused the ceremony to be abandoned.

Some parts of the ceremony had been determined by one or more mediums who had conveyed godly wishes. These practitioners had power and respect far beyond the mediums who dealt with family illness. Those through whom the gods spoke tranced in public and in daylight. Sometimes they responded to a question from community leaders, and sometimes the god took the initiative. Some mediums, when seeking the trance, drank large quantities of kava or gazed at an image of the god.

As the annual harvest season approached, warfare dwindled and finally stopped. It was much more than the practical need for farm labor. War was tapu during this time that the entire chiefdom devoted to ceremonial renewal of the land's fertility. First, the shedding of blood on the land polluted it and made it infertile. Second, the success of the ceremonies depended on the participation of everyone even if only by not distracting the gods with alternative activities.

Harvest ceremonies honored the greatest of the gods, those that were present when the world was created. It began when sky and earth were locked together in an embrace like that of a man and a woman. After the most important gods were born between them, they parted and made room for light and earthly life. One of their offspring became the god of light, and others took control of war, wind, thunder, crops, and the sea.

The harvest ceremonies took place at the greatest of the sacred grounds. Near the large platform that marked the most tapu part of the place, a pit held the refuse of previous ceremonies, including the remains of animal and human sacrifices. A little further on was the shrine devoted to the patron god of the site. He was represented by a piece of wood wrapped in cloth because high gods, unlike lower beings, did not have a humanlike form. They could possess humans or appear in the guise of a human, but neither was their natural state. The wrapping of the image, sometimes with braided cord, represented the binding of the god's mana. Godly power was dangerous unless contained by tapu.

The chief and high priests stood next to the platform, wrapped in mats to bind their mana, and performed the most important and esoteric rituals. As a direct descendant of the gods, the chief embodied their powers and served as their personal representative in the ceremony. At the same time, he stood for the people and the land for which they sought fertility. The chief had inherited mana from his ancestors, but it had increased through consecration rituals and the learning of sacred knowledge. The high priests were also born to mana but had acquired much of what they now had through consecration and frequent contact with the sacred. All of the nobility had mana in proportion to their closeness to the main line of descent from the gods. Commoners had little or none.

After the main rituals the people were free to feast, dance, and engage in sporting events. They enjoyed themselves, but they were aware that these were also religious acts. Feasting, as always, created rapport among the celebrants, the ancestors, and the gods. Many dances included erotic postures and movements that were intended to attract the gods and stimulate their procreative powers on behalf of the land.

The dancers formed a line to present their performance to the audience. They or a chorus intoned the chant that guided the music. Emphasizing movement of arms and hands, the dancers enacted the words of the chant or embellished them with gestures. Some singers provided a drone, a sustained single note that followed the basic rhythm. Other performers added rhythms with their bodies—clapping their hands, slapping their torsos and legs, slapping the ground. Drummers added greater complexity to the music, beating the membranes of cylindrical drums with their hands. In some performances men played nose flutes, creating melody by controlling exhalation from their nostrils.

Months before the performance a composer had begun the epic poem that shaped the chant. A traditional story provided the foundation, but innovative allusions linked it to the occasion at hand. Like most other chants, this one glorified the chief and the gods and ancestors from whom he derived his distinction. Chiefs from other politics received similar praise when they visited. Performers rehearsed for weeks or months before a major occasion.

The numerous sporting events also attracted, strengthened, and exhilarated the gods. Within a ring of spectators, men engaged in a series of wrestling or boxing bouts. Each began with one man striding around the enclosure to issue a general challenge and another rising to meet it. A wrestling match ended when one man threw the other on his back. In boxing, the opponents

In a public performance Polynesian dancers usually formed a line facing the audience (Hawaiian culture).

A man displays the stronger style of male dancing in Polynesia (Hawaiian culture).

approached each other with their fists bound by plant fibers and punched each other in the head and face, sometimes in the side, until one went down. Other sports included races on foot or in canoes and spear throwing. Competitions like these also took place at more ordinary gatherings than the harvest festival. In daily life people went beyond their regular bathing habits to enjoy swimming and body surfing.

Stories about the trickster and culture hero named Maui were another joy in life, especially for commoners. Though raised and taught by powerful gods, Maui came

European impression of a boxing match in traditional Polynesia (Hawaiian culture).

from a long human lineage and fully appreciated human pleasures. Due to his ambiguous origins, he felt the need to prove himself to both gods and humans. This he did with pranks on both, using his superior intellect as well as his ability to transform himself into any shape. His jokes were humorous, but sometimes harmful. Maui's rebelliousness was especially appealing to the disadvantaged: in many stories he represented the commoners against the elite and the weak against the strong. In addition, by daring to flout the most solemn tapus as well as ordinary social conventions, the trickster pleased all who chafed under the restrictions of society.

Sometimes Maui played the generous and gracious hero to humans. The fisherman that Maui tricked in one story might come from a village that the god saved in another tale by battling the raging sea. He also helped humans by providing them with some of the essentials of life. By hooking and pulling a giant fish-being deep under the sea, Maui created the land on which people lived. He slowed the sun, lengthening the day so that women had enough time to cook the food that people needed to survive. He stole fire from the underworld goddess and, when some of the sparks fell on trees, people learned that they could burn wood. Maui's end came when he failed in his attempt to destroy Death.

When the many pleasures of life ended, relatives of the dead person washed the body and covered it with cloth. As a result of this contact with death, they would be strictly tapu until ritually released. Objects in contact with the deceased would also be tapu. Some people feared the ghost because they had been personal enemies of the deceased. They tried to disguise themselves by wearing different clothes, cutting their hair, blackening their faces, or changing their names.

Relatives provided the soul with food, clothing, and possessions for its journey. Prayers and rituals strengthened the soul, gave it protection, and summoned the ancestors to help it. It would follow a well-defined path that had predictable resting places, but also unavoidable dangers such as demons and other monsters. Commoners went to an underworld that was like the surface or somewhat less desirable. Nobles went to the sky and enjoyed a life like that on earth or even better.

The soul was forever connected to its bones and concerned that relatives dispose of them properly. The soul was not settled in the other world until the flesh had left the bones. Some souls possessed the living to avenge an offense or to help them. The living summoned ancestral souls to help the newly dead and also held memorial festivals for those who had gone over long before. They honored their own ancestors and the god of the dead with offerings, chants, dancing, and feasting. These observances enhanced the soul's prestige in the afterworld.

A Closer Look

The Western Polynesian Region

Samoa and Tonga were the most populous archipelagoes in this geographically small part of Polynesia. Fiji had a great deal in common with them as a result of trading and military contacts. In what I call the Greater Polynesian Area, the designation of this centrally located Region as "Western" is somewhat misleading. I retain the term because it is so widely used in the literature for this part of the Area.

Several material items distinguished the Region. The Western Polynesians used composite fishhooks and cooked their starchy vegetables whole or in large pieces. Women made bark cloth by pasting strips together. They decorated a sheet by laying it over a tablet with a design carved in relief and rubbing it. Decoration of bark cloth for ceremonial presentation was a highly developed art while sculptures were rare and small. A prominent product of wood carving was a large bowl with legs used for making kava, a mildly soporific drink used in ceremonial contexts.

Emphasis on the brother–sister relationship pervaded social life. Kinship terminology distinguished the lines descending from a brother and sister. At the same time the role of the mother's brother linked the two lines. Siblings of different gender observed strict avoidance rules, and a man showed the greatest respect to his sister.

Male conceptualization of women as sisters, nonsexual partners imbued with mana, contributed to esteem for women and opportunities for them to occupy high public offices. A chief's sister (or her children) exceeded him in sanctity, although he held the greater political power. In accord with their spiritual role in society, women were less tattooed than men. Men were represented as secular warriors by tattoos from the waist to the knees, including the penis.

The sororal/spiritual model of women modified sexual openness by encouraging symbolic control of sex and reproduction. Virginity at marriage was preferred by all and considered essential in a leader's daughter. One daughter of a chieftain or chief occupied a ceremonial position on behalf of society that required perpetual celibacy. This binding of mana was essential to the fertility of land and sea. The ceremonial virgin (exemplified by the famous *taupou* of Samoa) also refrained from any productive activities and ate heavily in order to achieve corpulence (Shore 1989).

Western Polynesians viewed the sacred and the secular as complementary. People conceptualized hierarchy mainly in terms of finely graded personal ranks. They honored their chiefs with a special language that consisted of respectful euphemisms for both reference and direct address. People of rank regularly engaged in the kava ceremony, drinking ritually in a group.

Maintenance of high rank depended heavily on success in social exchange because the spiritual authority of men was limited (Thomas 1995a). The elaborate system emphasized the exchange of unlike things, such as food for durable items, often carried out in a single session. This contrasted with the alternating presentation of like items that characterized the rest of the Pacific (e.g., reciprocal feasts).

The chief played the most important role in ceremonial leadership. Mediums who also had ritual knowledge assisted him. The tomb of a deceased chief was the usual sacred ground for worship. Tangaloa stood alone among the gods as responsible for creation and continuing dominion over one or more great segments of the world, such as the sea or the sky. However, people originated from rocks or the earth with little or no help from any of the gods.

The Eastern Polynesian Region

This Region formed an arc around Western Polynesia in the north and east. Starting with Hawaii in the north, the large island groups included the Cooks, the Tuamotus, and the Society Islands (which contained Tahiti). The Maori of New Zealand are usually assigned to this Region, although it could be argued that they merit a Region of their own.

Eastern Polynesians mashed their starchy vegetables before cooking, using stone pounders that required a great deal of labor to make. To make cloth, women soaked the bark for a long time before beating it and joined the strips by felting. They impressed decorative patterns on the material with finely grooved beaters.

The conjugal pair provided the model for male–female relations, represented by a high level of freedom in erotic expression and sexual activity. According to Shore (1989) Eastern Polynesians shared the Pacific idea of women as ritually polluting and contact between the sexes as debilitating to men; they offset the effect of frequent sexual contact by a strict tapu on eating together. Other authorities argue that tapus on women arose not from pollution, but from their proximity to the powerful sacred world through reproduction (Hanson and Hanson 1983). Resolution of the apparent contradiction may lie in distinguishing the polluting blood involved in reproductive processes from the sacred nature of other aspects of reproduction. The blood of men, when spilled in war for example, also caused pollution.

With women less sacred than in the Western Polynesian Region, even if not especially polluting, the chief was the most sacred figure in society. As the sole representative of the generative powers of the gods, he wore a special loincloth to bind the power symbolized by his genitals. Sacred and political authority were combined rather than being complementary, and the hierarchy was graded from sacred to common. Among their powers chiefs held most of the authority over land tenure.

Kinship terminology represented the emphases on sexual relations and a unified hierarchy. Affinal relatives were prominent. Seniority characterized the classification of blood relatives, including distinction of elder generations from younger and elder siblings from younger.

Most worship took place at sacred grounds distinct from chiefs' tombs. These grounds were marked by stone constructions such as walls, terraces, and platforms. Sacred buildings were adjuncts to the open areas. Ritual priests were distinct from mediums and played a prominent role in ceremonies. They also served as repositories for myth and genealogy. Carved representations of the gods provided an important focus for rituals. Tangaloa shared his achievements and status with three similar gods.

A male god produced human beings through sex with the earth or with a woman that he formed from earth. From then on, the rest of the world developed through repeated acts of intercourse in which unlike beings produced offspring different from either of them. Thus the world took shape by a process of growth, upward and outward, and the people of today ascended from their beginnings.

Sculpted humanoid figures in various styles and sizes represented lesser gods, ancestors, and people. Elite men wore facial tattoos composed of triangles or diamonds accompanied by lines. Other than that, tattooing varied a great deal from one society to another.

The Micronesian Region

Although Micronesia was once considered a clear-cut culture area, the concept of Micronesia as a cultural unit is now ignored (Quanchi and Adams, eds. 1993) or explicitly rejected for too much internal diversity (Linnekin 1997a). Whether as an Area or a Region, Micronesia can be distinguished from its neighbors on the basis of some modal patterns. Lacking the mulberry tree, Micronesians could only produce cruder forms of bark cloth and often made their clothes from banana fiber instead. The closeness of island groups permitted a great deal of contact. Nearly every island or group produced a craft specialty for external trade. These included mats, dyes, and shell ornaments. Exchange was linked to focal islands: there was a tendency for one or two islands in a given area, usually the largest and richest, to exercise some kind of cultural dominance. They functioned as trade centers and hurricane refuges and often collected some kind of tribute (sometimes insignificant, sometimes really trade) from smaller islands.

Matrilineal groups held land and provided the basis for rank and chiefly office. Although tapus were important, beliefs about mana were weak. The high gods belonged entirely to mythology, and religious activity focused on spirits, ghosts, and ancestors. Personal ancestors helped or harmed the living, depending on their mode of death. The greatest supernatural beings were deified humans, either ancestors or exceptional individuals.

Traditional States in Polynesia?

Many people know that King Kamehameha I established a Hawaiian state with the help of European weapons. However, the state level of organization may have existed in the Hawaiian Islands before that time (Kirch 2000). By 1700 A.D. paramount chiefs had established four major polities on the largest islands in the group. These resulted from escalating territorial aggression and the amalgamation of earlier chiefdoms. In these polities the subordinate rulers served at the pleasure of their superiors. Chieftains, rather than descent groups, controlled community land and commoners had to exchange tribute and labor for the right to use the land. The social gap between commoners and aristocracy had also increased. Elite culture strongly encouraged class endogamy and placed great value on sumptuary symbols made by specialized craftsmen; for example, feathered belts, cloaks, and helmets. Intense social stratification, alienation of land from commoners, and military imperialism are characteristics widely associated with the state level of organization (Kirch 2000).

Similar trends have been noted in the traditional cultures of the Society Islands and Tonga (Oliver 1989c; Quanchi and Adams, eds. 1993). Wider kinship ties declined as affiliation with territorial groups became more important. Rank on the basis of kinship became less important than membership in increasingly rigid socioeconomic classes, and elite ranking increased in complexity. Ritual and political leadership separated into distinct power centers as organized priesthoods appropriated important ritual activities.

Increasingly large and complex political systems were associated with increasing emphasis on war and conquest, presumably in a feedback relationship. Warfare took on greater ideological significance along with greater intensity and complexity, including major pitched battles on land and sea. The probability of rebellion was heightened by the fact that a paramount chief's realm often contained districts that had been acquired by conquest.

These classic examples come from Eastern and Western Polynesia. Similar processes may have been underway in the Micronesian Region, represented by the island of Kosrae (Kusaie), where a paramount chief controlled the entire island. He was able to force his subordinate chiefs to live with him in a capital town where commoner labor had been mobilized to build megalithic structures (Kirch 2000).

MELANESIAN AREA

Examples:

New Guinea, New Britain, New Ireland, Solomon Islands, Vanuatu (formerly New Hebrides), New Caledonia

Melanesia was tucked into the southwestern corner of the Pacific Ocean, bounded by Asia, Australia, and Polynesia. New Guinea anchored the Area, geographically, demographically, and culturally. Located at the western end of Melanesia, New Guinea is the second largest island in the world (after Greenland), with an area of more than 300,000 square miles. Although many other Melanesian islands are large compared to those of Polynesia, their combined land area is only about 54,000 square miles.

All of Melanesia lay in the tropics, but there was a great deal of local variation based on rainfall, altitude, and terrain. Rain forest was the natural vegetation for most of the land, but savanna occurred in some places while others harbored permanent or temporary swamps. Temperate conditions prevailed in the mountainous interiors of the largest islands. Variety in flora and fauna generally declined from New Guinea eastward.

The population of New Guinea was about 2 million (more than all of Polynesia). A conventional estimate for the rest of the Area is about a half million (Hays 1991), but the populations of some southerly islands, most notably New Caledonia, may have been underestimated (Kirch 2000). No matter how this debate turns out, it is likely that New Guinea held at least half the population of Melanesia.

Finally, and most importantly for our purposes, the most distinctive features of Melanesian culture were concentrated in New Guinea and nearby islands. Eastward and southward, similarities to Polynesia became increasingly common. The description in this chapter emphasizes the culture of New Guinea and the islands closest to it.

Students of Melanesia have always stressed its diversity (Chowning 1977; Knauft 1993). Nevertheless, there were some modal patterns in the Area. They may not have had the generality of modal patterns in most other Areas, but they characterized a majority of the ethnic groups and the population.

The sago palm *(Metroxylon)* supplemented taro and yams in Melanesian subsistence. It provided food in every part of the Area where swampy soil gave it a home. The starch that filled the trunk, destined to fuel the tree's flowering process, provided people with an abundance of calories.

Practical trade was more prominent in Melanesia than in Polynesia. This was possible because islands and archipelagoes were closer together. It was desirable because of the greater variety in local resources. The latter applied to differences between coast and interior as well as differences between islands.

Another economic pattern shared with Polynesia was experienced more intensely in Melanesia. "Pigs are our hearts," said one New Guinea man (Oliver 1989a). In Vanuatu, near the other end of the Area, pigs were "the supreme objects of sacrifice" and commanded "a large amount of time, effort and resources" (Lane 1965:267). To a Melanesian, pigs were far more than an appropriate gift and the best feast food.

Various kinds of chieftains influenced community life in Melanesia (Godelier 1986). Ethnography has emphasized what I will call *wealth chieftains*, those who attained status by the manipulation of valuable goods. However, their apparent prominence may be an artifact of colonial pacification (Spriggs 1997). Other paths to influence included war leadership and ritual knowledge.

Terms such as "big man" and "great man" have been applied to these Melanesian leaders. I prefer my cross-cultural term "chieftain" for several reasons: (1) most obviously, the usage is consistent with the rest of this book; (2) arguments among specialists make it difficult to define "big man" or "great man" for the general reader; (3) the distinction between such figures and hereditary leaders has become obscure. In the description below, Melanesian communities were led by chieftains who attained influence by various means, including wealth, war, ritual, and heredity.

Melanesians tended to regard people other than their close kin with suspicion, an attitude that has been called the "paranoid ethos" (Schwartz 1973). The term "paranoid" is inappropriate because many Melanesians had reason to be suspicious of others. Economic competition was often intense, and frequent warfare often involved nearby communities. The situation was not uniform across the Area, but Melanesians on the whole probably did tend to regard more people as actual or potential enemies than was true among their Polynesian neighbors or in many other cultures in the world.

Melanesia differed sharply from Polynesia in many aspects of knowledge and expression. Melanesians perceived a constricted horizontal universe in which most of the important supernatural beings shared the physical world with humans. Ancestors were at least as important as gods. The main theme of Melanesian religion was "collective material welfare" (Swain and Trompf

1995). The men of a descent group or community all participated in ceremonies seeking practical help from the supernaturals.

Constriction also characterized the mythology of Melanesia, which began with a world that already existed. Culture heroes arranged the physical features and established human social life. The stories lacked time depth and did not form any sequence. In each tale the world lacked only the one innovation that the story explained.

Men completely dominated religion and carried out numerous secret rituals. A house dedicated to religious activity played an important role. In some cultures it was the men's house and in other cultures a separate one.

Music and dance contrasted with Polynesia in their relative simplicity and lack of specialization in performance. The simple songs did not shape music and dance as Polynesian chants did. The distinctive instrument of Melanesia was the slit drum.

Key features:

▶ Use of sago palm

▶ Special significance of pigs

▶ Extensive practical trade

▶ Leadership by variety of chieftains

▶ Men's house

▶ Importance of ancestral souls

▶ Constricted cosmology and mythology

▶ Secret rituals and religious house

▶ Simple song, music, dance

Modal Patterns in Melanesian Culture

Material Culture

The man sleeping on the floor of the house stirred as the early morning sun brushed his face. He adjusted his head on the wooden rest that preserved his elaborately treated hair during the night. His wife, with short, plain hair, did not use one. She rose and went to the platform against a wall to get a small piece of wood for the guttering fire. The platform stood about the height of a person. In addition to firewood it held dishes, baskets, and surplus food.

Soon the man was up and on his way to the men's house. His loincloth hung near his knees in front, and he wore fiber bands of varied colors on his arms and legs.

Often he used the armbands to carry small items. The other people he saw, men and women, wore similar bands, along with simple ornaments in the hair, ears, or nose, or at the neck or breast. It was a matter of personal taste. Patterns of scars also decorated people. The women wore knee-length skirts of shredded leaves or string attached to a cord or fiber band around the waist.

The men's house reared above the small dwellings nearby and conveyed its importance with huge posts, heavy beams, and special panels that were all elaborately carved. It was the place for many important male activities. Bachelors lived in the men's house; married men spent so much time in it, often overnight, that they kept weapons and personal possessions there.

When not working on his equipment in the men's house, a man often went fishing. Other than fishing, his main subsistence task was to obtain the pulp from sago trees. Whenever a sago palm approached the flowering stage, men cut it down with their adzes. It was hard work: the trees rose to heights of thirty feet or more and their trunks were twenty to thirty inches thick. Some men split the downed tree while others preferred to strip the bark. This was to gain access to the pulp, which they crushed with special choppers topped by stone or wooden heads. After the starch was washed out of the pulp fiber and dried, it could be stored for months. A single tree yielded an average of 300 pounds of starch, and some produced as much as 900 pounds. After a while people went back to the felled tree to gather the large and oily grubs that had grown there.

A man also cleared and fenced land for root crops and planned their production. He had to consider his obligations to particular relatives as well as his contributions to major exchanges. Often he allocated plots to specific people at the time of planting: his wife, his wife's relatives, members of his own family, and those who had helped him clear the land or assisted in other tasks. He notified these people of his intentions so that they could better plan for their own obligations. The man's wife performed most of the farm labor and also took care of his pigs. Occasionally a woman nursed a small pig. On many days a woman took her children to gather shellfish and use small hand nets to catch fish in shallow pools.

A woman went to one of the gardens nearly every day for fresh vegetables. Sometimes she weeded and cleaned while she was there. Back home, preparing for the evening meal, she scraped and often pared the vegetables with a bone or shell knife. If available, meat was cut with a bamboo knife. On some days the cook prepared a special side dish from sago starch. She made it into porridge, thickened soup with it, or baked it into pancakes that could be folded around meat, fish, or vegetables. Sometimes the woman made a different cake from roasted or baked taro. She mashed the cooked roots, mixed them with other ingredients such as grated nuts or coconut oil, and baked the dough in the earth oven. For seasoning a woman used salt water in her cooking. Interior people obtained sea water in bamboo tubes.

At regular intervals a group of women put fish in their net bags or baskets and, accompanied by armed men, they went inland to trade. In most cases the armed men were to protect against ambush by enemies along the way. However, some trade meetings took place between communities that were at best suspicious of one another and were sometimes at war.

At a fixed location the trading party met people from an interior community who had plant foods to exchange. Trade with bush people could also provide other materials if they were absent from the seaboard community's territory. These included meat from the hunting and trapping of birds and land animals; gathered fibers for bags and nets; and bamboo to make cooking vessels, water containers, carving knives, and torches. Where coastal communities had varying resources, they met in a similar manner.

The women often bargained a bit, but the relative value of various goods was well established. Many people expressed these values in terms of a common article such as dog teeth or a particular kind of ornament. In some instances, especially where the relationship was tense, women simply put down their goods and picked up those that their counterparts had deposited. Sometimes the men from both sides exchanged a few small gifts. Where hostility was greatest, including open warfare, the silent trade might be practiced. One group placed their goods at the appointed place and withdrew. Then the other group took what they wanted and left behind what they offered in return without ever being face to face with their enemies.

Some men, especially the more courageous and ambitious ones, went on trading expeditions to obtain practical goods or wealth or both. When a man arrived at his destination, his trading partner received him. Partners were obliged to give one another hospitality and protection. The latter was important because men often traded in communities that were past or potential enemies and in some cases were current enemies. Partners phrased their exchanges as gifts, avoiding any bargaining, but it was understood that the relationship depended on reciprocity. Partners accepted delayed return, sometimes extending to a year or more that separated trips. Some men inherited partnerships from their fathers. In some cases clan ties substituted for partnership.

An exchange between two communities was part of a larger network through which various goods circulated. Some of these networks approached two hundred miles in length and encompassed thousands of people. In the larger networks men from certain communities were active as intermediaries. The goods exchanged on this scale included axe stone, weapons, salt, lime, and pigments. The most desirable were shells or ornaments made from them—beads, necklaces, or bracelets. These constituted a category of wealth that rivaled or exceeded pigs.

A Melanesian trading canoe (Trobriand culture).

Some places played a central role in trade networks. Many of them were also manufacturing centers that produced special ornaments, weapons, pottery, and other objects. The men in these communities built the best canoes and took the longest voyages. However, even the largest outriggers were unsafe in rough water, and men would not go to sea if a storm threatened.

Social Relations

Though living in a small community, a man circulated through several different social spheres. One was the men's house that he shared with other adult males, married and unmarried. A member spent a large part of many days there, making and maintaining his equipment while socializing with the other occupants, discussing social and political issues, and planning and performing rituals. In the men's house there was no worry about sexual pollution because women were excluded. Whenever caution and desire were balanced, a man could visit his family dwelling for sex or companionship with his wife and play with his children.

Local patrilineal relatives composed another of the man's social spheres. In addition to holding land together, they formed a group that defended members against harm and loss of property or reputation. In case of injury or death, the group had the duty to seek compensation or vengeance. Elder members secured spouses for their juniors.

In everyday matters a man often received more help from a personal kindred composed of some patrilineal kin along with other relationships. This included many of his affines as well as friends and neighbors. Men who did reciprocal farm work together tended to feel a common bond with the land, which made them like kin, and they often solidified this connection by exchanging use rights to particular plots of land.

Beyond these kinship ties was a community that contained two or more descent groups. The potential for friction in this situation was in many cases defused by a system in which one group was dominant over the others by virtue of earlier settlement or conquest. Furthermore, everyone recognized that a heterogeneous community conferred advantages in conflict with other communities. In addition to providing more warriors, the presence of more than one descent group meant that many men could find their wives within the community. This was highly preferable because the shifting currents of warfare could quickly make enemies of their neighbors. Thus most wives from the outside came from groups that were past, present, or potential antagonists. Men feared that these women might spy for their home communities or practice witchcraft against their husbands.

When all was well in a new baby's social world, it received close attention from numerous people related to it in diverse ways. Nevertheless, there were always many

dangers, so caretakers began teaching a child about them at an early age. There were rough terrain and rough sea, distant sorcerers and enemies lurking in ambush, and supernatural beings prepared to punish people for transgressions or harm them for no good reason at all. The child also learned about using the resources in the environment for human benefit. Most of this practical knowledge came from the parent of the same sex. Everyone respected knowledge, so a child soon became eager to acquire it and put it on display. Most children were less enthusiastic about sharing food; however, they were often urged or forced to do so, because generosity within the community was a basic value.

Parents and senior kin sometimes subjected their young to physical punishment, but they objected strongly if any outsider did so. More often they stressed the consequences of bad behavior: physical or magical retaliation, withdrawal of social support and aid, and refusal to consider the offender as a possible affine. When children behaved well, it was to avoid censure rather than gain rewards. The young had few toys other than tops and swings made from bark or vines. They sang, danced, and played guessing games. Sometimes, especially on moonlit nights, they played more formal and elaborate games based on rhymes.

Expected to become warriors, older boys engaged in mock battles with grass stalks filling in for spears. They received many opportunities to develop independence and initiative. By the age of six, although not ready for the men's house, a boy made some provision to sleep apart from his mother and sisters. Their elders encouraged boys in exploits against people outside the small community. Stealing a pig was one of the more common and praiseworthy deeds. If the victims learned the identity of the thieves, they were likely to retaliate and warfare could result.

Throughout childhood small advances were marked by simple ceremonies in which close kin feasted and exchanged with one another. Such advances included naming, first haircut, first tooth, and first clothing. The assumption of regular clothing came late, but adults delighted in costuming children for special occasions. Sometimes they dressed the young in miniature versions of adult costumes.

As puberty approached, both boys and girls began to adopt adult standards of modesty in dress and behavior. They made sure of privacy or darkness for defecation, sexual play, and often for eating. For many young people the acceptance of these standards required little teaching or enforcement. During this time a young person underwent one or more body modifications, such as tooth blackening or the piercing of the ears or the nasal septum.

A girl was marriageable after her first menses. In addition to sexual maturity, she usually had her own garden and knew how to make all the standard woman's goods. She might have opportunities for premarital sex, but pregnancy was a serious risk. The father of her baby might be forced to marry her, even though it would be raised as her sibling, but she would bear all the shame.

A boy should have learned all the tasks of a man by late adolescence. These included magic for various everyday goals such as gardening, hunting, protecting property, curing, and success in love. He had also acquired the basic ritual knowledge of the men's house. However, he would go on learning and assuming more responsibility as his life continued, perhaps achieving full social maturity only in middle age.

The transition to adulthood differed drastically for girls and boys. A girl matured naturally, fitting into the mold provided by her mother. Although he had begun to learn some aspects of the male role in life, a maturing boy had to be decisively separated from the world of women and resocialized as a man. Accordingly, the men gathered a group of boys when enough were ready and put them through one or more periods of initiation.

Initiation began with complete separation from all females and everything feminine. This included foods that had female characteristics, such as softness or a color like menstrual blood. The segregation could last for months, and some limits on contact with the feminine could go on for years. During initiation, boys developed masculine strength and self-control by undergoing ordeals of pain, fear, endurance, and obedience. They learned or practiced male skills, those of hunting and war, and they began to acquire the religious knowledge of men. Boys who experienced initiation together established lifelong bonds and formed a kind of age set.

Most men married by age twenty-five and women by twenty. The parents or kinship group arranged a first marriage, often through child betrothal, in accord with exchange relationships and alliances. Marriage was the most important link between communities as well as between kin groups. Cross-cousin marriage often satisfied these social concerns.

After formal delivery of the bride, the groom's people presented her family with the first installment of bridewealth. It consisted of the items used in all important exchanges: pigs, pork, and shells or other portable wealth. Most people considered this to be compensation to the girl's group for loss of a valuable member and the children she would bear. The husband's side gave generously to maintain or enhance their prestige. This event was part of the larger cycle of social exchanges.

When he married, a man entered into formal relationships with close affines that approached total avoidance in some cases. Most people considered this a way to prevent friction. Some saw more significance in it, saying that a degree of avoidance forestalled enmity between people who should be friends and helpers.

Wives initiated the majority of divorces, many out of distaste for forced marriage or bullying by co-wives. Sometimes the husband failed to pay all of the bride-

wealth. A man was less likely to seek divorce. For one thing, with the option of spending much of his time in the men's house, the husband suffered less from bad marriage. Also, he had an economic stake in maintaining the relationship. When a man initiated divorce, he could not claim return of the bridewealth unless his wife had flagrantly misbehaved. If the marriage had lasted a long time and produced children, most people considered this to be sufficient compensation. A divorced woman was free to remarry, but her kin demanded bridewealth appropriate to her age and status. A widow had less freedom. She stayed with her late husband's people and mourned for a long time, as much as three years. Then she was free to remarry.

Men idealized unlimited polygyny, especially men who sought influence over others. Wives tended crops and raised pigs to be used in exchanges. They produced children, sons to provide support and daughters to bring bridewealth. The marriage of children also brought a man allies in other kin groups and localities.

Some men who aspired to leadership manipulated wealth in the form of pigs, produce, and valuables such as shell jewelry. A prospective wealth chieftain had to gain a following because community decisions came from discussion and consensus. One approach involved making loans to individuals, especially young men who needed bridewealth, land to farm, or pigs to start their own herds. Chieftains attracted the community at large by giving feasts of their own and by sponsoring larger feasts and ceremonies. They gained prestige for their ability to organize feasts and exchanges as well as for the wealth that they contributed. Having used external trade and personal connections to amass enough wealth for these purposes, a man faced the danger of physical attack or sorcery if he became selfish.

A Melanesian pig (Dani culture, New Guinea).

Some chieftains devoted their organizational abilities mainly to warfare, either coordinating the fighting or arranging truces and peace through compensatory exchange. Personal success in fighting enhanced a leader's reputation and influence. Ritual or magical knowledge—especially in relation to economic activities such as farming, fishing, and trade—brought leadership status to others. A reputation for sorcery impressed and intimidated people. Finally, since chieftains had to sway the opinions of others, oratorical ability was a major asset.

A hamlet or community contained a nonhereditary chieftain only when and if some individual had the necessary capabilities. If several emerged in the same group, they competed with one another for the greatest influence. Even where chieftainship was not hereditary, kinship often made a difference. Seniority in a large group provided a man with many reliable supporters. Many chieftains appointed a deputy who was likely to succeed to the position, and this was often a son or another close relative. Whether designated successor or not, the son of a leader usually acquired his father's special knowledge and inherited his wealth.

A man had affinal relatives and members of his own descent group in other communities. He invoked these ties for trade, ceremony, and personal aid, but he could not use them to arrange group actions. The presence of relatives in two communities did not prevent them from going to war, although relatives on the battlefield might avoid confronting one another. The situation arose often because war usually involved neighboring communities.

Conflicts began over offenses such as the kidnapping of a woman or theft of a pig, but fighting continued with both sides seeking revenge for previous killings. It was possible to make peace through the exchange of compensations, but the issue went beyond the mundane. Any group that lost a member to homicide suffered a spiritual decline and the ancestors demanded revenge. Raiding parties killed anyone of the enemy group, including women and children. Every death was celebrated, and those who killed gained prestige.

Knowledge and Expression

People lived in the midst of the supernatural. They shared the world with diverse spirits and with more powerful beings as well. Although there were a few gods in the sky, most of them resided on earth in special places like mountains or islands. The place of the dead was also on earth, and people knew its location. There were stories about a few people who had been there and returned. But the souls of the deceased were often closer than the land of the dead, watching the lives of their descendants. Still part of society, but imbued with superhuman powers, the ancestors were crucial for support of the living. They were at least as important as the gods.

Men joined together to communicate with the ancestors and gods. Although they took directions from some older men with greater knowledge of the rituals, interaction with the supernaturals was a group enterprise. Occasions for ceremonies included transitions in the lives of group members and phases in the annual cycle of subsistence. In giving the greater beings their due, people hoped to obtain specific and practical benefits. They sought fertility for crops and animals, success in manufacturing, social well-being, and protection and success in war. They hoped to receive occasional messages about important events in the future.

Every ceremony required that people from other descent groups or communities be invited. The hosts feasted their guests with pork and other special foods. They gave them pork, or live pigs, or other valuables to take home with them. Accumulation of the requisite food and goods required a great deal of work and self-restraint on the part of the hosts for weeks or months before the celebration. The greatest ceremonies took years to prepare. They were of special importance because people could be sure that their ancestral benefactors would return en masse to witness such an event.

During initiation, boys began to acquire the religious knowledge of men. They learned the symbols, many of them phallic, used in male rituals and saw the bull-roarer that gave men's rites their distinctive sound. Initiates heard the myth that epitomized the differences and tensions between men and women. The story concerned a god with exaggerated male traits, especially a long penis, whose prodigious sexual desires led him into situations where women shamed him. In his anger he cursed human beings with death, which had not previously existed.

The god who brought death to the world had traveled widely and created many local geographic features, such as lakes where he urinated. Other culture heroes, some in groups, had also passed through the world and provided people with ritual knowledge and the conditions of social life before going on to some distant unknown place.

When people gathered for a public ceremony or feast, they put on their best ornaments in great numbers. They wore nose and ear plugs, arm rings, leg rings, necklaces, belts, and disks on the head or chest. Most decorations were composed of objects connected by fiber bands. Men displayed more ornamentation than women. Chieftains wore the finest ornaments, especially those of seashell and turtle shell, or decided who would. People also wore painted designs on their faces and bodies. Red came from clay, black from soot, and white lime from burned shells or coral. The collective beauty of this display expressed the vitality and power of the group.

Men sang together during all of their ceremonies, secret and public. The words were repetitious and often made no sense to the singers because they were archaic or foreign. Even so, there were specific songs for different

Melanesian men dance and sing with hour-glass drums (New Guinea).

occasions, including trade, war, pig kills, and initiation rites. Men danced to the songs, using simple steps that everyone knew. In many dances the participants formed a single moving group, often going in a circle, sometimes in a straight line. Their swaying bodies called attention to their decorations, including elaborate headdresses. Some dancing men carried drums in one hand and beat them with the other. The drum was the shape of an hourglass, two to six feet long, with a grip across the middle. It had a single head made from the skin of a snake or lizard. Women sometimes joined the men in these ceremonies but danced separately. A few men on the sidelines provided rhythm with bamboo beaters while others played slit drums. A slit drum, several feet long, sat lengthwise on the ground or on supports. Made from a hollowed section of a log, it had a single longitudinal opening on top. The player beat the drum with a stick on the slit.

Men created numerous images to link themselves with the ancestors and the gods. They carved anthropomorphic wooden figures, including many ordinary-looking war gods, and painted them in black, white, and red. They also carved and painted elaborate masks of wood or bark and usually embellished them with a variety of materials such as flowers, feathers, shells, and leaves. Men wore the masks to dance in ceremonies and often donned costumes to go with them. Not only did these images represent the supernatural beings; some of them contained the power of those beings or even the beings

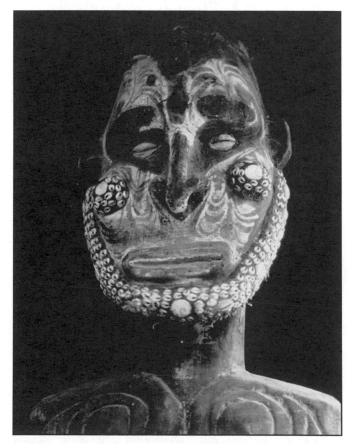

A sculpted figure with sea shells (Vanuatu).

themselves. Some became highly valuable items through repeated exchange.

Death provided yet another occasion for ceremony and exchange, especially when the deceased was a prominent man. The death of such a man disrupted all his exchange relationships, and others had to replace him, sometimes competing to do so. When any adult died, the body was specially dressed and ornamented for the attention of the mourners. They buried the person under or near the house, along with the most personal possessions. A man owned other property, some of which was divided equally among his sons. The mourners ate his pigs and food stores at the funeral feast. The soul that was satisfied with these attentions went to the place of the dead some distance away but continued to watch over those left behind and returned for the great feasts.

Relatives continued to mourn for several months. Many blackened their bodies with soot or charcoal. Others smeared themselves with mud or clay. After the bones of the deceased were recovered, the spouse or some other close relative wore the lower jaw for the remainder of the mourning period. It ended with a great feast, when the bones went to their final resting place in a cave or crevice. Thereafter, people commemorated the ancestor at other great feasts and made special offerings from time to time.

A Closer Look

Defining Regions within Melanesia is just as difficult as characterizing the Area as a whole. There is an obvious cultural division between the western and eastern ends of Melanesia, but a continuum lies between them with different traits shifting at different points. A similar problem applies to cultural variation associated with altitude in interior New Guinea. The Regions I describe below should be viewed as separated by unusually wide and fuzzy boundaries.

The New Guinea Lowland Region

This Region included the coastal plains of New Guinea and numerous small offshore islands, the Bismarck Archipelago (mainly New Britain and New Ireland), and the Admiralties. It was characterized by an unhealthy climate and relatively low population density (Kirch 2000). Taro was the leading staple, and people lived in houses with raised floors. They combined two plant products, areca palm nut and betel pepper, into a mildly stimulating chew (often confusingly called betel nut).

The Lowland Region contained the famous matrilineal chiefdoms of the Trobriand Islands, but they were not typical. Although matrilineal societies were rather common in the Region, an emphasis on patrilineal descent predominated. Full-fledged multicommunity chiefdoms were very rare. Hereditary community chieftains ruled in a number of Lowland cultures, but they shared influence with competitive leaders in many cases and were absent in many more.

A common practice in the Region was head-hunting, a pattern of warfare in which the primary or sole purpose of many expeditions was to obtain the head of an enemy. Although probably not a modal pattern, head-hunting demands mention because of its fame. In many Lowland cultures the capture of enemy heads brought a kind of spiritual energy or "life force" into the community (Knauft 1999). The need for this supernatural rejuvenation was expressed in myth and ritual. War cannibalism seems to have had similar significance for a number of peoples in the Region, a contrast with the more usual Pacific pattern of cannibalism for revenge. Head-hunting and cannibalism together might constitute a modal pattern for the Region in which people sought spiritual rejuvenation by incorporating physical parts of their enemies into the community.

Another famous but nonmodal feature of the New Guinea Lowlands was male homosexual behavior in connection with the initiation of boys (Herdt, ed. 1984; but compare Knauft 1993). The transfer of semen implanted more of the male essence into initiates, a response to the perceived need to resocialize boys. It also promoted maturation and growth. Men symbolically compared semen to mother's milk.

The recently dead regarded their living relatives with favor as long as they received proper ritual attention. To the living it was a relationship based on reciprocity. The costumed figures that represented supernatural beings included clowns. These disheveled or clumsy figures entertained onlookers but sometimes changed demeanor and terrorized them.

The New Guinea Highland Region

The mountains of New Guinea gave many people a healthy temperate climate. They had no contact with the sea and so lacked all the maritime characteristics of the Pacific Zone. They maintained the extensive trade and exchange networks by walking. Tropical crops do poorly in the mountains, so people came to depend on the sweet potato. This raises an important historical issue. According to Kirch (2000), the sweet potato is a recent introduction by Europeans. Scaglion argues that the plant reached the mountains hundreds of years before the Europeans arrived in the Region. The issue is important because many distinctive Highland features may have been based on using the sweet potato as the staple crop. Thus the description that follows may or may not pertain to the Highlands of 1700 A.D.

Production of sweet potatoes in the uneven mountain terrain demanded extensive use of techniques such as irrigation, drainage, terracing, ridging, and mounding.

However, because the crop does well in temperate conditions, the yield supported much higher population densities than those in the Lowlands. Sweet potato production may also have been partly responsible for the large herds of domestic pigs. Highlanders slaughtered numerous pigs at great feasts that were part of complex systems involving hundreds of people and having ecological, economic, social, political, and religious ramifications.

With hunting minor and fishing limited to fresh waters, cultivation by women took on greater importance. Despite (or because) of this, women experienced unusually poor social conditions in at least the eastern part of the Region. A high level of hostility between the sexes manifested itself in physical violence against women, disproportionate female suicide, and exclusion of women from initiation as well as other ceremonies (Gelber 1986). The initiation rituals were extremely harsh and instilled very negative attitudes toward women. Mothers resented this treatment of their sons and expressed their feelings in ritualized attacks on the men.

Men greatly feared witchcraft or sorcery from women, and they took the intensity of a widow's mourning as a measure of the probability that she had or had not poisoned her husband (Smart 1998). One possible reason for such distrust is that many women came from groups that were their husbands' potential or even current enemies in war. This situation arose because warfare was frequent among neighboring communities and because the communities were too small to provide appropriate marriage partners from within. The ideal community was composed of a single patrilineal descent group.

Highlanders believed that sex stunted the growth of children. They curtailed early sex play and adolescent sexual experience, allowing only formal, nonsexual courting ceremonies in supervised groups. Some men regarded sex with women as disgusting, as well as ritually dangerous.

The dead were exposed on a platform or in a tree until their bones were available for burial. To Highlanders the recently dead existed only as dangerous ghosts. For economic and other benefits they looked to their remote ancestors, who responded to bargaining and bribes.

Highland esthetic expression was devoted largely to body decoration. In addition to body painting and ornaments, they adorned themselves with elaborate wigs and with headdresses made from flowing bird-of-paradise feathers and iridescent beetle shells. These creations expressed pride in wealth and accomplishment (Newton et al. 1987).

The East Melanesia Region

This Region included the Solomon Islands, Vanuatu (New Hebrides), New Caledonia, and the Loyalty Islands. It was more southerly and temperate, healthier, and had higher population densities than the New Guinea Lowlands (Kirch 2000). The Region had some distinctive cultural traits of its own, but the predominant pattern was a west-to-east continuum of increasing similarity to Polynesia. The simplest and most sharply defined example of this transition was the replacement of seashells with mats as the primary portable valuable in social exchange.

Women had greater freedom and influence. Ritual pollution seems to have been treated as a symbolic boundary rather than a serious danger. Hereditary chieftains overshadowed competitive leaders or replaced them entirely. Some of these chieftains received first fruits and some of them had autocratic powers, ranging from the levy of fines to the pronouncement of a death sentence. Senior descent lines were considered closer to sources of supernatural power. In Vanuatu competitive leadership was institutionalized through the progressive purchase of ranked titles. By this typically Melanesian means, leaders acquired spiritual power much like that of the mana inherited by chieftains in Polynesia.

Attitudes toward the dead varied, and in some cultures they were simply regarded as dangerous. Many people in the Region turned to gods for help with their lives. Some gods of myth had specific connections with Polynesia. Tagaro Lowa of Vanuatu is obviously cognate with Tangaloa, and Maui was known by his Polynesian name.

Parallels to Polynesia appeared in the dances and songs of the Region. Some dances divided performers from the audience and required the performers to practice for as long as several months. Certain dances, including some by women, were acknowledged to have erotic appeal. Sitting dances emphasized movements of the arms and hands. Chants and songs in East Melanesia often narrated events to which the dancers alluded in their movements.

In some East Melanesian dances, people used every part of the body, even the eyes, and uttered loud, shrill cries or chants. These features differed from western Melanesia and most of Polynesia. However, they seem to have resembled performances of the Maori in New Zealand.

AUSTRALIAN ZONE

Areas:

- Australian Desert
- Australian Rim

Arnhem
Land

Rim

Area

Western
Desert
Region

Central
Desert
Region

Desert Area

Victoria
Region

Australian Zone
with Areas
and Regions

Previous page A native family of northern Australia (Tiwi culture,
Bathurst Island).

OVERVIEW OF THE ZONE

Examples:

Arrernte (Arunta, Aranda), Mardu, Walbiri, Yolngu (Murngin), Gidjingali, Tiwi

Between 300,000 and 1 million Native Australians, all of whom were foragers, inhabited a land roughly the size of the United States. These people are commonly called "Aborigines" although the word (without the capital letter) designates indigenous people anywhere. I consider Native Australian a more appropriate term.

Women provided the bulk of the food, as is generally true for foragers in tropical and moderate climates. However, they seem to have produced more protein than is typical by killing reptiles and by gathering nuts, seeds, and large grubs. Both women and men engaged in semi-agricultural practices that enhanced and renewed plant resources (Flood 1990).

Men hunted large animals, especially the emu and various kangaroos. The emu *(Dromaius)* is an ostrichlike flightless bird that averages eighty-five pounds and a height of almost five feet. The powerful thighs provided meat similar to beef. "Kangaroo" is a nonscientific term with many meanings. Here we make it synonymous with the newly expanded genus *Macropus* that includes kangaroos (strict sense), wallaroos, and wallabies (Nowak 1999). Marsupial grazers with great leaping ability, all are kangaroos in the popular mind (Tonkinson 1991). Most of the smaller species have a body length of two feet or so, with a tail about the same; they weigh between twenty-five and forty-five pounds. The body length in the large kangaroos ranges from three to four and one-half feet, the tail about the same, and the weight from forty to one hundred pounds.

Although all Australians were generalized foragers, groups with access to unusual resources specialized in extraction and often in related crafts. The resultant goods spread widely through trade and gift giving. Shell pendants, the most prized items, crossed the continent. One of the more distinctive items in the exchange system was *pituri*. This is a native term for two kinds of plants that contain nicotine. Numerous species belonged to *Nicotiana*, the same genus as New World tobacco. Two species belonged to *Duboisia*. Australians chewed pituri for pleasure, physiological support, and religious experience.

In social organization and religious thought, Native Australians had a culture more complex than that of most other foragers and many food producers. Their local and regional band organization is familiar from other foragers, but they belonged to a variety of other groups based on descent, marriage, and religion. The estate group was especially important and distinctive. Its members inherited responsibility for a set of sacred places and the rituals associated with them.

Social networks of unusual extent and complexity, perhaps unique among generalized foragers, connected regional bands and provided access to mates, resources, trading partners, and information. They also provided personnel for large and exciting ceremonial gatherings. Often several of these functions coincided in a single modestly sized network of about 400 people, which was commonly called a "tribe" in earlier literature. Intermarriage, highly permeable band boundaries, and sentiments about cultural unity usually characterized such a group. However, the term "tribe" is misleading because there was no political coordination of any kind.

Larger and more amorphous networks included thousands of people and extended across large portions of the continent (Lourandos 1997). In some cases members recognized such a network with a name. As in the case of "tribes," outsiders once gave these larger networks misleading political labels such as "nation" and "confederacy."

Australian totemism was "more highly elaborated than in any other known society" (Tonkinson 1991:22). Various groups of people viewed themselves as being born to important relationships with animal species and other natural phenomena. Social totems symbolized kinship affiliations while ritual totems were the focus of religious responsibilities. The word "totem" is often used loosely, sometimes denoting little more than an animal emblem, but Australian totemism was a profound feature of social and ritual life.

Native Australians explained their totems and every other important aspect of life in terms of an elaborate mythology about the Dreamtime (or Dreaming), when culture heroes turned the world into the one that people knew. This rich body of knowledge, including associated rituals, was imparted to young men in a long series of initiation ceremonies and other learning experiences.

Key features:

▶ Generalized foragers
▶ Spear-thrower, boomerang, pituri
▶ Enhancement and renewal of basic resources
▶ Specializations in extraction and related crafts
▶ Elaborate kinship systems
▶ Supraband social networks
▶ Long period of male initiation
▶ Totemism
▶ Dreamtime mythology

Modal Patterns in Native Australian Culture

Material Culture

The family slept on the ground behind a windbreak made of branches, brush, and grass. Among them small fires burned to keep them warm. The end of a stick rested in each fire; a person could push it further in whenever the flames died down. Occasionally there was a flurry of movement when part of a body touched a fire; everyone had scars from these unavoidable incidents. A person could call some dogs to act as living blankets when the fires were not enough, but this was rarely necessary except during winter.

As the sun rose and the people began to stir, they heard the murmurs of other families in their own sub-camps a dozen or more yards away. Then there was the sound of horseplay from the cluster of shelters where the young bachelors slept. On the fringe of this local band several elderly women had set up their own household. Sometimes elderly men did the same. As the people rose for the day, adjusting their few ornaments of twine, feathers, or shells, reddish and yellowish dingo dogs began to swarm through the camp in search of food and affection.

Women went out to gather food with numerous options in mind, mostly involving varied uses of the digging stick. The simplest use was to knock down fruits or nuts. If the women found a yam vine, they would follow it to the area where its tubers sprouted and unearth them with the stick. They usually left some tubers, or parts of them, on the vine to sprout again. Sometimes they buried a tuber or a cutting to start a new vine. A woman carried all these items in her *pichi*, a tray or bowl carved from wood or bark. Often she balanced the pichi on her head, cushioning it with a ring of grass that she fashioned quickly whenever she needed it.

The digging stick turned up many edible roots, and sometimes fat grubs attached to the roots. Witchetty grubs, the larvae of a particular moth, were one to three inches long. People prized them for their taste, and they provided a substantial amount of protein. Worms were similarly valuable. Women also extracted small mammals from their burrows and used their sticks to club snakes and lizards. Lizards, up to six feet in length, could supply a substantial amount of meat.

A hunter depended on extensive knowledge of winds, seasons, and the habits of the prey. He tracked animals by interpreting their varied marks, and he drew close to them by imitating their sounds or disguising himself and his scent with mud or ocher. When close enough, he threw his spear with a spear-thrower that in effect lengthened his arm and imparted greater velocity to the weapon. The ten-foot spear had a powerful

A woman holding a digging stick and carrying a pichi on her head (Arunta culture, Native Australia).

impact within forty yards and could travel as far as a hundred yards.

One man stalked an emu, slowly drawing close enough to see the dark brown feathers on its body, the long, blue neck, and the small, bald head. He stopped at a considerable distance from the bird, knowing that he had the advantage of its curiosity. Hiding behind a clump of brush, the hunter raised his spear-thrower and waved it. As the bird came near, the man fitted his spear into the thrower, rose quickly, and cast the weapon. He was happy to see it hit squarely because an emu not seriously injured could flee at a speed of thirty miles an hour. Sometimes they lost control and fell down, but this was not something to depend on. There was an easier way to take an emu, by putting pituri in a water source that it used, but this could only be done when all the conditions were right.

Another man had found a group of kangaroos resting at the edge of the scrubby, wooded area in which they lived. He approached them with the greatest care because they were extremely wary and lacked the emu's gullibility. Whenever one of the animals seemed suspicious, the hunter precisely imitated some appropriate element of

Emu, one of the larger game animals in the Australian Zone.

kangaroo behavior. Despite the man's care, the animals detected him and scrambled into their wooded refuge. Noticing the tracks of a fairly large bandicoot, the man gave up on the kangaroos. He followed the bandicoot to its burrow and dug it out.

During the course of the morning, several men took small animals with their boomerangs. This flat throwing stick was about three inches wide and three feet long, with a curve about nine inches from one end. The hunter grasped the uncurved end and threw the stick to hit his prey after a single bounce.

As the sun rose high, people straggled back into camp. Unless affected by a drought or some other disaster, people rarely needed more than half a day to find enough food. Men rested from the morning's pursuits, but the more industrious soon turned to other tasks. One completed a stone axe by hafting the chipped and ground head to a wooden handle. He glued it with tree gum and secured it with sinew. People used such an axe to cut wood and bark, shape wood, remove animals and beehives from trees, and butcher animals. Men also used it as a weapon in hunting and war.

Another man examined his spear-thrower for defects, a job that took a while because the device was actually a multipurpose tool. It included a small tray for mixing paint from ocher, a hook for obtaining fruits or other small out-of-reach objects, and a blade at one end that could be used as a knife or a scraper in butchering or woodworking. Such light multipurpose tools, most of

them made from wood, made it possible for people to carry a diversified technology despite their nomadic life. When the man found everything intact, he applied the blade to a pichi that he was carving for his wife.

Some of the women in camp began processing roots and nuts they had gathered to remove bitter substances that could be poisonous. The process entailed pounding or slicing of the food and repeated soakings. Other women, having brought different foods home, gathered firewood and then started the fires for the evening. Because the manufacture of fire by friction was a long and tedious process, women kept glowing sticks alive to light a fire whenever necessary. They even carried the lit sticks when the band was on the move.

With the fires ready, women began to cook the evening meal, the only one that people ate on a regular basis. Sometimes a woman roasted a piece of meat over an open fire. More often she cooked meat and plant foods in a shallow earth oven, mixed with embers, ashes, and sand. People preferred their meat very lightly cooked and often ate witchetty grubs raw.

A man who had killed a large animal cooked it himself with a certain amount of ceremony. He gave prescribed portions to his family and relatives, including in-laws if present, and distributed the rest throughout the camp. The hunter took only a small portion of poorer meat for himself and sometimes nothing at all.

If the evening meal had included fruit, people sometimes dispersed the seeds in an area made fertile by their activities: an area cleared by burning or a pile of refuse at the edge of the camp. Occasionally men encouraged the growth of fruit trees or bushes by diverting a small channel of water to pass near them.

The local band moved when resources dictated. As they left the old camp, most of the adults picked up fire sticks to carry with them. Women would use them when they settled down again, to start fires for cooking and warmth. Men used the sticks to set grass fires while they were traveling. The immediate result was to make many

One of the many kangaroo species hunted by Native Australians.

small animals available to hunt at one time. In the long run the regenerating vegetation would attract other animals that people ate.

One day several men left the group to get good stone for axes from a quarry a hundred miles away. They carried goods to trade with the people who worked the quarry, including wood tools, weapons, several kinds of ocher, and shell pendants that had ultimately come from seashore people. To ease the long walk with their burdens, the men chewed pituri along the way. They had made it before they left, mixing the leaves with ash from a particular bark. The pituri lessened their hunger, thirst, and fatigue on the long trip.

The men knew they were close to their destination when they first saw the long ridge that held the prized stone. Coming closer, they could make out the round and oval pits from which the stone was obtained. At the site they encountered many men. Some, like themselves, had come from near and far to trade. Others were local people who specialized in mining and trading the stone. As transactions took place at the foot of the ridge, men stood and knelt in the pits above, extracting the stone. Others made the blanks, pieces roughly the size of an axe head but still in need of shaping and sharpening.

After the long return journey, the men prepared to use the blanks that they had obtained. They made some of them into axe blades to be used by themselves and their families. Others they saved as gifts to various relatives when they met them or when a special occasion arose. Still other blanks were kept until a big ceremonial meeting where a man presented gifts to distant relatives and trading partners who would provide him with special gifts in return. All these exchanges, unlike the trading at the quarry, were based on reciprocity and emphasized alliances between individuals and groups.

Many of the goods that were exchanged on special occasions came from unusual sources like the stone quarries. Local people with distinctive resources specialized in extraction and associated craftwork. Sometimes people traveled more than a hundred miles to obtain such goods. The goods themselves went even farther in chains of exchanges. The most favored items, pearl shell pendants, crossed the continent.

Social Relations

The family of a mature man included more than one wife. An experienced woman exercised a great deal of autonomy within marriage, choosing the times, places, and company for her gathering expeditions. When dealing directly with her husband, she often expressed her opinions forcefully. Strong-willed and articulate wives cowed some husbands. Other men responded to conflict by beating their wives, but the male advantage in strength was offset by several factors. The man who attacked his wife faced intervention by her male relatives if they con-

sidered his violence to be excessive. There was also a significant threat of physical retaliation by the woman herself because she was strong and skilled with her digging stick. Women sometimes fought each other, usually in a duel in which the combatants alternated head blows until one was unwilling or unable to continue.

The fact that a woman provided most of her family's food gave her leverage in domestic conflicts. Her departure, even for a few days, could have a considerable effect on her husband's quality of life. If the local band contained one or more households of elderly women, a wife could conveniently take refuge in this women's camp. Another option was to visit relatives elsewhere.

A man could divorce his wife at any time without stating a reason, but a woman had no right to a divorce. The safest course of action for an unhappy wife was to go away for a legitimate reason, such as a visit to her parents, and stay away for a long time in the hope that her husband would lose interest and not force her to return. The dangerous alternative was to elope with another man, an act likely to provoke retaliation by the husband and men who supported him.

Because most of the older men had several wives, no brides were immediately available for younger men. Many parents arranged marriages for their daughters when they were infants. The hopeful husbands spent a long time waiting, worrying about a change of mind, and providing gifts and services to their prospective in-laws. Such men could be found in the bachelor camps of many local bands.

One consequence of the system was marriage between people of extremely disparate ages, resulting in drastic variation among the households in many local bands. An old man whose contemporary wives had died was left with vigorous young women beyond his control. A young man sometimes inherited old wives from a relative and neglected or rejected them. An elderly person in such a situation often withdrew from marital relationships and established a household with one or two similarly situated members of the same sex.

Beyond the household, people traced their personal relationships bilaterally. Most kinship terms were classificatory, covering several connected relatives such as a father and his brothers. Equivalence of siblings shaped many relationships. People expected brothers to be especially close; although they sometimes competed for the same potential wives, both kinship and religious interests bound them together. Sibling equivalence extended to the opposite sex, as in a man's close attachment to his father's sister.

Many other relationships were constricted to varying degrees, ranging from formal behavior to minimal communication to complete avoidance. Some avoidances represented sexual and marital prohibitions. Others emphasized the respect that one of the related people owed to the other. In either case, avoidance probably decreased the chances of conflict in potentially tense relationships.

A man was especially careful to avoid any intimacy with an actual or prospective mother-in-law. They were barred from face-to-face communication or any prolonged interaction. This was a matter of respect on the part of the man who received the woman's daughter. He supplied his mother-in-law with food, gave her gifts, defended her if she were abused, and avenged any injury to her.

A pregnant woman expected extra help from her husband, co-wives, and others in camp. She gave birth outside the camp with the aid of particular female relatives. Soon after birth the infant came into contact with the mother's sisters and other relatives considered to be the equivalent to the mother. They gave the baby care and affection, and sometimes one of them nursed it. A little bit later male relatives who were classified with the father began to play with the infant. After a few months the various caregivers began to teach the baby simple words, especially the kin terms for themselves and for others in the camp. They also introduced the child to some of the behavior that it owed to those people and could expect from them.

Young children played with each other, mixing together with little regard for the behavioral restrictions they would observe later in life. However, adults made sure that there was no contact between children in kinship categories that made the boy a potential son-in-law to the girl. Children had few toys other than the patient dogs that they mauled every day. This was the beginning of a lifelong affection for the animals, as shown by the many adults who stopped to pet and kiss them. The dogs had some use as scavengers in the camp, and some men used them to corner wounded prey. Their greatest value was as living blankets during cold winter nights. However, people tolerated far more dogs in the camp than they needed for any of these purposes. Being frequently underfoot, they were sometimes kicked, but people viewed their own dogs as almost family members, and adults sometimes came to blows over an offense against a dog.

When a boy began to display facial hair, he was ready for his major initiation ceremony. The ceremony called for a great deal of time and effort from many people, so it was often delayed until several boys were ready. The novices who shared an initiation entered into a lifelong bond with one another, which often connected men from different kinship groups and even different regional bands.

When they judged that the time was right, a group of men took control of the novices in a ritual manner as women put on a show of resistance and wept for the loss of their children. Several men went to other local bands to announce the ceremony and invite attendance. When visiting groups arrived, they received a formal welcome and then participated in a ceremonial combat to settle any outstanding disputes. With adult relationships in order, attention shifted to the boys to be initiated. The men subjected the novices to one or more public ceremonies witnessed by the women. Then they took the boys into seclusion away from the camp, not to be seen by any woman, and performed the most important ritual, which involved cutting some part of the body. After giving the initiates lengthy instruction in social customs and religion, the men returned the boys to the camp. When the boys arrived, they received a ritual welcome from the women.

This was just the beginning. Over a period of years an initiate would witness more secret rituals and learn more about religion. A youth saw his own future in the men conducting ceremonies. He expected to become an important participant during his middle years and hoped to become a leader. Eventually, as an elder and ultimate repository of belief and custom, he would share in the highest religious authority. A young man knew that at any age respect and authority came only to those who had something to offer the community.

The importance of religious knowledge in adult life gave older men control over younger ones. In some cases the men responsible for an initiation ceremony left out an eligible boy who had behaved badly. They could also withhold vital religious knowledge later on in the long learning process. Periods of ritual isolation, accompanied by exhortations to refrain from sex, kept young men away from their seniors' wives. Painful operations on the body may have had an intimidating effect.

During initiation and afterward, a boy acquired general knowledge of myth and ritual; he also learned the secrets of his own religious estate, which consisted of one or more sacred sites or tracts of land. A group of people, most of them patrilineal relatives, shared a spiritual connection with a particular estate and took responsibility for the performance of ceremonies associated with that estate.

Because kin preferred traveling together, most or all the male members of a local band belonged to same estate group. The women of the group were usually scattered, living with their husbands according to the patrilocal rule, and some had moved to other regional bands after marriage. However, no matter where they lived, all members of a religious group were bonded to each other by the common attachment to their estate.

People belonged to other social groups that were unequivocally based on descent. At a minimum a society was divided into moieties, either explicitly recognized or implicit in their marriage practices and kinship concepts. Social totems symbolized these exogamous groups. Because the social totem was considered to be of the same flesh as the associated people, they did not eat it.

Placing high value on harmony and cooperation, people tried to settle many conflicts with argument and negotiation. Often they voiced complaints among the campfires at night, appealing to the shame of the accused or the force of public opinion. Such tirades usually pertained to minor offenses or flimsy suspicions and provided entertainment for those not involved. Serious crimes included physical injury, blatant adultery, or the elopement of a wife or prospective wife with another man. Supported by his male kin, the victim sought revenge. When the victim was a mature man, often the case in sexual transgressions, other senior men supported him even if they were not close relatives. Confronted with the solidarity of community leaders, many an offender submitted to ritual punishment. At a prearranged place and time he faced a volley of spears, although he was allowed to dodge or even use a shield. As soon as he shed blood, the ordeal ended and the crime was expiated. However, repeated offenses of any kind often elicited lethal action from the community.

Some offenders fled and refused to give themselves up. Others, such as sorcerers, lived in other groups to begin with. Cases like these required a formal revenge expedition. A revenge expedition began with special rituals and/or decorations for the men. In some cases these parties seem to have entered other groups openly, and people other than the accused offered no resistance or even cooperated. However, there was a fine line between punitive expeditions and simple raiding parties. Sometimes the attackers set up ambushes, and sometimes they killed people in addition to the original offenders. In some cases they captured women or young boys to bring back to their own band.

Religious violations fell into a separate category. When a man violated sacred law, ritual leaders met secretly to decide his punishment. In extreme cases the verdict was death, inflicted by the leaders themselves or by their designated agents. A woman or child who saw a forbidden object or ritual, or who violated sacred ground in any other way, was subject to immediate death by spearing.

Large battles, some involving hundreds of men, were often prearranged and carried out in a formal way. Some of these were the outcome of numerous long-standing feuds and were intended to bring peace to an entire area. Even the largest resulted in only a dozen or so fatalities. In any fight the main weapons were those used in the hunt, the spear and the boomerang.

Relations beyond the regional band had a positive side that enmeshed people in a variety of social networks based on different kinds and combinations of bonds. Every regional band was linked to others by intermarriage, and the people considered themselves to be relatives. Sharing a dialect or language provided another source of solidarity, as did common cultural patterns, especially in religion.

Knowledge and Expression

Arriving at their destination, the members of the local band scattered to set up their separate subcamps. Their behavior was ordinary, but excited conversation and sidelong glances showed that the occasion was not. On the far side of the ridge near the campsite, there was a sacred place that housed souls of human beings and emus. The people and birds that derived their souls from this place shared a totemic relationship derived from the mythological era that people called the Dreamtime. During this period, supernatural beings traveled across the earth, creating natural features that still exist and presenting humans with every important aspect of their cultures. Because people owed everything to this sacred past, they idealized stability and continuity and held that the present should duplicate the essential features of the past.

The local band had come to this place by the ridge for a ceremony inspired by the Dreamtime. They would reenact and commemorate the earthly experiences and creative acts of the totemic being who had left the souls of humans and emus at this site. But they had more than a memorial on their minds. The Dreamtime was an eternal dimension, binding the past to the present and future in a dynamic way. The creative beings continued to exist at the same time as humans and concerned themselves with the well-being of their spiritual descendants. Rituals pleased the Dreamtime beings and ensured their help and protection in this world. People saw everything around them as parts of a continuum from mundane to sacred. All the sacred things, including behavior, objects, and people, were rooted in the Dreamtime. Ceremonies tapped directly into the ongoing power of the creative era.

As people set up camp, they shared an excitement that was social as well as religious. Soon several other local bands would arrive for the ceremonies. Many of the men in these bands shared the emu totem. They were spiritually connected to each other, to the living birds, and to the Dreamtime being who had left the souls of both at this particular site. Together these men constituted the core of a group associated with the religious estate of the emu totem. The estate included all the places and objects affected by the Dreamtime being as he passed through this region.

Bearing primary responsibility for ceremonies dedicated to their totem, men tried to stay in or near the estate. If conflicts or the pursuit of food had caused them to disperse in local bands, they were obligated to return for the rituals. Women also belonged to the estate and the group that administered it, although many went further away than the men because of patrilocal marriages. Even so, women tried to return for important ceremonies.

A person's membership in the estate group was established by a parent's religious experience; for example, the mother first realized she was pregnant when near a sacred site, or the father dreamed of a particular totem after he learned of the pregnancy. Although the main bond in an estate group was spiritual, most of the members were patrilineally related. Fathers preferred this and tried to arrange it. A man who expected his wife to conceive, for instance, made an effort to take his family to his own estate. A man who had just learned of his wife's pregnancy usually dreamed of his own totem. In some cases the nonpatrilineal members of a totemic group faced hostility from the core members. Core members often had greater opportunities for ritual leadership than did nonrelatives.

Some estate groups were larger than a single totemic group because the estate contained totemic centers and associated sites for several different species and the Dreamtime beings who created them. Most totemic species were mammals or reptiles, some were plants, and a few were phenomena such as thunder or lighting. Those who held the estate in common usually joined for the ceremonies devoted to any of their totems.

On the first night of ritual, men sat in one group and the women and children in another. Beating time on the ground with sticks, clubs, or boomerangs, the men began to sing. Their voices frequently became guttural or nasal, and they punctuated the words with screams, whoops, grunts, and falsetto ululations. Women and children thrilled at the performance, but the words meant little to them because they were heavily symbolic. For initiated men and a few knowledgeable old women, a single word could evoke a wide range of images from the Dreamtime story. Each song was short, but there were dozens appropriate for this occasion, as was the case for any ceremony.

With the singing going strongly, men began to leave the group in order to dance. Some performed alone and others with a companion or two. They used complicated steps and hand movements, simulating Dreamtime beings or related living animals. Each dance lasted only a minute or two but, as with the songs, there were many available. Some dances brought laughter because the Dreamtime beings they represented, apart from their heroic creations, had lived much as humans do including many foibles. Although it was not appropriate on this occasion, there were ceremonies in which women danced, sometimes simultaneously with the men and sometimes separately.

Next morning initiated men left the camp for a ceremonial ground forbidden to other people. They began by

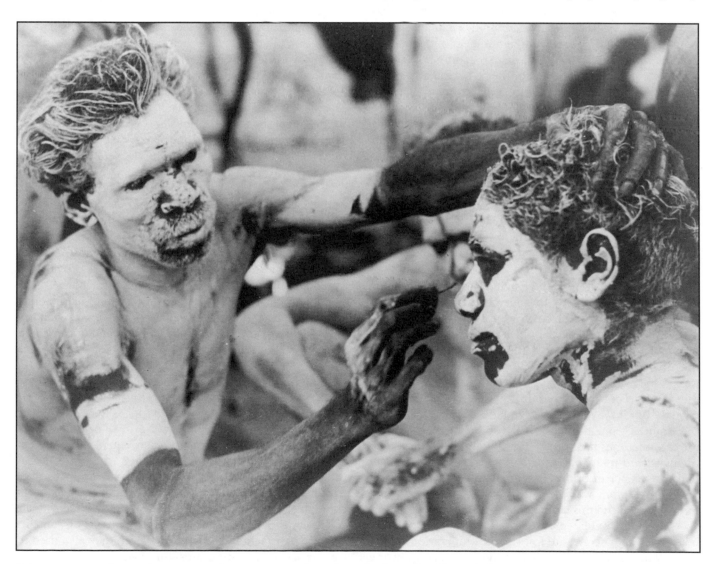

Painting was a vital part of preparation for a ceremony throughout the Australian Zone. In this case, clay is being applied before an initiation ritual (Arnhem Land).

singing and then, guided by the older men in charge of this ceremony, they prepared for the secret dances that were the most important part. Men who would represent mythical beings received body decorations that took hours to prepare. Various paints were applied to the body. Over a base of red ocher, tufts of down or wild cotton were attached with blood. The designs reached from the thighs across the upper body to the neck, where they were integrated with an elaborate headdress that in many cases represented a totemic animal. Here again, most of the dances were brief, and some elicited laughter. In the evening, finished with the secret rituals, men returned to the camp for another public performance. This provided greater excitement than the first night because the men continued to wear the decorations from the afternoon. The same daily cycle went on for a week. This was true for many such ceremonies, and some lasted longer.

Ritual totems had nothing to do with marriage regulation. The human caretakers were not of the same flesh as their ritual totem, so they could consume the animal or plant. Most of the relevant ceremonies had at least the tangential effect of increasing the numbers of the totemic species, and this was the primary goal of some rites.

It was a letdown when people had to pull away from the sacred life and resume the food quest, but the Dreamtime lived in stories told among the fires on an ordinary night. These were versions of the myths suitable for the uninitiated. Most of them related minor anecdotes from the lengthy travels and works of the Dreamtime culture heroes. People also narrated tales of tricksters, evil spirits, and human adventures in love and sex. Many of these came from personal experience, dreams, or imagination. They were mainly for pleasure but could provide some instruction for children. The nighttime camp was also a place for dancing and for singing songs that touched on every aspect of life.

People came close to the Dreamtime again when one or more boys were ready to undergo their first initiation ceremony and begin learning the enormous body of myth and ritual possessed by the older men. After the invited groups had assembled and settled in, the men subjected the novice boys to one or more of several preliminary rites. One was tossing the boys in the air and catching them. Everyone said that this was to promote their growth, but it may also have symbolized the transition of the novices from the hands of women to the hands of men. Sometimes men bit the boys' scalps until they bled; this was said to encourage the growth of hair, but blood had the deeper meaning of symbolizing life. Sometimes the nasal septum was pierced to hold an ornament, but many peoples did this before the first initiation ceremony.

After the public preliminaries, the men took the boys away to a secret site for a painful operation on the body. The most common was a genital operation; the main alternative, removal of a tooth. The operation gave the boys an opportunity to display courage, and it marked them as individuals who had begun to receive secret knowledge. It probably represented symbolic death, a necessary prelude to rebirth as an initiated man. The experience of pain has also been interpreted as part of the transition from childish egotism to disciplined adult altruism.

At some point in the period of isolation, the novices participated in the blood rite. Men drew blood from their own bodies and accumulated it in a container. After consecrating the blood with a special song, the men smeared it on themselves and the boys. Sometimes the participants drank from the blood. Human blood played a prominent role in all rituals, primarily symbolizing life. In the initiation ritual it also represented courage and strength. By partaking of the blood, the participants engaged in a spiritual communion with each other and with the Dreamtime beings that made their lives possible.

Another rite subjected the boys to an ordeal and purification by fire. They ran through embers or were showered with them or, at the very least, stared into a fire until dazed. Finally, the men washed the boys clean of all paint and any other signs of their initiation into the men's secret world except for the permanent scars of the body operations. The men returned the initiates to camp, where the women formally welcomed them. The youths looked forward to other occasions when they would learn more about the male relationship with the Dreamtime.

No single social group possessed the complete mythology because the supernaturals were not bound by the physical or social limits of humans. Men lived with the knowledge that parts of the Dreamtime epic were possessed by strangers, enemies, and people they would never meet. Sometimes neighboring groups met to perform complementary ritual enactments of their mythological knowledge. Great meetings, some bringing together more than a thousand people, provided a grander opportunity for the same kind of exchange.

At a great gathering young men would learn something about the totemic beings of other areas. They would also hear more than their fathers and uncles could tell them about the beings that had traveled far and wide during the Dreamtime, affecting the worlds of many different peoples. In addition to solemn ceremonies and increased knowledge, a great meeting gave everyone the chance to visit with relatives and friends long missed and to have a great deal of fun. It was also an occasion when old enemies might encounter each other, an event that sometimes turned deadly.

Women had rituals of their own, performed apart from men and also rooted in the Dreaming. These seem to have been concerned largely with sex and love. Women enhanced their attractiveness, largely by magic, to find satisfaction in affairs. However, they also tried to manage social relationships, for example, getting a man to marry. Furthermore, sex and love may often have been metaphors for larger values such as fertility.

Although women as well as men had secret rites, there were important asymmetries in the system. Women provided subsistence support for male-dominated ceremonies but received none for their own. Women played a subordinate role in some male rituals while men never assumed such a role. And women who violated men's secrets were subject to immediate punishments such as rape or death; a man who trespassed on women's ritual might sicken from supernatural punishment, but he feared no secular retaliation.

Men painted and incised various wood and stone surfaces, mainly for supernatural reasons, with designs that were symbolic rather than realistic. Rock and cave paintings illustrated stories or facilitated magic. Portable objects of stone or wood were used in rituals.

A Closer Look

The Most Primitive People

Native Australians have been characterized as the most "primitive" people in the world, largely on the basis of their technology. The value of such judgments is dubious, and the criterion chosen is ethnocentrically limited. Even in its own terms the judgment did not accurately assess all parts of the continent or all aspects of the technology. It is true that Australia was the only continent that lacked the bow, but this may have been related to the unusual fauna and the alternative weapons available. The large prey were thick-skinned and the spear, enhanced by the spear-thrower, was probably more effective than an arrow (Flood 1990). Hunters killed smaller mammals with a variety of boomerangs, a unique kind of throwing stick that they bounced off the ground (most of them, except for toys, were not designed to return). The club sufficed for reptiles and for the many small mammals that were dug from their burrows. This weaponry illustrates the more general point that Australian technology was sufficient for its purposes and in some cases was probably the best for unusual conditions.

Gender and Sexuality

Australians shared in the modal Oceanic view of sex as a healthy pleasure for both males and females, including the use of positions for intercourse that increased freedom and pleasure for the woman (Abbie 1970). This attitude was inculcated from an early age, but it conflicted with marriage arrangement and especially with infant betrothal. Young women married to much older men often sought affairs despite the threat of severe punishment (Hiatt 1996). Some eloped with young men, leading to revenge parties. A disproportionately high percent-

age of infanticides against firstborns may have reflected the resentment of young brides (Burbank 1989).

Although women valued sex with a desirable partner, they had to cope with situations in which men used it for dominance and intimidation. In some puberty rituals young girls were deflowered with a sharp instrument and then subjected to group sex with older men. Somewhat similarly, gang rape was a punishment for promiscuous women. A lone girl was subject to rape by any man who encountered her (Abbie 1970), perhaps to discourage young women from meeting lovers.

Men controlled the sexuality of women in other ways. A husband could offer his wife to a brother or a friend. Men also used women to expiate offenses against other men (Burbank 1989) and to deflect aggression (Berndt and Berndt 1985). However, according to Bell (1993), women may have had a say in these matters and in some cases may have enjoyed the sexual adventures.

The sacred estates belonged to all clan members, women as well as men. The rituals associated with the sites provided material and spiritual benefits to all. And yet women were excluded from the major ceremonies. Some clan women had little opportunity to participate because patrilocal marriages took them far from home. However, this does not explain the categorical exclusion of women from some rituals, their subordinate role in others, and their exclusion from initiated knowledge of such matters.

It has been suggested that the spiritual powers of women, related to reproduction, endangered the men's ceremonies (Abbie 1970; see also the Northern American Zone). Men considered menstrual blood to be especially dangerous, though not unclean. Occasionally old women were allowed to witness very sacred rituals. The secret ceremonies of men seem to have expressed the impact of women's reproductive power. In the initiation rites men symbolically killed the boys so that they could cause them to be reborn. Unclear about any physical role in conception, men compensated by assuming the exclusive right to bestow the supernatural component of new life. The belief that in the mythological past men stole the symbols of religious power from women suggests further male uncertainty connected with gender.

AUSTRALIAN DESERT AREA

Examples:

Arrernte (Arunta, Aranda), Mardu, Walbiri

The Desert Area covered the western two thirds of the continent. At the center of the Area was a habitat with average rainfall less than ten inches per year. It gradually gave way to an outer ring of dry grasslands that received less than twenty inches of rain per year. These long-term averages gloss over the fact that many years saw no precipitation at all. Summer temperatures ranged up to 150 degrees Fahrenheit, and a person could easily die of dehydration within eight hours (Abbie 1970).

The native people applied a wide variety of techniques to getting enough water. Desert Australians contrasted with the famous Kalahari foragers in that Australians ate (and drank) their way *into* the main water sources rather than out of them (Tonkinson 1991). As in other dry habitats, seeds played a vital role in subsistence because of their relative abundance and because they could be stored. They were worth a great deal of labor: a woman spent from seven to thirteen hours gathering and grinding enough seeds to make two pounds of flour.

The sparse and fluctuating resources of the Desert placed strong ecological pressures on its inhabitants. Although some infanticides may have stemmed from the resentment of manipulated young women, there is little doubt that the practice in the Desert was used to keep family size in balance with the availability of resources. Although the elderly were generally well treated, even they were sometimes abandoned out of necessity.

In social organization the Desert people elaborated the moiety principle by combining it with the distinction between generations. The basic system divided a society into four categories, called *sections*, that guided marriage choices and summarized a person's relatives. These sections are often called *marriage classes*, using the term "class" in a nonhierarchical sense. Some cultures went further and recognized eight classes, but only the basic system will be described below.

Like many other people in the world, Desert Australians regarded circumcision as vital to initiation (Abbie 1970). However, different cultures in Australia held varying ideas about the significance of the practice (Berndt and Berndt 1985). Some viewed it as punishment for a mythological act of incest. To others it symbolically separated the initiate from the world of women, the prepuce being likened to the umbilical cord. Some simply considered it essential to cleanliness. The Desert initiation process also included a unique operation called subincision, in which the bottom of the penis was slit to the urethra.

Key features:

► Water seeking crucial
► Seed grinding
► Section systems
► Circumcision and subincision

Modal Patterns in Australian Desert Culture

Material Culture

It was a very dry summer, and people in the small local band had used most of their water-getting techniques in different camps over the last few weeks. In a dry riverbed they had scooped out sand to reach the water below. They had recovered water from the hollows of trees and extracted it from tree roots. They had dug up small frogs

A hunter walking through an Australian desert. The land was arid but harbored a substantial amount of vegetation (Pitjandjara culture, Western Desert).

that bloated themselves with water before burrowing under the ground. After squeezing water from the frogs, people ate them.

Now, early in a morning that was already hot, the band prepared for a long walk to a usually reliable waterhole. This was one of the good sources that they saved for times of serious need. People plucked succulent plants that they would chew on during the walk. Women used small pichis to scoop the last dregs of water into larger ones. They covered the water with leaves and twigs, which diminished losses from spilling and evaporation, and then hoisted the pichis to their heads.

Toward midday the travelers sighted a large eucalyptus tree and felt grateful. They set their burdens down and dug holes among the roots of the tree. There they rested and hid from the worst of the sun. The shelter of the tree made it less likely that a small child or elderly person would die on this march.

They resumed the journey with the sun low in the sky and arrived at their destination in the evening. The first people to peer into the opening among the rocks voiced their disappointment. An animal had fallen into the hole and fouled the water. After pulling the carcass out and throwing it away, the people sat down, drank water from the pichis, and considered their options.

One way to get potable water was to enlarge the hole so that fresher water diluted the bad. Another possibility was to dig a hole parallel to the natural one so that the water filtered into it. Or they could scoop the foul water out and filter it through grass and twigs. One way or another, they would get the water that they needed as they had so many times before.

This little oasis was one of the localities where women had left millstones for grinding seeds into flour. These stones differed from those used to grind other plants or to powder ochers for paint making. The millstones were larger, flatter, and smoother. They had come from faraway places through exchange.

A man seeking water in a "soak."

In the early morning women went out and gathered seeds, pulling them off various bushes and grasses. They carried the seeds back to camp in their pichis and then winnowed them in the same vessels. Each woman found a smooth stone for a grinder, spread her seeds on the millstone, and began the tedious preparation. As she crushed the seeds, she repeatedly wetted the flour with squirts of water from her mouth. When she had the dough finished, she allowed her children to eat a few mouthfuls raw. Then she baked the rest in ashes to make a flat round loaf for the family's dinner. Women used string bags to carry food home from their gathering expeditions. Some were woven so tightly that they held honey or even water.

Social Relations

Men depended heavily on women for subsistence because game was scarce and the mainstay in plant food was the grass seeds that required long and arduous work to grind. The dependence of a particular husband on a particular wife was presumably heightened by the fact that polygynous men rarely had more than three wives. The loss of just one wife substantially diminished the family workforce.

The seed-grinding equipment itself may have influenced gender relations. Composed of heavy stone, it was not portable. Proximity to the wife's equipment often meant proximity to the wife's relatives, despite the preference for patrilocal residence. This meant stronger support and protection for the wife in disputes and an easier departure if she decided to leave her husband, whether temporarily or permanently.

Although young women suffered frustrations arising from infant betrothal, they benefited later in life. A mother had equal rights to the food and gifts provided by her daughter's prospective husband, and she played a role in choosing him. The boy's mother also influenced the arrangements. Although a man bestowed a daughter on a boy that he circumcised, the relationship was established by an antecedent women's ritual in which the boy's mother chose his mother-in-law. The two women enjoyed a close relationship thereafter, if not before.

Local bands were often small, sometimes no more than a single family. Scattered resources required that people disperse widely during parts of the year, although they might aggregate at major water sources at other times. Regional bands, on the other hand, tended to be large, many containing hundreds of people. Presumably this simplified access to a large resource area. Access to resources may also have been the primary reason for social networks beyond the band level.

In the same vein people rarely defended territorial boundaries or specific resources. Nevertheless, there were instances where a large contingent from one social network attacked the population of another and dispossessed them. The sparse evidence suggests that water was the most likely cause.

Desert societies were subdivided into sections based on descent and generation. Adjacent generations in each of the moieties formed four sections in a pattern that constantly repeated itself. People of different sections in the same generation married, and their children belonged to the other two sections. The sections provided a broad classification of relatives that simplified a very extensive kinship terminology.

Knowledge and Expression

The Dreamtime heroes of Desert mythology emphasized the totemic view of life. They possessed human and animal traits and could change their shapes. Operations on the penis were important in the initiation rituals. Circumcision, the more important act, linked initiation to the marriage system in that a man eventually bestowed one of his daughters on a boy that he circumcised.

Desert men also subincised the penis, slitting the underside lengthwise. This provided a ready source for ritual bloodletting throughout life, although the blood was less sacred than that taken from the arm. One explanation for the practice relates to the totemic world view connecting humans and animals. Kangaroos and some other marsupials have bifurcated penises that may have provided the model. At least one ethnic group explicitly connected subincision with a kangaroo hero in their Dreamtime mythology. However, not all Australian cultures had these particular heroes in their own myths.

Another interpretation connects the operation with Australian men's ritual concern about female reproductive powers. The distended halves of the subincised penis resemble the vulva, and some Australian cultures explicitly compared the ritual drawing of blood from the organ with menstruation. It may be that the marsupial model inspired the operation among some people while the resemblance to female genitals made it significant to others.

Women's ceremonies reflected their position in society. They affirmed the sexual rights of women and asserted relative equality of gender. Sexual components were often directed toward fertility, and there was considerable attention to land, health, and harmony. Female rites had extensive links to the Dreamtime.

Girls were subjected to ritual introcision at puberty. The initiator penetrated the hymen with a hot stick or sharp stone. This was compared to circumcision, though the ceremonial context was minimal. If outsiders see a paradox between the painful introcision ritual and the rights of women mentioned above, they should recall that Desert Area men underwent the painful operation of subincision, as well as circumcision.

A Closer Look

The Central Desert Region

The Central Desert is named for its location on the continent as a whole. It is the eastern half of the Australian desert. This Region was made famous by reports on the Aranda or Arunta, now called Arrernte by anthropologists (Morton 1999). Another important example is the Walbiri (Meggitt 1965), whose name has been spelled in a bewildering number of ways. We can think of Central Desert culture as the basic adaptation of Native Australian society to an arid environment: groupings such as totemic clans, regional bands, and ethnic populations were readily identifiable. The drier Western Desert was more distinctive in this respect.

The Western Desert Region

Western Desert peoples included those known to outsiders as the Mardu and the Pintupi. This habitat "epitomizes" arid Australia and, compared to dry locales such as the Great Basin in North America and the Kalahari in Africa, the Western Desert "stands out as a place that is exceedingly poor" in numbers and variety of edible plants and animals (Gould 1980:61). The sparsity of mammals under these conditions was compensated somewhat by one of the richest reptile faunas in the world (Tonkinson 1991). However, rainfall averaged five to ten inches a year, with extreme variation, and population densities dipped to half those of the Central Desert (Myers 1991).

Social groupings were vaguely defined and strongly egalitarian. Although the core members of an estate group were related patrilineally, the religious link was more important than kinship. Thus there were no real lineages or clans in the Western Desert (Tonkinson 1991). The essential connection to the totem was made by each individual rather than by a descent group (Myers 1991).

The regional band existed as a de facto network of kin and friends within a certain area of land, who interacted with each other more often than with outsiders (Tonkinson 1991). However, these networks were not a basis for self identification. People only referred to regional bands other than their own as units. Members of a regional band never came together as an exclusive group, and large gatherings usually included members of several different bands.

Similarly, Western Desert people did not distinguish themselves in ethnic terms. Populations such as Mardu and Pintupi represent some real cultural and linguistic variations, but they have been delineated by outsiders for their own convenience. People throughout the Region spoke mutually intelligible dialects and formed a single social network (Tonkinson 1991). Given these vagaries in group identification, there could be no traditional enemies and little basis for warfare or even feud. Individuals and families disputed with each other and phrased their conflicts in terms of kinship (Tonkinson 1991).

AUSTRALIAN RIM AREA

Examples:

Tiwi, Yolngu (Murngin), Gidjingali, Narrinyeri, Kurnai

The Rim Area formed a semicircle that encompassed the northern, eastern, and western margins of Australia. Although no more extensive than the Desert, it harbored much of the native population (Peterson 1999).

Annual rainfall ranged from forty to sixty inches (Abbie 1970), and the climates varied from temperate in the south to tropical in the north. A major unifying feature of the Rim was that it was not the Desert and, therefore, it released human beings from Desert constraints such as constant concern about drinking water. The Rim also provided food resources in its perennial streams and rivers. People in contact with the ocean were enriched even further (Lourandos 1997).

A river in eastern Australia represents the abundance of water in the Australian Rim Area (Barron River, Queensland).

The data for the Rim Area are very uneven. With regard to the southeast, where contact and destruction were early, records of native culture are very limited and highly biased. In the north, on the other hand, anthropologists have studied intact cultures.

Men made a greater contribution to subsistence in the Rim Area as compared to the Desert. There was better hunting in those well-watered lands and an abundance of aquatic animals ranging from dugong to fish. Rim leadership was individualized in the sense that, even among the older men, some had greater authority than others or at least achieved much greater influence.

Initiation rituals involved no genital cutting in traditional times, although circumcision has more recently spread into the northern part of the Rim Area. A variety of alternative operations were intermingled throughout the Area. One of the most common was tooth avulsion, the removal of one or two teeth, which was a secondary ritual in many parts of the Desert. The other common practice was the removal of hair from face and body. In a few cultures the body was scarified.

Rim religion recognized a higher god among the other Dreamtime beings. This god was male and lived in the sky. He surveyed human life and received the souls of the dead. It is possible that some or all of the beliefs about the higher god are the result of contact with Europeans. It is obvious that some could have been borrowed from Christianity, but Swain (1996) argues that they were indigenous formulations in response to the new situation. Beliefs about the making of shamans also differed from those in the Desert Area.

Key features:

- ▶ Use of aquatic resources
- ▶ Larger male contribution to subsistence
- ▶ Individualized leadership
- ▶ More intense warfare and large battles
- ▶ Absence of genital operations in initiation
- ▶ High god

Modal Patterns in Australian Rim Culture

Material Culture

During a large part of the year (or all of it in the best-favored places), people abandoned nomadic foraging to live in villages near the sea. They lived in substantial wooden huts, some of them plastered with clay. They found subsistence especially easy when they could combine the rich terrestrial resources of the wet season with the resources of the rivers and the sea. Women exploited an abundance of shellfish in addition to gathering plant foods. Men took large quantities of fish with large and small nets and with traps made from stones, grass, brush, or logs. They also hunted large aquatic mammals: dug-

Spearing fish from a tree, one example of the varied exploitation of aquatic resources in the Australian Rim Area.

ongs in the warmer waters toward the north and seals and sea lions in the south. Aquatic hunting was facilitated by rafts and by bark canoes sewn with fiber.

The relative abundance and reliability of the food supply allowed for smaller regional bands with smaller ranges. Many contained fewer than one hundred people, doing most of their foraging in a range of less than one hundred square miles. The same conditions allowed local bands to be larger than those of the desert, sometimes containing the whole population of the regional band.

Social Relations

Chieftains, individuals with unusual influence and even authority, arose from several factors. One was a hierarchical religious system in which some mature individuals could acquire more knowledge than others and take control of ceremonies. In many cases control was facilitated by personal ownership of the sites where ceremonies were held. These were usually places of recurring food abundance, especially seasonal runs of fish. As many as a thousand people came together for such a gathering, which offered a great deal in addition to the ceremonies. People feasted, socialized, exchanged goods, and played games. The games seem to have included sportive battles, some engaging hundreds of participants.

Knowledge and Expression

During a boy's initiation ceremonies, after the key ritual that marked his body, he learned the secret name of the god that rose above other Dreamtime beings. This god took responsibility for the major transformations that produced the world known to humans, including natural features and cultural institutions. Sometimes following behind the higher god, totemic beings established sites that linked them to particular clans. The Dreamtime heroes remained in human form during their activities, rather than shifting to animal characteristics.

The religious life of women seems to reflect a less favorable position than that of their Desert sisters. They had little or no secret ritual of their own, and the rites that they did perform were more narrowly focused on sex. Trying to turn the minds of bachelors from men's religious concerns to sex, the women's ceremonies may have been an attempt at undermining male dominance.

In the face of death people pondered the moon, who regularly died and came back to life. At one time the moon had offered humans a drink that would have given them the same kind of eternal life. Somehow, because of a mistake by women in many of the stories, people missed the opportunity. However, death was not the end. The soul went on a journey that included tests, ordeals, and dangers. Eventually it reached the land of the dead, where it dwelled with other souls and with the Dreamtime beings.

A Closer Look

The Arnhem Land Region

This Region coincided with, and is named for, the roughly oval peninsula that crowns the north central part of Australia. The most famous inhabitants of Arnhem Land are the Murngin, now called Yolngu in the anthropological literature. Two other important examples are the Gidjingali and Gunwinggu. High rainfall sustained various kinds of forests, some dominated by Eucalyptus and others full-fledged rain forests with closed canopies. The people made yams an important staple and learned to propagate them by leaving or replanting the top of the tuber in the ground (Lourandos 1997).

Leaders enhanced their position with polygyny. Some had ten or more wives, who provided an enormous supply of plant foods and of daughters to bestow on young men. The prospective husbands provided a steady supply of meat (Hart et al. 1988; Hiatt 1996).

The main god of the Dreamtime was a woman, often identified with the rainbow serpent in one way or another. In some mythologies several sisters replaced the single goddess, but in all cases they played the primary culture hero role. The female gods of Arnhem Land were strongly associated with fertility.

Arnhem Land was the "richest art area in Australia" (Elkin 1964:243). Men used the conventional ochers and pipe clay for paints but distinguished their work with techniques, surfaces, and a degree of elaboration not found elsewhere on the continent. Men painted their spears and shaped them esthetically to the point of losing some effectiveness. Even clubs and baskets were richly painted with various designs.

Caves contained numerous paintings with one overlaying another. In depicting animals, the artists used a technique that displayed the internal anatomy of the subjects. They extended the technique to mythical creatures and evil spirits but represented totemic and other mythical beings in a more conventional way.

Men also painted on bark. They removed square or rectangular sheets of bark from a eucalyptus tree and flattened them by exposure to heat and then pressing them under stones. For a brush the painter used a stick, root, or bamboo shoot with one end frayed by chewing. The main subject of this medium was clan designs based on myths.

Arnhem Landers elaborated music in several ways. First, they gave more attention to the ubiquitous clapping sticks, choosing the wood carefully for its sonic quality and carving or decorating the sticks. Second, they played a unique instrument known as the drone pipe (didjeridu). Hollowed from a straight branch, it was three to six feet long and two to four inches in diameter. A skilled player could vary the fundamental deep note somewhat and introduce overtones by manipulating the oral muscles and breathing. In effect the mouth and lungs became extensions of the instrument (Abbie 1970).

The body paint and tapping sticks are typical of the Australian Zone, but the didjeridu played by the man on the left represents the many artistic elaborations of the Arnhem Land Region.

After initial ceremonies the dead were exposed on platforms until eventually relatives collected the remains and buried them with additional ritual. As part of the inquest people placed a possession of the deceased flat on the ground and watched for any signs of the killer that the soul might place there. While some spiritual essence returned to the individual's totemic center, the soul journeyed to the Land of the Dead. It was across a river or the sea and could only be reached by canoe. The being who paddled the canoe either beat the soul during the voyage or extracted a reward when it was done.

The Victoria Region

This Region was centered on what is now the state of Victoria and extended into South Australia and New South Wales. It included the lower portion of the Murray-Darling river system. Three prominent ethnic groups were the Narrinyeri (including the Yaraldi regional band), the Kulin, and the Kurnai.

The role of women differentiated this Region. Marriage required the bride's consent, and in some cases a young woman took the initiative. A wife had the same right as her husband to expect sexual fidelity, aside from legitimate occasions for exchange or license. Although there were some customary preferences as to the remarriage of a widow, the woman had the right to make her own choice. Women also occupied a stronger position in public matters than elsewhere in Native Australia. They had much to say around the campfires at night (Massola 1971), and older women consulted with men on important issues. Some women became powerful as magicians, doctors, or rainmakers.

Nevertheless, men retained the preeminent position in public life. Compared to the rest of Australia, Victorian Region culture formalized authority. A single chieftain led each clan, and it appears that in some cases the regional band had a chieftain as well (Berndt and Berndt 1993; Fison and Howitt 1967). Elder men constituted councils for clans and for larger groups or gatherings. These institutions of governance dealt with disputes, scheduled major celebrations, and judged the appropriateness of marriage. They also made decisions about warfare, especially against other ethnic groups.

Regional bands defended their territorial boundaries and/or specific resource sites. The sites were in many cases locales where fish appeared in abundance on a regular seasonal basis. The value of these sites was often enhanced by the construction of fixed artifacts such as stone traps or drainage systems (Lourandos 1997). However, adjacent bands usually shared resources to at least some degree.

Beyond neighbors there were supraband networks at least as extensive and complex as those in the Desert. Since local resources sufficed, the main functions of these large networks must have been social, including ceremonies, economic exchange, and information. They may have mitigated potentially destructive competition among territorial bands (Lourandos 1997).

Initiation Operations

The distribution of initiation operations raises questions. Circumcision and subincision are both characteristic of the Desert Area. Rim physical operations other than tooth avulsion were less intrusive and intimate, the most common being scarification of the body and plucking hair from the face and/or body. In the light of political differences between the Areas, this variation in the initiation practices suggests that intimidation is a factor. Throughout the initiation sequence, the older men can threaten a recalcitrant subject with delay or termination of the process. Eventually, however, it must end. If the process includes painful and frightening procedures, this may establish a psychological advantage that persists beyond final initiation. Comparing the two Culture Areas, the older men of the Rim seem to have extra support from ownership of rich and stable resources. This may explain why they inflict relatively superficial injury on initiates while Desert men enthusiastically accepted a second and more drastic genital operation.

Glossary

Italicized terms are defined in the Glossary.

adolescence. The period of an individual's life between *childhood* and adulthood. It begins around the time of puberty but, especially for boys, is defined mainly by cultural criteria. It ends with marriage at about age seventeen for girls and eighteen or older for boys.

adze. A chopping tool in which the face of the blade is perpendicular to the handle.

afterlife. Existence of some spiritual part of the individual after the death of the physical body on earth. The existence may be in an *afterworld* separate from human life or near humans as a *ghost*.

afterworld. A supernatural place apart from the human world that is inhabited by souls of the dead.

agriculture. Mode of farming in which special techniques make permanent cultivation of the same land possible.

Area (cultural). In this book, a cultural unit that encompasses numerous neighboring societies sharing numerous *modal patterns*. A subdivision of a *Zone*.

arranged marriage. A *marriage* chosen and negotiated by parents or other relatives of the couple to be married.

authority. The right to command the behavior of others, regarded as legitimate within a particular cultural tradition.

axe. A chopping tool in which the face of the blade is parallel to the handle.

band. A *community* that is regularly subdivided into mobile components. It is held together by a common area of land and extensive kinship ties.

band organization. A full band community may be called a *regional band* while the subgroups are often termed *local bands*. Band organization is particularly associated with *foragers*.

bargaining. Form of economic transaction in which participants must reach an agreement on the terms of exchange.

basketry. (1) Creation of various artifacts by intertwining fibers; (2) the artifacts themselves.

bilateral kinship. Recognition of relatives on both the mother's and the father's side. In the strict sense, a system that places almost equal emphasis on both sides in contrast to a system based on *unilineal descent*.

bride service. Subsistence and other tasks performed by a new or prospective husband for his in-laws in return for his wife. It lasted for a specified period of time, usually a year or several years and required matrilocal residence.

bridewealth. A gift or series of gifts from a prospective husband or his family to the family of the intended bride. Sometimes called "bride price."

bureaucracy. Governance by sets of officials specialized for the purpose. The term is also used for the officials themselves. The concept of bureaucracy is closely associated with the definition of the *state*.

camp. A temporary settlement (lasting for a few days or weeks), marked by relatively flimsy shelters.

ceramics. (1) Production of various artifacts from clay, usually hardening them by firing; (2) the artifacts themselves.

chief. A leader of an aggregation of communities whose office is accessible only through heredity and entails special duties and privileges. A hereditary chief automatically inherits the office while an elective chief is chosen from among members of a particular kinship group. An appointed chief is a subordinate selected by one of the other kinds of chief. A chief has *authority* but may have little *power*.

chiefdom. A multicommunity political unit in which a single *chief* is the highest authority.

chieftain. Single highest leader of a community or subdivision of a community (such as a kinship group, neighborhood, or faction). The position entails multiple functions (vs. *situational leader*). There may or may not be a permanent office. If there is, it may or may not have a hereditary component.

childhood. The period of an individual's life between *infancy* and *adolescence*, marked by increasing imposition of social restrictions and responsibilities (very roughly six to thirteen years).

cicatrization.   Scarification of the body for esthetic or symbolic reasons.

clan.   A *unilineal descent* group in which not all members know their exact relationships with each other and, therefore, some consider themselves relatives solely on the basis of descent from the common ancestor that founded the clan.

community.   A relatively stable residential or territorial group, composed of more than one family, in which members regularly interact face to face. Includes *band, village,* and *neighborhood.*

concubine.   A female *slave* kept specifically for sexual and/or reproductive purposes. Concubines sometimes provided affection and companionship.

conquest.   Decisive victory in *warfare* that results in some kind of economic and/or political domination.

corporate group.   Group of relatives or nonrelatives that share in control over some kind of property.

cross-cousin.   Offspring of a person's parent's opposite-sex sibling; i.e., father's sister's offspring or mother's brother's offspring.

culture hero.   A (usually supernatural) being who provided humans with one or more essential features of life, such as fire, crops, or moral values.

digging stick.   A long stick with a sharpened end, a simple but extremely versatile tool used for digging and many other purposes.

divination.   Acquisition of information by supernatural means.

Domain (cultural).   The largest cultural units discussed in this book, each based on a few significant *modal patterns.* The Domains are the New World, the Old World, and Oceania.

dugout canoe.   Boat made by chopping out the interior of a log.

dwelling.   Roofed structure used for sleeping and other domestic purposes.

egalitarian.   Providing relatively equal opportunity for all members of the group in question to achieve desirable statuses. This characteristic is usually heavily qualified by gender, meaning that male statuses are about equally available for all males and likewise among females.

empire.   A political entity established when one polity conquers and controls others; characteristic of *chiefdoms* and *states.* The degree of control varies from a few tributary requirements to total administration. If the conquered polity is completely incorporated into the conqueror's system, then it has become part of the (conquering) state.

ethnicity.   Identification of a subcultural group based on external markers such as language, religion, or physical features.

exchange.   A transaction of goods and/or services.

exogamy.   Marriage to someone from outside a group.

extended family.   *See* family.

external trade.   Exchange between individuals belonging to different *communities.*

family.   Related people who live in the same *household* or nearby and cooperate on a regular basis. A nuclear family is composed of parents and offspring. An extended family is composed of more than one nuclear family.

farming.   Cultivation of crops. *See* agriculture and horticulture.

feast.   Ritualized communal meal to mark a special occasion.

festival.   A period of celebration set apart from ordinary life; often associated with major religious ceremonies, but also including various forms of recreation.

fields.   Cultivated areas outside a village, used for one or more staple and other important crops.

fishing.   Capture of fish by any of a wide variety of methods.

focal state.   A *state* that has only one center of population and power.

foragers.   People whose subsistence depends entirely on undomesticated food sources. Often referred to as hunter-gatherers or gatherer-hunters, alternatives that are enmeshed in an argument inspired by political correctness. More important, both of those terms slight the importance of fishing to many such people.

gardens.   Fairly small cultivated areas used for something other than staple crops. Some secondary crops and/or other plants are grown in a kitchen garden. A decorative garden is intended to beautify its location.

gathering.   Regular collection of wild plants for subsistence and other purposes.

ghost.   A *soul* or some other spiritual component of a human being that survives physical death and remains in the vicinity of living humans. Ghosts may be evil, neutral, or beneficent.

god.   An individualized and named supernatural being with substantial powers and usually headquartered in some realm other than the surface of the earth (*see* spirit). Spelled with a capital letter, God is the only god in a particular belief system or is in some way far superior to all the others.

hamlet.   A spatially distinct subdivision of a village. In contrast to *neighborhoods,* there is significant physical space between hamlets of the same village.

hearth.   A domestic fire enclosed by stones. More generally, any fire that played a central role in domestic life.

horticulture.   Simple farming methods that eventually exhausted the soil and required people to move to another location.

household.   People living together in a single dwelling or compound and cooperating for subsistence and other tasks.

hunting.   Vigorous pursuit and killing of large and/or elusive animals.

incest taboo.   Customary rule prohibiting sex between particular relatives.

infancy.   The earliest stage of life, up to about three years, ending with the completion of toilet training and weaning.

infanticide.   Killing of infants, usually newborns. Often done because the infants could not be supported.

influence.   The ability to modify the behavior of other people without coercion or official position. Influence usually comes from some combination of intellect, skill, rectitude, and force of personality.

kin.   Relatives of all kinds; a broader term than *family*. The term kin group refers to any relatives who are explicitly linked as a group, e.g., a *family* or a *lineage*.

king.   The head of a *state* who is made eligible by inheritance. As with a *chief*, accession may be direct or elective. The status of king is in other ways much like that of a chief, though it usually entails more *power* and *authority*. In addition, a king is more likely to face usurpations by others with valid or false claims to the position.

kinship terminology.   Words and concepts used by the individual in a culture to identify his or her personal relatives.

law.   Formal code of behavior, whether written or unwritten.

lineage.   A *unilineal descent* group in which all members know their exact kin relationships with all other members.

local bands.   Fluid subdivisions of a *regional band;* a component of *band organization*.

loincloth.   A brief garment that wraps around the waist and covers at least the pubic area.

magic.   Ritualized acts intended to produce an automatic result by compelling supernatural beings or impersonal forces.

marriage.   Relationship between a man and a woman based on economic cooperation and the production and support of children.

midwife.   Birth attendant with a great deal of experience, sometimes a professional.

mobilization.   Form of economic transaction in which a central authority collects units of value (money, food, etc.) from a population and then uses the wealth for its own purposes.

modal pattern.   The most common form of a cultural trait within a given cultural unit (*Domain, Zone, Area,* or *Region*).

mythology.   Stories about ancient beings, mostly supernatural, that explain how the world came to be as it is and justify various cultural practices.

neighborhood.   Subdivision of a large village, town, or city. An area that constitutes a *community*.

nuclear family.   *See* family.

offering.   Any object ritually presented to a supernatural being, even if consumed by humans afterward.

parallel cousin.   Offspring of a person's parent's same-sex sibling; i.e., father's brother's offspring or mother's sister's offspring.

paramount chief.   A *chief* who has the single highest rank in a political unit in which subdivisions are also headed by chiefs.

patrilocal residence.   Residence of a married couple with or near the husband's family.

peasants.   Farmers who support a *chiefdom* or *state* while being partially isolated from the centers of *power* and culture. They are unavoidably affected by central concerns such as taxes and conscription but have limited knowledge of or control over such processes.

political.   Having to do with internal social control or external social relations of a social unit.

polygyny.   Marriage of one man to more than one woman. By far the most common form of polygamy.

postpartum sex taboo.   Customary period of celibacy for a woman after giving birth.

power.   The ability to coerce the behavior of others. It may or may not be regarded as legitimate (*see* authority).

priest.   An individual who acts as the ritual leader of a group, guiding the members in worship or appeal to supernatural forces or interceding on their behalf. "Priest" is a distinct social status in many cultures, but the role may be filled by someone else, such as a *shaman* or a political leader.

raiding.   Isolated attacks made by relatively small and loosely coordinated parties.

rank.   A position of individual superiority or inferiority with respect to other individuals. It may be hereditary or achieved.

reciprocity.   Economic transaction in which the nature and amount given is determined by cultural traditions.

redistribution.   Economic transaction in which a central authority collects (or otherwise controls) valuables from a population (money, food, etc.) and returns the same valuables to the same population in some way.

Region (cultural).   In this book, a cultural unit within an *Area* that can be identified by *modal patterns*.

regional band.   A *community* that is regularly dispersed into fluid subgroups; a component of *band organization*.

regional state.   A *state* with more than one major urban center within a continuous area.

remnant state.   Small statelike polity (usually one of several) resulting from the disintegration of a full-fledged *state*.

ritual clown.   A performer in a ceremony who feigns erroneous, immoral, sacrilegious, and disgusting acts.

sacrifice.   An *offering* in the form of the death of an animal, including a human.

serf.   A farmer bound by law or custom to an area of land owned by another person and required to compensate the owner with produce.

servant.   A person who regularly performed domestic services for others. Some were *slaves* while others worked for wages or to discharge a more general obligation for service such as *tax* or *tribute*.

sexual division of labor.   Customary assignment of tasks primarily or entirely to one sex or the other.

shaman.   A religious practitioner with powers derived from direct contact with supernatural forces, usually one or more familiar *spirits*. Typically the contact is made while in a *trance*. The most common purpose of shamans is to heal afflicted individuals. Often they perform other services for individuals, e.g., *divination*.

shifting cultivation.   A pattern of farming in which the community must move from time to time in order to leave an area of exhausted fields to regenerate.

situational leader.   An individual who has assumed leadership of a particular activity (e.g., a raid or a hunt), usually because he or she is thought to have some special expertise in the matter.

slash-and-burn.   A pattern of farming in which a field is cleared and fertilized by cutting down natural vegetation and burning it.

slave.   A person whose labor is owned by someone else. In the extreme case of chattel slavery, the body is also owned and the slave can be bought or sold like an inanimate object.

sorcerer.   A human who used supernatural power to harm other people, often for profit. The *witch* constitutes a subcategory characterized by innate power requiring little ritual action.

soul.   A spiritual essence that may leave the body during life (e.g. in dreams) and after death.

spirit.   A supernatural being with limited powers and limited individuality, often a nameless member of a general category of such beings, and often tied to a particular locality. In some cases the distinction between spirit and *god* is not clear.

state.   A political unit that, regardless of the structure of higher leadership, has a *bureaucracy* as its foundation.

state religion.   Hierarchically organized religion that is intertwined with the government of a *state*.

stratification.   Division of a society into several layers, often referred to as classes. Stratification may involve little more than prestige (as in some *chiefdoms*), or it may involve extensive differentiation (as in most *states*).

tattoo.   Design on the body created by inserting a substance, usually soot, under the skin.

tax.   A regular payment owed by citizens to a ruler or government. May be rendered in goods, services, or money (contrast with *tribute*).

traditional culture.   In this book, a non-Western culture as it existed just before drastic alteration by European colonialism.

trance.   An altered state of consciousness in which the trancer makes contact with the supernatural. One kind is the communication trance, in which information is transferred between human and supernatural. The other is possession trance, in which the supernatural entity takes control of the human's body, often speaking through the trancer to other humans.

tribe.   A political unit composed of more than one *community*. A tribe can be a *chiefdom* although many tribes are relatively *egalitarian*.

tribute.   A regular payment owed by a conquered society or its people to the conquering ruler or government. May be rendered in goods, services, or money (contrast with *tax*).

trickster.   A mythological being devoted to satisfying lust, gluttony, and greed, and making mischief for other beings (including humans). Some tricksters are also *culture heroes*. Lesser tricksters appear in some nonmythological stories.

unilineal descent.   Affiliation with ancestors and a living group on the basis of inheritance through one sex only. In patrilineal descent (by far the most common) males transmit affiliation, and in matrilineal descent females transmit affiliation.

village.   A *community* that is relatively stable with regard to location and composition. Some villages exist for centuries, but others last for only a few months (in the latter case the village is usually one phase in the annual cycle of a regional *band*).

warfare.   Organized fighting between independent political units of any size (ranging from *community* to *state*).

weir.   An enclosure, usually of wood or stone, that traps fish or guides them to a particular spot.

Western culture.   The cultures of Europe and their offshoots, such as the United States.

witch.   A kind of sorcerer that possessed innate power to do supernatural harm. As a result witches used little magical ritual. Witches also tended to be evil in the sense of doing harm for its own sake, while the acts of other sorcerers were directed toward ultimate goals such as profit or revenge.

Zone (cultural).   In this book, a large cultural unit in which diverse cultures display some significant *modal patterns*. A subdivision of a *Domain*.

Bibliography

General

Andrews, Anthony P. 1983. *Maya Salt Production and Trade*. Tucson: University of Arizona Press.

Aveni, Anthony F. 1993. *Ancient Astronomers*. Montreal: St. Remy Press.

Barber, Elizabeth Wayland. 1994. *Women's Work*. New York: W. W. Norton.

Barfield, Thomas J. 1993. *The Nomadic Alternative*. Englewood Cliffs, NJ: Prentice-Hall.

Bates, Daniel G. 1998. *Human Adaptive Strategies*. Needham Heights, MA: Allyn and Bacon.

Betzig, Laura. 1989. Causes of Conjugal Dissolution: A Cross-Cultural Study. *Current Anthropology* 30:654–676.

Bodley, John H. 1997. *Cultural Anthropology: Tribes, States, and the Global System*, 2nd ed. Mountain View, CA: Mayfield

Bourguignon, Erika, and Greenbaum, Lenora S. 1973. *Diversity and Homogeneity in World Societies*. New Haven, CT: HRAF Press.

Brain, Robert. 1979. *The Decorated Body*. New York: Harper & Row.

Broude, Gwen J. 1995. *Growing Up: A Cross-cultural Encyclopedia*. Santa Barbara, CA: ABC-CLIO.

Brown, Donald E. 1991. *Human Universals*. Philadelphia: Temple University Press.

Buckley, Thomas, and Gottlieb, Alma (eds.). 1988. *Blood Magic*. Berkeley: University of California Press.

Caras, Roger A. 1996. *A Perfect Harmony*. New York: Fireside.

Child, Alice B., and Child, Irvin L. 1993. *Religion and Magic in the Life of Traditional Peoples*. Englewood Cliffs, NJ: Prentice-Hall.

Christen, Kimberly A. 1998. *Clowns and Tricksters, an Encyclopedia of Tradition and Culture*. Santa Barbara, CA: ABC-CLIO.

Counts, Dorothy A., and Counts, David R. 1985. Introduction to Dorothy A. Counts and David R. Counts (eds.), *Aging and Its Transformations*. Pittsburgh, PA: University of Pittsburgh Press.

Critchfield, Richard. 1983. *Villages*. New York: Anchor.

Davies, Nigel. 1981. *Human Sacrifice*. New York: Dorset.

Drescher, Seymour, and Engerman, Stanley L. (eds.). 1998. *A Historical Guide to World Slavery*. New York: Oxford University Press.

Duley, Margot I., and Edwards, Mary I. (eds.). 1986. *The Cross-cultural Study of Women*. New York: Feminist Press.

Earhart, H. Byron (ed.). 1993. *Religious Traditions of the World*. New York: HarperCollins.

Earle, Timothy. 1997. *How Chiefs Come to Power*. Stanford, CA: Stanford University Press.

——— (ed.). 1991. *Chiefdoms: Power, Economy, and Ideology*. New York: Cambridge University Press.

Ebin, Victoria. 1979. *The Body Decorated*. New York: Thames and Hudson.

Eliade, Mircea. 1964. *Shamanism*. Princeton, NJ: Princeton University Press.

Ember, Carol, and Ember, Melvin. 1999. *Cultural Anthropology*. Upper Saddle River, NJ: Prentice-Hall.

Fagan, Brian M., et al. (eds.). 1996. *The Oxford Companion to Archaeology*. New York: Oxford University Press.

Feinman, Gary M., and Marcus, Joyce (eds.). 1998. *Archaic States*. Santa Fe, NM: School of American Research.

Frayser, Suzanne G. 1985. *Varieties of Human Experience: An Anthropological Perspective on Human Sexuality*. New Haven, CT: HRAF Press.

Gamst, Frederick C. 1974. *Peasants in Complex Society*. New York: Holt, Rinehart, and Winston.

Habenstein, Robert W., and Lamers, William M. 1974. *Funeral Customs the World Over*, 3rd ed. Milwaukee, WI: Bullfin.

Hynes, William J., and Doty, William G. (eds.). 1993. *Mythical Trickster Figures*. Tuscaloosa: University of Alabama Press.

Ingold, Tim, Riches, David, and Woodburn, James (eds.). 1991. *Hunters and Gatherers*. 2 vols. New York: Berg.

Jankowiak, William (ed.). 1995. *Romantic Passion*. New York: Columbia University Press.

Johnson, Dennis. 1995. *Tropical Palms*. Rome: Food and Agriculture Organization of the United Nations.

Jordan, Michael. 1993. *Myths of the World*. London: Kyle Cathie.

Karolyi, Otto. 1998. *Traditional African & Oriental Music*. New York: Penguin.

Konner, Melvin. 1991. *Childhood*. Boston: Little Brown.

Lefkowitz, Mary. 1996. *Not Out of Africa*. New York: Basic.

Levinson, David. 1989. *Family Violence in Cross-cultural Perspective*. Newbury Park, CA: Sage.

———. 1994. *Ethnic Relations: A Cross-cultural Encyclopedia*. Santa Barbara, CA: ABC-CLIO.

———. 1995. *Human Environments: A Cross-cultural Encyclopedia*. Santa Barbara, CA: ABC-CLIO.

———, and Christensen, Karen (eds.). 1996. *Encyclopedia of World Sport: From Ancient Times to the Present*. New York: Oxford University Press.

————, and Ember, Melvin (eds.). 1996. *Encyclopedia of Cultural Anthropology.* 4 vols. New York: Henry Holt.

Malm, William P. 1967. *Music Cultures of the Pacific, the Near East, and Asia.* Englewood Cliffs, NJ: Prentice-Hall.

Metcalf, Peter, and Huntington, Richard. 1991. *Celebrations of Death,* 2nd ed. New York: Cambridge University Press.

Morgen, Sandra (ed.). 1989. *Gender and Anthropology.* Washington, DC: American Anthropological Association.

Newton, Douglas, Jones, Julie, and Ezra, Kate. 1987. *The Pacific Islands, Africa, and the Americas.* New York: Metropolitan Museum of Art.

Nichols, Deborah L., and Charlton, Thomas H. (eds.). 1997. *The Archaeology of City-States.* Washington, DC: Smithsonian.

North, Jane, and North, Steve. n.d. Tattoo History Source Book. *Tatoos.Com* (ezine).

Nowak, Ronald M. 1999. *Walker's Mammals of the World,* 6th ed. 2 vols. Baltimore, MD: Johns Hopkins University Press.

Palgi, Phyllis, and Abramovitch, Henry. 1984. Death: A Cross-Cultural Perspective. *Annual Reviews in Anthropology* 13:385–417.

Rubin, Arnold (ed.). 1988. *Marks of Civilization.* Los Angeles: Museum of Cultural History, University of California.

Schlegel, Alice, and Barry, Herbert, III. 1991. *Adolescence: An Anthropological Inquiry.* New York: Free Press.

Scupin, Raymond. 1995. *Cultural Anthropology,* 2nd ed. Englewood Cliffs, NJ: Prentice-Hall.

———— (ed.). 2000. *Religion and Culture: An Anthropological Focus.* Upper Saddle River, NJ: Prentice-Hall.

Seaman, Gary, and Day, Jane S. (eds.). 1994. *Ancient Traditions: Shamanism in Central Asia and the Americas.* Niwot: University Press of Colorado.

Service, Elman R. 1971. *Primitive Social Organization,* 2nd ed. New York: Random House.

————. 1978. *Profiles in Ethnology,* 3rd ed. New York: Harper & Row.

Short, John Rennie (ed.). 1992. *Human Settlement.* New York: Oxford University Press.

Sjoberg, Gideon. 1960. *The Preindustrial City.* New York: Free Press.

Smart, Ninian. 1998. *The World's Religions,* 2nd ed. New York: Cambridge University Press.

Southall, Aidan. 1998. *The City in Space and Time.* New York: Cambridge University Press.

Stone, Linda. 1997. *Kinship and Gender.* Boulder, CO: Westview.

Strauss, Neil. 1998, May 27. Girl Power Is Squelched. *New York Times,* E2.

Strouthes, Daniel P. 1995. *Law and Politics: A Cross-cultural Encyclopedia.* Santa Barbara, CA: ABC-CLIO.

Suggs, David N., and Miracle, Andrew W. (eds.). 1993. *Culture and Human Sexuality.* Pacific Grove, CA: Brooks/Cole.

Sullivan, Lawrence E. (ed.). 1989. *Death, Afterlife, and the Soul.* New York: Macmillan.

Trevathan, Wenda. 1987. *Human Birth: An Evolutionary Perspective.* New York: Aldine de Gruyter.

Weiner, Annette B., and Schneider, Jane (eds.). 1989. *Cloth and Human Experience.* Washington, DC: Smithsonian.

Wilkins, Sally. 2002. *Sports and Games of Medieval Cultures.* Westport, CT: Greenwood.

Willis, Roy (ed.). 1993. *World Mythology.* New York: Henry Holt.

Winthrop, Robert H. 1991. *Dictionary of Concepts in Cultural Anthropology.* Westport, CT: Greenwood.

Wolf, Eric R. 1966. *Peasants.* Englewood Cliffs, NJ: Prentice-Hall.

The New World

Adams, E. Charles. 1991. *The Origin and Development of the Pueblo Katsina Cult.* Tucson: University of Arizona Press.

Adams, Richard E. W. 1991. *Prehistoric Mesoamerica.* Norman: University of Oklahoma Press.

————. 1997. *Ancient Civilizations of the New World.* Boulder, CO: Westview.

Albers, Patricia C. 1989. From Illusion to Illumination: Anthropological Studies of American Indian Women. In Sandra Morgen (ed.), *Gender and Anthropology.* Washington, DC: American Anthropological Association.

Allaire, Louis. 1999. Archaeology of the Caribbean Region. In Frank Salomon and Stuart B. Schwartz (eds.), *South America, Part 1.* Vol. 3 of *Cambridge History of the Native Peoples of the Americas.* New York: Cambridge University Press.

Allen, Catherine J. 1988. *The Hold Life Has: Coca and Cultural Identity in an Andean Community.* Washington, DC: Smithsonian.

Arens, W. 1979. *The Man-eating Myth.* New York: Oxford University Press.

Ascher, Marcia, and Ascher, Robert. 1997. *Mathematics of the Incas.* New York: Dover.

Axtell, James (ed.). 1981. *The Indian Peoples of Eastern America.* New York: Oxford University Press.

Baldwin, Gordon C. 1973. *Indians of the Southwest.* New York: Capricorn.

Basso, Ellen B. 1988. *The Kalapalo Indians of Central Brazil.* Prospect Heights, IL: Waveland Press.

Bauer, Brian S. 1992. *The Development of the Inca State.* Austin: University of Texas Press.

————. 1998. *The Sacred Landscape of the Inca, the Cusco Ceque System.* Austin: University of Texas Press.

————, and Dearborn, David S. P. 1995. *Astronomy and Empire in the Ancient Andes.* Austin: University of Texas Press.

Bean, Lowell John. 1976. Power and Its Applications in Native California. In Lowell John Bean and Thomas C. Blackburn (eds.), *Native Californians: A Theoretical Perspective.* Socorro, NM: Ballena.

————. 1978. Social Organization. In Robert F. Heizer (ed.), *California.* Vol. 8 of *Handbook of North American Indians.* Washington, DC: Smithsonian.

————, and Blackburn, Thomas C. (eds.). 1976. *Native Californians: A Theoretical Perspective.* Socorro, NM: Ballena.

Beckman, Tad. 1996. *Indians of the Great Basin.* http://www4.hmc.edu:800.

————. *The View from Native California: Lifeways of California's Indigenous People.* http://www4.hmc.edu:800.

Berdan, Frances F. 1982. *The Aztecs of Central Mexico.* New York: Holt, Rinehart, and Winston.

Berlo, Janet C., and Phillips, Ruth B. 1998. *Native North American Art.* New York: Oxford University Press.

Bierhorst, John. 1979. *A Cry from the Earth.* Santa Fe, NM: Ancient City.

————. 1985. *The Mythology of North America.* New York: William Morrow.

————. 1988. *The Mythology of South America.* New York: William Morrow.

Bingham, Marjorie Wall, and Gross, Susan Hill. 1986. *Women in Latin America.* St. Louis Park, MN: Glenhurst.

Blanton, Richard E., et al. 1993. *Ancient Mesoamerica.* New York: Cambridge University Press.

Borrero, Luis Alberto. 1997. The Origins of Ethnographic Subsistence Patterns in Fuego-Patagonia. In Colin McEwan et al. (eds.), *Patagonia.* Princeton, NJ: Princeton University Press.

Bragdon, Kathleen J. 1996. *Native People of Southern New England, 1500–1650.* Norman: University of Oklahoma Press.

Braun, Barbara (ed.). 1995. *Arts of the Amazon.* London: Thames and Hudson.

Bray, Warwick. 1987. *Everyday Life of the Aztecs.* New York: Dorset.

Brody, Hugh. 1987. *Living Arctic: Hunters of the Canadian North.* Seattle: University of Washington Press.

Bruhns, Karen Olson. 1994. *Ancient South America.* New York: Cambridge University Press.

Burland, Cottie. 1996. *North American Indian Mythology.* New York: Barnes & Noble.

Calero, Luis F. 1997. *Chiefdoms Under Siege.* Albuquerque: University of New Mexico Press.

Callaway, Donald G., Janetski, Joel C., and Stewart, Omer C. 1986. Ute. In Warren L. D'Azevedo (ed.), *Great Basin.* Vol. 11 of *Handbook of North American Indians.* Washington, DC: Smithsonian.

Callender, Charles, and Kochems, Lee M. 1993. The North American Berdache. In David M. Suggs and Andrew W. Miracle (eds.), *Culture and Human Sexuality.* Pacific Grove, CA: Brooks/Cole.

Carmack, Robert M. 1996. Mesoamerica at Spanish Contact. In Robert M. Carmack et al. (eds.), *The Legacy of Mesoamerica.* Upper Saddle River, NJ: Prentice-Hall.

————, Gasco, Janine, and Gossen, Gary H. (eds.). 1996. *The Legacy of Mesoamerica.* Upper Saddle River, NJ: Prentice-Hall.

Carneiro, Robert. 1990. Chiefdom-level Warfare as Exemplified in Fiji and the Cauca Valley. In Jonathan Haas (ed.), *The Anthropology of War.* New York: Cambridge University Press.

Carrasco, Davíd. 1998. Religions of Mesoamerica. In H. Byron Earhart (ed.), *Religious Traditions of the World.* New York: HarperCollins, 1990. Reprint, Prospect Heights, IL: Waveland Press.

Carrasco, Pedro. 1982. The Political Economy of the Aztec and Inca States. In George A. Collier et al. (eds.), *The Inca and Aztec States, 1400–1800.* New York: Academic.

Chagnon, Napoleon. 1997. *Yanomamo,* 5th ed. Fort Worth, TX: Harcourt Brace Jovanovich.

Chapman, Anne. 1982. *Drama and Power in a Hunting Society.* Cambridge: Cambridge University Press.

————. 1997. The Great Ceremonies of the Selk'nam and the Yamana. In Colin McEwan et al. (eds.), *Patagonia.* Princeton, NJ: Princeton University Press.

Chase, Diane Z., and Chase, Arlen R. 1992. *Mesoamerican Elites.* Norman: University of Oklahoma Press.

Classen, Constance. 1993. *Inca Cosmology and the Human Body.* Salt Lake City: University of Utah Press.

Clastres, Hélène. 1995. *The Land-Without-Evil.* Urbana: University of Illinois Press.

Coe, Michael D. 1993. *The Maya,* 5th ed. New York: Thames and Hudson.

————. 1994. *Mexico,* 4th ed. New York: Thames and Hudson.

Coe, Sophie D. 1994. *America's First Cuisines.* Austin: University of Texas Press.

Collier, George A. 1982. Introduction to George A. Collier et al. (eds.), *The Inca and Aztec States, 1400–1800.* New York: Academic.

————, Rosaldo, Renato I., and Wirth, John (eds.). 1982. *The Inca and Aztec States, 1400–1800.* New York: Academic.

Conklin, Beth. 2001. *Consuming Grief: Compassionate Cannibalism in an Amazonian Society.* Austin: University of Texas Press.

Crocker, William, and Crocker, Jean. 1994. *The Canela.* Fort Worth, TX: Harcourt Brace.

Culin, Stewart. 1992. *Games of the North American Indians.* 2 vol. Lincoln: University of Nebraska Press.

Damas, David (ed.). 1984. *Arctic.* Vol. 5 of *Handbook of North American Indians.* Washington, DC: Smithsonian.

Davies, Nigel. 1995. *The Incas.* Niwot: University Press of Colorado.

D'Azevedo, Warren L. (ed.). 1986. *Great Basin.* Vol. 11 of *Handbook of North American Indians.* Washington, DC: Smithsonian.

de Rios, Marlene. [1990] 1996. *Hallucinogens.* Prospect Heights, IL: Waveland Press.

Dole, Gertrude E. [1974] 1985. Endocannibalism Among the Amahuaca Indians. In Patricia J. Lyon (ed.), *Native South Americans: Ethnology of the Least Known Continent.* Prospect Heights, IL: Waveland Press.

Donald, Leland. 1997. *Aboriginal Slavery on the Northwest Coast of North America.* Berkeley: University of California Press.

Dozier, Edward P. [1970] 1983. *The Pueblo Indians of North America.* Prospect Heights, IL: Waveland Press.

Driver, Harold. 1969. *Indians of North America.* Chicago: University of Chicago Press.

Drucker, Philip. 1963. *Indians of the Northwest Coast.* Garden City, NY: Natural History.

Dye, David H., and Cox, Cheryl Anne. 1990. *Towns and Temples Along the Mississippi.* Tuscaloosa: University of Alabama Press.

Fabian, Stephen Michael. 1992. *Space-Time of the Bororo of Brazil.* Gainesville: University Press of Florida.

Fagan, Brian M. 1991. *Kingdoms of Gold, Kingdoms of Jade.* New York: Thames and Hudson.

————. 1995. *Ancient North America.* New York: Thames and Hudson.

Feder, Kenneth L. 1996. *Frauds, Myths, and Mysteries.* Mountain View, CA: Mayfield.

Feest, Christian F. 1993. The Pervasive World of Arts. In Alvin M. Josephy (ed.), *America in 1492.* New York: Vintage.

Flannery, Kent V., Marcus, Joyce, and Reynolds, Robert G. 1989. *The Flocks of the Wamani.* New York: Academic.

Fowler, Catherine S., and Liljeblad, Sven. 1986. Northern Paiute. In Warren L. D'Azevedo (ed.), Vol. 11 of *Handbook of North American Indians.* Washington, DC: Smithsonian.

Fowler, William R., Jr. 1989. *The Cultural Evolution of Ancient Nahua Civilizations.* Norman: University of Oklahoma Press.

Furst, Peter T. (ed.). [1972] 1990. *Flesh of the Gods.* Prospect Heights, IL: Waveland Press.

Gabriel, Kathryn. 1996. *Gambler Way.* Boulder, CO: Johnson.

Garbarino, Merwin S., and Sasso, Robert F. 1994. *Native American Heritage,* 3rd ed. Prospect Heights, IL: Waveland Press.

Gill, Sam D. 1993. Religious Forms and Themes. In Alvin M. Josephy (ed.), *America in 1492.* New York: Vintage.

———, and Sullivan, Irene F. 1992. *Dictionary of Native American Mythology.* New York: Oxford University Press.

Goldman, Irving. 1963. *The Cubeo.* Illinois Studies in Anthropology, no. 2. Urbana: University of Illinois Press.

Gossen, Gary H. (ed.). 1986. *Symbol and Meaning Beyond the Closed Community.* Albany: State University of New York Press.

———. 1997. *South and Meso-American Native Spirituality.* New York: Crossroad.

Graham, Mark Miller (ed.). 1993. *Reinterpreting Prehistory of Central America.* Niwot: University Press of Colorado.

Gregor, Thomas. 1985. *Anxious Pleasures: The Sexual Lives of an Amazonian People.* Chicago: University of Chicago Press.

Grieder, Terence. 1993. A Global View of Central America. In Mark Miller Graham (ed.), *Reinterpreting Prehistory of Central America.* Niwot: University Press of Colorado.

Griffen, William B. 1983. Southern Periphery: East. In Alfonso Ortiz (ed.), *Southwest.* Vol. 10 of *Handbook of North American Indians.* Washington, DC: Smithsonian.

Harner, Michael J. 1972. *The Jivaro.* Garden City, NY: Anchor.

———. 1977. The Ecological Basis for Aztec Sacrifice. *American Ethnologist* 4(1): 117–135.

Hassig, Ross. 1988. *Aztec Warfare.* Norman: University of Oklahoma Press.

———. 1992. *War and Society in Ancient Mesoamerica.* Berkeley: University of California Press.

Heizer, Robert F. (ed.). 1978. *California.* Vol. 8 of *Handbook of North American Indians.* Washington, DC: Smithsonian.

Helm, June (ed.). 1981. *Subarctic.* Vol. 6 of *Handbook of North American Indians.* Washington, DC: Smithsonian.

Helms, Mary W. 1979. *Ancient Panama.* Austin: University of Texas Press.

Hill, Kim, and Hurtado, A. Magdalena. 1996. *Ache Life History.* Hawthorne, NY: Aldine de Gruyter.

Hill, Robert M. 1992. *Colonial Cakchiquels.* Fort Worth, TX: Harcourt Brace.

———, and Monaghan, John. 1987. *Continuities in Highland Maya Social Organization.* Philadelphia: University of Pennsylvania Press.

Hodge, Mary G., and Smith, Michael E. (eds.). 1994. *Economies and Polities in the Aztec Realm.* Albany: State University of New York Press.

Hudson, Charles. 1976. *The Southeastern Indians.* Knoxville: University of Tennessee Press.

Hultkrantz, Åke. 1979. *The Religions of the American Indians.* Berkeley: University of California Press.

Huxley, Francis. 1966. *Affable Savages.* New York: Capricorn.

Hyslop, John. 1990. *Inka Settlement Planning.* Austin: University of Texas Press.

Jacobs, Sue-Ellen, Thomas, Wesley, and Lang, Sabine. 1997. Introduction to Sue-Ellen Jacobs et al. (eds.), *Two-Spirit People.* Urbana: University of Illinois Press.

——— (eds.). 1997. *Two-Spirit People.* Urbana: University of Illinois Press.

Josephy, Alvin M. (ed.). 1993. *America in 1492.* New York: Vintage.

Karsten, Rafael. 1979. *Indian Tribes of the Argentine and Bolivian Gran Chaco.* New York: AMS (reprint).

Keegan, William F. 1992. *The People Who Discovered Columbus.* Gainesville: University Press of Florida.

Keeley, Lawrence H. 1996. *War Before Civilization.* New York: Oxford University Press.

Kehoe, Alice B. 1992. *North American Indians,* 2nd ed. Englewood Cliffs, NJ: Prentice-Hall.

Kelekna, Pita. 1994. Farming, Feuding and Female Status: The Achuar Case. In Anna Roosevelt (ed.), *Amazonian Indians from Prehistory to the Present.* Tucson: University of Arizona Press.

Kelly, Isabel T., and Fowler, Catherine S. 1986. Southern Paiute. In Warren L. D'Azevedo (ed.), *Great Basin.* Vol. 11 of *Handbook of North American Indians.* Washington, DC: Smithsonian.

Kendall, Ann. 1989. *Everyday Life of the Incas.* New York: Dorset.

Kensinger, Kenneth M. 1995. *How Real People Ought to Live: The Cashinahua of Eastern Peru.* Prospect Heights, IL: Waveland Press.

Kidwell, Clara Sue. 1993. Systems of Knowledge. In Alvin M. Josephy (ed.), *America in 1492.* New York: Vintage.

Killion, Thomas W. (ed.). 1992. *Gardens of Prehistory.* Tuscaloosa: University of Alabama Press.

Klein, Laura F., and Ackerman, Lillian A. (eds.). 1995. *Women and Power in Native North America.* Norman: University of Oklahoma Press.

Knack, Martha C. 1995. The Dynamics of Southern Paiute Women's Roles. In Laura F. Klein and Lillian A. Ackerman (eds.), *Woman and Power in Native North America.* Norman: University of Oklahoma Press.

Kroeber, A. L. 1976. *Handbook of the Indians of California.* New York: Dover.

Kuznar, Lawrence A. 1995. *Awatimarka.* Fort Worth, TX: Harcourt Brace.

Lange, Frederick W. 1993. The Conceptual Structure in Lower Central American Studies: A Central American View. In Mark Miller Graham (ed.), *Reinterpreting Prehistory of Central America.* Niwot: University Press of Colorado.

———. 1996a. Gaps in Our Databases and Blanks in Our Syntheses: The Potential for Central American Archeology in the Twenty-first Century. In Frederick W. Lange (ed.), *Paths to Central American Prehistory.* Niwot: University Press of Colorado.

———. 1996b. *Paths to Central American Prehistory.* Niwot: University Press of Colorado.

Lantis, Margaret. 1984. Aleut. In David Damas (ed.), *Arctic.* Vol. 5 of *Handbook of North American Indians.* Washington, DC: Smithsonian.

Leeming, David, and Page, Jake. 1998. *The Mythology of Native North America.* Norman: University of Oklahoma Press.

Lery, Jean de. 1990. *History of a Voyage to the Land of Brazil.* Trans. Janet Whatley. Berkeley: University of California Press.

Liljeblad, Sven. 1986. Oral Tradition: Content and Style of Verbal Arts. In Warren L. D'Azevedo (ed.), *Great Basin.* Vol. 11 of *Handbook of North American Indians.* Washington, DC: Smithsonian.

Lockhart, James. 1992. *The Nahuas After the Conquest.* Stanford, CA: Stanford University Press.

Lowie, Robert H. 1948. The Tropical Forests: An Introduction. In Julian Steward (ed.), *Tropical Forest Tribes.* Vol. 3 of *Handbook of South American Indians.* Washington, DC: U.S. Government Printing Office.

Lyon, Patricia J. (ed.). [1974] 1985. *Native South Americans: Ethnology of the Least Known Continent.* Prospect Heights, IL: Waveland Press.

Malmstrom, Vincent H. 1997. *Cycles of the Sun, Mysteries of the Moon*. Austin: University of Texas Press.

Malpass, Michael A. 1996. *Daily Life in the Inca Empire*. Westport, CT: Greenwood.

Mason, Otis Tufton. 1988. *American Indian Basketry*. New York: Dover.

Maybury-Lewis, David. 1967. *Akwe-Shavante Society*. Oxford, UK: Clarendon.

——— (ed.). 1979. *Dialectical Societies*. Cambridge, MA: Harvard University Press.

McCafferty, Sharisse D., and McCafferty, Geoffrey G. 1996. Spinning and Weaving as Female Gender Identity in Post-Classic Mexico. In Margo Blum Scheville, Janet Catherine Berlo, and Edward B. Dwyer (eds.), *Textile Traditions of Mesoamerica and the Andes*. Austin: University of Texas Press.

McDowell, Jim. 1997. *Hamatsa, the Enigma of Cannibalism on the Pacific Northwest Coast*. Vancouver: Ronsdale Press.

McEwan, Colin, Borrero, Luis A., and Prieto, Alfredo (eds.). 1997. *Patagonia*. Princeton, NJ: Princeton University Press.

McMillan, Alan D. 1995. *Native Peoples and Cultures of Canada*, 2nd ed. Vancouver: Douglas & McIntyre.

Meggers, Betty. 1996. *Amazonia*, rev. ed. Washington, DC: Smithsonian.

Métraux, Alfred. 1948. The Tupinamba. In Julian Steward (ed.), *Tropical Forest Tribes*. Vol. 3 of *Handbook of South American Indians*. Washington, DC: U.S. Government Printing Office.

Miller, Jay. 1993. A Kinship of Spirit. In Alvin M. Josephy (ed.), *America in 1492*. New York: Vintage.

Miller, Mary, and Taube, Karl. 1993. *The Gods and Symbols of Ancient Mexico and the Maya*. London: Thames and Hudson.

Moran, Emilio F. 1993. *Through Amazonian Eyes*. Iowa City: University of Iowa Press.

Moseley, Michael E. 1992. *The Incas and Their Ancestors*. New York: Thames and Hudson.

Murdock, George P. [1974] 1985. South American Culture Areas. In Patricia J. Lyon (ed.), *Native South Americans: Ethnology of the Least Known Continent*. Prospect Heights, IL: Waveland Press.

Murphy, Yolanda, and Murphy, Robert F. 1985. *Women of the Forest*, 2nd ed. New York: Columbia University Press.

Nabokov, Peter, with Dean Snow. 1993. Farmers of the Woodlands. In Alvin M. Josephy (ed.), *America in 1492*. New York: Vintage.

Newcomb, William W., Jr. 1974. *North American Indians*. Pacific Palisades, CA: Goodyear.

Newson, Linda A. 1987. *Indian Survival in Colonial Nicaragua*. Norman: University of Oklahoma Press.

Nichols, Deborah L., and Charlton, Thomas H. (eds.). 1997. *The Archeology of City-States*. Washington, DC: Smithsonian.

Niethammer, Carolyn. 1977. *Daughters of the Earth*. New York: Collier.

Nimuendaju, Curt. 1967. *The Apinaye*. New York: Humanities Press (reprint).

Orlove, Benjamin S. 1981. Native Andean Pastoralists: Traditional Adaptations and Recent Changes. In Philip Carl Salzman (ed.), *Contemporary Nomadic and Pastoral Peoples: Africa and Latin America*. Studies in Third World Societies, no. 17. Williamsburg, VA: College of William and Mary.

Ortiz, Alfonso (ed.). 1979. *Southwest*. Vol. 9 of *Handbook of North American Indians*. Washington, DC: Smithsonian.

———. 1983. *Southwest*. Vol. 10 of *Handbook of North American Indians*. Washington: DC: Smithsonian.

Ortiz de Montellano, Bernard R. 1990. *Aztec Medicine, Health, and Nutrition*. New Brunswick, NJ: Rutgers University Press.

Oswalt, Wendell H. 1967. *Alaskan Eskimos*. Scranton, PA: Chandler.

Paper, Jordan. 1988. *Offering Smoke*. Moscow: University of Idaho Press.

Patterson, Thomas C. 1991. *The Inca Empire*. New York: Berg.

Pollard, Helen Perlstein. 1993. *Tariacuri's Legacy*. Norman: University of Oklahoma Press.

Porro, Antonio. 1994. Social Organization and Political Power in the Amazon Floodplain: The Ethnohistorical Sources. In Anna Roosevelt (ed.), *Amazonian Indians From Prehistory to the Present*. Tucson: University of Arizona Press.

Potter, Stephen R. 1993. *Commoners, Tribute, and Chiefs*. Charlottesville: University Press of Virginia.

Radin, Paul. 1969. *Indians of South America*. New York: Greenwood.

Ralegh, Sir Walter. 1997. *The Discoverie of the Large, Rich and Bewtiful Empyre of Guiana*. With commentary by Neil Whitehead. Norman: University of Oklahoma Press.

Redmond, Elsa M. 1994. *Tribal and Chiefly Warfare in South America*. Ann Arbor: Memoirs of the Museum of Anthropology, no. 28, University of Michigan.

———. 1998. Introduction to Elsa Redmond (ed.), *Chiefdoms and Chieftaincy in the Americas*. Gainesville: University Press of Florida.

——— (ed.). 1998. *Chiefdoms and Chieftaincy in the Americas*. Gainesville: University Press of Florida.

Restall, Matthew. 1997. *The Maya World*. Stanford, CA: Stanford University Press.

Ridington, Robin. 1991. Northern Hunters. In Alvin M. Josephy (ed.), *America in 1492*. New York: Vintage.

Rogers, Daniel J., and Smith, Bruce D. (eds.). 1995. *Mississippian Communities and Households*. Tuscaloosa: University of Alabama Press.

Rogers, Edward S., and Smith, James G. E. 1981. Environment and Culture in the Shield and Mackenzie Borderlands. In June Helm (ed.), *Subarctic*. Vol. 6 of *Handbook of North American Indians*. Washington, DC: Smithsonian.

Roosevelt, Anna. 1994. Amazonian Anthropology: Strategy for a New Synthesis. In Anna Roosevelt (ed.), *Amazonian Indians From Prehistory to the Present*. Tucson: University of Arizona Press.

——— (ed.). 1994. *Amazonian Indians From Prehistory to the Present*. Tucson: University of Arizona Press.

Roscoe, Will. 1998. *Changing Ones: Third and Fourth Genders in Native North America*. New York: St. Martin's Press.

Rosman, Abraham, and Rubel, Paula G. [1971] 1986. *Feasting with Mine Enemy: Rank and Exchange among Northwest Coast Societies*. Prospect Heights, IL: Waveland Press.

Rostworowski de Diez Canseco, Maria. 1999. *History of the Inca Realm*. New York: Cambridge University Press.

Rountree, Helen C. 1989. *The Powatan Indians of Virginia*. Norman: University of Oklahoma Press.

———, and Davidson, Thomas E. 1997. *Eastern Shore Indians of Virginia and Maryland*. Charlottesville: University Press of Virginia.

Rouse, Irving. 1992. *The Tainos*. New Haven, CT: Yale University Press.

Rowe, John Howland. 1946. *Inca Culture at the Time of the Spanish Conquest*. Washington, DC: U.S. Government Printing Office.

Russell, Howard S. 1980. *Indian New England Before the Mayflower.* Hanover, NH: University Press of New England.

Sabloff, Jeremy A. 1997. *The Cities of Ancient Mexico,* rev. ed. New York: Thames and Hudson.

Salomon, Frank, and Schwartz, Stuart B. (eds.). 1999. *South America, Part 1.* Vol. 3 of *Cambridge History of the Native Peoples of the Americas.* New York: Cambridge University Press.

Salzman, Philip Carl. 1981. *Contemporary Nomadic and Pastoral Peoples: Africa and Latin America.* Studies in Third World Societies, no. 17. Williamsburg, VA: College of William and Mary.

Scarborough, Vernon L., and Wilcox, David R. (eds.). 1991. *The Mesoamerican Ballgame.* Tucson: University of Arizona Press.

Schevill, Margot Blum, Berlo, Janet Catherine, and Dwyer, Edward B. (eds.), *Textile Traditions of Mesoamerica and the Andes.* Austin: University of Texas Press.

Schroeder, Susan, Wood, Stephanie, and Haskett, Robert (eds.). 1997. *Indian Women of Early Mexico.* Norman: University of Oklahoma Press.

Sharer, Robert J. 1994. *The Ancient Maya,* 5th ed. Stanford, CA: Stanford University Press.

Shein, Max. 1992. *The Precolumbian Child.* Culver City, CA: Labyrinthos.

Silverblatt, Irene. 1987. *Moon, Sun, and Witches.* Princeton, NJ: Princeton University Press.

Siskind, Janet. 1973. *To Hunt in the Morning.* New York: Oxford University Press.

Soustelle, Jacques. 1970. *Daily Life of the Aztecs.* Stanford, CA: Stanford University Press.

Steward, Julian (ed.). 1946. *The Marginal Tribes.* Vol. 1 of *Handbook of South American Indians.* Washington, DC: U.S. Government Printing Office.

———. 1948. *Tropical Forest Tribes.* Vol. 3 of *Handbook of South American Indians.* Washington, DC: U.S. Government Printing Office.

———. 1949. *The Comparative Ethnology of South American Indians.* Vol. 5 of *Handbook of South American Indians.* Washington, DC: U.S. Government Printing Office.

———, and Faron, Louis C. 1959. *Native Peoples of South America.* New York: McGraw-Hill.

Sturtevant, William C. 1998. Tupinamba Chiefdoms? In Elsa M. Redmond (ed.), *Chiefdoms and Chieftaincy in the Americas.* Gainesville: University Press of Florida.

Sullivan, Lawrence E. 1988. *Icanchu's Drum.* New York: Macmillan.

Suttles, Wayne (ed.). 1990. *Northwest Coast.* Vol. 7 of *Handbook of North American Indians.* Washington, DC: Smithsonian.

Swanton, John R. 1979. *The Indians of the Southeastern United States.* Washington, DC: Smithsonian (orig. 1946).

Taube, Karl. 1992. *The Major Gods of Ancient Yucatan.* Washington, DC: Dumbarton Oaks Research Laboratory.

———. 1993. *Aztec and Maya Myths.* Austin: University of Texas Press.

Townsend, Richard F. 1992. *The Aztecs.* New York: Thames and Hudson.

Trigger, Bruce G. 1990. *The Huron,* 2nd ed. Fort Worth, TX: Harcourt Brace Jovanovich.

———. 1993. *Early Civilizations.* Cairo: The American University in Cairo Press.

——— (ed.). 1978. *Northeast.* Vol. 15 of *Handbook of North American Indians.* Washington, DC: Smithsonian.

———, and Washburn, Wilcomb E. (eds.). 1996. *North America.* Vol. 1 of *The Cambridge History of the Native Peoples of the Americas.* New York: Cambridge University Press.

Underhill, Ruth Murray. 1965. *Red Man's Religion.* Chicago: University of Chicago Press.

———. 1971. *Red Man's America,* rev. ed. Chicago: University of Chicago Press.

Urton, Gary. 1999. *Inca Myths.* Austin: University of Texas Press.

Vanstone, James W. 1974. *Athapaskan Adaptations.* Chicago: Aldine.

Vennum, Thomas, Jr. 1994. *American Indian Lacrosse.* Washington, DC: Smithsonian.

Villamarin, Juan, and Villamarin, Judith. 1999. Chiefdoms. In Frank Salomon and Stuart B. Schwartz (eds.), *South America, Part 1.* Vol. 3 of *The Cambridge History of the Native Peoples of the Americas.* New York: Cambridge University Press.

Von Graeve, Bernard. 1989. *The Pacaa Nova.* Lewiston, NY: Broadview.

Von Hagen, Adriana, and Morris, Craig. 1998. *The Cities of the Ancient Andes.* New York: Thames and Hudson.

Walker, Deward E., Jr. (ed.). 1989. *Witchcraft and Sorcery of the American Native Peoples.* Moscow: University of Idaho Press.

Whitehead, Neil Lancelot. 1994. The Ancient Amerindian Polities of the Amazon, the Orinoco, and the Atlantic Coast: A Preliminary Analysis of Their Passage From Antiquity to Extinction. In Anna Roosevelt (ed.), *Amazonian Indians From Prehistory to the Present.* Tucson: University of Arizona Press.

Whitlock, Ralph. 1987. *Everyday Life of the Maya.* New York: Dorset.

Wilbert, Johannes. 1987. *Tobacco and Shamanism in South America.* New Haven, CT: Yale University Press.

Williams, Marc. 1995. Chiefly Compounds. In Daniel J. Rogers and Bruce D. Smith (eds.), *Mississippian Communities and Households.* Tuscaloosa: University of Alabama Press.

Williams, Walter L. 1986. *The Spirit and the Flesh.* Boston: Beacon.

Wilson, David J. 1999. *Indigenous South Americans of the Past and Present: An Ecological Perspective.* Boulder: Westview Press.

Wilson, Samuel M. 1990. *Hispaniola.* Tuscaloosa: University of Alabama Press.

——— (ed.). 1997. *The Indigenous Peoples of the Caribbean.* Gainesville: University Press of Florida.

Wust, Irmhild. 1994. The Eastern Bororo From an Archeological Perspective. In Anna Roosevelt (ed.), *Amazonian Indians From Prehistory to the Present.* Tucson: University of Arizona Press.

The Old World

Anagnost, Ann. 1986. Transformations of Gender in Modern China. In Sandra Morgen (ed.), *Gender and Anthropology.* Washington, DC: American Anthropological Association.

Anonymous. 1987. *A Handbook of Korea.* Seoul: Seoul International.

Balikci, Asen. [1970] 1989. *The Netsilik Eskimo.* Prospect Heights, IL: Waveland Press.

Bartholomew, Alan A. 1995. Turks. In John Middleton and Amal Rassam (eds.), *Africa and the Middle East.* Vol. 9 of *Encyclopedia of World Cultures.* Boston: G. K. Hall.

Bascom, William R., and Herskovits, Melville J. (eds.). 1959. *Continuity and Change in African Cultures.* Chicago: University of Chicago Press.

Bates, Daniel, and Rassam, Amal. 1983. *Peoples and Cultures of the Middle East.* Englewood Cliffs, NJ: Prentice-Hall.

Beals, Alan R. 1962. *Gopalpur, a South Indian Village.* New York: Holt, Rinehart, and Winston.

———. 1974. *Village Life in South India.* Chicago: Aldine.

Black, Lydia T. 1988. Peoples of the Amur and Maritime Regions. In William W. Fitzhugh and Aron Crowell (eds.), *Crossroads of Continents.* Washington, DC: Smithsonian.

Bohannan, Paul, and Curtin, Phillip. 1995. *Africa and Africans,* 4th ed. Prospect Heights, IL: Waveland Press.

Boord, Martin. 1993. Tibet and Mongolia. In Roy Willis (ed.), *World Mythology.* New York: Henry Holt.

Brandt, Vincent S. R. 1990. *A Korean Village.* Prospect Heights, IL: Waveland Press.

Brenner, Suzanne A. 1995. Why Women Rule the Roost: Rethinking Javanese Ideologies of Gender and Self-control. In Aihwa Ong and Michael G. Peletz (eds.), *Bewitching Women, Pious Men.* Berkeley: University of California Press.

Burling, Robbins. 1965. *Hill Farms and Padi Fields.* Englewood Cliffs, NJ: Prentice-Hall.

Caplan, Lionel. 1980. Power and Status in South Asian Slavery. In James L. Watson (ed.), *Asian and African Systems of Slavery.* Berkeley: University of California Press.

Carrasco, Pedro. 1959. *Land and Polity in Tibet.* Seattle: University of Washington Press.

Ch'en, Kenneth K. S. 1968. *Buddhism, the Light of Asia.* Woodbury, NY: Barron's.

Clammer, John. 1993. Fishermen, Forest-eaters, Peddlers, Peasants, and Pastoralists: Economic Anthropology. In Grant Evans (ed.), *Asia's Cultural Mosaic.* Englewood Cliffs, NJ: Prentice-Hall.

Cohen, Paul T. 1993. Order Under Heaven: Anthropology and the State. In Grant Evans (ed.), *Asia's Cultural Mosaic.* Englewood Cliffs, NJ: Prentice-Hall.

Coquery-Vidrovitch, Catherine. 1997. *African Women: A Modern History.* Boulder, CO: Westview.

Cordwell, Justine M. 1959. African Art. In William R. Bascom and Melville J. Herskovits (eds.), *Continuity and Change in African Cultures.* Chicago: University of Chicago Press.

Dillon, Richard G. 1990. *Ranking and Resistance: A Precolonial Cameroonian Polity in Regional Perspective.* Stanford, CA: Stanford University Press.

Dirks, Nicholas B. 1993. *The Hollow Crown,* 2nd ed. Ann Arbor: University of Michigan Press.

Dorjahn, Vernon R. 1959. The Factor of Polygyny in African Demography. In William R. Bascom and Melville J. Herskovits (eds.), *Continuity and Change in African Cultures.* Chicago: University of Chicago Press.

Duley, Margot I. 1986a. Women in China. In Margot I. Duley and Mary I. Edwards (eds.), *The Cross-cultural Study of Women.* New York: Feminist Press.

———. 1986b. Women in India. In Margot I. Duley and Mary I. Edwards (eds.), *The Cross-cultural Study of Women.* New York: Feminist Press.

———. 1986c. Women in the Islamic Middle East and North Africa. In Margot I. Duley and Mary I. Edwards (eds.), *The Cross-cultural Study of Women.* New York: Feminist Press.

Dunn, Charles J. 1972. *Everyday Life in Traditional Japan.* Rutland, VT: Tuttle.

Eickelmann, Dale F. 1998. *The Middle East and Central Asia,* 3rd ed. Upper Saddle River, NJ: Prentice-Hall.

Ekvall, Robert B. 1983. *Fields on the Hoof.* Prospect Heights, IL: Waveland Press.

Evans, Grant. 1993. Hierarchy and Dominance: Class, Status and Caste. In Grant Evans (ed.), *Asia's Cultural Mosaic.* Englewood Cliffs, NJ: Prentice-Hall.

——— (ed.). 1993. *Asia's Cultural Mosaic.* Englewood Cliffs, NJ: Prentice-Hall.

Fee, Lian Kwen, and Rajah, Ananda. 1993. The Ethnic Mosaic. In Grant Evans (ed.), *Asia's Cultural Mosaic.* Englewood Cliffs, NJ: Prentice-Hall.

Fienup-Riordan, Ann. 1995. Eskimo. In Timothy J. O'Leary and David Levinson (eds.), *North America.* Vol. 1 of *Encyclopedia of World Cultures.* Boston: G. K. Hall.

Fitzhugh, William W., and Crowell, Aron (eds.). 1988. *Crossroads of Continents.* Washington, DC: Smithsonian.

Fraser, Thomas M., Jr. [1966] 1984. *Fishermen of South Thailand.* Prospect Heights, IL: Waveland Press.

Geertz, Clifford. 1960. *The Religion of Java.* New York: Free Press of Glencoe.

Gelb, Joyce, and Palley, Marian Lief. 1994. Introduction to Joyce Gelb and Marian Lief Palley (eds.), *Women of Japan and Korea.* Philadelphia: Temple University Press.

——— (eds.). 1994. *Women of Japan and Korea.* Philadelphia: Temple University Press.

Goldstein, Melvyn C., and Beall, Cynthia M. 1990. *Nomads of Western Tibet.* Berkeley: University of California Press.

Goody, Jack. 1980. Slavery in Time and Space. In James L. Watson (ed.), *Asian and African Systems of Slavery.* Berkeley: University of California Press.

Gordon, April A. and Gordon, Donald L. (eds.). 1996. *Understanding Contemporary Africa.* Boulder, CO: Lienne Rienner.

Graburn, Nelson H. H., and Strong, B. Stephen. 1973. *Circumpolar Peoples.* Pacific Palisades, CA: Goodyear.

Gulick, John. 1976. *The Middle East.* Pacific Palisades, CA: Goodyear.

Hambly, Wilfrid D. 1930. *Ethnology of Africa.* Chicago: Field Museum of Natural History.

Helliwell, Christine. 1993. Women in Asia: Anthropology and the Study of Women. In Grant Evans (ed.), *Asia's Cultural Mosaic.* Englewood Cliffs, NJ: Prentice-Hall.

Herbert, Eugenia W. 1984. *Red Gold of Africa.* Madison: University of Wisconsin Press.

Herskovits, Melville J. 1960. Negro Folklore. In Simon Ottenberg and Phoebe Ottenberg (eds.), *Cultures and Societies of Africa.* New York: Random House.

Hiskett, Mervyn. 1994. *The Course of Islam in Africa.* Edinburgh, Scotland: University of Edinburgh Press.

Hockings, Paul (ed.). 1992. *South Asia.* Vol. 3 of *Encyclopedia of World Cultures.* Boston: G. K. Hall.

Iliffe, John. 1995. *Africans: The History of a Continent.* New York: Cambridge University Press.

Isichei, Elizabeth. 1997. *A History of African Societies to 1870.* New York: Cambridge University Press.

Issenman, Betty Kobayashi. 1997. *Sinews of Survival.* Vancouver: UBC Press.

July, Robert W. 1998. *A History of the African People,* 5th ed. Prospect Heights, IL: Waveland Press.

Kawagley, A. Oscar. 1995. *A Yupiaq Worldview: A Pathway to Ecology and Spirit.* Prospect Heights, IL: Waveland Press.

Keim, Curtis A. 1995. Africa and Europe Before 1900. In Phyllis M. Martin and Patrick O'Meara (eds.), *Africa,* 3rd ed. Bloomington: Indiana University Press.

Kendall, Laurel. 1985. *Shamans, Housewives, and Other Restless Spirits.* Honolulu: University of Hawaii Press.

Keyes, Charles F. 1995. *The Golden Peninsula.* Honolulu: University of Hawaii Press.

Khazanov, Anatoly M. 1994. *Nomads and the Outside World,* 2nd ed. Madison: University of Wisconsin Press.

Knappert, Jan. 1995. *Indian Mythology.* London: Diamond.

Koentjaraningrat, R. M. 1975. *Introduction to the Peoples and Cultures of Indonesia and Malaysia.* Menlo Park, CA: Cummings.

Kopytoff, Igor. 1987. Introduction to Igor Kopytoff (ed.), *The African Frontier: The Reproduction of Traditional African Societies.* Bloomington: Indiana University Press.

———. 1999. Permutations in Patrimonialism and Populism: The Afghem Chiefdoms of Western Cameroon. In Susan McIntosh Keech (ed.), *Beyond Chiefdoms: Pathways to Complexity in Africa.* New York: Cambridge University Press.

——— (ed.). 1987. *The African Frontier: The Reproduction of Traditional African Societies.* Bloomington: Indiana University Press.

Krupnick, Igor. 1993. *Arctic Adaptations.* Hanover, NH: University Press of New England.

Kusimba, Chapurukha. 1999. *The Rise and Fall of Swahili States.* Walnut Creek, CA: Altamira.

Laughlin, William S. 1980. *Aleuts: Survivors of the Bering Land Bridge.* New York: Holt, Rinehart and Winston.

Lamphear, John, and Falola, Toyin. 1995. Aspects of Early African History. In Phyllis M. Martin and Patrick O'Meara (eds.), *Africa,* 3rd ed. Bloomington: Indiana University Press.

Lester, Robert C. 1987. *Buddhism, the Path to Nirvana.* Prospect Heights, IL: Waveland Press.

Levin, M. G., and Potapov, L. P. (eds.). 1964. *The Peoples of Siberia.* Chicago: University of Chicago Press.

Levine, Donald N. 1974. *Wax and Gold.* Chicago: University of Chicago Press.

LeVine, Robert, et al. 1994. *Child Care and Culture: Lessons From Africa.* New York: Cambridge University Press.

Lewis, Bernard. 1963. *Istanbul and the Civilization of the Ottoman Empire.* Norman: University of Oklahoma Press.

———. 1990. *Race and Slavery in the Middle East.* New York: Oxford University Press.

Lewis, Herbert S. 1965. *A Galla Monarchy.* Madison: University of Wisconsin Press.

Lewis, Oscar. 1965. *Village Life in Northern India.* New York: Vintage.

Lindholm, Charles. 1996. *The Islamic Middle East.* Cambridge, MA: Blackwell.

Littleton, C. Scott (ed.). 1996. *The Sacred East.* London: Macmillan.

Lodrick, Deryck. 1981. *Sacred Cows, Sacred Places.* Berkeley: University of California Press.

Mackey, Sandra. 1996. *The Iranians.* New York: Dutton.

Mair, Lucy. 1977. *African Kingdoms.* Oxford: Oxford University Press.

Maloney, Clarence. 1974. *Peoples of South Asia.* New York: Holt, Rinehart and Winston.

Mandelbaum, David G. 1988. *Women's Seclusion and Men's Honor.* Tucson: University of Arizona Press.

Mann, Susan. 1997. *Precious Records.* Stanford, CA: Stanford University Press.

Marcus, Abraham. 1989. *The Middle East on the Eve of Modernity.* New York: Columbia University Press.

Martin, Phyllis M., and O'Meara, Patrick (eds.). 1995. *Africa,* 3rd ed. Bloomington: Indiana University Press.

Matsunosuke, Nishiyama. 1997. *Edo Culture.* Honolulu: University of Hawaii Press.

Mauet, Jacques. 1972. *Civilizations of Black Africa.* New York: Oxford University Press.

McCall, John C. 1995. Social Organization in Africa. In Phyllis M. Martin and Patrick O'Meara (eds.), *Africa,* 3rd ed. Bloomington: Indiana University Press.

McIntosh, Susan Keech (ed.). 1999. *Beyond Chiefdoms: Pathways to Complexity in Africa.* New York: Cambridge University Press.

McNaughton, Patrick R., and Pelrine, Diane. 1995. African Art. In Phyllis M. Martin and Patrick O'Meara (eds.), *Africa,* 3rd ed. Bloomington: Indiana University Press.

Meeker, Michael E. 1989. *The Pastoral Son and the Spirit of Patriarchy.* Madison: University of Wisconsin Press.

Merkur, Daniel. 1991. *Powers Which We Do Not Know: The Gods and Spirits of the Inuit.* Moscow: University of Idaho Press.

Middleton, John. 1992. *The World of the Swahili, an African Mercantile Civilization.* New Haven, CT: Yale University Press.

———, and Rassam, Amal (eds.). 1995. *Africa and the Middle East.* Vol. 9 of *Encyclopedia of World Cultures.* Boston: G. K. Hall.

Miyazaki, Ichisada. 1981. *China's Examination Hell.* New Haven, CT: Yale University Press.

Morrow, Lance. 1986. Women in Sub-Saharan Africa. In Margot I. Duley and Mary I. Edwards (eds.), *The Cross-cultural Study of Women.* New York: Feminist Press.

Moyo, Ambrose. 1996. Religion in Africa. In April A. Gordon and Donald L. Gordon, *Understanding Contemporary Africa.* Boulder, CO: Lienne Rienner.

Murdock, George Peter. 1959. *Africa.* New York: McGraw-Hill.

Naquin, Susan, and Rawski, Evelyn S. 1987. *Chinese Society in the Eighteenth Century.* New Haven, CT: Yale University Press.

Nashat, Guity, and Tucker, Judith E. 1999. *Women in the Middle East and North Africa.* Bloomington: Indiana University Press.

Nasr, Seyyed Hossein. 1992. *Science and Civilization in Islam.* New York: Barnes & Noble.

Netting, Robert McC. 1968. *Hill Farmers of Nigeria.* Seattle: University of Washington.

Norbeck, Edward. 1976. *Changing Japan,* 2nd ed. New York: Holt, Rinehart and Winston.

Oakes, Jill, and Riewe, Rick. 1998. *Spirit of Siberia: Traditional Native Life, Clothing, and Footwear.* Washington, DC: Smithsonian.

Ogot, B. A. (ed.). 1992. *Africa From the Sixteenth to the Eighteenth Century.* Berkeley: University of California Press.

Ohnuki-Tierney, Emiko. 1974. *The Ainu of the Northwest Coast of Southern Sakhalin.* New York: Holt, Rinehart and Winston.

O'Leary, Timothy J., and Levinson, David (eds.), *Encyclopedia of World Cultures.* Vol. 1. Boston: G. K. Hall.

Ong, Aihwa. 1989. Center, Periphery, and Hierarchy: Gender in Southeast Asia. In Sandra Morgen (ed.), *Gender and Anthropology.* Washington, DC: American Anthropological Association.

———, and Peletz, Michael G. (eds.). 1995. *Bewitching Women, Pious Men.* Berkeley: University of California Press.

Osgood, Cornelius. 1951. *The Koreans and Their Culture.* New York: Ronald.

Ottenberg, Simon, and Ottenberg, Phoebe. 1960. *Cultures and Societies of Africa.* New York: Random House.

Pandian, Jacob. 1995. *The Making of India and Indian Traditions.* Englewood Cliffs, NJ: Prentice-Hall.

Peacock, James L. 1973. *Indonesia.* Pacific Palisades, CA: Goodyear.

Price, Pamela. 1996. *Kingship and Political Practice in Colonial India.* New York: Cambridge University Press.

Provencher, Ronald. 1973. *Mainland Southeast Asia.* Pacific Palisades, CA: Goodyear.

Reid, Anthony. 1988. Vol. 1 of *Southeast Asia in the Age of Commerce, 1450–1680.* New Haven, CT: Yale University Press.

Reischauer, Edwin O. 1988. *The Japanese Today.* Cambridge, MA: Belknap.

Riches, David, and Vitebsky, Piers. 1993. The Arctic Regions. In Roy Willis (ed.), *World Mythology.* New York: Henry Holt.

Ritzenthaler, Robert, and Ritzenthaler, Pat. 1962. *Cameroons Village: An Ethnography of the Bafut.* Milwaukee, WI: Milwaukee Public Museum Publications in Anthropology, no. 8.

Samuel, Geoffrey. 1993. *Civilized Shamans.* Washington, DC: Smithsonian.

Scarce, Jennifer. 1996. *Domestic Culture in the Middle East.* Edinburgh, Scotland: National Museums of Scotland.

Schneider, Harold K. 1981. *The Africans.* Englewood Cliffs, NJ: Prentice-Hall.

Schwartz, Theodore. 1973. Cult and Context: The Paranoid Ethos in Melanesia. *Ethos* 1: 153–174.

Siegel, Brian. 1996. Family and Kinship. In April A. Gordon and Donald L. Gordon (eds.), *Understanding Contemporary Africa.* Boulder, CO: Lienne Rienner.

Sinclair, Karen. 1986. Women in Oceania. In Margot I. Duley and Mary I. Edwards (eds.), *The Cross-cultural Study of Women.* New York: Feminist Press.

Smith, Andrew B. 1992. *Pastoralism in Africa: Origins and Development Ecology.* Athens: Ohio University Press.

Smith, Richard J. 1994. *China's Cultural Heritage,* 2nd ed. Boulder, CO: Westview.

Smith, Robert J. 1983. *Japanese Society.* New York: Cambridge University Press.

Sorenson, Clark W. 1993a. Ancestors and In-laws: Kinship Beyond the Family. In Grant Evans (ed.), *Asia's Cultural Mosaic.* Englewood Cliffs, NJ: Prentice-Hall.

———. 1993b. Asian Families: Domestic Group Formation. In Grant Evans (ed.), *Asia's Cultural Mosaic.* Englewood Cliffs, NJ: Prentice-Hall.

Steinberg, David Joel (ed.). 1987. *In Search of Southeast Asia,* rev. ed. Honolulu: University of Hawaii Press.

Stone, Ruth M. 1995. African Music Performed. In Phyllis M. Martin and Patrick O'Meara (eds.), *Africa,* 3rd ed. Bloomington: Indiana University Press.

Stover, Leon E., and Stover, Takeko K. 1976. *China.* Pacific Palisades, CA: Goodyear.

Tapp, Nicholas. 1993. Karma and Cosmology: Anthropology and Religion. In Grant Evans (ed.), *Asia's Cultural Mosaic.* Englewood Cliffs, NJ: Prentice-Hall.

Temple, Robert. 1998. *The Genius of China.* London: Prion.

Thornton, John K. 1983. *The Kingdom of Kongo: Civil War and Transition, 1641–1718.* Madison: University of Wisconsin Press.

Turton, Andrew. 1980. Thai Institutions of Slavery. In James L. Watson (ed.), *Asian and African Systems of Slavery.* Berkeley: University of California Press.

Tyler, Stephen. [1973] 1986. *India: An Anthropological Perspective.* Prospect Heights, IL: Waveland Press.

Turnbull, Colin M. 1977. *Man in Africa.* Garden City, NY: Anchor.

Twedell, Colin E., and Kimball, Linda Amy. 1985. *Introduction to the Peoples and Cultures of Asia.* Englewood Cliffs, NJ: Prentice-Hall.

Vansina, Jan. 1966. *Kingdoms of the Savanna.* Madison: University of Wisconsin Press.

———. 1990. *Paths in the Rainforests.* Madison: University of Wisconsin Press.

———. 1999. Pathways of Political Development in Equatorial Africa and Neo-Evolutionary Theory. In Susan Keech McIntosh (ed.), *Beyond Chiefdoms: Pathways to Complexity in Africa.* New York: Cambridge University Press.

Vogel, Joseph O. (ed.). 1997. *Encyclopedia of Precolonial Africa.* Walnut Creek, CA: Altamira.

Walters, Derek. 1995. *Chinese Mythology.* London: Diamond.

Watson, James L. 1980a. Slavery as an Institution: Open and Closed Systems. In James L. Watson (ed.), *Asian and African Systems of Slavery.* Berkeley: University of California Press.

———. 1980b. Transactions in People: The Chinese Market in Slaves, Servants, and Heirs. In James L. Watson (ed.), *Asian and African Systems of Slavery.* Berkeley: University of California Press.

——— (ed.). 1980. *Asian and African Systems of Slavery.* Berkeley: University of California Press.

Webb, James L. A. 1995. *Desert Frontier . . . The Western Sahel.* Madison. University of Wisconsin Press.

Wiser, William, and Wiser, Charlotte. 1971. *Behind Mud Walls, 1930–1960,* rev. and enl. ed. Berkeley: University of California Press.

Wolpert, Stanley. 1991. *India.* Berkeley: University of California Press.

Yang, C. K. [1961] 1991. *Religion in Chinese Society.* Prospect Heights, IL: Waveland Press.

Zaslavsky, Claudia. 1990. *Africa Counts.* New York: Lawrence Hill.

Oceania

Abbie, A. A. 1970. *The Original Australians.* New York: American Elsevier.

Alkire, William H. 1977. *An Introduction to the Peoples and Cultures of Micronesia,* 2nd ed. Menlo Park, CA: Cummings.

Allen, M. R. 1967. *Male Cults and Secret Initiations in Melanesia.* New York: Cambridge University Press.

Allen, Tricia, and Gilbert, Steve. n.d. Tattoo history source book: Polynesia. *Tattoos. Com Ezine.* http://tattoos.com/jane/steve/polynesia.htm

Ammann, Raymond. 1997. *Kanak Dance and Music.* New York: Columbia University Press.

Bell, Diane. 1993. *Daughters of the Dreaming,* 2nd ed. Minneapolis: University of Minnesota Press.

Bellwood, Peter, Fox, James J., and Tryon, Darrell (eds.). 1995. *The Austronesians.* Canberra: Australian National University.

Berndt, Ronald M., and Berndt, Catherine H. 1970. *Man, Land & Myth in North Australia.* East Lansing: Michigan State University Press.

————. 1985. *The World of the First Australians,* 4th ed. New York: Rigby.

————. 1993. *A World That Was.* Vancouver: UBC Press.

———— (eds.). 1980. *Aborigines of the West,* rev. ed. Perth: University of Western Australia Press.

Best, Elsdon. 1952. *The Maori as He Was,* rev. ed. Wellington, NZ: R. E. Owen.

Brown, Paula. 1978. *Highland Peoples of New Guinea.* New York: Cambridge University Press.

Burbank, Victoria K. 1989. Gender and the Anthropology Curriculum: Aboriginal Australia. In Sandra Morgen (ed.), *Gender and Anthropology.* Washington, DC: American Anthropological Association.

————. 1994. *Fighting Women.* Berkeley: University of California Press.

Carrier, James G. (ed.). 1992. *History and Tradition in Melanesian Anthropology.* Berkeley: University of California Press.

Carroll, Vern (ed.). 1970. *Adoption in Eastern Oceania.* Honolulu: University of Hawaii Press.

Chowning, Ann. 1977. *An Introduction to the Peoples and Cultures of Melanesia,* 2nd ed. Menlo Park, CA: Cummings.

Codrington, R. H. 1972. *The Melanesians.* New York: Dover Reprint.

Counts, Dorothy Ayers, and Counts, David R. (eds.). 1985. *Aging and Its Transformations.* Pittsburgh, PA: University of Pittsburgh Press.

D'Alleva, Anne. 1998. *Art of the Pacific.* London: Calmann and King.

Denoon, Donald. 1997a. Human Settlement. In Donald Denoon (ed.), *The Cambridge History of the Pacific Islanders.* New York: Cambridge University Press.

————. 1997b. Pacific Edens? Myths and Realities of Primitive Affluence. In Donald Denoon (ed.), *The Cambridge History of the Pacific Islanders.* New York: Cambridge University Press.

———— (ed.). 1997. *The Cambridge History of the Pacific Islanders.* New York: Cambridge University Press.

Elkin, A. P. 1964. *The Australian Aborigines.* Garden City, NY: Anchor.

Ferdon, Edwin N. 1981. *Early Tahiti as the Explorers Saw It, 1767–1797.* Tucson: University of Arizona Press.

————. 1987. *Early Tonga as the Explorers Saw It, 1616–1810.* Tucson: University of Arizona Press.

————. *Early Observations of Marquesan Culture, 1595–1813.* Tucson: University of Arizona Press.

Fison, K., and Howitt, A. W. 1968. *Kamilaroi and Kurnai.* Oosterhout N.B., The Netherlands: Anthropological Publications (reprint of 1880 edition).

Flood, Josephine. 1990. *Archaeology of the Dreamtime.* New Haven, CT: Yale University Press.

Gale, Faye (ed.). 1974. *Woman's Role in Aboriginal Society.* Canberra: Australian Institute of Aboriginal Studies.

Gelber, Marilyn G. 1986. *Gender and Society in the New Guinea Highlands.* Boulder, CO: Westview.

Gell, Alfred. 1993. *Wrapping in Images.* New York: Oxford University Press.

Godelier, Maurice. 1986. *The Making of Great Men.* New York: Cambridge University Press.

————, and Strathern, Marilyn (eds.). 1991. *Big Men and Great Men.* New York: Cambridge University Press.

Goldman, Irving. 1970. *Ancient Polynesian Society.* Chicago: University of Chicago Press.

Gould, Richard A. 1969. *Yiwara.* New York: Scribner's.

————. 1980. *Living Archaeology.* New York: Cambridge University Press.

Handy, E. S. Craighill. 1985. *Polynesian Religion.* Millwood, NY: Kraus Reprint (orig. 1927).

Hanson, F. Allan. 1970. *Rapan Lifeways.* Boston: Little, Brown.

————, and Hanson, Louise. 1983. *Counterpoint in Maori Culture.* Boston: Routledge & Kegan Paul.

Hays, Terence E. 1991. Introduction to Terence E. Hays (ed.), *Oceania.* Vol. 2 of *Encyclopedia of World Cultures.* Boston: G. K. Hall.

———— (ed.). 1991. *Oceania.* Vol. 2 of *Encyclopedia of World Cultures.* Boston: G. K. Hall.

Hart, C. W. M., Pilling, Arnold R., and Goodale, Jane C. 1988. *The Tiwi of North Australia,* 3rd ed. New York: Holt, Rinehart and Winston.

Herdt, Gilbert H. (ed.). 1984. *Ritualized Homosexuality in Melanesia.* Berkeley: University of California Press.

Hiatt, L. R. 1996. *Arguments About Aborigines.* New York: Cambridge University Press.

Holmes, Lowell D., and Holmes, Ellen Rhoads. 1992. *Samoan Village Then and Now,* 2nd ed. Fort Worth, TX: Harcourt Brace Jovanovich.

Horton, David (ed.). 1994. *The Encyclopaedia of Aboriginal Australia.* 2 vols. Canberra: Aboriginal Studies Press.

Howard, Alan, and Borofsky, Robert (eds.). 1989. *Developments in Polynesian Ethnology.* Honolulu: University of Hawaii Press.

Huntsman, Judith, and Hooper, Anthony. 1996. *Tokelau.* Honolulu: University of Hawaii Press.

Kaeppler, Adrienne L. 1989. Art and Aesthetics. In Alan Howard and Robert Borofsky (eds.), *Developments in Polynesian Ethnology.* Honolulu: University of Hawaii Press.

Kane, Herb Kawainui. 1997. *Ancient Hawai'i.* Captain Cook, HI: Kawainui Press.

Keesing, Roger M. 1984. Rethinking *Mana. Journal of Anthropological Research* 40: 137–156.

Kirch, Patrick Vinton. 1984. *The Evolution of the Polynesian Chiefdoms.* New York: Cambridge University Press.

————. 2000. *On the Road of the Winds.* Berkeley: University of California Press.

Knappert, Jan. 1995. *Pacific Mythology.* London: Diamond.

Knauft, Bruce M. 1993. *South Coast New Guinea Cultures.* New York: Cambridge University Press.

————. 1999. *From Primitive to Postcolonial.* Ann Arbor: University of Michigan Press.

Lane, R. B. 1965. The Melanesians of South Pentecost, New Hebrides. In P. Lawrence and M. J. Meggitt (eds.), *Gods, Ghosts, and Men in Melanesia: Some Religions of Australia, New Guinea, and the New Hebrides.* Melbourne: Oxford University Press.

Leenhardt, Maurice. 1979. *Do Kamo.* Chicago: University of Chicago Press.

Lewis, Albert B. 1932. *Ethnology of Melanesia.* Chicago: Field Museum of Natural History.

Linnekin, Jocelyn. 1990. *Sacred Queens and Women of Consequence.* Ann Arbor: University of Michigan Press.

————. 1997a. Contending Approaches. In Donald Denoon (ed.), *The Cambridge History of the Pacific Islanders.* New York: Cambridge University Press.

————. 1997b. Gender Division of Labour. In Donald Denoon (ed.), *The Cambridge History of the Pacific Islanders.* New York: Cambridge University Press.

Linton, Ralph. 1926. *Ethnology of Polynesia and Micronesia.* Chicago: Field Museum of Natural History.

Lourandos, Harry. 1997. *Continent of Hunter-Gatherers.* New York: Cambridge University Press.

Maddock, Kenneth. 1982. *The Australian Aborigines,* 2nd ed. New York: Penguin Books.

Marshall, Mac (ed.). 1983. *Siblingship in Oceania.* Lanham, MD: University Press of America.

Massola, Aldo. 1971. *The Aborigines of South-eastern Australia As They Were.* Melbourne: William Heinemann.

Meggitt, M. J. 1965. *Desert People.* Chicago: University of Chicago Press.

Metge, Joan. 1967. *The Maoris of New Zealand.* London: Routledge & Kegan Paul.

Morton, John. 1999. The Arrernte of Central Australia. In Richard B. Lee and Richard Daly (eds.), *The Cambridge Encyclopedia of Hunters and Gatherers.* New York: Cambridge University Press.

Myers, Fred R. 1991. *Pintupi Country, Pintupi Self.* Berkeley: University of California Press.

O'Brien, Denise, and Tiffany, Sharon W. (eds.). 1984. *Rethinking Women's Roles: Perspectives from the Pacific.* Berkeley: University of California Press.

Oliver, Douglas L. 1989a. *Native Cultures of the Pacific Islands.* Honolulu: University of Hawaii Press.

———. 1989b. *The Pacific Islands,* 3rd ed. Honolulu: University of Hawaii Press.

———. 1989c. *Oceania.* 2 vols. Honolulu: University of Hawaii Press.

Parmentier, Richard J. 1987. *The Sacred Remains.* Chicago: University of Chicago Press.

Petersen, Glenn. 1982. *One Man Cannot Rule a Thousand.* Ann Arbor: University of Michigan Press.

Peterson, Nicolas. 1999. Introduction: Australia. In Richard B. Lee and Richard Daly (eds.), *The Cambridge Encyclopedia of Hunters and Gatherers.* New York: Cambridge University Press.

Quanchi, Max, and Adams, Ron (eds.). 1993. *Culture Contact in the Pacific.* New York: Cambridge University Press.

Ritchie, Jane, and Ritchie, James. 1979. *Growing Up in Polynesia.* North Sydney, Australia: Allen & Unwin.

———. 1989. Socialization and Character Development. In Alan Howard and Robert Borofsky (eds.), *Developments in Polynesian Ethnology.* Honolulu: University of Hawaii Press.

Roth, G. K. 1973. *Fijian Way of Life,* 2nd ed. London: Oxford University Press.

Shore, Bradd. 1989. Mana and Tapu. In Alan Howard and Robert Borofsky (eds.), *Developments in Polynesian Ethnology.* Honolulu: University of Hawaii Press.

Sillitoe, Paul. 1998. *An Introduction to the Anthropology of Melanesia.* New York: Cambridge University Press.

Smith, DeVerne Reed. 1983. *Palauan Social Structure.* New Brunswick, NJ: Rutgers University Press.

Spriggs, Matthew. 1997. *The Island Melanesians.* Cambridge, MA: Blackwell.

Stephen, Michele (ed.). 1987. *Sorcerer and Witch in Melanesia.* New Brunswick, NJ: Rutgers University Press.

Swain, Tony. 1993. *A Place for Strangers, Towards a History of Australian Aboriginal Being.* New York: Cambridge University Press.

———, and Trompf, Garry. 1995. *The Religions of Oceania.* New York: Routledge.

Thomas, Nicholas. 1995a. Exchange Systems, Political Dynamics, and Colonial Transformations in Nineteenth-century Oceania. In Peter Bellwood et al. (eds.), *The Austronesians.* Canberra: Australian National University.

———. 1995b. *Oceanic Art.* London: Thames and Hudson.

Thompson, Laura. 1971. *Southern Lau, Fiji.* New York: Kraus Reprint.

Tonkinson, Robert. 1991. *The Mardu Aborigines,* 2nd ed. Fort Worth, TX: Harcourt Brace Jovanovich.

Valeri, Valerio. 1985. *Kingship and Sacrifice.* Chicago: University of Chicago Press.

Index